THE RISE

OF THE

DUTCH REPUBLIC.

A History.

BY JOHN LOTHROP MOTLEY.

IN THREE VOLUMES.

VOL. II.

NEW YORK:
HARPER & BROTHERS,
329 & 331 PEARL STREET.
1868.

THE

RISE OF THE DUTCH REPUBLIC.

CHAPTER VIII.

Secret policy of the government—Berghen and Montigny in Spain—Debates at Segovia—Correspondence of the Duchess with Philip—Procrastination and dissimulation of the King—Secret communication to the Pope—Effect in the provinces of the King's letters to the government—Secret instructions to the Duchess—Desponding statements of Margaret—Her misrepresentations concerning Orange, Egmont, and others—Wrath and duplicity of Philip—Egmont's exertions in Flanders—Orange returns to Antwerp—His tolerant spirit—Agreement of 2d September—Horn at Tournay—Excavations in the Cathedral—Almost universal attendance at the preaching—Building of temples commenced—Difficult position of Horn—Preaching in the Clothiers' Hall—Horn recalled—Noircarmes at Tournay—Friendly correspondence of Margaret with Orange, Egmont, Horn, and Hoogstraaten—Her secret defamation of these persons. .

EGMONT in Flanders, Orange at Antwerp, Horn at Tournay, Hoogstraaten at Mechlin, were exerting themselves to suppress insurrection and to avert ruin.* What, meanwhile, was the policy of the government? The secret course pursued both at Brussels and at Madrid may be condensed into the usual formula—dissimulation, procrastination, and again dissimulation.

It is at this point necessary to take a rapid survey of the open and the secret proceedings of the King and his repre-

---

* Pontus Payen MS. La Défense de Messire Antoine de Lalaing, Compte de Hocstrate, etc., etc., Mons (republished by M. Gachard). Letter of Horn to Montigny. Foppens, ii. 480. Bor, ii. 84–86. Wesenbecke.

sentatives from the moment at which Berghen and Montigny arrived in Madrid. Those ill-fated gentlemen had been received with apparent cordiality, and admitted to frequent, but unmeaning, interviews with his Majesty. The current upon which they were embarked was deep and treacherous, but it was smooth and very slow. They assured the King that his letters, ordering the rigorous execution of the inquisition and edicts, had engendered all the evils under which the provinces were laboring. They told him that Spaniards and tools of Spaniards had attempted to govern the country, to the exclusion of native citizens and nobles, but that it would soon be found that Netherlanders were not to be trodden upon like the abject inhabitants of Milan, Naples, and Sicily.* Such words as these struck with an unaccustomed sound upon the royal ear, but the envoys, who were both Catholic and loyal, had no idea, in thus expressing their opinions, according to their sense of duty, and in obedience to the King's desire, upon the causes of the discontent, that they were committing an act of high treason.

When the news of the public preaching reached Spain, there were almost daily consultations at the grove of Segovia. The eminent personages who composed the royal council were the Duke of Alva, the Count de Feria, Don Antonio de Toledo, Don Juan Manrique de Lara, Ruy Gomez, Quixada, Councillor Tisnacq, recently appointed President of the State Council, and Councillor Hopper.† Six Spaniards and two Netherlanders, one of whom, too, a man of dull intellect and thoroughly subservient character, to deal with the local affairs of the Netherlands in a time of intense excitement ! The instructions of the envoys had been to represent the necessity of according three great points—abolition of the inquisition, moderation of the edicts, according to the draft prepared in Brussels, and an ample pardon for past transactions. There was much debate upon all these propositions.‡ Philip said little, but he listened

---

* Hopper, Rec. et Mem., 78–80.   † Ibid., 88.

‡ Ibid., 81, sqq. 88, sqq.

attentively to the long discourses in council, and he took an incredible quantity of notes. It was the general opinion that this last demand on the part of the Netherlanders was the fourth link in the chain of treason. The first had been the cabal by which Granvelle had been expelled ; the second, the mission of Egmont, the main object of which had been to procure a modification of the state council, in order to bring that body under the control of a few haughty and rebellious nobles ; the third had been the presentation of the insolent and seditious Request ; and now, to crown the whole, came a proposition embodying the three points—abolition of the inquisition, revocation of the edicts, and a pardon to criminals, for whom death was the only sufficient punishment.*

With regard to these three points, it was, after much wrangling, decided to grant them under certain restrictions. To abolish the inquisition would be to remove the only instrument by which the Church had been accustomed to regulate the consciences and the doctrines of its subjects. It would be equivalent to a concession of religious freedom, at least to individuals within their own domiciles, than which no concession could be more pernicious.† Nevertheless, it might be advisable to permit the temporary cessation of the papal inquisition, now that the episcopal inquisition had been so much enlarged and strengthened in the Netherlands, on the condition that this branch of the institution should be maintained in energetic condition.‡ With regard to the Moderation, it was thought better to defer that matter till the proposed visit of his Majesty to the provinces. If, however, the Regent should think it absolutely necessary to make a change, she must cause a new draft to be made, as that which had been sent was not found admissible.§ Touching the pardon general, it would be necessary to make many conditions and restrictions before it could be granted. Provided these were sufficiently minute to exclude all persons whom it might be found desirable to

---

* Hopper, 81–83.   † Ibid., 86.   ‡ Ibid.   § Ibid., 87.

chastise, the amnesty was possible. Otherwise it was quite out of the question.

Meantime, Margaret of Parma had been urging her brother to come to a decision, painting the distracted condition of the country in the liveliest colors, and insisting, although perfectly aware of Philip's private sentiments, upon a favorable decision as to the three points demanded by the envoys. Especially she urged her incapacity to resist any rebellion, and demanded succor of men and money in case the "Moderation" were not accepted by his Majesty.

It was the last day of July before the King wrote at all, to communicate his decisions upon the crisis which had occurred in the first week of April. The disorder for which he had finally prepared a prescription had, before his letter arrived, already passed through its subsequent stages of the field-preaching and the image-breaking. Of course these fresh symptoms would require much consultation, pondering, and note-taking before they could be dealt with. In the mean time they would be considered as not yet having happened. This was the masterly procrastination of the sovereign, when his provinces were in a blaze.

His masterly dissimulation was employed in the direction suggested by his councillors. Philip never originated a thought, nor laid down a plan, but he was ever true to the falsehood of his nature, and was indefatigable in following out the suggestions of others. No greater mistake can be made than to ascribe talent to this plodding and pedantic monarch. The man's intellect was contemptible, but malignity and duplicity, almost superhuman, have effectually lifted his character out of the regions of the common-place. He wrote accordingly to say that the pardon, under certain conditions, might be granted, and that the papal inquisition might cease—the bishops now being present in such numbers, "to take care of their flocks," and the episcopal inquisition being therefore established upon so secure a basis.* He added, that if a moderation of the

---

* Correspondance de Marg. d'Autriche, 100–103, sqq.

edicts were still desired, a new project might be sent to Madrid, as the one brought by Berghen and Montigny was not satisfactory.* In arranging this wonderful scheme for composing the tumults of the country, which had grown out of a determined rebellion to the inquisition in any form, he followed not only the advice, but adopted the exact language of his councillors.

Certainly, here was not much encouragement for patriotic hearts in the Netherlands. A pardon, so restricted that none were likely to be forgiven save those who had done no wrong ; an episcopal inquisition stimulated to renewed exertions, on the ground that the papal functionaries were to be discharged; and a promise that, although the proposed Moderation of the edicts seemed too mild for the monarch's acceptance, yet at some future period another project would be matured for settling the matter to universal satisfaction—such were the propositions of the Crown. Nevertheless, Philip thought he had gone too far, even in administering this meagre amount of mercy, and that he had been too frank in employing so slender a deception, as in the scheme thus sketched. He therefore summoned a notary, before whom, in presence of the Duke of Alva, the Licentiate Menchaca and Dr. Velasco, he declared that, although he had just authorized Margaret of Parma, by force of circumstances, to grant pardon to all those who had been compromised in the late disturbances of the Netherlands, yet as he had not done this spontaneously nor freely, he did not consider himself bound by the authorization, but that, on the contrary, he reserved his right to punish all the guilty, and particularly those who had been the authors and encouragers of the sedition.†

So much for the *pardon* promised in his official correspondence.

With regard to the concessions, which he supposed himself to have made in the matter of the inquisition and the edicts,

---

* Correspondance de Marg. d'Autriche, 100–103, sqq.
† Correspondance de Philippe II., i. 443.

he saved his conscience by another process.   Revoking with his right hand all which his left had been doing, he had no sooner despatched his letters to the Duchess Regent than he sent off another to his envoy at Rome.* In this despatch he instructed Requesens to inform the Pope as to the recent royal decisions upon the three points, and to state that there had not been time to consult his Holiness beforehand.   Nevertheless, continued Philip " the prudent," *it was perhaps better thus*, since the *abolition could have no force*, unless the Pope, by whom the institution had been established, consented to its suspension. This *matter, however, was to be kept a profound secret*.†   So much for the inquisition matter.   The papal institution, notwithstanding the official letters, was to exist, unless the Pope chose to destroy it ; and his Holiness, as we have seen, had sent the Archbishop of Sorrento, a few weeks before, to Brussels, for the purpose of concerting secret measures for strengthening the " Holy Office" in the provinces.

With regard to the proposed moderation of the edicts, Philip informed Pius the Fifth, through Requesens, that the project sent by the Duchess not having been approved, orders had been transmitted for a new draft, in which all the articles providing for *the severe punishment of heretics were to be retained*, while alterations, to be agreed upon by the state and privy councils, and the knights of the Fleece, were to be adopted—certainly in no sense of clemency.   On the contrary, the King assured his Holiness, that if the *severity of chastisement should be mitigated* the least in the world by the new articles, they would in no case receive the royal approbation. Philip further implored the Pope " not to be scandalized" with regard to the proposed pardon, as it would be by no means extended to offenders against religion.   All this was to be kept entirely secret.   The King added, that rather than permit the least prejudice to the ancient religion, he would sacrifice all his states, and lose a hundred lives if he had so many ; for he would never consent to be the sovereign of

---

* Correspondance de Philippe II., i. 445, 446.   † Ibid.

heretics. He said he would arrange the troubles of the Netherlands, without violence, if possible, because forcible measures would cause the entire destruction of the country. Nevertheless they should be employed, if his purpose could be accomplished in no other way. In that case the King would himself be the executor of his own design, without allowing the peril which he should incur, nor the ruin of the provinces, nor that of his other realms, to prevent him from doing all which a Christian prince was bound to do, to maintain the Catholic religion and the authority of the Holy See, as well as to testify his personal regard for the reigning pontiff, whom he so much loved and esteemed.*

Here was plain speaking. Here were all the coming horrors distinctly foreshadowed. Here was the truth told to the only being with whom Philip ever was sincere. Yet even on this occasion, he permitted himself a falsehood by which his Holiness was not deceived. Philip had no intention of going to the Netherlands in person, and the Pope knew that he had none. "I feel it in my bones," said Granvelle, mournfully, "that nobody in Rome believes in his Majesty's journey to the provinces."† From that time forward, however, the King began to promise this visit, which was held out as a panacea for every ill, and made to serve as an excuse for constant delay.

It may well be supposed that if Philip's secret policy had been thoroughly understood in the Netherlands, the outbreak would have come sooner. On the receipt, however, of the public despatches from Madrid, the administration in Brussels made great efforts to represent their tenor as highly satisfactory. The papal inquisition was to be abolished, a pardon was to be granted, a new moderation was to be arranged at some indefinite period ; what more would men have ? Yet without seeing the face of the cards, the people suspected the real truth, and Orange was convinced of it. Viglius wrote that if the King did not make his intended visit soon, he

---

* Correspondance de Philippe II., ii. 445, 446.

† Siento en los huessos."—Ibid., 318.

would come too late, and that every week more harm was done by procrastination than could be repaired by months of labor and perhaps by torrents of blood.* What the precise process was, through which Philip was to cure all disorders by his simple presence, the President did not explain.

As for the measures propounded by the King after so long a delay, they were of course worse than useless ; for events had been marching while he had been musing. The course suggested was, according to Viglius, but " a plaster for a wound, but a drag-chain for the wheel."† He urged that the convocation of the states-general was the only remedy for the perils in which the country was involved, unless the King should come in person. He however expressed the hope that by general consultation some means would be devised by which, if not a good, at least a less desperate aspect would be given to public affairs, " so that the commonwealth, if fall it must, might at least fall upon its feet like a cat, and break its legs rather than its neck."‡

Notwithstanding this highly figurative view of the subject, and notwithstanding the urgent representations of Duchess Margaret to her brother, that nobles and people were all clamoring about the necessity of convening the states-general,§ Philip was true to his instincts on this as on the other questions. He knew very well that the states-general of the Netherlands and Spanish despotism were incompatible ideas, and he recoiled from the idea of the assembly with infinite aversion. At the same time a little wholesome deception could do no harm. He wrote to the Duchess, therefore, that he was determined *never to allow the* states-general to be convened. He forbade her to consent to the step under any circumstances, but ordered her to *keep his prohibition a profound secret.* He wished, he said, the people to think that it was only for the moment that the convocation was forbidden,

---

* Ep. ad Joach. Hopperum, 366, 367.

† Ibid., 376.   ‡ Ibid.

§ Unpublished letter of Margaret of Parma (13th Sept., 1566). Brussels Archives, before cited.

and that the Duchess was expecting to receive the necessary permission at another time. It was his desire, he distinctly stated, that the people should not despair of obtaining the assembly, but *he was resolved never to consent* to the step, for he knew very well what was meant by a meeting of the states-general.* Certainly after so ingenuous but secret a declaration from the disciple of Macchiavelli, Margaret might well consider the arguments to be used afterward by herself and others, in favor of the ardently desired measure, as quite superfluous.

Such then was the policy secretly resolved upon by Philip, even before he heard of the startling events which were afterwards to break upon him. He would maintain the inquisition and the edicts; he would exterminate the heretics, even if he lost all his realms and his own life in the cause; he would never hear of the national representatives coming together. What then were likely to be his emotions when he should be told of twenty thousand armed heretics assembling at one spot, and fifteen thousand at another, in almost every town in every province, to practice their blasphemous rites; when he should be told of the whirlwind which had swept all the ecclesiastical accumulations of ages out of existence; when he should read Margaret's despairing letters, in which she acknowledged that she had at last committed an act unworthy of God, of her King, and of herself,† in permitting liberty of worship to the renegades from the ancient church!

The account given by the Duchess was in truth very dismal. She said that grief consumed her soul and crimson suffused her cheeks while she related the recent transactions. She took God to witness that she had resisted long, that she had past many sleepless nights, that she had been wasted with fever and grief.‡ After this penitential preface she confessed that, being a prisoner and almost besieged in her palace, sick in body and soul, she had promised pardon and security to the

---

* Correspondance de Philippe II., i. 439.   † Strada, v. 222, 223.

‡ Ibid. Compare Correspondance de Marg. d'Autriche, 187–200. Correspondance de Philippe II., i. 452–454

confederates, with liberty of holding assemblies to heretics in places where the practice had already obtained. These concessions had been made valid until the King by and with the consent of the states-general, should definitely arrange the matter. She stated, however, that she had given her consent to these two demands, not in the royal name, but in her own. The King was not bound by her promise, and she *expressed the hope that he would have no regard* to any such obligation. She further implored her brother to come forth as soon as possible to avenge the injuries inflicted upon the ancient church, adding, that if deprived of that consolation, she should incontinently depart this life. That hope alone would prevent her death.*

This was certainly strong language. She was also very explicit in her representations of the influence which had been used by certain personages to prevent the exercise of any authority upon her own part. "Wherefore," said Margaret, " I eat my heart, and shall never have peace till the arrival of your Majesty."†

There was no doubt who those personages were who, as it was pretended, had thus held the Duchess in bondage, and compelled her to grant these infamous concessions. In her secret Italian letters, she furnished the King with a tissue of most extravagant and improbable falsehoods, supplied to her mainly by Noircarmes and Mansfeld, as to the course pursued at this momentous crisis by Orange, Egmont, Horn, and Hoogstraaten. They had all, she said, declared against God and against religion.‡ Horn, at least, was for killing all the priests and monks in the country, if full satisfaction were not given to the demands of the heretics. Egmont had declared openly for the beggars, and was levying troops in Germany. Orange had the firm intention of making himself master of

---

* Strada, ubi sup. Correspondance de Marg. d'Autriche, ubi sup. Correspondance de Philippe II., i. ubi sup.

† "Pourquoy je me mange le cœur, et n'en serois quitte sans la presence de Vostre Majesté."—Correspondance de Marg. d'Autriche, 202.

‡ Correspondance de Philippe II., i. 452–454.

the whole country, and of dividing it among the other
seigniors and himself.* The Prince had said that if she took
refuge in Mons, as she had proposed, they would instantly
convoke the states-general, and take all necessary measures.
Egmont had held the same language, saying that he would
march at the head of forty thousand men to besiege her in
that city.† All these seigniors, however, had avowed their
determination to prevent her flight, to assemble the estates,
and to drag her by force before the assembly, in order to compel her consent to every measure which might be deemed
expedient.‡ Under all these circumstances, she had been
obliged to defer her retreat, and to make the concessions which
had overwhelmed her with disgrace.

With such infamous calumnies, utterly disproved by every
fact in the case, and unsupported by a tittle of evidence, save
the hearsay reports of a man like Noircarmes, did this " woman,
nourished at Rome, in whom no one could put confidence,"§
dig the graves of men who were doing their best to serve her.

Philip's rage at first hearing of the image-breaking has
been indicated. He was ill of an intermittent fever at the
wood of Segovia when the news arrived,‖ and it may well be
supposed that his wrath at these proceedings was not likely to
assuage his malady. Nevertheless, after the first burst of
indignation, he found relief in his usual deception. While
slowly maturing the most tremendous vengeance which
anointed monarch ever deliberately wreaked upon his people,
he wrote to say, that it was " his intention to treat his vassals
and subjects in the provinces like a good and clement prince,
not to ruin them nor to put them into servitude, but to exercise all humanity, sweetness, and grace, avoiding all harsh-
ness."¶ Such were the avowed intentions of the sovereign
towards his people at the moment when the terrible Alva,
who was to be the exponent of all this " humanity, sweetness,

---

* Correspondance de Philippe II., i. 452–454.   † Ibid.   ‡ Ibid.
§ Groen v. Prinst., Archives, etc., ii. 401.   Expression of Egmont's.
‖ Hopper, Rec. et Mem., 104.
¶ Correspondance de Marg. d'Autriche, 206, 207.—Letter of Nov. 27, 1566.

and grace," was already beginning the preparations for his famous invasion of the Netherlands.

The essence of the compact agreed to upon the 23d August between the confederates and the Regent, was that the preaching of the reformed religion should be tolerated in places where it had previously to that date been established. Upon this basis Egmont, Horn, Orange, Hoogstraaten, and others, were directed once more to attempt the pacification of the different provinces.

Egmont departed for his government of Flanders, and from that moment vanished all his pretensions, which at best had been slender enough, to the character of a national chieftain. During the whole of the year his course had been changeful. He had felt the influence of Orange ; he had generous instincts ; he had much vanity ; he had the pride of high rank, which did not easily brook the domination of strangers, in a land which he considered himself and his compeers entitled by their birth to rule. At this juncture, however, particularly when in the company of Noircarmes, Berlaymont, and Viglius, he expressed, notwithstanding their calumnious misstatements, the deepest detestation of the heretics.* He was a fervent Catholic, and he regarded the image-breaking as an unpardonable crime. "We must take up arms," said he, "sooner or later, to bring these Reformers to reason, or they will end by laying down the law for us."† On the other hand, his anger would be often appeased by the grave but gracious remonstrances of Orange. During a part of the summer, the Reformers had been so strong in Flanders that upon a single day sixty thousand armed men had been assembled at the different field-preachings within that province. "All they needed was a Jacquemart, or a Philip van Artevelde," says a Catholic contemporary, "but they would have scorned to march under the banner of a brewer ; having dared to raise their eyes for a chief, to the most illustrious warrior of his age.‡ No doubt, had Egmont ever listened to these aspirations,

---

* Pontus Payen MS.   † Ibid.   ‡ Ibid.

he might have taken the field against the government with an invincible force, seized the capital, imprisoned the Regent, and mastered the whole country, which was entirely defenceless, before Philip would have had time to write more than ten despatches upon the subject.

These hopes of the Reformers, if hopes they could be called, were now destined to be most bitterly disappointed. Egmont entered Flanders, not as a chief of rebels—not as a wise pacificator, but as an unscrupulous partisan of government, disposed to take summary vengeance on all suspected persons who should fall in his way. He ordered numerous executions of image-breakers and of other heretics. The whole province was in a state of alarm; for, although he had not been furnished by the Regent with a strong body of troops, yet the name of the conqueror at Saint Quentin and Gravelines was worth many regiments. His severity was excessive.* His sanguinary exertions were ably seconded also by his secretary Bakkerzeel, a man who exercised the greatest influence over his chief, and who was now fiercely atoning for having signed the Compromise by persecuting those whom that league had been formed to protect. "Amid all the perplexities of the Duchess Regent," says a Walloon historian, "this virtuous princess was consoled by the exploits of Bakkerzeel, gentleman in Count Egmont's service. On one occasion he hanged twenty heretics, including a minister, at a single heat."†

Such achievements as these by the hands or the orders of the distinguished general who had been most absurdly held up as a possible protector of the civil and religious liberties of the country, created profound sensation. Flanders and Artois were filled with the wives and children of suspected thousands who had fled the country to escape the wrath of Egmont.‡ The cries and piteous lamentations of these unfortunate creatures were heard on every side. Count Louis was

---

* Pontus Payen MS. Compare Groen v. Prinst., Archives, etc., ii. 282–297.
† Renom de France MS., l. 33.
‡ Groen v. Prinst., Archives, etc., ii. 296, 297.

earnestly implored to intercede for the persecuted Reformers. " You who have been so nobly gifted by Heaven, you who have good will and singular bounty written upon your face," said Utenhove to Louis, " have the power to save these poor victims from the throats of the ravenous wolves."* The Count responded to the appeal, and strove to soften the severity of Egmont, without, however, producing any very signal effect. Flanders was soon pacified, nor was that important province permitted to enjoy the benefits of the agreement which had been extorted from the Duchess. The preachings were forbidden, and the ministers and congregations arrested and chastised, even in places where the custom had been established previously to the 23d August.† Certainly such vigorous exertions upon the part both of master and man did not savor of treason to Philip, and hardly seemed to indicate the final doom of Egmont and Bakkerzeel.

The course of Orange at Antwerp was consistent with his whole career. He honestly came to arrange a pacification, but he knew that this end could be gained only by loyally maintaining the Accord which had been signed between the confederates and the Regent. He came back to the city on the 26th August,‡ and found order partially re-established. The burghers having at last become thoroughly alarmed, and the fury of the image-breakers entirely appeased, it had been comparatively easy to restore tranquillity. The tranquillity, however, rather restored itself, and when the calm had succeeded to the tempest, the placid heads of the burgomasters once more emerged from the waves.

Three image-breakers, who had been taken in the act, were hanged by order of the magistrates upon the 28th of August.§

---

* Groen v. Prinst., Archives, etc., ii. 296, 297.
† Ibid.   ‡ Ibid, ii. 261.
§ This is the account of Hoofd, iii. 110, 111. The three rioters were executed, not by command of the Prince (as stated by M. Groen v. Prinsterer, Archives, et Correspondance, ii. 261,) but by that of the civic authorities—"en alstoen moedt geschept hebbende, ten derden daaghen daar naa, drie van de gevange beeldstormers met de galge, de rest met ballingshap oft anders straften."—Hoofd, ubi sup.

The presence of Orange gave them courage to achieve these executions which he could not prevent, as the fifth article of the Accord enjoined the chastisement of the rioters. The magistrates chose that the " chastisement" on this occasion should be exemplary, and it was not in the power of Orange to interfere with the regular government of the city when acting according to its laws. The deed was not his, however, and he hastened, in order to obviate the necessity of further violence, to prepare articles of agreement, upon the basis of Margaret's concessions. Public preaching, according to the Reformed religion, had already taken place within the city. Upon the 22d, possession had been taken of at least three churches. The senate had deputed pensionary Wesenbeck to expostulate with the ministers, for the magistrates were at that moment not able to command. Taffin, the Walloon preacher, had been tractable, and had agreed to postpone his exercises. He furthermore had accompanied the pensionary to the cathedral, in order to persuade Herman Modet that it would be better for him likewise to defer his intended ministrations.* They had found that eloquent enthusiast already in the great church, burning with impatience to ascend upon the ruins, and quite unable to resist the temptation of setting a Flemish psalm and preaching a Flemish sermon within the walls which had for so many centuries been vocal only to the Roman tongue and the Roman ritual. All that he would concede to the entreaties of his colleague and of the magistrate, was that his sermon should be short. In this, however, he had over-rated his powers of retention, for the sermon not only became a long one, but he had preached another upon the afternoon of the same day. The city of Antwerp, therefore, was clearly within the seventh clause of the treaty of the 24th August, for preaching had taken place in the cathedral, previously to the signing of that Accord.†

Upon the 2d September, therefore, after many protracted

---

* Bor, ii. 85. Hoofd, iii. 102. Wesenbeck.
† Bor, ii. 85, 86. Hoofd, iii. 102. Wesenbeck.

interview with the heads of the Reformed religion, the Prince drew up sixteen articles of agreement between them, the magistrates and the government, which were duly signed and exchanged.* They were conceived in the true spirit of statesmanship, and could the rulers of the land have elevated themselves to the mental height of William de Nassau, had Philip been able of comprehending such a mind, the Prince, who alone possessed the power in those distracted times of governing the wills of all men, would have enabled the monarch to transmit that beautiful cluster of provinces, without the loss of a single jewel, to the inheritors of his crown.

If the Prince were playing a game, he played it honorably. To have conceived the thought of religious toleration in an age of universal dogmatism ; to have labored to produce mutual respect among conflicting opinions, at a period when many Dissenters were as bigoted as the orthodox, and when most Reformers fiercely proclaimed not liberty for every Christian doctrine, but only a new creed in place of all the rest,† to have admitted the possibility of several roads to heaven, when zealots of all creeds would shut up all pathways but their own ; if such sentiments and purposes were sins, they would have been ill-exchanged for the best virtues of the age. Yet, no doubt, this was his crying offence in the opinion of many contemporaries. He was now becoming apostate from the ancient Church, but he had long thought that Emperors, Kings, and Popes had taken altogether too much care of men's souls in times past, and had sent too many of them prematurely to their great account. He was equally indisposed to grant full powers for the same purpose to Calvinists, Lutherans, or Anabaptists. "He censured the severity of our theologians," said a Catholic contemporary, accumulating all the religious offences of the Prince in a single paragraph, "because they keep strictly the constitutions of the Church without conceding a single point to their adversaries ; he blamed the Calvinists as seditious and unruly people, yet

---

* Bor, iii. 98, 99, gives the articles.   † Pontus Payen MS.

nevertheless had a horror for the imperial edicts which condemned them to death; he said it was a cruel thing to take a man's life for sustaining an erroneous opinion; in short, he fantasied in his imagination a kind of religion, half Catholic, half Reformed, in order to content all persons; a system which would have been adopted could he have had his way."* This picture, drawn by one of his most brilliant and bitter enemies, excites our admiration while intended to inspire aversion.

The articles of agreement at Antwerp thus promulgated assigned three churches to the different sects of reformers, stipulated that no attempt should be made by Catholics or Protestants to disturb the religious worship of each other, and provided that neither by mutual taunts in their sermons, nor by singing street ballads, together with improper allusions and overt acts of hostility, should the good-fellowship which ought to reign between brethren and fellow-citizens, even although entertaining different opinions as to religious rites and doctrines, be for the future interrupted.†

This was the basis upon which the very brief religious peace, broken almost as soon as established, was concluded by William of Orange, not only at Antwerp, but at Utrecht,‡ Amsterdam,§ and other principal cities within his government.

The Prince, however, notwithstanding his unwearied exertions, had slender hopes of a peaceful result. He felt that the last step taken by the Reformation had been off a precipice. He liked not such rapid progress. He knew that the King would never forgive the image-breaking. He felt that he would never recognize the Accord of the 24th August. Sir Thomas Gresham, who, as the representative of the Protestant Queen of England in the great commercial metropolis of Europe, was fully conversant with the turn things were taking, was already advising some other place for the sale of English commodities. He gave notice to his government that commerce would have no security at Antwerp " in those

---

* Pontus Payen MS.
‡ Bor, ii. 101, 102.

† Articles in Bor, ii. 98, 99.
§ Ibid., ii., 101.

brabbling times." He was on confidential terms with the Prince, who invited him to dine upon the 4th September, and caused pensionary Wesenbeck, who was also present, to read aloud the agreement which was that day to be proclaimed at the town-house. Orange expressed himself, however, very doubtfully as to the future prospects of the provinces, and as to the probable temper of the King. " In all his talke," says Gresham, " the Prince saide unto me, ' I know this will nothing contente the King.' "*

While Egmont had been thus busied in Flanders, and Orange at Antwerp, Count Horn had been doing his best in the important city of Tournay.† The Admiral was not especially gifted with intellect, nor with the power of managing men, but he went there with an honest purpose of seeing the Accord executed, intending, if it should prove practicable, rather to favor the Government than the Reformers. At the same time, for the purpose of giving satisfaction to the members of " the religion," and of manifesting his sincere desire for a pacification, he accepted lodgings which had been prepared for him at the house of a Calvinist merchant in the city,‡ rather than take up his quarters with fierce old governor Moulbais in the citadel. This gave much offence to the Catholics, and inspired the Reformers, with the hope of having their preaching inside the town. To this privilege they were entitled, for the practice had already been established there, previously to the 24th October.§ Nevertheless, at first he was disposed to limit them, in accordance with the wishes of the Duchess, to extra-mural exercises.

Upon his arrival, by a somewhat ominous conjuncture, he had supped with some of the leading citizens in the hall of the " gehenna" or torture room,‖ certainly not a locality calculated to inspire a healthy appetite. On the following Sunday he had been entertained with a great banquet, at

---

* Burgon, ii. 161, 162.   † Groen v. Prinst., Archives, etc., ii. 362, note.
‡ Pasquier de la Barre MS., 36ᵛᵒ.
§ Letter of Horn to Duchess of Parma in Foppens, Supplément, ii. 393.
‖ Pasquier de la Barre MS., 36ᵛᵒ.

which all the principal burghers were present, held in a house on the market-place.*　The festivities had been interrupted by a quarrel, which had been taking place in the cathedral. Beneath the vaults of that edifice, tradition said that a vast treasure was hidden, and the canons had been known to boast that this buried wealth would be sufficient to rebuild their temple more magnificently than ever, in case of its total destruction.†　The Admiral had accordingly placed a strong guard in the church as soon as he arrived, and commenced very extensive excavations in search of this imaginary mine.　The Regent informed her brother that the Count was prosecuting this work with the view of appropriating whatever might be found to his own benefit.‡　As she knew that he was a ruined man, there seemed no more satisfactory mode of accounting for these proceedings.　Horn had, however, expressly stated to her that every penny which should come into his possession from that or any other source would carefully be restored to the rightful owners.§　Nothing of consequence was ever found to justify the golden legends of the monks, but in the mean time the money-diggers gave great offence.　The canons, naturally alarmed for the safety of their fabulous treasure, had forced the guard, by surreptitiously obtaining the countersign from a certain official of the town.‖　A quarrel ensued which ended in the appearance of this personage, together with the commander of the military force on guard in the cathedral, before the banqueting company.　The Count, in the rough way habitual with him, gave the culprit a sound rebuke for his intermeddling, and threatened, in case the offence were repeated, to have him instantly bound, gagged, and forwarded to Brussels for further punishment.¶　The matter thus satisfactorily adjusted, the banquet proceeded, the merchants present being all delighted at seeing the said

---

* De la Barre MS. 42vo.   † Ibid.

‡ Correspondance de Philippe II., i. 466–468.

§ Letter of Horn to Duchess of Parma.　Foppens, Supplément, ii. 427.　Compare letter of Duchess to Horn, p. 408.

‖ De la Barre MS. 42vo   ¶ Ibid.

official, who was exceedingly unpopular, " so well huffed by the Count."* The excavations were continued for a long time, until there seemed danger of destroying the foundation of the church, but only a few bits of money were discovered, with some other articles of small value.†

Horn had taken his apartments in the city in order to be at hand to suppress any tumults, and to inspire confidence in the people. He had come to a city where five sixths of the inhabitants‡ were of the reformed religion, and he did not, therefore, think it judicious to attempt violently the suppression of their worship. Upon his arrival he had issued a proclamation, ordering that all property which might have been pillaged from the religious houses should be instantly restored to the magistracy, under penalty that all who disobeyed the command should " be forthwith strangled at the gibbet." Nothing was brought back, however, for the simple reason that nothing had been stolen.§ There was, therefore, no one to be strangled.

The next step was to publish the Accord of 24th August, and to signify the intention of the Admiral to enforce its observance. The preachings were as enthusiastically attended as ever, while the storm which had been raging among the images had in the mean time been entirely allayed. Congregations of fifteen thousand were still going to hear Ambrose Wille in the suburbs, but they were very tranquil in their demeanor.‖ It was arranged between the Admiral and the leaders of the reformed consistories, that three places, to be selected by Horn, should be assigned for their places of worship.¶ At these spots, which were outside the walls, permission was given the Reformers to build meeting-houses.** To this arrangement the Duchess formally gave her consent.††

Nicholas Taffin, councillor, in the name of the Reformers,

---

* " Fort joyeulx que le contente avoit ainsi espouffé le dict procureur."—Ibid.

† Letter of Horn. Foppens, Supplément, 396.

‡ De la Barre MS., f. 46–60. Foppens, Supplément, 396.

§ Foppens, Supplément, ii. 382.   ‖ De la Barre MS., 38, sqq.

¶ De la Barre MS., 44.   ** Ibid.   †† Foppens, Supplément, ii. 407.

made " a brave and elegant harangue" before the magistrates, representing that, as on the most moderate computation, three quarters of the population were dissenters, as the Regent had ordered the construction of the new temples, and as the Catholics retained possession of all the churches in the city, it was no more than fair that the community should bear the expense of the new buildings. It was indignantly replied, however, that Catholics could not be expected to pay for the maintenance of heresy, particularly when they had just been so much exasperated by the image-breaking. Councillor Taffin took nothing, therefore by his " brave and elegant harangue," saving a small vote of forty livres.

The building was, however, immediately commenced. Many nobles and rich citizens contributed to the work ; some making donations in money ; others giving quantities of oaks, poplars, elms, and other timber trees, to be used in the construction. The foundation of the first temple outside the Porte de Cocquerel was immediately laid. Vast heaps of broken images and other ornaments of the desecrated churches were most unwisely used for this purpose, and the Catholics were exceedingly enraged at beholding those male and female saints, who had for centuries been placed in such " reverend and elevated positions," fallen so low as to be the foundation-stones of temples whose builders denounced all those holy things as idols.*

As the autumn began to wane, the people were clamorous for permission to have their preaching inside the city. The new buildings could not be finished before the winter ; but in the mean time the camp-meetings were becoming, in the stormy seasons fast approaching, a very inconvenient mode of worship. On the other hand, the Duchess was furious at the proposition, and commanded Horn on no account to consent that the interior of Tournay should be profaned by these heretical rites.†
It was in vain that the Admiral represented the justice of the

---

* De la Barre MS., 46, sqq.
† Letter of Duchess of Parma.   Foppens, Supplément, ii. 406.

claim, as these exercises had taken place in several of the city churches previously to the Accord of the 24th of August.* That agreement had been made by the Duchess only to be broken. She had already received money and the permission to make levies, and was fast assuming a tone very different from the abject demeanor which had characterized her in August. Count Horn had been used even as Egmont, Orange and Hoogstraaten had been employed, in order that their personal influence with the Reformers might be turned to account. The tools and the work accomplished by them were to be thrown away at the most convenient opportunity.

The Admiral was placed in a most intolerable position. An honest, common-place, sullen kind of man, he had come to a city full of heretics, to enforce concessions just made by the government to heresy. He soon found himself watched, paltered with, suspected by the administration at Brussels. Governor Moulbais in the citadel, who was nominally under his authority, refused obedience to his orders, was evidently receiving secret instructions from the Regent, and was determined to cannonade the city into submission at a very early day. Horn required him to pledge himself that no fresh troops should enter the castle. Moulbais swore he would make no such promise to a living soul. The Admiral stormed with his usual violence, expressed his regret that his brother Montigny had so bad a lieutenant in the citadel, but could make no impression upon the determined veteran, who knew, better than Horn, the game which was preparing.† Small reinforcements were daily arriving at the castle ; the soldiers of the garrison had been heard to boast " that they would soon carve and eat the townsmen's flesh on their dressers,"‡ and all the good effect from the Admiral's proclamation on arriving, had completely vanished.

Horn complained bitterly of the situation in which he was placed. He knew himself the mark of incessant and calum-

---

* Foppens, Supplément, ii. 393.   † De la Barre MS., 50ʳᵒ.
‡ " Ils mengheroient leur chair sur leur trestchoir."—Ibid., 24.

nious misrepresentation both at Brussels and Madrid. He had been doing his best, at a momentous crisis, to serve the government without violating its engagements, but he declared himself to be neither theologian nor jurist, and incapable, while suspected and unassisted, of performing a task which the most learned doctors of the council would find impracticable. He would rather, he bitterly exclaimed, endure a siege in any fortress by the Turks, than be placed in such a position. He was doing all that he was capable of doing, yet whatever he did was wrong. There was a great difference, he said, between being in a place and talking about it at a distance.*

In the middle of October he was recalled by the Duchess, whose letters had been uniformly so ambiguous that he confessed he was quite unable to divine their meaning.† Before he left the city, he committed his most unpardonable crime. Urged by the leaders of the reformed congregations to permit their exercises in the Clothiers' Hall until their temples should be finished, the Count accorded his consent provisionally, and subject to revocation by the Regent, to whom the arrangement was immediately to be communicated.

Horn departed, and the Reformers took instant possession of the hall. It was found in a very dirty and disorderly condition, encumbered with benches, scaffoldings, stakes, gibbets, and all the machinery used for public executions upon the market-place. A vast body of men went to work with a will ; scrubbing, cleaning, whitewashing, and removing all the foul lumber of the hall ; singing in chorus, as they did so, the hymns of Clement Marot. By dinner-time the place was ready.‡ The pulpit and benches for the congregation had taken the place of the gibbet timber. It is difficult to comprehend that such work as this was a deadly crime. Nevertheless, Horn, *who was himself a sincere Catholic*, had committed the most mortal of all his offences against Philip and

---

* Letter to Duchess of Parma; Foppens, Supplément, ii. 412, 413.

† Letter of Horn to Philip II., in Foppens, Supplément, ii. 499–506.

‡ De la Barre MS., 50ᵛ⁰.

against God, by having countenanced so flagitious a transaction.

The Admiral went to Brussels. Secretary de la Torre,* a very second-rate personage, was despatched to Tournay to convey the orders of the Regent. Governor Moulbais, now in charge of affairs both civil and military, was to prepare all things for the garrison, which was soon to be despatched under Noircarmes. The Duchess had now arms in her hands, and her language was bold. La Torre advised the Reformers to be wise " while the rod was yet green and growing, lest it should be gathered for their backs ; for it was unbecoming in subjects to make bargains with their King."† There was hardly any decent pretext used in violating the Accord of the 24th August, so soon as the government was strong enough to break it. It was always said that the preachings suppressed, had not been established previously to that arrangement ; but the preachings had in reality obtained almost every where, and were now universally abolished. The ridiculous quibble was also used that, in the preachings other religious exercises were not included, whereas it was notorious that they had never been separated. It is, however, a gratuitous task to unravel the deceptions of tyranny when it hardly deigns to disguise itself. The dissimulations which have resisted the influence of centuries are more worthy of serious investigation, and of these the epoch offers us a sufficient supply.

At the close of the year, the city of Tournay was completely subjugated and the reformed religion suppressed. Upon the 2nd day of January, 1567, the Seignior de Noircarmes arrived before the gates at the head of eleven com-

---

* La Torre arrived in Tournay upon the 28th October, 1566, according to the narrative of De la Barre. That manuscript (now in the Brussels Archives, and the only copy known to exist) was afterwards laid before the Blood Council. Secretary La Torre has noticed in several places on the margin, "the author lies," (l'autheur ment.) The passages thus discredited by this very common-place tool of tyranny have only reference to himself.—Pasquier de la Barre MS., f°. 57ᵛᵒ., 59.   † Renom de France MS., i. c. 23.

panies, with orders from Duchess Margaret to strengthen the garrison and disarm the citizens.* He gave the magistrates exactly one hour and a half to decide whether they would submit without a murmur.† He expressed an intention of maintaining the Accord of 24th August; a ridiculous affectation under the circumstances, as the event proved. The notables were summoned, submission agreed upon, and within the prescribed time the magistrates came before Noircarmes, with an unconditional acceptance of his terms.‡ That truculent personage told them, in reply, that they had done wisely, for if they had delayed receiving the garrison a minute longer, he would have instantly *burned the city to ashes and put every one of the inhabitants to the sword.*§ He had been fully authorized to do so, and subsequent events were to show, upon more than one dreadful occasion, how capable Noircarmes would have been of fulfilling this menace.

The soldiers, who had made a forced march all night, and who had been firmly persuaded that the city would refuse the terms demanded, were excessively disappointed at being obliged to forego the sack and pillage upon which they had reckoned.‖ Eight or nine hundred rascally peasants, too, who had followed in the skirts of the regiments, each provided with a great empty bag, which they expected to fill with booty which they might purchase of the soldiers, or steal in the midst of the expected carnage and rapine, shared the discontent of the soldiery, by whom they were now driven ignominiously out of the town.¶ The citizens were immediately disarmed. All the fine weapons which they had been obliged to purchase at their own expense, when they had been arranged by the magistrates under eight banners, for defence of the city against tumult and invasion, were taken from them; the most beautiful cutlasses, carbines,

---

* Pasquier de la Barre MS.

† De la Barre MS., 77ᵛᵒ., 78.   ‡ Ibid., 78ᵛᵒ.

§ "Disant que la ville estait bien conseillée d'avoir obey à Sa Maj. sans avᵣ fait quelqᵉ rebellion, ajoutant que si quelque resistance luy heust este donnée à introduire la garnison, qu'il avoit charge expresse de luy bouter par forche et mettre la ville en feu et tous les manans et habitans au fil de l'espée."—De la Barre MS., 78ᵛᵒ.   ‖ Ibid., 79.   ¶ Ibid., 81.

poniards, and pistols, being divided by Noircarmes among his officers.* Thus Tournay was tranquillized.

During the whole of these proceedings in Flanders, and at Antwerp, Tournay, and Mechlin, the conduct of the Duchess had been marked with more than her usual treachery. She had been disavowing acts which the men upon whom she relied in her utmost need had been doing by her authority ; she had been affecting to praise their conduct, while she was secretly misrepresenting their actions and maligning their motives, and she had been straining every nerve to make foreign levies, while attempting to amuse the confederates and sectaries with an affectation of clemency.

When Orange complained that she had been censuring his proceedings at Antwerp, and holding language unfavorable to his character, she protested that she thoroughly approved his arrangements—excepting only the two points of the intramural preachings and the permission to heretics of other exercises than sermons—and that if she were displeased with him he might be sure that she would rather tell him so than speak ill of him behind his back.† The Prince, who had been compelled by necessity, and fully authorized by the terms of the " Accord," to grant those two points which were the vital matter in his arrangements,. answered very calmly, that he was not so frivolous as to believe in her having used language to his discredit had he not been quite certain of the fact, as he would soon prove by evidence.‡ Orange was not the man to be deceived as to the position in which he stood, nor as to the character of those with whom he dealt. Margaret wrote, however, in the same vein concerning him to Hoogstraaten, affirming that nothing could be further from her intention than to characterize the proceedings of " her cousin, the Prince of Orange, as contrary to the service of his Majesty; knowing, as she did, how constant had been his affection, and how diligent his actions, in the cause of God and the King."§

---

* De la Barre MS., 91.
† Correspondance de Guillaume le Tacit, ii. 233–235.   ‡ Ibid., 239.
§ La défense du Comte de Hocstrate, 95.

She also sent councillor d'Assonleville on a special mission to the Prince, instructing that smooth personage to inform her said cousin of Orange that he was and always had been "loved and cherished by his Majesty, and that for herself she had ever loved him like a brother or a child."*

She wrote to Horn, approving of his conduct in the main, although in obscure terms, and expressing great confidence in his zeal, loyalty, and good intentions.† She accorded the same praise to Hoogstraaten, while as to Egmont she was perpetually reproaching him for the suspicions which he seemed obstinately to entertain as to her disposition and that of Philip, in regard to his conduct and character.‡

It has already been partly seen what were her private sentiments and secret representations as to the career of the distinguished personages thus encouraged and commended. Her pictures were painted in daily darkening colors. She told her brother that Orange, Egmont, and Horn were about to place themselves at the head of the confederates, who were to take up arms and had been levying troops ; that the Lutheran religion was to be forcibly established, that the whole power of the government was to be placed in the triumvirate thus created by those seigniors, and that Philip was in reality to be excluded entirely from those provinces which were his ancient patrimony.§ All this information she had obtained from Mansfeld, at whom the nobles were constantly sneering as at a faithful valet who would never receive his wages.‖

She also informed the King that the scheme for dividing the country was already arranged : that Augustus of Saxony was to have Friesland and Overyssel ; Count Brederode, Holland ; the Dukes of Cleves and Lorraine, Gueldres ; the King of France, Flanders, Artois, and Hainault, of which territories Egmont was to be perpetual stadholder ; the Prince of Orange, Brabant ; and so on indefinitely.¶ A general massacre of all

---

* Correspondance de Guillaume le Tacit., ii. 391–397.
⌐ Foppens, Supplément, ii. 420, 421, 436.
‡ Correspondance de Philippe II., i. 493.
§ Ibid., i. 460, 461, 455, 456.   ‖ Ibid.   ¶ Ibid., i. 473–476.

the Catholics had been arranged by Orange, Horn, and Egmont, to commence as soon as the King should put his foot on shipboard to come to the country.* This last remarkable fact Margaret reported to Philip, upon the respectable authority of Noircarmes.†

She apologized *for having employed the service of these nobles, on the ground of necessity.* Their proceedings in Flanders, at Antwerp, Tournay, Mechlin, had been highly reprehensible, and she had been obliged to disavow them in the most important particulars. As for Egmont, she had most unwillingly entrusted forces to his hands for the purpose of putting down the Flemish sectaries. She had been afraid to show a want of confidence in his character, but at the same time she believed that all soldiers under Egmont's orders would be so many enemies to the king.‡ Notwithstanding his protestations of fidelity to the ancient religion and to his Majesty, she feared that he was busied with some great plot against God and the King.§ When we remember the ruthless manner in which the unfortunate Count had actually been raging against the sectaries, and the sanguinary proofs which he had been giving of his fidelity to " God and the King," it seems almost incredible that Margaret could have written down all these monstrous assertions.

The Duchess gave, moreover, repeated warnings to her brother, that the nobles were in the habit of obtaining possession of all the correspondence between Madrid and Brussels, and that they spent a vast deal of money in order to read her own and Philip's most private letters.‖ She warned him therefore, to be upon his guard, for she believed that almost all their despatches were read.¶ Such being the case, and the tenor of those documents being what we have seen it to be, her complaints as to the incredulity** of those seigniors to her affectionate protestations, seem quite wonderful.

---

* Correspondance de Philippe II., i. 484.
† Ibid.   ‡ Ibid., i. 459.   § Ibid.   ‖ Ibid., i. 475.   ¶ Ibid., i. 393.
** Correspondance de Philippe II., i.   Correspondance de Guillaume le Tacit., ii. passim.

CHAPTER IX.

IT is necessary to allude to certain important events contemporaneous with those recorded in the last chapter, that the
reader may thoroughly understand the position of the leading
personages in this great drama at the close of the year 1566.

The Prince of Orange had, as we have seen, been exerting
all his energies faithfully to accomplish the pacification of the
commercial metropolis, upon the basis assented to beforehand by the Duchess. He had established a temporary
religious peace, by which alone at that crisis the gathering
tempest could be averted ; but he had permitted the law to
take its course upon certain rioters, who had been regularly
condemned by courts of justice. He had worked day and
night—notwithstanding immense obstacles, calumnious mis-

statements, and conflicting opinions—to restore order out of chaos ; he had freely imperilled his own life—dashing into a tumultuous mob on one occasion, wounding several with the halberd which he snatched from one of his guard,* and dispersing almost with his single arm a dangerous and threatening insurrection—and he had remained in Antwerp, at the pressing solicitations of the magistracy, who represented that the lives of not a single ecclesiastic would be safe as soon as his back was turned, and that all the merchants would forthwith depart from the city.† It was nevertheless necessary that he should make a personal visit to his government of Holland, where similar disorders had been prevailing, and where men of all ranks and parties were clamoring for their stadholder.

Notwithstanding all his exertions however, he was thoroughly aware of the position in which he stood towards the government. The sugared phrases of Margaret, the deliberate commendation of the " benign and debonair" Philip, produced no effect upon this statesman, who was accustomed to look through and through men's actions to the core of their hearts. In the hearts of Philip and Margaret he already saw treachery and revenge indelibly imprinted. He had been especially indignant at the insult which the Duchess Regent had put upon him, by sending Duke Eric of Brunswick with an armed force into Holland in order to protect Gouda, Woerden, and other places within the Prince's own government.‡ He was thoroughly conversant with the general tone in which the other seigniors and himself were described to their sovereign. He was already convinced that the country was to be conquered by foreign mercenaries, and that his own life, with those of many other nobles, was to be sacrificed.§ The moment had arrived in which he was justified in looking about him for means of defence, both for himself and his country, if the King should be so insane as to carry out the purposes which the

---

* Antwerpsch Chronykje, p. 96; cited by Groen van Prinsterer, ii. 310.

† Correspondance de Guillaume le Tacit., ii. 239.

‡ Groen v. Prinst., Archives, ii. 322–326.

§ Correspondance de Guillaume le Tacit., ii. 391–397.

Prince suspected. The time was fast approaching in which a statesman placed upon such an elevation before the world as that which he occupied, would be obliged to choose his part for life. To be the unscrupulous tool of tyranny, a rebel, or an exile, was his necessary fate. To a man so prone to read the future, the moment for his choice seemed already arrived. Moreover, he thought it doubtful, and events were most signally to justify his doubts, whether he could be accepted as the instrument of despotism, even were he inclined to prostitute himself to such service. At this point, therefore, undoubtedly began the treasonable thoughts of William the Silent, if it be treason to attempt the protection of ancient and chartered liberties against a foreign oppressor. He despatched a private envoy to Egmont,* representing the grave suspicions manifested by the Duchess in sending Duke Eric into Holland, and proposing that means should be taken into consideration for obviating the dangers with which the country was menaced. Catholics as well as Protestants, he intimated, were to be crushed in one universal conquest as soon as Philip had completed the formidable preparations which he was making for invading the provinces. For himself, he said, he would not remain in the land to witness the utter desolation of the people, nor to fall an unresisting victim to the vengeance which he foresaw. If, however, he might rely upon the co-operation of Egmont and Horn, he was willing, with the advice of the states-general, to risk preparations against the armed invasion of Spaniards by which the country was to be reduced to slavery. It was incumbent, however, upon men placed as they were, "not to let the grass grow under their feet ;" and the moment for action was fast approaching.†

This was the scheme which Orange was willing to attempt. To make use of his own influence and that of his friends, to interpose between a sovereign insane with bigotry, and a people in a state of religious frenzy, to resist brutal violence if need should be by force, and to compel the sovereign to

---

* Groen v. Prinst., Archives, etc., ii. 323–326.   † Ibid.

respect the charters which he had sworn to maintain, and which were far more ancient than his sovereignty ; so much of treason did William of Orange already contemplate, for in no other way could he be loyal to his country and his own honor.

Nothing came of this secret embassy, for Egmont's heart and fate were already fixed. Before Orange departed, however, for the north, where his presence in the Dutch provinces was now imperatively required, a memorable interview took place at Dendermonde between Orange, Horn, Egmont, Hoogstraaten, and Count Louis.* The nature of this conference was probably similar to that of the secret mission from Orange to Egmont just recorded. It was not a long consultation. The gentlemen met at eleven o'clock, and conversed until dinner was ready, which was between twelve and one in the afternoon. They discussed the contents of a letter recently received by Horn from his brother Montigny at Segovia, giving a lively picture of Philip's fury at the recent events in the Netherlands, and expressing the Baron's own astonishment and indignation that it had been impossible for the seigniors to prevent such outrages as the public preaching, the image-breaking and the Accord. They had also some conversation concerning the dissatisfaction manifested by the Duchess at the proceedings of Count Horn at Tournay, and they read a very remarkable letter which had been furnished them, as having been written by the Spanish envoy in Paris, Don Francis of Alava, to Margaret of Parma. This letter was forged. At least the Regent, in her Italian correspondence, asserted it to be fictitious,† and in those secret letters to Philip she usually told the truth. The astuteness of William of Orange had in this instance been deceived. The striking

---

* Foppens, Supplément, i. (Procès d'Egmont) 73–76 and 166–170 (Procès de Hornes). Groen v. Prinst., ii. 360, sqq. Correspondance de Guillaume le Tacit. ii. Introduction of Gachard, 74, sqq. Compare Bor, ii. 108; Hoofd, ii. 114; Strada v. 230, sqq.; Bentivoglio, iii. 42, sqq. Correspondance de Philippe II., i. 474–476.

† Correspondance de Philippe II., i. 476.

fidelity, however, with which the present and future policy of the government was sketched, the accuracy with which many unborn events were foreshadowed, together with the minute touches which gave an air of genuineness to the fictitious despatch, might well deceive even so sagacious an observer as the Prince.

The letters* alluded to the deep and long-settled hostility of Philip to Orange, Horn, and Egmont, as to a fact entirely within the writer's knowledge, and that of his correspondent, but urged upon the Duchess the assumption of an extraordinary degree of apparent cordiality in her intercourse with them. It was the King's intention to use them and to destroy them, said the writer, and it was the Regent's duty to second the design. "The tumults and troubles have not been without their secret concurrence," said the supposititious Alava, "and your Highness may rest assured that they will be the first upon whom his Majesty will seize, not to confer benefits, but to chastise them as they deserve. Your Highness, however, should show no symptom of displeasure, but should constantly maintain in their minds the idea that his Majesty considers them as the most faithful of his servants. While they are persuaded of this, they can be more easily used, but when the time comes, they will be treated in another manner. Your Highness may rest assured that his Majesty is not less inclined than your Highness that they should receive the punishment which they merit."† The Duchess was furthermore recommended "to deal with the three seigniors according to the example of the Spanish Governments in its intercourse with the envoys, Bergen and Montigny, who are met with a smiling face, but who are closely watched, and who will never be permitted to leave Spain alive."‡ The remainder of the letter alludes to supposed engagements between France and Spain for the extirpation of heresy, from

---

* The letters are given by Bor, ii. 109, 110, without a doubt as to their genuineness.

† Bor, ubi sup. ‡ Ibid.

which allusion to the generally accepted but mistaken notion as to the Bayonne conference, a decided proof seems to be furnished that the letter was not genuine. Great complaints, however, are made, as to the conduct of the Queen Regent, who is described as "a certain lady well known to her Highness, and as a person without faith, friendship, or truth; the most consummate hypocrite in the world." After giving instances of the duplicity manifested by Catherine de Medici, the writer continues: "She sends her little black dwarf to me upon frequent errands, in order that by means of this spy she may worm out my secrets. I am, however, upon my guard, and flatter myself that I learn more from him than she from me. She shall never be able to boast of having deceived a Spaniard."*

An extract or two from this very celebrated document seemed indispensable, because of the great importance attached to it, both at the Dendermonde Conference, and at the trials of Egmont and Horn. The contemporary writers of Holland had no doubt of its genuineness, and what is more remarkable, Strada, the historiographer of the Farnese family, after quoting Margaret's denial of the authenticity of the letter, coolly observes: "Whether this were only an invention of the conspirators, or actually a despatch from Alava, I shall not decide. It is certain, however, that the Duchess *declared* it to be false."†

Certainly, as we read the epistles, and observe how profoundly the writer seems to have sounded the deep guile of the Spanish Cabinet, and how distinctly events, then far in the future, are indicated, we are tempted to exclaim: "aut Alava, aut Diabolus;" either the envoy wrote the despatch, or Orange. Who else could look into the future, and into Philip's heart so unerringly?

As the charge has never been made, so far as we are aware, against the Prince, it is superfluous to discuss the amount of

---

* Bor, ubi sup.　　　　　　　† Strada, v. 231.

immorality which should belong to such a deception. A tendency to employ stratagem in his warfare against Spain was, no doubt, a blemish upon his high character. Before he is condemned, however, in the Court of Conscience, the ineffable wiles of the policy with which he had to combat must be thoroughly scanned, as well as the pure and lofty purpose for which his life's long battle was fought.

There was, doubtless, some conversation at Dendermonde on the propriety or possibility of forcible resistance to a Spanish army, with which it seemed probable that Philip was about to invade the provinces, and take the lives of the leading nobles. Count Louis was in favor of making provision in Germany for the accomplishment of this purpose. It is also highly probable that the Prince may have encouraged the proposition. In the sense of his former communication to Egmont, he may have reasoned on the necessity of making levies to sustain the decisions of the states-general against violence. There is, however, no proof of any such fact. Egmont, at any rate, opposed the scheme, on the ground that "it was wrong to entertain any such ill opinion of so good a king as Philip, that he had never done any thing unjust towards his subjects, and that if any one was in fear, he had better leave the country."* Egmont, moreover, doubted the authenticity of the letters from Alava, but agreed to carry them to Brussels, and to lay them before the Regent. That lady, when she saw them, warmly assured the Count that they were inventions.†

The Conference broke up after it had lasted an hour and a half. The nobles then went to dinner, at which other persons appear to have been present, and the celebrated Dendermonde meeting was brought to a close. After the repast was finished, each of the five nobles mounted his horse, and departed on his separate way.‡

---

* Procès d'Egmont (Foppens, i. 75).
† Letter of Egmont in Groen v. Prinst., Archives, ii. 400, 401.
‡ Procès d'Egmont, 73–76. Procès de Hornes, 166–170 (Foppens, Supplé-

From this time forth the position of these leading seigniors became more sharply defined. Orange was left in almost complete isolation. Without the assistance of Egmont, any effective resistance to the impending invasion from Spain seemed out of the question. The Count, however, had taken his irrevocable and fatal resolution. After various oscillations during the stormy period which had elapsed, his mind, notwithstanding all the disturbing causes by which it had hitherto been partially influenced, now pointed steadily to the point of loyalty. The guidance of that pole star was to lead him to utter shipwreck. The unfortunate noble, entrenched against all fear of Philip by the brazen wall of an easy conscience, saw no fault in his past at which he should grow pale with apprehension. Moreover, he was sanguine by nature, a Catholic in religion, a royalist from habit and conviction. Henceforth he was determined that his services to the crown should more than counterbalance any idle speeches or insolent demonstrations of which he might have been previously guilty.

Horn pursued a different course, but one which separated him also from the Prince, while it led to the same fate which Egmont was blindly pursuing. The Admiral had committed no act of treason. On the contrary, he had been doing his best, under most difficult circumstances, to avert rebellion and save the interests of a most ungrateful sovereign. He was now disposed to wrap himself in his virtue, to retreat from a court life, for which he had never felt a vocation,* and to resign all connection with a government by which he felt himself very badly treated. Moody, wrathful, disappointed, ruined, and calumniated, he would no longer keep terms with King or Duchess. He had griefs of long standing against the

---

ment). Correspondance de Guillaume le Tacit. ii. Introduction of M. Gachard, lxxiv. sqq. Compare Bor. ii. 108; Hoofd, iii. 114; Strada, v. 230, sqq.; Bentivoglio, iii. 42, sqq.; Correspondance de Philippe II., i. 474–476.

* "Aiant par trop cognu n'estre ma vocation estre en court," etc., etc.—Letter of Horn to his secretary, Alonzo de la Loo. Foppens, ii. 470, 471.

whole of the royal family. He had never forgiven the Emperor for refusing him, when young, the appointment of chamberlain.* He had served Philip long and faithfully, but he had never received a stiver of salary or "merced," notwithstanding all his work as state councillor, as admiral, as superintendent in Spain ; while his younger brother had long been in receipt of nine or ten thousand florins yearly. He had spent four hundred thousand florins in the King's service ; his estates were mortgaged to their full value ; he had been obliged to sell his family plate.† He had done his best in Tournay to serve the Duchess, and he had averted the "Sicilian vespers," which had been imminent at his arrival.‡ He had saved the Catholics from a general massacre, yet he heard nevertheless from Montigny, that all his actions were distorted in Spain, and his motives blackened.§ His heart no longer inclined him to continue in Philip's service, even were he furnished with the means of doing so. He had instructed his secretary, Alonzo de la Loo, whom he had despatched many months previously to Madrid, that he was no longer to press his master's claims for a "merced," but to signify that he abandoned all demands and resigned all posts. He could turn hermit for the rest of his days, as well as the Emperor Charles.‖ If he had little, he could live upon little. It was in this sense that he spoke to Margaret of Parma, to Assonleville, to all around him. It was precisely in this strain and temper that he wrote to Philip, indignantly defending his course at Tournay, protesting against the tortuous conduct of the Duchess, and bluntly declaring that he would treat no longer with ladies upon matters which concerned a man's honor.¶

Thus, smarting under a sense of gross injustice, the Admiral expressed himself in terms which Philip was not likely

---

* Renom de France MS., i. c. 31

† Ibid.   ‡ Ibid.   § Ibid.

‖ Ibid. Foppens. Supplément, ii. 506–509.

¶ Foppens, Supplément, ii. 501–505.

to forgive. He had undertaken the pacification of Tournay, because it was Montigny's government, and he had promised his services whenever they should be requisite. Horn was a loyal and affectionate brother, and it is pathetic to find him congratulating Montigny on being, after all, better off in Spain than in the Netherlands.* Neither loyalty nor the sincere Catholicism for which Montigny at this period commended Horn in his private letters,† could save the two brothers from the doom which was now fast approaching.

Thus Horn, blind as Egmont—not being aware that a single step beyond implicit obedience had created an impassable gulf between Philip and himself—resolved to meet his destiny in sullen retirement. Not an entirely disinterested man, perhaps, but an honest one, as the world went, mediocre in mind, but brave, generous, and direct of purpose, goaded by the shafts of calumny, hunted down by the whole pack which fawned upon power as it grew more powerful, he now retreated to his "desert," as he called his ruined home at Weert,‡ where he stood at bay, growling defiance at the Regent, at Philip, at all the world.

Thus were the two prominent personages upon whose co-operation Orange had hitherto endeavored to rely, entirely separated from him. The confederacy of nobles, too, was dissolved, having accomplished little, notwithstanding all its noisy demonstrations, and having lost all credit with the people by the formal cassation of the Compromise in conse-

---

* "Pour fasché que estes là, estes plus à votre aise que ici."—Letter to Montigny. Foppens, ii. 496.

† "J'ai reçu ung grand contentement de l'assurance que me donnez, que nuls ne basteront de vous faire changer d'opinion, en chose qui touche le fait de la religion ancienne, qui est certes conforme à ce que j'en ay tousjours ferement pensé et cru, ors que le diable est subtil, et ses ministres. Je n'ay failly de le faire entendre aux lieux que m'avez escrit."—Montigny to Horn, 26th May, 1567.

The whole letter is published in Willems, Mengelingen van Historisch Vaderlandschen Inhoud (Antwerpen, 1827–1830), pp. 325–334.

‡ Procès de Hornes. Foppens, Supplément.

quence of the Accord of August.* As a body, they had justified the sarcasm of Hubert Languet, that "the confederated nobles had ruined their country by their folly and incapacity." They had profaned a holy cause by indecent orgies, compromised it by seditious demonstrations, abandoned it when most in need of assistance. Bakkerzeel had distinguished himself by hanging sectaries in Flanders. "Golden Fleece" de Hammes, after creating great scandal in and about Antwerp, since the Accord, had ended by accepting an artillery commission in the Emperor's army, together with three hundred crowns for convoy from Duchess Margaret.† Culemburg was serving the cause of religious freedom by defacing the churches within his ancestral domains, pulling down statues, dining in chapels, and giving the holy wafer to his parrot.‡ Nothing could be more stupid than these acts of irreverence, by which Catholics were offended and honest patriots disgusted. Nothing could be more opposed to the sentiments of Orange, whose first principle was abstinence by all denominations of Christians from mutual insults. At the same time, it is somewhat revolting to observe the indignation with which such offences were regarded by men of the most abandoned character. Thus, Armenteros, whose name was synonymous with government swindling, who had been rolling up money year after year, by peculations, auctioneering of high posts in church and state, bribes, and all kinds of picking and stealing, could not contain his horror as he referred to wafers eaten by parrots, or "toasted on forks"§ by renegade

---

* Groen v. Prinst., ii. 282.

† Unpublished Letter, 13th September, Margaret of Parma to Philip II. Brussels Archives MS.—The Duchess expressed great regret that she was prohibited by the statutes of the order to which De Hammes was a servant or official, from arresting and punishing him for his crimes. Her legal advisers, Viglius, Assonleville, and the rest, were to make new discoveries with regard to these privileges, when not servants merely, but illustrious chevaliers of the order were to be put to death.—Compare Correspondance de Philippe II., 463.

‡ Ibid., i. 472, 480, 481.

§ "Asar en un asador."—Correspondance de Philippe II., i. 480, 481. Tomas Armenteros to Antonio Perez.

priests ; and poured out his emotions on the subject into the
faithful bosom of Antonio Perez, the man with whose de-
baucheries, political villanies, and deliberate murders all
Europe was to ring.

No doubt there were many individuals in the confederacy
for whom it was reserved to render honorable service in the
national cause. The names of Louis Nassau, Marnix of St.
Aldegonde, Bernard de Merode, were to be written in golden
letters in their country's rolls ; but at this moment they were
impatient, inconsiderate, out of the control of Orange. Louis
was anxious for the King to come from Spain with his army,
and for "the bear dance to begin."* Brederode, noisy, bawl-
ing, and absurd as ever, was bringing ridicule upon the
national cause by his buffoonery, and endangering the whole
people by his inadequate yet rebellious exertions.

What course was the Prince of Orange to adopt ? He could
find no one to comprehend his views. He felt certain at the
close of the year that the purpose of the government was fixed.
He made no secret of his determination never to lend himself
as an instrument for the contemplated subjugation of the
people. He had repeatedly resigned all his offices. He was
now determined that the resignation once for all should be
accepted. If he used dissimulation, it was because Philip's
deception permitted no man to be frank. If the sovereign
constantly disavowed all hostile purposes against his people,
and manifested extreme affection for the men whom he had
already doomed to the scaffold, how could the Prince openly
denounce him ? It was his duty to save his country and his
friends from impending ruin. He preserved, therefore, an
attitude of watchfulness. Philip, in the depth of his cabinet,
was under a constant inspection by the sleepless Prince. The
sovereign assured his sister that her apprehensions about their
correspondence was groundless. He always locked up his
papers, and took the key with him.† Nevertheless, the key

---

* Archives et Correspondance, ii. 309.   † Foppens, Supplément, ii. 512.

was taken out of his pocket and the papers read. Orange was accustomed to observe, that men of leisure might occupy themselves with philosophical pursuits and with the secrets of nature, but that it was his business to study the hearts of kings.* He knew the man and the woman with whom he had to deal. We have seen enough of the policy secretly pursued by Philip and Margaret to appreciate the accuracy with which the Prince, groping as it were in the dark, had judged the whole situation. Had his friends taken his warnings, they might have lived to render services against tyranny. Had he imitated their example of false loyalty, there would have been one additional victim, more illustrious than all the rest, and a whole country hopelessly enslaved.

It is by keeping these considerations in view, that we can explain his connection with such a man as Brederode. The enterprises of that noble, of Tholouse, and others, and the resistance of Valenciennes, could hardly have been prevented even by the opposition of the Prince. But why should he take the field against men who, however rashly or ineffectually, were endeavoring to oppose tyranny, when he knew himself already proscribed and doomed by the tyrant? Such loyalty he left to Egmont. Till late in the autumn, he had still believed in the possibility of convoking the states-general, and of making preparations in Germany to enforce their decrees.

The confederates and sectaries had boasted that they could easily raise an army of sixty thousand men within the provinces,† that twelve hundred thousand florins monthly would be furnished by the rich merchants of Antwerp,‡ and that

---

* Strada, v. 234.

† "Mesmes osent aucuns des confederez et sectaires menasser d'oser d'armes et force contre moi —— Se vantans que l'on fera venir en armes contre moy cinquante ou soixante mil hommes de ces pays sans les estrangiers."—Unpublished letter of Margaret of Parma, heretofore cited. Brussels Archives MS.

‡ "Disans avoir les bourses des marchans d'Anvers qui en ce cas leur furniront par mois plus de xii² mil florins," etc., etc.—Ibid.

it was ridiculous to suppose that the German mercenaries enrolled by the Duchess in Saxony, Hesse, and other Protestant countries, would ever render serious assistance against the adherents of the reformed religion.* Without placing much confidence in such exaggerated statements, the Prince might well be justified in believing himself strong enough, if backed by the confederacy, by Egmont, and by his own boundless influence, both at Antwerp and in his own government, to sustain the constituted authorities of the nation even against a Spanish army, and to interpose with legitimate and irresistible strength between the insane tyrant and the country which he was preparing to crush. It was the opinion of the best informed Catholics that, if Egmont should declare for the confederacy, he could take the field with sixty thousand men, and make himself master of the whole country at a blow.† In conjunction with Orange, the moral and physical force would have been invincible.

It was therefore not Orange alone, but the Catholics and Protestants alike, the whole population of the country, and the Duchess Regent herself, who desired the convocation of the estates. Notwithstanding Philip's deliberate but secret determination never to assemble that body, although the hope was ever to be held out that they should be convened, Margaret had been most importunate that her brother should permit the measure. "There was less danger," she felt herself compelled to say, "in assembling than in not assembling the States ; it was better to preserve the Catholic religion for a part of the country, than to lose it altogether."‡ "The more

---

* "Que en fait de la religion les dits Alemans les favoriseront oires qu'ilz soient en la soulde de V^re. Mat^s. et consequemment oseront plus tot barbouiller quelque chose."—Ibid.

† "Vous l'eussiez veu marcher en campaigne avec une armée de 60,000 hommes et avoir reduict en sa puissance la ville de Bruxelles ——. par un exploit soudain se fust aisement emparé de la principaulté du Pays Bas," etc., etc. —Pontus Payen MS.

‡ " C'est moins mal les assembler que point assembler," etc., etc.—Unpublished Letter of Duchess of Parma.

it was delayed," she said, "the more ruinous and desperate became the public affairs. If the measure were postponed much longer, all Flanders, half Brabant, the whole of Holland, Zeland, Gueldres, Tournay, Lille, Mechlin, would be lost forever, without a chance of ever restoring the ancient religion."* The country, in short, was "without faith, King, or law,"† and nothing worse could be apprehended from any deliberation of the states-general. These being the opinions of the Duchess, and according to her statement those of nearly all the good Catholics in the country, it could hardly seem astonishing or treasonable that the Prince should also be in favor of the measure.

As the Duchess grew stronger, however, and as the people, aghast at the fate of Tournay and Valenciennes, began to lose courage, she saw less reason for assembling the states. Orange, on the other hand, completely deserted by Egmont and Horn, and having little confidence in the characters of the ex-confederates, remained comparatively quiescent but watchful.

At the close of the year, an important pamphlet‡ from his hand was circulated, in which his views as to the necessity of allowing some degree of religious freedom were urged upon the royal government with his usual sagacity of thought, moderation of language, and modesty in tone. The man who had held the most important civil and military offices in the country almost from boyhood, and who was looked up to by friend and foe as the most important personage in the three millions of its inhabitants, apologized for his "presumption" in coming forward publicly with his advice. "I would not," he said, "in matters of such importance, affect to be wiser or to make greater pretensions

---

* Unpublished letter of Duchess of Parma.

† "Estant quasi tout le pays sans foy, roy et loy, et le peu que demeure entier s'en va journellement empirant."—Ibid.

‡ Archives et Correspondance, ii. 429–450. Compare Hopper, Rec. et Mem., iii. It is also given in Bor, iii. 131–133.

than my age or experience warrants, yet seeing affairs in such perplexity, I will rather incur the risk of being charged with forwardness than neglect that which I consider my duty."*

This, then, was the attitude of the principal personages in the Netherlands, and the situation of affairs at the end of the eventful year 1566, the last year of peace which the men then living or their children were to know. The government, weak at the commencement, was strong at the close. The confederacy was broken and scattered. The Request, the beggar banquets, the public preaching, the image-breaking, the Accord of August, had been followed by reaction. Tournay had accepted its garrison. Egmont, completely obedient to the crown, was compelling all the cities of Flanders and Artois to receive soldiers sufficient to maintain implicit obedience, and to extinguish all heretical demonstrations, so that the Regent was at comparative leisure to effect the reduction of Valenciennes.

This ancient city, in the province of Hainault, and on the frontier of France, had been founded by the Emperor Valentinian, from whom it had derived its name.† Originally established by him as a city of refuge, it had received the privilege of affording an asylum to debtors, to outlaws, and even to murderers. This ancient right had been continued, under certain modifications, even till the period with which we are now occupied.‡ Never, however, according to the government, had the right of asylum, even in the wildest times, been so abused by the city before. What were debtors, robbers, murderers, compared to heretics ? yet these worst enemies of their race swarmed in the rebellious city, practising even now the foulest rites of Calvin, and obeying those most pestilential of all preachers, Guido de Bray, and Peregrine de la Grange. The place was the hot-bed of heresy and sedition, and it seemed to be agreed, as by common

---

* Archives et Correspondance, ii. 430, 431.
† Guicciardini, 458, sqq.   ‡ Ibid.

accord, that the last struggle for what was called the new religion, should take place beneath its walls.*

Pleasantly situated in a fertile valley, provided with very strong fortifications and very deep moats, Valenciennes, with the Scheld flowing through its centre, and furnishing the means of laying the circumjacent meadows under water, was considered in those days almost impregnable.† The city was summoned, almost at the same time as Tournay, to accept a garrison. This demand of government was met by a peremptory refusal. Noircarmes, towards the middle of December, ordered the magistrates to send a deputation to confer with him at Condé. Pensionary Outreman accordingly repaired to that neighboring city, accompanied by some of his colleagues.‡ This committee was not unfavorable to the demands of government. The magistracies of the cities, generally, were far from rebellious; but in the case of Valenciennes the real power at that moment was with the Calvinist consistory and the ministers. The deputies, after their return from Condé, summoned the leading members of the reformed religion, together with the preachers. It was urged that it was their duty forthwith to use their influence in favor of the demand made by the government upon the city.§

"May I grow mute as a fish!" answered de la Grange, stoutly, "may the tongue cleave to the roof of my mouth, before I persuade my people to accept a garrison of cruel mercenaries, by whom their rights of conscience are to be trampled upon!"‖

Councillor Outreman reasoned with the fiery minister, that if he and his colleague were afraid of their own lives, ample provision should be made with government for their departure under safe conduct. La Grange replied that he had no fears for himself, that the Lord would protect those who preached

---

* "—— Il sembloit que de la fortune de Valenciennes dependoit celle de toute la gueuserie."—Valenciennes MS.

† Guicciardini, ubi supra.   ‡ Valenciennes MS.
§ Ibid.   ‡ Ibid.   Pontus Payen MS.

and those who believed in his holy word, but that He would not forgive them should they now bend their necks to His enemies.*

It was soon very obvious that no arrangement could be made. The magistrates could exert no authority, the preachers were all-powerful, and the citizens, said a Catholic inhabitant of Valenciennes, "allowed themselves to be led by their ministers like oxen."† Upon the 17th December, 1566, a proclamation was accordingly issued by the Duchess Regent, declaring the city in a state of siege, and all its inhabitants rebels.‡ The crimes for which this penalty was denounced, were elaborately set forth in the edict. Preaching according to the reformed religion had been permitted in two or three churches, the sacrament according to the Calvinistic manner had been publicly administered, together with a renunciation by the communicants of their adhesion to the Catholic Church, and now a rebellious refusal to receive the garrison sent to them by the Duchess had been added to the list of their iniquities. For offences like these the Regent deemed it her duty to forbid all inhabitants of any city, village, or province of the Netherlands holding communication with Valenciennes, buying or selling with its inhabitants, or furnishing them with provisions, on pain of being considered accomplices in their rebellion, and as such of being executed with the halter.§

The city was now invested by Noircarmes with all the troops which could be spared. The confederates gave promises of assistance to the beleaguered citizens, Orange privately encouraged them to hold out in their legitimate refusal;‖ Brederode and others busied themselves with hostile demonstrations which were destined to remain barren; but in the mean time the inhabitants had nothing to rely upon save their own stout hearts and arms.

At first, the siege was sustained with a light heart.

---

* Valenciennes MS.   Pontus Payen MS.   † Valenciennes MS.
‡ The proclamation is given in Bor, iii. 134–136.
§ Proclamation in Bor, ubi sup.
‖ Correspondance de Guillaume le Tacit, preface, cxlix, cl., notes.

Frequent sallies were made, smart skirmishes were ventured, in which the Huguenots, on the testimony of a most bitter Catholic contemporary, conducted themselves with the bravery of veteran troops, and as if they had done nothing all their lives but fight ;* forays were made upon the monasteries of the neighborhood for the purpose of procuring supplies, and the broken statues of the dismantled churches were used to build a bridge across an arm of the river, which was called in derision the Bridge of Idols.† Noircarmes and the six officers under him, who were thought to be conducting their operations with languor, were christened the Seven Sleepers.‡ Gigantic spectacles, three feet in circumference, were planted derisively upon the ramparts, in order that the artillery, which it was said that the papists of Arras were sending, might be seen, as soon as it should arrive.§ Councillor Outreman, who had left the city before the siege, came into it again, on commission from Noircarmes. He was received with contempt, his proposals on behalf of the government were answered with outcries of fury ; he was pelted with stones, and was very glad to make his escape alive.‖ The pulpits thundered with the valiant deeds of Joshua, Judas Maccabeus, and other bible heroes.¶ The miracles wrought in their behalf served to encourage the enthusiasm of the people, while the movements making at various points in the neighborhood encouraged a hope of a general rising throughout the country.

Those hopes were destined to disappointment. There were large assemblages made, to be sure, at two points. Nearly three thousand sectaries had been collected at Lannoy under Pierre

---

* "Sortoient journellement aux escarmouches combattans avec hardiesse et dexterité comme si toutte leur vie n'eussent faict aultre chose que porter les armes."—Pontus Payen MS.   † Ibid.

‡ "Les gueux les appelloient les sept dormans."—Valenciennes MS.

§ "Ils avoient fichez sur leurs ramparts de fort longues picques et au bout d'icelles attaché de fort grandes lunettes aintes trois pieds en diametre, et quand on leur demandoit à quoy elles servaient, respondaient joyeusement que c'estoit pour descouvir de plus long l'artillerie que les papistes d'Arras debvoient envoier," etc., etc.—Pontus Payen MS.

‖ Valenciennes MS.   ¶ Ibid.

Cornaille, who, having been a locksmith and afterwards a Calvinist preacher, was now disposed to try his fortune as a general.* His band was, however, disorderly. Rustics armed with pitchforks, young students and old soldiers out of employment, furnished with rusty matchlocks, pikes and halberds, composed his force.† A company similar in character, and already amounting to some twelve hundred in number, was collecting at Watrelots.‡ It was hoped that an imposing array would soon be assembled, and that the two bands, making a junction, would then march to the relief of Valenciennes. It was boasted that in a very short time, thirty thousand men would be in the field.§ There was even a fear of some such result felt by the Catholics.

It was then that Noircarmes and his "seven sleepers" showed that they were awake. Early in January, 1567, that fierce soldier, among whose vices slothfulness was certainly never reckoned before or afterwards, fell upon the locksmith's army at Lannoy, while the Seigneur de Rassinghem attacked the force at Watrelots on the same day.‖ Noircarmes destroyed half his enemies at the very first charge. The ill-assorted rabble fell asunder at once. The preacher fought well, but his undisciplined force fled at the first sight of the enemy. Those who carried arquebusses threw them down without a single discharge, that they might run the faster. At least a thousand were soon stretched dead upon the field; others were hunted into the river. Twenty-six hundred, according to the Catholic accounts, were exterminated in an hour.¶

Rassinghem, on his part, with five or six hundred regulars, attacked Teriel's force, numbering at least twice as many. Half of these were soon cut to pieces and put to flight. Six hundred, however, who had seen some service, took refuge in

---

* Valenciennes MS. Pontus Payen MS.
† Pontus Payen MS.   ‡ Ibid.   § Ibid.
‖ Ibid. Valenciennes MS. Compare Hoofd, iii. 125; Strada, vi. 256, 257.
Vit. Viglii, 49.
  ¶ Groen v. Prinst., Archives, etc., iii. 7, 8. Compare Strada, ubi sup.; Hoofd, ubi sup.; Pontus Payen MS.

the cemetery of Watrelots. Here, from behind the stone wall of the inclosure, they sustained the attack of the Catholics with some spirit.* The repose of the dead in the quiet country church-yard was disturbed by the uproar of a most sanguinary conflict. The temporary fort was soon carried, and the Huguenots retreated into the church. A rattling arquebusade was poured in upon them as they struggled in the narrow doorway.† At least four hundred corpses were soon strewn among the ancient graves. The rest were hunted into the church, and from the church into the belfry. A fire was then made in the steeple and kept up till all were roasted or suffocated.‡ Not a man escaped.

This was the issue in the first stricken field in the Netherlands, for the cause of religious liberty. It must be confessed that it was not very encouraging to the lovers of freedom. The partisans of government were elated, in proportion to the apprehension which had been felt for the result of this rising in the Walloon country. "These good hypocrites," wrote a correspondent of Orange, "are lifting up their heads like so many dromedaries. They are becoming unmanageable with pride."§ The Duke of Aerschot and Count Meghem gave great banquets in Brussels, where all the good chevaliers drank deep in honor of the victory, and to the health of his Majesty and Madame. "I saw Berlaymont just go by the window," wrote Schwartz to the Prince. "He was coming from Aerschot's dinner with a face as red as the Cardinal's new hat."‖

On the other hand, the citizens of Valenciennes were depressed in equal measure with the exultation of their antagonists. There was no more talk of seven sleepers now, no more lunettes stuck upon lances, to spy the coming forces of the enemy. It was felt that the government was wide awake, and that the city would soon see the impending horrors with-

---

* Pontus Payen MS.   † Ibid.   ‡ Ibid.
§ "Haulcent pour l'heure la teste comme trommetaires, et ne sont quacy plus traictables d'orgueil."—Archives et Correspondance, iii. 13. ‖ Ibid., 9.

out telescopes. The siege was pressed more closely. Noir-carmes took up a commanding position at Saint Armand, by which he was enabled to cut off all communication between the city and the surrounding country. All the villages in the neighborhood were pillaged ; all the fields laid waste. All the infamies which an insolent soldiery can inflict upon help-less peasantry were daily enacted. Men and women who attempted any communication with the city, were murdered in cold blood by hundreds.* The villagers were plundered of their miserable possessions, children were stripped naked in the midst of winter for the sake of the rags which covered them ; matrons and virgins were sold at public auction by the tap of drum ;† sick and wounded wretches were burned over slow fires, to afford amusement to the soldiers.‡ In brief, the whole unmitigated curse which military power inflamed by religious bigotry can embody, had descended upon the heads of these unfortunate provincials who had dared to worship God in Christian churches without a Roman ritual.

Meantime the city maintained a stout heart still. The whole population were arranged under different banners. The rich and poor alike took arms to defend the walls which sheltered them.§ The town paupers were enrolled in three companies, which bore the significant title of the " Tous-nuds" or the " Stark-nakeds,"‖ and many was the fierce conflict delivered outside the gates by men, who, in the words of a Catholic then in the city, might rather be taken for " expe-rienced veterans than for burghers and artisans."¶ At the same time, to the honor of Valenciennes, it must be stated, upon the same incontestable authority, that not a Catholic in the city was injured or insulted. The priests who had remained there were not allowed to say mass, but they

---

* Remonstrance addressed by the inhabitants of Valenciennes to the Knights of the Fleece.—§ 9, apud Bor, iii. 136–141.   † Ibid.   ‡ Ibid.

§ Valenciennes MS.   ‖ Ibid.

¶ " Qu'on eut pris tous pour de vieux routiers et soldats experimentes, et non pas pour des bourgeois et artisans de prime abord."—Ibid.

never met with an opprobrious word or look from the people.*

The inhabitants of the city called upon the confederates for assistance. They also issued an address to the Knights of the Fleece ;† a paper which narrated the story of their wrongs in pathetic and startling language. They appealed to those puissant and illustrious chevaliers to prevent the perpetration of the great wrong which was now impending over so many innocent heads. "Wait not," they said, "till the thunderbolt has fallen, till the deluge has overwhelmed us, till the fires already blazing have laid the land in coals and ashes, till no other course be possible, but to abandon the country in its desolation to foreign barbarity. Let the cause of the oppressed come to your ears. So shall your conscience become a shield of iron; so shall the happiness of a whole country witness before the angels, of your truth to his Majesty, in the cause of his true grandeur and glory."‡

These stirring appeals to an order of which Philip was chief, Viglius chancellor, Egmont, Mansfeld, Aerschot, Berlaymont, and others, chevaliers, were not likely to produce much effect. The city could rely upon no assistance in those high quarters.

Meantime, however, the bold Brederode was attempting a very extensive diversion, which, if successful, would have saved Valenciennes and the whole country beside. That eccentric personage, during the autumn and winter had been creating disturbances in various parts of the country. Wherever he happened to be established, there came from the windows of his apartments a sound of revelry and uproar. Suspicious characters in various costumes thronged his door and dogged his footsteps.§ At the same time the authorities felt themselves obliged to treat him with respect. At Horn he had entertained many of the leading citizens at a great

---

* "Si ne recuerent ils toutes fois aucunes injures ny fascherie excepté qu'on leur defendit de dire la messe, laquelle le bon Prélat de S. Jean disoit secrettement en sa chambre pour sa consolation."—Ibid.

† Ante, page 50.   ‡ Remonstrance, etc., ubi sup.   § Bor, iii. 147, 148.

banquet. The health of the beggars had been drunk in
mighty potations, and their shibboleth had resounded through
the house. In the midst of the festivities, Brederode had
suspended a beggar's medal around the neck of the burgomaster, who had consented to be his guest upon that occasion,
but who had no intention of enrolling himself in the frater-
nities of actual or political mendicants. The excellent magistrate, however, was near becoming a member of both. The
emblem by which he had been conspicuously adorned proved
very embarrassing to him upon his recovery from the effects of
his orgies with the "great beggar," and he was subsequently
punished for his imprudence by the confiscation of half his
property.*

Early in January, Brederode had stationed himself in his
city of Viane. There, in virtue of his seignorial rights, he
had removed all statues and other popish emblems from
the churches, performing the operation, however, with much
quietness and decorum. He had also collected many disorderly
men at arms in this city, and had strengthened its fortifications, to resist, as he said, the threatened attacks of
Duke Eric of Brunswick and his German mercenaries.†
A printing-press was established in the place, whence satir-
ical pamphlets, hymn-books, and other pestiferous productions, were constantly issuing to the annoyance of government.‡ Many lawless and uproarious individuals enjoyed the
Count's hospitality. All the dregs and filth of the provinces,
according to Doctor Viglius, were accumulated at Viane as
in a cesspool.§ Along the placid banks of the Lech, on which
river the city stands, the "hydra of rebellion"‖ lay ever coiled
and threatening.

Brederode was supposed to be revolving vast schemes,
both political and military, and Margaret of Parma was

* Velius Hoorn, bl. 298; cited by Wagenaar, vi. 189.
† Correspondance de Guillaume le Tacit. ii. 255–257.—Compare Bor, iii. 147,
148; Bentivoglio, iii. 46.
‡ Bor, ubi sup. Correspondance de Guillaume le Tacit. ii. 328–331.
§ Vigl. ad J. Hopperum, 418–424.   ‖ Ibid., 425.

kept in continual apprehension by the bravado of this very noisy conspirator. She called upon William of Orange, as usual, for assistance. The Prince, however, was very ill-disposed to come to her relief. An extreme disgust for the policy of the government already began to characterize his public language. In the autumn and winter he had done all that man could do for the safety of the monarch's crown, and for the people's happiness. His services in Antwerp have been recorded. As soon as he could tear himself from that city, where the magistrates and all classes of citizens clung to him as to their only saviour, he had hastened to tranquillize the provinces of Holland, Zeland, and Utrecht. He had made arrangements in the principal cities there upon the same basis which he had adopted in Antwerp, and to which Margaret had consented in August. It was quite out of the question to establish order without permitting the reformers, who constituted much the larger portion of the population, to have liberty of religious exercises at some places, not consecrated, within the cities.

At Amsterdam, for instance, as he informed the Duchess, there were swarms of unlearned, barbarous people, mariners and the like,[*] who could by no means perceive the propriety of doing their preaching in the open country, seeing that the open country, at that season, was quite under water.[†] Margaret's gracious suggestion that, perhaps, something might be done with boats, was also considered inadmissible. " I know not," said Orange, " who could have advised your highness to make such a proposition."[‡] He informed her, likewise, that the barbarous mariners had a clear right to their preaching, for the custom had already been established previously to the August treaty, at a place called the " Lastadge," among the wharves. " In the name of God, then," wrote Margaret, " let them continue to preach in the Lastadge."[§]   This being

---

* Correspondance de Guillaume le Tacit. ii. 283, 284.—"Maronniers et gens indoctz, barbares."   † Ibid.   ‡ Ibid.
§ " Au nom de Dieu qu'ils ayent leurs presches au dict Lastaige."—Correspondance de Guillaume le Tacit. ii. 296.

all the barbarians wanted, an Accord, with the full consent of
the Regent, was drawn up at Amsterdam and the other
northern cities. The Catholics kept churches and cathedrals,
but in the winter season, the greater part of the population
obtained permission to worship God upon dry land, in ware-
houses and dock-yards.

Within a very few weeks, however, the whole arrangement
was coolly cancelled by the Duchess, her permission revoked,
and peremptory prohibition of all preaching within or without
the walls proclaimed.*   The government was growing stronger.
Had not Noircarmes and Rassinghem cut to pieces three
or four thousand of these sectaries marching to battle
under parsons, locksmiths, and similar chieftains?   Were
not all lovers of good government "erecting their heads like
dromedaries?"

It may easily be comprehended that the Prince could not
with complacency permit himself to be thus perpetually
stultified by a weak, false, and imperious woman. She had
repeatedly called upon him when she was appalled at the tempest
and sinking in the ocean; and she had as constantly disavowed
his deeds and reviled his character when she felt herself in
safety again.   He had tranquillized the old Batavian provinces,
where the old Batavian spirit still lingered, by his personal
influence and his unwearied exertions. Men of all ranks and
religions were grateful for his labors. The Reformers had
not gained much, but they were satisfied. The Catholics
retained their churches, their property, their consideration.
The states of Holland had voted him fifty thousand florins,†
as an acknowledgment of his efforts in restoring peace. He
had refused the present. He was in debt, pressed for money,
but he did not choose, as he informed Philip, "that men should
think his actions governed by motives of avarice or particular
interest, instead of the true affection which he bore to his
Majesty's service and the *good of the country.*"‡   Nevertheless,

---

* Correspondance de Guillaume le Tacit. ii. 351–353.
† Bor, iii. 147.   Hoofd, iv. 129.
‡ Correspondance de Guillaume le Tacit. ii. 360–365.

his back was hardly turned before all his work was undone by the Regent.

A new and important step on the part of the government had now placed him in an attitude of almost avowed rebellion.   All functionaries, from governors of provinces down to subalterns in the army, were required to take a new oath of allegiance, "novum et hactenus inusitatum religionis juramentum,"* as the Prince characterized it, which was, he said, quite equal to the inquisition. Every man who bore his Majesty's commission was ordered solemnly to pledge himself to obey the orders of government, every where, and against every person, without limitation or restriction.† Count Mansfeld, now "factotum at Brussels,"‡ had taken the oath with great fervor. So had Aerschot, Berlaymont, Meghem, and, after a little wavering, Egmont.§ Orange spurned the proposition. He had taken oaths enough which he had never broken, nor intended now to break. He was ready still to do every thing conducive *to the real interest* of the monarch. Who dared do more was no true servant to the government, no true lover of the country. He would never disgrace himself by a blind pledge, through which he might be constrained to do acts detrimental, in his opinion, to the safety of the crown, the happiness of the commonwealth, and his own honor. The alternative presented he willingly embraced.|| He renounced all his offices, and desired no longer to serve a government whose policy he did not approve, a King by whom he was suspected.

His resignation was not accepted by the Duchess, who still made efforts to retain the services of a man who was necessary to her administration. She begged him, notwithstanding the purely defensive and watchful attitude which he had now

---

* Archives et Correspondance, iii. 29.

† Groen v. Prinst., Archives, etc., iii. 26–31.   Correspondance de Guillaume le Tacit. ii. 312, 313, 317–321, 416–418.

‡ Expression of Orange.   Archives et Correspondance, iii. 40.

§ Correspondance de Guillaume le Tacit. ii. 312, 313.   Strada, vi. 264.

|| Renom de France MS., i. c. 39.

assumed, to take measures that Brederode should abandon his mischievous courses. She also reproached the Prince with having furnished that personage with artillery for his fortifications. Orange answered, somewhat contemptuously, that he was not Brederode's keeper, and had no occasion to meddle with his affairs.* He had given him three small field-pieces, promised long ago ; not that he mentioned that circumstance as an excuse for the donation. " Thank God," said he, " we have always had the liberty in this country of making to friends or relatives what presents we liked, and methinks that things have come to a pretty pass when such trifles are scrutinized."† Certainly, as Suzerain of Viane, and threatened with invasion in his seignorial rights, the Count might think himself justified in strengthening the bulwarks of his little stronghold, and the Prince could hardly be deemed very seriously to endanger the safety of the crown by the insignificant present which had annoyed the Regent.

It is not so agreeable to contemplate the apparent intimacy which the Prince accorded to so disreputable a character, but Orange was now in hostility to the government, was convinced by evidence, whose accuracy time was most signally to establish, that his own head, as well as many others, were already doomed to the block, while the whole country was devoted to abject servitude, and he was therefore disposed to look with more indulgence upon the follies of those who were endeavoring, however weakly and insanely, to avert the horrors which he foresaw. The time for reasoning had passed. All that true wisdom and practical statesmanship could suggest, he had already placed at the disposal of a woman who stabbed him in the back even while she leaned upon his arm— of a King who had already drawn his death warrant, while reproaching his " cousin of Orange" for want of confidence in the royal friendship. Was he now to attempt the subjugation of his country by interfering with the proceedings of men whom he had no power to command, and who, at

---

* Correspondance de Guillaume le Tacit. ii. 339–340·   † Ibid.

least, were attempting to oppose tyranny? Even if he should do so, he was perfectly aware of the reward reserved for his loyalty. He liked not such honors as he foresaw for all those who had ever interposed between the monarch and his vengeance. For himself he had the liberation of a country, the foundation of a free commonwealth to achieve. There was much work for those hands before he should fall a victim to the crowned assassin.

Early in February, Brederode, Hoogstraaten, Horn, and some other gentlemen, visited the Prince at Breda.* Here it is supposed the advice of Orange was asked concerning the new movement contemplated by Brederode. He was bent upon presenting a new petition to the Duchess with great solemnity. There is no evidence to show that the Prince approved the step, which must have seemed to him superfluous, if not puerile. He probably regarded the matter with indifference. Brederode, however, who was fond of making demonstrations, and thought himself endowed with a genius for such work, wrote to the Regent for letters of safe conduct that he might come to Brussels with his petition. The passports were contemptuously refused. He then came to Antwerp, from which city he forwarded the document to Brussels in a letter.

By this new Request, the exercise of the reformed religion was claimed as a right, while the Duchess was summoned to disband the forces which she had been collecting, and to maintain in good faith the "August" treaty.† These claims were somewhat bolder than those of the previous April, although the liberal party was much weaker and the confederacy entirely disbanded. Brederode, no doubt, thought it good generalship to throw the last loaf of bread into the enemy's camp before the city should surrender. His haughty tone was at once taken down by Margaret of Parma. "She wondered," she said, "what manner of nobles these were, who,

---

* Correspondance de Guillaume le Tacit. ii. 404, sqq.
† Ibid. Bor, iii. 149–151.

after requesting, a year before, to be saved only from the inquisition, now presumed to talk about preaching in the cities. The concessions of August had always been odious, and were now canceled. "As for you and your accomplices," she continued to the Count, "you will do well to go to your homes at once without meddling with public affairs, for, in case of disobedience, I shall deal with you as I shall deem expedient."*

Brederode, not easily abashed, disregarded the advice, and continued in Antwerp. Here, accepting the answer of the Regent as a formal declaration of hostilities, he busied himself in levying troops in and about the city.†

Orange had returned to Antwerp early in February. During his absence, Hoogstraaten had acted as governor at the instance of the Prince and of the Regent. During the winter that nobleman, who was very young and very fiery, had carried matters with a high hand, whenever there had been the least attempt at sedition. Liberal in principles, and the devoted friend of Orange, he was disposed however to prove that the champions of religious liberty were not the patrons of sedition. A riot occurring in the cathedral, where a violent mob were engaged in defacing whatever was left to deface in that church, and in heaping insults on the papists at their worship, the little Count, who, says a Catholic contemporary, "had the courage of a lion," dashed in among them, sword in hand, killed three upon the spot, and, aided by his followers, succeeded in slaying, wounding, or capturing all the rest.‡ He had also tracked the ringleader of the tumult to his lodging, where he had caused him to be arrested at midnight, and hanged at once in his shirt without any form of trial.§ Such rapid proceedings little resembled the calm and judicious moderation of Orange upon all occasions, but they certainly might have sufficed to con-

---

* Bor, iii. 149–151. Archives et Correspondance, iii. 31.
† Correspondance de Guillaume le Tacit. ii. 410, 411.
‡ Pontus Payen MS. § Ibid.

vince Philip that all antagonists of the inquisition were not heretics and outlaws. Upon the arrival of the Prince in Antwerp, it was considered advisable that Hoogstraaten should remain associated with him in the temporary government of the city.*

During the month of February, Brederode remained in Antwerp, secretly enrolling troops. It was probably his intention—if so desultory and irresponsible an individual could be said to have an intention—to make an attempt upon the Island of Walcheren. If such important cities as Flushing and Middelburg could be gained, he thought it possible to prevent the armed invasion now soon expected from Spain. Orange had sent an officer to those cities, who was to reconnoitre their condition, and to advise them against receiving a garrison from government without his authority.† So far he connived at Brederode's proceedings, as he had a perfect right to do, for Walcheren was within what had been the Prince's government, and he had no disposition that these cities should share the fate of Tournay, Valenciennes, Bois le Duc, and other towns which had already passed or were passing under the spears of foreign mercenaries.

It is also probable that he did not take any special pains to check the enrolments of Brederode. The peace of Antwerp was not endangered, and to the preservation of that city the Prince seemed now to limit himself. He was hereditary burgrave of Antwerp, but officer of Philip's never more. Despite the shrill demands of Duchess Margaret, therefore, the Prince did not take very active measures by which the crown of Philip might be secured. He, perhaps, looked upon the struggle almost with indifference. Nevertheless, he issued a formal proclamation by which the Count's enlistments were forbidden. Van der Aà, a gentleman who had been active in making these levies, was compelled to leave the

---

* Bor, iii. 153.

† Gachard, Preface to Correspondance de Guillaume le Tacit. ii. cxliv. sqq.— Compare Groen v. Prinst., Archives, etc., iii. 48–50; Bor, iii. 156; Meteren, ii. 45; Hoofd, iii. 120.

city.* Brederode was already gone to the north to busy himself with further enrolments.†

In the mean time there had been much alarm in Brussels. Egmont, who omitted no opportunity of manifesting his loyalty, offered to throw himself at once into the Isle of Walcheren, for the purpose of dislodging any rebels who might have effected an entrance.‡ He collected accordingly seven or eight hundred Walloon veterans, at his disposal in Flanders, in the little port of Sas de Ghent, prepared at once to execute his intention, "worthy," says a Catholic writer, "of his well-known courage and magnanimity.§ The Duchess expressed gratitude for the Count's devotion and loyalty, but his services in the sequel proved unnecessary. The rebels, several boat-loads of whom had been cruising about in the neighborhood of Flushing during the early part of March, had been refused admittance into any of the ports on the island. They therefore sailed up the Scheld, and landed at a little village called Ostrawell, at the distance of somewhat more than a mile from Antwerp.‖

The commander of the expedition was Marnix of Tholouse, brother to Marnix of Saint Aldegonde. This young nobleman, who had left college to fight for the cause of religious liberty, was possessed of fine talents and accomplishments.¶ Like his illustrious brother, he was already a sincere convert to the doctrines of the reformed Church.** He had nothing, however, but courage to recommend him as a leader in a military expedition. He was a mere boy, utterly without experience in the field.†† His troops were raw levies, vagabonds, and outlaws.

Such as it was, however, his army was soon posted at Ostrawell in a convenient position, and with considerable judgment. He had the Scheld and its dykes in his rear, on his right and left the dykes and the village. In front he threw up a breastwork and sunk a trench.‡‡ Here then was set up the standard of rebellion, and hither flocked daily many

---

* Bor, iii. 156.   † Ibid.   ‡ Pontus Payen MS.
§ Ibid.   ‖ Bor, iii. 156. Hoofd, iii. 120. Meteren, ii. 45.
¶ Pontus Payen MS.   ** Ibid.   †† Ibid.   ‡‡ Ibid.

malcontents from the country round.   Within a few days
three thousand men were in his camp.   On the other hand,
Brederode was busy in Holland, and boasted of taking the
field ere long with six thousand soldiers at the very least.
Together they would march to the relief of Valenciennes, and
dictate peace in Brussels.*

It was obvious that this matter could not be allowed to go
on.   The Duchess, with some trepidation, accepted the offer
made by Philip de Lannoy, Seigneur de Beauvoir, commander
of her body-guard in Brussels, to destroy this nest of rebels
without delay.†   Half the whole number of these soldiers was
placed at his disposition, and Egmont supplied De Beauvoir
with four hundred of his veteran Walloons.‡

With a force numbering only eight hundred, but all picked
men, the intrepid officer undertook his enterprise, with great
despatch and secrecy.   Upon the 12th March, the whole troop
was sent off in small parties, to avoid suspicion, and armed only
with sword and dagger.   Their helmets, bucklers, arquebusses,
corselets, spears, standards and drums, were delivered to their
officers, by whom they were conveyed noiselessly to the place
of rendezvous.§   Before daybreak, upon the following morning,
De Beauvoir met his soldiers at the abbey of Saint Bernard,
within a league of Antwerp.   Here he gave them their arms,
supplied them with refreshments, and made them a brief
speech.|| He instructed them that they were to advance,
with furled banners and without beat of drum, till within sight
of the enemy, that the foremost section was to deliver its fire,
retreat to the rear and load, to be followed by the next, which
was to do the same, and above all, that not an arquebus
should be discharged till the faces of the enemy could be distinguished.¶

The troop started.   After a few minutes' march they were
in full sight of Ostrawell.   They then displayed their flags

---

* Pontus Payen MS.   † Ibid.   ‡ Ibid.
§ Pontus Payen MS.   Compare Gachard, Preface to Guillaume le Tacit. ii.
cxxiv.–cxxx. || Pontus Payen MS.
¶ Ibid.—Compare the Letters of De Beauvoir, published by M. Gachard,
Preface, etc., ubi supra.

and advanced upon the fort with loud huzzas. Tholouse was as much taken by surprise as if they had suddenly emerged from the bowels of the earth.* He had been informed that the government at Brussels was in extreme trepidation. When he first heard the advancing trumpets and sudden shouts, he thought it a detachment of Brederode's promised force. The cross on the banners† soon undeceived him. Nevertheless "like a brave and generous young gentleman as he was,"‡ he lost no time in drawing up his men for action, implored them to defend their breastworks, which were impregnable against so small a force, and instructed them to wait patiently with their fire, till the enemy were near enough to be marked.

These orders were disobeyed. The " young scholar," as De Beauvoir had designated him, had no power to infuse his own spirit into his rabble rout of followers. They were already panic-struck by the unexpected appearance of the enemy. The Catholics came on with the coolness of veterans, taking as deliberate aim as if it had been they, not their enemies, who were behind breastworks. The troops of Tholouse fired wildly, precipitately, quite over the heads of the assailants. Many of the defenders were slain as fast as they showed themselves above their bulwarks. The ditch was crossed, the breastwork carried at a single determined charge. The rebels made little resistance, but fled as soon as the enemy entered their fort. It was a hunt, not a battle. Hundreds were stretched dead in the camp ; hundreds were driven into the Scheld ; six or eight hundred took refuge in a farm-house ; but De Beauvoir's men set fire to the building, and every rebel who had entered it was burned alive or shot. No quarter was given. Hardly a man of the three thousand who had held the fort escaped. The body of Tholouse was cut into a hundred pieces.§ The Seigneur

---

* Pontus Payen MS.

† Letter of De Beauvoir, ubi sup.   ‡ Pontus Payen MS.

§ " Le Sʳ de Tholouze qui at esté haché en cent pièces, non obstant l'offre de deux mil escus qu'il faisoit pour ranson," etc.—Letter of De Beauvoir in Gachard, ubi sup.

de Beauvoir had reason, in the brief letter which gave an account of this exploit, to assure her Highness that there were "some very valiant fellows in his little troop." Certainly they had accomplished the enterprise entrusted to them with promptness, neatness, and entire success. Of the great rebellious gathering, which every day had seemed to grow more formidable, not a vestige was left.[*]

This bloody drama had been enacted in full sight of Antwerp. The fight had lasted from daybreak till ten o'clock in the forenoon, during the whole of which period, the city ramparts looking towards Ostrawell, the roofs of houses, the towers of churches had been swarming with eager spectators. The sound of drum and trumpet, the rattle of musketry, the shouts of victory, the despairing cries of the vanquished were heard by thousands who deeply sympathized with the rebels thus enduring so sanguinary a chastisement.[†]   In Antwerp there were forty thousand people opposed to the Church of Rome.[‡]   Of this number the greater proportion were Calvinists, and of these Calvinists there were thousands looking down from the battlements upon the disastrous fight. .

The excitement soon became uncontrollable. Before ten o'clock vast numbers of sectaries came pouring towards the Red Gate, which afforded the readiest egress to the scene of action ; the drawbridge of the Ostrawell Gate having been destroyed the night before by command of Orange.[§]   They came from every street and alley of the city. Some were armed with lance, pike, or arquebus ; some bore sledge-hammers ; others had the partisans, battle-axes, and huge two-handed swords of the previous century ;[||] all were determined upon issuing forth to the rescue of their friends in the fields outside the town. The wife of Tholouse, not yet aware of her husband's death, although his defeat was obvious, flew from street to street,

---

[*] Gachard, Preface, ubi sup. Pontus Payen MS.—Compare Bor, iii. 157; Meteren, f. 45.   Strada vi, 250, 251.

[†] Strada, Bor, Meteren, ubi supra.

[‡] Letter of Sir T. Gresham in Burgon, ii. 195.

[§] Bor, iii. 157   Hoofd, iii. 121.   [||] Pontus Payen MS.

calling upon the Calvinists to save or to avenge their perishing brethren.*

A terrible tumult prevailed. Ten thousand men were already up and in arms. It was then that the Prince of Orange, who was sometimes described by his enemies as timid and pusillanimous by nature, showed the mettle he was made of. His sense of duty no longer bade him defend the crown of Philip—which thenceforth was to be entrusted to the hirelings of the Inquisition—but the vast population of Antwerp, the women, the children, and the enormous wealth of the richest city in the world had been confided to his care, and he had accepted the responsibility. Mounting his horse, he made his appearance instantly at the Red Gate, before as formidable a mob as man has ever faced.† He came there almost alone, without guards. Hoogstraaten arrived soon afterwards with the same intention. The Prince was received with howls of execration. A thousand hoarse voices called him the Pope's servant, minister of Antichrist, and lavished upon him many more epithets of the same nature.‡ His life was in imminent danger. A furious clothier levelled an arquebus full at his breast. "Die, treacherous villain !" he cried ; "thou who art the cause that our brethren have perished thus miserably in yonder field."§ The loaded weapon was struck away by another hand in the crowd, while the Prince, neither daunted by the ferocious demonstrations against his life, nor enraged by the virulent abuse to which he was subjected, continued tranquilly, earnestly, imperatively to address the crowd. William of Orange had that in his face and tongue "which men willingly call master—authority." With what other talisman could he, without violence and without soldiers, have quelled even for a moment ten thousand furious Calvinists, armed, enraged against his person, and thirsting for vengeance on Catholics. The postern of the Red Gate had already been broken through before Orange and his

---

* Strada, vi. 252.

† Bor, iii. 157.   Hoofd, iii. 121.—Compare Strada, vi. 252-253.

‡ Pontus Payen MS.   § Bor, iii. 157.   Hoofd, iii. 121.

colleague, Hoogstraaten, had arrived. The most excited of
the Calvinists were preparing to rush forth upon the enemy at
Ostrawell. The Prince, after he had gained the ear of the
multitude, urged that the battle was now over, that the
reformers were entirely cut to pieces, the enemy retiring,
and that a disorderly and ill-armed mob would be unable to
retrieve the fortunes of the day. Many were persuaded to
abandon the design. Five hundred of the most violent, however, insisted upon leaving the gates, and the governors, distinctly warning these zealots that their blood must be upon
their own heads, reluctantly permitted that number to issue
from the city. The rest of the mob, not appeased, but uncertain, and disposed to take vengeance upon the Catholics
within the walls, for the disaster which had been occurring
without, thronged tumultuously to the long, wide street,
called the Mere, situate in the very heart of the city.*

Meantime the ardor of those who had sallied from the gate
grew sensibly cooler, when they found themselves in the open
fields. De Beauvoir, whose men, after the victory, had scattered in pursuit of the fugitives, now heard the tumult in the
city. Suspecting an attack, he rallied his compact little
army again for a fresh encounter. The last of the vanquished
Tholousians who had been captured, more fortunate than their
predecessors, had been spared for ransom. There were three
hundred of them ; rather a dangerous number of prisoners for
a force of eight hundred, who were just going into another
battle. De Beauvoir commanded his soldiers, therefore, to
shoot them all.† This order having been accomplished, the
Catholics marched towards Antwerp, drums beating, colors
flying. The five hundred Calvinists, not liking their appearance, and being in reality outnumbered, retreated within the
gates as hastily as they had just issued from them. De Beauvoir advanced close to the city moat, on the margin of which
he planted the banners of the unfortunate Tholouse, and

---

* Bor, iii. 157, sqq. Pontus Payen MS. Letter of Sir T. Gresham.

† Pontus Payen MS.—"Leur commanda de tuer sur le champ tous leurs
prisonniers."—"Qui fust aussitòt executé que commande."

sounded a trumpet of defiance. Finding that the citizens had apparently no stomach for the fight, he removed his trophies, and took his departure.*

On the other hand, the tumult within the walls had again increased. The Calvinists had been collecting in great numbers upon the Mere. This was a large and splendid thoroughfare, rather an oblong market-place than a street, filled with stately buildings, and communicating by various cross streets with the Exchange and with many other public edifices. By an early hour in the afternoon twelve or fifteen thousand Calvinists,† all armed and fighting men, had assembled upon the place. They had barricaded the whole precinct with pavements and upturned wagons. They had already broken into the arsenal and obtained many field-pieces, which were planted at the entrance of every street and by-way. They had stormed the city jail and liberated the prisoners, all of whom, grateful and ferocious, came to swell the numbers who defended the stronghold on the Mere. A tremendous mischief was afoot. Threats of pillaging the churches and the houses of the Catholics, of sacking the whole opulent city, were distinctly heard among this powerful mob, excited by religious enthusiasm, but containing within one great heterogeneous mass the elements of every crime which humanity can commit. The alarm throughout the city was indescribable. The cries of women and children, as they remained in trembling expectation of what the next hour might bring forth, were, said one who heard them, "enough to soften the hardest hearts."‡

Nevertheless the diligence and courage of the Prince kept pace with the insurrection. He had caused the eight companies of guards enrolled in September, to be mustered upon the square in front of the city hall, for the protection of that building and of the magistracy. He had summoned the

---

* Pontus Payen MS.

† Correspondance de Marg. d'Autriche, 226, 227.

‡ Bor. iii. 159, who has incorporated into his work the "justification" published cotemporaneously by the magistracy of Antwerp.

senate of the city, the board of ancients, the deans of guilds, the ward masters, to consult with him at the council-room. At the peril of his life he had again gone before the angry mob in the Mere, advancing against their cannon and their outcries, and compelling them to appoint eight deputies to treat with him and the magistrates at the town-hall. This done, quickly but deliberately he had drawn up six articles, to which those deputies gave their assent, and in which the city government cordially united. These articles provided that the keys of the city should remain in the possession of the Prince and of Hoogstraaten, that the watch should be held by burghers and soldiers together, that the magistrates should permit the entrance of no garrison, and that the citizens should be entrusted with the care of the charters, especially with that of the joyful entrance.*

These arrangements, when laid before the assembly at the Mere by their deputies, were not received with favor. The Calvinists demanded the keys of the city. They did not choose to be locked up at the mercy of any man. They had already threatened to blow the city hall into the air if the keys were not delivered to them.† They claimed that burghers, without distinction of religion, instead of mercenary troops, should be allowed to guard the market-place in front of the town-hall.

It was now nightfall, and no definite arrangement had been concluded. Nevertheless, a temporary truce was made, by means of a concession as to the guard. It was agreed that the burghers, Calvinists and Lutherans, as well as Catholics, should be employed to protect the city. By subtlety, however, the Calvinists detailed for that service, were posted not in the town-house square, but on the ramparts and at the gates.‡

A night of dreadful expectation was passed. The army of fifteen thousand mutineers remained encamped and barricaded on the Mere, with guns loaded and artillery pointed. Fierce

---

* Bor. iii. 157.
† Letter of Sir T. Gresham.　Bor, ubi sup.　　　　　‡ Bor.

cries of "Long live the beggars," "Down with the papists,"
and other significant watchwords, were heard all night long,
but no more serious outbreak occurred.*

During the whole of the following day, the Calvinists
remained in their encampment, the Catholics and the city
guardsmen at their posts near the city hall. The Prince was
occupied in the council-chamber from morning till night with
the municipal authorities, the deputies of "the religion," and
the guild officers, in framing a new treaty of peace. Towards
evening fifteen articles were agreed upon, which were to be
proposed forthwith to the insurgents, and in case of non-
acceptance to be enforced. The arrangement provided that
there should be no garrison ; that the September contracts
permitting the reformed worship at certain places within the
city should be maintained ; that men of different parties should
refrain from mutual insults ; that the two governors, the Prince
and Hoogstraaten, should keep the keys ; that the city should
be guarded by both soldiers and citizens, without distinction
of religious creed ; that a band of four hundred cavalry and a
small flotilla of vessels of war should be maintained for the
defence of the place, and that the expenses to be incurred
should be levied upon all classes, clerical and lay, Catholic and
Reformed, without any exception.†

It had been intended that the governors, accompanied by
the magistrates, should forthwith proceed to the Mere, for the
purpose of laying these terms before the insurgents. Night
had, however, already arrived, and it was understood that the
ill-temper of the Calvinists had rather increased than diminished, so that it was doubtful whether the arrangement
would be accepted. It was, therefore, necessary to await the
issue of another day, rather than to provoke a night battle in
the streets.‡

During the night the Prince labored incessantly to provide
against the dangers of the morrow. The Calvinists had

---

* Bor, ubi. sup. Hoofd, iii. 121, sqq.

† Bor, iii. 158.   ‡ Ibid., 158ᵇ.

fiercely expressed their disinclination to any reasonable arrangement. They had threatened, without further pause, to plunder the religious houses and the mansions of all the wealthy Catholics, and to drive every papist out of town.* They had summoned the Lutherans to join with them in their revolt, and menaced them, in case of refusal, with the same fate which awaited the Catholics.† The Prince, who was himself a Lutheran, not entirely free from the universal prejudice against the Calvinists, whose sect he afterwards embraced, was fully aware of the deplorable fact, that the enmity at that day between Calvinists and Lutherans was as fierce as that between Reformers and Catholics. He now made use of this feeling, and of his influence with those of the Augsburg Confession, to save the city. During the night he had interviews with the ministers and notable members of the Lutheran churches, and induced them to form an alliance upon this occasion with the Catholics and with all friends of order, against an army of outlaws who were threatening to burn and sack the city. The Lutherans, in the silence of night, took arms and encamped, to the number of three or four thousand, upon the river side, in the neighborhood of Saint Michael's cloister. The Prince also sent for the deans of all the foreign mercantile associations—Italian, Spanish, Portuguese, English, Hanseatic, engaged their assistance also for the protection of the city, and commanded them to remain in their armor at their respective factories, ready to act at a moment's warning. It was agreed that they should be informed at frequent intervals as to the progress of events.‡

On the morning of the 15th, the city of Antwerp presented a fearful sight. Three distinct armies were arrayed at different points within its walls. The Calvinists, fifteen thousand strong, lay in their encampment on the Mere; the Lutherans, armed, and eager for action, were at St. Michael's; the Catholics

---

* Bor, iii., 158ᵇ.   † Ibid.

‡ Ibid., iii. 158, 159.   Strada, vi. 252, 253.   Hoofd, iii. 120, 122.   Letter of Sir T. Gresham.

and the regulars of the city guard were posted on the square. Between thirty-five and forty thousand men were up, according to the most moderate computation.* All parties were excited, and eager for the fray. The fires of religious hatred burned fiercely in every breast. Many malefactors and outlaws, who had found refuge in the course of recent events at Antwerp, were in the ranks of the Calvinists, profaning a sacred cause, and inspiring a fanatical party with bloody resolutions. Papists, once and forever, were to be hunted down, even as they had been for years pursuing Reformers. Let the men who had fed fat on the spoils of plundered Christians be dealt with in like fashion. Let their homes be sacked, their bodies given to the dogs—such were the cries uttered by thousands of armed men.

On the other hand, the Lutherans, as angry and as rich as the Catholics, saw in every Calvinist a murderer and a robber. They thirsted after their blood; for the spirit of religious frenzy, the characteristic of the century, can with difficulty be comprehended in our colder and more sceptical age. There was every probability that a bloody battle was to be fought that day in the streets of Antwerp—a general engagement, in the course of which, whoever might be the victors, the city was sure to be delivered over to fire, sack, and outrage. Such would have been the result, according to the concurrent testimony of eye-witnesses, and contemporary historians of every country and creed, but for the courage and wisdom of one man. William of Orange knew what

---

* The government estimate, as to the numbers of the armed Calvinists alone, was fourteen thousand.—Correspondance de M. d'Autriche, 226, 227. Sir Thomas Gresham estimated them at ten thousand armed and fighting men, while he placed the total numbers upon both sides as high as fifty thousand. "So that, sir, by credible report, there rose up all sorts above fyftie thousand menne very well armed."—Letter of March 17, 1566, in Burgon.

The Prince of Orange, who was always moderate in his computations on such occasions, stated the whole force on both sides at twenty-eight thousand only— "Dan E. L. mögen uns vertrauen das zu baiden seiten in die acht und zwantig thausend bewerter man gewesen seindt."—Letter to Landgrave William. Archives et Correspondance, iii. 59. This applies exclusively to armed and fighting men.

would be the consequence of a battle, pent up within the walls of Antwerp. He foresaw the horrible havoc which was to be expected, the desolation which would be brought to every hearth in the city. "Never were men so desperate and so willing to fight,"* said Sir Thomas Gresham, who had been expecting every hour his summons to share in the conflict. If the Prince were unable that morning to avert the impending calamity, no other power, under heaven, could save Antwerp from destruction.

The articles prepared on the 14th had been already approved by those who represented the Catholic and Lutheran interests. They were read early in the morning to the troops assembled on the square and at St. Michael's, and received with hearty cheers.† It was now necessary that the Calvinists should accept them, or that the quarrel should be fought out at once. At ten o'clock, William of Orange, attended by his colleague, Hoogstraaten, together with a committee of the municipal authorities, and followed by a hundred troopers, rode to the Mere. They wore red scarfs over their armor,‡ as symbols by which all those who had united to put down the insurrection were distinguished. The fifteen thousand Calvinists, fierce and disorderly as ever, maintained a threatening aspect. Nevertheless, the Prince was allowed to ride into the midst of the square. The articles were then read aloud by his command, after which, with great composure, he made a few observations. He pointed out that the arrangement offered them was founded upon the September concessions, that the right of worship was conceded, that the foreign garrison was forbidden, and that nothing further could be justly demanded or honorably admitted. He told them that a struggle upon their part would be hopeless, for the Catholics and Lutherans, who were all agreed as to the justice of the treaty, outnumbered them by nearly two to one. He, therefore, most earnestly and affectionately adjured them to testify their acceptance to the peace offered by repeating the words

---

* Letter in Burgon, 17th March.   † Bor. Letter of Sir T. Gresham.   ‡ Ibid.

with which he should conclude. Then, with a firm voice, the Prince exclaimed, " God save the King !" It was the last time that those words were ever heard from the lips of the man already proscribed by Philip. The crowd of Calvinists hesitated an instant, and then, unable to resist the tranquil influence, convinced by his reasonable language, they raised one tremendous shout of " Vive le Roi !"

The deed was done, the peace accepted, the dreadful battle averted, Antwerp saved. The deputies of the Calvinists now formally accepted and signed the articles. Kind words were exchanged among the various classes of fellow-citizens, who but an hour before had been thirsting for each other's blood, the artillery and other weapons of war were restored to the arsenals, Calvinists, Lutherans, and Catholics, all laid down their arms, and the city, by three o'clock, was entirely quiet. Fifty thousand armed men had been up, according to some estimates, yet, after three days of dreadful expectation, not a single person had been injured, and the tumult was now appeased.*

The Prince had, in truth, used the mutual animosity of Protestant sects to a good purpose ; averting bloodshed by the very weapons with which the battle was to have been waged. Had it been possible for a man like William the Silent to occupy the throne where Philip the Prudent sat, how different might have been the history of Spain and the fate of the Netherlands. Gresham was right, however, in his conjecture that the Regent and court would not " take the business well." Margaret of Parma was incapable of comprehending such a mind as that of Orange, or of appreciating its efforts. She was surrounded by unscrupulous and mercenary soldiers, who hailed the coming civil war as the most profitable of speculations. " Factotum" Mansfeld, the Counts Aremberg and Meghem, the Duke of Aerschot, the sanguinary Noircarmes, were already counting their share in the coming confiscations. In the internecine conflict approaching, there

---

* Bor. iii. 159. Hoofd, iv. 121, 122. Strada vi. 252, 253. Archives et Correspondance, iii. 48–52, 58. 59.

would be gold for the gathering, even if no honorable laurels would wreath their swords. " Meghen with his regiment is desolating the country," wrote William of Orange to the Land-grave of Hesse, "and reducing many people to poverty. Aremberg is doing the same in Friesland. They are only thinking how, under the pretext of religion, they may grind the poor Christians, and grow rich and powerful upon their estates and their blood."*

The Seignior de Beauvoir wrote to the Duchess, claiming all the estates of Tholouse, and of his brother St. Aldegonde, as his reward for the Ostrawell victory,† while Noircarmes was at this very moment to commence at Valenciennes that career of murder and spoliation which, continued at Mons a few years afterwards, was to load his name with infamy.

From such a Regent, surrounded by such councillors, was the work of William de Nassau's hands to gain applause ? What was it to them that carnage and plunder had been spared in one of the richest and most populous cities in Christendom? Were not carnage and plunder the very elements in which they disported themselves ? And what more dreadful offence against God and Philip could be committed than to permit, as the Prince had just permitted, the right of worship in a Christian land to Calvinists and Lutherans ? As a matter of course, therefore, Margaret of Parma denounced the terms by which Antwerp had been saved as a "novel and exorbitant capitulation," and had no intention of signifying her appro-bation either to prince or magistrate.‡

---

* Archives et Correspondance, iii. 39.
† Correspondance de Philippe II., i. 546.
‡ Correspondance de Marg. d'Autriche, 227.

CHAPTER X.

VALENCIENNES, whose fate depended so closely upon the issue of these various events, was now trembling to her fall. Noircarmes had been drawing the lines more and more closely about the city, and by a refinement of cruelty had compelled many Calvinists from Tournay to act as pioneers in the trenches against their own brethren in Valenciennes.* After the defeat of Tholouse, and the consequent frustration of all Brederode's arrangements to relieve the siege, the Duchess had sent a fresh summons to Valenciennes, together with letters acquainting the citizens with the results of the Ostrawell battle. The intelligence was not believed. Egmont and Aerschot, however, to whom Margaret had entrusted this last

---

* Pasquier de la Barre MS., f. 92.

mission to the beleaguered town, roundly rebuked the deputies who came to treat with them, for their insolence in daring to doubt the word of the Regent. The two seigniors had established themselves in the Chateau or Beusnage, at a league's distance from Valenciennes. Here they received commissioners from the city, half of whom were Catholics appointed by the magistrates, half Calvinists deputed by the consistories. These envoys were informed that the Duchess would pardon the city for its past offences, provided the gates should now be opened, the garrison received, and a complete suppression of all religion except that of Rome acquiesced in without a murmur. As nearly the whole population was of the Calvinist faith, these terms could hardly be thought favorable. It was, however, added, that fourteen days should be allowed to the Reformers for the purpose of converting their property, and retiring from the country.*

The deputies, after conferring with their constituents in the city, returned on the following day with counter-propositions, which were not more likely to find favor with the government. They offered to accept the garrison, provided the soldiers should live at their own expense, without any tax to the citizens for their board, lodging, or pay. They claimed that all property which had been seized should be restored, all persons accused of treason liberated. They demanded the unconditional revocation of the edict by which the city had been declared rebellious, together with a guarantee from the Knights of the Fleece and the state council that the terms of the proposed treaty should be strictly observed.†

As soon as these terms had been read to the two seigniors, the Duke of Aerschot burst into an immoderate fit of laughter. He protested that nothing could be more ludicrous than such propositions, worthy of a conqueror dictating a peace, thus offered by a city closely beleaguered,

---

* Pontus Payen MS. Valenciennes MS.
† Pontus Payen MS.

and entirely at the mercy of the enemy. The Duke's hilarity was not shared by Egmont, who, on the contrary, fell into a furious passion. He swore that the city should be burned about their ears, and that every one of the inhabitants should be put to the sword for the insolent language which they had thus dared to address to a most clement sovereign. He ordered the trembling deputies instantly to return with this peremptory rejection of their terms, and with his command that the proposals of government should be accepted within three days' delay.

The commissioners fell upon their knees at Egmont's feet, and begged for mercy. They implored him at least to send this imperious message by some other hand than theirs, and to permit them to absent themselves from the city. They should be torn limb from limb, they said, by the enraged inhabitants, if they dared to present themselves with such instructions before them. Egmont, however, assured them that they should be sent into the city, bound hand and foot, if they did not instantly obey his orders. The deputies, therefore, with heavy hearts, were fain to return home with this bitter result to their negotiations. The terms were rejected, as a matter of course, but the gloomy forebodings of the commissioners, as to their own fate at the hands of their fellow-citizens, were not fulfilled.*

Instant measures were now taken to cannonade the city. Egmont, at the hazard of his life, descended into the foss, to reconnoitre the works, and to form an opinion as to the most eligible quarter at which to direct the batteries.† Having communicated the result of his investigations to Noircarmes, he returned to report all these proceedings to the Regent at Brussels. Certainly the Count had now separated himself far enough from William of Orange, and was manifesting an energy in the cause of tyranny which was sufficiently unscrupulous. Many people who had been deceived by his more

---

* Pontus Payen MS.   Valenciennes MS.   † Ibid.

generous demonstrations in former times, tried to persuade themselves that he was acting a part. Noircarmes, however —and no man was more competent to decide the question,— distinctly expressed his entire confidence in Egmont's loyalty.[*] Margaret had responded warmly to his eulogies, had read with approbation secret letters from Egmont to Noircarmes, and had expressed the utmost respect and affection for "the Count." Egmont had also lost no time in writing to Philip, informing him that he had selected the most eligible spot for battering down the obstinate city of Valenciennes, regretting that he could not have had the eight or ten military companies, now at his disposal, at an earlier day, in which case he should have been able to suppress many tumults, but congratulating his sovereign that the preachers were all fugitive, the reformed religion suppressed, and the people disarmed. He assured the King that he would neglect no effort to prevent any renewal of the tumults, and expressed the hope that his Majesty would be satisfied with his conduct, notwithstanding the calumnies of which the times were full.[†]

Noircarmes meanwhile, had unmasked his batteries, and opened his fire exactly according to Egmont's suggestions.[‡] The artillery played first upon what was called the "White Tower," which happened to bear this ancient, rhyming inscription :—

> "When every man receives his own,
> And justice reigns for strong and weak,
> Perfect shall be this tower of stone,
> And—all the dumb will learn to speak."[§]

For some unknown reason, the rather insipid quatrain was

---

[*] Correspondance de Guillaume le Tacit. ii. 502.
[†] Correspondance de Philippe II., i. 524.
[‡] Pontus Payen MS.　Correspondance de Philippe II., i. ubi sub.
[§] 　　　"Quand chacun sera satisfaict,
　　　　Et la justice regnera,
　　　　Ce boulevard sera parfaict,
　　　　　Et—la muette parlera."—Valenciennes MS.

tortured into a baleful prophecy. It was considered very ominous that the battery should be first opened against this Sibylline tower. The chimes, too, which had been playing, all through the siege, the music of Marot's sacred songs, happened that morning to be sounding forth from every belfry the twenty-second psalm : " My God, my God, why hast thou forsaken me ?"*

It was Palm Sunday, 23d of March. The women and children were going mournfully about the streets, bearing green branches in their hands, and praying upon their knees, in every part of the city. Despair and superstition had taken possession of citizens, who up to that period had justified La Noue's assertion, that none could endure a siege like Huguenots. As soon as the cannonading began, the spirit of the inhabitants seemed to depart. The ministers exhorted their flocks in vain as the tiles and chimneys began to topple into the streets, and the concussions of the artillery were responded to by the universal wailing of affrighted women.†

Upon the very first day after the unmasking of the batteries, the city sent to Noircarmes, offering almost an unconditional surrender. Not the slightest breach had been effected—not the least danger of an assault existed—yet the citizens, who had earned the respect of their antagonists by the courageous manner in which they had sallied and skirmished during the siege, now in despair at any hope of eventual succor, and completely demoralized by the course of recent events outside their walls, surrendered ignominiously, and at discretion.‡ The only stipulation agreed to by Noircarmes was, that the city should not be sacked, and that the lives of the inhabitants should be spared.§

This pledge was, however, only made to be broken. Noircarmes entered the city and closed the gates. All the richest citizens, who of course were deemed the most

---

* Valenciennes MS.　　　　　　　† Pontus Payen MS.
‡ Ibid.　Valenciennes MS.　Bor, iii. 142.
§ Bor, iii. 142.　Hoofd, iv. 129 (bis.)

criminal, were instantly arrested. The soldiers, although not permitted formally to sack the city, were quartered upon the inhabitants, whom they robbed and murdered, according to the testimony of a Catholic citizen, almost at their pleasure.*

Michael Herlin, a very wealthy and distinguished burgher, was arrested upon the first day. The two ministers, Guido de Bray and Peregrine de la Grange, together with the son of Herlin, effected their escape by the water-gate. Having taken refuge in a tavern at Saint Arnaud, they were observed, as they sat at supper, by a peasant, who forthwith ran off to the mayor of the borough with the intelligence that some individuals, who looked like fugitives, had arrived at Saint Arnaud. One of them, said the informer, was richly dressed, and wore a gold-hilted sword with velvet scabbard. By the description, the mayor recognized Herlin the younger, and suspected his companions. They were all arrested, and sent to Noircarmes. The two Herlins, father and son, were immediately beheaded.† Guido de Bray and Peregrine de la Grange were loaded with chains, and thrown into a filthy dungeon, previously to their being hanged.‡ Here they were visited by the Countess de Roeulx, who was curious to see how the Calvinists sustained themselves in their martyrdom. She asked them how they could sleep, eat, or drink, when covered with such heavy fetters. "The cause, and my good conscience," answered De Bray, "make me eat, drink, and sleep better than those who are doing me wrong. These shackles are more honorable to me than golden rings and chains. They are more useful to me, and as I hear their clank, methinks I hear the music of sweet voices and the tinkling of lutes."§

This exultation never deserted these courageous enthusiasts. They received their condemnation to death "as if it had been

---

* Valenciennes MS.   † Pontus Payen MS.
‡ Brandt, Reformatie, i. 448, 449.
§ Ibid.   Hist. des Mart., f. 661, 662, apud Brandt.

an invitation to a marriage feast."* They encouraged the friends who crowded their path to the scaffold with exhortations to remain true in the Reformed faith. La Grange, standing upon the ladder, proclaimed with a loud voice, that he was slain for having preached the pure word of God to a Christian people in a Christian land. De Bray, under the same gibbet, testified stoutly that he, too, had committed that offence alone. He warned his friends to obey the magistrates, and all others in authority, except in matters of conscience ; to abstain from sedition, but to obey the will of God. The executioner threw him from the ladder while he was yet speaking. So ended the lives of two eloquent, learned, and highly-gifted divines.†

Many hundreds of victims were sacrificed in the unfortunate city. "There were a great many other citizens strangled or beheaded," says an aristocratic Catholic historian of the time, " but they were mostly personages of little quality, whose names are quite unknown to me."‡ The franchises of the city were all revoked. There was a prodigious amount of property confiscated to the benefit of Noircarmes and the rest of the " Seven Sleepers." Many Calvinists were burned, others were hanged. " *For two whole years,*" says another Catholic, who was a citizen of Valenciennes at the time, " *there was scarcely a week in which several citizens were not executed and often a great number were despatched at a time.* All this gave so much alarm to the good and innocent, that many quitted the city as fast as they could."§ If the good and innocent happened to be rich, they might be sure that Noircarmes would deem that a crime for which no goodness and innocence could atone.

---

* "En schickten sich soo blij moedelijk tot sterven als of ze ter bruiloft gingen." —Brandt, ubi sup.

† Brandt. Hist. des Martyrs, ubi sup.

‡ Pontus Payen MS.—" Beaucoup d'autres bourgeois receurent depuis pareil traictement, qui estoient personnages de petite qualité et à moy incognus."

§ Valenciennes MS.

Upon the fate of Valenciennes had depended, as if by common agreement, the whole destiny of the anti-Catholic party. "People had learned at last," says another Walloon, "that the King had long arms, and that he had not been enlisting soldiers to string beads. So they drew in their horns and their evil tempers, meaning to put them forth again, should the government not succeed at the siege of Valenciennes."* The government had succeeded, however, and the consternation was extreme, the general submission immediate and even abject. "The capture of Valenciennes," wrote Noircarmes to Granvelle, "has worked a miracle. The other cities all come forth to meet me, putting the rope around ●their own necks."† No opposition was offered any where. Tournay had been crushed ; Valenciennes, Bois le Duc, and all other important places, accepted their garrisons without a murmur. Even Antwerp had made its last struggle, and as soon as the back of Orange was turned, knelt down in the dust to receive its bridle. The Prince had been able, by his courage and wisdom, to avert a sanguinary conflict within its walls, but his personal presence alone could guarantee any thing like religious liberty for the inhabitants, now that the rest of the country was subdued. On the 26th April, sixteen companies of infantry, under Count Mansfeld, entered the gates.‡ On the 28th the Duchess made a visit to the city, where she was received with respect, but where her eyes were shocked by that which she termed the "abominable, sad, and hideous spectacle of the desolated churches."§

To the eyes of all who loved their fatherland and their race, the sight of a desolate country, with its ancient charters superseded by brute force, its industrious population swarming from the land in droves, as if the pestilence were raging, with

---

* Renom de France MS., i. 35, 37.
† Gachard, Preface to Guillaume le Tacit. ii. clxi., note 2.
‡ Gachard, Preface, etc., lxxxix.
§ Correspondance de Guillaume le Tacit. ii. 383-386.

gibbets and scaffolds erected in every village, and with a
sickening and universal apprehension of still darker disasters
to follow, was a spectacle still more sad, hideous, and
abominable.

For it was now decided that the Duke of Alva, at the head
of a Spanish army, should forthwith take his departure for
the Netherlands. A land already subjugated was to be
crushed, and every vestige of its ancient liberties destroyed.
The conquered provinces, once the abode of municipal liberty,
of science, art, and literature, and blessed with an unexampled
mercantile and manufacturing prosperity, were to be placed
in absolute subjection to the cabinet council at Madrid. A
dull and malignant bigot, assisted by a few Spanish grandees,
and residing at the other extremity of Europe, was thenceforth to exercise despotic authority over countries which for
centuries had enjoyed a local administration, and a system
nearly approaching to complete self-government. Such was
the policy devised by Granvelle and Spinosa,* which the
Duke of Alva, upon the 15th April, had left Madrid to
enforce.

It was very natural that Margaret of Parma should be
indignant at being thus superseded. She considered herself
as having acquired much credit by the manner in which the
latter insurrectionary movements had been suppressed, so soon
as Philip, after his endless tergiversations, had supplied her
with arms and money. Therefore she wrote in a tone of
great asperity to her brother, expressing her discontent. She
had always been trammelled in her action, she said, by his
restrictions upon her authority. She complained that he had
no regard for her reputation or her peace of mind. Notwithstanding all impediments and dangers, she had at last settled
the country, and now another person was to reap the honor.†
She also despatched the Seigneur de Billy to Spain, for the

* Confessions of Del Rio.
† Correspondance de Philippe II., i. 523.

purpose of making verbal representations to his Majesty upon the inexpediency of sending the Duke of Alva to the Netherlands at that juncture with a Spanish army.*

Margaret gained nothing, however, by her letters and her envoy, save a round rebuke from Philip, who was not accustomed to brook the language of remonstrance, even from his sister. His purpose was fixed. Absolute submission was now to be rendered by all. "He was highly astonished and dissatisfied," he said, "that she should dare to write to him with so much passion, and in so resolute a manner. If she received no other recompence, save the glory of having restored the service of God, she ought to express her gratitude to the King for having given her the opportunity of so doing."†

The affectation of clement intentions was still maintained, together with the empty pretence of the royal visit. Alva and his army were coming merely to prepare the way for the King, who still represented himself as "debonair and gentle, slow to anger, and averse from bloodshed." Superficial people believed that the King was really coming, and hoped wonders from his advent. The Duchess knew better. The Pope never believed in it, Granvelle never believed in it, the Prince of Orange never believed in it, Councillor d'Assonleville never believed in it. "His Majesty," says the Walloon historian, who wrote from Assonleville's papers, "had many imperative reasons for not coming. He was fond of quiet, he was a great negotiator, distinguished for phlegm and modesty, disinclined to long journeys, particularly to sea voyages, which were very painful to him. Moreover, he was then building his Escorial with so much taste and affection that it was impossible for him to leave home."‡ These excellent reasons sufficed to detain the monarch, in whose place a general was appointed, who, it must be confessed, was neither phlegmatic nor modest, and whose energies were quite equal to the work required.

---

* Pontus Payen MS. Correspondance de Philippe II., i. 536.
† Correspondance de Philippe II., i. 540.
‡ Renom de France MS., i. 29.

There had in truth never been any thing in the King's project of visiting the Netherlands but pretence."*

On the other hand, the work of Orange for the time was finished. He had saved Antwerp, he had done his best to maintain the liberties of the country, the rights of conscience, and the royal authority, so far as they were compatible with each other. The alternative had now been distinctly forced upon every man, either to promise blind obedience or to accept the position of a rebel. William of Orange had thus become a rebel. He had been requested to sign the new oath, greedily taken by the Mansfelds, the Berlaymonts, the Aerschots, and the Egmonts, to obey every order which he might receive, against every person and in every place, without restriction or limitation,† and he had distinctly and repeatedly declined the demand. He had again and again insisted upon resigning all his offices. The Duchess, more and more anxious to gain over such an influential personage to the cause of tyranny, had been most importunate in her requisitions. "A man with so noble a heart," she wrote to the Prince, "and with a descent from such illustrious and loyal ancestors, can surely not forget his duties to his Majesty and the country."‡

William of Orange knew his duty to both better than the Duchess could understand. He answered this fresh summons by reminding her that he had uniformly refused the new and extraordinary pledge required of him. He had been true to his old oaths, and therefore no fresh pledge was necessary. Moreover, a pledge without limitation he would never take. The case might happen, he said, that he should be ordered to do things contrary to his conscience, prejudicial to his Majesty's service, and in violation of his oaths to maintain the laws of the country. He therefore once more resigned all his offices, and signified his intention of leaving the provinces.§

---

* Nihil profectionis inerat, præter speciem," says Strada, vi. 280.
† Groen v. Prinst., Archives, iii. 43–48.   ‡ Ibid.
§ Ibid.

Margaret had previously invited him to an interview at Brussels, which he had declined, because he had discovered a conspiracy in that place to "play him a trick." Assonleville had already been sent to him without effect. He had refused to meet a deputation of Fleece Knights at Mechlin, from the same suspicion of foul play. After the termination of the Antwerp tumult, Orange again wrote to the Duchess, upon the 19th March, repeating his refusal to take the oath, and stating that he considered himself as at least suspended from all his functions, since she had refused, upon the ground of incapacity, to accept his formal resignation. Margaret now determined, by the advice of the state council, to send Secretary Berty, provided with an ample letter of instructions, upon a special mission to the Prince at Antwerp. That respectable functionary performed his task with credit, going through the usual formalities, and adducing the threadbare arguments in favor of the unlimited oath, with much adroitness and decorum. He mildly pointed out the impropriety of laying down such responsible posts as those which the Prince now occupied at such a juncture. He alluded to the distress which the step must occasion to the debonair sovereign.

William of Orange became somewhat impatient under the official lecture of this secretary to the privy council, a mere man of sealing-wax and protocols. The slender stock of platitudes with which he had come provided was soon exhausted. His arguments shrivelled at once in the scorn with which the Prince received them. The great statesman, who, it was hoped, would be entrapped to ruin, dishonor, and death by such very feeble artifices, asked indignantly whether it were really expected that he should acknowledge himself perjured to his old obligations by now signing new ones; that he should disgrace himself by an unlimited pledge which might require him to break his oaths to the provincial statutes and to the Emperor; that he should consent to administer the religious edicts which he abhorred; that he should act as executioner of Christians on account of their religious opinions, an office against which his soul revolted; that he should bind himself by an unlimited promise which might require him to put his own wife to death, because she was a Lutheran?   Moreover, was it to be supposed that he would obey without restriction any orders issued to him in his Majesty's name, when the King's representative might be a person whose supremacy it ill became one of his race to acknowledge?   Was William of Orange to receive absolute commands from the Duke of Alva?   Having mentioned that name with indignation, the Prince became silent.*

It was very obvious that no impression was to be made upon the man by formalists.   Poor Berty having conjugated his paradigm conscientiously through all its moods and tenses, returned to his green board in the council-room with his procès verbal of the conference.   Before he took his leave, however, he prevailed upon Orange to hold an interview with the Duke of Aerschot, Count Mansfeld, and Count Egmont.†

This memorable meeting took place at Willebroek, a village midway between Antwerp and Brussels, in the first week of April.   The Duke of Aerschot was prevented from attending, but Mansfeld and Egmont—accompanied by the faithful Berty, to make another procès verbal—duly made their appearance.‡   The Prince had never felt much sympathy with Mansfeld, but a tender and honest friendship had always existed between himself and Egmont, notwithstanding the difference of their characters, the incessant artifices employed by the Spanish court to separate them, and the impassable chasm which now existed between their respective positions towards the government.

The same common-places of argument and rhetoric were now discussed between Orange and the other three personages, the Prince distinctly stating, in conclusion, that he considered himself as discharged from all his offices, and

---

* Strada, vi. 265–268.   Hoofd, iv. 130.   Corresp. de Guillaume le Tacit, ii. 354, 355–369, 370, 391–417.   † Strada, 268.

‡ Correspondance de Guillaume le Tacit ii. 416–418.—The procès verbal made by Berty upon this occasion has been lost.   Gachard, note, p. 417.   Guillaume le Tacit., ii.—Compare Strada, vi. 268, 269.

that he was about to leave the Netherlands for Germany. The interview, had it been confined to such formal conversation, would have but little historic interest. Egmont's choice had been made. Several months before he had signified his determination to hold those for enemies who should cease to conduct themselves as faithful vassals, declared himself to be without fear that the country was to be placed in the hands of Spaniards, and disavowed all intention, in any case whatever, of taking arms against the King.* His subsequent course, as we have seen, had been entirely in conformity with these solemn declarations. Nevertheless, the Prince, to whom they had been made, thought it still possible to withdraw his friend from the precipice upon which he stood, and to save him from his impending fate. His love for Egmont had, in his own noble and pathetic language, "struck its roots too deeply into his heart" to permit him, in this their parting interview, to neglect a last effort, even if this solemn warning were destined to be disregarded.

By any reasonable construction of history, Philip was an unscrupulous usurper, who was attempting to convert himself from a Duke of Brabant and a Count of Holland into an absolute king. It was William who was maintaining, Philip who was destroying ; and the monarch who was thus blasting the happiness of the provinces, and about to decimate their population, was by the same process to undermine his own power forever, and to divest himself of his richest inheritance. The man on whom he might have leaned for support, had he been capable of comprehending his character, and of understanding the age in which he had himself been called upon to reign, was, through Philip's own insanity, converted into the instrument by which his most valuable provinces were to be taken from him, and eventually re-organized into an independent commonwealth. Could a vision, like that imagined by the immortal dramatist for another tyrant and murderer,

---

* Gachard, preface to vol. ii.   Guillaume le Tacit., cix.

have revealed the future to Philip, he, too, might have beheld
his victim, not crowned himself, but pointing to a line of
kings, even to some who *two-fold balls and treble sceptres carried*, and smiling on them for his.   But such considerations as
these had no effect upon the Prince of Orange.   He knew himself already proscribed, and he knew that the secret condemnation had extended to Egmont also.   He was anxious that his
friend should prefer the privations of exile, with the chance of
becoming the champion of a struggling country, to the wretched
fate towards which his blind confidence was leading him.   Even
then it seemed possible that the brave soldier, who had been
recently defiling his sword in the cause of tyranny, might become mindful of his brighter and earlier fame.   Had Egmont
been as true to his native land as, until " the long divorce of
steel fell on him," he was faithful to Philip, he might yet have
earned brighter laurels than those gained at St. Quentin and
Gravelingen.   Was he doomed to fall, he might find a glorious
death upon freedom's battle-field, in place of that darker departure then so near him, which the prophetic language of
Orange depicted, but which he was too sanguine to fear.   He
spoke with confidence of the royal clemency.   " Alas, Egmont,"
answered the Prince, " the King's clemency, of which you
boast, will destroy you.   Would that I might be deceived,
but I foresee too clearly that you are to be the bridge which
the Spaniards will destroy so soon as they have passed over it
to invade our country."*   With these last, solemn words he
concluded his appeal to awaken the Count from his fatal
security.   Then, as if persuaded that he was looking upon
his friend for the last time, William of Orange threw his arms
around Egmont, and held him for a moment in a close embrace.
Tears fell from the eyes of both at this parting moment—
and then the brief scene of simple and lofty pathos terminated
—Egmont and Orange separated from each other, never to
meet again on earth.†

---

* Strada, vi. 286.   Compare Bentivoglio, iii. 55.

† Ibid.—Hoofd alludes to a rumor, according to which Egmont said to
Orange at parting, " Adieu, landless Prince !" and was answered by his friend

A few days afterwards, Orange addressed a letter to Philip, once more resigning all his offices, and announcing his intention of departing from the Netherlands for Germany. He added, that he should be always ready to place himself and his property at the King's orders in every thing which he believed conducive *to the true* service of his Majesty.* The Prince had already received a remarkable warning from old Landgrave Philip of Hesse, who had not forgotten the insidious manner in which his own memorable captivity had been brought about by the arts of Granvelle and of Alva. "Let them not smear your mouths with honey," said the Landgrave. "If the three seigniors, of whom the Duchess Margaret has had so much to say, are invited to court by Alva, under pretext of friendly consultation, let them be wary, and think twice ere they accept. I know the Duke of Alva and the Spaniards, and how they dealt with me."†

The Prince, before he departed, took a final leave of Horn and Egmont, by letters, which, as if aware of the monumental character they were to assume for posterity, he drew up in Latin.‡ He desired, now that he was turning his back upon the country, that those two nobles who had refused to imitate, and had advised against his course, should remember that he was acting deliberately, conscientiously, and in pursuance of a long-settled plan.

To Count Horn he declared himself unable to connive longer at the sins daily committed against the country and his own conscience. He assured him that the government

---

with "Adieu, headless Count!" "Men voeght'er by dat zy voorts elkandre, Prins zonder goedt, Graaf zonder hooft, zouden adieu gezeit hebben." The story has been often repeated, yet nothing could well be more insipid than such an invention. Hoofd observes that the whole conversation was reported by a person whom the Calvinists had concealed in the chimney of the apartment where the interview took place. It would be difficult to believe in such epigrams even had the historian himself been in the chimney. He, however, only gives the anecdote as a rumor, which he does not himself believe. "Twelk ik nochtans niet zoo zeeker houde," etc.—Hoofd, Nederl. Hist. iv. 131.

  * Archives et Correspondance, iii. 64, 65.   † Ibid., iii. 42.

  ‡ Ibid., iii. 69–73.

had been accustoming the country to panniers, in order that it might now accept patiently the saddle and bridle. For himself, he said, his back was not strong enough for the weight already imposed upon it, and he preferred to endure any calamity which might happen to him in exile, rather than be compelled by those whom they had all condemned to acquiesce in the object so long and steadily pursued.*

He reminded Egmont, who had been urging him by letter to remain, that his resolution had been deliberately taken, and long since communicated to his friends. He could not, in conscience, take the oath required ; nor would he, now that all eyes were turned upon him, remain in the land, the only recusant. He preferred to encounter all that could happen, rather than attempt to please others by the sacrifice of liberty, of his fatherland, of his own conscience. "I hope, therefore," said he to Egmont in conclusion, "that you, after weighing my reasons, will not disapprove my departure. The rest I leave to God, who will dispose of all as may most conduce to the glory of his name. For yourself, I pray you to believe that you have no more sincere friend than I am. My love for you has struck such deep root into my heart, that it can be lessened by no distance of time or place, and I pray you in return to maintain the same feelings towards me which you have always cherished."†

The Prince had left Antwerp upon the 11th April, and had written these letters from Breda, upon the 13th of the same month. Upon the 22d, he took his departure for Dillenburg, the ancestral seat of his family in Germany, by the way of Grave and Cleves.‡

It was not to be supposed that this parting message would influence Egmont's decision with regard to his own movements, when his determination had not been shaken at his memorable interview with the Prince. The Count's fate was sealed. Had he not been praised by Noircarmes ; had he not

---

* Archives et Correspondance, iii. 69–73.   † Ibid.
‡ Ibid., iii. 73, 74.

earned the hypocritical commendations of Duchess Margaret ; nay more, had he not just received a most affectionate letter of thanks and approbation from the King of Spain himself? This letter, one of the most striking monuments of Philip's cold-blooded perfidy, was dated the 26th of March. " I am pleased, my cousin," wrote the monarch to Egmont, " that you have taken the new oath, *not that I considered it at all necessary* so far as regards yourself, but for the example which you have thus given to others, and which I hope they will all follow. I have received not less pleasure in hearing of the excellent manner in which you are doing your duty, the assistance you are rendering, and the offers which you are making to my sister, for which I thank you, and request you to continue in the same course."*

The words were written by the royal hand which had already signed the death-warrant of the man to whom they were addressed. Alva, who came provided with full powers to carry out the great scheme resolved upon, unrestrained by provincial laws or by the statutes of the Golden Fleece, had left Madrid to embark for Carthagena, at the very moment when Egmont was reading the royal letter.† " The Spanish honey," to use once more old Landgrave Philip's homely metaphor, had done its work, and the unfortunate victim was already entrapped.

Count Horn remained in gloomy silence in his lair at Weert, awaiting the hunters of men, already on their way. It seemed inconceivable that he, too, who knew himself suspected and disliked, should have thus blinded himself to his position. It will be seen, however, that the same perfidy was to be employed to ensnare him which proved so successful with Egmont.

As for the Prince himself, he did not move too soon. Not long after his arrival in Germany, Vandenesse, the King's private secretary, but Orange's secret agent, wrote him word that he had read letters from the King to Alva, in which the

---

* Foppens, Supplément, ii. 544.
† Correspondance de Philippe II., i. 528, 15th April, 1567.

Duke was instructed to "arrest the Prince as soon as he could lay hands upon him, and not to let *his trial last more than twenty-four hours.*"*

Brederode had remained at Viane, and afterwards at Amsterdam, since the ill-starred expedition of Tholouse, which he had organized, but at which he had not assisted. He had given much annoyance to the magistracy of Amsterdam, and to all respectable persons, Calvinist or Catholic. He made much mischief, but excited no hopes in the minds of reformers. He was ever surrounded by a host of pot companions, swaggering nobles disguised as sailors, bankrupt tradesmen, fugitives and outlaws of every description, excellent people to drink the beggars' health and to bawl the beggars' songs, but quite unfit for any serious enterprise.† People of substance were wary of him, for they had no confidence in his capacity, and were afraid of his frequent demands for contributions to the patriotic cause. He spent his time in the pleasure gardens, shooting at the mark with arquebuss or crossbow, drinking with his comrades, and shrieking " Vivent les gueux."‡

The Regent, determined to dislodge him, had sent Secretary La Torre to him in March, with instructions that if Brederode refused to leave Amsterdam, the magistracy were to call for assistance upon Count Meghem, who had a regiment at Utrecht.§ This clause made it impossible for La Torre to

---

* This appears in a document, never yet published, in the Royal Archives at Dresden. It is a report drawn up by Captain von Berlepsch, of an interview held with the Prince of Orange, to whom he had been deputed by the Elector Augustus of Saxony. It is to be remarked, moreover, that Augustus at this period (November, 1567,) declined receiving the Prince at Dresden, while professing the greatest interest in his welfare!—Unpublished letter from Elector Augustus to Prince W. of Orange, 10th Nov., 1567, in Dresden Archives. So hatte auch des Konnings Vortrauter Kemmerling Signor Vandenes auch in grosser geheim warnen laszen dasz ehr hette aufs Konnings tische briefe gesehen ahn Hertzogen von Alba, darin bewohlen, s. fg. nachzutrachten und wan man ihn bekeme, seinen procesz nicht uber 24 Stunden zuvorlengern."—Bericht von Hauptm. v. Berlepsch.

† Correspondance de Guillaume le Tacit. ii. 434, 454. Bor, iii. 161. Hoofd, v. 127. ‡ Ibid.

§ Correspondance de Guillaume le Tacit. ii. 439, 440. Bor, iii. 161, 162.

exhibit his instructions to Brederode. Upon his refusal, that personage, although he knew the secretary as well as he knew his own father, coolly informed him that he knew nothing about him ; that he did not consider him as respectable a person as he pretended to be ; that he did not believe a word of his having any commission from the Duchess, and that he should therefore take no notice whatever of his demands. La Torre answered meekly, that he was not so presumptuous, nor so destitute of sense as to put himself into comparison with a gentleman of Count Brederode's quality, but that as he had served as secretary to the privy council for twenty-three years, he had thought that he might be believed upon his word. Hereupon La Torre drew up a formal protest, and Brederode drew up another. La Torre made a procès verbal of their interview, while Brederode stormed like a madman, and abused the Duchess for a capricious and unreasonable tyrant. He ended by imprisoning La Torre for a day or two, and seizing his papers. By a singular coincidence, these events took place on the 13th, 24th, and 15th of March,* the very days of the great Antwerp tumult. The manner in which the Prince of Orange had been dealing with forty or fifty thousand armed men, anxious to cut each other's throats, while Brederode was thus occupied in browbeating a pragmatical but decent old secretary, illustrated the difference in calibre of the two men.

This was the Count's last exploit. He remained at Amsterdam some weeks longer, but the events which succeeded changed the Hector into a faithful vassal. Before the 12th of April, he wrote to Egmont, begging his intercession with Margaret of Parma, and offering "carte blanche" as to terms, if he might only be allowed to make his peace with government.† It was, however, somewhat late in the

---

* Correspondance de Guillaume le Tacit. ii. 444-454.

† " —— Brederode ha suplicado de ser perdonado y embiado à Monsieur d'Egmont carta blanca."—MS. Letter of Granvelle to Alba. Bibl. de Bourg.

day for the "great beggar" to make his submission. No
terms were accorded him, but he was allowed by the Duchess
to enjoy his revenues provisionally, subject to the King's
pleasure. Upon the 25th April, he entertained a select circle
of friends at his hotel in Amsterdam, and then embarked
at midnight for Embden. A numerous procession of his adherents escorted him to the ship, bearing lighted torches, and
singing bacchanalian songs. He died within a year afterwards,
of disappointment and hard drinking, at Castle Hardenberg,
in Germany, after all his fretting and fury, and notwithstanding his vehement protestations to die a poor soldier at the feet
of Louis Nassau.*

That "good chevalier and good Christian," as his brother
affectionately called him, was in Germany, girding himself for
the manly work which Providence had destined him to perform.
The life of Brederode, who had engaged in the early struggle,
perhaps from the frivolous expectation of hearing himself
called Count of Holland, as his ancestors had been, had contributed nothing to the cause of freedom, nor did his death
occasion regret. His disorderly band of followers dispersed in
every direction upon the departure of their chief. A vessel
in which Batenburg, Galaina, and other nobles, with their
men-at-arms, were escaping towards a German port, was carried
into Harlingen, while those gentlemen, overpowered by sleep
and wassail, were unaware of their danger, and delivered over
to Count Meghem, by the treachery of their pilot. The soldiers were immediately hanged. The noblemen were reserved
to grace the first great scaffold which Alva was to erect upon
the horse-market in Brussels.†

The confederacy was entirely broken to pieces. Of the
chieftains to whom the people had been accustomed to look
for support and encouragement, some had rallied to the
government, some were in exile, some were in prison. Mon-

---

* Bor, iii. 168. Hoofd, iv. 135. Vit. Viglii, 51.—Compare Bor, Hoofd,
ubi sup.

† Pontus Payen MS.

tigny, closely watched in Spain, was virtually a captive, pining
for the young bride to whom he had been wedded amid such
brilliant festivities but a few months before his departure, and
for the child which was never to look upon its father's face.*
His colleague, Marquis Berghen, more fortunate, was already
dead. The excellent Viglius seized the opportunity to put in
a good word for Noircarmes, who had been grinding Tournay
in the dust, and butchering the inhabitants of Valenciennes.
"We have heard of Berghen's death," wrote the President to
his faithful Joachim. "The Lord of Noircarmes, who has
been his substitute in the governorship of Hainault, has given
a specimen of what he can do. Although I have no private
intimacy with that nobleman, I can not help embracing him
with all my benevolence. Therefore, oh my Hopper, pray do
your best to have him appointed governor."†

With the departure of Orange, a total eclipse seemed to
come over the Netherlands. The country was absolutely help-
less, the popular heart cold with apprehension. All persons
at all implicated in the late troubles, or suspected of heresy,
fled from their homes. Fugitive soldiers were hunted into
rivers, cut to pieces in the fields, hanged, burned, or drowned,
like dogs, without quarter, and without remorse. The most
industrious and valuable part of the population left the land
in droves. The tide swept outwards with such rapidity that
the Netherlands seemed fast becoming the desolate waste
which they had been before the Christian era. Throughout
the country, those Reformers who were unable to effect their
escape betook themselves to their old lurking-places. The
new religion was banished from all the cities, every convent-
icle was broken up by armed men, the preachers and leading
members were hanged, their disciples beaten with rods, reduced to beggary, or imprisoned, even if they sometimes escaped
the scaffold. An incredible number, however, were executed
for religious causes. Hardly a village so small, says the Ant-

---

* The child was baptized at Tournay on the 1st December, 1566.—Pasquier
de la Barre MS. f. 73.   † Foppens, Supplément, ii. 552.

werp chronicler, but that it could furnish one, two, or three hundred victims to the executioner.* The new churches were levelléd to the ground, and out of their timbers gallows were constructed.† It was thought an ingenious pleasantry to hang the Reformers upon the beams under which they had hoped to worship God. The property of the fugitives was confiscated. The beggars in name became beggars in reality. Many who felt obliged to remain, and who loved their possessions better than their creed, were suddenly converted into the most zealous of Catholics. Persons who had for years not gone to mass, never omitted now their daily and nightly visits to the churches.‡ Persons who had never spoken to an ecclesiastic but with contumely, now could not eat their dinners without one at their table.§ Many who were suspected of having participated in Calvinistic rites, were foremost and loudest in putting down and denouncing all forms and shows of the reformation. The country was as completely "pacified," to use the conqueror's expression, as Gaul had been by Cæsar.

The Regent issued a fresh edict upon the 24th May, to refresh the memories of those who might have forgotten previous statutes, which were, however, not calculated to make men oblivious. By this new proclamation, all ministers and teachers were sentenced to the gallows. All persons who had suffered their houses to be used for religious purposes were sentenced to the gallows. All parents or masters whose children or servants had attended such meetings were sentenced to the gallows, while the children and servants were only to be beaten with rods. All people who sang hymns at the burial of their relations were sentenced to the gallows. Parents who allowed their newly-born children to be baptized by other hands than those of the Catholic priest were sentenced to the gallows. The same punishment was denounced against the persons who should christen the child or act as its sponsors. Schoolmasters who should teach any error or false doctrine

---

* Meteren, ii. f. 45.

† De la Barre MS., 96.   Hoofd, iv. 138.   Strada, vi. 278.

‡ Bor, iii. 174.   § Ibid.

were likewise to be punished with death. Those who infringed the statutes against the buying and selling of religious books and songs were to receive the same doom, after the first offence. All sneers or insults against priests and ecclesiastics were also made capital crimes. Vagabonds, fugitives, apostates, runaway monks, were ordered forthwith to depart from every city on pain of death. In all cases confiscation of the whole property of the criminal was added to the hanging.*

This edict, says a contemporary historian, increased the fear of those professing the new religion to such an extent that they left the country "in great heaps."† It became necessary, therefore, to issue a subsequent proclamation forbidding all persons, whether foreigners or natives, to leave the land or to send away their property, and prohibiting all shipmasters, wagoners, and other agents of travel, from assisting in the flight of such fugitives, all upon pain of death.‡

Yet will it be credited that the edict of 24th May, the provisions of which have just been sketched, actually excited the wrath of Philip on *account* of *their clemency?* He wrote to the Duchess, expressing the pain and dissatisfaction which he felt, that an edict so indecent, so illegal, so contrary to the Christian religion, should have been published. Nothing, he said, could offend or distress him more deeply, than any outrage whatever, even the slightest one, offered to God and to His Roman Catholic Church. He therefore commanded his sister instantly to revoke the edict.§ One might almost imagine from reading the King's letter that Philip was at last appalled at the horrors committed in his name. Alas, he was only indignant that heretics had been suffered to hang who ought to have been burned, and that a few narrow and almost impossible loopholes had been left through which those who had offended might effect their escape.

And thus, while the country is paralyzed with present and expected woe, the swiftly advancing trumpets of the Spanish

---

* The edict is published in Bor, iii. 170, 171.   † Ibid., 171.
‡ Ibid., 175.   § Correspondance de Philippe II., i. 550–552.

army resound from beyond the Alps. The curtain is falling upon the prelude to the great tragedy which the prophetic lips of Orange had foretold. When it is again lifted, scenes of disaster and of bloodshed, battles, sieges, executions, deeds of unfaltering but valiant tyranny, of superhuman and successful resistance, of heroic self-sacrifice, fanatical courage and insane cruelty, both in the cause of the Wrong and the Right, will be revealed in awful succession—a spectacle of human energy, human suffering, and human strength to suffer, such as has not often been displayed upon the stage of the world's events.

PART III.

ALVA.

1567—1573.

CHAPTER I.

THE armed invasion of the Netherlands was the necessary
consequence of all which had gone before. That the inevitable
result had been so long deferred lay rather in the incompre-
hensible tardiness of Philip's character than in the circumstances of the case. Never did a monarch hold so steadfastly
to a deadly purpose, or proceed so languidly and with so much

circumvolution to his goal. The mask of benignity, of possible clemency, was now thrown off, but the delusion of his intended visit to the provinces was still maintained. He assured the Regent that he should be governed by her advice, and as she had made all needful preparations to receive him in Zeland, that it would be in Zeland he should arrive.*

The same two men among Philip's advisers were prominent as at an earlier day—the Prince of Eboli and the Duke of Alva. They still represented entirely opposite ideas, and in character, temper, and history, each was the reverse of the other. The policy of the Prince was pacific and temporizing ; that of the Duke uncompromising and ferocious. Ruy Gomez was disposed to prevent, if possible, the armed mission of Alva, and he now openly counselled the King to fulfil his long-deferred promise, and to make his appearance in person before his rebellious subjects. The jealousy and hatred which existed between the Prince and the Duke—between the man of peace and the man of wrath—were constantly exploding, even in the presence of the King. The wrangling in the council was incessant. Determined, if possible, to prevent the elevation of his rival, the favorite was even for a moment disposed to ask for the command of the army himself. There was something ludicrous in the notion, that a man whose life had been pacific, and who trembled at the noise of arms, should seek to supersede the terrible Alva, of whom his eulogists asserted, with Castilian exaggeration, that the very name of fear inspired him with horror. But there was a limit beyond which the influence of Anna de Mendoza and her husband did not extend. Philip was not to be driven to the Netherlands against his will, nor to be prevented from assigning the command of the army to the most appropriate man in Europe for his purpose.†

It was determined at last that the Netherland heresy should

---

* Correspondance de Philippe II., i. 550.

† Cabrera, l. 7, c. vii., p. 414. Strada, i. 282, 283. Hist. du duc d'Albe, ii. 155, 242.

be conquered by force of arms. The invasion resembled both a crusade against the infidel, and a treasure-hunting foray into the auriferous Indies, achievements by which Spanish chivalry had so often illustrated itself. The banner of the cross was to be replanted upon the conquered battlements of three hundred infidel cities, and a torrent of wealth, richer than ever flowed from Mexican or Peruvian mines, was to flow into the royal treasury from the perennial fountains of confiscation. Who so fit to be the Tancred and the Pizarro of this bicolored expedition as the Duke of Alva, the man who had been devoted from his earliest childhood, and from his father's grave, to hostility against unbelievers, and who had prophesied that treasure would flow in a stream, a yard deep, from the Netherlands as soon as the heretics began to meet with their deserts. An army of chosen troops was forthwith collected, by taking the four legions, or terzios, of Naples, Sicily, Sardinia, and Lombardy, and filling their places in Italy by fresh levies. About ten thousand picked and veteran soldiers were thus obtained, of which the Duke of Alva was appointed general-in-chief.[*]

Ferdinando Alvarez de Toledo, Duke of Alva, was now in his sixtieth year. He was the most successful and experienced general of Spain, or of Europe. No man had studied more deeply, or practised more constantly, the military science. In the most important of all arts at that epoch he was the most consummate artist. In the only honorable profession of the age, he was the most thorough and the most pedantic professor. Since the days of Demetrius Poliorcetes, no man had besieged so many cities. Since the days of Fabius Cunctator, no general had avoided so many battles, and no soldier, courageous as he was, ever attained to a more sublime indifference to calumny or depreciation. Having proved in his boyhood, at Fontarabia, and in his maturity at Mühlberg, that he could exhibit heroism and headlong courage, when necessary,

---

[*] Brandt, Hist. der Ref., i. 496. De Thou, v., l. 41, pp. 289, 290. Bern°. de Mendoza. Guerras de los payses baxos, etc., 20, 21, 29.

he could afford to look with contempt upon the witless gibes which his enemies had occasionally perpetrated at his expense. Conscious of holding his armies in his hand, by the power of an unrivalled discipline, and the magic of a name illustrated by a hundred triumphs, he could bear with patience and benevolence the murmurs of his soldiers when their battles were denied them.

He was born in 1508, of a family which boasted imperial descent. A Palæologus, brother of a Byzantine emperor, had conquered the city of Toledo, and transmitted its appellation as a family name.* The father of Ferdinando, Don Garcia, had been slain on the isle of Gerbes, in battle with the Moors, when his son was but four years of age.† The child was brought up by his grandfather, Don Frederic, and trained from his tenderest infancy to arms. Hatred to the infidel, and a determination to avenge his father's blood, crying to him from a foreign grave, were the earliest of his instincts. As a youth he was distinguished for his prowess. His maiden sword was fleshed at Fontarabia, where, although but sixteen years of age, he was considered, by his constancy in hardship, by his brilliant and desperate courage, and by the example of military discipline which he afforded to the troops, to have contributed in no small degree to the success of the Spanish arms.

In 1530, he accompanied the Emperor in his campaign against the Turk. Charles, instinctively recognizing the merit of the youth who was destined to be the life-long companion of his toils and glories, distinguished him with his favor at the opening of his career. Young, brave, and enthusiastic, Ferdinand de Toledo at this period was as interesting a hero as ever illustrated the pages of Castilian romance. His mad ride from Hungary to Spain and back again, accomplished in seventeen days, for the sake of a brief visit to his newly-married wife, is not the least attractive episode in the history

---

* De la Roca. Resultas de la Vida de Don F. A. de T. Duque de Alva, p. 3. Hist. du Duc d'Albe, i. 5.   † Hist. du Duc d'Albe, i. 8.

of an existence which was destined to be so dark and sanguinary. In 1535, he accompanied the Emperor on his memorable expedition to Tunis. In 1546 and 1547 he was generalissimo in the war against the Smalcaldian league. His most brilliant feat of arms—perhaps the most brilliant exploit of the Emperor's reign—was the passage of the Elbe and the battle of Mühlberg, accomplished in spite of Maximilian's bitter and violent reproaches, and the tremendous possibilities of a defeat.* That battle had finished the war. The gigantic and magnanimous John Frederic, surprised at his devotions in the church, fled in dismay, leaving his boots behind him, which for their superhuman size, were ridiculously said afterwards to be treasured among the trophies of the Toledo house.† The rout was total. "I came, I saw, and God conquered," said the Emperor, in pious parody of his immortal predecessor's epigram. Maximilian, with a thousand apologies for his previous insults, embraced the heroic Don Ferdinand over and over again, as, arrayed in a plain suit of blue armor, unadorned save with streaks of his enemies' blood, he returned from pursuit of the fugitives. So complete and so sudden was the victory, that it was found impossible to account for it, save on the ground of miraculous interposition. Like Joshua, in the vale of Ajalon, Don Ferdinand was supposed to have commanded the sun to stand still for a season, and to have been obeyed. Otherwise, how could the passage of the river, which was only concluded at six in the evening, and the complete overthrow of the Protestant forces, have all been accomplished within the narrow space of an

---

* Hist. du Duc d'Albe, liv. i. c. vii.   De Thou, liv. iv.

† Hist. du Duc d'Albe, i. 274.   Brantome, Hom. Illust., etc. (ch. v.), says that one of the boots was "large enough to hold a camp bedstead," p. 11.   I insert the anecdote only as a specimen of the manner in which similar absurdities, both of great and of little consequence, are perpetuated by writers in every land and age.   The armor of the noble-hearted and unfortunate John Frederic may still be seen in Dresden.   Its size indicates a man very much above the average height, while the external length of the iron shoe, on the contrary, is less than eleven inches.

April twilight ? The reply of the Duke to Henry the Second of France, who questioned him subsequently upon the subject, is well known. " Your Majesty, I was too much occupied that evening with what was taking place on the earth beneath, to pay much heed to the evolutions of the heavenly bodies." Spared as he had been by his good fortune from taking any part in the Algerine expedition, or in witnessing the ignominious retreat from Innspruck, he was obliged to submit to the intercalation of the disastrous siege of Metz in the long history of his successes. Doing the duty of a field-marshal and a sentinel, supporting his army by his firmness and his discipline when nothing else could have supported them, he was at last enabled, after half the hundred thousand men with whom Charles had begun the siege had been sacrificed, to induce his imperial master to raise the siege before the remaining fifty thousand had been frozen or starved to death.[*]

The culminating career of Alva seemed to have closed in the mist which gathered around the setting star of the empire. Having accompanied Philip to England in 1554, on his matrimonial expedition, he was destined in the following years, as viceroy and generalissimo of Italy, to be placed in a series of false positions. A great captain engaged in a little war, the champion of the cross in arms against the successor of St. Peter, he had extricated himself, at last, with his usual adroitness, but with very little glory.[†] To him had been allotted the mortification, to another the triumph. The lustre of his own name seemed to sink in the ocean while that of a hated rival, with new spangled ore, suddenly " flamed in the forehead of the morning sky." While he had been paltering with a dotard, whom he was forbidden to crush, Egmont had struck down the chosen troops of France, and conquered her most illustrious commanders. Here was the unpardonable crime which could only be expiated by the blood of the victor.

---

[*] Hist. du Duc d'Albe, i. 272–283, liv. iii., chaps. 21–24.

[†] Ibid., liv. iv. et v. De Thou, liv. xviii. De la Roca, Resultas, etc., 68–72.

Unfortunately for his rival, the time was now approaching when the long-deferred revenge was to be satisfied.

On the whole, the Duke of Alva was inferior to no general of his age. As a disciplinarian he was foremost in Spain, perhaps in Europe. A spendthrift of time, he was an economist of blood, and this was, perhaps, in the eye of humanity, his principal virtue. Time and myself are two, was a frequent observation of Philip, and his favorite general considered the maxim as applicable to war as to politics. Such were his qualities as a military commander. As a statesman, he had neither experience nor talent. As a man his character was simple. He did not combine a great variety of vices, but those which he had were colossal, and he possessed no virtues. He was neither lustful nor intemperate, but his professed eulogists admitted his enormous avarice, while the world has agreed that such an amount of stealth and ferocity, of patient vindictiveness and universal bloodthirstiness, were never found in a savage beast of the forest, and but rarely in a human bosom. His history was now to show that his previous thrift of human life was not derived from any love of his kind. Personally he was stern and overbearing. As difficult of access as Philip himself, he was even more haughty to those who were admitted to his presence. He addressed every one with the depreciating second person plural.* Possessing the right of being covered in the presence of the Spanish monarch, he had been with difficulty brought to renounce it before the German Emperor.† He was of an illustrious family, but his territorial possessions were not extensive. His duchy was a small one, furnishing him with not more than fourteen thousand crowns of annual income, and with four hundred soldiers.‡ He had, however, been a thrifty financier all his life, never having been without a handsome sum of ready money at interest. Ten years before his arrival in the Netherlands, he was supposed to have already increased his income to forty thousand a year by the proceeds of his investments at Ant-

---

* V. d. Vynckt, ii. 41.   † Ibid., 42.
                        ‡ Badovaro MS.

werp.* As already intimated, his military character was sometimes profoundly misunderstood. He was often considered rather a pedantic than a practical commander, more capable to discourse of battles than to gain them. Notwithstanding that his long life had been an almost unbroken campaign, the ridiculous accusation of timidity was frequently made against him.† A gentleman at the court of the Emperor Charles once addressed a letter to the Duke with the title of " General of his Majesty's armies in the Duchy of Milan in time of peace, and major-domo of the household in the time of war."‡ It was said that the lesson did the Duke good, but that he rewarded very badly the nobleman who gave it, having subsequently caused his head to be taken off.§ In general, however, Alva manifested a philosophical contempt for the opinions expressed concerning his military fame, and was especially disdainful of criticism expressed by his own soldiers. " Recollect," said he, at a little later period, to Don John of Austria, " that the first foes with whom one has to contend are one's own troops, with their clamors for an engagement at this moment, and their murmurs about results at another ; with their ' I thought that the battle should be fought ;' or, ' it was my opinion that the occasion ought not to be lost.' Your highness will have opportunity enough to display valor, and will never be weak enough to be conquered by the babble of soldiers."‖

* "Ha d'entrata come Duca $\frac{m}{14}$ scudi, ma fino a $\frac{m}{40}$ per danari investiti in Anversa et se stima che egli si trova sempre buona somma di contanti."—Badovaro MS·

† "Ha visto et maneggiato molte guerre et per la prattica che ha discorre meglio che io habbia mai conosciuto in quella corte—ma le due oppositioni l'una che facci le provisioni sue con troppo reservato et cauto et quasi timido nell' imprese."—Suriano MS.

Badovaro is much more severe; " nella guerra mostra timidità et poca intelligenza et poco stimato nella corte come per persona avara, superba et ambitiosa; adulatore et invido molto et di puochissimo cuore."

‡ This anecdote is attributed by Dom l'Evesque and by M. Gachard to Badovaro. It is, however, not to be found in the copy of his Manuscript in the Bibliothèque de Bourgogne.

§ Dom l'Evesque, Mem. de Granvelle, i. 26, sqq.—The Benedictine does not further indicate the author of the pleasantry. One is disposed to imagine it to have been Egmont. Nevertheless, the Duke caused the heads of so many gentlemen to be taken off, that the description is sufficiently vague.

‖ Documentos ineditos para la historia de España, iii. 273–283.

In person he was tall, thin, erect, with a small head, a long visage, lean yellow cheek, dark twinkling eyes, adust complexion, black bristling hair, and a long sable-silvered beard, descending in two waving streams upon his breast.[*]

Such being the design, the machinery was well selected. The best man in Europe to lead the invading force was placed at the head of ten thousand picked veterans. The privates in this exquisite little army,[†] said the enthusiastic connoisseur Brantôme, who travelled post into Lorraine expressly to see them on their march, all wore engraved or gilded armor, and were in every respect equipped like captains. They were the first who carried muskets, a weapon which very much astonished the Flemings when it first rattled in their ears. The musketeers, he observed, might have been mistaken for princes, with such agreeable and graceful arrogance did they present themselves. Each was attended by his servant or esquire, who carried his piece for him, except in battle, and all were treated with extreme deference by the rest of the army, as if they had been officers.[‡] The four regiments of Lombardy, Sardinia, Sicily, and Naples, composed a total of not quite nine thousand of the best foot soldiers in Europe. They were commanded respectively by Don Sancho de Lodroño, Don Gonzalo de Bracamonte, Julien Romero, and Alfonso de Ulloa, all distinguished and experienced generals.[§] The cavalry, amounting to about twelve hundred, was under the command of the natural son of the Duke, Don Ferdinando de Toledo, Prior of the Knights of St. John. Chiapin Vitelli, Marquis of Cetona, who had served the King in many a campaign, was appointed Maréchal de camp, and Gabriel Cerbelloni was placed in command of the artillery. On the way the

---

[*] "Di persona grande, magra, piccola testa, collerico et adusto."—Badovaro MS.

There is a very good contemporary portrait of the Duke, by Barends, in the Royal gallery at Amsterdam, which accords very exactly with the descriptions preserved concerning his person.

[†] "Gentille et gaillarde armée."

[‡] Brantôme, Grandes Capitaines étrangers, etc. (usâ 75). (Duc d'Albe).

[§] Mendoza, Guerras de los payses baxos, fol. 20, 21, 29, 30.

Duke received, as a present from the Duke of Savoy, the services of the distinguished engineer, Pacheco, or Paciotti,* whose name was to be associated with the most celebrated citadel of the Netherlands, and whose dreadful fate was to be contemporaneous with the earliest successes of the liberal party.

With an army thus perfect, on a small scale, in all its departments, and furnished, in addition, with a force of two thousand prostitutes, as regularly enrolled, disciplined, and distributed† as the cavalry or the artillery, the Duke embarked upon his momentous enterprise, on the 10th of May, at Carthagena. Thirty-seven galleys, under command of Prince Andrea Doria, brought the principal part of the force to Genoa, the Duke being delayed a few days at Nice by an attack of fever. On the 2d of June, the army was mustered at Alexandria de Palla, and ordered to rendezvous again at San Ambrosio at the foot of the Alps. It was then directed to make its way over Mount Cenis and through Savoy, Burgundy, and Lorraine, by a regularly arranged triple movement. The second division was each night to encamp on the spot which had been occupied upon the previous night by the vanguard, and the rear was to place itself on the following night in the camp of the corps de bataille.‡ Thus coiling itself along almost in a single line by slow and serpentine windings, with a deliberate, deadly, venomous purpose, this army, which was to be the instrument of Philip's long deferred vengeance, stole

---

* Hoofd, iv. 148.

† Ibid. Correspondance de Philippe II., i. 565.—"On dit qu'ils ont plus de deux milles putaines avecques eux, tellement que nous ne serons en faulte des putaines avecq ceulx que nous avons."—Lett. de Jean de Hornes à Arnoul Munten.

Brantôme particularly commends the organization of this department. "De plus il y avoit quatre cens courtezanes à cheval, *belles et braves comme princesses*, et huit cens à pied, *bien à point aussi*."—Vie des Grands Hommes, etc. (usâ p. 80). (d'Albe).

Such was the moral physiognomy of the army which came to enforce the high religious purposes of Philip. In such infamous shape was the will of God supposed to manifest itself before the eyes of the heretics in the Netherlands

‡ B. de Mendoza, 30.

through narrow mountain pass and tangled forest. So close and intricate were many of the defiles through which the journey led them* that, had one tithe of the treason which they came to punish, ever existed, save in the diseased imagination of their monarch, not one man would have been left to tell the tale. Egmont, had he really been the traitor and the conspirator he was assumed to be, might have easily organized the means of cutting off the troops before they could have effected their entrance into the country which they had doomed to destruction. His military experience, his qualifications for a daring stroke, his great popularity, and the intense hatred entertained for Alva, would have furnished him with a sufficient machinery for the purpose.

Twelve days' march carried the army through Burgundy, twelve more through Lorraine. During the whole of the journey they were closely accompanied by a force of cavalry and infantry, ordered upon this service by the King of France, who, for fear of exciting a fresh Huguenot demonstration, had refused the Spaniards a passage through his dominions. This reconnoitring army kept pace with them like their shadow, and watched all their movements. A force of six thousand Swiss, equally alarmed and uneasy at the progress of the troops, hovered likewise about their flanks, without, however, offering any impediment to their advance. Before the middle of August they had reached Thionville, on the Luxemburg frontier, having on the last day marched a distance of two leagues through a forest, which seemed expressly arranged to allow a small defensive force to embarrass and destroy an invading army. No opposition, however, was attempted, and the Spanish soldiers encamped at last within the territory of the Netherlands, having accomplished their adventurous journey in entire safety, and under perfect discipline.†

The Duchess had in her secret letters to Philip continued to express her disapprobation of the enterprise thus committed to Alva. She had bitterly complained that now when the country

---

* B. de Mendoza, 30, 31.   † Ibid.

had been pacified by her efforts, another should be sent to reap all the glory, or perhaps to undo all that she had so painfully and so successfully done. She stated to her brother, in most unequivocal language, that the name of Alva was odious enough to make the whole Spanish nation detested in the Netherlands. She could find no language sufficiently strong to express her surprise that the King should have decided upon a measure likely to be attended with such fatal consequences without consulting her on the subject, and in opposition to what had been her uniform advice. She also wrote personally to Alva, imploring, commanding, and threatening, but with equally ill success.* The Duke knew too well who was sovereign of the Netherlands now, his master's sister or himself. As to the effects of his armed invasion upon the temper of the provinces, he was supremely indifferent. He came as a conqueror not as a mediator. "I have tamed people of iron in my day," said he, contemptuously, "shall I not easily crush these men of butter?"†

At Thionville he was, however, officially waited upon by Berlaymont and Noircarmes, on the part of the Regent. He at this point, moreover, began to receive deputations from various cities, bidding him a hollow and trembling welcome, and deprecating his displeasure for any thing in the past which might seem offensive. To all such embassies he replied in vague and conventional language ; saying, however, to his confidential attendants : I am here,—so much is certain,— whether I am welcome or not is to me a matter of little consequence.‡ At Tirlemont, on the 22d August, he was met by Count Egmont, who had ridden forth from Brussels to show him a becoming respect, as the representative of his sovereign. The Count was accompanied by several other noblemen, and brought to the Duke a present of several beautiful horses.§

---

* Correspondance de Philippe II., i. 546, 556, etc.   Strada, i. 289.   Hoofd, iv. 148.   Strada, i. 292.

† Hoofd, iv. 148.   ‡ Bor, iv. 182.

§ MS., 12–941. Bib. de Bourg.—Troubles des Pays Bas de Jean de Grutere Extraits par M. Emile Gachet (1st Août, 1847.)

Alva received him, however, but coldly, for he was unable at first to adjust the mask to his countenance as adroitly as was necessary. Behold the greatest of all the heretics, he observed to his attendants, as soon as the nobleman's presence was announced, and in a voice loud enough for him to hear.* Even after they had exchanged salutations, he addressed several remarks to him in a half jesting, half biting tone, saying among other things, that his countship might have spared him the trouble of making this long journey in his old age.† There were other observations in a similar strain which might have well aroused the suspicion of any man not determined, like Egmont, to continue blind and deaf. After a brief interval, however, Alva seems to have commanded himself. He passed his arm lovingly over that stately neck,‡ which he had already devoted to the block, and—the Count having resolved beforehand to place himself, if possible, upon amicable terms with the new Viceroy—the two rode along side by side in friendly conversation, followed by the regiment of infantry and three companies of light horse, which belonged to the Duke's immediate command.§ Alva, still attended by Egmont, rode soon afterwards through the Louvain gate into Brussels, where they separated for a season. Lodgings had been taken for the Duke at the house of a certain Madame de Jasse,‖ in the neighborhood of Egmont's palace. Leaving here the principal portion of his attendants, the Captain-General, without alighting, forthwith proceeded to the palace to pay his respects to the Duchess of Parma.

For three days the Regent had been deliberating with her council as to the propriety of declining any visit from the man whose presence she justly considered a disgrace and an insult to herself.¶ This being the reward of her eight years' devotion to her brother's commands ; to be superseded by a

* Bor, iv. 182.   Hoofd, iv. 150.

† Jean de Grutere MS   Extraits de M. Gachet.

‡ Hoofd, 150.   § Jean de Grutere MS.   Extraits de M. Gachet

‖ Ibid.   ¶ Correspondance de Philippe II., i. 631.

subject, and one too who came to carry out a policy which she had urgently deprecated, it could hardly be expected of the Emperor's daughter that she should graciously submit to the indignity, and receive her successor with a smiling countenance. In consequence, however, of the submissive language with which the Duke had addressed her in his recent communications, offering with true Castilian but empty courtesy, to place his guards, his army, and himself at her feet, she had consented to receive his visit with or without his attendants.*

On his appearance in the court-yard, a scene of violent altercation and almost of bloodshed took place between his body-guard and the archers of the Regent's household, who were at last, with difficulty, persuaded to allow the mercenaries of the hated Captain-General to pass.† Presenting himself at three o'clock in the afternoon, after these not very satisfactory preliminaries, in the bed-chamber of the Duchess, where it was her habit to grant confidential audiences, he met, as might easily be supposed, with a chilling reception. The Duchess, standing motionless in the centre of the apartment, attended by Berlaymont, the Duke of Aerschot, and Count Egmont, acknowledged his salutations with calm severity. Neither she nor any one of her attendants advanced a step to meet him. The Duke took off his hat, but she, calmly recognizing his right as a Spanish grandee, insisted upon his remaining covered. A stiff and formal conversation of half an hour's duration then ensued, all parties remaining upon their feet.‡ The Duke, although respectful, found it difficult to conceal his indignation and his haughty sense of approaching triumph. Margaret was cold, stately, and forbidding, disguising her rage and her mortification under a veil of imperial pride.§ Alva, in a letter to Philip, describing the interview, assured his Majesty that he had treated the Duchess with as much deference as he could have shown to the Queen,‖ but it is probable, from other contemporaneous accounts, that an ill-disguised and even angry

---

* Correspondance de Philippe II., i. 631.   † Ibid.   ‡ Ibid.
§ Strada, i. 297.   ‖ Correspondance de Philippe II., i. 636.

arrogance was at times very visible in his demeanor. The state council had advised the Duchess against receiving him until he had duly exhibited his powers. This ceremony had been waived, but upon being questioned by the Duchess at this interview as to their nature and extent, he is reported to have coolly answered that he really did not exactly remember, but that he would look them over, and send her information at his earliest convenience.[*]

The next day, however, his commission was duly exhibited. In this document, which bore date 31st January, 1567, Philip appointed him to be Captain-General " in correspondence with his Majesty's dear sister of Parma, who was occupied with other matters belonging to the government," begged the Duchess to co-operate with him and to command obedience for him, and ordered all the cities of the Netherlands to receive such garrisons as he should direct.[†]

At the official interview between Alva and Madame de Parma, at which these powers were produced, the necessary preliminary arrangements were made regarding the Spanish troops, which were now to be immediately quartered in the principal cities. The Duke, however, informed the Regent that as these matters were not within her province, he should take the liberty of arranging them with the authorities, without troubling her in the matter, and would inform her of the result of his measures at their next interview, which was to take place on the 26th August.[‡]

Circular letters signed by Philip, which Alva had brought with him, were now despatched to the different municipal bodies of the country. In these the cities were severally commanded to accept the garrisons, and to provide for the armies whose active services the King hoped would not be required, but which he had sent beforehand to prepare a peaceful entrance for himself. He enjoined the most absolute obedience to the Duke of Alva until his own arrival, which was to be almost

---

[*] V. de Vynckt, ii. 53.   [†] Bor. iv. 182, 183.
[‡] Correspondance de Philippe II., i. 632.

immediate. These letters were dated at Madrid on the 28th February, and were now accompanied by a brief official circular, signed by Margaret of Parma, in which she announced the arrival of her dear cousin of Alva, and demanded unconditional submission to his authority.*

Having thus complied with these demands of external and conventional propriety, the indignant Duchess unbosomed herself, in her private Italian letters to her brother, of the rage which had been hitherto partially suppressed. She reiterated her profound regret that Philip had not yet accepted the resignation which she had so recently and so earnestly offered. She disclaimed all jealousy of the supreme powers now conferred upon Alva, but thought that his Majesty might have allowed her to leave the country before the Duke arrived with an authority which was so extraordinary, as well as so humiliating to herself. Her honor might thus have been saved. She was pained to perceive that she was like to furnish a perpetual example to all others, who considering the manner in which she had been treated by the King, would henceforth have but little inducement to do their duty. At no time, on no occasion, could any person ever render him such services as hers had been. For nine years she had enjoyed not a moment of repose. If the King had shown her but little gratitude, she was consoled by the thought that she had satisfied her God, herself, and the world. She had compromised her health, perhaps her life, and now that she had pacified the country, now that the King was more absolute, more powerful than ever before, another was sent to enjoy the fruit of her labors and her sufferings.†

The Duchess made no secret of her indignation at being thus superseded, and as she considered the matter, outraged. She openly avowed her displeasure. She was at times almost beside herself with rage. There was universal sympathy with her emotions, for all hated the Duke, and shuddered at the

---

* Bor, iv. 183, 184.
† Correspondance de Philippe II., i. 635. Strada, i. 298.

arrival of the Spaniards. The day of doom for all the crimes which had ever been committed in the course of ages, seemed now to have dawned upon the Netherlands. The sword which had so long been hanging over them, seemed now about to descend. Throughout the provinces, there was but one feeling of cold and hopeless dismay. Those who still saw a possibility of effecting their escape from the fated land, swarmed across the frontier. All foreign merchants deserted the great marts. The cities became as still as if the plague-banner had been unfurled on every house-top.

Meantime the Captain-General proceeded methodically with his work. He distributed his troops through Brussels, Ghent, Antwerp, and other principal cities. As a measure of necessity and mark of the last humiliation, he required the municipalities to transfer their keys to his keeping. The magistrates of Ghent humbly remonstrated against the indignity, and Egmont was imprudent enough to make himself the mouth-piece of their remonstrance, which, it is needless to add, was unsuccessful.* Meantime his own day of reckoning had arrived.

As already observed, the advent of Alva at the head of a foreign army was the natural consequence of all which had gone before. The delusion of the royal visit was still maintained, and the affectation of a possible clemency still displayed, while the monarch sat quietly in his cabinet without a remote intention of leaving Spain, and while the messengers of his accumulated and long-concealed wrath were already descending upon their prey. It was the deliberate intention of Philip, when the Duke was despatched to the Netherlands, that all the leaders of the anti-inquisition party, and all who had, at any time or in any way, implicated themselves in opposition to the government, or in censure of its proceedings, should be put to death. It was determined that the provinces should be subjugated to the absolute domination of the council of Spain, a small body of foreigners sitting at

---

* Bor, iv. 184.   Hoofd, iv. 150.

the other end of Europe, a junta in which Netherlanders were to have no voice and exercise no influence. The despotic government of the Spanish and Italian possessions was to be extended to these Flemish territories, which were thus to be converted into the helpless dependencies of a *foreign and an absolute crown.** There was to be a re-organization of the inquisition, upon the same footing claimed for it before the outbreak of the troubles, together with a re-enactment and vigorous enforcement of the famous edicts against heresy.†

Such was the scheme recommended by Granvelle and Espinosa, and to be executed by Alva.‡ As part and parcel of this plan, it was also arranged at secret meetings at the house of Espinosa, before the departure of the Duke, that all the seigniors against whom the Duchess Margaret had made so many complaints, especially the Prince of Orange, with the Counts Egmont, Horn, and Hoogstraaten, should be immediately arrested and brought to chastisement. The Marquis Berghen and the Baron Montigny, being already in Spain, could be dealt with at pleasure. It was also decided that the gentlemen implicated in the confederacy or compromise, should at once be proceeded against for high treason, without any regard to the promise of pardon granted by the Duchess.

---

* "—— touchant l'ordre qu'il debvoit tenir audict pays —— l'on s'est peu appercevoir que *l'intention estait de mectre avec* le temps l'ordre de l'administration de justice et *gouvernement à la façon d'Espagne,* en quoy le feu Courtewille et moy avons toujours resisté."—Confessions of Counselor Louis del Ryo.

† Correspondance de Philippe II., i. 562

‡ "Et que *mesmement le Cardinal Granvelle et President Viglius, M. de Berlaymont et Noircarmes* auraient à sa Majesté conseillé le même. Voires expressement qu'il *convenoit une armée d'espaignolz* avecq quelque chef pour maintenir le pays en l'obeissance de sa Majesté et en la religion Catholique. Et que le Duc d'Alve fut envoyé pour chef par conseil du Cardinal Spinosa et *advis du Cardinal de Granvelle,* comme il est assez apparu par *plusieurs lettres escriptes* en ce temps là à ses amys, et tout cecy est aussy selon *la commune opinion* —— Sur le second scavoir les motifs et raisons qui en ont esté pour persuader au Roy de l'envoyer, ne puis dire aultre sinon que leur sembloit selon que j'ay peu entendre que le Roy par ce *moyen se debvroit faire absolut Roy* et restablir la religion Catholique."—Confessions of Del Rio.

The general features of the great project having been thus mapped out, a few indispensable preliminaries were at once executed. In order that Egmont, Horn, and other distinguished victims might not take alarm, and thus escape the doom deliberately arranged for them, royal assurances were despatched to the Netherlands, cheering their despondency and dispelling their doubts. With his own hand Philip wrote the letter, full of affection and confidence, to Egmont, to which allusion has already been made. He wrote it *after* Alva had left Madrid upon his mission of vengeance. The same stealthy measures were pursued with regard to others. The Prince of Orange was not capable of falling into the royal trap, however cautiously baited. Unfortunately he could not communicate his wisdom to his friends

It is difficult to comprehend so very sanguine a temperament as that to which Egmont owed his destruction. It was not the Prince of Orange alone who had prophesied his doom. Warnings had come to the Count from every quarter, and they were now frequently repeated. Certainly he was not without anxiety, but he had made his decision ; determined to believe in the royal ·word, and in the royal gratitude for his services rendered, not only against Montmorency and De Thermes, but against the heretics of Flanders. He was, however, much changed. He had grown prematurely old. At forty-six years his hair was white, and he never slept without pistols under his pillow.* Nevertheless he affected, and sometimes felt, a light-heartedness which surprised all around him. The Portuguese gentleman Robles, Seigneur de Billy, who had returned early in the summer from Spain, whither he had been sent upon a confidential mission by Madame de Parma, is said to have made repeated communications to Egmont as to the dangerous position in which he stood.† Immediately after his arrival in Brussels he had visited the Count, then confined to his house by an injury

---

* Groen v. Prinst., Archives, etc. Supplément, 35, 36.
† Pontus Payen MS.

caused by the fall of his horse. "Take care to get well very fast," said De Billy, "for there are very bad stories told about you in Spain." Egmont laughed heartily at the observation, as if nothing could well be more absurd than such a warning. His friend—for De Billy is said to have felt a real attachment to the Count—persisted in his prophecies, telling him that "birds in the field sang much more sweetly than those in cages," and that he would do well to abandon the country before the arrival of Alva.*

These warnings were repeated almost daily by the same gentleman, and by others, who were more and more astonished at Egmont's infatuation. Nevertheless, he had disregarded their admonitions, and had gone forth to meet the Duke at Tirlemont. Even then he might have seen, in the coldness of his first reception, and in the disrespectful manner of the Spanish soldiers, who not only did not at first salute him, but who murmured audibly that he was a Lutheran and traitor, that he was not so great a favorite with the government at Madrid as he desired to be.

After the first few moments, however, Alva's manner had changed, while Chiappin Vitelli, Gabriel de Serbelloni, and other principal officers, received the Count with great courtesy, even upon his first appearance. The grand prior, Ferdinando de Toledo, natural son of the Duke, and already a distinguished soldier, seems to have felt a warm and unaffected friendship for Egmont, whose brilliant exploits in the field had excited his youthful admiration, and of whose destruction he was, nevertheless, compelled to be the unwilling instrument.† For a few days, accordingly, after the arrival of the new Governor-General all seemed to be going smoothly. The grand prior and Egmont became exceedingly intimate, passing their time together in banquets, masquerades, and play,‡ as joyously as if the merry days which had succeeded the treaty of Cateau Cambresis were returned. The Duke,

---

* Pontus Paren MS.   † Correspondance de Philippe II., i. 574.
‡ Pontus Payen MS.

too, manifested the most friendly dispositions, taking care to send him large presents of Spanish and Italian fruits, received frequently by the government couriers.*

Lapped in this fatal security, Egmont not only forgot his fears, but unfortunately succeeded in inspiring Count Horn with a portion of his confidence. That gentleman had still remained in his solitary mansion at Weert, notwithstanding the artful means which had been used to lure him from that "desert." It is singular that the very same person who, according to a well-informed Catholic contemporary, had been most eager to warn Egmont of his danger, had also been the foremost instrument for effecting the capture of the Admiral. The Seigneur de Billy, on the day after his arrival from Madrid, had written to Horn, telling him that the King was highly pleased with his services and character. De Billy also stated that he had been commissioned by Philip to express distinctly the royal gratitude for the Count's conduct, adding that his Majesty was about to visit the Netherlands in August, and would probably be preceded or accompanied by Baron Montigny.†

Alva and his son Don Ferdinando had soon afterwards addressed letters from Gerverbiller (dated 26th and 27th July) to Count Horn, filled with expressions of friendship and confidence.‡ The Admiral, who had sent one of his gentlemen to greet the Duke, now responded from Weert that he was very sensible of the kindness manifested towards him, but that for reasons which his secretary Alonzo de la Loo would more fully communicate, he must for the present beg to be excused from a personal visit to Brussels. The secretary was received by Alva with extreme courtesy.§ The Duke expressed infinite pain that the King had not yet rewarded Count Horn's services according to their merit, said that a year before he had told his brother Montigny how very much

---

* Pontus Payen MS.

† Foppens. Suppl. à Strada, ii. 553, sqq.

‡ Correspondance de Philippe II., i. 563, note.

§ Letter of Alonzo de la Loo in Correspondance de Philippe II., i. 563, 564.

he was the Admiral's friend, and begged La Loo to tell his master that he should not doubt the royal generosity and gratitude. The governor added, that if he could see the Count in person he could tell him things which would please him, and which would prove that he had not been forgotten by his friends. La Loo had afterward a long conversation with the Duke's secretary Albornoz, who assured him that his master had the greatest affection for Count Horn, and that since his affairs were so much embarrassed, he might easily be provided with the post of governor at Milan, or viceroy of Naples, about to become vacant. The secretary added, that the Duke was much hurt at receiving no visits from many distinguished nobles whose faithful friend and servant he was, and that Count Horn ought to visit Brussels, if not to treat of great affairs, at least to visit the Captain-General as a friend. "After all this," said honest Alonzo, "I am going immediately to Weert, to urge his lordship to yield to the Duke's desires."*

This scientific manoeuvring, joined to the urgent representations of Egmont, at last produced its effect. The Admiral left his retirement at Weert to fall into the pit which his enemies had been so skilfully preparing at Brussels. On the night of the 8th September, Egmont received another most significative and mysterious warning. A Spaniard, apparently an officer of rank, came secretly into his house, and urged him solemnly to effect his escape before the morrow. The Countess, who related the story afterwards, always believed, without being certain, that the mysterious visitor was Julian Romero, maréchal de camp.† Egmont, however, continued as blindly confident as before.

---

* Letter of Alonzo de la Loo in Correspondance de Philippe II., i. 563, 564. —Compare "La deduction de l'innocence du Comte de Hornes" (1568), pp. 33–35.

† "Voires le *jour précédent*, quelque Seigneur du conseil l'avoit préadverti, aiant Madame sa femme souvent declaré que ung capitaine Espagnol qu'on soubçonnoit avoir este Julian Romero, étoit venu de nuict en son logis lui conseiller la retraicte, mais la confidence de ses services, l'espoir de son innocence le fit desmeurer."—Renom de France MS., ji., c. i.

On the following day, September 9th, the grand prior, Don Ferdinando, gave a magnificent dinner, to which Egmont and Horn, together with Noircarmes, the Viscount of Ghent, and many other noblemen were invited. The banquet was enlivened by the music of Alva's own military band, which the Duke sent to entertain the company. At three o'clock he sent a message begging the gentlemen, after their dinner should be concluded, to favor him with their company at his house (the maison de Jassey), as he wished to consult them concerning the plan of the citadel, which he proposed erecting at Antwerp.*

At this moment, the grand prior who was seated next to Egmont, whispered in his ear; "Leave this place, Signor Count, instantly; take the fleetest horse in your stable and make your escape without a moment's delay." Egmont, much troubled, and remembering the manifold prophecies and admonitions which he had passed by unheeded, rose from the table and went into the next room. He was followed by Noircarmes and two other gentlemen, who had observed his agitation, and were curious as to its cause. The Count repeated to them the mysterious words just whispered to him by the grand prior, adding that he was determined to take the advice without a moment's delay. "Ha! Count," exclaimed Noircarmes, "do not put lightly such implicit confidence in this stranger who is counselling you to your destruction. What will the Duke of Alva and all the Spaniards say of such a precipitate flight? Will they not say that your Excellency has fled from the consciousness of guilt? Will not your escape be construed into a confession of high treason?"†

If these words were really spoken by Noircarmes, and that they were so, we have the testimony of a Walloon gentleman in constant communication with Egmont's friends and with the whole Catholic party, they furnish another proof of the malignant and cruel character of the man. The advice fixed

---

* Pontus Payen MS., book iv.   † Ibid.

forever the fate of the vacillating Egmont. He had risen from table determined to take the advice of a noble-minded Spaniard, who had adventured his life to save his friend He now returned in obedience to the counsel of a fellow-country-man, a Flemish noble, to treat the well-meant warning with indifference, and to seat himself again at the last banquet which he was ever to grace with his presence.

At four o'clock, the dinner being finished, Horn and Egmont, accompanied by the other gentlemen, proceeded to the "Jassy" house, then occupied by Alva, to take part in the deliberations proposed.* They were received by the Duke with great courtesy. The engineer, Pietro Urbino, soon appeared and laid upon the table a large parchment containing the plan and elevation of the citadel to be erected at Ant-werp.† A warm discussion upon the subject soon arose, Egmont, Horn, Noircarmes and others, together with the engineers Urbino and Pacheco, all taking part in the debate.‡ After a short time, the Duke of Alva left the apartment, on pretext of a sudden indisposition, leaving the company still warmly engaged in their argument.§ The council lasted till near seven in the evening. As it broke up, Don Sancho d'Avila, captain of the Duke's guard, requested Egmont to remain for a moment after the rest, as he had a communica-tion to make to him. After an insignificant remark or two, the Spanish officer, as soon as the two were alone, requested Egmont to surrender his sword. The Count, agitated, and notwithstanding every thing which had gone before, still taken by surprise, scarcely knew what reply to make.|| Don Sancho repeated that he had been commissioned to arrest him, and again demanded his sword. At the same moment the doors of the adjacent apartment were opened, and Egmont saw him-self surrounded by a company of Spanish musqueteers and halberdmen. Finding himself thus entrapped, he gave up

---

* Pontus Payen MS.   † Ibid.
‡ Ibid.—Compare Correspondance de Philippe II., i. 573.
§ Pontus Payen MS. || Correspondance de Philippe II., i. 573.

his sword, saying bitterly, as he did so, that it had at least rendered some service to the King in times which were past. He was then conducted to a chamber, in the upper story of the house, where his temporary prison had been arranged. The windows were barricaded, the daylight excluded, the whole apartment hung with black. Here he remained fourteen days (from the 9th to 23d September). During this period, he was allowed no communication with his friends. His room was lighted day and night with candles, and he was served in strict silence by Spanish attendants, and guarded by Spanish soldiers. The captain of the watch drew his curtain every midnight, and aroused him from sleep that he might be identified by the relieving officer.[*]

Count Horn was arrested upon the same occasion by Captain Salinas, as he was proceeding through the court-yard of the house, after the breaking up of the council. He was confined in another chamber of the mansion, and met with a precisely similar treatment to that experienced by Egmont. Upon the 23d September, both were removed under a strong guard to the castle of Ghent.[†]

On this same day, two other important arrests, included and arranged in the same program, had been successfully accomplished. Bakkerzeel, private and confidential secretary of Egmont, and Antony Van Straalen, the rich and influential burgomaster of Antwerp, were taken almost simultaneously.[‡] At the request of Alva, the burgomaster had been invited by the Duchess of Parma to repair on business to Brussels. He seemed to have feared an ambuscade, for as he got into his coach to set forth upon the journey, he was so muffled in a multiplicity of clothing, that he was scarcely to be recognized.[§] He was no sooner, however, in the open country and upon a spot remote from human habitations, than

---

[*] Pontus Payen MS.

[†] Ibid.—Compare Bor, iv. 184; Hoofd, iv. 150, 151; Strada, vi. 298–300; Correspondance de Philippe II., ubi sup.

[‡] Ibid., i. 637–638.

[§] Strada, i. 299.

he was suddenly beset by a band of forty soldiers under command of Don Alberic Lodron and Don Sancho de Lodroño.* These officers had been watching his movements for many days. The capture of Bakkerzeel was accomplished with equal adroitness at about the same hour.

Alva, while he sat at the council board with Egmont and Horn, was secretly informed that those important personages, Bakkerzeel and Straalen, with the private secretary of the Admiral, Alonzo de la Loo, in addition, had been thus successfully arrested. He could with difficulty conceal his satisfaction, and left the apartment immediately that the trap might be sprung upon the two principal victims of his treachery. He had himself arranged all the details of these two important arrests, while his natural son, the Prior Don Ferdinando, had been compelled to superintend the proceedings.† The plot had been an excellent plot, and was accomplished as successfully as it had been sagaciously conceived. None but Spaniards had been employed in any part of the affair.‡ Officers of high rank in his Majesty's army had performed the part of spies and policemen with much adroitness, nor was it to be expected that the duty would seem a disgrace, when the Prior of the Knights of Saint John was superintendent of the operations, when the Captain-General of the Netherlands had arranged the whole plan, and when all, from subaltern to viceroy, had received minute instructions as to the contemplated treachery from the great chief of the Spanish police, who sat on the throne of Castile and Aragon.

No sooner were these gentlemen in custody than the secretary Albornoz was dispatched to the house of Count Horn, and to that of Bakkerzeel, where all papers were immediately seized, inventoried, and placed in the hands of the Duke.§ Thus, if amid the most secret communications of Egmont and

---

* Correspondance de Philippe II., i., ubi sup.
† Ibid.—Compare Hoofd, iv. 151.   Strada, i. 299.
‡ Correspondance de Philippe II., i. 638.   § Ibid.

Horn or their correspondents, a single treasonable thought should be lurking, it was to go hard but it might be twisted into a cord strong enough to strangle them all.

The Duke wrote a triumphant letter to his Majesty that very night. He apologized that these important captures had been deferred so long but, stated that he had thought it desirable to secure all these leading personages at a single stroke. He then narrated the masterly manner in which the operations had been conducted. Certainly, when it is remembered that the Duke had only reached Brussels upon the 23d August, and that the two Counts were securely lodged in prison on the 9th of September, it seemed a superfluous modesty upon his part thus to excuse himself for an apparent delay. At any rate, in the eyes of the world and of posterity, his zeal to carry out the bloody commands of his master was sufficiently swift.

The consternation was universal throughout the provinces when the arrests became known. Egmont's great popularity and distinguished services placed him so high above the mass of citizens, and his attachment to the Catholic religion was moreover so well known, as to make it obvious that no man could now be safe, when men like him were in the power of Alva and his myrmidons. The animosity to the Spaniards increased hourly.* The Duchess affected indignation† at the arrest of the two nobles, although it nowhere appears that she attempted a word in their defence, or lifted, at any subsequent moment, a finger to save them. She was not anxious to wash her hands of the blood of two innocent men ; she was only offended that they had been arrested without her permission. The Duke had, it is true, sent Berlaymont and Mansfeld to give her information of the fact, as soon as the capture had been made, with the plausible excuse that he preferred to save her from all the responsibility and all the unpopularity of the measure.‡ Nothing, however, could appease her wrath at

---

* Bor, iv. 185.   † Strada, i. 301.
‡ Bor, iv. 185.   Strada, i. 300, 301.

this and every other indication of the contempt in which he appeared to hold the sister of his sovereign. She complained of his conduct daily to every one who was admitted to her presence. Herself oppressed by a sense of personal indignity, she seemed for a moment to identify herself with the cause of the oppressed provinces. She seemed to imagine herself the champion of their liberties, and the Netherlanders, for a moment, seemed to participate in the delusion. Because she was indignant at the insolence of the Duke of Alva to herself, the honest citizens began to give her credit for a sympathy with their own wrongs. She expressed herself determined to move about from one city to another, until the answer to her demand for dismissal should arrive.* She allowed her immediate attendants to abuse the Spaniards in good set terms upon every occasion. Even her private chaplain permitted himself, in preaching before her in the palace chapel, to denounce the whole nation as a race of traitors and ravishers, and for this offence was only reprimanded, much against her will, by the Duchess, and ordered to retire for a season to his convent.† She did not attempt to disguise her dissatisfaction at every step which had been taken by the Duke. In all this there was much petulance, but very little dignity, while there was neither a spark of real sympathy for the oppressed millions, nor a throb of genuine womanly emotion for the impending fate of the two nobles. Her principal grief was that she had pacified the provinces, and that another had now arrived to reap the glory ; but it was difficult, while the unburied bones of many heretics were still hanging, by her decree, on the rafters of their own dismantled churches, for her successfully to enact the part of a benignant and merciful Regent. But it is very true that the horrors of the Duke's administration have been propitious to the fame of Margaret, and perhaps more so to that of Cardinal Granvelle. The faint and struggling rays of humanity

---

* Correspondance de Philippe II., i. 631   † Ibid.

which occasionally illumined the course of their government, were destined tô be extinguished in a chaos so profound and dark, that these last beams of light seemed clearer and more bountiful by the contrast.

The Count of Hoogstraaten, who was on his way to Brussels, had, by good fortune, injured his hand through the accidental discharge of a pistol. Detained by this casualty at Cologne, he was informed, before his arrival at the capital, of the arrest of his two distinguished friends, and accepted the hint to betake himself at once to a place of safety.*

The loyalty of the elder Mansfeld was beyond dispute even by Alva. His son Charles had, however, been imprudent, and, as we have seen, had even affixed his name to the earliest copies of the Compromise. He had retired, it is true, from all connexion with the confederates, but his father knew well that the young Count's signature upon that famous document would prove his death-warrant, were he found in the country. He therefore had sent him into Germany before the arrival of the Duke.†

The King's satisfaction was unbounded when he learned this important achievement of Alva, and he wrote immediately to express his approbation in the most extravagant terms.‡ Cardinal Granvelle, on the contrary, affected astonishment at a course which he had secretly counselled. He assured his Majesty that he had never believed Egmont to entertain sentiments opposed to the Catholic religion, nor to the interests of the Crown, up to the period of his own departure from the Netherlands. He was persuaded, he said, that the Count had been abused by others, *although, to be sure, the Cardinal had learned with regret what Egmont had written on the occasion of the baptism of Count Hoogstraaten's child.* As to the other persons arrested, he said that no one regretted their fate. The Cardinal added, that he was *supposed to be himself the instigator of these captures*, but that he was not disturbed by that, or by other imputations of a similar nature.§

---

* Bor, iv. 185   † Ibid., iv. 185.   Correspondance de Philippe II., i. 647.
‡ Correspondance de Philippe II., i. 666.   § Ibid., 674.

In conversation with those about him, he frequently expressed regret that the Prince of Orange had been too crafty to be caught in the same net in which his more simple companions were so inextricably entangled. Indeed, on the first arrival of the news, that men of high rank had been arrested in Brussels, the Cardinal eagerly inquired if the Taciturn had been taken, for by that term he always characterized the Prince. Receiving a negative reply, he expressed extreme disappointment, adding, that if Orange had escaped, they had taken nobody, and that his capture would have been more valuable than that of every man in the Netherlands.*

Peter Titelmann, too, the famous inquisitor, who retired from active life, was then living upon Philip's bounty, and encouraged by friendly letters from that monarch,† expressed the same opinion. Having been informed that Egmont and Horn had been captured, he eagerly inquired if "wise William" had also been taken. He was, of course, answered in the negative. "Then will our joy be but brief," he observed. "Woe unto us for the wrath to come from Germany."‡

On the 12th of July, of this year, Philip wrote to Granvelle to inquire the particulars of a letter which the Prince of Orange, *according to a previous communication of the Cardinal,* had written to Egmont on the occasion of the baptism of Count Hoogstraaten's child.§ On the 17th of August, the Cardinal replied, by setting the King right as to the error which he had committed. The letter, as he had already stated, was not written by Orange, *but by Egmont,* and he expressed his astonishment that Madame de Parma had not yet sent it to his Majesty. The Duchess must have seen it, because her confessor had shown it to the person who was Granvelle's informant. In this letter, the Cardinal continued,

---

* Hoofd, iv. 151. Strada, i. 300. Meteren 50.

† Correspondance de Philippe II., i. 523.

‡ " —— si (inquit) astutus Gulielmus (Aurantius) evasit non erunt solida gaudia nostra, væ nobis à bello Germanico."—Pandoræ sive veniæ Hispanicæ editæ Anatomia. Prometheo auctore, 1574.

§ Correspondance de Philippe II., i. 564–610.

the statement had been made by Egmont to the Prince of Orange *that their plots were discovered*, that the King was making armaments, that they were unable to resist him, and that therefore it had become necessary *to dissemble* and to accommodate themselves as well as possible to the present situation, while *waiting for other circumstances under which to accomplish their designs*. Granvelle advised, moreover, that Straalen, who had been privy to the letter, and perhaps the amanuensis, should be forthwith arrested.*

The Cardinal was determined not to let the matter sleep, notwithstanding his protestation of a kindly feeling towards the imprisoned Count. Against the statement that he knew of a letter which amounted to a full confession of treason, out of Egmont's own mouth—a fact which, if proved, and perhaps, if even insinuated, would be sufficient with Philip to deprive Egmont of twenty thousand lives—against these constant recommendations to his suspicious and sanguinary master, to ferret out this document, if it were possible, it must be confessed that the churchman's vague and hypocritical expressions on the side of mercy were very little worth.

Certainly these seeds of suspicion did not fall upon a barren soil. Philip immediately communicated the information thus received to the Duke of Alva, charging him on repeated occasions to find out what was written, either by Egmont or by Straalen, at Egmont's instigation, stating that such a letter was written at the time of the Hoogstraaten baptism, that it would probably illustrate the opinions of Egmont at that period, and that the letter itself, which the confessor of Madame de Parma had once had in his hands, ought, if possible, to be procured.† Thus the very language used by Granvelle to Philip was immediately repeated by the monarch to his representative in the Netherlands, at the moment when all Egmont's papers were in his possession, and when Egmont's private secretary was undergoing the torture,‡ in order that secrets

---

* Correspondance de Philippe II., i. 624.   † Ibid., i. 666–702.

‡ Vigl. Epist. ad Hopp., xxvi. 406. V. d. Vynckt, ii. 82. Correspondance de Philippe II., i. 671.

might be wrenched from him which had never entered his brain. The fact that no such letter was found, that the Duchess had never alluded to any such document, and that neither a careful scrutiny of papers, nor the application of the rack,* could elicit any satisfactory information on the subject, leads to the conclusion that no such treasonable paper had ever existed, save in the imagination of the Cardinal. At any rate, it is no more than just to hesitate before affixing a damning character to a document, in the absence of any direct proof that there ever was such a document at all. The confessor of Madame de Parma told another person, who told the Cardinal, that either Count Egmont, or Burgomaster Straalen, by command of Count Egmont, wrote to the Prince of Orange thus and so. What evidence was this upon which to found a charge of high treason against a man whom Granvelle affected to characterize as otherwise neither opposed to the Catholic religion, nor to the true service of the King? What vulpine kind of mercy was it on the part of the Cardinal, while making such deadly insinuations, to recommend the imprisoned victim to clemency?

The unfortunate envoys, Marquis Bergen and Baron Montigny, had remained in Spain under close observation. Of those doomed victims who, in spite of friendly remonstrances and of ominous warnings, had thus ventured into the lion's den, no retreating footmarks were ever to be seen. Their fate, now that Alva had at last been despatched to the Netherlands, seemed to be sealed, and the Marquis Bergen, accepting the augury in its most evil sense, immediately afterwards had sickened unto death. Whether it were the sickness of hope deferred, suddenly changing to despair, or whether it were a still more potent and unequivocal poison which came to the relief of the unfortunate nobleman, will perhaps never be ascertained with certainty.† The secrets of those terrible prison-houses of Spain, where even the eldest begotten son,

---

* Correspondance de Philippe II., i. 671.
† Strada, i. 290. Hoofd, iv. 146,

and the wedded wife of the monarch, were soon afterwards believed to have been the victims of his dark revenge, can never perhaps be accurately known, until the grave gives up its dead, and the buried crimes of centuries are revealed.

It was very soon after the departure of Alva's fleet from Carthagena, that the Marquis Bergen felt his end approaching. He sent for the Prince of Eboli, with whom he had always maintained intimate relations, and whom he believed to be his disinterested friend. Relying upon his faithful breast, and trusting to receive from his eyes alone the pious drops of sympathy which he required, the dying noble poured out his long and last complaint. He charged him to tell the man whom he would no longer call his king, that he had ever been true and loyal, that the bitterness of having been constantly suspected, when he was conscious of entire fidelity, was a sharper sorrow than could be lightly believed, and that he hoped the time would come when his own truth and the artifices of his enemies would be brought to light. He closed his parting message by predicting that after he had been long laid in the grave, the impeachments against his character would be at last, although too late, retracted.*

So spake the unhappy envoy, and his friend replied with words of consolation. It is probable that he even ventured, in the King's name, to grant him the liberty of returning to his home; the only remedy, as his physicians had repeatedly stated, which could possibly be applied to his disease. But the devilish hypocrisy of Philip, and the abject perfidy of Eboli, at this juncture, almost surpass belief. The Prince came to press the hand and to close the eyes of the dying man whom he called his friend, having first carefully studied a billet of most minute and secret instructions from his master as to the deportment he was to observe upon this solemn occasion and afterwards. This paper, written in Philip's own hand, had been delivered to Eboli on the very day of his visit to Bergen, and bore the superscription that it was not to be

---

* Strada, i. 290.

read nor opened till the messenger who brought it had left his presence. It directed the Prince, if it should be evident that the Marquis was past recovery, to promise him, in the King's name, the permission of returning to the Netherlands. Should, however, a possibility of his surviving appear, Eboli was only to hold out a hope that such permission might eventually be obtained. In case of the death of Bergen, the Prince was immediately to confer with the Grand Inquisitor and with the Count of Feria, upon the measures to be taken for his obsequies. It might seem advisable, in that event to exhibit the regret which the King and his ministers felt for his death, and the great esteem in which they held the nobles of the Netherlands. At the same time, Eboli was further instructed to confer with the same personages as to the most efficient means for preventing the escape of Baron Montigny ; to keep a vigilant eye upon his movements, and to give general directions to governors and to postmasters to intercept his flight, should it be attempted. Finally, in case of Bergen's death, the Prince was directed to despatch a special messenger, apparently on his own responsibility, and as if in the absence and without the knowledge of the King, to inform the Duchess of Pàrma of the event, and to urge her immediately to take possession of the city of Bergen-op-Zoom, and of all other property belonging to the Marquis, until it should be ascertained whether it were not possible to convict him, after death, of treason, and to confiscate his estates accordingly.*

Such were the instructions of Philip to Eboli, and precisely in accordance with the program, was the horrible comedy enacted at the death-bed of the envoy. Three days after his parting interview with his disinterested friend, the Marquis was a corpse.† Before his limbs were cold, a messenger was on his way to Brussels, instructing the Regent to *sequestrate his property, and to arrest, upon suspicion of heresy, the youthful kinsman and niece, who, by the*

---

* Correspondance de Philippe II., i. 572.   † Strada, i. 290.

will of the Marquis, were to be united in marriage and to share his estate.* The whole drama, beginning with the death scene, was enacted according to order. Before the arrival of Alva in the Netherlands, the property of the Marquis was in the hands of the Government, awaiting the confiscation,† which was but for a brief season delayed, while on the other hand, Baron Montigny, Bergen's companion in doom, who was not, however, so easily to be carried off by home-sickness, was closely confined in the alcazar of Segovia, never to leave a Spanish prison alive.‡ There is something pathetic in the delusion in which Montigny and his brother, the Count Horn, both indulged, each believing that the other was out of harm's way, the one by his absence from the Netherlands, the other by his absence from Spain, while both, involved in the same meshes, were rapidly and surely approaching their fate.§

In the same despatch of the 9th September, in which the Duke communicated to Philip the capture of Egmont and Horn, he announced to him his determination to establish a new court for the trial of crimes committed during the recent period of troubles.‖ This wonderful tribunal was accordingly created with the least possible delay. It was called the Council of Troubles, but it soon acquired the terrible name, by which it will be forever known in history, of the Blood-Council.¶ It superseded all other institutions. Every court, from those of the municipal magistracies up to the supreme councils of the provinces, were forbidden to take cognizance in future of any cause growing out of the late troubles.** The council of state, although it was not formally disbanded, fell into complete desuetude, its members being occasionally summoned

---

* Correspondance de Philippe II., i. 547–590, Strada, i. 291, and note of M. Gachard.   † V. d. Vynckt, ii. 77.

‡ Hoofd, iv. 172, 173.   Correspondance de Philippe II., i. 648, 654, 666.

§ Vide Déduction de l'Innocence du Comte de Hornes, pp. 203, 204.

‖ Correspondance de Philippe II., i. 637.

¶ Hoofd, iv. 153.   Bor, iv. 185, 186.   Meteren, f. 49.   Reidani, Ann Belg., p. 5.   ** Bor, iv. 185, 186.

into Alva's private chambers in an irregular manner, while its principal functions were usurped by the Blood-Council. Not only citizens of every province, but the municipal bodies and even the sovereign provincial estates themselves, were compelled to plead, like humble individuals, before this new and extraordinary tribunal.* It is unnecessary to allude to the absolute violation which was thus committed of all charters, laws and privileges, because the very creation of the council was a bold and brutal proclamation that those laws and privileges were at an end. The constitution or maternal principle of this suddenly erected court was of a twofold nature. It defined and it punished the crime of treason. The definitions, couched in eighteen articles, declared it to be treason to have delivered or signed any petition against the new bishops, the Inquisition, or the Edicts ; to have tolerated public preaching under any circumstances ; to have omitted resistance to the image-breaking, to the field-preaching, or to the presentation of the Request by the nobles, and "either through sympathy or surprise" to have asserted that the King did not possess the right to deprive all the provinces of their liberties, or to have maintained that this present tribunal was bound to respect in any manner any laws or any charters.† In these brief and simple, but comprehensive terms, was the crime of high treason defined. The punishment was still more briefly, simply, and comprehensively stated, for it was instant death in all cases.‡ So well too did this new and terrible engine perform its work, that in less than three months from the time of its erection, eighteen hundred human beings had suffered death§ by its summary proceedings ; some of the highest, the noblest, and the most virtuous in the land among the number ; nor had it then manifested the slightest indication of faltering in its dread career.

Yet, strange to say, this tremendous court, thus established upon the ruins of all the ancient institutions of the country,

---

* Bor, Hoofd, Meteren, ubi sup.   † Meteren, 49

‡ Hoofd, Bor, ubi supra. Meteren.

§ Brandt, Hist. de Ref., i. 468. Bor, iv. 116.

had not been provided with even a nominal authority from any source whatever. The King had granted it no letters patent or charter, nor had even the Duke of Alva thought it worth while to grant any commissions either in his own name or as Captain-General, to any of the members composing the board.* The Blood-Council was merely an informal club, of which the Duke was perpetual president, while the other members were all appointed by himself.

Of these subordinate councillors, two had the right of voting, subject, however, in all cases to his final decision, while the rest of the number did not vote at all.† It had not, therefore, in any sense, the character of a judicial, legislative, or executive tribunal, but was purely a board of advice by which the bloody labors of the duke were occasionally lightened as to detail, while not a feather's weight of power or of responsibility was removed from his shoulders. He reserved for himself the final decision upon all causes which should come before the council, and stated his motives for so doing with grim simplicity. "Two reasons," he wrote to the King, " have determined me thus to limit the power of the tribunal ; the first that, not knowing its members, I might be easily deceived by them ; the second, that *the men of law* only condemn *for crimes which are proved ;* whereas your Majesty knows that affairs of state are governed by very different rules from *the laws which they have here.*"‡

It being, therefore, the object of the Duke to compose a body of men who would be of assistance to him in condemning for crimes which could *not* be proved, and in slipping over statutes which were not to be recognized, it must be confessed that he was not unfortunate in the appointments which he

---

* V. Notice sur le Cons. des Troubles, par M. Gachard, p. 7.   MS. Letters of Requesens, 30th December, 1573, and of Geron. de Roda, 18th May, 1576.

† Gachard.   Notice, etc., 8 and 9, with the letters cited from Alva, 14th September, 1567, and from Requesens, 30th December, 1573.

‡ Gachard, Notice, etc., p. 5.—" La otra es que letrados no sentencian sino en casos probados; y como V. M. sabe, los negocios de Estado son muy differentes de las leyes que ellos tienen."—Lett. of 9th Sept., 1567.

made to the office of councillors. In this task of appointment he had the assistance of the experienced Viglius.* That learned jurisconsult, with characteristic lubricity, had evaded the dangerous honor for himself, but he nominated a number of persons from whom the Duke selected his list. The sacerdotal robes which he had so recently and so "craftily" assumed, furnished his own excuse, and in his letters to his faithful Hopper he repeatedly congratulated himself upon his success in keeping himself at a distance from so bloody and perilous a post.†

It is impossible to look at the conduct of the distinguished Frisian at this important juncture without contempt. Bent only upon saving himself, his property, and his reputation, he did not hesitate to bend before the "most illustrious Duke," as he always denominated him, with fulsome and fawning homage.‡ While he declined to dip his own fingers in the innocent blood which was about to flow in torrents, he did not object to officiate at the initiatory preliminaries of the great Netherland holocaust. His decent and dainty demeanor seems even more offensive than the jocularity of the real murderers. Conscious that no man knew the laws and customs of the Netherlands better than himself, he had the humble effrontery to observe that it was necessary for him at that moment silently to submit his own unskilfulness to the superior judgment and knowledge of others.§ Having at last been relieved from the stone of Sisyphus, which, as he plaintively expressed himself, he had been rolling for twenty years ;‖ having, by the arrival of Tisnacq, obtained his discharge as President of the state council, he was yet not unwilling to retain the emoluments and the rank of President of the privy council, although both offices had become sinecures since the erection of the Council of Blood. Although

---

* Correspondance de Philippe II., i. 637.   Vigl. Epist. ad Hopp., xli. 441–442; xxvii. 410.

† Vigl. ad Hopp. Epist. 27 et 41.   ‡ Ibid., 26, etc.

§ Ibid., 26.   ‖ Vita Viglii, cxi.

his life had been spent in administrative and judicial employments, he did not blush upon a matter of constitutional law to defer to the authority of such jurisconsults as the Duke of Alva and his two Spanish bloodhounds, Vargas and Del Rio. He did not like, he observed, in his confidential correspondence, to gainsay the Duke, when maintaining, that in cases of treason, the privileges of Brabant were powerless, although he mildly doubted whether the Brabantines would agree with the doctrine.* He often thought, he said, of remedies for restoring the prosperity of the provinces, but in action he only assisted the Duke, to the best of his abilities, in arranging the Blood-Council. He wished well to his country, but he was more anxious for the favor of Alva. "I rejoice," said he, in one of his letters, "that the most illustrious Duke has written to the King in praise of my obsequiousness ; when I am censured here for so reverently cherishing him, it is a consolation that my services to the King and to the governor are not unappreciated there."† Indeed the Duke of Alva, who had originally suspected the President's character, seemed at last overcome by his indefatigable and cringing homage. He wrote to the King, in whose good graces the learned Doctor was most anxious at that portentous period to maintain himself, that the President was very serviceable and diligent, and that he deserved to receive a crumb of comfort from the royal hand.‡ Philip, in consequence, wrote in one of his letters a few lines of vague compliment, which could be shown to Viglius, according to Alva's suggestion. It is, however, not a little characteristic of the Spanish court and of the Spanish monarch, that, on the very day before, he had sent to the Captain-General a few documents of very different import. In order, as he said, that the Duke might be ignorant of nothing which related to the Netherlands, he forwarded to him copies of the letters written by Margaret of Parma from Brussels, three years before. These letters, as it will be recollected, con-

---

* Vigl. ad Hopp., Epist., 24.   † Ibid., 26.
‡ Correspondance de Philippe II., i. 647.

tained an account of the secret investigations which the Duchess had made as to the private character and opinions of Viglius—at the very moment when he apparently stood highest in her confidence—and charged him with heresy, swindling, and theft. Thus the painstaking and time-serving President, with all his learning and experience, was successively the dupe of Margaret and of Alva, whom he so obsequiously courted, and always of Philip, whom he so feared and wor-shipped.*

With his assistance, the list of blood-councillors was quickly completed. No one who was offered the office refused it. Noircarmes and Berlaymont accepted with very great eager-ness.† Several presidents and councillors of the different provincial tribunals were appointed, but all the Netherlanders were men of straw. Two Spaniards, Del Rio and Vargas, were the only members who could vote; while their decisions, as already stated, were subject to reversal by Alva. Del Rio was a man without character or talent, a mere tool in the hands of his superiors, but Juan de Vargas was a terrible reality.

No better man could have been found in Europe for the post to which he was thus elevated. To shed human blood was, in his opinion, the only important business and the only exhilarating pastime of life. His youth had been stained with other crimes. He had been obliged to retire from Spain, because of his violation of an orphan child to whom he was guardian,‡ but, in his manhood, he found no pleasure but in murder. He executed Alva's bloody work with an industry which was almost superhuman, and with a merriment which would have shamed a demon. His execrable jests ring through the blood and smoke and death-cries of those days of per-

---

* Correspondance de Philippe II., i. 666.

† "Norcarme y Barlemon —— no solo no han rehusado, pero me parece lo han acetado de muy buena gana."—MS. Letter of Alba, 10th September, 1567; cited in Gachard, Notice sur le Conseil des Troubles, p. 7, note.

‡ Hoofd, iv. 152.—See Correspondance de Philippe II., ii. 713, 731, also La Déduction de l'Innocence du Comte de Hornes, pp. 60, 61.

petual sacrifice. He was proud to be the double of the iron-hearted Duke, and acted so uniformly in accordance with his views, that the right of revision remained but nominal. There could be no possibility of collision where the subaltern was only anxious to surpass an incomparable superior. The figure of Vargas rises upon us through the mist of three centuries with terrible distinctness. Even his barbarous grammar has not been forgotten, and his crimes against syntax and against humanity have acquired the same immortality. "Heretici fraxerunt templa, boni nihili faxerunt contra, ergo debent omnes patibulare," was the comprehensive but barbarous formula of a man who murdered the Latin language as ruthlessly as he slaughtered his contemporaries.*

Among the ciphers who composed the rest of the board, the Flemish Councillor Hessels was the one whom the Duke most respected. He was not without talent or learning, but the Duke only valued him for his cruelty. Being allowed to take but little share in the deliberations, Hessels was accustomed to doze away his afternoon hours at the council table, and when awakened from his nap in order that he might express an opinion on the case then before the court, was wont to rub his eyes and to call out "Ad patibulum, ad patibulum," ("to the gallows with him, to the gallows with him,") with great fervor, but in entire ignorance of the culprit's name or the merits of the case. His wife, naturally disturbed that her husband's waking and sleeping hours were alike absorbed with this hangman's work, more than once ominously expressed her hope to him, that he, whose head and heart were thus engrossed with the gibbet, might not one day come to hang upon it himself; a gloomy prophecy which the Future most terribly fulfilled.†

The Council of Blood, thus constituted, held its first session on the 20th September, at the lodgings of Alva.‡ Springing

---

* V. d. Vynckt, ii. 75, 76, 77; Brandt, i. 465, 466; Reidani, p. 5; Hoofd, 152. "The heretics destroyed the temples, the good men did nothing to prevent it, therefore they should all be hanged."

† Hoofd, xiv. 594. Brandt, 494.　　　‡ Gachard. Notice, etc., 9.

completely grown and armed to the teeth from the head of its inventor, the new tribunal—at the very outset in possession of all its vigor—forthwith began to manifest a terrible activity in accomplishing the objects of its existence. The councillors having been sworn to "eternal secrecy as to any thing which should be transacted at the board, and having likewise made oath to denounce any one of their number who should violate the pledge," the court was considered as organized. Alva worked therein seven hours daily.* It may be believed that the subordinates were not spared, and that their office proved no sinecure. Their labors, however, were not encumbered by antiquated forms. As this supreme and only tribunal for all the Netherlands had no commission or authority save the will of the Captain-General, so it was also thought a matter of supererogation to establish a set of rules and orders such as might be useful in less independent courts. The forms of proceeding were brief and artless. There was a rude organization by which a crowd of commissioners, acting as inferior officers of the council, were spread over the provinces, whose business was to collect information concerning all persons who might be incriminated for participation in the recent troubles.† The greatest crime, however, was to be rich, and one which could be expiated by no virtues, however signal. Alva was bent upon proving himself as accomplished a financier as he was indisputably a consummate commander, and he had promised his master an annual income of 500,000 ducats from the confiscations which were to accompany the executions.‡

It was necessary that the blood torrent should flow at once through the Netherlands, in order that the promised golden river, a yard deep, according to his vaunt,§ should begin to irrigate the thirsty soil of Spain. It is obvious, from the fundamental laws which were made to define treason at the

---

* Gachard. Notice, etc., 10.   † Ibid., 14, etc.

‡ Ibid., 22.—Compare Brandt, i. 475: Meteren, 29; Hoofd, iv.; V. d. Vynckt, ii. 81, et alios.   § Brandt, i. 496.

same moment in which they established the council, that any man might be at any instant summoned to the court. Every man, whether innocent or guilty, whether Papist or Protestant, felt his head shaking on his shoulders. If he were wealthy, there seemed no remedy but flight, which was now almost impossible, from the heavy penalties affixed by the new edict upon all carriers, shipmasters, and wagoners, who should aid in the escape of heretics.*

A certain number of these commissioners were particularly instructed to collect information as to the treason of Orange, Louis Nassau, Brederode, Egmont, Horn, Culemberg, Vanden Berg, Bergen, and Montigny. Upon such information the proceedings against those distinguished seigniors were to be summarily instituted. Particular councillors of the Court of Blood were charged with the arrangement of these important suits, but the commissioners were to report in the first instance to the Duke himself, who afterwards returned the paper into the hands of his subordinates.†

With regard to the inferior and miscellaneous cases which were daily brought in incredible profusion before the tribunal, the same preliminaries were observed, by way of aping the proceedings in courts of justice. Alva sent the cart-loads of information which were daily brought to him, but which neither he nor any other man had time to read, to be disposed of by the board of councillors. It was the duty of the different subalterns, who, as already stated, had no right of voting, to prepare reports upon the cases. Nothing could be more summary. Information was lodged against a man, or against a hundred men, in one document. The Duke sent the papers to the council, and the inferior councillors reported at once to Vargas. If the report concluded with a recommendation of death to the man, or the hundred men in question, Vargas instantly approved it, and execution was done upon the man, or the hundred men, within forty-eight hours. If the report *had any other conclusion*, it was imme-

---

* Bor, iii. 175, 176.   † Gachard, Notice, etc., 10, 11.

diately sent back for revision, and the reporters were overwhelmed with reproaches by the President.*

Such being the method of operation, it may be supposed
that the councillors were not allowed to slacken in their
terrible industry. The register of every city, village, and
hamlet throughout the Netherlands showed the daily lists
of men, women, and children thus sacrificed at the shrine
of the demon who had obtained the mastery over this unhappy land.† It was not often that an individual was of
sufficient importance to be tried—if trial it could be called—
by himself.‡ It was found more expeditious to send them in
batches to the furnace. Thus, for example, on the 4th of
January, eighty-four inhabitants of Valenciennes were condemned ; on another day, ninety-five miscellaneous individuals, from different places in Flanders ; on another, forty-
six inhabitants of Malines ; on another, thirty-five persons
from different localities, and so on.§

The evening of Shrovetide, a favorite holiday in the
Netherlands, afforded an occasion for arresting and carrying off
a vast number of doomed individuals at a single swoop.‖ It
was correctly supposed that the burghers, filled with wine and
wassail, to which perhaps the persecution under which they
lived lent an additional and horrible stimulus, might be easily
taken from their beds in great numbers, and be delivered over
at once to the council. The plot was ingenious, the net was

---

* Gachard, Notice, etc., 19, 20.—"En siendo el aviso de condenaer à muerte
se decia que estaba muy bien y no habia mas que ver ; empero, si el aviso era de
menor pena, no se estaba à lo que ellos decian, sino tornabase à ver el proceso, y
decian les sobre ellos malas palabras y hacian les ruin tratamiento," etc.—Official
document cited by M. Gachard in Notice sur le Conseil, etc.

† Hoofd, iv.   Brandt, ix.

‡ See in particular the "Sententien van Alva gezammelt van J. Markus,"
passim; a work in which a few thousand sentences of death upon men and
women still in the Netherlands, or of banishment under pain of death upon such
as had escaped, have been collected and published. The sentences were given
mainly upon the culprits in lots or gangs.—See also the Correspondance de Philippe II., ii., passim, and the "Registre des Condamnés et Bannis à Cause des
Troubles des Pays Bas."—3 vols. MS. Brussels Archives.

§ Hoofd, iv. 157, 158.   Meteren, 49.   Gachard, 15, 16.

‖ Hoofd, iv. 157, 158.   Brandt, i. 471.   Bor, iv. 230.   Gachard, 14.

spread accordingly. Many of the doomed were, however, luckily warned of the terrible termination which was impending over their festival, and bestowed themselves in safety for a season. A prize of about five hundred prisoners was all which rewarded the sagacity of the enterprise.* It is needless to add that they were all immediately executed. It is a wearisome and odious task to ransack the mouldy records of three centuries ago, in order to reproduce the obscure names of the thousands who were thus sacrificed. The dead have buried their dead, and are forgotten. It is likewise hardly necessary to state that the proceedings before the council were all *ex parte*, and that an information was almost inevitably followed by a death-warrant. It sometimes happened even that the zeal of the councillors outstripped the industry of the commissioners. The sentences were occasionally in advance of the docket. Thus upon one occasion a man's case was called for trial, but before the investigation was commenced it was discovered that he had been already executed. A cursory examination of the papers proved, moreover, as usual, that the culprit had committed no crime. " No matter for that," said Vargas, jocosely, " if he has died innocent, it will be all the better for him when he takes his trial in the other world."†

But, however the councillors might indulge in these gentle jests among themselves, it was obvious that innocence was in reality impossible, according to the rules which had been laid down regarding treason. The practice was in accordance with the precept, and persons were daily executed with senseless pretexts, which was worse than executions with no pretexts at all. Thus Peter de Witt of Amsterdam was beheaded, because at one of the tumults in that city he had persuaded a rioter *not to fire* upon a magistrate. This was taken as sufficient proof that he was a man in authority among the rebels, and he was accordingly put to death.‡ Madame Juriaen, who, in 1566, had struck with

---

* Hoofd, Brandt, Bor, Gachard, ubi supra.
† Brandt, i. 494. Hoofd, v. 191　　　　‡ Hoofd, v. 183. Brandt, i. 488.

her slipper a little wooden image of the Virgin, together with her maid-servant, who had witnessed without denouncing the crime, were both drowned by the hangman in a hogshead placed on the scaffold.*

Death, even, did not in all cases place a criminal beyond the reach of the executioner. Egbert Meynartzoon, a man of high official rank, had been condemned, together with two colleagues, on an accusation of collecting money in a Lutheran church. He died in prison of dropsy. The sheriff was indignant with the physician, because, in spite of cordials and strengthening prescriptions, the culprit had slipped through his fingers before he had felt those of the hangman. He consoled himself by placing the body on a chair, and having the dead man beheaded in company with his colleagues.†

Thus the whole country became a charnel-house ; the death-bell tolled hourly in every village ; not a family but was called to mourn for its dearest relatives, while the survivors stalked listlessly about, the ghosts of their former selves, among the wrecks of their former homes. The spirit of the nation, within a few months after the arrival of Alva, seemed hopelessly broken. The blood of its best and bravest had already stained the scaffold ; the men to whom it had been accustomed to look for guidance and protection, were dead, in prison, or in exile. Submission had ceased to be of any avail, flight was impossible, and the spirit of vengeance had alighted at every fireside. The mourners went daily about the streets, for there was hardly a house which had not been made desolate. The scaffolds, the gallows, the funeral piles, which had been sufficient in ordinary times, furnished now an entirely inadequate machinery for the incessant executions. Columns and stakes in every street, the door-posts of private houses, the fences in the fields were laden with human carcasses, strangled, burned, beheaded. The orchards in the country bore on many a tree the hideous fruit of human bodies.‡

---

* Brandt, i. 488.   Reael, 43.   Hist. des Martyrs, 449.
† Brandt, 488.   Reael, 60, 6.   Hoofd, v. 181, 182.   ‡ Hoofd, iv. 153.

Thus the Netherlands were crushed, and but for the stringency of the tyranny which had now closed their gates, would have been depopulated. The grass began to grow in the streets of those cities which had recently nourished so many artisans. In all those great manufacturing and industrial marts, where the tide of human life had throbbed so vigorously, there now reigned the silence and the darkness of midnight. It was at this time that the learned Viglius wrote to his friend Hopper, that all venerated the prudence and gentleness of the Duke of Alva.* Such were among the first-fruits of that prudence and that gentleness.

The Duchess of Parma had been kept in a continued state of irritation. She had not ceased for many months to demand her release from the odious position of a cipher in a land where she had so lately been sovereign, and she had at last obtained it. Philip transmitted his acceptance of her resignation by the same courier who brought Alva's commission to be governor-general in her place.† The letters to the Duchess were full of conventional compliments for her past services, accompanied, however, with a less barren and more acceptable acknowledgment, in the shape of a life income of 14,000 ducats instead of the 8000 hitherto enjoyed by her Highness.‡

In addition to this liberal allowance, of which she was never to be deprived, except upon receiving full payment of 140,000 ducats, she was presented with 25,000 florins by the estates of Brabant, and with 30,000 by those of Flanders.§

With these substantial tokens of the success of her nine years' fatigue and intolerable anxiety, she at last took her departure from the Netherlands, having communicated the dissolution of her connexion with the provinces by a farewell letter to the Estates dated 9th December, 1567.‖ Within a

* Vigl. ad Hopp. Ep. xlvi. 451.
† Correspondance de Philippe II., i. 658, 662, 680, etc.
‡ Ibid., 658. Strada, i. 305.
§ Vigl. ad Hopp., Ep. xlv. Correspondance de Philippe II., ii. 715.
‖ See it in Bor, iv. 186, 187.

few weeks afterwards, escorted by the Duke of Alva across the frontier of Brabant, attended by a considerable deputation of Flemish nobility into Germany, and accompanied to her journey's end at Parma by the Count and Countess of Mansfeld, she finally closed her eventful career in the Netherlands.*

The horrors of the succeeding administration proved beneficial to her reputation. Upon the dark ground of succeeding years the lines which recorded her history seemed written with letters of light. Yet her conduct in the Netherlands offers but few points for approbation, and many for indignant censure. That she was not entirely destitute of feminine softness and sentiments of bounty, her parting despatch to her brother proved. In that letter she recommended to him a course of clemency and forgiveness, and reminded him that the nearer kings approach to God in station, the more they should endeavor to imitate him in his attributes of benignity.† But the language of this farewell was more tender than had been the spirit of her government. One looks in vain, too, through the general atmosphere of kindness which pervades the epistle, for a special recommendation of those distinguished and doomed seigniors, whose attachment to her person and whose chivalrous and conscientious endeavors to fulfil her own orders, had placed them upon the edge of that precipice from which they were shortly to be hurled. The men who had restrained her from covering herself with disgrace by a precipitate retreat from the post of danger, and who had imperilled their lives by obedience to her express instructions, had been long languishing in solitary confinement, never to be terminated except by a traitor's death—yet we search in vain for a kind word in their behalf.

Meantime the second civil war in France had broken out. The hollow truce by which the Guise party and the Huguenots had partly pretended to deceive each other was hastened to its

---

* Vigl. ad Hopp., xiv. xlvi. Strada, i. 305, 306.
† Correspondance de Philippe II., 687.

end, among other causes, by the march of Alva to the Netherlands. The Huguenots had taken alarm, for they recognized the fellowship which united their foes in all countries against the Reformation, and Condé and Coligny knew too well that the same influence which had brought Alva to Brussels would soon create an exterminating army against their followers. Hostilities were resumed with more bitterness than ever. The battle of St. Denis—fierce, fatal, but indecisive—was fought. The octogenarian hero, Montmorency, fighting like a foot soldier, refusing to yield his sword, and replying to the respectful solicitations of his nearest enemy by dashing his teeth down his throat with the butt-end of his pistol, the hero of so many battles, whose defeat at St. Quintin had been the fatal point in his career, had died at last in his armor, bravely but not gloriously, in conflict with his own countrymen, led by his own heroic nephew.* The military control of the Catholic party was completely in the hand of the Guises ; the Chancellor de l'Hôpital had abandoned the court after a last and futile effort to reconcile contending factions, which no human power could unite ; the Huguenots had possessed themselves of Rochelle and of other strong places, and, under the guidance of adroit statesmen and accomplished generals, were pressing the Most Christian monarch hard in the very heart of his kingdom.†

As early as the middle of October, while still in Antwerp, Alva had received several secret agents of the French monarch, then closely beleaguered in his capital. Cardinal Lorraine offered to place several strong places of France in the hands of the Spaniard, and Alva had written to Philip that he was disposed to accept the offer, and to render the service. The places thus held would be a guarantee for his expenses, he said, while in case King Charles and his brother should die, " their possession would enable Philip to assert his own claim to the French crown in right of his wife, the *Salic law being merely a pleasantry.*"‡

---

* De Thou, 374, et seq., liv. xli. t. 5.   † Ibid., 378.
‡ Correspondance de Philippe II., i. 593, 594.

The Queen Dowager, adopting now a very different tone from that which characterized her conversation at the Bayonne interview, wrote to Alva, that, if for want of 2000 Spanish musketeers, which she requested him to furnish, she should be obliged to succumb, she chose to disculpate herself in advance before God and Christian princes for the peace which she should be obliged to make.* The Duke wrote to her in reply, that it was much better to have a kingdom ruined in preserving it for God and the king by war, than to have it kept entire without war, to the profit of the devil and of his followers.† He was also reported on another occasion to have reminded her of the Spanish proverb—that the head of one salmon is worth those of a hundred frogs.‡ The hint, if it were really given, was certainly destined to be acted upon.

The Duke not only furnished Catherine with advice, but with the musketeers which she had solicited. Two thousand foot and fifteen hundred horse, under the Count of Aremberg, attended by a choice band of the Catholic nobility of the Netherlands, had joined the royal camp at Paris before the end of the year, to take their part in the brief hostilities by which the second treacherous peace was to be preceded.§

Meantime, Alva was not unmindful of the business which had served as a pretext in the arrest of the two Counts. The fortifications of the principal cities were pushed on with great rapidity. The memorable citadel of Antwerp in particular had already been commenced in October under the superintendence of the celebrated engineers, Pacheco and Gabriel de Cerbelloni.‖ In a few months it was completed, at a cost of one million four hundred thousand florins, of which sum the citizens, in spite of their remonstrances, were compelled to contribute more than one quarter. The sum of four hundred thousand florins was forced from the burghers by a tax upon all hereditary property within the municipality.¶

---

* Correspondance de Philippe II., i. 694.   † Ibid., i. 696.

‡ De Thou, t. v., liv. xliv., 515.   Hug. Grot. Annal., lib. ii. 40.   Bor. iv. 219.

§ Ibid., iv. 219.

‖ Correspondance de Philippe II., ii. 725, 726. Bor, iv.   ¶ Ibid., iv. 219.

Two thousand workmen were employed daily in the construction of this important fortress, which was erected, as its position most plainly manifested, not to protect, but to control the commercial capital of the provinces. It stood at the edge of the city, only separated from its walls by an open esplanade. It was the most perfect pentagon in Europe,[*] having one of its sides resting on the Scheld, two turned towards the city, and two towards the open country. Five bastions, with walls of hammered stone, connected by curtains of turf and mason-ry, surrounded by walls measuring a league in circumference, and by an outer moat fed by the Scheld, enclosed a spacious enceinte, where a little church with many small lodging-houses, shaded by trees and shrubbery, nestled among the bristling artillery, as if to mimic the appearance of a peaceful and pastoral village. To four of the five bastions, the Captain-General, with characteristic ostentation, gave his own names and titles. One was called the Duke, the second Ferdinando, a third Toledo, a fourth Alva, while the fifth was baptized with the name of the ill-fated engineer, Pacheco. The water-gate was decorated with the escutcheon of Alva, surrounded by his Golden Fleece collar, with its pendant lamb of God ; a symbol of blasphemous irony, which still remains upon the fortress, to recal the image of the tyrant and murderer. Each bastion was honeycombed with casemates and subterranean storehouses, and capable of containing within its bowels a vast supply of provisions, munitions, and soldiers. Such was the celebrated citadel built to tame the turbulent spirit of Antwerp, at the cost of those whom it was to terrify and to insult.[†]

---

[*] "La nompareille forteresse du monde."—Brantôme. Vie de Don Sancho d'Avila.

[†] De Thou, v. 300.   Bor. iv. 219.   Hoofd, iv. 154.   Bentivoglio, iv. 58.

CHAPTER II.

LATE in October, the Duke of Alva made his triumphant
entry into the new fortress. During his absence, which was to
continue during the remainder of the year, he had ordered
the Secretary Courteville and the Councillor del Rio to super-

intend the commission, which was then actually engaged in collecting materials for the prosecutions to be instituted against the Prince of Orange and the other nobles who had abandoned the country.* Accordingly, soon after his return, on the 19th of January, 1568, the Prince, his brother Louis of Nassau, his brother-in-law, Count Van den Berg, the Count Hoogstraaten, the Count Culemburg, and the Baron Montigny, were summoned in the name of Alva to appear before the Blood-Council, within thrice fourteen days from the date of the proclamation, under pain of perpetual banishment with confiscation of their estates.† It is needless to say that these seigniors did not obey the summons. They knew full well that their obedience would be rewarded only by death.

The charges against the Prince of Orange, which were drawn up in ten articles, stated, chiefly and briefly, that he had been, and was, the head and front of the rebellion; that as soon as his Majesty had left the Netherlands, he had begun his machinations to make himself master of the country and to expel his sovereign by force, if he should attempt to return to the provinces; that he had seduced his Majesty's subjects by false pretences that the Spanish inquisition was about to be introduced; that he had been the secret encourager and director of Brederode and the confederated nobles; and that when sent to Antwerp, in the name of the Regent, to put down the rebellion, he had encouraged heresy and accorded freedom of religion to the Reformers.‡

The articles against Hoogstraaten and the other gentlemen were of similar tenor. It certainly was not a slender proof of the calm effrontery of the government thus to see Alva's proclamation charging it as a crime upon Orange that he had inveigled the lieges into revolt by a false assertion that the inquisition was about to be established, when letters from the Duke to Philip, and from Granvelle to Philip, dated upon nearly the same day, advised the immediate restoration of

---

* Gachard. Notice, etc., 10, 11.
† Bor, iv. 220, 221, 222. Meteren, 50. V. de Vynckt, ii. 77.
‡ See the document condensed in Bor, ubi supra.

the inquisition as soon as an adequate number of executions had paved the way for the measure.* It was also a sufficient indication of a reckless despotism, that while the Duchess, who had made the memorable Accord with the Religionists, received a flattering letter of thanks and a farewell pension of fourteen thousand ducats yearly, those who, by her orders, had acted upon that treaty as the basis of their negotiations, were summoned to lay down their heads upon the block.

The Prince replied to this summons by a brief and somewhat contemptuous plea to the jurisdiction. As a Knight of the Fleece, as a member of the Germanic Empire, as a sovereign prince in France, as a citizen of the Netherlands, he rejected the authority of Alva and of his self-constituted tribunal. His innocence he was willing to establish before competent courts and righteous judges. As a Knight of the Fleece, he said he could be tried only by his peers, the brethren of the Order, and, for that purpose, he could be summoned only by the King as Head of the Chapter, with the sanction of at least six of his fellow-knights. In conclusion, he offered to appear before his Imperial Majesty, the Electors, and other members of the Empire, or before the Knights of the Golden Fleece. In the latter case, he claimed the right, under the statutes of that order, to be placed while the trial was pending, not in a solitary prison, as had been the fate of Egmont and of Horn, but under the friendly charge and protection of the brethren themselves. The letter was addressed to the procurator-general, and a duplicate was forwarded to the Duke.†

From the general tenor of the document, it is obvious both that the Prince was not yet ready to throw down the gauntlet to his sovereign, nor to proclaim his adhesion to the new religion. On departing from the Netherlands in the spring, he had said openly that he was still in possession of sixty thousand florins yearly, and that he should commence no hostilities against Philip, so long as he did not disturb him in his

---

* Correspondance de Philippe II., i. 624.
† See the letter in Bor, iv. 222, 223, 224.

honor or his estates.* Far-seeing politician, if man ever were, he knew the course whither matters were inevitably tending, but he knew how much strength was derived from putting an adversary irretrievably in the wrong. He still maintained an attitude of dignified respect towards the monarch, while he hurled back with defiance the insolent summons of the viceroy. Moreover, the period had not yet arrived for him to break publicly with the ancient faith. Statesman, rather than religionist, at this epoch, he was not disposed to affect a more complete conversion than the one which he had experienced. He was, in truth, not for a new doctrine, but for liberty of conscience. His mind was already expanding beyond any dogmas of the age. The man whom his enemies stigmatized as atheist and renegade, was really in favor of toleration, and, therefore, the more deeply criminal in the eyes of all religious parties.

Events, personal to himself, were rapidly to place him in a position from which he might enter the combat with honor. His character had already been attacked, his property threatened with confiscation. His closest ties of family were now to be severed by the hand of the tyrant. His eldest child, the Count de Buren, torn from his protection, was to be carried into indefinite captivity in a foreign land. It was a remarkable oversight, for a person of his sagacity, that, upon his own departure from the provinces, he should leave his son, then a boy of thirteen years, to pursue his studies at the college of Louvain. Thus exposed to the power of the government, he was soon seized as a hostage for the good behavior of the father. Granvelle appears to have been the first to recommend the step in a secret letter to Philip,† but Alva scarcely needed prompting. Accordingly, upon the 13th of February, 1568, the Duke sent the Seignior de Chassy to Louvain, attended by four officers and by twelve archers. He was furnished with a letter to the Count de Buren, in which that young nobleman was requested to place implicit confi-

---

* Reidani, i. 5.   † Correspondance de Philippe II., i. 701.

dence in the bearer of the despatch, and was informed that the desire which his Majesty had to see him educated for his service, was the cause of the communication which the Seignior de Chassy was about to make.*

That gentleman was, moreover, minutely instructed as to his method of proceeding in this memorable case of kidnapping. He was to present the letter to the young Count in presence of his tutor. He was to invite him to Spain in the name of his Majesty. He was to assure him that his Majesty's commands were solely with a view to his own good, and that he was not commissioned to arrest, but only to escort him. He was to allow the Count to be accompanied only by two valets, two pages, a cook, and a keeper of accounts. He was, however, to induce his tutor to accompany him, at least to the Spanish frontier. He was to arrange that the second day after his arrival at Louvain, the Count should set out for Antwerp, where he was to lodge with Count Lodron, after which they were to proceed to Flushing, whence they were to embark for Spain. At that city he was to deliver the young Prince to the person whom he would find there, commissioned for that purpose by the Duke. As soon as he had made the first proposition at Louvain to the Count, he was, with the assistance of his retinue, to keep the most strict watch over him day and night, but without allowing the supervision to be perceived.†

The plan was carried out admirably, and in strict accordance with the program. It was fortunate, however, for the kidnappers, that the young Prince proved favorably disposed to the plan. He accepted the invitation of his captors with alacrity. He even wrote to thank the governor for his friendly offices in his behalf.‡ He received with boyish gratification the festivities with which Lodron enlivened his brief sojourn at Antwerp, and he set forth without reluctance for that gloomy and terrible land of Spain, whence so rarely

---

* Correspondance de Philippe II., ii. 730.   † Ibid, ii. 729.
‡ Ibid., ii. 734.

a Flemish traveller had returned.* A changeling, as it were, from his cradle, he seemed completely transformed by his Spanish tuition, for he was educated and not sacrificed by Philip. When he returned to the Netherlands, after a twenty years' residence in Spain, it was difficult to detect in his gloomy brow, saturnine character, and Jesuistical habits, a trace of the generous spirit which characterized that race of heroes, the house of Orange-Nassau.

Philip had expressed some anxiety as to the consequences of this capture upon the governments of Germany.† Alva, however, re-assured his sovereign upon that point, by reason of the extreme docility of the captive, and the quiet manner in which the arrest had been conducted. At that particular juncture, moreover, it would have been difficult for the government of the Netherlands to excite surprise any where, except by an act of clemency. The president and the deputation of professors from the university of Louvain waited upon Vargas, by whom, as acting president of the Blood-Council, the arrest had nominally been made, with a remonstrance that the measure was in gross violation of their statutes and privileges. That personage, however, with his usual contempt both for law and Latin, answered brutally, " Non curamus vestros privilegios," and with this memorable answer, abruptly closed his interview with the trembling pedants.‡

Petitions now poured into the council from all quarters, abject recantations from terror-stricken municipalities, humble intercessions in behalf of doomed and imprisoned victims. To a deputation of the magistracy of Antwerp, who came with a prayer for mercy in behalf of some of their most distinguished fellow-citizens, then in prison, the Duke gave a most passionate and ferocious reply. He expressed his wonder that the citizens of Antwerp, that hotbed of treason, should dare to approach him in behalf of traitors and heretics. Let them

---

* Correspondance de Philippe II., ii. 729, 730, 733, 734, 735, 737.—Compare Strada, i. 311, 312. Hoofd, iv. 152. Brandt, i. 468. Bor, iv. 222. V. d. Vynckt, ii. 97, 98.

† Corresp. Phil. II., i. 731.   ‡ Bor, iv. 222. V. d. Vynckt, ii. 98.

look to it in future, he continued, or he would hang every man
in the whole city, to set an example to the rest of the country ;
for his Majesty would rather the whole land should become an
uninhabited wilderness, than that a single Dissenter should
exist within its territory.*

Events now marched with rapidity. The monarch seemed
disposed literally to execute the threat of his viceroy. Early
in the year, the most sublime sentence of death was promulgated which has ever been pronounced since the creation of the
world. The Roman tyrant wished that his enemies' heads
were all upon a single neck, that he might strike them off at a
blow ; the inquisition assisted Philip to place the heads of all
his Netherland subjects upon a single neck for the same fell
purpose. Upon the 16th February, 1568, a sentence of the
Holy Office condemned *all the inhabitants* of the Netherlands
to death as heretics. From this universal doom *only a few
persons, especially named,* were excepted.† A proclamation of
the King, dated ten days later, confirmed this decree of the
inquisition, and ordered it to be carried into instant execution,
without regard to age, sex, or condition.‡ This is probably
the most concise death-warrant that was ever framed. Three
millions of people, men, women, and children, were sentenced
to the scaffold in three lines ; and, as it was well known that
these were not harmless thunders, like some bulls of the Vatican, but serious and practical measures, which it was intended
should be enforced, the horror which they produced may be
easily imagined. It was hardly the purpose of Government
to compel the absolute completion of the wholesale plan in all
its length and breadth, yet in the horrible times upon which
they had fallen, the Netherlanders might be excused for
believing that no measure was too monstrous to be fulfilled.
At any rate, it was certain that when *all* were condemned,
any might at a moment's warning be carried to the scaffold,
and this was precisely the course adopted by the authorities.

---

* Hoofd, iv. 157.   Bor, iv. 215, 216, 217.
† Ibid. iv. 226.   Hoofd, iv. 158.   Meteren, 49.
‡ Bor, Hoofd, Meteren, ubi sup.

Under this universal decree the industry of the Blood-Council might now seem superfluous. Why should not these mock prosecutions be dispensed with against individuals, now that a common sentence had swallowed the whole population in one vast grave ? Yet it may be supposed that if the exertions of the commissioners and councillors served no other purpose, they at least furnished the Government with valuable evidence as to the relative wealth and other circumstances of the individual victims. The leading thought of the Government being that persecution, judiciously managed, might fructify into a golden harvest,* it was still desirable to persevere in the cause in which already such bloody progress had been made.

And under this new decree, the executions certainly did not slacken. Men in the highest and the humblest positions were daily and hourly dragged to the stake. Alva, in a single letter to Philip, coolly estimated the number of executions which were to take place immediately after the expiration of holy week, "*at eight hundred heads.*"† Many a citizen, convicted of a hundred thousand florins and of no other crime, saw himself suddenly tied to a horse's tail, with his hands fastened behind him, and so dragged to the gallows.‡ But although wealth was an unpardonable sin, poverty proved rarely a protection. Reasons sufficient could always be found for dooming the starveling laborer as well as the opulent burgher. To avoid the disturbances created in the streets by the frequent harangues or exhortations addressed to the bystanders by the victims on their way to the scaffold, a new gag was invented. The tongue of each prisoner was screwed into an iron ring, and then seared with a hot iron. The swelling and inflammation which were the immediate result, prevented the tongue from slipping through the ring, and of course effectually precluded all possibility of speech.§

---

* "Hem (den Koning) opvullende met de hoope van een ander Indie in 't aenslaen der verbeurde goederen opgedaen te hebben; hoewel 't nergens 200 breedt uitviel. — Brandt, i. 475. Batavishe Arcadia, 577. Meteren, 50, et mult. al.

† Correspondance de Philippe II., i. 754. ‡ Meteren, 50.

§ Ibid., 54. Hoofd, v. 173.

Although the minds of men were not yet prepared for concentrated revolt against the tyranny under which they were languishing, it was not possible to suppress all sentiments of humanity, and to tread out every spark of natural indignation. Unfortunately, in the bewilderment and misery of this people, the first development of a forcible and organized resistance was of a depraved and malignant character. Extensive bands of marauders and highway robbers sprang into existence, who called themselves the Wild Beggars,* and who, wearing the mask and the symbols of a revolutionary faction, committed great excesses in many parts of the country, robbing, plundering, and murdering. Their principal wrath was exercised against religious houses and persons. Many monasteries were robbed, many clerical persons maimed and maltreated. It became a habit to deprive priests of their noses or ears, and to tie them to the tails of horses.† This was the work of ruffian gangs, whose very existence was engendered out of the social and moral putrescence to which the country was reduced, and who were willing to profit by the deep and universal hatred which was felt against Catholics and monks. An edict thundered forth by Alva,‡ authorizing and commanding all persons to slay the wild beggars at sight, without trial or hangman, was of comparatively slight avail. An armed force of veterans actively scouring the country was more successful, and the freebooters were, for a time, suppressed.§

Meantime the Counts Egmont and Horn had been kept in rigorous confinement at Ghent. Not a warrant had been read or drawn up for their arrest. Not a single preliminary investigation, not the shadow of an information had preceded the long imprisonment of two men so elevated in rank, so distinguished in the public service.‖ After the expiration of two months, however, the Duke condescended to commence a mock process against them. The councillors appointed to this

---

* Bor, iv. 224. Hoofd.   † Bor, iv. 224.
‡ Dated 27th March, 1568. Bor, iv. 225.   § Ibid.
‖ La déduction de l'innocence du Comte de Hornes, A. D. 1568, etc., 35, 36
Bor, iv. 195.

work were Vargas and Del Rio, assisted by Secretary Praets. These persons visited the Admiral on the 10th, 11th, 12th and 17th of November, and Count Egmont on the 12th, 13th, 14th, and 16th, of the same month ; requiring them to respond to a long, confused, and rambling collection of interrogatories.* They were obliged to render these replies in prison, unassisted by any advocates, on penalty of being condemned *in contumaciam.*† The questions, awkwardly drawn up as they seemed, were yet tortuously and cunningly arranged with a view of entrapping the prisoners into self-contradiction. After this work had been completed, all the papers by which they intended to justify their answers were taken away from them.‡ Previously, too, their houses and those of their secretaries, Bakkerzeel and Alonzo de la Loo, had been thoroughly ransacked, and every letter and document which could be found placed in the hands of government. Bakkerzeel, moreover, as already stated, had been repeatedly placed upon the rack, for the purpose of extorting confessions which might implicate his master. These preliminaries and precautionary steps having been taken, the Counts had again been left to their solitude for two months longer. On the 10th January, each was furnished with a copy of the declarations or accusations filed against him by the procurator-general. To these documents, drawn up respectively in sixty-three, and in ninety articles,§ they were required, within five days' time, without the assistance of an advocate, and without consultation with any human being, to deliver a written answer, on pain, as before, of being proceeded against and condemned by default.‖

This order was obeyed within nearly the prescribed period and here, it may be said, their own participation in their trial ceased ; while the rest of the proceedings were buried in the deep bosom of the Blood-Council. After their answers had been delivered, and not till then, the prisoners were, by an additional

---

* Bor, iv. 190   † La Déduction, etc., 36, 37.
‡ La Déduction de l'Innocence, etc., 39.
§ Foppens, Supp. à l'Hist. de Strada, etc., i. 24–63.
‖ Bor, iv. 195. La Déduction, etc., 39–41.

mockery, permitted to employ advocates.* These advocates, however, were allowed only occasional interviews with their clients, and always in the presence of certain persons, especially deputed for that purpose by the Duke.† They were also allowed commissioners to collect evidence and take depositions, but before the witnesses were ready, a purposely premature day, 8th of May, was fixed upon for declaring the case closed, and not a single tittle of their evidence, personal or documentary, was admitted.‡ Their advocates petitioned for an exhibition of the evidence prepared by government, and were refused.§ Thus, they were forbidden to use the testimony in their favor, while that which was to be employed against them was kept secret. Finally, the proceedings were formally concluded on the 1st of June, and the papers laid before the Duke.‖ The mass of matter relating to these two monster processes was declared, *three days* afterwards to have been examined—a physical impossibility in itself¶—and judgment was pronounced upon the 4th of June. This issue was precipitated by the campaign of Louis Nassau in Friesland, forming a series of important events which it will be soon our duty to describe. It is previously necessary, however, to add a few words in elucidation of the two mock trials which have been thus briefly sketched.

The proceedings had been carried on, from first to last, under protest by the prisoners, under a threat of contumacy on the part of the government.** Apart from the totally irresponsible and illegal character of the tribunal before which they were summoned—the Blood-Council being a private institution of Alva's without pretext or commission—these nobles acknowledged the jurisdiction of but three courts.

---

* La Déduction, etc., 42, 43. Compare Vigl. ad Hopp. Ep. 44 and 45.

† La Déduction de l'Innocence, etc., 42, 43.

‡ La Déduction, etc., 43, 44. In the case of Egmont, he was declared " exclus et debarté," and therefore deprived of all right to make defence, on the 14th May.
—V. Supp. to Strada, i. 102, 193. Appointment of Alva.

§ La Déduction, etc., 43.   ‖ Bor. iv. 239.

¶ Ibid. La Déduction, etc., 45, 46.   ** Ibid., 40, 41.

As Knights of the Golden Fleece, both claimed the privilege of that Order to be tried by its statutes. As a citizen and noble of Brabant, Egmont claimed the protection of the "Joyeuse Entrée," a constitution which had been sworn to by Philip and his ancestors, and by Philip more amply than by all his ancestors. As a member and Count of the Holy Roman Empire, the Admiral claimed to be tried by his peers, the electors and princes of the realm.*

The Countess Egmont, since her husband's arrest, and the confiscation of his estates before judgment, had been reduced to a life of poverty as well as agony. With her eleven children, all of tender age, she had taken refuge in a convent. Frantic with despair, more utterly desolate, and more deeply wronged than high-born lady had often been before, she left no stone unturned to save her husband from his fate, or at least to obtain for him an impartial and competent tribunal. She addressed the Duke of Alva, the King, the Emperor, her brother the Elector Palatine, and many leading Knights of the Fleece.† The Countess Dowager of Horn, both whose sons now lay in the jaws of death, occupied herself also with the most moving appeals to the same high personages.‡ No pains were spared to make the triple plea to the jurisdiction valid. The leading Knights of the Fleece, Mansfeld, whose loyalty was unquestioned, and Hoogstraaten, although himself an outlaw, called upon the King of Spain to protect the statutes of the illustrious order of which he was the chief.§ The estates of Brabant, upon the petition of Sabina, Countess Egmont, that they would take to heart the privileges of the province, so that her husband might enjoy that protection of which the meanest citizen in the land could not be justly deprived, addressed a feeble and trembling protest to Alva, and enclosed to him the lady's petition.‖ The Emperor, on behalf

---

* Bor, iv. 195.　　　　　　　　　　　† Ibid., iv. 188, 189, 190.
‡ La Déduction, etc., 605–642.　Bor, ubi sup.
§ La Déduction, etc., ubi sup.
‖ Bor, iv. 189.　Foppens, Supp. de Strada, i. 16–22.

of Count Horn, wrote personally to Philip, to claim for him a trial before the members of the realm.*

It was all in vain. The conduct of Philip and his Viceroy coincided in spirit with the honest brutality of Vargas. "*Non curamus vestros privilegios*," summed up the whole of the proceedings. *Non curamus vestros privilegios* had been the unanswerable reply to every constitutional argument which had been made against tyranny since Philip mounted his father's throne. It was now the only response deemed necessary to the crowd of petitions in favor of the Counts, whether they proceeded from sources humble or august. Personally, the King remained silent as the grave. In writing to the Duke of Alva, he observed that "the Emperor, the Dukes of Bavaria and Lorraine, the Duchess and the Duchess-dowager, had written to him many times, and in the most pressing manner, in favor of the Counts Horn and Egmont." He added, that he had made no reply to them, nor to other Knights of the Fleece who had implored him to respect the statutes of the order, and he begged Alva "to hasten the process as fast as possible." To an earnest autograph letter, in which the Emperor, on the 2nd of March, 1568, made a last effort to save the illustrious prisoners, he replied, that "the whole world would at last approve his conduct, but that, at any rate, he would not act differently, even if he should risk the loss of the provinces, and if *the sky should fall on his head*."†

But little heed was paid to the remonstrances in behalf of the imperial Courts, or the privileges of Brabant. These were but cobweb impediments which, indeed, had long been brushed away. President Viglius was even pathetic on the subject of Madame Egmont's petition to the council of Brabant. It

---

* The letter is published in the Déduction de l'Innocence, etc., 609. It is dated 20th October, 1567. The Emperor claims for the Admiral, as member of the Empire, a trial before the electors and princes of the holy realm, speaks of his distinguished services, and implores his release from a confinement "the reasons for which are entirely concealed and unknown."

† "Y me viniesse   caer el mundo encima."—Correspondance de Philippe II. ii. 762. See also Ibid., 738, 739, 746, 750.

was so bitter, he said, that the Duke was slightly annoyed, and took it ill that the royal servants in that council should have his Majesty's interests so little at heart.* It seemed indecent in the eyes of the excellent Frisian, that a wife pleading for her husband, a mother for her eleven children, so soon to be fatherless, should indulge in strong language !

The statutes of the Fleece were obstacles somewhat more serious. As, however, Alva had come to the Netherlands† pledged to accomplish the destruction of these two nobles, as soon as he should lay his hands upon them, it was only a question of form, and even that question was, after a little reflection, unceremoniously put aside.

To the petitions in behalf of the two Counts, therefore, that they should be placed in the friendly keeping of the Order, and be tried by its statutes, the Duke replied, peremptorily, that he had undertaken the cognizance of this affair by commission of his Majesty, as sovereign of the land, not as head of the Golden Fleece, that he should carry it through as it had been commenced, and that the Counts should discontinue presentations of petitions upon this point.‡

In the embarrassment created by the stringent language of these statutes, Doctor Viglius found an opportunity to make himself very useful. Alva had been turning over the laws and regulations of the Order, but could find no loophole. The President, however, came to his rescue, and announced it as his legal opinion that the Governor need concern himself no further on the subject, and that the code of the Fleece offered no legal impediment to the process.§ Alva immediately wrote to communicate this opinion to Philip, adding, with great satisfaction, that he should immediately make it known to the brethren of the Order, a step which was the more necessary

---

* Vigl. ad Hopp., Epist., xxiv. 400.

† V. Gachard. Notice sur le Conseil des Troubles, 13, 14. Wagenaer Vaderl. Hist. Deel, vi. 278. Hoofd, iv.

‡ Bor, iv. 189. La Déduction, etc., 642. Suppl. à l'Hist. de Strada, i. 11–16.

§ "La chose ne laisse rien à désirer."— Correspondance de Philippe II., ii. 712.

because Egmont's advocate had been making great trouble with these privileges, and had been protesting at every step of the proceedings.* In what manner the learned President argued these troublesome statutes out of the way, has nowhere appeared ; but he completely reinstated himself in favor, and the King wrote to thank him for his legal exertions.

It was now boldly declared that the statutes of the Fleece did not extend to such crimes as those with which the prisoners were charged. Alva, moreover, received an especial patent, ante-dated eight or nine months, by which Philip empowered him to proceed against all persons implicated in the troubles, and particularly against Knights of the Golden Fleece.†

It is superfluous to observe that these were merely the arbitrary acts of a despot. It is hardly necessary to criticise such proceedings. The execution of the nobles had been settled before Alva left Spain. As they were inhabitants of a constitutional country, it was necessary to stride over the constitution. As they were Knights of the Fleece, it was necessary to set aside the statutes of the Order. The Netherland constitutions seemed so entirely annihilated already, that they could hardly be considered obstacles ; but the Order of the Fleece was an august little republic of which Philip was the hereditary chief, of which emperors, kings, and great seigniors were the citizens. Tyranny might be embarrassed by such subtle and golden filaments as these, even while it crashed through municipal charters as if they had been reeds and bulrushes. Nevertheless, the King's course was taken. Although the thirteenth, fourteenth, and fifteenth chapters of the Order expressly provided for the trial and punishment of brethren who had been guilty of rebellion, heresy, or treason ;‡ and

---

* Correspondance de Philippe II., ii. 712.

† Ibid., i. 553, 705; and ii. 731.

‡ Vide "Réponse en Forme de Missive faite par Monseigneur le Comte de Hochstrate au Procureur-Général du Conseil de Crime, 28th Feb., 1568," with a letter of same date from that nobleman to the Duke of Alva, enclosing copies of the text of all the statutes of the Golden Fleece bearing upon these questions, with the addition of copious citations from the text of the "Joyeuse Entrée"— Byv. Van. Auth. Stukken tot de Hist. van. P. Bor, 17–32

although the eleventh chapter, perpetual and immutable, of additions to that constitution by the Emperor Charles,* conferred on the Order exclusive jurisdiction over all crimes whatever committed by the knights, yet it was coolly proclaimed by Alva, that the crimes for which the Admiral and Egmont had been arrested, were beyond the powers of the tribunal.

So much for the plea to the jurisdiction. It is hardly worth while to look any further into proceedings which were initiated and brought to a conclusion in the manner already narrated. Nevertheless, as they were called a process, a single glance at the interior of that mass of documents can hardly be superfluous.

The declaration against Count Horn, upon which, supported by invisible witnesses, he was condemned, was in the nature of a narrative. It consisted in a rehearsal of circumstances, some true and some fictitious, with five inferences. These five inferences amounted to five crimes—high treason, rebellion, conspiracy, misprision of treason, and breach of trust.† The proof of these crimes was evolved, in a dim and misty manner, out of a purposely confused recital. No events, however, were recapitulated which have not been described in the course of this history. Setting out with a general statement, that the Admiral, the Prince of Orange, Count

---

* See the text of this chapter of additions in the pamphlet above cited. The manner of proceeding against a knight is therein minutely prescribed.

His arrest required a warrant, signed by at least six knights, and he was afterwards to be kept, not in prison, but in "the amiable company of the said Order" ("amiable compagnie du dit Ordre") while the process, according to the proper form, was taking its course. These details are curious. The cause of the Golden Fleece is not one of universal interest, but the stringent and imperious character of the statutes, which were thus boldly and contemptuously violated, seemed a barrier which would have resisted even the attacks of the destroyer of the Brabant constitution. Philip had no more difficulty in violating his oath as head of the Fleece than he had as Duke of Brabant. The charter of the "Joyeuse Entrée" and its annihilation deserve a memorable place in the history of constitutional liberty. The article xvii. alone, was a sufficient shield to protect not only a grand seignior like Egmont, but the humblest citizen of the province.—Déduction de l'Innocence, etc., 581–590.

† La Déduction. etc., 72, 73.

Egmont, and other lords had organized a plot to expel his Majesty from the Netherlands, and to divide the provinces among themselves ; the declaration afterwards proceeded to particulars.   Ten of its sixty-three articles were occupied with the Cardinal Granvelle, who, by an absurd affectation, was never directly named, but called "a certain personage—a principal personage—a grand personage, of his Majesty's state-council."*   None of the offences committed against him were forgotten : the 11th of March letter, the fool's-cap, the livery, were reproduced in the most violent colors, and the cabal against the minister was quietly assumed to constitute treason against the monarch.

The Admiral, it was further charged, had advised and consented to the fusion of the finance and privy councils with that of state, a measure which was clearly treasonable.   He had, moreover, held interviews with the Prince of Orange, with Egmont, and other nobles, at Breda and at Hoogstraaten, at which meetings the confederacy and the petition had been engendered.   That petition had been the cause of all the evils which had swept the land.   "It had scandalously injured the King, by affirming that the inquisition was a tyranny to humanity, *which was an infamous and unworthy proposition.*"†   The confederacy, with his knowledge and countenance, had enrolled 30,000 men.   He had done nothing, any more than Orange or Egmont, to prevent the presentation of the petition.   In the consultation at the state-council which ensued, both he and the Prince were for leaving Brussels at once, while Count Egmont expressed an intention of going to Aix to drink the waters.   Yet Count Egmont's appearance (proceeded this *indictment against another individual*) exhibited not a single sign of sickness.‡   The Admiral had, moreover,

---

* Interrogatories of Count Horn, in Bor, iv. 190 and seq.

† Charges against Count Horn, art. xv.   Bor, iv. 191.—The same words occur also in the charges against Count Egmont.—Procès d'Egmont, art. xii. "Scavoir de proposer par jurement que l'inquisition contient en soi tyrannie impassant toute barbarie, qui sont parolles infames et indignes d'être pensez."—Supp. de Strada, i. 31.

‡ Charges against Count Horn, art. xx

drank the toast of " Vivent les gueux" on various occasions, at the Culemberg House banquet, at the private table of the Prince of Orange, at a supper at the monastery of Saint Bernard's, at a dinner given by Burgomaster Straalen. He had sanctioned the treaties with the rebels at Duffel, *by which he had clearly rendered himself guilty of high treason.* He had held an interview with Orange, Egmont, and Hoogstraaten, at Denremonde, for the treasonable purpose of arranging a levy of troops to prevent his Majesty's entrance into the Netherlands. He had refused to come to Brussels at the request of the Duchess of Parma, when the rebels were about to present the petition. He had written to his secretary that he was thenceforth resolved to serve neither King nor Kaiser. He had received from one Taffin, with marks of approbation, a paper, stating that the assembling of the states-general was the only remedy for the troubles in the land. He had repeatedly affirmed that the inquisition and edicts ought to be repealed.

On his arrival at Tournay in August, 1566, the people had cried "Vivent les gueux ;" a proof that he liked the cry. All his transactions at Tournay, from first to last, had been criminal. He had tolerated Reformed preaching, he had forbidden Catholics and Protestants to molest each other, he had omitted to execute heretics, he had allowed the religionists to erect an edifice for public worship outside the walls. He had said, at the house of Prince Espinoy, that if the King should come into the provinces with force, he would oppose him with 15,000 troops. He had said, if his brother Montigny should be detained in Spain, he would march to his rescue at the head of 50,000 men whom he had at his command. He had on various occasions declared that "men should live according to their consciences"—as if divine and human laws were dead, and men, like wild beasts, were to follow all their lusts and desires. Lastly, he had encouraged the rebellion in Valenciennes.*

---

* Charges against Count Horn, v. Bor, iv. 190–195.

Of all these crimes and misdeeds the procurator declared himself sufficiently informed, and the aforesaid defendant entirely, commonly, and publicly defamed.*

Wherefore, that officer terminated his declaration by claiming " that the cause should be concluded summarily, and without figure or form of process ; and that therefore, by his Excellency or his sub-delegated judges, the aforesaid defendant should be declared to have in diverse ways committed high treason, should be degraded from his dignities, and should be condemned to death, with confiscation of all his estates."†

The Admiral, thus peremptorily summoned, within five days, without assistance, without documents, and from the walls of a prison, to answer to these charges, *solus ex vinculis causam dicere*, undertook his task with the boldness of innocence.‡ He protested, of course, to the jurisdiction, and complained of the want of an advocate, not in order to excuse any weakness in his defence, but only any inelegance in his statement. He then proceeded flatly to deny some of the facts, to admit others, and to repel the whole treasonable inference.§ His answer in all essential respects was triumphant. Supported by the evidence which, alas ! was not collected and published till after his death, it was impregnable.

He denied that he had ever plotted against his King, to whom he had ever been attached, but admitted that he had desired the removal of Granvelle, to whom he had always been hostile. He had, however, been an open and avowed enemy to the Cardinal, and had been engaged in no secret conspiracy against his character or against his life.‖ He denied that the livery (for which, however, he was not responsible) had been intended to ridicule the Cardinal, but asserted that it was intended to afford an example of economy to an extravagant nobility.¶ He had met Orange and Egmont at Breda

---

* Charges against Count Horn, v. Bor, iv. 195.   † Ibid.

‡ Ibid. La Déduction, etc., 57, 68.

§ Answer of Count Horn to the charges of the procureur-général, in Bor, iv. 195–209.   ‖ Ibid., 196, 197.   ¶ Ibid., art. v. Bor, 197.

and Hoogstraaten, and had been glad to do so, for he had
been long separated from them. These interviews, however,
had been social, not political, for good cheer and merry-
making,* not for conspiracy and treason. He had never had
any connection with the confederacy ; he had neither advised
nor protected the petition, but, on the contrary, after hearing
of the contemplated movement, had written to give notice
thereof to the Duchess. He was in no manner allied with
Brederode, but, on the contrary, for various reasons, was not
upon friendly terms with him.†   He had not entered his
house since his return from Spain.‡   He had not been a party
to the dinner at Culemburg House. Upon that day he had
dined with the Prince of Orange, with whom he was lodging.
and, after dinner, they had both gone together to visit Mansfeld, who was confined with an inflamed eye. There they
had met Egmont, and the three had proceeded together to
Culemburg House in order to bring away Hoogstraaten, whom
the confederates had compelled to dine with them ; and also
to warn the nobles not to commit themselves by extravagant
and suspicious excesses. They had remained in the house but
a few minutes, during which time the company had insisted
upon their drinking a single cup to the toast of " Vivent le roy
et les gueux." They had then retired, taking with them
Hoogstraaten, and all thinking that they had rendered a
service to the government by their visit, instead of having
made themselves liable to a charge of treason.§ As to the
cries of " Vivent les gueux" at the tables of Orange, of the
Abbot of Saint Bernard, and at other places, those words had
been uttered by simple, harmless fellows ; and as he considered
the table a place of freedom, he had not felt himself justified
in rebuking the manners of his associates, particularly in
houses where he was himself but a guest.|| As for committing
treason at the Duffel meeting, he had not been there at all.¶

---

* Answer of Count Horn, art. xiii., xiv., 198.
† Ibid., art. xxi., 199, 200.   ‡ Ibid.   § Ibid., art. xxii.
|| Ibid., art. xxiv. xxv., 200.   ¶ Ibid. art. xxvi.

He thanked God that, at that epoch, he had been absent from Brussels, for had he, as well as Orange and Egmont, been commissioned by the Duchess to arrange those difficult matters, he should have considered it his duty to do as they did.* He had never thought of levying troops against his Majesty. The Denremonde meeting had been held to consult upon four subjects : the affairs of Tournay ; the intercepted letters of the French ambassador, Alava ; the letter of Montigny, in which he warned his brother of the evil impression which the Netherland matters were making in Spain ; and the affairs of Antwerp, from which city the Prince of Orange found it necessary at that moment to withdraw.† With regard to his absence from Brussels, he stated that he had kept away from the Court because he was ruined. He was deeply in debt, and so complete was his embarrassment, that he had been unable in Antwerp to raise 1000 crowns upon his property, even at an interest of one hundred per cent.‡ So far from being able to levy troops, he was hardly able to pay for his daily bread. With regard to his transactions at Tournay, he had, throughout them all, conformed himself to the instructions of Madame de Parma. As to the cry of " *Vivent les gueux*," he should not have cared at that moment if the populace had cried *Vive* Comte Horn, for his thoughts were then occupied with more substantial matters. He had gone thither under a special commission from the Duchess, and had acted under instructions daily received by her own hand. He had, by her orders, effected a temporary compromise between the two religious parties, on the basis of the Duffel treaty. He had permitted the public preaching to continue, but had not introduced it for the first time. He had allowed temples to be built outside the gates, but it was by express command of Madame, as he could prove by her letters. She had even reproved him before the council, because the work had not been accomplished with sufficient despatch.§ With regard to

---

* Answer of Count Horn, etc., art. xxx.   † Ibid., art. xxxiii.
‡ Ibid., art. xxxiv.   § Ibid., art. xxxix. xlvii.

his alleged threat, that he would oppose the King's entrance with 15,000 men, he answered, with astonishing simplicity, that he did not remember making any such observation, but it was impossible for a man to retain in his mind all the nonsense which he might occasionally utter.* The honest Admiral thought that his poverty, already pleaded, was so notorious that the charge was not worthy of a serious answer. He also treated the observation which he was charged with having made, relative to his marching to Spain with 50,000 men to rescue Montigny as "frivolous and ridiculous."† He had no power to raise a hundred men. Moreover he had rejoiced at Montigny's detention, for he had thought that to be out of the Netherlands was to be out of harm's way.‡ On the whole, he claimed that in all those transactions of his which might be considered anti-Catholic, he had been governed entirely by the instructions of the Regent, and by her Accord with the nobles. That Accord, as she had repeatedly stated to him, was to be kept sacred until his Majesty, by advice of the states-general, should otherwise ordain.§

Finally, he observed, that law was not his vocation. He was no pettifogger, but he had endeavored loyally to conform himself to the broad and general principles of honor, justice, and truth. In a very few and simple words, he begged his judges to have regard to his deeds, and to a life of loyal service. If he had erred occasionally in those times of tumult, his intentions had ever been faithful and honorable.‖

The charges against Count Egmont were very similar to those against Count Horn. The answers of both defendants were nearly identical. Interrogations thus addressed to two different persons, as to circumstances which had occurred long before, could not have been thus separately, secretly, but simultaneously answered in language substantially the same, had not that language been the words of truth. Egmont was

---

* "Niet moglijk te gedenken van alle sulke kleine proposten."—Answer of Count Horn, art. i. 205   † Ibid., art. iii.

‡ Ibid.   § Ibid., passim, but particularly art. iv., 206.

‖ Ibid. Conclusion, 208, 209.

accused generally of plotting with others to expel the King from the provinces, and to divide the territory among themselves. Through a long series of ninety articles, he was accused of conspiring against the character and life of Cardinal Granvelle. He was the inventor, it was charged, of the fool's-cap livery. He had joined in the letters to the King, demanding the prelate's removal. He had favored the fusion of the three councils. He had maintained that the estates-general ought to be forthwith assembled, that otherwise the debts of his Majesty and of the country could never be paid, and that the provinces would go to the French, to the Germans, or to the devil.* He had asserted that he would not be instrumental in burning forty or fifty thousand men, in order that the inquisition and the edicts might be sustained.† He had declared that the edicts were rigorous. He had advised the Duchess to moderate them, and remove the inquisition, saying that these measures, with a pardon general in addition, were the only means of quieting the country. He had advised the formation of the confederacy, and promised to it his protection and favor. He had counselled the presentation of the petition. He had arranged all these matters, in consultation with the other nobles, at the interviews at Breda and Hoogstraaten. He had refused the demand of Madame de Parma, to take arms in her defence. He had expressed his intention, at a most critical moment, of going to the baths of Aix for his health, although his personal appearance gave no indication of any malady whatever.‡ He had countenanced and counselled the proceedings of the rebel nobles at Saint Trond. He had made an accord with those of "the religion" at Ghent, Bruges, and other places. He had advised the Duchess to grant a pardon to those who had taken up arms. He had maintained, in common with the Prince of Orange, at a session of the state council, that if Madame should leave

---

* Interrogatoires de Comte d'Egmont, 315.   † Ibid.

‡ Procès d'Egmont, art. xx. Supp. Strada, i. 34. This remark of Egmont's was deemed so treasonable that, as already stated, it was brought most superfluously into the indictment against Horn.

Brussels, they would assemble the states-general of their own authority, and raise a force of forty thousand men.* He had plotted treason, and made arrangements for the levy of troops at the interview at Denremonde, with Horn, Hoogstraaten, and the Prince of Orange. He had taken under his protection on the 20th April, 1566, the confederacy of the rebels ; had promised that they should never be molested, for the future, on account of the inquisition or the edicts, and that so long as they kept within the terms of the Petition and the Compromise, he would defend them with his own person. He had granted liberty of preaching outside the walls in many cities within his government. He had said repeatedly, that if the King desired to introduce the inquisition into the Netherlands, he would sell all his property and remove to another land ; thus declaring with how much contempt and detestation he regarded the said inquisition.† He had winked at all the proceedings of the sectaries. He had permitted the cry of " *Vivent les gueux*" at his table. He had assisted at the banquet at Culemburg House.‡

These were the principal points in the interminable act of accusation. Like the Admiral, Egmont admitted many of the facts, and flatly denied the rest. He indignantly repelled the possibility of a treasonable inference from any of, or all, his deeds. He had certainly desired the removal of Granvelle, for he believed that the King's service would profit by his recal. He replied, almost in the same terms as the Admiral had done, to the charge concerning the livery, and asserted that its principal object had been to set an example of economy. The fool's-cap and bells had been changed to a bundle of arrows, *in consequence of a certain rumor which became rife in Brussels,* and in obedience to an ordinance of Madame de Parma.§ As to the assembling of the states-general, the fusion of the councils, the moderation of the edicts, he had certainly been in favor of these measures, which he considered to be wholesome

---

* Procès d'Egmont, 326.　　　　　† Ibid., art. lxxiii., 54.
‡ Interrogatoires d'Egmont, 327–348.　Procès d'Egmont, 24–63.
§ Interrogatoires, 314.　Procès d'Egmont, 65

and lawful, not mischievous or treasonable.* He had certainly maintained that the edicts were rigorous, and had advised the Duchess, under the perilous circumstances of the country, to grant a temporary modification until the pleasure of his Majesty could be known. With regard to the Compromise, he had advised all his friends to keep out of it, and many in consequence had kept out of it.† As to the presentation of the petition, he had given Madame de Parma notice thereof, so soon as he had heard that such a step was contemplated.‡ He used the same language as had been employed by Horn, with regard to the interview at Breda and Hoogstraaten—that they had been meetings of "good cheer" and good fellowship.§ He had always been at every moment at the command of the Duchess, save when he had gone to Flanders and Artois to suppress the tumults, according to her express orders. He had no connexion with the meeting of the nobles at Saint Trond. He had gone to Duffel as special envoy from the Duchess, to treat with certain plenipotentiaries appointed at the Saint Trond meeting.‖ He had strictly conformed to the letter of instructions, drawn up by the Duchess, which would be found among his papers,¶ but he had never promised the nobles his personal aid or protection. With regard to the Denremonde meeting, he gave almost exactly the same account as Horn had given. The Prince, the Admiral, and himself, had conversed between a quarter past eleven and dinner time, which was twelve o'clock, on various matters, particularly upon the King's dissatisfaction with recent events in the Netherlands, and upon a certain letter from the ambassador Alava in Paris to the Duchess of Parma.** He had, however, expressed his opinion to Madame that the letter was a forgery. He had permitted public preaching in certain cities, outside the walls, where it had already been established, because this was in accordance with the treaty which Madame had made at Duffel, which she had ordered

---

* Interrogatoires, 312.　　† Ibid., 317.　　‡ Ibid., 318.
§ Ibid., 319.　Procès d'Egmont, 78.　　‖ Ibid., 330, 331.
¶ Ibid., 330.　　** Ibid., 326, 327.

him honorably to maintain. He had certainly winked at the
religious exercises of the Reformers, because he had been expressly commanded to do so, and because the government at
that time was not provided with troops to suppress the new
religion by force. He related the visit of Horn, Orange, and
himself to Culemburg House, at the memorable banquet, in
almost the same words which the Admiral had used. He had
done all in his power to prevent Madame from leaving Brussels, in which effort he had been successful, and from which
much good had resulted to the country. He had never recommended that a pardon should be granted to those who had
taken up arms, but on the contrary, had advised their chastisement, as had appeared in his demeanor towards the rebels at
Osterwel, Tournay, and Valenciennes. He had never permitted the cry of " *Vivent les gueux*" at his own table, nor encouraged it in his presence any where else.*

Such were the leading features in these memorable cases of
what was called high treason. Trial there was none. The
tribunal was incompetent ; the prisoners were without advocates ; the government evidence was concealed ; the testimony
for the defence was excluded ; and the cause was finally decided before a thousandth part of its merits could have been
placed under the eyes of the judge who gave the sentence.†

But it is almost puerile to speak of the matter in the
terms usually applicable to state trials. The case had been
settled in Madrid long before the arrest of the prisoners in
Brussels. The sentence, signed by Philip in blank, had been
brought in Alva's portfolio from Spain.‡ The proceedings
were a mockery, and, so far as any effect upon public opinion

---

* Interrogatoires, 327–346. Procès d'Egmont, 74, 75, sqq.

† La Déduction de l'Innocence du Comte de Hornes, 57, 58, 59.

‡ Hoofd, v. 168, who relates the fact on the authority of Simon de Rycke,
Councillor of Amsterdam, who had it from Philip, eldest son of Count Egmont.—
Compare Address of the estates of Holland to the states-general ; " om dat u den
Hertog somwijlen een blank signet met des Coninx hand getekend laet sien,
schrijvende daer in wat hem gelust en gelieft en seggende dat het al versch, uit
Spangien komt," etc., etc.—Bor, vi. 463. Wagenaer, Vaderl. Hist., vi. 278.
Gachard, Notice sur le Conseil des Troubles. 13

was concerned, might as well have been omitted. If the gentlemen had been shot in the court-yard of Jasse-house, by decree of a drum-head court-martial, an hour after their arrest, the rights of the provinces and the sentiments of humanity would not have been outraged more utterly. Every constitutional and natural right was violated from first to last. This certainly was not a novelty. Thousands of obscure individuals, whose relations and friends were not upon thrones and in high places, but in booths and cellars, and whose fate therefore did not send a shudder of sympathy throughout Europe, had already been sacrificed by the Blood tribunal. Still this great case presented a colossal emblem of the condition in which the Netherlands were now gasping. It was a monumental exhibition of the truth which thousands had already learned to their cost, that law and justice were abrogated throughout the land. The country was simply under martial law—the entire population under sentence of death. The whole civil power was in Alva's hand; the whole responsibility in Alva's breast. Neither the most ignoble nor the most powerful could lift their heads in the sublime desolation which was sweeping the country. This was now proved beyond peradventure. A miserable cobbler or weaver might be hurried from his shop to the scaffold, invoking the *jus de non evocando* till he was gagged, but the Emperor would not stoop from his throne, nor electors palatine and powerful nobles rush to his rescue; but in behalf of these prisoners the most august hands and voices of Christendom had been lifted up at the foot of Philip's throne; and their supplications had proved as idle as the millions of tears and death-cries which had been shed or uttered in the lowly places of the land. It was obvious, then, that all intercession must thereafter be useless. Philip was fanatically impressed with his mission. His viceroy was possessed by his loyalty as by a demon. In this way alone, that conduct which can never be palliated may at least be comprehended. It was Philip's enthusiasm to embody the wrath of God against heretics. It was Alva's enthusiasm to embody the wrath of Philip. Narrow-minded, isolated, seeing only that section of the world which was visible through the loop-hole of the fortress in which Nature had imprisoned him for life, placing his glory in unconditional obedience to his superior, questioning nothing, doubting nothing, fearing nothing, the viceroy accomplished his work of hell with all the tranquillity of an angel. An iron will, which clove through every obstacle ; adamantine fortitude, which sustained without flinching a mountain of responsibility sufficient to crush a common nature, were qualities which, united to his fanatical obedience, made him a man for Philip's work such as could not have been found again in the world.

The case, then, was tried before a tribunal which was not only incompetent, under the laws of the land, but not even a court of justice in any philosophical or legal sense. Constitutional and municipal law were not more outraged in its creation, than all national and natural maxims.

The reader who has followed step by step the career of the two distinguished victims through the perilous days of Margaret's administration, is sufficiently aware of the amount of treason with which they are chargeable. It would be an insult to common sense for us to set forth, in full, the injustice of their sentence. Both were guiltless towards the crown ; while the hands of one, on the contrary, were deeply dyed in the blood of the people. This truth was so self-evident, that even a member of the Blood-Council, Pierre Arsens, president of Artois, addressed an elaborate memoir to the Duke of Alva, criticising the case according to the rules of law, and maintaining that Egmont, instead of deserving punishment, was entitled to a signal reward.*

So much for the famous treason of Counts Egmont and Horn, so far as regards the history of the proceedings and the merits of the case. The last act of the tragedy was precipitated by occurrences which must be now narrated.

The Prince of Orange had at last thrown down the gauntlet.

---

* Van der Vynckt, ii. 92, 93.

Proscribed, outlawed, with his Netherland property confiscated, and his eldest child kidnapped, he saw sufficient personal justification for at last stepping into the lists, the avowed champion of a nation's wrongs. Whether the revolution was to be successful, or to be disastrously crushed ; whether its result would be to place him upon a throne or a scaffold, not even he, the deep-revolving and taciturn politician, could possibly foresee. The Reformation, in which he took both a political and a religious interest, might prove a sufficient lever in his hands for the overthrow of Spanish power in the Netherlands. The inquisition might roll back upon his country and himself, crushing them forever. The chances seemed with the inquisition. The Spaniards, under the first chieftain in Europe, were encamped and entrenched in the provinces. The Huguenots had just made their fatal peace in France, to the prophetic dissatisfaction of Coligny.* The leading men of liberal sentiments in the Netherlands were captive or in exile. All were embarrassed by the confiscations which, in anticipation of sentence, had severed the nerves of war. The country was terror-stricken, paralyzed, motionless, abject, forswearing its convictions, and imploring only life. At this moment William of Orange reappeared upon the scene.

He replied to the act of condemnation, which had been pronounced against him in default, by a published paper, of moderate length and great eloquence. He had repeatedly offered to place himself, he said, upon trial before a competent court. As a Knight of the Fleece, as a member of the Holy Roman Empire, as a sovereign prince, he could acknowledge no tribunal save the chapters of the knights or of the realm. The Emperor's personal intercession with Philip had been employed in vain, to obtain the adjudication of his case by either.† It would be both death and degradation on his part to acknowledge the jurisdiction of the infamous Council of Blood. He scorned, he said, to plead his cause "before he knew not what

---

* De Thou, v. 414–417   † Hoofd, iv. 159.   De Thou, v. 362, 363, 369.

base knaves, not fit to be the valets of his companions and himself."*

He appealed therefore to the judgment of the world. He published not an elaborate argument, but a condensed and scathing statement of the outrages which had been practised upon him.† He denied that he had been a party to the Compromise. He denied that he had been concerned in the Request, although he denounced with scorn the tyranny which could treat a petition to government as an act of open war against the sovereign. He spoke of Granvelle with unmeasured wrath. He maintained that his own continuance in office had been desired by the cardinal, in order that his personal popularity might protect the odious designs of the government. The edicts, the inquisition, the persecution, the new bishoprics, had been the causes of the tumults. He concluded with a burst of indignation against Philip's conduct toward himself. The monarch had forgotten his services and those of his valiant ancestors. He had robbed him of honor, he had robbed him of his son—both dearer to him than life. By thus doing he had degraded himself more than he had injured him, for he had broken all his royal oaths and obligations.‡

The paper was published early in the summer of 1568. At about the same time, the Count of Hoogstraaten published a similar reply to the act of condemnation with which he had been visited. He defended himself mainly upon the ground, that all the crimes of which he stood arraigned had been committed in obedience to the literal instructions of the Duchess of Parma, after her accord with the confederates.§

The Prince now made the greatest possible exertions to raise funds and troops. He had many meetings with influential individuals in Germany. The Protestant princes, particularly the Landgrave of Hesse and the Elector of Saxony, promised him assistance. He brought all his powers of eloquence and

---

* Apologie d'Orange, 64, 65.

† Bor, iv. 227, 227; and the text of the Justification in Byv. Aut. Stukk i. 3, et seq.   ‡ Ibid., Bor, i. 3, sqq.   § Bor, iv. 224.

of diplomacy to make friends for the cause which he had now boldly espoused. The high-born Demosthenes electrified large assemblies by his indignant invectives against the Spanish Philip.* He excelled even his royal antagonist in the industrious subtlety with which he began to form a thousand combinations. Swift, secret, incapable of fatigue, this powerful and patient intellect sped to and fro, disentangling the perplexed skein where all had seemed so hopelessly confused, and gradually unfolding broad schemes of a symmetrical and regenerated polity. He had high correspondents and higher hopes in England. He was already secretly or openly in league with half the sovereigns of Germany. The Huguenots of France looked upon him as their friend, and on Louis of Nassau as their inevitable chieftain, were Coligny destined to fall.† He was in league with all the exiled and outlawed nobles of the Netherlands.‡ By his orders recruits were daily enlisted, without sound of drum. He granted a commission to his brother Louis, one of the most skilful and audacious soldiers of the age, than whom the revolt could not have found a more determined partisan, nor the Prince a more faithful lieutenant.

This commission, which was dated Dillenburg, 6th April, 1568, was a somewhat startling document. It authorized the Count to levy troops and wage war against Philip, strictly for Philip's good. The fiction of loyalty certainly never went further. The Prince of Orange made known to all "to whom those presents should come," that through the affection which he bore the gracious King, he purposed to expel his Majesty's forces from the Netherlands. "To show our love for the monarch and his hereditary provinces," so ran the commission, "to prevent the desolation hanging over the country by the ferocity of the Spaniards, to maintain the privileges sworn to by his Majesty and his predecessors, to prevent the extirpation

---

* Hoofd, v. 161–163. Bentivoglio, lib. iv. 62–64.

† De Thou, vi. 36.

‡ Hoofd, v. 163, 164. Wagenaer, Vad. Hist. 266–268. Van. d. Vynckt, ii. 23, 24. Bor, iv. 227. De Thou, vi. 36.

of all religion by the edicts, and to save the sons and daughters of the land from abject slavery, we have requested our dearly beloved brother Louis Nassau to enrol as many troops as he shall think necessary.[*]

Van der Bergh, Hoogstraaten, and others, provided with similar powers, were also actively engaged in levying troops ;[†] but the right hand of the revolt was Count Louis, as his illustrious brother was its head and heart. Two hundred thousand crowns was the sum which the Prince considered absolutely necessary for organizing the army with which he contemplated making an entrance into the Netherlands. Half this amount had been produced by the cities of Antwerp, Amsterdam, Leyden, Harlem, Middelburg, Flushing, and other towns, as well as by refugee merchants in England. The other half was subscribed by individuals. The Prince himself contributed 50,000 florins, Hoogstraaten 30,000, Louis of Nassau 10,000, Culemberg 30,000, Van der Bergh 30,000, the Dowager-countess Horn 10,000, and other persons in less proportion.[‡] Count John of Nassau also pledged his estates to raise a large sum for the cause. The Prince himself sold all his jewels, plate, tapestry, and other furniture, which were of almost regal magnificence.[§] Not an enthusiast, but a deliberate, cautious man, he now staked his all upon the hazard, seemingly so desperate. The splendor of his station has been sufficiently depicted. His luxury, his fortune, his family, his life, his children, his honor, all were now ventured, not with the recklessness of a gambler, but with the calm conviction of a statesman.

A private and most audacious attempt to secure the person of Alva and the possession of Brussels had failed.[||] He was soon, however, called upon to employ all his energies against the open warfare which was now commenced.

According to the plan of the Prince, the provinces were to

---

[*] Bor, iv. 233, 234.   [†] Ibid. 234.

[‡] Confession of the Seigneur de Villars.—Vide Correspondance de Philippe II., ii. 757.   [§] Hoofd, v. 163.

[||] Meteren, 51. Hoofd, v. 163, 164. Mendoza, ii. 39, 40.

be attacked simultaneously, in three places, by his lieutenants, while he himself was waiting in the neighborhood of Cleves, ready for a fourth assault. An army of Huguenots and refugees was to enter Artois upon the frontier of France ; a second, under Hoogstraaten, was to operate between the Rhine and the Meuse ; while Louis of Nassau was to raise the standard of revolt in Friesland.*

The two first adventures were destined to be signally unsuccessful. A force under Seigneur de Cocqueville, latest of all, took the field towards the end of June. It entered the bailiwick of Hesdin in Artois, was immediately driven across the frontier by the Count de Roeulx, and cut to pieces at St. Valery by Maréchal de Cossè, governor of Picardy. This action was upon the 18th July. Of the 2500 men who composed the expedition, scarce 300 escaped. The few Netherlanders who were taken prisoners were given to the Spanish government, and, of course, hanged.†

The force under the Seigneur de Villars was earlier under arms, and the sooner defeated. This luckless gentleman, who had replaced the Count of Hoogstraaten, crossed the frontier of Juliers, in the neighborhood of Maestricht, by the 20th April. His force, infantry and cavalry, amounted to nearly three thousand men. The object of the enterprise was to raise the country, and, if possible, to obtain a foothold by securing an important city. Roermonde was the first point of attack, but the attempts, both by stratagem and by force, to secure the town, were fruitless. The citizens were not ripe for revolt, and refused the army admittance. While the invaders were, therefore, endeavoring to fire the gates, they were driven off by the approach of a Spanish force.

The Duke, so soon as the invasion was known to him, had acted with great promptness. Don Sancho de Lodroño and Don Sancho de Avila, with five vanderas‡ of Spanish infantry, three

---

* Bor, iv. 233, 234. Hoofd, v. 164, 165. Mendoza, f. 39, et seq.

† Bor, iv. 238. Hoofd, 164. Mendoza. Gachard, Correspondance du Duc d'Albe sur l'Invasion du Comte L. de Nassau en Frise, etc., pp. 10, 11.

‡ A vandera in Alva's army amounted, on an average, to 170 men.

companies of cavalry, and about three hundred pikemen under Count Eberstein, a force amounting in all to about 1600 picked troops, had been at once despatched against Villars. The rebel chieftain, abandoning his attempt upon Roermonde, advanced towards Erkelens. Upon the 25th April, between Erkelens and Dalem, the Spaniards came up with him, and gave him battle. Villars lost all his cavalry and two vanderas of his infantry in the encounter. With the remainder of his force, amounting to 1300 men, he effected his retreat in good order to Dalem. Here he rapidly entrenched himself. At four in the afternoon, Sancho de Lodroño, at the head of 600 infantry, reached the spot. He was unable to restrain the impetuosity of his men, although the cavalry under Avila, prevented by the difficult nature of the narrow path through which the rebels had retreated, had not yet arrived. The enemy were two to one, and were fortified ; nevertheless, in half an hour the entrenchments were carried, and almost every man in the patriot army put to the sword. Villars himself, with a handful of soldiers, escaped into the town, but was soon afterwards taken prisoner, with all his followers. He sullied the cause in which he was engaged by a base confession of the designs formed by the Prince of Orange—a treachery, however, which did not save him from the scaffold. In the course of this day's work, the Spanish lost twenty men, and the rebels nearly 200. This portion of the liberating forces had been thus disastrously defeated on the eve of the entrance of Count Louis into Friesland.[*]

As early as the 22d April, Alva had been informed, by the lieutenant-governor of that province, that the beggars were mustering in great force in the neighborhood of Embden. It was evident that an important enterprise was about to be attempted.[†] Two days afterwards, Louis of Nassau entered the provinces, attended by a small body of

---

[*] Bor, iv. 234. Hoofd, v. 164. Mendoza, 40–46. Gachard, Correspondance du Duc d'Albe, 7, 8. Cabrera, lib. viii. c. i. 483, 484. Correspondance de Philippe II., ii. 756, 757.

[†] Correspondance du Duc d'Albe, 13–16.

troops. His banners blazed with patriotic inscriptions. *Nunc aut nunquam, Recuperare aut mori*, were the watchwords of his desperate adventure : " Freedom for fatherland and conscience" was the device which was to draw thousands to his standard.*
On the western wolds of Frisia, he surprised the castle of Wedde, a residence of the absent Aremberg, stadholder of the province. Thence he advanced to Appingadam, or Dam, on the tide waters of the Dollart. Here he was met by his younger brother, the gallant Adolphus, whose days were so nearly numbered, who brought with him a small troop of horse.† At Wedde, at Dam, and at Slochteren, the standard was set up. At these three points there daily gathered armed bodies of troops, voluntary adventurers, peasants with any rustic weapon which they could find to their hand. Lieutenant-governor Groesbeck wrote urgently to the Duke, that the beggars were hourly increasing in force ; that the leaders perfectly understood their game ; that they kept their plans a secret, but were fast seducing the heart of the country.‡

On the 4th May, Louis issued a summons to the magistracy of Groningen, ordering them to send a deputation to confer with him at Dam. He was prepared, he said, to show the commission with which he was provided. He had not entered the country on a mere personal adventure, but had received orders to raise a sufficient army. By the help of the eternal God, he was determined, he said, to extirpate the detestable tyranny of those savage persecutors who had shed so much Christian blood. He was resolved to lift up the down-trod privileges, and to protect the fugitive, terror-stricken Christians and patriarchs of the country.§ If the magistrates were disposed to receive him with friendship, it was well.   Otherwise, he should, with regret, feel himself

---

* Hoofd, v. 164, 165.   Brandt, i. 477. Meurs, Gul. Aur. iv. 44.

† Bor, 235.   Mendoza, 46.   Correspondance du Duc d'Albe, 15, 16.

‡ Ibid., 15–17.

§ Address of Louis Nassau to the Burgomasters and Magistracy of Groningen, 4th May, 1568, in Gachard, Correspondance du Duc d'Albe, 21, 22.

obliged to proceed against them, as enemies of his Majesty and of the common weal.

As the result of this summons, Louis received a moderate sum of money, on condition of renouncing for the moment an attack upon the city. With this temporary supply he was able to retain a larger number of the adventurers, who were daily swarming around him.[*]

In the mean time Alva was not idle. On the 30th April, he wrote to Groesbeck, that he must take care not to be taken napping ; that he must keep his eyes well open until the arrival of succor, which was already on the way.[†] He then immediately ordered Count Aremberg, who had just returned from France on conclusion of hostilities, to hasten to the seat of war. Five vanderas of his own regiment, a small body of cavalry, and Braccamonte's Sardinian legion, making in all a force of nearly 2500 men, were ordered to follow him with the utmost expedition. Count Meghem, stadholder of Gueldres, with five vanderas of infantry, three of light horse, and some artillery, composing a total of about 1500 men, was directed to co-operate with Aremberg.[‡] Upon this point the orders of the Governor-general were explicit. It seemed impossible that the rabble rout under Louis Nassau could stand a moment before nearly 4000 picked and veteran troops, but the Duke was earnest in warning his generals not to undervalue the enemy.[§]

On the 7th May, Counts Meghem and Aremberg met and conferred at Arnheim, on their way to Friesland. It was fully agreed between them, after having heard full reports of the rising in that province, and of the temper throughout the eastern Netherlands, that it would be rash to attempt any separate enterprise. On the 11th, Aremberg reached Vollen-hoven, where he was laid up in his bed with the gout.[||] Bodies of men, while he lay sick, paraded hourly with fife and drum before his windows, and discharged pistols and arquebuses across the ditch of the blockhouse where he was

---

[*] Bor, iv. 235.   [†] Correspondance du Duc d'Albe, 17–20.
[‡] Ibid., 29.   Mendoza, 46. 47.   Bor, iv. 235.
[§] Correspondance du Duc d'Albe, 49.   [||] Ibid., 33–37.

quartered.* On the 18th, Braccamonte, with his legion, arrived by water at Harlingen. Not a moment more was lost. Aremberg, notwithstanding his gout, which still confined him to a litter, started at once in pursuit of the enemy.† Passing through Groningen, he collected all the troops which could be spared. He also received six pieces of artillery. Six cannon, which the lovers of harmony had baptized with the notes of the gamut, *ut, re, mi, fa, sol, la,* were placed at his disposal by the authorities, and have acquired historical celebrity.‡ It was, however, ordained that when those musical pieces piped, the Spaniards were not to dance. On the 22d, followed by his whole force, consisting of Braccamonte's legion, his own four vanderas, and a troop of Germans, he came in sight of the enemy at Dam. Louis of Nassau sent out a body of arquebusiers, about one thousand strong, from the city. A sharp skirmish ensued, but the beggars were driven into their entrenchments, with a loss of twenty or thirty men, and nightfall terminated the contest.

It was beautiful to see, wrote Aremberg to Alva, how brisk and eager were the Spaniards, notwithstanding the long march which they had that day accomplished.§ Time was soon to show how easily immoderate valor might swell into a fault. Meantime, Aremberg quartered his troops in and about Wittewerum Abbey, close to the little unwalled city of Dam.

On the other hand, Meghem, whose co-operation had been commanded by Alva, and arranged personally with Aremberg a fortnight before, at Arnheim, had been delayed in his movements. His troops, who had received no wages for a long time had mutinied.|| A small sum of money, however, sent from Brussels, quelled this untimely insubordination. Meghem then set forth to effect his junction with his colleague, having assured the Governor-general that the war would be ended in six days. The beggars had not a stiver, he said, and

---

* Correspondance du Duc d'Albe, 59, 69.   † Ibid., 73, 74.
‡ Hoofd, v. 166. Strada, i. 320.
§ Correspondance du Duc d'Albe, 87, 88. Bor, iv. 235. || Ibid., 39.

must disband or be beaten to pieces as soon as Aremberg and he had joined forces. Nevertheless he admitted that these same "master-beggars," as he called them, might prove too many for either general alone.*

Alva, in reply, expressed his confidence that four or five thousand choice troops of Spain would be enough to make a short war of it, but nevertheless warned his officers of the dangers of overweening confidence.† He had been informed that the rebels had assumed the red scarf of the Spanish uniform. He hoped the stratagem would not save them from broken heads, but was unwilling that his Majesty's badge should be altered.‡ He reiterated his commands that no enterprise should be undertaken, except by the whole army in concert ; and enjoined the generals incontinently to hang and strangle all prisoners the moment they should be taken.§

Marching directly northward, Meghem reached Coeverden, some fifty miles from Dam, on the night of the 22d. He had informed Aremberg that he might expect him with his infantry and his light horse in the course of the next day. On the following morning, the 23d, Aremberg wrote his last letter to the Duke, promising to send a good account of the beggars within a very few hours.||

Louis of Nassau had broken up his camp at Dam about midnight. Falling back, in a southerly direction, along the Wold-weg, or forest road, a narrow causeway through a swampy district, he had taken up a position some three leagues from his previous encampment. Near the monastery of Heiliger Lee, or the "Holy Lion," he had chosen his ground.¶ A little money in hand, ample promises, and the hopes of booty, had effectually terminated the mutiny, which had also broken out in his camp. Assured that Meghem had not yet effected his junction with Aremberg, prepared to strike, at last, a telling blow for freedom and fatherland, Louis awaited the arrival of his eager foe.

His position was one of commanding strength and fortunate augury. Heiliger Lee was a wooded eminence, arti-

---

* Correspondance du Duc d'Albe, 43–45, etc.   † Ibid., 49.

‡ Ibid., 77.   § Ibid. || Ibid., 92.   ¶ Bor, iv. 235. Mendoza, 47.

ficially reared by Premonstrant monks. It was the only rising ground in that vast extent of watery pastures, enclosed by the Ems and Lippe*—the "fallacious fields" described by Tacitus. Here Hermann, first of Teutonic heroes, had dashed out of existence three veteran legions of tyrant Rome. Here the spectre of Varus, begrimed and gory, had risen from the morass to warn Germanicus,† who came to avenge him, that Gothic freedom was a dangerous antagonist.‡ And now, in the perpetual reproductions of history, another German warrior occupied a spot of vantage in that same perilous region. The tyranny with which he contended strove to be as universal as that of Rome, and had stretched its wings of conquest into worlds of which the Cæsars had never dreamed. It was in arms, too, to crush not only the rights of man, but the rights of God. The battle of freedom was to be fought not only for fatherland, but for conscience. The cause was even holier than that which had inspired the arm of Hermann.

Although the swamps of that distant age had been transformed into fruitful pastures, yet the whole district was moist, deceitful, and dangerous. The country was divided into squares, not by hedges but by impassable ditches.§ Agricultural entrenchments had long made the country almost impregnable, while its defences against the ocean rendered almost as good service against a more implacable human foe.

Aremberg, leading his soldiers along the narrow causeway, in hot pursuit of what they considered a rabble rout of fugitive beggars, soon reached Winschoten. Here he became aware of the presence of his despicable foe. Louis and Adolphus of Nassau, while sitting at dinner in the convent of the "Holy Lion," had been warned by a friendly peasant of the approach of the Spaniards. The opportune intelligence had given the patriot general time to make his preparations. His earnest entreaties had made his troops ashamed of their mutinous

---

* Bor, iv. 235.   De Thou, v. 445–448.   † Tacit. Ann. i.   ‡ Ibid.
§ Mendoza, 52.   Guicciardini, Belg. Descript. De Thou, ubi sup.

conduct on the preceding day, and they were now both ready and willing to engage.* The village was not far distant from the abbey, and in the neighborhood of the abbey Louis of Nassau was now posted. Behind him was a wood, on his left a hill of moderate elevation, before him an extensive and swampy field. In the front of the field was a causeway leading to the abbey. This was the road which Aremberg was to traverse. On the plain which lay between the wood and the hill, the main body of the beggars were drawn up. They were disposed in two squares or squadrons, rather deep than wide, giving the idea of a less number than they actually contained. The lesser square, in which were two thousand eight hundred men, was partially sheltered by the hill. Both were flanked by musketeers. On the brow of the hill was a large body of light armed troops, the *enfans perdus* of the army. The cavalry, amounting to not more than three hundred men, was placed in front, facing the road along which Aremberg was to arrive.†

That road was bordered by a wood extending nearly to the front of the hill. As Aremberg reached its verge, he brought out his artillery, and opened a fire upon the body of light troops. The hill protected a large part of the enemy's body from this attack. Finding the rebels so strong in numbers and position, Aremberg was disposed only to skirmish. He knew better than did his soldiers the treacherous nature of the ground in front of the enemy. He saw that it was one of those districts where peat had been taken out in large squares for fuel, and where a fallacious and verdant scum upon the surface of deep pools simulated the turf that had been removed. He saw that the battle-ground presented to him by his sagacious enemy was one great sweep of traps and pitfalls.‡ Before he could carry the position, many men must necessarily be engulfed.

He paused for an instant. He was deficient in cavalry, having only Martinengo's troop, hardly amounting to four

---

* Détails sur la bataille de Heyliger Lee.   Groen van Prinst., iii. 220–223.

† Mendoza, 48, 49.   De Thou, v. 445, 446.   ‡ Mendoza, 49.

hundred men.* He was sure of Meghem's arrival within twenty-four hours. If, then, he could keep the rebels in check, without allowing them any opportunity to disperse, he should be able, on the morrow, to cut them to pieces, according to the plan agreed upon a fortnight before. But the Count had to contend with a double obstacle. His soldiers were very hot, his enemy very cool. The Spaniards, who had so easily driven a thousand musketeers from behind their windmill, the evening before, who had seen the whole rebel force decamp in hot haste on the very night of their arrival before Dam, supposed themselves in full career of victory. Believing that the name alone of the old legions had stricken terror to the hearts of the beggars, and that no resistance was possible to Spanish arms, they reviled their general for his caution. His reason for delay was theirs for hurry. Why should Meghem's loitering and mutinous troops, arriving at the eleventh hour, share in the triumph and the spoil ? No man knew the country better than Aremberg, a native of the Netherlands, the stadholder of the province. Cowardly or heretical motives alone could sway him, if he now held them back in the very hour of victory.† Inflamed beyond endurance by these taunts, feeling his pride of country touched to the quick, and willing to show that a Netherlander would lead wherever Spaniards dared to follow, Aremberg allowed himself to commit the grave error for which he was so deeply to atone. Disregarding the dictates of his own experience and the arrangements of his superior, he yielded to the braggart humor of his soldiers, which he had not, like Alva, learned to moderate or to despise.

In the mean time, the body of light troops which had received the fire from the musical pieces of Groningen was seen to waver. The artillery was then brought beyond the cover of the wood, and pointed more fully upon the two main squares of the enemy. A few shots told. Soon afterward the *enfans perdus* retreated helter-skelter, entirely deserting their position.

---

* Bor, iv. 235.

† Mendoza, 49, 50.   Bor, iv. 235, 236.   Hoofd, v. 165, 166.

This apparent advantage, which was only a preconcerted stratagem, was too much for the fiery Spaniards. They rushed merrily* forward to attack the stationary squares, their general being no longer able to restrain their impetuosity. In a moment the whole van-guard had plunged into the morass. In a few minutes more they were all helplessly and hopelessly struggling in the pools, while the musketeers of the enemy poured in a deadly fire upon them, without wetting the soles of their own feet. The pikemen, too, who composed the main body of the larger square, now charged upon all who were extricating themselves from their entanglement, and drove them back again to a muddy death. Simultaneously, the lesser patriot squadron, which had so long been sheltered, emerged from the cover of the hill, made a detour around its base, enveloped the rear-guard of the Spaniards before they could advance to the succor of their perishing comrades, and broke them to pieces almost instantly.† Gonzalo de Braccamonte, the very Spanish colonel who had been foremost in denunciation of Aremberg, for his disposition to delay the contest, was now the first to fly. To his bad conduct was ascribed the loss of the day. The anger of Alva was so high, when he was informed of the incident, that he would have condemned the officer to death but for the intercession of his friends and countrymen.‡ The rout was sudden and absolute. The foolhardiness of the Spaniards had precipitated them into the pit which their enemies had dug. The day was lost. Nothing was left for Aremberg but to perish with honor.

---

* "Lustig aangetogen." Bor, iv. 235.

† Mendoza, 50. Hoofd, v. 166. Bor, 235, 236. Correspondance du Duc d'Albe, 92–97.

‡ This at least is the statement made by the author of the MS. heretofore cited, "Pièces concernant les Troubles des Pays Bas," etc. The writer adds, that Alphonse d'Ulloa had taken good care not to mention the circumstance, as telling too hard upon the Spaniards. It is remarkable, however, that Ulloa does distinctly state that Alva, upon arriving in Amsterdam after the battle of Jemmingen, caused the captains and colonels of the Sardinian regiment to be beheaded, for having been the cause of Aremberg's defeat and death. Braccamonte was the "Maestro de campo" of the Tercio of Sardinia.—Commentaire du Seigneur A. d'Ulloa, i. 57. Mendoza, ii. 28ᵛᵒ.

Placing himself at the head of his handful of cavalry, he dashed into the mêlée. The shock was sustained by young Adolphus of Nassau, at the head of an equal number of riders. Each leader singled out the other. They met as "captains of might" should do, in the very midst of the affray.* Aremberg, receiving and disregarding a pistol shot from his adversary, laid Adolphus dead at his feet, with a bullet through his body and a sabre cut on his head. Two troopers in immediate attendance upon the young Count shared the same fate from the same hand. Shortly afterward, the horse of Aremberg, wounded by a musket ball, fell to the ground. A few devoted followers lifted the charger to his legs and the bleeding rider to his saddle. They endeavored to bear their wounded general from the scene of action. The horse staggered a few paces and fell dead. Aremberg disengaged himself from his body, and walked a few paces to the edge of a meadow near the road. Here, wounded in the action, crippled by the disease which had so long tormented him, and scarcely able to sustain longer the burthen of his armor, he calmly awaited his fate. A troop of the enemy advanced soon afterwards, and Aremberg fell, covered with wounds, fighting like a hero of Homer, single-handed, against a battalion, with a courage worthy a better cause and a better fate. The sword by which he received his final death-blow was that of the Seigneur de Haultain.† That officer having just seen his brother slain before his eyes, forgot the respect due to unsuccessful chivalry.‡

---

* This hotly contested field, with the striking catastrophe of Adolphus and Aremberg, suggests the chivalrous pictures in "Chevy Chase:"

> "At last these two stout earls did meet,
> Like captains of great might,
> Like lions wode, they laid on lode,
> And made a cruel fight," etc., etc.

† Meteren, f. 52. De Thou, v. 447.

‡ The principal authority followed in the foregoing description of the first victory gained by the rebels in the eighty years' war, which had now fairly commenced, is the Spaniard Mendoza, who fought through this whole campaign in Friesland. Other historians give a still more picturesque aspect to the main incident of the battle. According to Strada, i. 320 (who gives as his autho-

The battle was scarcely finished when an advancing trumpet was heard. The sound caused the victors to pause in their pursuit, and enabled a remnant of the conquered Spaniards to escape. Meghem's force was thought to be advancing. That general had indeed arrived, but he was alone. He had reached Zuidlaren, a village some four leagues from the scene of action, on the noon of that day. Here he had found a letter from Aremberg, requesting him to hasten. He had done so. His troops, however, having come from Coevorden that morning, were unable to accomplish so long a march in addition. The Count, accompanied by a few attendants, reached the neighborhood of Heiliger Lee only in time to meet with some of the camp sutlers and other fugitives, from whom he learned the disastrous news of the defeat. Finding that all was lost, he very properly returned to Zuidlaren, from which place he made the best of his way to Groningen. That important city, the key of Friesland, he was thus enabled to secure. The troops which he brought, in addition to the four German vanderas of Schaumburg, already quartered there, were sufficient to protect it against the ill-equipped army of Louis Nassau.*

The patriot leader had accomplished, after all, but a barren

---

rity a letter from Mic. Barbanson to Margaret of Parma, 30th May, 1568), Adolphus and Aremberg fell by each other's hands, and lay dead side by side. The story is adopted with some hesitation by Hoofd and Bentivoglio. Cabrera, lib. viii. 486, 487, follows Mendoza literally, and ascribes the death of Adolphus to the hand of Aremberg, who in his turn was slain afterward in the mêlée. Meteren, on the contrary, seeming to think, as well as the Spaniards, that the honor of the respective nations was at stake, on the individual prowess of the champions, prefers to appear ignorant that this striking single combat had taken place. He mentions the death of Adolphus as having occurred in the mêlée, and ascribes Aremberg's death-blow to the Sieur de Haultain. Amelis van Amstel, in a report to the council of Gueldres, relates, on the authority of a prisoner taken in the battle, that the body of Aremberg was brought before Count Louis after the fight, and that the unfortunate but chivalrous officer had been shot through the throat, through the body, and through the head; or, in his own respectful language, "his lordship was shot through the windpipe of his lordship's throat, in his side through and through again, and likewise his lordship's forehead, above his eyes, was very valiantly wounded."

* Correspondance du Duc d'Albe, 94–98.

victory. He had, to be sure, destroyed a number of Spaniards, amounting, according to the different estimates, from five hundred to sixteen hundred men.* He had also broken up a small but veteran army. More than all, he had taught the Netherlanders, by this triumphant termination to a stricken field, that the choice troops of Spain were not invincible. But the moral effect of the victory was the only permanent one. The Count's badly paid troops could with difficulty be kept together. He had no sufficient artillery to reduce the city whose possession would have proved so important to the cause. Moreover, in common with the Prince of Orange and all his brethren, he had been called to mourn for the young and chivalrous Adolphus, whose life-blood had stained the laurels of this first patriot victory.† Having remained, and thus wasted the normal three days upon the battle-field, Louis now sat down before Groningen, fortifying and entrenching himself in a camp within cannon-shot of the city.‡

On the 23rd we have seen that Aremberg had written, full of confidence, to the Governor-general, promising soon to send him good news of the beggars. On the 26th, Count Meghem wrote that, having spoken with a man who had helped to place Aremberg in his coffin, he could hardly entertain any farther doubt as to his fate.§

The wrath of the Duke was even greater than his surprise. Like Augustus, he called in vain on the dead commander for his legions, but prepared himself to inflict a more rapid and more terrible vengeance than the Roman's. Recognizing the gravity of his situation, he determined to take the field in person, and to annihilate this insolent chieftain who had dared not only to cope with, but to conquer his veteran regiments. But before he could turn his back upon Brussels, many deeds were to be done. His measures now followed each other in breath-

---

* Correspondance du Duc d'Albe, 111. Mendoza only allows 450 Spaniards killed. Compare Hoofd, v. 166. Cabrera, lib. viii. 485–487. Meteren, 52, et alios.   † Hoofd, v. 166. Bor, iv. 236.

‡ Hoofd, Bor, ubi sup.   § Correspondance du Duc d'Albe, 102.

less succession, fulminating and blasting at every stroke. On the 28th May, he issued an edict, banishing, on pain of death, the Prince of Orange, Louis Nassau, Hoogstraaten, Van den Berg, and others, with confiscation of all their property.* At the same time he razed the Culemburg Palace to the ground, and erected a pillar upon its ruins, commemorating the accursed conspiracy which had been engendered within its walls.† On the 1st June, eighteen prisoners of distinction, including the two barons Batenburg, Maximilian Kock, Blois de Treslong and others, were executed upon the Horse Market, in Brussels. In the vigorous language of Hoogstraaten, this horrible tragedy was enacted directly before the windows of that "cruel animal, Noircarmes," who, in company of his friend, Berlaymont, and the rest of the Blood-Council, looked out upon the shocking spectacle.‡ The heads of the victims were exposed upon stakes, to which also their bodies were fastened. Eleven of these victims were afterward deposited, uncoffined, in unconsecrated ground ; the other seven were left unburied to moulder on the gibbet.§ On the 2d June, Villars, the leader in the Daalem rising, suffered on the scaffold, with three others.‖ On the 3d, Counts Egmont and Horn were brought in a carriage from Ghent to Brussels, guarded by ten companies of infantry and one of cavalry. They were then lodged in the "Broodhuis" opposite the Town Hall, on the great square of Brussels.¶ On the 4th, Alva having, as he solemnly declared before God and the world, examined thoroughly the mass of documents appertaining to those two great prosecutions which had only been closed three days before, pronounced sentence against the illustrious prisoners.** These documents of iniquity signed and sealed by the Duke, were sent to the Blood-Council,

---

* Bor, iv. 238.   † Meteren. 50. Bor, iv. 248. Hoofd, v. 167.
‡ Groen v. Prinst., Archives, iii. 239.
§ Bor, iv. 238. Hoofd, v. 167, 168.   ‖ Bor, Hoofd, ubi sup.
¶ Bor, v. 238, 239. Hoofd, v. 168. The building is now called the "Maison du Roi."
** Bor, Hoofd, ubi sup. Meteren, 52, 53.

where they were read by Secretary Praets.* The signature of
Philip was not wanting, for the sentences had been drawn
upon blanks signed by the monarch, of which the Viceroy
had brought a whole trunk full from Spain. The sentence
against Egmont declared very briefly that the Duke of Alva,
having read all the papers and evidence in the case, had found
the Count guilty of high treason. It was proved that Egmont
had united with the confederates ; that he had been a party to
the accursed conspiracy of the Prince of Orange ; that he had
taken the rebel nobles under his protection, and that he had
betrayed the Government and the Holy Catholic Church by
his conduct in Flanders. Therefore the Duke condemned him
to be executed by the sword on the following day, and decreed
that his head should be placed on high in a public place,
there to remain until the Duke should otherwise direct. The
sentence against Count Horn was similar in language and
purport.†

That afternoon the Duke sent for the Bishop of Ypres.
The prelate arrived at dusk. As soon as he presented himself,
Alva informed him of the sentence which had just been pronounced, and ordered him to convey the intelligence to the
prisoners. He further charged him with the duty of shriving
the victims, and preparing their souls for death. The bishop
fell on his knees, aghast at the terrible decree. He implored
the Governor-General to have mercy upon the two unfortunate
nobles. If their lives could not be spared, he prayed him at
any rate to grant delay. With tears and earnest supplications
the prelate endeavored to avert or to postpone the doom
which had been pronounced. It was in vain. The sentence,

---

* Bor, v. 239. " Les procès instruits furent lus et visitez au Conseil des
Troubles y assistans journellement le Ducq comme President avec les seigneurs
de Berlaymont et de Noircarmes—trop bien le Ducq se feit delivrer par escript
leurs opinions secrètes de chacune, la pluralité desquelles inclina à la condemnation."—Renom de France MS., ii. c. 5. The same writer adds that the sentence, drawn up by Hessels, and signed by the Duke, was read two or three
days afterward in presence of Berlaymont and Noircarmes; "Par où l'on a
présumé, à bonne raison, que la résolution venait d'Espagne."—Ibid.

† Bor, iv. 289.

inflexible as destiny, had been long before ordained. Its
execution had been but hastened by the temporary triumph of
rebellion in Friesland. Alva told the Bishop roughly that he
had not been summoned to give advice. Delay or pardon
was alike impossible. He was to act as confessor to the
criminals, not as councillor to the Viceroy. The Bishop, thus
rebuked, withdrew to accomplish his melancholy mission.*
Meanwhile, on the same evening, the miserable Countess of
Egmont had been appalled by rumors, too vague for belief,
too terrible to be slighted. She was in the chamber of
Countess Aremberg, with whom she had come to condole for
the death of the Count, when the order for the immediate
execution of her own husband was announced to her.† She
hastened to the presence of the Governor-General. The Princess Palatine, whose ancestors had been emperors, remembered
only that she was a wife and a mother. She fell at the feet of
the man who controlled the fate of her husband, and implored
his mercy in humble and submissive terms. The Duke, with
calm and almost incredible irony, reassured the Countess by
the information that, on the morrow, her husband was certainly to be released.‡ With this ambiguous phrase, worthy
the paltering oracles of antiquity, the wretched woman was
obliged to withdraw. Too soon afterward the horrible truth
of the words was revealed to her—words of doom, which she
had mistaken for consolation.

An hour before midnight the Bishop of Ypres reached
Egmont's prison. The Count was confined in a chamber on
the second story of the Brood-huis, the mansion of the cross-
bowmen's guild, in that corner of the building which rests on
a narrow street running back from the great square.§ He
was aroused from his sleep by the approach of his visitor.
Unable to speak, but indicating by the expression of his

---

* Bor, iv. 239.   Hoofd, 168, 169.   Strada, i. 327, et multi alii.

† Brantôme, Hommes Illustres, etc., usâ ii. 176.

‡ Hoofd, v. 169, who is the only authority for an anecdote which, for the honor
of humanity, one wishes to think false.

§ Bruxelles et ses Environs, par Alphonse Wauters, 93.

features the occurrence of a great misfortune, the Bishop, soon after his entrance, placed the paper given to him by Alva in Egmont's hands. The unfortunate noble thus suddenly received the information that his death-sentence had been pronounced, and that its execution was fixed for the next morning. He read the paper through without flinching, and expressed astonishment rather than dismay at its tidings.* Exceedingly sanguine by nature, he had never believed, even after his nine months' imprisonment, in a fatal termination to the difficulties in which he was involved. He was now startled both at the sudden condemnation which had followed his lingering trial, and at the speed with which his death was to fulfil the sentence. He asked the Bishop, with many expressions of amazement, whether pardon was impossible; whether delay at least might not be obtained? The prelate answered by a faithful narrative of the conversation which had just occurred between Alva and himself.† Egmont, thus convinced of his inevitable doom, then observed to his companion, with exquisite courtesy, that, since he was to die, he rendered thanks both to God and to the Duke that his last moments were to be consoled by so excellent a father confessor.‡

Afterwards, with a natural burst of indignation, he exclaimed that it was indeed a cruel and unjust sentence. He protested that he had never in his whole life wronged his Majesty; certainly never so deeply as to deserve such a punishment. All that he had done had been with loyal intentions. The King's true interest had been his constant

---

* "Met grooter Verwondering dan Versleegenheit."—Hoofd, v. 169.

† Hoofd, ubi sup. Bor, iv. 239.

‡ Ibid., iv. 239. Hoofd, v. 169.—It is painful to reflect that, notwithstanding the kind words exchanged between the Bishop and Egmont upon this melancholy occasion, the prelate expressed to others his *entire approbation of the Count's execution.* "Ypres considers the punishment of Egmont as *very just and necessary* for an example," wrote Morillon to Granvelle a week after the murder. "To try the bishop farther," he continued, "I observed that the King was very near giving Egmont the office which he had since bestowed upon Alva; upon which he replied that it would have been our ruin," etc., etc.—Groen v. Prinst., Archives, etc. Supplément, 83.

aim. Nevertheless, if he had fallen into error, he prayed
to God that his death might wipe away his misdeeds, and
that his name might not be dishonored, nor his children
brought to shame. His beloved wife and innocent children
were to endure misery enough by his death and the confiscation of his estates. It was at least due to his long
services that they should be spared further suffering.* He
then asked his father confessor what advice he had to give
touching his present conduct. The Bishop replied by an
exhortation, that he should turn himself to God ; that he
should withdraw his thoughts entirely from all earthly interests,
and prepare himself for the world beyond the grave. He
accepted the advice, and kneeling before the Bishop, confessed
himself. He then asked to receive the sacrament, which the
Bishop administered, after the customary mass. Egmont
asked what prayer would be most appropriate at the hour of
execution. His confessor replied that there was none more
befitting than the one which Jesus had taught his disciples—
Our Father, which art in heaven.

Some conversation ensued, in which the Count again expressed his gratitude that his parting soul had been soothed
by these pious and friendly offices. By a revulsion of feeling,
he then bewailed again the sad fate of his wife and of his young
children. The Bishop entreated him anew to withdraw his
mind from such harrowing reflections, and to give himself entirely to God. Overwhelmed with grief, Egmont exclaimed
with natural and simple pathos—"Alas ! how miserable and
frail is our nature, that, when we should think of God only,
we are unable to shut out the images of wife and children."†

Recovering from his emotion, and having yet much time,
he sat down and wrote with perfect self-possession two letters,
one to Philip and one to Alva. The celebrated letter to the
King was as follows :—

---

* Bor, Hoofd, ubi sup. Meteren, 53. Pièces concernant les Troubles, etc.
331vo. MS.

† Bor, iv. 240. Hoofd, v. 169. Pièces concernant les Troubles des Pays Bas,
332vo. MS. Gérard Collection. Archives of the Hague.

"SIRE,—I have learned, this evening, the sentence which your Majesty has been pleased to pronounce upon me. Although I have never had a thought, and believe myself never to have done a deed, which could tend to the prejudice of your Majesty's person or service, or to the detriment of our true ancient and Catholic religion, nevertheless I take patience to bear that which it has pleased the good God to send. If, during these troubles in the Netherlands, I have done or permitted aught which had a different appearance, it has been with the true and good intent to serve God and your Majesty, and the necessity of the times. Therefore, I pray your Majesty to forgive me, and to have compassion on my poor wife, my children, and my servants; having regard to my past services. In which hope I now commend myself to the mercy of God.

"From Brussels,
"*Ready to die*, this 5th June, 1568,
" Your Majesty's very humble and loyal vassal and servant,
"LAMORAL D'EGMONT."*

Having thus kissed the murderous hand which smote him, he handed the letter, stamped rather with superfluous loyalty than with Christian forgiveness, to the Bishop, with a request that he would forward it to its destination, accompanied by a letter from his own hand. This duty the Bishop solemnly promised to fulfil.†

Facing all the details of his execution with the fortitude which belonged to his character, he now took counsel with his confessor as to the language proper for him to hold from the scaffold to the assembled people. The Bishop, however, strongly dissuaded him from addressing the multitude at all.

---

* Bor, iv. 240. Hoofd, 169, 170. Strada, i. 327, 328, et alii.—See also Gachard, Correspondance de Philippe II., ii. 764. Foppens, Supplément, i. 261.

† Hoofd, v. 170.—According to Bor, iv. 240, Egmont also wrote a letter to the Duke; according to Meteren, 53, he wrote one to his wife.—Compare Strada, i. 327, 328. Haraens, Ann. Tum. Belgic, iii. 90. Foppens, Supplément, i. 260.

The persons farthest removed, urged the priest, would not hear the words, while the Spanish troops in the immediate vicinity would not understand them. It seemed, therefore, the part of wisdom and of dignity for him to be silent, communing only with his God. The Count assented to this reasoning, and abandoned his intention of saying a few farewell words to the people, by many of whom he believed himself tenderly beloved.* He now made many preparations for the morrow, in order that his thoughts, in the last moments, might not be distracted by mechanical details, cutting the collar from his doublet and from his shirt with his own hands,† in order that those of the hangman might have no excuse for contaminating his person. The rest of the night was passed in prayer and meditation.

Fewer circumstances concerning the last night of Count Horn's life have been preserved. It is, however, well ascertained that the Admiral received the sudden news of his condemnation with absolute composure. He was assisted at his devotional exercises in prison by the curate of La Chapelle.‡

During the night, the necessary preparations for the morning tragedy had been made in the great square of Brussels. It was the intention of government to strike terror to the heart of the people by the exhibition of an impressive and appalling spectacle. The absolute and irresponsible destiny which ruled them was to be made manifest by the immolation of these two men, so elevated by rank, powerful connexion, and distinguished service.

The effect would be heightened by the character of the locality where the gloomy show was to be presented. The great square of Brussels had always a striking and theatrical aspect. Its architectural effects, suggesting in some degree the meretricious union between Oriental and a corrupt Grecian art, accomplished in the mediæval midnight, have amazed the eyes of many generations. The splendid Hotel de Ville, with

---

* Bor, iv. 240.   Hoofd, v. 170.

† Bor, Hoofd, ubi. sup.   Pièces concernant l'Hist. des Troubles, MS. f. 333.

‡ Letter of Alva to Philip.   Correspondance de Marg. d'Autriche, 252.

its daring spire and elaborate front, ornamented one side of
the place ; directly opposite was the graceful but incoherent
façade of the Brood-huis, now the last earthly resting-place
of the two distinguished victims, while grouped around these
principal buildings rose the fantastic palaces of the Archers,
Mariners, and of other guilds, with their festooned walls
and toppling gables bedizened profusely with emblems, statues, and quaint decorations. The place had been alike the
scene of many a brilliant tournament and of many a bloody
execution. Gallant knights had contended within its pre-
cincts, while bright eyes rained influence from all those
picturesque balconies and decorated windows. Martyrs to
religious and to political liberty had, upon the same spot,
endured agonies which might have roused every stone of
its pavement to mutiny or softened them to pity. Here
Egmont himself, in happier days, had often borne away the
prize of skill or of valor, the cynosure of every eye ; and
hence, almost in the noon of a life illustrated by many brilliant actions, he was to be sent, by the hand of tyranny, to
his great account.

On the morning of the 5th of June, three thousand Spanish
troops* were drawn up in battle array around a scaffold which
had been erected in the centre of the square. Upon this
scaffold, which was covered with black cloth, were placed two
velvet cushions, two iron spikes, and a small table. Upon the
table was a silver crucifix. The provost-marshal, Spelle, sat
on horseback below, with his red wand in his hand, little dreaming that for him a darker doom was reserved than that of
which he was now the minister. The executioner was concealed beneath the draperies of the scaffold.†

At eleven o'clock, a company of Spanish soldiers, led by
Julian Romero and Captain Salinas, arrived at Egmont's
chamber. The Count was ready for them. They were about

---

* Nineteen vanderas occupied the square, two were left to guard the palace,
and one went the rounds of the city during the execution.—Bor, Hoofd, ubi. sup.
Compare Ulloa, Commentaire, premier et second (Paris, 1570), i. 43.

† Bor, iv. 240. Hoofd, v. 170, 171. Strada, i. 328.

to bind his hands, but he warmly protested against the indignity, and, opening the folds of his robe, showed them that he had himself shorn off his collars, and made preparations for his death. His request was granted. Egmont, with the Bishop at his side, then walked with a steady step the short distance which separated him from the place of execution. Julian Romero and the guard followed him. On his way, he read aloud the fifty-first Psalm : " Hear my cry, O God, and give ear unto my prayer !" He seemed to have selected these scriptural passages as a proof that, notwithstanding the machinations of his enemies, and the cruel punishment to which they had led him, loyalty to his sovereign was as deeply rooted and as religious a sentiment in his bosom as devotion to his God. " Thou wilt prolong the King's life ; and his years as many generations. He shall abide before God for ever ! O prepare mercy and truth which may preserve him." Such was the remarkable prayer of the condemned traitor on his way to the block.

Having ascended the scaffold, he walked across it twice or thrice. He was dressed in a tabard or robe of red damask, over which was thrown a short black mantle, embroidered in gold. He had a black silk hat, with black and white plumes, on his head, and held a handkerchief in his hand. As he strode to and fro, he expressed a bitter regret that he had not been permitted to die, sword in hand, fighting for his country and his king. Sanguine to the last, he passionately asked Romero, whether the sentence was really irrevocable, whether a pardon was not even then to be granted. The marshal shrugged his shoulders, murmuring a negative reply. Upon this, Egmont gnashed his teeth together, rather in rage than despair. Shortly afterward commanding himself again, he threw aside his robe and mantle, and took the badge of the Golden Fleece from his neck. Kneeling, then, upon one of

---

* Chronike oft Journal van het gene in de Nederlanden en namentlyk tot Antwerpen is voorgerallen ten tyde der Troublen van den Jaer, 1566 tot 1593, door N. de Weert.—MS. Coll. Gérard. Library of the Hague.—Compare Hoofd; Meteren, 53.   Ulloa, i. 42.

the cushions, he said the Lord's Prayer aloud, and requested the Bishop, who knelt at his side, to repeat it thrice. After this, the prelate gave him the silver crucifix to kiss, and then pronounced his blessing upon him. This done, the Count rose again to his feet, laid aside his hat and handkerchief, knelt again upon the cushion, drew a little cap over his eyes, and, folding his hands together, cried with a loud voice, "Lord, into Thy hands I commit my spirit." The executioner then suddenly appeared, and severed his head from his shoulders at a single blow.*

A moment of shuddering silence succeeded the stroke. The whole vast assembly seemed to have felt it in their own hearts. Tears fell from the eyes even of the Spanish soldiery, for they knew and honored Egmont as a valiant general. The French embassador, Mondoucet, looking upon the scene from a secret place, whispered that he had now seen the head fall before which France had twice trembled. Tears were even seen upon the iron cheek of Alva, as, from a window in a house directly opposite the scaffold, he looked out upon the scene.†

A dark cloth was now quickly thrown over the body and the blood, and, within a few minutes, the Admiral was seen advancing through the crowd. His bald head was uncovered,

---

* Bor, iv. 240. Hoofd, v. 170, 171. Strada, i. 328.

† "En hem niet bet door den hals, dan den omstanderen in 't hart sneed," says Hoofd, v. 170, 171. Even Bentivoglio becomes softened in relating the pathetic scene. "E veramente parve," says the Cardinal, "che sotto il suo collo n' havesse come un altro la Fiandra tutta, si grande fù il senso, che mostrò allora del suo supplicio."—Liv. iv. 69. Compare Strada, i. 329. Meteren, 53. Bor, 241. "I hear," wrote Morillon to Granvelle (June 7th, 1567,) "that his Excellency shed tears *as big as pease* during the execution." (At jecté des larmes aussi grosses que poix.)—Groen v. Prinst., Archives, Supplément, 81. Certainly, if the fable of the crocodile had never before been heard of, it would have been necessary to invent it then. The prebendary goes on to say that "he had caused the story of the Duke's tenderness to be trumpeted in many places, "à faict sonner où il luy a semblé convenir, quia multorum animi exacerbeti."— Ibid. Morillon also quotes Alva as having had the effrontery to say that he desired a mitigation of the punishment, but that the King had answered, "he could forgive offences against himself, but the crimes committed against God were unpardonable ! ! !"—Ibid.

his hands were unbound. He calmly saluted such of his acquaintances as he chanced to recognize upon his path.* Under a black cloak, which he threw off when he had ascended the scaffold, he wore a plain, dark doublet, and he did not, like Egmont, wear the insignia of the Fleece. Casting his eyes upon the corpse, which lay covered with the dark cloth, he asked if it were the body of Egmont. Being answered in the affirmative, he muttered a few words in Spanish, which were not distinctly audible. His attention was next caught by the sight of his own coat of arms reversed, and he expressed anger at this indignity to his escutcheon, protesting that he had not deserved the insult.† He then spoke a few words to the crowd below, wishing them happiness, and begging them to pray for his soul. He did not kiss the crucifix, but he knelt upon the scaffold to pray, and was assisted in his devotions by the Bishop of Ypres. When they were concluded, he rose again to his feet. Then drawing a Milan cap completely over his face, and uttering, in Latin, the same invocation which Egmont had used, he submitted his neck to the stroke.‡

Egmont had obtained, as a last favor, that his execution should precede that of his friend. Deeming himself in part to blame for Horn's reappearance in Brussels after the arrival of Alva, and for his death, which was the result, he wished to be spared the pang of seeing him dead. Gemma Frisius, the astrologer who had cast the horoscope of Count Horn at his birth, had come to him in the most solemn manner to warn him against visiting Brussels. The Count had answered stoutly that he placed his trust in God, and that, moreover, his friend Egmont was going thither also, who had engaged that no worse fate should befal the one of them than the other.§

---

* Foppens Supplément, i. 264.　　　　† N. de Weert Chronyk MS.

‡ The Duke of Alva assured Philip that both the Counts "sont morts fort catholiquement et modestement."—Compare Bor, iv. 240; Hoofd, v. 171; Meteren, f. 53; Ulloa, i. 43; De Weert MS.

§ Bor, iv. 241. Hoofd, v. 170.

The heads of both sufferers were now exposed for two hours upon the iron stakes. Their bodies, placed in coffins, remained during the same interval upon the scaffold. Meantime, notwithstanding the presence of the troops, the populace could not be restrained from tears and from execrations. Many crowded about the scaffold, and dipped their handkerchiefs in the blood, to be preserved afterwards as memorials of the crime and as ensigns of revenge.*

The bodies were afterwards delivered to their friends. A stately procession of the guilds, accompanied by many of the clergy, conveyed their coffins to the church of Saint Gudule. Thence the body of Egmont was carried to the convent of Saint Clara, near the old Brussels gate, where it was embalmed.† His escutcheon and banners were hung upon the outward wall of his residence, by order of the Countess. By command of Alva they were immediately torn down.‡ His remains were afterwards conveyed to his city of Sottegem, in Flanders, where they were interred. Count Horn was entombed at Kempen. The bodies had been removed from the scaffold at two o'clock. The heads remained exposed between burning torches for two hours longer. They were then taken down, enclosed in boxes, and, as it was generally supposed, despatched to Madrid.§ The King was thus enabled to look upon the

---

* Bor, Hoofd, Meteren, Strada, i. 328.   Bentivoglio, liv. iv. 69.

† Bor, iv. 241. Ulloa, i. 44.—The latter writer, who was maréchal-de-camp in Alva's army, and had commanded the citadel of Ghent during the imprisonment of the Counts, observes that the coffin of Egmont, after its removal to St. Clara, was visited by crowds of people, all bathed in tears, who kissed it as if it had been the shrine of saintly remains, offering up prayers the while for the repose of the departed soul. He adds that the same devotion was not paid to the body of Horn, which remained almost deserted in the great church. There is something pathetic in this image of the gloomy, melancholy Horn lying thus in his bloody shroud as solitary and deserted as he had been in the latter years of his life in his desolate home. Certainly the Admiral deserved as much popular sympathy as Egmont.

‡ Bor, iv. 241. Hoofd, v. 171. Meteren, f. 53.

§ Ibid.—"Te vier uren werden de hoofden gesloten elk besundere in een houten kiste d'welck by de Spangaerden was daer toe gemaekt, want de selve

dead faces of his victims without the trouble of a journey to the provinces.

Thus died Philip Montmorency, Count of Horn, and Lamoral of Egmont, Prince of Gaveren. The more intense sympathy which seemed to attach itself to the fate of Egmont, rendered the misfortune of his companion in arms and in death comparatively less interesting.*

Egmont is a great historical figure, but he was certainly not a great man. His execution remains an enduring monument not only of Philip's cruelty and perfidy but of his dulness. The King had everything to hope from Egmont and nothing to fear. Granvelle knew the man well, and, almost to the last, could not believe in the possibility of so unparalleled a blunder as that which was to make a victim, a martyr, and a popular idol of a personage brave indeed, but incredibly vacillating and inordinately vain, who, by a little management, might have been converted into a most useful instrument for the royal purposes.

It is not necessary to recapitulate the events of Egmont's career. Step by step we have studied his course, and at no single period have we discovered even a germ of those elements which make the national champion. His pride of order rendered him furious at the insolence of Granvelle, and caused him to chafe under his dominion. His vanity of high rank and of distinguished military service made him covet the highest place under the Crown, while his hatred of those by whom he considered himself defrauded of his claims, converted

---

naer Spaengnien werdden gesonden, soo men seyde." The author of this manuscript, which contains many curious details, was a contemporary, and occupied a place under government afterward at Antwerp.—Compare the letter of Geronimo de Roda in Gachard, Notice sur le Conseil des Troubles, page 29. (Bulletins de l'Acad. Roy. de Belg., xvi. 6.) "Y preguntàron si era verdad que Julian habia tomado las cabezas y echado las no sè donde; que aunque en esto hablò Berleymonte creo quisò dar à entender que las debian haber guardado."

* "Defleri," says Strada, (i. 330), "profecto haud modice potuisset hujus viri (Hornani) mors, si non Egmontius omnium lacrymas consumpsisset."—Compare Ulloa, i. 44.

him into a malcontent. He had no sympathy with the people, but he loved, as a grand Seignior, to be looked up to and admired by a gaping crowd. He was an unwavering Catholic, held sectaries in utter loathing, and, after the image-breaking, took a positive pleasure in hanging ministers, together with their congregations, and in pressing the besieged Christians of Valenciennes to extremities. Upon more than one occasion he pronounced his unequivocal approval of the infamous edicts, and he exerted himself at times to enforce them within his province. The transitory impression made upon his mind by the lofty nature of Orange was easily effaced in Spain by court flattery and by royal bribes. Notwithstanding the coldness, the rebuffs, and the repeated warnings which might have saved him from destruction, nothing could turn him at last from the fanatic loyalty towards which, after much wavering, his mind irrevocably pointed. His voluntary humiliation as a general, a grandee, a Fleming, and a Christian before the insolent Alva upon his first arrival, would move our contempt were it not for the gentler emotions suggested by the infatuated nobleman's doom. Upon the departure of Orange, Egmont was only too eager to be employed by Philip in any work which the monarch could find for him to do. Yet this was the man whom Philip chose, through the executioner's sword, to convert into a popular idol, and whom Poetry has loved to contemplate as a romantic champion of freedom.

As for Horn, details enough have likewise been given of his career to enable the reader thoroughly to understand the man. He was a person of mediocre abilities and thoroughly commonplace character. His high rank and his tragic fate are all which make him interesting. He had little love for court or people. Broken in fortunes, he passed his time mainly in brooding over the ingratitude of Charles and Philip, and in complaining bitterly of the disappointments to which their policy had doomed him. He cared nothing for Cardinalists or confederates. He disliked Brederode, he detested Granvelle. Gloomy and morose, he went to bed, while the men who were called his fellow-conspirators were dining and making merry in the same house with himself. He had as little sympathy with the cry of "Vivent les gueux" as for that of "Vive le Roy." The most interesting features in his character are his generosity toward his absent brother and the manliness with which, as Montigny's representative at Tournay, he chose rather to confront the anger of the government, and to incur the deadly revenge of Philip, than make himself the executioner of the harmless Christians in Tournay. In this regard, his conduct is vastly more entitled to our respect than that of Egmont, and he was certainly more deserving of reverence from the people, even though deserted by all men while living, and left headless and solitary in his coffin at Saint Gudule.

The hatred for Alva, which sprang from the graves of these illustrious victims, waxed daily more intense. "Like things of another world," wrote Hoogstraaten,* "seem the cries, lamentations, and just compassion which all the inhabitants of Brussels, noble or ignoble, feel for such barbarous tyranny, while this Nero of an Alva is boasting that he will do the same to all whom he lays his hands upon." No man believed that the two nobles had committed a crime, and many were even disposed to acquit Philip of his share in the judicial murder. The people ascribed the execution solely to the personal jealousy of the Duke. They discoursed to each other not only of the envy with which the Governor-general had always regarded the military triumphs of his rival, but related that Egmont had at different times won large sums of Alva at games of hazard, and that he had moreover, on several occasions, carried off the prize from the Duke in shooting at the popinjay.† Nevertheless, in spite of all these absurd rumors, there is no doubt that Philip and Alva must share equally in the guilt of the transaction, and that the "chastisement" had been arranged before Alva had departed from Spain.

---

* Groen van Prinsterer, Archives, etc., iii. 240, 241.
† Strada, i. 326.

The Countess Egmont remained at the convent of Cambre with her eleven children, plunged in misery and in poverty. The Duke wrote to Philip, that he doubted if there were so wretched a family in the world. He, at the same time, congratulated his sovereign on the certainty that the more intense the effects, the more fruitful would be the example of this great execution. He stated that the Countess was considered a most saintly woman, and that there had been scarcely a night in which, attended by her daughters, she had not gone forth bare-footed to offer up prayers for her husband in every church within the city. He added, that it was doubtful whether they had money enough to buy themselves a supper that very night, and he begged the King to allow them the means of supporting life. He advised that the Countess should be placed, without delay in a Spanish convent, where her daughters might at once take the vail, assuring his Majesty that her dower was entirely inadequate to her support. Thus humanely recommending his sovereign to bestow an alms on the family which his own hand had reduced from a princely station to beggary, the Viceroy proceeded to detail the recent events in Friesland, together with the measures which he was about taking to avenge the defeat and death of Count Aremberg.*

---

* Correspondance de Philippe, ii. 765–774.

CHAPTER III.

THOSE measures were taken with the precision and promptness which marked the Duke's character, when precision and promptness were desirable. There had been a terrible energy in his every step, since the successful foray of Louis Nassau. Having determined to take the field in person with nearly all the Spanish veterans, he had at once acted upon the necessity of making the capital secure, after his back should be turned. It was impossible to leave three thousand choice troops to guard Count Egmont. A less number seemed insufficient to prevent a rescue. He had, therefore, no longer delayed the chastisement which had already been determined, but which the events in the north had precipitated. Thus the only positive result of Louis Nassau's victory was the execution of his imprisoned friends.

The expedition under Aremberg had failed from two causes.

The Spanish force had been inadequate, and they had attacked the enemy at a disadvantage. The imprudent attack was the result of the contempt with which they had regarded their antagonist. These errors were not to be repeated. Alva ordered Count Meghem, now commanding in the province of Groningen, on no account to hazard hostilities until the game was sure.* He also immediately ordered large reinforcements to move forward to the seat of war. The commanders intrusted with this duty were Duke Eric of Brunswick, Chiappin Vitelli, Noircarmes, and Count de Roeulx. The rendezvous for the whole force was Deventer, and here they all arrived on the 10th July. On the same day the Duke of Alva himself entered Deventer, to take command in person.† On the evening of the 14th July he reached Rolden, a village three leagues distant from Groningen, at the head of three terzios of Spanish infantry, three companies of light horse, and a troop of dragoons.‡ His whole force in and about Groningen amounted to fifteen thousand choice troops besides a large but uncertain number of less disciplined soldiery.§

Meantime, Louis of Nassau, since his victory, had accomplished nothing. For this inactivity there was one sufficient excuse, the total want of funds. His only revenue was the amount of black mail which he was able to levy upon the inhabitants of the province. He repeated his determination to treat them all as enemies, unless they furnished him with the means of expelling their tyrants from the country.‖ He obtained small sums in this manner from time to time. The inhabitants were favorably disposed, but they were timid and

---

* Correspondance du Duc d'Albe, 136.
† Mendoza, 56, 57.   ‡ Correspondance du Duc d'Albe, 154.
§ Mendoza, 53–55. Correspondance du Duc d'Albe, 102, 106, 138, 152. The Netherland historians give him 17,000 foot and 3000 horse. Hoofd, v. 174, Bor, iv. 243, 244.—Compare Bentivoglio, liv. iv. 70, and Strada, i. 331, who gives Alva 12,000 foot, and 3000 horse, and to Louis of Nassau an equal number of infantry with an inferior force of cavalry.
‖ Correspondance du Duc d'Albe, 114, 115, 123, 124.

despairing. They saw no clear way towards the accomplishment of the result concerning which Louis was so confident.
They knew that the terrible Alva was already on his way.
They felt sure of being pillaged by both parties, and of being
hanged as rebels, besides, as soon as the Governor-general
should make his appearance.

Louis had, however, issued two formal proclamations for two
especial contributions. In these documents he had succinctly
explained that the houses of all recusants should be forthwith
burned about their ears,* and in consequence of these peremptory measures, he had obtained some ten thousand florins.
Alva ordered counter-proclamations to be affixed to church
doors and other places, forbidding all persons to contribute
to these forced loans of the rebels, on penalty of paying twice
as much to the Spaniards, with arbitrary punishment in addition, after his arrival.† The miserable inhabitants, thus placed
between two fires, had nothing for it but to pay one-half of
their property to support the rebellion in the first place, with
the prospect of giving the other half as a subsidy to tyranny
afterwards; while the gibbet stood at the end of the vista to
reward their liberality. Such was the horrible position of the
peasantry in this civil conflict. The weight of guilt thus
accumulated upon the crowned head which conceived, and
upon the red right hand which wrought all this misery, what
human scales can measure?

With these precarious means of support, the army of Louis
of Nassau, as may easily be supposed, was anything but
docile. After the victory of Heiliger Lee there had seemed to
his German mercenaries a probability of extensive booty,
which grew fainter as the slender fruit of that battle became
daily more apparent. The two abbots of Wittewerum and of
Heiliger Lee, who had followed Aremberg's train in order to
be witnesses of his victory, had been obliged to pay to the
actual conqueror a heavy price for the entertainment to which

---

* Proclamation of Count Louis, dated Dam, 5th June, 1568. Correspondance
du Duc d'Albe, 124, 125.   † Ibid., 144, 145.

they had invited themselves,* and these sums, together with the amounts pressed from the reluctant estates, and the forced contributions paid by luckless peasants, enabled him to keep his straggling troops together a few weeks longer. Mutiny, however, was constantly breaking out, and by the eloquent expostulations and vague promises of the Count, was with difficulty suppressed.†

He had, for a few weeks immediately succeeding the battle, distributed his troops in three different stations. On the approach of the Duke, however, he hastily concentrated his whole force at his own strongly fortified camp, within half cannon shot of Groningen. His army, such as it was, numbered from 10,000 to 12,000 men.‡ Alva reached Groningen early in the morning, and without pausing a moment, marched his troops directly through the city. He then immediately occupied an entrenched and fortified house, from which it was easy to inflict damage upon the camp. This done, the Duke, with a few attendants, rode forward to reconnoitre the enemy in person. He found him in a well fortified position, having the river on his front, which served as a moat to his camp, and with a deep trench three hundred yards beyond, in addition. Two wooden bridges led across the river ; each was commanded by a fortified house, in which was a provision of pine torches, ready at a moment's warning, to set fire to the bridges. Having thus satisfied himself, the Duke rode back to his army, which had received strict orders not to lift a finger till his return. He then despatched a small force of five hundred musketeers, under Robles, to skirmish with the enemy, and, if possible, to draw them from their trenches.§

The troops of Louis, however, showed no greediness to engage. On the contrary, it soon became evident that their dispositions were of an opposite tendency. The Count him-

---

* Bor. iv. 236.   † Ibid., iv. 236–244, etc.   Hoofd, v. 175.
‡ Ibid. v. 174.   According to Groen van Prinsterer, only 7000 to 8000 against 17,000 foot and 3000 horse, iii. 265.
§ Mendoza, 59.   Correspondance du Duc d'Albe, 154.

self, not at that moment trusting his soldiery, who were in an extremely mutinous condition, was desirous of falling back before his formidable antagonist. The Duke, faithful, however, to his life-long principles, had no intentions of precipitating the action in those difficult and swampy regions. The skirmishing, therefore, continued for many hours, an additional force of 1000 men being detailed from the Spanish army. The day was very sultry, however, the enemy reluctant, and the whole action languid. At last, towards evening, a large body, tempted beyond their trenches, engaged warmly with the Spaniards. The combat lasted but a few minutes, the patriots were soon routed, and fled precipitately back to their camp. The panic spread with them, and the whole army was soon in retreat. On retiring, they had, however, set fire to the bridges, and thus secured an advantage at the outset of the chase. The Spaniards were no longer to be held. Vitelli obtained permission to follow with 2000 additional troops. The fifteen hundred who had already been engaged, charged furiously upon their retreating foes. Some dashed across the blazing bridges, with their garments and their very beards on fire.* Others sprang into the river. Neither fire nor water could check the fierce pursuit. The cavalry dismounting, drove their horses into the stream, and clinging to their tails, pricked the horses forward with their lances. Having thus been dragged across, they joined their comrades in the mad chase along the narrow dykes, and through the swampy and almost impassable country where the rebels were seeking shelter. The approach of night, too soon advancing, at last put an end to the hunt. The Duke with difficulty recalled his men, and compelled them to restrain their eagerness until the morrow. Three hundred of the patriots were left dead upon the field, besides at least an equal number who perished in the river and canals. The army of Louis was entirely routed, and the Duke considered it virtually destroyed. He

---

* Mendoza, 61.

THE RISE OF THE DUTCH REPUBLIC.   [1568.

wrote to the state council that he should pursue them the next day, but doubted whether he should find anybody to talk with him. In this the Governor-general soon found himself delightfully disappointed.*

Five days later, the Duke arrived at Reyden, on the Ems. Owing to the unfavorable disposition of the country people, who were willing to protect the fugitives by false information to their pursuers, he was still in doubt as to the position then occupied by the enemy.† He had been fearful that they would be found at this very village of Reyden. It was a fatal error on the part of Count Louis that they were not.‡ Had he made a stand at this point, he might have held out a long time. The bridge which here crossed the river would have afforded him a retreat into Germany at any moment, and the place was easily to be defended in front.§ Thus he might have maintained himself against his fierce but wary foe, while his brother Orange, who was at Strasburg watching the progress of events, was executing his own long-planned expedition into the heart of the Netherlands. With Alva thus occupied in Friesland, the results of such an invasion might have been prodigious. It was, however, not on the cards for that campaign. The mutinous disposition of the mercenaries under his command‖ had filled Louis with doubt and disgust. Bold and sanguine, but always too fiery and impatient, he saw not much possibility of paying his troops any longer with promises. Perhaps he was not unwilling to place them in a position where they would be obliged to fight or to perish. At any rate, such was their present situation. Instead of halting at Reyden, he had made his stand at Jemmingen, about four leagues distant from that place, and a little further down the river.¶ Alva discovered this important fact soon after his

---

* Mendoza, 59–63. Alva's Letter to the State Council. Correspondance du Duc d'Albe, 154, 155. Compare Bor, iv. 244; Hoofd, v. 174, 175.

† Mendoza, 63.   ‡ Ibid., 63, 64. Hoofd, v. 174.

§ Mendoza, Hoofd, ubi sup.

‖ Bor, iv. 236, 244. Hoofd, v. 175.

¶ Ibid., v. 174, 175. Bor, iv. 244. Mendoza, 64.

arrival at Reyden, and could not conceal his delight. Already
exulting at the error made by his adversary, in neglecting the
important position which he now occupied himself, he was
doubly delighted at learning the nature of the place which he
had in preference selected. He saw that Louis had completely
entrapped himself.

Jemmingen was a small town on the left bank of the Ems.
The stream here very broad and deep, is rather a tide inlet than
a river, being but a very few miles from the Dollart. This
circular bay, or ocean chasm, the result of the violent inundation of the 13th century, surrounds, with the river, a narrow
peninsula. In the corner of this peninsula, as in the bottom
of a sack, Louis had posted his army. His infantry, as usual,
was drawn up in two large squares, and still contained ten
thousand men. The rear rested upon the village, the river
was upon his left ; his meagre force of cavalry upon the right.
In front were two very deep trenches. The narrow road,
which formed the only entrance to his camp, was guarded by a
ravelin on each side, and by five pieces of artillery.*

The Duke having reconnoitred the enemy in person, rode
back, satisfied that no escape was possible. The river was too
deep and too wide for swimming or wading, and there were
but very few boats. Louis was shut up between twelve
thousand Spanish veterans and the river Ems. The rebel
army, although not insufficient in point of numbers, was in a
state of disorganization. They were furious for money and
reluctant to fight. They broke out into open mutiny upon
the very verge of battle, and swore that they would instantly
disband, if the gold, which, as they believed, had been recently
brought into the camp, were not immediately distributed
among them.† Such was the state of things on the eventful
morning of the 21st July. All the expostulations of Count
Louis seemed powerless. His eloquence and his patience, both
inferior to his valor, were soon exhausted. He peremptorily
refused the money for which they clamored, giving the most

---

* Mendoza, 68, 69.   † Bor, iv. 244, 245. Hoofd, v. 175.

cogent of all reasons, an empty coffer. He demonstrated plainly that they were in that moment to make their election, whether to win a victory or to submit to a massacre. Neither flight nor surrender was possible. They knew how much quarter they could expect from the lances of the Spaniards or the waters of the Dollart. Their only chance of salvation lay in their own swords. The instinct of self-preservation, thus invoked, exerted a little of its natural effect.*

Meantime, a work which had been too long neglected, was then, if possible, to be performed. In that watery territory, the sea was only held in check by artificial means. In a very short time, by the demolition of a few dykes and the opening of a few sluices, the whole country through which the Spaniards had to pass could be laid under water. Believing it yet possible to enlist the ocean in his defence, Louis, having partially reduced his soldiers to obedience, ordered a strong detachment upon this important service. Seizing a spade, he commenced the work himself,† and then returned to set his army in battle array. Two or three tide gates had been opened, two or three bridges had been demolished, when Alva, riding in advance of his army, appeared within a mile or two of Jemmingen.‡ It was then eight o'clock in the morning. The patriots redoubled their efforts. By ten o'clock the waters were already knee high, and in some places as deep as to the waist. At that hour, the advanced guard of the Spaniards arrived. Fifteen hundred musketeers were immediately ordered forward by the Duke. They were preceded by a company of mounted cara-bineers, attended by a small band of volunteers of distinction. This little band threw themselves at once upon the troops engaged in destroying the dykes. The rebels fled at the first onset, and the Spaniards closed the gates.§ Feeling the full importance of the moment, Count Louis ordered a large force of musketeers to recover the position, and to complete the

---

* Hoofd, v. 175, 176.   † Meteren, 54. Hoofd, v. 175.
‡ Mendoza, 67. Correspondance du Duc d'Albe.
§ Mendoza, 67, 68. Correspondance du Duc d'Albe, 157, 158.

work of inundation. It was too late. The little band of
Spaniards held the post with consummate tenacity. Charge
after charge, volley after volley, from the overwhelming force
brought against them, failed to loosen the fierce grip with
which they held this key to the whole situation. Before they
could be driven from the dykes, their comrades arrived, when
all their antagonists at once made a hurried retreat to their
camp.*

Very much the same tactics were now employed by the
Duke, as in the engagement near Selwaert Abbey. He was
resolved that this affair, also, should be a hunt, not a battle,
but foresaw that it was to be a more successful one. There
was no loophole of escape, so that after a little successful
baiting, the imprisoned victims would be forced to spring from
their lurking-place, to perish upon his spears. On his march
from Reyden that morning, he had taken care to occupy
every farm-house, every building of whatever description along
the road, with his troops. He had left a strong guard on the
bridge at Reyden, and had thus closed carefully every avenue.†
The same fifteen hundred musketeers were now advanced
further towards the camp. This small force, powerfully but
secretly sustained, was to feel the enemy ; to skirmish with
him, and to draw him as soon as possible out of his trenches.‡
The plan succeeded. Gradually the engagements between
them and the troops sent out by Count Louis grew more
earnest. Finding so insignificant a force opposed to them,
the mutinous rebels took courage. The work waxed hot.
Lodroño and Romero, commanders of the musketeers, becoming alarmed, sent to the Duke for reinforcements. He
sent back word in reply, that if they were not enough to
damage the enemy, they could, at least, hold their own for the
present. So much he had a right to expect of Spanish
soldiers.§ At any rate, he should send no reinforcements.

---

* Mendoza, who was himself one of the Spartan band which held the dyke,
states the number of rebels thus repulsed by less than 200 Spaniards, at 4000
all musketeers.—67, 68.

† Mendoza, 66, 67.   ‡ Ibid., 69.   § Ibid.

Again they were more warmly pressed, again their messenger returned with the same reply. A third time they send the most urgent entreaties for succour. The Duke was still inexorable.*

Meantime the result of this scientific angling approached. By noon the rebels, not being able to see how large a portion of the Spanish army had arrived, began to think the affair not so serious. Count Louis sent out a reconnoitring party upon the river in a few boats. They returned without having been able to discover any large force. It seemed probable, therefore, that the inundation had been more successful in stopping their advance than had been supposed.† Louis, always too rash, inflamed his men with temporary enthusiasm. Determined to cut their way out by one vigorous movement, the whole army at last marched forth from their entrenchments, with drums beating, colors flying ; but already the concealed reinforcements of their enemies were on the spot. The patriots met with a warmer reception than they had expected. Their courage evaporated. Hardly had they advanced three hundred yards, when the whole body wavered and then retreated precipitately towards the encampment,‡ having scarcely exchanged a shot with the enemy. Count Louis, in a frenzy of rage and despair, flew from rank to rank, in vain endeavouring to rally his terror-stricken troops. It was hopeless. The battery which guarded the road was entirely deserted. He rushed to the cannon himself, and fired them all with his own hand.§ It was their first and last discharge. His single arm, however bold, could not turn the tide of battle, and he was swept backwards with his coward troops. In a moment afterwards, Don Lope de Figueroa, who led the van of the Spaniards, dashed upon the battery, and secured it, together with the ravelins.‖ Their own artillery was turned against the rebels, and the road was

---

* Mendoza, 69.
† Hoofd, v. 175, 176. Mendoza, 70.   ‡ Mendoza, 70. Hoofd, v. 176
§ Bor, iv. 245. Hoofd. v. 176.   ‖ Mendoza, 70.

soon swept. The Spaniards in large numbers now rushed
through the trenches in pursuit of the retreating foe. No
resistance was offered, nor quarter given. An impossible
escape was all which was attempted. It was not a battle, but
a massacre. Many of the beggars in their flight threw
down their arms ; all had forgotten their use. Their antagonists butchered them in droves, while those who escaped the
sword were hurled into the river. *Seven* Spaniards were
killed, and *seven thousand* rebels.* The swift ebb-tide swept
the *hats* of the perishing wretches in such numbers down the
stream, that the people at Embden knew the result of the
battle in an incredibly short period of time.† The skirmishing
had lasted from ten o'clock till one,‡ but the butchery continued much longer. It took time to slaughter even unresisting victims. Large numbers obtained refuge for the night
upon an island in the river. At low water next day the
Spaniards waded to them, and slew every man.§ Many
found concealment in hovels, swamps, and thickets, so that
the whole of the following day was occupied in ferreting out
and despatching them. There was so much to be done, that
there was work enough for all. "Not a soldier," says, with
great simplicity, a Spanish historian who fought in the
battle, "not a soldier, nor even a lad, who wished to share in
the victory, but could find somebody to wound, to kill, to
burn, or to drown."‖ The wounding, killing, burning,
drowning lasted two days, and very few escaped. The landward pursuit extended for three or four leagues around,¶ so
that the roads and pastures were covered with bodies, with
corslets, and other weapons. Count Louis himself stripped
off his clothes, and made his escape, when all was over, by

---

* Letter of Alva to the Council of State. Correspondance du Duc d'Albe,
158. The same letter is published in Bor, iv. 245, 246. All writers allow
seven thousand to have been killed on the patriot side, and the number of
Spaniards slain is not estimated at more than eighty, even by the patriotic
Meteren, 55. Compare Bor, iv. 245–246 ; Herrera, xv. 696 ; Hoofd, v. 176,
and Mendoza, 72.

† Mendoza, 71,   ‡ Correspondance du Duc d'Albe, 157.
§ Mendoza. 71.   ‖ Ibid., 72.   ¶ Ibid., 71.

swimming across the Ems.* With the paltry remnant of his troops he again took refuge in Germany.

The Spanish army, two days afterwards, marched back to Groningen. The page which records their victorious campaign is foul with outrage and red with blood. None of the horrors which accompany the passage of hostile troops through a defenceless country were omitted. Maids and matrons were ravished in multitudes ; old men butchered in cold blood. As Alva returned, with the rear-guard of his army, the whole sky was red with a constant conflagration ; the very earth seemed changed to ashes.† Every peasant's hovel, every farm-house, every village upon the road had been burned to the ground. So gross and so extensive had been the outrage, that the commander-in-chief felt it due to his dignity to hang some of his own soldiers who had most distinguished themselves in this work.‡ Thus ended the campaign of Count Louis in Friesland. Thus signally and terribly had the Duke of Alva vindicated the supremacy of Spanish discipline and of his own military skill.

On his return to Groningen, the estates were summoned, and received a severe lecture for their suspicious demeanour in regard to the rebellion.§ In order more effectually to control both province and city, the Governor-general ordered the construction of a strong fortress,‖ which was soon begun but never completed. Having thus furnished himself with a key to this important and doubtful region, he returned by way of Amsterdam to Utrecht. There he was met by his son Frederic with strong reinforcements.¶ The Duke reviewed his whole army, and found himself at the head of 30,000 infantry and 7,000 cavalry.** Having fully subdued the province, he had no occupation for such a force, but he improved

---

* Correspondance du Duc d'Albe, 158; or "in a boat," Bor, iv. 245. Meteren, 55; or "partly by swimming and partly in a boat," Mendoza, 72. Compare Hoofd, v. 176; De Thou, v. 458–462, etc., etc.

† Bor, iv. 245. Mendoza, 73. ‡ Ibid.

§ Bor, iv. 246. Hoofd, v. 176, 177.

‖ Bor, iv. 246; v. 260. ¶ De Thou, v. 462. Vie du Duc d'Albe, ii. 323.

** De Thou, v. 462, but compare Mendoza, 76, 77.

the opportunity by cutting off the head of an old woman in Utrecht. The Vrow van Diemen, eighteen months previously, had given the preacher Arendsoon a night's lodging in her house.* The crime had, in fact, been committed by her son-in-law, who dwelt under her roof, and who had himself, without her participation, extended this dangerous hospitality to a heretic ; but the old lady, although a devout Catholic, was rich. Her execution would strike a wholesome terror into the hearts of her neighbours. The confiscation of her estates would bring a handsome sum into the government coffers. It would be made manifest that the same hand which could destroy an army of twelve thousand rebels at a blow could inflict as signal punishment on the small delinquencies of obscure individuals. The old lady, who was past eighty-four years of age, was placed in a chair upon the scaffold. She met her death with heroism, and treated her murderers with contempt. "I understand very well," she observed, "why my death is considered necessary. The calf is fat and must be killed." To the executioner she expressed a hope that his sword was sufficiently sharp, " as he was likely to find her old neck very tough." With this grisly parody upon the pathetic dying words of Anne Boleyn, the courageous old gentlewoman submitted to her fate.†

The tragedy of Don Carlos does not strictly belong to our subject, which is the rise of the Netherland commonwealth— not the decline of the Spanish monarchy, nor the life of Philip the Second. The thread is but slender which connects the unhappy young prince with the fortunes of the northern republic. He was said, no doubt with truth, to desire the government of Flanders. He was also supposed to be in secret correspondence with the leaders of the revolt in the provinces. He appeared, however, to possess very little of their confidence. His name is only once mentioned by William of Orange, who said in a letter that " the Prince

---

* Brandt, i. 480. Hoofd.

† Brandt, Hist. de Reformatie, D. i. 480. Reael's Mem., 36. Hoofd v. 177.

of Spain had lately eaten sixteen pounds of fruit, including four pounds of grapes at a single sitting, and had
become ill in consequence."* The result was sufficiently
natural, but it nowhere appears that the royal youth, born to
consume the fruits of the earth so largely, had ever given the
Netherlanders any other proof of his capacity to govern them.
There is no doubt that he was a most uncomfortable personage
at home, both to himself and to others, and that he hated his
father very cordially. He was extremely incensed at the
nomination of Alva to the Netherlands, because he had hoped
that either the King would go thither or entrust the mission
to him, in either of which events he should be rid for a time
of the paternal authority, or at least of the paternal presence.
It seems to be well ascertained that Carlos nourished towards
his father a hatred which might lead to criminal attempts,
but there is no proof that such attempts were ever made. As
to the fabulous amours of the Prince and the Queen, they had
never any existence save in the imagination of poets, who
have chosen to find a source of sentimental sorrow for the
Infante in the arbitrary substitution of his father for himself
in the marriage contract with the daughter of Henry the
Second. As Carlos was but twelve or thirteen years of age
when thus deprived of a bride whom he had never seen, the
foundation for a passionate regret was but slight. It would
hardly be a more absurd fantasy, had the poets chosen to
represent Philip's father, the Emperor Charles, repining in
his dotage for the loss of "bloody Mary," whom he had so
handsomely ceded to his son. Philip took a bad old woman
to relieve his father ; he took a fair young princess at his son's
expense ; but similar changes in state marriages were such
matters of course, that no emotions were likely to be created
in consequence. There is no proof whatever, nor any reason
to surmise, that any love passages ever existed between Don
Carlos and his step-mother.

---

* Groen v. Prinst., Archives, i. 434, but see Correspondance de Guillaume le
Tacit. iii. 12.

As to the process and the death of the Prince, the mystery has not yet been removed, and the field is still open to conjecture. It seems a thankless task to grope in the dark after the truth at a variety of sources, when the truth really exists in tangible shape if profane hands could be laid upon it. The secret is buried in the bosom of the Vatican. Philip wrote two letters on the subject to Pius V. The contents of the first (21st January, 1568) are known. He informed the pontiff that he had been obliged to imprison his son, and promised that he would, in the conduct of the affair, omit nothing which could be expected of a father and of a just and prudent king.* The second letter, in which he narrated, or is supposed to have narrated, the whole course of the tragic proceedings, down to the death and burial of the Prince, has never yet been made public. There are hopes that this secret missive, after three centuries of darkness, may soon see the light.†

As Philip generally told the truth to the Pope, it is probable that the secret, when once revealed, will contain the veritable solution of the mystery. Till that moment arrives, it seems idle to attempt fathoming the matter. Nevertheless, it may be well briefly to state the case as it stands. As against the King, it rests upon no impregnable, but certainly upon respectable authority. The Prince of Orange, in his famous Apology, calls Philip the murderer of his wife and of his son, and says that there was proof of the facts in France.‡ He alludes to the violent death of Carlos almost as if it were an indisputable truth. "As for Don Charles," he says, "was he not our future sovereign? And if the father could allege

---

* De Thou, v. 436. Liv. xliii.

† I am assured by Mr. Gachard that a copy of this important letter is confidently expected by the Commission Royale d'Histoire.

‡ "A cruellement meudri sa femme, fille et seur des Rois de France! comme j'entends qu'on en a en France les informations —— sa femme legitime, mère de deux filles vraies héritieres d'Espaigne."—Apologie, 34, sqq. The part of this accusation relative to the Queen is entirely disproved by the letters of the French envoy Fourquevaulx. Vide Von Raumer, Gesch. Europas, iii. 129–132, and Hist. Briefe, i. 113–157.

against his son fit cause for death, was it not rather for us to judge him than for three or four monks or inquisitors of Spain?"*

The historian, P. Matthieu, relates that Philip assembled his council of conscience; that they recommended mercy; that hereupon Philip gave the matter to the inquisition, by which tribunal Carlos was declared a heretic on account of his connexion with Protestants, and for his attempt against his father's life was condemned to death, and that the sentence was executed by four slaves, two holding the arms, one the feet, while the fourth strangled him.†

De Thou gives the following account of the transaction, having derived many of his details from the oral communications of Louis de Foix :‡

---

* "Mais il a en dispense. De qui? du pape du Rome qui est un Dieu en terre. Certes c'est ce que je croi: car le Dieu du ciel ne l'auroit jamais accordé —— voilà pourquoi à esté adjousté à ces horribles faultes précédentes un cruel parricide, le père meurdrissant inhumainement son enfant et son héritier, affin que par ce moien le pape eut overture de dispense d'un si execrable inceste. Si doncq nous disons que nous rejettons le gouvernement d'un tel roi incestueus, parricide et meurdrier de sa femme, qui nous pourroit accuser justement? —— Quant à Don Charles, n'estoit il pas notre seigneur futur et maistre presumptif? Et si le père pouvoit alleguer contre son fils cause idoine de mort, estoit ce point à nous qui avions tant d'intérest, plustot à le juger, qu' à trois ou quatre moines ou Inquisiteurs d'Espaigne ?"—Apologie, 35, 36.

† Hist. de France et des choses mémorables advenues aux provinces étrangères durant sept années de paix (Paris, 1606) 1598–1604.—Compare the admirable article by the historian Ranke; "Zur Geschichte des Don Carlos." (Aus dem 46ten Bande der Wiener Jahrbücher der Litteratur besonders abgedruckt). Wien. 1829. Carl Gerold.

‡ It is surprising that the illustrious historian Ranke, to whose pamphlet on this subject we are under deep obligations, should undervalue the testimony of this personage. He calls him, "a certain Foix, who had known the Prince and had arranged the lock of his door," adding, that "the evidence of a man belonging only to an inferior class of society is of course not conclusive." "Das Zeugnis eines Menschen der nur einem untergeordneten Kreise der Gesellschaft angehörte reicht wie sich versteht nicht aus.") Certainly one would suppose the man, from this contemptuous notice, a mere locksmith. Even had he been but a mechanic, his testimony would seem to us much more valuable in such an age of dissimulation than if he had been a prime minister, a cardinal, or a king; always supposing that he testified to things within his knowledge. Louis de Foix was no mechanic, however, but a celebrated engineer, a native of Paris, the architect of the palace and monastery of the Escorial, and the inventor of

Philip imagined that his son was about to escape from Spain, and to make his way to the Netherlands. The King also believed himself in danger of assassination from Carlos, his chief evidence being that the Prince always carried pistols in the pockets of his loose breeches. As Carlos wished always to be alone at night without any domestic in his chamber, de Foix had arranged for him a set of pulleys, by means of which he could open or shut his door without rising from his bed. He always slept with two pistols and two drawn swords under his pillow, and had two loaded arquebusses in a wardrobe close at hand. These remarkable precautions would seem rather to indicate a profound fear of being himself assassinated; but they were nevertheless supposed to justify Philip's suspicions, that the Infante was meditating parricide. On Christmas eve, however (1567), Don Carlos told his confessor that he had determined to kill a man. The priest, in consequence, refused to admit him to the communion. The Prince demanded, at least, a wafer which was not consecrated, in order that he might seem to the people to be participating in the sacrament. The confessor declined the proposal, and immediately repairing to the King, narrated the whole story. Philip exclaimed that he was himself the man whom the Prince intended to kill, but that measures should be forthwith taken to prevent such a design. The monarch then consulted the Holy Office of the inquisition, and the resolution was taken to arrest his son. De Foix was compelled to alter the pulleys of the door to the Prince's chamber in such a manner that it could be opened without the usual noise, which was almost sure to awaken him. At midnight, accordingly, Count Lerma entered the room so stealthily that the arms were all removed from the Prince's pillow and the wardrobe, without awakening the sleeper. Philip, Ruy Gomez, the Duke de Feria, and two

---

the machinery by which the water of the Tagus was carried to the highest parts of the city of Toledo. On his return to France, he distinguished himself by constructing a new harbour at Bayonne, and by other works of public utility. Certainly it is hardly fair to depreciate the statements of such a man upon the ground of his inferiority in social position.

other nobles, then noiselessly crept into the apartment. Carlos still slept so profoundly that it was necessary for Lerma to shake him violently by the arm before he could be aroused. Starting from his sleep in the dead of night, and seeing his father thus accompanied, before his bed, the Prince cried out that he was a dead man, and earnestly besought the bystanders to make an end of him at once. Philip assured him, however, that he was not come to kill him, but to chastise him paternally, and to recal him to his duty. He then read him a serious lecture, caused him to rise from his bed, took away his servants, and placed him under guard. He was made to array himself in mourning habiliments, and to sleep on a truckle bed. The Prince was in despair. He soon made various attempts upon his own life. He threw himself into the fire, but was rescued by his guards, with his clothes all in flames. He passed several days without taking any food, and then ate so many patties of minced meat that he nearly died of indigestion. He was also said to have attempted to choke himself with a diamond, and to have been prevented by his guard ; to have filled his bed with ice ; to have sat in cold draughts ; to have gone eleven days without food, the last method being, as one would think, sufficiently thorough. Philip, therefore, seeing his son thus desperate, consulted once more with the Holy Office, and came to the decision that it was better to condemn him legitimately to death than to permit him to die by his own hand. In order, however, to save appearances, the order was secretly carried into execution. Don Carlos was made to swallow poison in a bowl of broth, of which he died in a few hours. This was at the commencement of his twenty-third year. The death was concealed for several months, and was not made public till after Alva's victory at Jemmingen.*

Such was the account drawn up by de Thou from the oral communications of de Foix, and from other sources not indicated. Certainly, such a narrative is far from being entitled

---

* De Thou, v. Liv. xliii. 433–437.

to implicit credence. The historian was a contemporary, but he was not in Spain, and the engineer's testimony is, of course, not entitled to much consideration on the subject of the process and the execution (if there were an execution) ; although conclusive as to matters which had been within his personal knowledge. For the rest, all that it can be said to establish is the existence of the general rumor, that Carlos came to his death by foul means and in consequence of advice given by the inquisition.

On the other hand, in all the letters written at the period by persons in Madrid most likely, from their position, to know the truth, not a syllable has been found in confirmation of the violent death said to have been suffered by Carlos.* Secretary Erasso, the papal nuncio Castagna, the Venetian envoy Cavalli, all express a conviction that the death of the prince had been brought about by his own extravagant conduct and mental excitement ; by alternations of starving and voracious eating, by throwing himself into the fire, by icing his bed, and by similar acts of desperation. Nearly every writer alludes to the incident of the refusal of the priest to admit Carlos to communion, upon the ground of his confessed deadly hatred to an individual whom all supposed to be the King. It was also universally believed that Carlos meant to kill his father. The nuncio asked Spinosa (then president of Castile) if this report were true. "If nothing more were to be feared," answered the priest, "the King would protect himself by other measures, but the matter was worse, if worse could be."† The King, however, summoned all the *foreign diplomatic body* and assured them that *the story was false.*‡ After his arrest, the Prince, according to Castagna, attempted

---

* "In allen diesen Schreiben," says Ranke, "so verschiedener Menschen habe ich niemals auch nur eine leise Andeutung von einem Schriftlichen oder mündlichen Spruche, nirgends auch nur eine geringe Spur von einer gewaltsamen Herbeiführung dieses Todes gefunden. Sie wissen vielmehr sämtlich nur von einem sehr erklärlichen Verlaufe der Krankheit, auf welche ein naturliches Verscheiden folgte."—Zur Geschichte, etc.

† Ranke. Zur Geschichte, etc. ‡ Ibid.

various means of suicide, abstaining, at last, many days from food, and dying in consequence, "discoursing, upon his death-bed, gravely and like a man of sense."[*]

The historian Cabrera, official panegyrist of Philip the Second, speaks of the death of Carlos as a natural one, but leaves a dark kind of mystery about the symptoms of his disease. He states, that the Prince was tried and condemned by a commission or junta, consisting of Spinosa, Ruy Gomez, and the Licentiate Virviesca, but that he was carried off by an illness, the nature of which he does not describe.[†]

Llorente found nothing in the records of the Inquisition to prove that the Holy Office had ever condemned the Prince or instituted any process against him. He states that he was condemned by a commission, but that he died of a sickness which supervened. It must be confessed that the illness was a convenient one, and that such diseases are very apt to attack individuals whom tyrants are disposed to remove from their path, while desirous, at the same time, to save appearances. It would certainly be presumptuous to accept implicitly the narrative of de Thou, which is literally followed by Hoofd,[‡] and by many modern writers. On the other hand, it would be an exaggeration of historical scepticism to absolve Philip from the murder of his son, solely upon negative testimony. The people about court did not believe in the crime. They saw no proofs of it. Of course they saw none. Philip would take good care that there should be none if he had made up his mind that the death of the Prince should be considered a natural one. An à priori argument, which omits the character of the suspected culprit, and the extraordinary circumstances of time and place, is not satisfactory. Philip thoroughly understood the business of secret midnight murder. We shall soon have occasion to relate the elaborate and ingenious method by which the assassination of Montigny was accom-

---

* "Pero che prima sempre pareva che nel suo parlar dicesse cose vane e di poco fondamento et allora principio a discorrere gravemente e di huomo prudente."—Zur Geschichte, etc., 26.

† Cabrera. Felipe el prudente, lib. viii.   ‡ Nederl. Hist., 179, 180.

plished and kept a profound secret from the whole world, until
the letters of the royal assassin, after three centuries' repose,
were exhumed, and the foul mystery revealed.   Philip was capable of any crime.   Moreover, in his letter to his aunt,
Queen Catharine of Portugal,* he distinctly declares himself,
like Abraham, prepared to go all lengths in obedience to the
Lord.   "I have chosen in this matter," he said, "to *make
the sacrifice* to God of my *own flesh and blood*, and to prefer
His service and the universal welfare to all other human considerations."†   Whenever the letter to Pius V. sees the light,
it will appear whether the sacrifice which the monarch thus
made to his God proceeded beyond the imprisonment and condemnation of his son, or was completed by the actual immolation of the victim.

With regard to the Prince himself, it is very certain that,
if he had lived, the realms of the Spanish Crown would have
numbered one tyrant more.   Carlos from his earliest youth,
was remarkable for the ferocity of his character.   The Emperor Charles was highly pleased with him, then about fourteen years of age, upon their first interview after the abdica-
tion.   He flattered himself that the lad had inherited his own
martial genius together with his name.   Carlos took much interest in his grandfather's account of his various battles, but
when the flight from Innspruck was narrated, he repeated many
times, with much vehemence, that he never would have fled ;
to which position he adhered, notwithstanding all the arguments of the Emperor, and very much to his amusement.‡
The young Prince was always fond of soldiers, and listened
eagerly to discourses of war.   He was in the habit also of

---

* And not the Empress, wife of Maximilian II., as stated by Cabrera, who
publishes the letter of January 21, 1568 (l. vii. c. xxii. 475).   Ranke has correct-
ed this error.—Zur Geschichte des Don Carlos, etc.

† "Mas en fin yo e querido hazer en esta parte sacrificio a Dios de mi propria
carne i sangre, i preferir su servicio i el beneficio i bien universal à las otras con-
sideraciones umanas," etc. etc.—Letter of Philip, apud Cabrera, vii. xxii. 475.   V.
lib. viii. 405–501.

‡ "—— et egli in colera reitero con mariviglia e riso di S. Mᵗᵃ e de circonstanti
che egli mai non sarebbe fuggito."—Badovaro MS.

recording the names of any military persons who, according to custom, frequently made offers of their services to the heir apparent, and of causing them to take a solemn oath to keep their engagements.* No other indications of warlike talent, however, have been preserved concerning him. "He was crafty, ambitious, cruel, violent," says the envoy Suriano, "a hater of buffoons, a lover of soldiers."† His natural cruelty seems to have been remarkable from his boyhood. After his return from the chase, he was in the habit of cutting the throats of hares and other animals, and of amusing himself with their dying convulsions.‡ He also frequently took pleasure in roasting them alive.§ He once received a present of a very large snake from some person who seemed to understand how to please this remarkable young prince. After a time, however, the favorite reptile allowed itself to bite its master's finger, whereupon Don Carlos immediately retaliated by biting off its head.‖

He was excessively angry at the suggestion that the prince who was expected to spring from his father's marriage with the English queen, would one day reign over the Netherlands, and swore he would challenge him to mortal combat in order to prevent such an infringement of his rights. His father and grandfather were both highly diverted with this manifestation of spirit,¶ but it was not decreed that the world should witness the execution of these fraternal intentions against the babe which was never to be born.

Ferocity, in short, seems to have been the leading characteristic of the unhappy Carlos. His preceptor, a man of

---

* Badovaro MS.

† E animoso, accorto, crudele, ambitioso, inimicissimo di buffoni, amicissimo di soldati."—Suriano MS.

‡ Strada, viii. 313.

§ "Dimostra di haver an animo fiero, et tra li effetti che si raccontavano uno é che alle volte che da la caccia li veniva portato lepre o simili animali, si diletta di veder li arrostiti vivi."—Badovaro MS.

‖ "Et essendo li donato una biscia scodarella molto grande, et essa havendo li dato un morso à un dito egli subitamente co denti gli spicco la testa."—Ibid.

¶ "Con somma allegrezza inteso."—Ibid.

learning and merit, who was called "the honorable John,"* tried to mitigate this excessive ardor of temperament by a course of Cicero de Officiis, which he read to him daily.† Neither the eloquence of Tully, however, nor the precepts of the honorable John made the least impression upon this very savage nature. As he grew older he did not grow wiser nor more gentle. He was prematurely and grossly licentious. All the money which as a boy, he was allowed, he spent upon women of low character, and when he was penniless, he gave them his chains, his medals, even the clothes from his back.‡ He took pleasure in affronting respectable females when he met them in the streets, insulting them by the coarsest language and gestures.§ Being cruel, cunning, fierce and licentious, he seemed to combine many of the worst qualities of a lunatic. That he probably was one is the best defence which can be offered for his conduct. In attempting to offer violence to a female, while he was at the university of Alcalà he fell down a stone staircase, from which cause he was laid up for a long time with a severely wounded head, and was supposed to have injured his brain.‖

The traits of ferocity recorded of him during his short life are so numerous that humanity can hardly desire that it should have been prolonged. A few drops of water having once fallen upon his head from a window, as he passed through the street, he gave peremptory orders to his guard to burn the house to the ground, and to put every one of its inhabitants to the sword. The soldiers went forthwith to execute the order, but more humane than their master, returned with the excuse that the Holy Sacrament of the Viaticum had that moment been carried into the house. This appeal to the superstition of the Prince successfully suspended the execution of the crime

---

* " Il precettore suo è nominato l'honorato Giovanni, che e di quelli belli costumi che si possano desiderar in alcun altro spagnuolo."—Badovaro MS.

† Ibid.   ‡ Ibid.   § Brantôme (usâ), ii. 117.

‖ Hoofd, v. 179. Compare Strada, i. 213. See also "Relacion de lo sucedido en la enfermedad del principe, nuestro Señor, por el Doctor Olivares, medico de su camara."—Papiers d'Etat de Granvelle, vi. 587, sqq.

which his inconceivable malignity had contemplated.* On another occasion, a nobleman, who slept near his chamber, failed to answer his bell on the instant. Springing upon his dilatory attendant, as soon as he made his appearance, the Prince seized him in his arms and was about to throw him from the window, when the cries of the unfortunate chamberlain attracted attention, and procured a rescue.†

The Cardinal Espinoza had once accidentally detained at his palace an actor who was to perform a favorite part by express command of Don Carlos. Furious at this detention, the Prince took the priest by the throat as soon as he presented himself at the palace, and plucking his dagger from its sheath, swore, by the soul of his father, that he would take his life on the spot. The grand inquisitor fell on his knees and begged for mercy, but it is probable that the entrance of the King alone saved his life.‡

There was often something ludicrous mingled with the atrocious in these ungovernable explosions of wrath. Don Pedro Manuel, his chamberlain, had once, by his command, ordered a pair of boots to be made for the Prince. When brought home, they were, unfortunately, too tight. The Prince after vainly endeavouring to pull them on, fell into a blazing passion. He swore that it was the fault of Don Pedro, who always wore tight boots himself, but he at the same time protested that his father was really at the bottom of the affair. He gave the young nobleman a box on the ear for thus conspiring with the King against his comfort, and then ordered the boots to be chopped into little pieces, stewed and seasoned. Then sending for the culprit shoemaker, he ordered him to eat his own boots, thus converted into a pottage ; and with this punishment the unfortunate mechanic, who had thought his life forfeited, was sufficiently glad to comply.§

Even the puissant Alva could not escape his violence. Like all the men in whom his father reposed confidence, the Duke

---

* Cabrera, lib. vii. c. xxii. p. 470.   † Ibid., ibid.   ‡ Cabrera, ubi sup.
§ Ibid., vii. 470.   Brantôme.   Art. Philippe II. ii. 115.

was odious to the heir apparent. Don Carlos detested him with the whole force of his little soul. He hated him as only a virtuous person deserved to be hated by such a ruffian. The heir apparent had taken the Netherlands under his patronage. He had even formed the design of repairing secretly to the provinces, and could not, therefore, disguise his wrath at the appointment of the Duke. It is doubtful whether the country would have benefited by the gratification of his wishes. It is possible that the pranks of so malignant an ape might have been even more mischievous than the concentrated and vigorous tyranny of an Alva. When the new Captain-general called, before his departure, to pay his respects to the Infante, the Duke seemed, to his surprise, to have suddenly entered the den of a wild beast. Don Carlos sprang upon him with a howl of fury, brandishing a dagger in his hand. He uttered reproaches at having been defrauded of the Netherland government. He swore that Alva should never accomplish his mission, nor leave his presence alive. He was proceeding to make good the threat with his poniard, when the Duke closed with him. A violent struggle succeeded. Both rolled together on the ground, the Prince biting and striking like a demoniac, the Duke defending himself as well as he was able, without attempting his adversary's life. Before the combat was decided, the approach of many persons put an end to the disgraceful scene.* As decent a veil as possible was thrown over the transaction, and the Duke departed on his mission. Before the end of the year, the Prince was in the prison whence he never came forth alive.

The figure of Don Carlos was as misshapen as his mind. His head was disproportionately large, his limbs were rickety, one shoulder was higher, one leg longer than the other.†

---

* Cabrera, lib. vii. c. xiii. 442, 443.

† "Ha la testa di grandezza sproportionata al corpo, di pelo nero et di debole complessione."—Badovaro MS.

"Se bene e simile al padre di faccia e pero dissimil di costumi."—Suriano MS.

"Carolus, præter colorem et capillum, ceterum corpore mendosus: quippe humero elatior et tibiâ alterâ longior erat, nec minus dehonestamentum ab indole feroci et contumaci."—Strada, x. 509.

With features resembling those of his father, but with a swarthy instead of a fair complexion, with an expression of countenance both fierce and foolish, and with a character such as we have sketched it, upon the evidence of those who knew him well, it is indeed strange that he should ever have been transformed by the magic of poetry into a romantic hero. As cruel and cunning as his father, as mad as his great-grandmother, he has left a name, which not even his dark and mysterious fate can render interesting.

CHAPTER IV.

THE Duke having thus crushed the project of Count Louis, and quelled the insurrection in Friesland, returned in triumph to Brussels. Far from softened by the success of his arms, he renewed with fresh energy the butchery which, for a brief season, had been suspended during his brilliant campaign in the north. The altars again smoked with victims; the hanging, burning, drowning, beheading, seemed destined to be the perpetual course of his administration, so long as human bodies remained on which his fanatical vengeance could be wreaked.* Four men of eminence were executed soon after his return to the capital. They had previously suffered such intense punishment on the rack, that it was necessary to carry them to the scaffold and bind them upon chairs, that they might be beheaded.† These four sufferers were a Frisian nobleman, named Galena, the secretaries of Egmont and Horn, Bakkerzeel and La Loo, and the distinguished burgomaster of Antwerp, Antony Van Straalen. The arrest of the three last-mentioned individuals, simultaneously with that of the two Counts, has been related in a previous chapter. In the case of Van Straalen, the services rendered by him to the provinces during his long and honorable career, had been so remarkable, that even the Blood-Council, in sending his case to Alva for his sentence, were inspired by a humane feeling. They felt so much compunction at the impending fate of a man who, among other meritorious acts, had furnished nearly all the funds for the brilliant campaign in Picardy, by which the opening years of Philip's reign had been illustrated, as to hint at the propriety of a pardon.‡ But the recommendation to mercy, though it came from the lips of tigers, dripping with human blood, fell unheeded on the tyrant's ear. It seemed meet that the man who had supplied the nerves of war in that unforgiven series of triumphs, should share the fate of the hero who had won the laurels.§

Hundreds of obscure martyrs now followed in the same path to another world, where surely they deserved to find their recompense, if steadfast adherence to their faith, and a tranquil trust in God amid tortures and death too horrible to be related, had ever found favor above. The "Red-Rod," as the provost of Brabant was popularly designated, was never idle. He flew from village to village throughout the province, executing the bloody behests of his

---

* Bor, iv. 248.

† J. P. van Cappelle, Bijdragen tot de Geschich. d. Nederl, 231. Meteren, f. 61.   ‡ Bor, 247, 248.

§ Bor, Cappelle, Hoofd, ubi sup. The last words of the Burgomaster as he bowed his neck to the executioner's stroke were, " " Voor wel gedaan, kwaclyk beloud," "For faithful service, evil recompense."—Cappelle, 232.

masters with congenial alacrity.* Nevertheless his career was soon destined to close upon the same scaffold where he had so long officiated. Partly from caprice, partly from an uncompromising and fantastic sense of justice, his master now hanged the executioner whose industry had been so untiring. The sentence which was affixed to his breast, as he suffered, stated that he had been guilty of much malpractice ; that he had executed many persons without a warrant, and had suffered many guilty persons for a bribe, to escape their doom.† The reader can judge which of the two clauses constituted the most sufficient reason.

During all these triumphs of Alva, the Prince of Orange had not lost his self-possession. One after another, each of his bold, skilfully-conceived and carefully-prepared plans had failed. Villers had been entirely discomfited at Dalhem, Cocqueville had been cut to pieces in Picardy, and now the valiant and experienced Louis had met with an entire overthrow in Friesland. The brief success of the patriots at Heiliger Lee had been washed out in the blood-torrents of Jemmingen. Tyranny was more triumphant, the provinces more timidly crouching, than ever. The friends on whom William of Orange relied in Germany, never enthusiastic in his cause, although many of them true-hearted and liberal, now grew cold and anxious. For months long, his most faithful and affectionate allies, such men as the Elector of Hesse and the Duke of Wirtemberg, as well as the less trustworthy Augustus of Saxony, had earnestly expressed their opinion that, under the circumstances, his best course was to sit still and watch the course of events.

It was known that the Emperor had written an urgent letter to Philip on the subject of his policy in the Netherlands in general, and concerning the position of Orange in particular. All persons, from the Emperor down to the pettiest potentate, seemed now of opinion that the Prince had better pause ; that he was, indeed, bound to wait the issue of that

---

* Bor, iv. 248.   † Ibid., v. 269, 270. Hoofd, v. 191.

remonstrance.* "Your highness must sit still," said Landgrave William. "Your highness must sit still," said Augustus of Saxony. "You must move neither hand nor foot in the cause of the perishing provinces," said the Emperor. "Not a soldier—horse, foot, or dragoon—shall be levied within the Empire. If you violate the peace of the realm, and embroil us with our excellent brother and cousin Philip, it is at your own peril. You have nothing to do but to keep quiet and await his answer to our letter."† But the Prince knew how much effect his sitting still would produce upon the cause of liberty and religion. He knew how much effect the Emperor's letter was like to have upon the heart of Philip. He knew that the more impenetrable the darkness now gathering over that land of doom which he had devoted his life to defend, the more urgently was he forbidden to turn his face away from it in its affliction. He knew that thousands of human souls, nigh to perishing, were daily turning towards him as their only hope on earth, and he was resolved, so long as he could dispense a single ray of light, that his countenance should never be averted. It is difficult to contemplate his character, at this period, without being infected with a perhaps dangerous enthusiasm. It is not an easy task coldly to analyse a nature which contained so much of the self-sacrificing and the heroic, as well as of the adroit and the subtle ; and it is almost impossible to give utterance to the emotions which naturally swell the heart at the contemplation of so much active virtue, without rendering oneself liable to the charge of excessive admiration. Through the mists of adversity, a human form may dilate into proportions which are colossal and deceptive. Our judgment may thus, perhaps, be led captive, but at any rate the sentiment excited is more healthful than that inspired by the mere shedder of blood, by the merely selfish conqueror. When the cause of the champion is that of

---

* Correspondance de Philippe II., ii. 786. Archives et Correspondance, iii. 130–136, 144, 145, 214–219.

† Correspondance de Guillaume le Tacit., iii. 1–19. Archives et Correspondance, iii. 130, et sqq.

human right against tyranny, of political and religious freedom against an all-engrossing and absolute bigotry, it is still
more difficult to restrain veneration within legitimate bounds.
To liberate the souls and bodies of millions, to maintain for a
generous people, who had well-nigh lost their all, those free
institutions which their ancestors had bequeathed, was a
noble task for any man.   But here stood a Prince of ancient
race, vast possessions,* imperial blood, one of the great ones
of the earth, whose pathway along the beaten track would
have been smooth and successful, but who was ready to
pour out his wealth like water, and to coin his heart's blood,
drop by drop, in this virtuous but almost desperate cause. He
felt that of a man to whom so much had been entrusted,
much was to be asked.   God had endowed him with an incisive and comprehensive genius, unfaltering fortitude, and
with the rank and fortune which enable a man to employ his
faculties, to the injury or the happiness of his fellows, on the
widest scale.   The Prince felt the responsibility, and the world
was to learn the result.

It was about this time that a deep change came over his
mind. Hitherto, although nominally attached to the communion of the ancient Church, his course of life and habits
of mind had not led him to deal very earnestly with things
beyond the world. The severe duties, the grave character of
the cause to which his days were henceforth to be devoted,
had already led him to a closer inspection of the essential
attributes of Christianity. He was now enrolled for life as a
soldier of the Reformation.†   The Reformation was hence-

---

* "Le Prince d'Orange avait 152,785 florins de revenu: ses charges étaient
de 98,366 florins."—Relation des Revenus des Seigneurs dont les biens ont été
confisqués, 12th Décembre, 1569.—Correspondance de Philippe II., ii. 115.

On his departure from the Netherlands in 1567, he said he had still 60,000
guldens per annum left—net income; and should undertake nothing against the
King, if he did not attack him in his honour and property.—Wagenaer, Vad.
Histor., vi. 228.   Reyd. ı. 1.

† The Prince went into the Reformed worship step by step, and it was not
until the 23rd October, 1573, that he publicly attended communion at a Calvinist meeting, but where ıs not mentioned."—Vide Van Wyn op Wagenaer,
vi. 73, and Van der Wall. Privilegie van Dort, bl. 149, No. 7.

forth his fatherland, the sphere of his duty and his affection. The religious Reformers became his brethren, whether in France, Germany, the Netherlands, or England. Yet his mind had taken a higher flight than that of the most eminent Reformers. His goal was not a new doctrine, but religious liberty. In an age when to think was a crime, and when bigotry and a persecuting spirit characterized Romanists and Lutherans, Calvinists and Zwinglians, he had dared to announce freedom of conscience as the great object for which noble natures should strive. In an age when toleration was a vice, he had the manhood to cultivate it as a virtue. His parting advice to the Reformers of the Netherlands, when he left them for a season in the spring of 1567, was to sink all lesser differences in religious union. Those of the Augsburg Confession and those of the Calvinistic Church, in their own opinion as incapable of commingling as oil and water, were, in his judgment, capable of friendly amalgamation.* He appealed eloquently to the good and influential of all parties to unite in one common cause against oppression. Even while favoring daily more and more the cause of the purified Church, and becoming daily more alive to the corruption of Rome, he was yet willing to tolerate all forms of worship, and to leave reason to combat error.

Without a particle of cant or fanaticism, he had become a deeply religious man. Hitherto he had been only a man of the world and a statesman, but from this time forth he began calmly to rely upon God's providence in all the emergencies of his eventful life. His letters written to his most confidential friends, to be read only by themselves, and which have been gazed upon by no other eyes until after the lapse of nearly three centuries, abundantly prove his sincere and simple trust. This sentiment was not assumed for effect to delude others, but cherished as a secret support for himself. His religion was not a cloak to his designs, but a consolation in his disasters. In his letter of instruction to his

---

* Wagenaer, Vaderl. Hist., vi. 227, 228. Hoofd, iv. 132, 133.

most confidential agent, John Bazius, while he declared himself frankly in favor of the Protestant principles, he expressed his extreme repugnance to the persecution of Catholics. "Should we obtain power over any city or cities," he wrote, "let the communities of papists be as much respected and protected as possible. Let them be overcome, not by violence, but with gentle-mindedness and virtuous treatment."* After the terrible disaster at Jemmingen, he had written to Louis, consoling him, in the most affectionate language, for the unfortunate result of his campaign. Not a word of reproach escaped from him, although his brother had conducted the operations in Friesland, after the battle of Heiliger Lee, in a manner quite contrary to his own advice. He had counselled against a battle, and had foretold a defeat;† but after the battle had been fought and a crushing defeat sustained, his language breathed only unwavering submission to the will of God, and continued confidence in his own courage. "You may be well assured, my brother," he wrote, "that I have never felt anything more keenly than the pitiable misfortune which has happened to you, for many reasons which you can easily imagine. Moreover, it hinders us much in the levy which we are making, and has greatly chilled the hearts of those who otherwise would have been ready to give us assistance. Nevertheless, since it has thus pleased God, it is necessary to have patience and to lose not courage ; conforming ourselves to His divine will, as for my part I have determined to do in everything which may happen, still proceeding onward in our work with his Almighty aid.‡ *Soevis tranquillus in undis,* he was never more placid than when the storm was wildest and the night darkest. He drew his consolations and refreshed his courage at the never-failing fountains of Divine mercy.

"I go to-morrow," he wrote to the unworthy Anne of Saxony ; "but when I shall return, or when I shall see you, I cannot, on my honor, tell you with certainty. I have resolved to place myself in the hands of the Almighty, that he may

---

* "Sacht moedigheyt ende deuchtsamkeit."—Archives, etc., iii. 196–200.

† Archives et Correspondance, etc., 257–261.   ‡ Ibid., iii. 276.

guide me whither it is His good pleasure that I should go. *I see well enough that I am destined to pass this life in misery and labor, with which I am well content, since it thus pleases the Omnipotent,* for I know that I have merited still greater chastisement. I only implore Him graciously to send me strength to endure with patience."*

Such language, in letters the most private, never meant to be seen by other eyes than those to which they were addressed, gives touching testimony to the sincere piety of his character. No man was ever more devoted to a high purpose, no man had ever more right to imagine himself, or less inclination to pronounce himself, entrusted with a divine mission. There was nothing of the charlatan in his character. His nature was true and steadfast. No narrow-minded usurper was ever more loyal to his own aggrandisement than this large-hearted man to the cause of oppressed humanity. Yet it was inevitable that baser minds should fail to recognise his purity. While he exhausted his life for the emancipation of a people, it was easy to ascribe all his struggles to the hope of founding a dynasty. It was natural for grovelling natures to search in the gross soil of self-interest for the sustaining roots of the tree beneath whose branches a nation found its shelter. What could they comprehend of living fountains and of heavenly dews ?

In May, 1568, the Emperor Maximilian had formally issued a requisition to the Prince of Orange to lay down his arms, and to desist from all levies and machinations against the King of Spain and the peace of the realm. This summons he was commanded to obey on pain of forfeiting all rights, fiefs, privileges and endowments bestowed by imperial hands on himself or his predecessors, and of incurring the heaviest disgrace, punishment, and penalties of the Empire.†

To this document the Prince replied in August, having paid in the meantime but little heed to its precepts. Now that

---

* Archives, etc., de la maison d'Orange Nassau, iii. 327–331.

† See the letter in Gachard, Correspondance de Guillaume le Tacit., iii. 1–5.

the Emperor, who at first was benignant, had begun to frown
on his undertaking, he did not slacken in his own endeavours
to set his army on foot. One by one, those among the princes
of the empire who had been most stanch in his cause, and
were still most friendly to his person, grew colder as tyranny
became stronger ; but the ardor of the Prince was not more
chilled by their despair than by the overthrow at Jemmingen,
which had been its cause. In August, he answered the letter
of the Emperor, respectfully but warmly. He still denounced
the tyranny of Alva and the arts of Granvelle with that
vigorous eloquence which was always at his command, while,
as usual, he maintained a show of almost exaggerated respect
for their monarch. It was not to be presumed, he said, that
his Majesty, "a king debonair and bountiful," had ever intended such cruelties as those which had been rapidly retraced
in the letter, but it was certain that the Duke of Alva had
committed them all of his own authority. He trusted,
moreover, that the Emperor, after he had read the "Justification" which the Prince had recently published, would appreciate the reason for his taking up arms. He hoped that his
Majesty would now consider the resistance just, Christian,
and conformable to the public peace. He expressed the belief
that rather than interpose any hindrance, his Majesty would
thenceforth rather render assistance " to the poor and desolate
Christians," even as it was his Majesty's office and authority
to be the last refuge of the injured.*

The "Justification against the false blame of his calum-
niators by the Prince of Orange," to which the Prince thus
referred, has been mentioned in a previous chapter. This
remarkable paper had been drawn up at the advice of his
friends, Landgrave William and Elector Augustus,† but it
was not the only document which the Prince caused to
be published at this important epoch. He issued a formal
declaration of war against the Duke of Alva ; he addressed a

---

* See the letter in Gachard, Correspondance de Guillaume le Tacit., iii. 5–19.

† Archives, etc., de la maison d'Orange, iii. 183–186.

solemn and eloquent warning or proclamation to all the inhabitants of the Netherlands.* These documents are all extremely important and interesting. Their phraseology shows the intentions and the spirit by which the Prince was actuated on first engaging in the struggle. Without the Prince and his efforts at this juncture, there would probably have never been a free Netherland commonwealth. It is certain, likewise, that without an enthusiastic passion for civil and religious liberty throughout the masses of the Netherland people, there would have been no successful effort on the part of the Prince. He knew his countrymen ; while they, from highest to humblest, recognised in him their saviour. There was, however, no pretence of a revolutionary movement. The Prince came to maintain, not to overthrow. The freedom which had been enjoyed in the provinces until the accession of the Burgundian dynasty, it was his purpose to restore. The attitude which he now assumed was a peculiar one in history. This defender of a people's cause set up no revolutionary standard. In all his documents he paid apparent reverence to the authority of the King. By a fiction, which was not unphilosophical, he assumed that the monarch was incapable of the crimes which he charged upon the Viceroy. Thus he did not assume the character of a rebel in arms against his prince, but in his own capacity of sovereign he levied troops and waged war against a satrap whom he chose to consider false to his master's orders. In the interest of Philip, assumed to be identical with the welfare of his people, he took up arms against the tyrant who was sacrificing both. This mask of loyalty would never save his head from the block, as he well knew, but some spirits lofty as his own, might perhaps be influenced by a noble sophistry, which sought to strengthen the cause of the people by attributing virtue to the King.

And thus did the sovereign of an insignificant little principality stand boldly forth to do battle with the most powerful monarch in the world. At his own expense, and by almost

---

* The Declaration is published in Bor, iv. 253–254.

superhuman exertions, he had assembled nearly thirty thousand men. He now boldly proclaimed to the world, and especially to the inhabitants of the provinces, his motives, his purposes, and his hopes.

"We, by God's grace Prince of Orange," said his declaration of 31st August, 1568, "salute all faithful subjects of his Majesty. To few people is it unknown that the Spaniards have for a long time sought to govern the land according to their pleasure. Abusing his Majesty's goodness, they have persuaded him to decree the introduction of the inquisition into the Netherlands. They well understood, that in case the Netherlanders could be made to tolerate its exercise, they would lose all protection to their liberty ; that if they opposed its introduction, they would open those rich provinces as a vast field of plunder. We had hoped that his Majesty, taking the matter to heart, would have spared his hereditary provinces from such utter ruin. We have found our hopes futile. We are unable, by reason of our loyal service due to his Majesty, and of our true compassion for the faithful lieges, to look with tranquillity any longer at such murders, robberies, outrages, and agony. We are, moreover, certain that his Majesty has been badly informed upon Netherland matters. We take up arms, therefore, to oppose the violent tyranny of the Spaniards, by the help of the merciful God, who is the enemy of all blood-thirstiness. Cheerfully inclined to wager our life and all our worldly wealth on the cause, we have now, God be thanked, an excellent army of cavalry, infantry, and artillery, raised all at our own expense. We summon all loyal subjects of the Netherlands to come and help us. Let them take to heart the uttermost need of the country, the danger of perpetual slavery for themselves and their children, and of the entire overthrow of the Evangelical religion. Only when Alva's blood-thirstiness shall have been at last overpowered, can the provinces hope to recover their pure administration of justice, and a prosperous condition for their commonwealth."*

---

* Bor, iv. 253, 254.

In the "warning" or proclamation to all the inhabitants of the Netherlands, the Prince expressed similar sentiments. He announced his intention of expelling the Spaniards forever from the country. To accomplish the mighty undertaking, money was necessary. He accordingly called on his countrymen to contribute, the rich out of their abundance, the poor even out of their poverty, to the furtherance of the cause. To do this, while it was yet time, he solemnly warned them "before God, the fatherland, and the world." After the title of this paper were cited the 28th, 29th, and 30th verses of the tenth chapter of Proverbs. The favorite motto of the Prince, "*pro lege, rege, grege,*" was also affixed to the document.[*]

These appeals had, however, but little effect. Of three hundred thousand crowns, promised on behalf of leading nobles and merchants of the Netherlands by Marcus Perez, but ten or twelve thousand came to hand.[†] The appeals to the gentlemen who had signed the Compromise, and to many others who had, in times past, been favorable to the liberal party were powerless. A poor Anabaptist preacher collected a small sum from a refugee congregation on the outskirts of Holland, and brought it, at the peril of his life, into the Prince's camp. It came from people, he said, whose will was better than the gift. They never wished to be repaid, he said, except by kindness, when the cause of reform should be triumphant in the Netherlands. The Prince signed a receipt for the money, expressing himself touched by this sympathy from these poor outcasts.[‡] In the course of time, other contributions from similar sources, principally collected by dissenting preachers, starving and persecuted church communities, were received.[§] The poverty-stricken exiles contri-

---

[*] The "Waarschouwing" is published in full in the Byvoegsel van Authentik. Stuk., tot P. Bor, Hist., 121-123.

[†] Bor, iv. 251, 252.   Hoofd, v. 183.

[‡] Brandt, Hist. der Reformatie, i. 526.   Letter of P. W. Boomgaerdt to C. P. Hoofd, 7th August, 1606.   [§] Brandt, i. 516.

buted far more, in proportion, for the establishment of civil and religious liberty, than the wealthy merchants or the haughty nobles.*

Late in September, the Prince mustered his army in the province of Treves, near the monastery of Romersdorf.† His force amounted to nearly thirty thousand men, of whom nine thousand were cavalry.‡ Lumey, Count de la Marck, now joined him at the head of a picked band of troopers ; a bold, ferocious partisan, descended from the celebrated Wild Boar of Ardennes. Like Civilis, the ancient Batavian hero, he had sworn to leave hair and beard unshorn till the liberation of the country was achieved, or at least till the death of Egmont, whose blood relation he was, had been avenged.§ It is probable that the fierce conduct of this chieftain, and particularly the cruelties exercised upon monks and papists‖ by his troops, dishonored the cause more than their valor could advance it. But in those stormy times such rude but incisive instruments were scarcely to be neglected, and the name of Lumey was to be forever associated with the earliest and most important triumphs of the liberal cause.

It was fated, however, that but few laurels should be won by the patriots in this campaign. The Prince crossed the Rhine at Saint Feit, a village belonging to himself.¶ He descended along the banks as far as the neighbourhood of Cologne. Then, after hovering in apparent uncertainty about the territories of Juliers and Limburg, he suddenly, on a bright moonlight night, crossed the Meuse with his whole army, in the neighbourhood of Stochem.** The operation was

---

* Bor, v. 312.   † Hoofd, v. 183.

‡ Hoofd, v. 183.—Compare Strada, vii. 338; Bentivoglio, v. 77, 78; Wagenaer, vi. 286; Grot. Ann., i. 32; Meteren, ii. 55.

§ Bor, iv. 256.   Strada, l. vii. 338.   Wagenaer, Vaderl. Hist. vi. 286.

‖ Bor, iv. 256.   Hoofd, v. 183.

¶ Bor, iv. 256.   Wagenaer, Vaderl. Hist., vi. 286.   Meteren, 55.

** "Relation de l'Expédition du Prince d'Orange en 1568," by the Secretary of State, Courteville, who accompanied the Duke of Alva during the campaign; in Gachard, Correspondance de Guillaume le Tacit., iii. 319-337.

brilliantly effected. A compact body of cavalry, according to the plan which had been more than once adopted by Julius Cæsar, was placed in the midst of the current, under which shelter the whole army successfully forded the river.* The Meuse was more shallow than usual, but the water was as high as the soldiers' necks. This feat was accomplished on the night and morning of the 4th and 5th of October. It was considered so bold an achievement that its fame spread far and wide. The Spaniards began to tremble at the prowess of a Prince whom they had affected to despise. The very fact of the passage was flatly contradicted. An unfortunate burgher at Amsterdam was scourged at the whipping-post, because he mentioned it as matter of common report.† The Duke of Alva refused to credit the tale when it was announced to him. "Is the army of the Prince of Orange a flock of wild geese," he asked, "that it can fly over rivers like the Meuse?"‡ Nevertheless it was true. The outlawed, exiled Prince stood once more on the borders of Brabant, with an army of disciplined troops at his back. His banners bore patriotic inscriptions. " Pro Lege, Rege, Grege," was emblazoned upon some. A pelican tearing her breast to nourish her young with her life-blood was the pathetic emblem of others.§ It was his determination to force or entice the Duke of Alva into a general engagement. He was desirous to wipe out the disgrace of Jemmingen. Could he plant his victorious standard thus in the very heart of the country, he felt that thousands would rally around it. The country would rise almost to a man, could he achieve a victory over the tyrant, flushed as he was with victory, and sated with blood.

With banners flying, drums beating, trumpets sounding, with all the pomp and defiance which an already victorious general could assume, Orange marched into Brabant, and took up a position within six thousand paces of Alva's encampment. His

---

* Hoofd, v. 185.   Meteren, f. 56.   † Hoofd, v. 185.
‡ Ibid., v. 185.   Strada, liv. vii. 340.
§ Bor, iv. 255.   Hoofd. v. 184.

plan was at every hazard to dare or to decoy his adversary into the chances of a stricken field. The Governor was entrenched at a place called Keiserslager, which Julius Cæsar had once occupied. The city of Maestricht was in his immediate neighbourhood, which was thus completely under his protection, while it furnished him with supplies.* The Prince sent to the Duke a herald, who was to propose that all prisoners who might be taken in the coming campaign should be exchanged instead of being executed.† The herald, booted and spurred, even as he had dismounted from his horse, was instantly hanged.‡ This was the significant answer to the mission of mercy. Alva held no parley with rebels before a battle, nor gave quarter afterwards.

In the meantime, the Duke had carefully studied the whole position of affairs, and had arrived at his conclusion. He was determined not to fight. It was obvious that the Prince would offer battle eagerly, ostentatiously, frequently, but the Governor was resolved never to accept the combat. Once taken, his resolution was unalterable. He recognized the important difference between his own attitude at present, and that in which he had found himself during the past summer in Friesland. There a battle had been necessary, now it was more expedient to overcome his enemy by delay. In Friesland, the rebels had just achieved a victory over the choice troops of Spain. Here they were suffering from the stigma of a crushing defeat. Then, the army of Louis Nassau was swelling daily by recruits, who poured in from all the country round. Now, neither peasant nor noble dared lift a finger for the Prince. The army of Louis had been sustained by the one which his brother was known to be preparing. If their movements had not been checked, a junction would have been effected. The armed revolt would then have assumed so

---

* Bor, iv. 255. Meteren, 56. Hoofd, iv. 185.

† "Aqui llegò un trompeta cò una carta, que algunos dixerò que era del Principe d'Orange, en que pedia, que no matassen los prisioneros que se tomassen en esta guerra," etc.—Herrera, lib. xv. c. xi. 701.

‡ Mendoza, 78. Meteren, 56.

formidable an aspect, that rebellion would seem, even for the timid, a safer choice than loyalty. The army of the Prince, on the contrary, was now the last hope of the patriots. The three by which it had been preceded had been successively and signally vanquished.*

Friesland, again, was on the outskirts of the country. A defeat sustained by the government there did not necessarily imperil the possession of the provinces. Brabant, on the contrary, was the heart of the Netherlands. Should the Prince achieve a decisive triumph then and there, he would be master of the nation's fate. The Viceroy knew himself to be odious, and he reigned by terror. The Prince was the object of the people's idolatry, and they would rally round him if they dared. A victory gained by the liberator over the tyrant, would destroy the terrible talisman of invincibility by which Alva governed. The Duke had sufficiently demonstrated his audacity in the tremendous chastisement which he had inflicted upon the rebels under Louis. He could now afford to play that scientific game of which he was so profound a master, without risking any loss of respect or authority. He was no enthusiast. Although he doubtless felt sufficiently confident of overcoming the Prince in a pitched battle, he had not sufficient relish for the joys of contest to be willing to risk even a remote possibility of defeat. His force, although composed of veterans and of the best musketeers and pikemen in Europe, was still somewhat inferior in numbers to that of his adversary. Against the twenty thousand foot and eight thousand horse of Orange, he could oppose only fifteen or sixteen thousand foot and fifty-five hundred riders.† Moreover, the advantage which he had possessed in Friesland, a country only favorable to infantry, in which he had been stronger than his opponent, was now transferred to his new enemy. On the plains of Brabant,

---

* Relation du Secrétaire Courteville. Guillaume le Tacit., iii. 323–326. V. d. Vynckt, ii. 113, 114. Bor, iv. 256, 257. Hoofd, v. 186.

† Strada, lib. vii. 338. Mendoza, f. 77. V. d. Vynckt, ii. 113.—Compare Hoofd, v. 186. Meteren, 56. Bentivoglio, lib. v. 77, 78.

the Prince's superiority in cavalry was sure to tell. The season of the year, too, was an important element in the calculation. The winter alone would soon disperse the bands of German mercenaries, whose expenses Orange was not able to support, even while in active service. With unpaid wages and disappointed hopes of plunder, the rebel army would disappear in a few weeks as totally as if defeated in the open field. In brief, Orange by a victory would gain new life and strength, while his defeat could no more than anticipate, by a few weeks, the destruction of his army, already inevitable. Alva, on the contrary, might lose the mastery of the Netherlands if unfortunate, and would gain no solid advantage if triumphant. The Prince had everything to hope, the Duke everything to fear, from the result of a general action.*

The plan, thus deliberately resolved upon, was accomplished with faultless accuracy. As a work of art, the present campaign of Alva against Orange was a more consummate masterpiece than the more brilliant and dashing expedition into Friesland. The Duke had resolved to hang upon his adversary's skirts, to follow him move by move, to check him at every turn, to harass him in a hundred ways, to foil all his enterprises, to parry all his strokes, and finally to drive him out of the country, after a totally barren campaign, when, as he felt certain, his ill-paid hirelings would vanish in all directions, and leave their patriot Prince a helpless and penniless adventurer. The scheme thus sagaciously conceived, his adversary, with all his efforts, was unable to circumvent.

The campaign lasted little more than a month. Twenty-nine times the Prince changed his encampment,† and at every remove the Duke was still behind him, as close and seemingly as impalpable as his shadow. Thrice they were within cannon-shot of each other, twice without a single trench or rampart between them.‡ The country people refused the Prince sup-

---

* Bor. iv. 256.   Hoofd.   V. d. Vynckt.   Courteville.   Meteren, ubi sup.

† V. d. Vynckt, ii. 114.   Strada, vii. 346.

† Hoofd, v. 187.   Letter of Duke of Alva to the Council of State from Cateau Cambresis, 22d November, 1568, in Bor. iv. 257.   Correspondance de Philippe II., ii. 808.

plies, for they trembled at the vengeance of the Governor.
Alva had caused the irons to be removed from all the mills, so
that not a bushel of corn could be ground in the whole province.* The country thus afforded but little forage for the
thirty thousand soldiers of the Prince. The troops, already
discontented, were clamorous for pay and plunder. During
one mutinous demonstration, the Prince's sword was shot
from his side, and it was with difficulty that a general outbreak was suppressed.† The soldiery were maddened and
tantalized by the tactics of Alva. They found themselves
constantly in the presence of an enemy, who seemed to court
a battle at one moment and to vanish like a phantom at the
next. They felt the winter approaching, and became daily
more dissatisfied with the irritating hardships to which they
were exposed. Upon the night of the 5th and 6th of October
the Prince had crossed the Meuse at Stochem.‡ Thence he
had proceeded to Tongres, followed closely by the enemy's
force, who encamped in the immediate neighbourhood. From
Tongres he had moved to Saint Trond, still pursued and still
baffled in the same cautious manner. The skirmishing at the
outposts was incessant, but the main body was withdrawn as
soon as there seemed a chance of its becoming involved.

From Saint Trond, in the neighbourhood of which he had
remained several days, he advanced in a southerly direction
towards Jodoigne. Count de Genlis, with a reinforcement
of French Huguenots, for which the Prince had been waiting,
had penetrated through the Ardennes, crossed the Meuse at
Charlemont, and was now intending a junction with him at
Waveron.§ The river Geta flowed between them. The Prince
stationed a considerable force upon a hill near the stream to protect the passage, and then proceeded leisurely to send his army
across the river. Count Hoogstraaten, with the rear-guard,

---

* Bor, iv. 256. Hoofd, v. 186.   † Strada, lib. vii. 342.

‡ Hoofd, v. 185. Courteville, 323. Compare Mendoza, f. 79. Wagenaer,
vi. 288.

§ Relation de Courtville, 327–329. Meteren, 56. Mendoza, 87. 88.

consisting of about three thousand men, were alone left upon the hither bank, in order to provoke or to tempt the enemy, who, as usual, was encamped very near. Alva refused to attack the main army, but rapidly detached his son, Don Frederic, with a force of four thousand foot and three thousand horse, to cut off the rear-guard. The movement was effected in a masterly manner, the hill was taken, the three thousand troops which had not passed the river were cut to pieces, and Vitelli hastily despatched a gentleman named Barberini to implore the Duke to advance with the main body, cross the river, and, once for all, exterminate the rebels in a general combat. Alva, inflamed, not with ardor for an impending triumph, but with rage, that his sagely-conceived plans could not be comprehended even by his son and by his favorite officers, answered the eager messenger with peremptory violence. "Go back to Vitelli," he cried. "Is he, or am I, to command in this campaign? Tell him not to suffer a single man to cross the river. Warn him against sending any more envoys to advise a battle; for should you or any other man dare to bring me another such message, I swear to you, by the head of the King, that you go not hence alive."*

With this decisive answer the messenger had nothing for it but to gallop back with all haste, in order to participate in what might be left of the butchery of Count Hoogstraaten's force, and to prevent Vitelli and Don Frederic in their ill-timed ardor, from crossing the river. This was properly effected, while in the meantime the whole rear-guard of the patriots had been slaughtered. A hundred or two, the last who remained, had made their escape from the field, and had taken refuge in a house in the neighbourhood. The Spaniards set the buildings on fire, and standing around with lifted lances, offered the fugitives the choice of being consumed in the flames or of springing out upon their spears. Thus entrapped some chose the one course, some the other. A few, to escape the fury of the fire and the brutality of the Spaniards, stabbed themselves

---

* Strada, lib. vii. 344.

with their own swords. Others embraced, and then killed each other, the enemies from below looking on, as at a theatrical exhibition ; now hissing and now applauding, as the death struggles were more or less to their taste.* In a few minutes all the fugitives were dead. Nearly three thousand of the patriots were slain in this combat, including those burned or butchered after the battle was over.† The Sieur de Louverwal was taken prisoner, and soon afterwards beheaded in Brussels ; but the greatest misfortune sustained by the liberal party upon this occasion was the death of Antony de Lalaing, Count of Hoogstraaten. This brave and generous nobleman, the tried friend of the Prince of Orange, and his colleague during the memorable scenes at Antwerp, was wounded in the foot during the action, by an accidental discharge of his own pistol. The injury, although apparently slight, caused his death in a few days.‡ There seemed a strange coincidence in his good and evil fortunes. A casual wound in the hand from his own pistol while he was on his way to Brussels, to greet Alva upon his first arrival, had saved him from the scaffold. And now in his first pitched battle with the Duke, this seemingly trifling injury in the foot was destined to terminate his existence. Another peculiar circumstance had marked the event. At a gay supper in the course of this campaign, Hoogstraaten had teased Count Louis, in a rough, soldierly way, with his disaster at Jemmingen. He had affected to believe that the retreat upon that occasion had been unnecessary. " We have been now many days in the Netherlands," said he, " and we have seen nothing of the Spaniards but their backs." " And when the Duke does break loose," replied Louis, somewhat nettled, " I warrant you will see their faces soon enough, and remember them for the rest of your life."§ The half-jesting remark was thus destined to become a gloomy prophecy.

---

* Strada, lib. vii. 345.

† Mendoza, 88–92. Bor. iv. 256, 257. Relation de Courteville, etc., 329–331.

‡ Hoofd, v. 187. Mendoza, 88–92. § Ibid., 92.

This was the only important action during the campaign. Its perfect success did not warp Alva's purpose, and, notwithstanding the murmurs of many of his officers, he remained firm in his resolution. After the termination of the battle on the Geta, and the Duke's obstinate refusal to pursue his advantage, the Baron de Chevreau dashed his pistol to the ground, in his presence, exclaiming that the Duke would never fight.[*] The Governor smiled at the young man's chagrin, seemed even to approve his enthusiasm, but reminded him that it was the business of an officer to fight, of a general to conquer. If the victory were bloodless, so much the better for all.[†]

This action was fought on the 20th of October. A few days afterwards, the Prince made his junction with Genlis at Waveren, a place about three leagues from Louvain and from Brussels.[‡] This auxiliary force was, however, insignificant. There were only five hundred cavalry and three thousand foot, but so many women and children, that it seemed rather an emigrating colony than an invading army.[§] They arrived late. If they had come earlier, it would have been of little consequence, for it had been written that no laurels were to be gathered in that campaign. The fraternal spirit which existted between the Reformers in all countries was all which could be manifested upon the occasion. The Prince was frustrated in his hopes of a general battle, still more bitterly disappointed by the supineness of the country. Not a voice was raised to welcome the deliverer. Not a single city opened its gates. All was crouching, silent, abject. The rising, which perhaps would have been universal had a brilliant victory been obtained, was, by the masterly tactics of Alva, rendered an almost inconceivable idea. The mutinous demonstrations in the Prince's camp became incessant ; the soldiers were discontented and weary. What the Duke had foretold was coming to pass, for the Prince's army was already dissolving.

---

* Hoofd, v. 187.   Mendoza, 90.   † Ibid., ibid.
‡ Relation de Courteville, etc., 332, 333.
§ Ibid., 331

Genlis and the other French officers were desirous that the Prince should abandon the Netherlands for the present, and come to the rescue of the Huguenots, who had again renewed the religious war under Condé and Coligny.* The German soldiers, however, would listen to no such proposal. They had enlisted to fight the Duke of Alva in the Netherlands, and would not hear of making war against Charles IX. in France.† The Prince was obliged to countermarch towards the Rhine. He recrossed the Geta, somewhat to Alva's astonishment,‡ and proceeded in the direction of the Meuse. The autumn rains, however, had much swollen that river since his passage at the beginning of the month, so that it could no longer be forded. He approached the city of Liege, and summoned their Bishop, as he had done on his entrance into the country, to grant a free passage to his troops. The Bishop who stood in awe of Alva, and who had accepted his protection again refused.§ The Prince had no time to parley. He was again obliged to countermarch, and took his way along the high road to France, still watched and closely pursued by Alva, between whose troops and his own daily skirmishes took place. At Le Quesnoy, the Prince gained a trifling advantage over the Spaniards ; at Cateau Cambresis he also obtained a slight and easy victory ; but by the 17th of November the Duke of Alva had entered Cateau Cambresis, and the Prince had crossed the frontier of France.‖

The Maréchal de Cossé, who was stationed on the boundary of France and Flanders, now harassed the Prince by very similar tactics to those of Alva.¶ He was, however, too weak to inflict any serious damage, although strong enough to create perpetual annoyance. He also sent a secretary to the Prince,

---

* Bor, iv. 256, 227. Archives et Correspondance, iii. 303–310.

† Bor, ubi sup. Archives et Correspondance, ubi sup.

‡ Courteville, Relation, etc., 333

§ Gachard, Correspondance de Guillaume le Tacit., iii. 19–34, and 338–366.

‖ Courteville, Relation, etc., 333, et seq. Bor, iv. 256, 257. Mendoza, 92–98.

¶ Bor, iv. 257. Hoofd. v· 188* De Thou, v. 467–472.

with a formal prohibition, in the name of Charles IX., against his entering the French territory with his troops.*

Besides these negotiations, conducted by Secretary Favelles on the part of Maréchal de Cossé, the King, who was excessively alarmed, also despatched the Maréchal Gaspar de Schomberg on the same service. That envoy accordingly addressed to the Prince a formal remonstrance in the name of his sovereign. Charles IX., it was represented, found it very strange that the Prince should thus enter the French territory. The King was not aware that he had ever given him the least cause for hostile proceedings, could not therefore take it in good part that the Prince should thus enter France with a "large and puissant army ;" because no potentate, however humble, could tolerate such a proceeding, much less a great and powerful monarch. Orange was therefore summoned to declare his intentions, but was at the same time informed, that if he merely desired " to pass amiably through the country," and would give assurance, and request permission to that effect, under his hand and seal, his Majesty would take all necessary measures to secure that amiable passage.†

The Prince replied by a reference to the statements which he had already made to Maréchal de Cossé. He averred that he had not entered France with evil intent, but rather with a desire to render very humble service to his Majesty, so far as he could do so with a clear conscience.

Touching the King's inability to remember having given any occasion to hostile proceedings on the part of the Prince, he replied that he would pass that matter by. Although he could adduce many, various, and strong reasons for violent measures, he was not so devoid of understanding as not to recognize the futility of attempting anything, by his own personal means, against so great and powerful a King, in comparison with whom he was "but a petty companion."

" Since the true religion," continued Orange, " is a public

* Groen v. Prinst., Archives, etc., iii. 313, 314.

† Pièces concernant les Troubles des Pays Bas, Coll. Gerard. b. 95. Archives of the Hague MS. 360, 361.

and general affair, which ought to be preferred to all private matters ; since the Prince, as a true Christian, is held by his honor and conscience to procure, with all his strength, its advancement and establishment in every place whatever ; since, on the other hand, according to the edict published in September last by his Majesty, attempts have been made to force in their consciences all those who are of the Christian religion ; and since it has been determined to exterminate the pure word of God, and the entire exercise thereof, and to permit no other religion than the Roman Catholic, a thing very prejudicial to the neighbouring nations where there is a free exercise of the Christian religion, therefore the Prince would put no faith in the assertions of his Majesty, that it was not his Majesty's intentions to force the consciences of any one."

Having given this very deliberate and succinct contradiction to the statements of the French King, the Prince proceeded to express his sympathy for the oppressed Christians everywhere. He protested that he would give them all the aid, comfort, counsel, and assistance that he was able to give them. He asserted his conviction that the men who professed "the religion" demanded nothing else than the glory of God and the advancement of His word, while in all matters of civil polity they were ready to render obedience to his Majesty. He added that all his doings were governed by a Christian and affectionate regard for the King and his subjects, whom his Majesty must be desirous of preserving from extreme ruin. He averred, moreover, that if he should perceive any indication that those of the religion were pursuing any other object than liberty of conscience and security for life and property, he would not only withdraw his assistance from them, but would use the whole strength of his army to exterminate them. In conclusion, he begged the King to believe that the work which the Prince had undertaken was a Christian work, and that his intentions were good and friendly towards his Majesty.[*]

---

[*] This very eloquently written letter was dated Cissonne, December 3rd, 1568. It has never been published. It is in the Collection of MSS. last cited (Pièces concernant, etc.), Hague Archives.

It was, however, in vain that the Prince endeavoured to induce his army to try the fortunes of the civil war in France. They had enlisted for the Netherlands, the campaign was over, and they insisted upon being led back to Germany.* Schomberg, secretly instructed by the King of France, was active in fomenting the discontent,† and the Prince was forced to yield. He led his army through Champagne and Lorraine to Strasburg, where they were disbanded.‡ All the money which the Prince had been able to collect was paid them. He pawned all his camp equipage, his plate, his furniture.§ What he could not pay in money he made up in promises, sacredly to be fulfilled, when he should be restored to his possessions. He even solemnly engaged, should he return from France alive, and be still unable to pay their arrears of wages, to surrender his person to them as a hostage for his debt.||

Thus triumphantly for Alva, thus miserably for Orange, ended the campaign. Thus hopelessly vanished the army to which so many proud hopes had attached themselves. Eight thousand men had been slain in paltry encounters,¶ thirty thousand were dispersed, not easily to be again collected. All the funds which the Prince could command had been wasted without producing a result. For the present, nothing seemed to afford a ground of hope for the Netherlands, but the war of freedom had been renewed in France. A band of twelve hundred mounted men-at-arms were willing to follow the fortunes of the Prince. The three brothers accordingly, William, Louis, and Henry—a lad of eighteen, who had abandoned his studies at the university to obey the chivalrous instincts of his race—set forth early in the following spring to join the banner of Condé.**

---

* Meteren, 56.   † De Thou, Hoofd.   ‡ Bor, iv. 257. Hoofd, v. 188.

§ Hoofd, v. 188. || Archives, etc., de la maison d'Orange, iii. 334–338, 355–360.

¶ Letter of Alva from Cateau Cambresis, in Bor, iv. 257. Mendoza, 98, 99, says 5000. Herrera (part i. lib. xv. cap. xii. p. 705) says 6000. All writers agree that the Duke sustained absolutely no loss throughout the campaign. Compare Herrera, lib. xiv. cap. xi. and xii. p. 700–706; and Cabrera, lib. viii. cap. viii. and ix. 505–513.

** Hoofd, v. 188. Langueti, Ep. Secret, i. 117. Groen v. Prinst., Archives etc., iii. 323. Meteren, 57.

Cardinal Granvelle, who had never taken his eyes or thoughts from the provinces during his residence at Rome, now expressed himself with exultation. He had predicted, with cold malice, the immediate results of the campaign, and was sanguine enough to believe the contest over, and the Prince for ever crushed. In his letters to Philip he had taken due notice of the compliments paid to him by Orange in his Justification, in his Declaration, and in his letter to the Emperor. He had declined to make any answer to the charges, in order to enrage the Prince the more. He had expressed the opinion, however, that this publication of writings was not the business of brave soldiers, but of cowards.* He made the same reflection upon the alleged intrigues by Orange to procure an embassy on his own behalf from the Emperor to Philip—a mission which was sure to end in smoke, while it would cost the Prince all credit, not only in Germany but the Netherlands.† He felt sure, he said, of the results of the impending campaign. The Duke of Alva was a man upon whose administrative prudence and military skill his sovereign could implicitly rely, nor was there a person in the ranks of the rebels capable of conducting an enterprise of such moment.‡ Least of all had the Prince of Orange sufficient brains for carrying on such weighty affairs, according to the opinion which he had formed of him during their long intercourse in former days.§

When the campaign had been decided, and the Prince had again become an exile, Granvelle observed that it was now proved how incompetent he and all his companions were to contend in military skill with the Duke of Alva.‖ With a cold sneer at motives which he assumed, as a matter of course, to be purely selfish, he said that the Prince had not taken the proper road to recover his property, and that he would now be much embarrassed to satisfy his creditors.¶ Thus must those ever fall, he moralized, who would fly higher than they ought ; adding, that henceforth the Prince would have enough

---

* Correspondance de Philippe II., ii. 795.   † Ibid.
‡ Ibid., ii. 792.   § Ibid.   ‖ Ibid., ii. 812.   ¶ Ibid.

to do in taking care of madam his wife, if she did not change soon in humor and character.*

Meantime the Duke of Alva, having despatched from Cateau Cambresis a brief account of the victorious termination of the campaign, returned in triumph to Brussels.† He had certainly amply vindicated his claim to be considered the first warrior of the age. By his lieutenants he had summarily and rapidly destroyed two of the armies sent against him ; he had annihilated in person the third, by a brilliantly successful battle, in which he had lost seven men, and his enemies seven thousand ; and he had now, by consummate strategy, foiled the fourth and last under the idolized champion of the Netherlands, and this so decisively that, without losing a man, he had destroyed eight thousand rebels, and scattered to the four winds the remaining twenty thousand. Such signal results might well make even a meeker nature proud. Such vast and fortunate efforts to fix for ever an impregnable military tyranny upon a constitutional country, might cause a more modest despot to exult. It was not wonderful that the haughty, and now apparently omnipotent Alva, should almost assume the god. On his return to Brussels he instituted a succession of triumphant festivals.‡ The people were called upon to rejoice and to be exceeding glad, to strew flowers in his path, to sing Hosannas in his praise who came to them covered with the blood of those who had striven in their defence. The holiday was duly culled forth ; houses, where funeral hatchments for murdered inmates had been perpetually suspended, were decked with garlands ; the bells, which had hardly once omitted their daily knell for the victims of an incredible cruelty, now rang their merriest peals ; and in the very square where so lately Egmont and Horn, besides many other less distinguished martyrs, had suffered an ignominious death, a gay tournament§ was held, day after day, with all

---

* Correspondance de Philippe II., ii. 812.

† Bor, iv. 257.　　Correspondance de Philippe II., ii. 808.

‡ Bor, iv. 257.

§ Ibid.

the insolent pomp which could make the exhibition most galling.

But even these demonstrations of hilarity were not sufficient. The conqueror and tamer of the Netherlands felt that a more personal and palpable deification was necessary for his pride. When Germanicus had achieved his last triumph over the ancient freedom of those generous races whose descendants, but lately in possession of a better organized liberty, Alva had been sent by the second and the worse Tiberius to insult and to crush, the valiant but modest Roman erected his trophy upon the plains of Idistavisus. " The army of Tiberius Cæsar having subdued the nations between the Rhine and the Elbe, dedicate this monument to Mars, to Jupiter, and to Augustus." * So ran the inscription of Germanicus, without a word of allusion to his own name. The Duke of Alva, on his return from the battle-fields of Brabant and Friesland, reared a colossal statue of himself, and upon its pedestal caused these lines to be engraved : " To Ferdinand Alvarez de Toledo, Duke of Alva, Governor of the Netherlands under Philip the Second, for having extinguished sedition, chastised rebellion, restored religion, secured justice, established peace ; to the King's most faithful minister this monument is erected."†

So pompous a eulogy, even if truthful and merited, would be sufficiently inflated upon a tombstone raised to a dead chieftain by his bereaved admirers. What shall we say of such false and fulsome tribute, not to a god, not to the memory of departed greatness, but to a living, mortal man, and offered not by his adorers but by himself ? Certainly, self-worship never went farther than in this remarkable monument, erected in Alva's honor, by Alva's hands. The statue was colossal, and was placed in the citadel of Antwerp. Its bronze was furnished by the cannon captured at Jemmingen.‡ It repre-

---

* Tacit. Ann., lib. iv.

† Bor, iv. 257, 258. Meteren, 61. De Thou, v. 471–473, who saw it after it was overthrown, and who was "as much struck by the beauty of the work as by the insane pride of him who ordered it to be made."

‡ Bor, iv. 257. Meteren, 61.

sented the Duke trampling upon a prostrate figure with two heads, four arms, and one body. The two heads were interpreted by some to represent Egmont and Horn, by others, the two Nassaus, William and Louis. Others saw in them an allegorical presentment of the nobles and commons of the Netherlands, or perhaps an impersonation of the Compromise and the Request. Besides the chief inscription on the pedestal, were sculptured various bas-reliefs; and the spectator, whose admiration for the Governor-general was not satiated with the colossal statue itself, was at liberty to find a fresh personification of the hero, either in a torch-bearing angel or a gentle shepherd. The work, which had considerable æsthetic merit, was executed by an artist named Jacob Jongeling. It remained to astonish and disgust the Netherlanders until it was thrown down and demolished by Alva's successor, Requesens.*

It has already been observed that many princes of the Empire had, at first warmly and afterwards, as the storm darkened around him, with less earnestness, encouraged the efforts of Orange. They had, both privately and officially, urged the subject upon the attention of the Emperor, and had solicited his intercession with Philip. It was not an interposition to save the Prince from chastisement, however the artful pen of Granvelle might distort the facts. It was an address in behalf of religious liberty for the Netherlands, made by those who had achieved it in their own persons, and who were at last enjoying immunity from persecution. It was an appeal which they who made it were bound to make, for the Netherland commissioners had assisted at the consultations by which the Peace of Passau had been wrung from the reluctant hand of Charles.†

These applications, however, to the Emperor, and through him to the King of Spain, had been, as we have seen, accompanied by perpetual advice to the Prince of Orange, that

---

* Bor, iv. 257, 258. Meteren, 61. De Thou, v. 471—473. Bentivoglio, lib. v. 186.

† Correspondance de Philippe II., ii. 791.

he should " sit still." The Emperor had espoused his cause with apparent frankness, so far as friendly mediation went, but in the meantime had peremptorily commanded him to refrain from levying war upon Alva, an injunction which the Prince had as peremptorily declined to obey. The Emperor had even sent especial envoys to the Duke and to the Prince, to induce them to lay down their arms, but without effect.* Orange knew which course was the more generous to his oppressed country ; to take up arms, now that hope had been converted into despair by the furious tyranny of Alva, or to " sit still" and await the result of the protocols about to be exchanged between king and kaiser. His arms had been unsuccessful indeed, but had he attended the issue of this sluggish diplomacy, it would have been even worse for the cause of freedom. The sympathy of his best friends, at first fervent then lukewarm, had, as disasters thickened around him, grown at last stone-cold. From the grave, too, of Queen Isabella arose the most importunate phantom in his path. The King of Spain was a widower again, and the Emperor among his sixteen children had more than one marriageable daughter. To the titles of " beloved cousin and brother-in-law," with which Philip had always been greeted in the Imperial proclamations, the nearer and dearer one of son-in-law was prospectively added.

The ties of wedlock were sacred in the traditions of the Habsburg house, but still the intervention was nominally made. As early as August, 1568, the Emperor's minister at Madrid had addressed a memorial to the King.† He had spoken in warm and strong language of the fate of Egmont and Horn, and had reminded Philip that the executions which were constantly taking place in the provinces were steadily advancing the Prince of Orange's cause. On the 22nd September, 1568, the six electors had addressed a formal memorial to the Emperor.‡ They thanked him for his previous interposition

---

* Instructions for the Archduke Charles. Correspondance de Philippe II., ii
797   † Ibid., ii. 786.   ‡ Ibid., ii. 791.

in favor of the Netherlands, painted in lively colors the cruelty
of Alva, and denounced the unheard-of rigor with which he
had massacred, not only many illustrious seigniors, but people
of every degree. Notwithstanding the repeated assurances
given by the King to the contrary, they reminded the
Emperor, that the *inquisition, as well as the Council of Trent,
had now been established in the Netherlands in full vigor.*[*]
They maintained that the provinces had been excluded from
the Augsbürg religious peace, to which their claim was perfect.
Nether Germany was entitled to the same privileges as Upper
Germany. They begged the Emperor to make manifest his
sentiments and their own. It was fitting that his Catholic
Majesty should be aware that the princes of the Empire were
united for the conservation of fatherland and of tranquillity.
To this end they placed in the Emperor's hands their estates,
their fortunes, and their lives.

Such was the language of that important appeal to the
Emperor in behalf of oppressed millions in the Netherlands,
an appeal which Granvelle had coldly characterized as an intrigue contrived by Orange to bring about his own restoration
to favor ! [†]

The Emperor, in answer, assured the electoral envoys that
he had taken the affair to heart, and had resolved to despatch
his own brother, the Archduke Charles, on a special mission
to Spain.[‡]

Accordingly, on the 21st October, 1568, the Emperor presented his brother with an ample letter of instructions.[§] He
was to recal to Philip's memory the frequent exhortations
made by the Emperor concerning the policy pursued in the
Netherlands. He was to mention the urgent interpellations
made to him by the electors and princes of the Empire in
their recent embassy. He was to state that the Emperor had
recently deputed commissioners to the Prince of Orange and
the Duke of Alva, in order to bring about, if possible, a sus-

---

* Correspondance de Philippe II., ii. 791.   † Ibid., ii. 795.
‡ Ibid., ii. 793   § Ibid., ii. 767.

pension of arms. He was to represent that the great number of men raised by the Prince of Orange in Germany, showed the powerful support which he had found in the country. Under such circumstances he was to show that it had been impossible for the Emperor to decree the ban against him, as the Duke of Alva had demanded. The Archduke was to request the King's consent to the reconciliation of Orange, on honorable conditions. He was to demand the substitution of clemency in the government of the Netherlands for severity, and to insist on the recal of the foreign soldiery from the Netherlands.*

Furnished with this very warm and stringent letter, the Archduke arrived in Madrid on the 10th December, 1568.† A few days later he presented the King with a copy of the instructions; those brave words upon which the Prince of Orange was expected to rely instead of his own brave heart and the stout arms of his followers. Philip having examined the letter, expressed his astonishment that such propositions should be made to him, and by the agency, too, of such a personage as the Archduke.‡ He had already addressed a letter to the Emperor, expressing his dissatisfaction at the step now taken.§ He had been disturbed at the honor thus done to the Prince of Orange, and at this interference with his own rights.‖ It was, in his opinion, an unheard-of proceeding thus to address a monarch of his quality upon matters in which he could accept the law from no man. He promised, however, that a written answer should be given to the letter of instructions.

On the 20th of January, 1569, that answer was placed in the hands of the Archduke.¶ It was intimated that the paper was a public one, fit to be laid by the Emperor before the electors; but that the King had also caused a confidential one** to be prepared, in which his motives and private griefs were indicated to Maximilian.

---

* Correspondance de Philippe II., ii. 797.

† Ibid., ii. 835.   ‡ Ibid.

§ See the letter in the Correspondance, etc., 807.   ‖ Ibid.

¶ Correspondance de Philippe II., ii. 818.   ** Ibid.. 819.

In the more public document, Philip observed that he had never considered himself obliged to justify his conduct, in his own affairs, to others.   He thought, however, that his example of severity would have been received with approbation by princes whose subjects he had thus taught obedience.   He could not admit that, on account of the treaties which constituted the Netherlands a circle of the Empire, he was obliged to observe within their limits the ordinances of the imperial diet.*   As to the matter of religion, his principal solicitude, since his accession to the crown, had been to maintain the Catholic faith throughout all his states.   In things sacred he could admit no compromise.   The Church alone had the right to prescribe rules to the faithful.   As to the chastisement inflicted by him upon the Netherland rebels, it would be found that he had not used rigor, as had been charged against him, *but, on the contrary, great clemency and gentleness.*†   He had made no change in the government of the provinces, certainly none in the edicts, the only statutes binding upon princes.   He had appointed the Duke of Alva to the regency, because it was his royal will and pleasure so to appoint him. The Spanish soldiery were necessary for the thorough chastisement of the rebels, and could not be at present removed.   As to the Prince of Orange, whose case seemed the principal motive for this embassy, and in whose interest so much had been urged, his crimes were so notorious that it was impossible even to attempt to justify them.   He had been, in effect, the author of all the conspiracies, tumults, and seditions which had taken place in the Netherlands.   All the thefts, sacrileges, violations of temples, and other misdeeds of which these provinces had been the theatre, were, with justice, to be imputed to him.   He had, moreover, levied an army and invaded his Majesty's territories.   Crimes so enormous had closed the gate to all clemency.   Notwithstanding his respect for the intercession made by the Emperor and the princes of the Empire, the King could not condescend to grant what was now asked of

---

* Correspondance de Philippe II., ii. 818.

† "Se hallarà aver usado S. M. Catolica no de rigor como se le imputa sino de mucha clemencia i piedad."—Correspondance de Philippe II., ii. 818.

him in regard to the Prince of Orange. As to a truce between him and the Duke of Alva, his Imperial Majesty ought to reflect upon the difference between a sovereign and his rebellious vassal, and consider how indecent and how prejudicial to the King's honor such a treaty must be esteemed.*

So far the public letter, of which the Archduke was furnished with a copy, both in Spanish and in Latin. The private memorandum was intended for the Emperor's eyes alone and those of his envoy. In this paper the King expressed himself with more warmth and in more decided language.† He was astonished, he said, that the Prince of Orange, in levying an army for the purpose of invading the states of his natural sovereign, should have received so much aid and comfort in Germany. It seemed incredible that this could not have been prevented by imperial authority. He had been pained that commissioners had been sent to the Prince. He regretted such a demonstration in his favor as had now been made by the mission of the Archduke to Madrid. That which, however, had caused the King the deepest sorrow was, that his Imperial Majesty should wish to persuade him in religious matters to proceed with mildness. The Emperor ought to be aware that no human consideration, no regard for his realms, nothing in the world which could be represented or risked, would cause him to swerve by a single hair's breadth from his path in the matter of religion.‡ This path was the same throughout all his kingdoms. He had ever trod in it faithfully, and he meant to keep in it perpetually. He would admit neither counsel nor persuasion to the contrary, and should take it ill if counsel or persuasion should be offered. He could not but consider the terms of the instructions given to the Archduke as exceeding the limits of amicable suggestion. They in effect amounted to a menace, and he was

---

* Correspondance de Philippe II., ii. 818. See also Cabrera; Vita de Filipo 2°, lib. viii. The whole instruction to the Archduke is there given, 518–530. The answer of Philip is also published in full, 578–592. See also the communication made by Luis Venegas, Philip's ambassador at the Imperial court, concerning the mission of the Archduke.—Ibid., 534–536.

† Correspondance de Philippe II., ii. 819.   ‡ Ibid.

astonished that a menace should be employed, because, with princes constituted like himself, such means could have but little success.*

On the 23rd of January, 1569, the Archduke presented the King with a spirited reply to the public letter. It was couched in the spirit of the instructions, and therefore need not be analysed at length. He did not believe that his Imperial Majesty would admit any justification of the course pursued in the Netherlands. The estates of the Empire would never allow Philip's reasoning concerning the connexion of those countries with the Empire, nor that they were independent, except in the particular articles expressed in the treaty of Augsburg. In 1555, when Charles the Fifth and King Ferdinand had settled the religious peace, they had been assisted by envoys from the Netherlands. The princes of the Empire held the ground, therefore, that the religious peace, which alone had saved a vestige of Romanism in Germany, should of right extend to the provinces. As to the Prince of Orange, the Archduke would have preferred to say nothing more, but the orders of the Emperor did not allow him to be silent. It was now necessary to put an end to this state of things in Lower Germany. The princes of the Empire were becoming exasperated. He recalled the dangers of the Smalcaldian war—the imminent peril in which the Emperor had been placed by the act of a single elector. They who believed that Flanders could be governed in the same manner as Italy and Spain were greatly mistaken, and Charles the Fifth had always recognised that error.†

This was the sum and substance of the Archduke's mission to Madrid, so far as its immediate objects were concerned. In the course, however, of the interview between this personage and Philip, the King took occasion to administer a rebuke to his Imperial Majesty for his general negligence in religious matters. It was a matter which lay at his heart, he said, that

---

* Correspondance de Philippe II., ii. 819.   † Ibid., ii. 820.

the Emperor, although, as he doubted not, a Christian and Catholic prince, was from policy unaccustomed to make those exterior demonstrations which matters of faith required. He therefore begged the Archduke to urge this matter upon the attention of his Imperial Majesty.*

The Emperor, despite this solemn mission, had become more than indifferent before his envoy had reached Madrid. For this indifference there were more reasons than one. When the instructions had been drawn up, the death of the Queen of Spain had not been known in Vienna.† The Archduke had even been charged to inform Philip of the approaching marriages of the two Archduchesses, that of Anne with the King of France, and that of Isabella with the King of Portugal. A few days later, however, the envoy received letters from the Emperor, authorizing him to offer to the bereaved Philip the hand of the Archduchess Anne.‡ The King replied to the Archduke, when this proposition was made, that if he had regard only to his personal satisfaction, he should remain as he was. As however he had now no son, he was glad that the proposition had been made, and would see how the affair could be arranged with France.§

Thus the ill success of Orange in Brabant, so disheartening to the German princes most inclined to his cause, and still more the widowhood of Philip, had brought a change over the views of Maximilian. On the 17th of January, 1569,

---

* Correspondance de Philippe II., ii. 835.　　　　　　　　† Ibid.

‡ Ibid. According to Cabrera, the Archduke learned the news of Queen Isabella's death on his journey to Madrid. Felipe II., lib. viii. 517.

Herrera (lib. xv. 707) erroneously states that the Archduke was, at the outset, charged with these two commissions by the Emperor; namely, to negotiate the marriage of the Archduchess Anne with Philip, and to arrange the affairs of the Netherlands. On the contrary, he was empowered to offer Anne to the King of France, and had already imparted his instructions to that effect to Philip, before he received letters from Vienna, written after the death of Isabella had become known. At another interview, he presented this new matrimonial proposition to Philip. These facts are important, for they indicate how completely the objects of the embassy, the commencement of which was so pretentious, were cast aside, that a more advantageous marriage for one of the seven Austrian Archduchesses might be secured.—Compare Correspondance de Philippe II., ii. 535.　　　　　　　　§ Ibid.

three days before his ambassador had entered upon his negotiations, he had accordingly addressed an autograph letter to his
Catholic Majesty. In this epistle, by a few cold lines, he entirely
annihilated any possible effect which might have been produced by the apparent earnestness of his interposition in favor
of the Netherlands. He informed the King that the Archduke had been sent, not to vex him, but to convince him of his
friendship. He assured Philip that he should *be satisfied with
his response, whatever it might be.* He entreated only that it
might be drawn up in such terms that the princes and electors
to whom it must be shown, might not be inspired with suspicion.*

The Archduke left Madrid on the 4th of March, 1569.
He retired, well pleased with the results of his mission, not
because its ostensible objects had been accomplished, for those
had signally failed, but because the King had made him
a present of one hundred thousand ducats, and had promised to espouse the Archduchess Anne.† On the 26th of
May, 1569, the Emperor addressed a final reply to Philip, in
which *he expressly approved the King's justification* of his conduct.‡ It was founded, he thought, in reason and equity.
Nevertheless, it could hardly be shown, as it was, to the
princes and electors, and he *had therefore modified many points*
which he thought might prove offensive.§

Thus ended "in smoke," as Granvelle had foretold, the
famous mission of Archduke Charles. The Holy Roman Emperor withdrew from his pompous intervention, abashed by a
rebuke, but consoled by a promise. If it were good to be
guardian of religious freedom in Upper and Nether Germany,
it was better to be father-in-law to the King of Spain and
both the Indies. Hence the lame and abrupt conclusion.

Cardinal Granvelle had been very serviceable in this juncture.
He had written to Philip to assure him that, in his opinion,
the Netherlands had no claim, under the transaction of Augs-

---

* Correspondance de Philippe II., ii. 817.   † Ibid., ii. 835.
‡ Ibid., ii. 874.   § Ibid.

burg, to require the observance within their territory of the decrees of the Empire.* He added, that Charles the Fifth had only agreed to the treaty of Passau to save his brother Ferdinand from ruin ; that he had only consented to it as Emperor, and had neither directly nor indirectly included the Netherlands within its provisions. He stated, moreover, *that the Emperor had revoked the treaty by an act which was never published, in consequence of the earnest solicitations of Ferdinand.†*

It has been seen that the King had used this opinion of Granvelle in the response presented to the Archduke. Although he did not condescend to an argument, he had laid down the fact as if it were indisputable. He was still more delighted to find that Charles had revoked the treaty of Passau, and eagerly wrote to Granvelle to inquire where the secret instrument was to be found.‡ The Cardinal replied that it was probably among his papers at Brussels, but that he doubted whether *it would be possible to find it in his absence.*§ Whether such a document ever existed, it is difficult to say. To perpetrate such a fraud would have been worthy of Charles ; to fable its perpetration not unworthy of the Cardinal. In either case, the transaction was sufficiently high-handed and exceedingly disgraceful.

---

* Correspondance de Philippe, II., ii. 800.   Gachard's Introduction to tom. i. clxxxvii.

† Correspondance de Philippe II., ii. 800.   ‡ Ibid., ii. 842.
§ Ibid., ii. 860.

CHAPTER V.

Quarrel between Alva and Queen Elizabeth of England—Spanish funds seized
by the English government—Non-intercourse between England and the
Netherlands—Stringent measures against heresy—Continued persecution—
Individual cases—Present of hat and sword to Alva from the Pope—
Determination of the Governor-general to establish a system of arbitrary
taxation in the provinces—Assembly of estates at Brussels—Alva's decrees
laid before them—The hundredth, tenth, and fifth pence—Opposition of
Viglius to the project—Estates of various provinces give a reluctant consent—Determined resistance of Utrecht—The city and province cited
before the Blood Council—Sentence of confiscation and disfranchisement
against both—Appeal to the King—Difficulty of collecting the new tax—
Commutation for two years—Projects for a pardon-general—Growing dis-
favour of the Duke—His desire to resign his post—Secret hostility between
the Governor and Viglius—Altered sentiments of the President—Opinions expressed by Granvelle—The pardon pompously proclaimed by the
Duke at Antwerp—Character of the amnesty—Dissatisfaction of the
people with the act—Complaints of Alva to the King—Fortunes and fate
of Baron Montigny in Spain—His confinement at Segovia—His attempt
to escape—Its failure—His mock trial—His wife's appeal to Philip—His
condemnation—His secret assassination determined upon—Its details, as
carefully prescribed and superintended by the King—Terrible inundation
throughout the Netherlands—Immense destruction of life and property in
Friesland—Lowestein Castle taken by De Ruyter, by stratagem—Recap-
ture of the place by the Spaniards—Desperate resistance and death of De
Ruyter.

It was very soon after the Duke's return to Brussels that a
quarrel between himself and the Queen of England took place.
It happened thus. Certain vessels, bearing roving commissions from the Prince of Condé, had chased into the ports of
England some merchantmen coming from Spain with supplies

in specie for the Spanish army in the Netherlands.* The trading ships remained in harbor, not daring to leave for their destination, while the privateers remained in a neighbouring port ready to pounce upon them should they put to sea. The commanders of the merchant fleet complained to the Spanish ambassador in London. The envoy laid the case before the Queen. The Queen promised redress, and, almost as soon as the promise had been made, seized upon all the specie in the vessels, amounting to about eight hundred thousand dollars, and appropriated the whole to her own benefit.† The pretext for this proceeding was twofold. In the first place, she assured the ambassador that she had taken the money into her possession in order that it might be kept safe for her royal brother of Spain. In the second place, she affirmed that the money did not belong to the Spanish government at all, but that it was the property of certain Genoese merchants, from whom, as she had a right to do, she had borrowed it for a short period.‡ Both these positions could hardly be correct, but either furnished an excellent reason for appropriating the funds to her own use.

The Duke of Alva being very much in want of money, was furious when informed of the circumstance. He immediately despatched Councillor d'Assonleville with other commissioners on a special embassy to the Queen of England.§ His envoys were refused an audience, and the Duke was taxed with presumption in venturing, as if he had been a sovereign, to send a legation to a crowned head.‖ No satisfaction was given to Alva, but a secret commissioner was despatched to Spain to discuss the subject there. The wrath of Alva was not appeased by this contemptuous treatment. Chagrined at the loss of his funds, and stung to the quick by a rebuke which his arrogance had merited, he resorted to a high-handed measure. He issued a proclamation commanding the personal arrest of every Englishman

---

* Bor, v. 272, 273   ‡ Bor, Meteren, ubi supra.
† Ibid. Meteren, 57.   ‖ Ibid., v. 277. Meteren, 57, 58.
§ Bor, v. 272, 273.

within the territory of the Netherlands, and the seizure of every article of property which could be found belonging to individuals of that nation.* The Queen retaliated by measures of the same severity against Netherlanders in England.† The Duke followed up his blow by a proclamation (of March 31st, 1569), in which the grievance was detailed, and strict non-intercourse with England enjoined.‡ While the Queen and the Viceroy were thus exchanging blows, the real sufferers were, of course, the unfortunate Netherlanders. Between the upper and nether millstones of Elizabeth's rapacity and Alva's arrogance, the poor remains of Flemish prosperity were well nigh crushed out of existence. Proclamations and commissions followed hard upon each other, but it was not till April 1573, that the matter was definitely arranged.§ Before that day arrived, the commerce of the Netherlands had suffered, at the lowest computation, a dead loss of two million florins, not a stiver of which was ever reimbursed to the sufferers by the Spanish government.‖

Meantime, neither in the complacency of his triumph over William of Orange, nor in the torrent of his wrath against the English Queen, did the Duke for a moment lose sight of the chief end of his existence in the Netherlands. The gibbet and the stake were loaded with their daily victims. The records of the period are foul with the perpetually renewed barbarities exercised against the new religion. To the magistrates of the different cities were issued fresh instructions, by which all municipal officers were to be guided in the discharge of their great duty. They were especially enjoined by the Duke to take heed that Catholic midwives, and none other, should be provided for every parish, duly sworn to give notice within twenty-four hours of every birth which occurred, in order that the curate might instantly proceed to baptism.¶ They were

---

* See the proclamation in Bor, v. 277–279.
† Bor, Meteren, ubi sup.   ‡ Ibid.
§ Bor, v. 279, 280.   Meteren, 57, 58.   ‖ Meteren, 58.
¶ Instructions from the Duke of Alva to Jacques de Blondel, Seigneur de Cuinchy, gouverneur et bailli de Tournay et Tournaisis.—Extraits des Registres de Tournay, par Gachard, 107, 108.

also ordered to appoint certain spies who should keep watch at every administration of the sacraments, whether public or private, whether at the altar or at death-beds, and who should report for exemplary punishment (that is to say, death by fire) all persons who made derisive or irreverential gestures, or who did not pay suitable honor to the said sacraments.* Furthermore, in order that not even death itself should cheat the tyrant of his prey, the same spies were to keep watch at the couch of the dying, and to give immediate notice to government of all persons who should dare to depart this life without previously receiving extreme unction and the holy wafer. The estates of such culprits, it was ordained, should be confiscated, and their bodies dragged to the public place of execution.†

An affecting case occurred in the north of Holland, early in this year, which, for its peculiarity, deserves brief mention. A poor Anabaptist, guilty of no crime but his fellowship with a persecuted sect, had been condemned to death. He had made his escape, closely pursued by an officer of justice, across a frozen lake. It was late in the winter, and the ice had become unsound. It trembled and cracked beneath his footsteps, but he reached the shore in safety. The officer was not so fortunate. The ice gave way beneath him, and he sank into the lake, uttering a cry for succor. There were none to hear him, except the fugitive whom he had been hunting. Dirk Willemzoon, for so was the Anabaptist called, instinctively obeying the dictates of a generous nature, returned, crossed the quaking and dangerous ice, at the peril of his life, extended his hand to his enemy, and saved him from certain death. Unfortunately for human nature, it cannot be added that the generosity of the action was met by a corresponding heroism. The officer was desirous, it is true, of avoiding the responsi-

---

* "—— a commettre certains personnages pour être présents au port et administration des Saints Sacrements, tant de l'autel que de l'extrême onction, à l'effet de remarquer ceux qui feraient gestes ou mines dérisoires ou irrévérencieux —— et d'en provoquer la punition exemplaire," etc.—Extraits des Registres de Tournay, par Gachard, 107, 108.

† "2. à dénoncer ceux qui décéderaient sans s'être fait administrer les Saints Sacrements, leurs *biens devant être confisqués et leurs corps portés au lieu public destiné pour la justice.*"—Ibid.

bility of sacrificing the preserver of his life, but the burgo-master of Asperen sternly reminded him to remember his oath. He accordingly arrested the fugitive, who, on the 16th of May following, was burned to death under the most lingering tortures.[*]

Almost at the same time four clergymen, the eldest seventy years of age, were executed at the Hague, after an imprisonment of three years. All were of blameless lives, having committed no crime save that of having favored the Reformation. As they were men of some local eminence, it was determined that they should be executed with solemnity. They were condemned to the flames, and as they were of the ecclesiastical profession, it was necessary before execution that their personal sanctity should be removed. Accordingly, on the 27th May, attired in the gorgeous robes of high mass, they were brought before the Bishop of Bois le Duc. The prelate, with a pair of scissors, cut a lock of hair from each of their heads. He then scraped their crowns and the tips of their fingers with a little silver knife very gently, and without inflicting the least injury. The mystic oil of consecration was thus supposed to be sufficiently removed. The prelate then proceeded to disrobe the victims, saying to each one as he did so, "*Eximo tibi vestem justitiae, quem volens abjecisti;*" to which the oldest pastor, Arent Dirkzoon, stoutly replied, "*imo vestem injustitiae.*" The bishop having thus completed the solemn farce of desecration, delivered the prisoners to the Blood Council, begging that they might be handled very gently. Three days afterwards they were all executed at the stake, having, however, received the indulgence of being strangled before being thrown into the flames.[†]

It was precisely at this moment, while the agents of the Duke's government were thus zealously enforcing his decrees, that a special messenger arrived from the Pope, bringing as a present to Alva a jewelled hat and sword.[‡] It was a gift

* Gerard Brandt Hist. der Reformatie, sect. i. b. x. 500.

† Bor, v. 312, 313. Hoofd, v. 199, 200.

‡ Bor, v. 270. Strada, lib. vii. 347.

rarely conferred by the Church, and never save upon the highest dignitaries, or upon those who had merited her most signal rewards by the most shining exploits in her defence.[*] The Duke was requested, in the autograph letter from his Holiness which accompanied the presents, " to remember, when he put the hat upon his head, that he was guarded with it as with a helmet of righteousness, and with the shield of God's help, indicating the heavenly crown which was ready for all princes who support the Holy Church and the Roman Catholic faith."[†]   The motto on the sword ran as follows, "*Accipe sanctum gladium, munus a Deo in quo dejicies adversarios populi mei Israel.*"[‡]

The Viceroy of Philip, thus stimulated to persevere in his master's precepts by the Vicegerent of Christ, was not likely to swerve from his path, nor to flinch from his work.   It was beyond the power of man's ingenuity to add any fresh features of horror to the religious persecution under which the provinces were groaning, but a new attack could be made upon the poor remains of their wealth.

The Duke had been dissatisfied with the results of his financial arrangements.   The confiscation of banished and murdered heretics had not proved the inexhaustible mine he had boasted.   The stream of gold which was to flow perennially into the Spanish coffers, soon ceased to flow at all.   This was inevitable.   Confiscations must, of necessity, offer but a precarious supply to any treasury.   It was only the frenzy of an Alva which could imagine it possible to derive a permanent revenue from such a source.   It was, however, not to be expected that this man, whose tyranny amounted to insanity, could comprehend the intimate connection between the interests of a people and those of its rulers, and he was determined to exhibit, by still more fierce and ludicrous experiments, how easily a great soldier may become a very paltry financier.

He had already informed his royal master that, after a very

---

* Strada, lib. vii. 347, 348.   † Bor, v. 270, 271.   ‡ Mendoza, 100.

short time, remittances would no longer be necessary from
Spain to support the expenses of the army and government
in the Netherlands.* He promised, on the contrary, that
at least two millions yearly should be furnished by the provinces, over and above the cost of their administration, to
enrich the treasury at home.† Another Peru had already
been discovered by his ingenuity, and one which was not
dependent for its golden fertility on the continuance of that
heresy which it was his mission to extirpate. His boast had
been much ridiculed in Madrid, where he had more enemies
than friends, and he was consequently the more eager to convert
it into reality. Nettled by the laughter with which all his
schemes of political economy had been received at home,‡ he
was determined to show that his creative statesmanship was no
less worthy of homage than his indisputable genius for destruction.

His scheme was nothing more than the substitution of an
arbitrary system of taxation by the Crown, for the legal and
constitutional right of the provinces to tax themselves. It
was not a very original thought, but it was certainly a bold
one. For although a country so prostrate might suffer the
imposition of any fresh amount of tyranny, yet it was doubtful whether she had sufficient strength remaining to bear the
weight after it had been imposed. It was certain, moreover,
that the new system would create a more general outcry than
any which had been elicited even by the religious persecution.
There were many inhabitants who were earnest and sincere
Catholics, and who therefore considered themselves safe from
the hangman's hands, while there were none who could
hope to escape the gripe of the new tax-gatherers. Yet the
Governor was not the man to be daunted by the probable unpopularity of the measure. Courage he possessed in more than
mortal proportion. He seemed to have set himself to the
task of ascertaining the exact capacity of the country for

---

* Correspondance de Philippe II., ii. 836, 837.   † Ibid., ii. 970.
‡ Vide V. d. Vynckt, ii. 118.

wretchedness. He was resolved accurately to gauge its width and its depth ; to know how much of physical and moral misery might be accumulated within its limits, before it should be full to overflowing. Every man, woman, and child in the country had been solemnly condemned to death ; and arbitrary executions, in pursuance of that sentence, had been daily taking place. Millions of property had been confiscated, while the most fortunate and industrious, as well as the bravest of the Netherlanders, were wandering penniless in distant lands. Still the blows, however recklessly distributed, had not struck every head. The inhabitants had been decimated, not annihilated, and the productive energy of the country, which for centuries had possessed so much vitality, was even yet not totally extinct. In the wreck of their social happiness, in the utter overthrow of their political freedom, they had still preserved the shadow, at least, of one great bulwark against despotism. The king could impose no tax.[*]

The "Joyeuse Entrée" of Brabant, as well as the constitutions of Flanders, Holland, Utrecht, and all the other provinces, expressly prescribed the manner in which the requisite funds for government should be raised. The sovereign or his stadholder was to appear before the estates in person, and make his request for money. It was for the estates, after consultation with their constituents, to decide whether or not this petition (Bede) should be granted, and should a single branch decline compliance, the monarch was to wait with patience for a more favorable moment.[†] Such had been the regular practice in the Netherlands, nor had the reigning houses often had occasion to accuse the estates of parsimony. It was, however, not wonderful that the Duke of Alva should be impatient at the continued existence of this provincial privilege. A country of condemned criminals, a nation whose universal neck might at any moment be laid upon the block without ceremony, seemed hardly fit

---

[*] Bentivoglio, lib. v. 82.   See also Introduction to this work.

[†] Ibid., ibid.—See also Kluit, Hist. der Holl. Staatsregering, and Viglii Comment. rerum actarum super imp. Dec. Den., c. vi.

to hold the purse-strings, and to dispense alms to its monarch. The Viceroy was impatient at this arrogant vestige of constitutional liberty. Moreover, although he had taken from the Netherlanders nearly all the attributes of freemen, he was unwilling that they should enjoy the principal privilege of slaves, that of being fed and guarded at their master's expense. He had therefore summoned a general assembly of the provincial estates in Brussels, and on the 20th of March, 1569, had caused the following decrees to be laid before them.*

A tax of the hundredth penny, or one per cent., was laid upon all property, real and personal, to be collected instantly. This impost, however, was not perpetual, but only to be paid once, unless, of course, it should suit the same arbitrary power by which it was assessed to require it a second time.

A tax of the twentieth penny, or five per cent., was laid upon every transfer of real estate. This imposition was perpetual.

Thirdly, a tax of the tenth penny, or ten per cent., was *assessed upon every article of merchandise or personal property, to be paid as often as it should be sold.* This tax was likewise to be perpetual.†

The consternation in the assembly when these enormous propositions were heard, can be easily imagined. People may differ about religious dogmas. In the most bigoted persecutions there will always be many who, from conscientious although misguided motives, heartily espouse the cause of the bigot. Moreover, although resistance to tyranny in matters of faith, is always the most ardent of struggles, and is supported by the most sublime principle in our nature, yet all men are not of the sterner stuff of which martyrs are fashioned. In questions relating to the world above, many may be seduced from their convictions by interest, or forced into apostasy by violence. Human nature is often malleable or fusible, where religious interests are concerned, but in affairs material and financial opposition to tyranny is apt to be unanimous.

* Bor, v. 279, 280.   † Ibid.

The interests of commerce and manufacture, when brought into conflict with those of religion, had often proved victorious in the Netherlands. This new measure, however—this arbitrary and most prodigious system of taxation, struck home to every fireside. No individual, however adroit or time-serving, could parry the blow by which all were crushed.

It was most unanswerably maintained in the assembly, that this tenth and twentieth penny would utterly destroy the trade and the manufactures of the country.* The hundredth penny, or the one per cent. assessment on all property throughout the land, although a severe subsidy, might be borne with for once. To pay, however, a twentieth part of the full value of a house to the government as often as the house was sold, was a most intolerable imposition. A house might be sold twenty times in a year, and in the course, therefore, of the year be confiscated in its whole value. It amounted either to a prohibition of all transfers of real estate, or to an eventual surrender of its price.

As to the tenth penny upon articles of merchandise, to be paid by the vendor at every sale, the scheme was monstrous. All trade and manufactures must, of necessity, expire, at the very first attempt to put it in execution.† The same article might be sold ten times in a week, and might therefore pay one hundred per cent. weekly. An article, moreover, was frequently compounded of ten different articles, each of which might pay one hundred per cent., and therefore the manufactured article, if ten times transferred, one thousand per cent. weekly. Quick transfers and unfettered movements being the nerves and muscles of commerce, it was impossible for it long to survive the paralysis of such a tax. The impost could never be collected, and would only produce an entire prostration of industry. It could by no possibility enrich the government.‡

---

* Bor, v. 283–285. Viglii Comm. Dec. Denarii, s. v. † Ibid.

‡ While occupied with his attempts to enforce this tax, the Duke established a commission to inquire into the value of the manufacturing industry of the provinces. In the year 1570, the aggregate annual value of manufactured

The King could not derive wealth from the ruin of his subjects ; yet to establish such a system was the stern and absurd determination of the Governor-general. The infantine simplicity of the effort seemed incredible. The ignorance was as sublime as the tyranny. The most lucid arguments and the most earnest remonstrances were all in vain. Too opaque to be illumined by a flood of light, too hard to be melted by a nation's tears, the Viceroy held calmly to his purpose. To the keen and vivid representations of Viglius, who repeatedly exhibited all that was oppressive and all that was impossible in the tax, he answered simply that it was nothing more nor less than the Spanish " alcabala," and that he derived 50,000 ducats yearly from its imposition in his own city of Alva.*

Viglius was upon this occasion in opposition to the Duke. It

---

articles was calculated at forty-five millions of florins (44,864,883 fl.) From this estimate, however, Luxemburg, Gueldres, Zeland, and the provinces beyond the Meuse, were excluded.

The returns for the others were thus stated:—

Brabant	11,197,416	florins.
Flanders	10,407,891	..
Valenciennes	5,223,980	..
Tournay	2,369,200	..
Holland	2,029,148	..
Lille, Douay, and Orchies	8,883,698	..
Hainault	1,982,540	..
Malines	262,880	..
Utrecht	734,900	..
Overyssel	1,610,260	..
Namur	454,980	..
Friesland	196,200	..
Artois	1,718,790	..

—Renom de France MS., ii. c. x. Upon this flourishing state of the manufacturing interest, notwithstanding the oppression to which the country had so long been subjected, the Duke indulged in golden dreams. "Oires le ducq considerant par ce calcul l'importance du dixième denier, *chatouillé doucement* de l'espérance ou de l'imagination du prouffit, pressa fort en l'année 1570 les états sur le 10eme denier.—Ibid.

The author shows that the tax would be paid at least seven times by cloth as well as by various other commodities.—Ibid. It would be easy to show, that if the tax were literally enforced, it would amount to seventy times seven, upon all manufactured wares.

* Viglii. Comm. Dec. Denarii, s. 6.

is but justice to state that the learned jurisconsult manfully and repeatedly confronted the wrath of his superior in many a furious discussion in council upon the subject. He had never essayed to snatch one brand from the burning out of the vast holocaust of religious persecution, but he was roused at last by the threatened destruction of all the material interests of the land. He confronted the tyrant with courage, sustained perhaps by the knowledge that the proposed plan was not the King's, but the Governor's. He knew that it was openly ridiculed in Madrid,* and that Philip, although he would probably never denounce it in terms, was certainly not eager for its execution. The President enlarged upon the difference which existed between the condition of a sparsely-peopled country of herdsmen and laborers in Spain, and the densely-thronged and bustling cities of the Netherlands. If the Duke collected 50,000 ducats yearly from the alcabala in Alva, he could only offer him his congratulations, but could not help assuring him that the tax would prove an impossibility in the provinces.† To his argument, that the impost would fall with severity not upon the highest nor the lowest classes of society, neither upon the great nobility and clergy nor on the rustic population, but on the merchants and manufacturers, it was answered by the President that it was not desirable to rob Saint Peter's altar in order to build one to Saint Paul.‡ It might have been simpler to suggest that the consumer would pay the tax, supposing it were ever paid at all, but the axiom was not so familiar three centuries ago as now.

Meantime, the report of the deputies to the assembly on their return to their constituents had created the most intense excitement and alarm. Petition after petition, report after report, poured in upon the government. There was a cry of despair, and almost of defiance, which had not been elicited by former agonies. To induce, however, a more favorable disposition on the part of the Duke, the hundredth

---

* V. d. Vynckt, Dl. ii. 118.
† Viglii. Comm. dec. Den. s. vii. 10.   ‡ Ibid., s. 9

penny, once for all, was conceded by the estates.* The tenth
and twentieth occasioned severe and protracted struggles,
until the various assemblies of the patrimonial provinces, one
after another, exhausted, frightened, and hoping that no
serious effort would be made to collect the tax, consented,
under certain restrictions, to its imposition.† The principal
conditions were a protest against the legality of the proceeding, and the provision that the consent of no province should
be valid until that of all had been obtained.‡ Holland, too,
was induced to give in its adhesion, although the city of
Amsterdam long withheld its consent; but the city and province of Utrecht were inexorable.§ They offered a handsome
sum in commutation, increasing the sum first proposed from
70,000 to 200,000 florins, but they resolutely refused to be
saddled with this permanent tax. Their stout resistance was
destined to cost them dear. In the course of a few months
Alva, finding them still resolute in their refusal, quartered
the regiment of Lombardy upon them, and employed other
coercive measures to bring them to reason.‖ The rude, insolent, unpaid and therefore insubordinate soldiery were billeted
in every house in the city, so that the insults which the population were made to suffer by the intrusion of these ruffians at
their firesides would soon, it was thought, compel the assent
of the province to the tax.¶ It was not so, however. The
city and the province remained stanch in their opposition.
Accordingly, at the close of the year (15th December, 1569)
the estates were summoned to appear within fourteen days
before the Blood Council.** At the appointed time the
procureur-general was ready with an act of accusation,
accompanied, as was usually the case, with a simultaneous
sentence of condemnation. The indictment revived and recapitulated all previous offences committed in the city and
the province, particularly during the troubles of 1566, and
at the epoch of the treaty with Duchess Margaret. The

---

* Bor, v. 286.　　　† Ibid.　　　‡ Ibid.　　　§ Ibid., v. 286, 287.
‖ Bor, v. 288.　　　¶ Ibid.　　　** Hoofd, v. 196. Bor, v. 291.

inhabitants and the magistrates, both in their individual and public capacities, were condemned for heresy, rebellion, and misprision. The city and province were accordingly pronounced guilty of high treason, were deprived of all their charters, laws, privileges, freedoms, and customs, and were declared to have forfeited all their property, real and personal, together with all tolls, rents, excises, and imposts, the whole being confiscated to the benefit of his Majesty.*

The immediate execution of the sentence was, however, suspended, to allow the estates opportunity to reply. An enormous mass of .pleadings, replies, replications, rejoinders, and apostilles was the result, which few eyes were destined to read, and least of all those to whom they were nominally addressed.† They were of benefit to none save in the shape of fees which they engendered to the gentlemen of the robe. It was six months, however, before the case was closed. As there was no blood to be shed, a summary process was not considered necessary. At last, on the 14th July, the voluminous pile of documents was placed before Vargas. It was the first time he had laid eyes upon them, and they were, moreover, written in a language of which he did not understand a word.‡ Such, however, was his capacity for affairs, that a glance only at the outside of the case enabled him to form his decision. Within half an hour afterwards, booted and spurred, he was saying mass in the church of Saint Gudule, on his way to pronounce sentence at Antwerp.§ That judgment was rendered the same day, and confirmed the preceding act of condemnation.‖ Vargas went to his task as cheerfully as if it had been murder. The act of outlawry and beggary was fulminated against the city and province, and a handsome amount of misery for others, and of plunder for himself, was

---

* See all the documents in Bor, v. 151, et seq.

† Bor, v. 290–319.—Compare Hoofd, v. 194–196; Wagenaer, Vaderl. Hist., vi. 293–304; Viglii Com. dec. Den., passim.

‡ Translations, however, were appended, which had only been completed that morning.—Bor, v. 319.

§ Bor, v. 319.   ‖ Ibid. Hoofd, Wagenaer, ubi sup.

the result of his promptness. Many thousand citizens were ruined, many millions of property confiscated.

Thus was Utrecht deprived of all its ancient liberties, as a punishment for having dared to maintain them. The clergy, too, of the province, having invoked the bull "*in Cœna Domini*," by which clerical property was declared exempt from taxation, had excited the wrath of the Duke.* To wield so slight a bulrush against the man who had just been girded with the consecrated and jewelled sword of the Pope, was indeed but a feeble attempt at defence. Alva treated the *Cœna Domini* with contempt, but he imprisoned the printer who had dared to republish it at this juncture. Finding, moreover, that it had been put in press by the orders of no less a person than Secretary La Torre, he threw that officer also into prison, besides suspending him from his functions for a year.†

The estates of the province and the magistracy of the city appealed to his Majesty from the decision of the Duke. The case did not directly concern the interests of religion, for although the heretical troubles of 1566 furnished the nominal motives of the condemnation, the resistance to the tenth and twentieth penny was the real crime for which they were suffering. The King, therefore, although far from clement, was not extremely rigorous. He refused the object of the appeal, but he did not put the envoys to death by whom it was brought to Madrid. This would have certainly been the case in matters strictly religious, or even had the commissioners arrived two years before, but even Philip believed, perhaps, that for the moment almost enough innocent blood had been shed. At any rate he suffered the legates from Utrecht to return,‡ not with their petition granted, but at least with their heads upon their shoulders. Early in the following year, the provinces still remaining under martial law, all the Utrecht charters were taken into the possession of

---

* Bor, v. 287. Hoofd, v. 195. † Ibid.
‡ Bor, v. 326–328 et seq.

government, and deposited in the castle of Vredenberg.* It was not till after the departure of Alva, that they were restored, according to royal command, by the new governor, Requesens.†

By the middle of the year 1569, Alva wrote to the King, with great cheerfulness of tone, announcing that the estates of the provinces had all consented to the tax. He congratulated his Majesty upon the fact that this income might thenceforth be enjoyed in perpetuity, and that it would bring at least two millions yearly into his coffers, over and above the expenses of government. The hundredth penny, as he calculated, would amount to at least five millions.‡

He was, however, very premature in his triumph, for the estates were not long in withdrawing a concession which had either been wrung from them by violence or filched from them by misrepresentation. Taking the ground that the assent of all had been stipulated before that of any one should be esteemed valid, every province now refused to enforce or to permit the collection of the tenth or the twentieth penny within their limits. Dire were the threatenings and the wrath of the Viceroy, painfully protracted the renewed negotiations with the estates. At last, a compromise was effected, and the final struggle postponed. Late in the summer it was agreed that the provinces should pay two millions yearly for the two following years, the term to expire in the month of August, 1571. Till that period, therefore, there was comparative repose upon the subject.§

The question of a general pardon had been agitated for more than a year, both in Brussels and Madrid. Viglius, who knew his countrymen better than the Viceroy knew them, had written frequently to his friend Hopper, on the propriety of at once proclaiming an amnesty.‖ There had also been many conferences between himself and the Duke of Alva, and he

---

* Bor, vi. 357–361.   † Bor, vi. 360, 361.

‡ Correspondance de Philippe II.,ii. 882.

§ Bor, v. 288, et seq.   Hoofd, v. 195.

‖ Epist. ad Joach. Hopp., 82–110.

had furnished more than one draught for the proposed measure.* The President knew full well that the point had been reached beyond which the force of tyranny could go no further. All additional pressure, he felt sure, could only produce reaction, the effect of which might be to drive the Spaniards from the Netherlands. There might then be another game to play. The heads of those who had so assiduously served the government throughout its terrible career might, in their turn, be brought to the block, and their estates be made to enrich the Treasury. Moreover, there were symptoms that Alva's favor was on the wane. The King had not been remarkably struck with the merits of the new financial measures, and had expressed much anxiety lest the trade of the country should suffer.† The Duke was known to be desirous of his recal. His health was broken, he felt that he was bitterly detested throughout the country, and he was certain that his enemies at Madrid were fast undermining his credit. He seemed also to have a dim suspicion that his mission was accomplished in the Netherlands; that as much blood had been shed at present as the land could easily absorb. He wrote urgently and even piteously to Philip, on the subject of his return. "Were your Majesty only pleased to take me from this country," he said, "I should esteem it as great a favor as if your Majesty had given me life."‡ He swore "by the soul of the Duchess," that he "would rather be cut into little pieces" than retire from his post were his presence necessary,§ but he expressed the opinion that through his exertions affairs had been placed in such train that they were sure to roll on smoothly to the end of time. "At present, and for the future," he wrote, "your Majesty is and will be more strictly obeyed than any of your predecessors;" adding, with insane self-complacency, "and all this has been *accomplished without violence.*"|| He also assured his Majesty as to the prosperous condition of financial affairs. His tax was to work

---

* Epist. ad Hopp., 110.   † Correspondance de Philippe II., ii. 896.
‡ Ibid., ii. 908.   § Ibid., ii. 951.
|| Ibid.

wonders. He had conversed with capitalists who had offered him four millions yearly for the tenth penny, but he had refused, because he estimated the product at a much higher figure.* The hundredth penny could not be rated lower than five millions. It was obvious, therefore, that instead of remitting funds to the provinces, his Majesty would, for the future, derive from them a steady and enormous income.† Moreover, he assured the King that there was at present no one to inspire anxiety from within or without. The only great noble of note in the country was the Duke of Aerschot, who was devoted to his Majesty, and who, moreover, "amounted to very little," as the King well knew.‡ As for the Prince of Orange, he would have business enough in keeping out of the clutches of his creditors. They had nothing to fear from Germany. England would do nothing as long as Germany was quiet ; and France was sunk too low to be feared at all.§

Such being the sentiments of the Duke, the King was already considering the propriety of appointing his successor. All this was known to the President. He felt instinctively that more clemency was to be expected from that successor, whoever he might be ; and he was satisfied, therefore, that he would at least not be injuring his own position by inclining at this late hour to the side of mercy. His opposition to the tenth and twentieth penny had already established a breach between himself and the Viceroy, but he felt secretly comforted by the reflection that the King was probably on the same side with himself. Alva still spoke of him, to be sure, both in public and private, with approbation ; taking occasion to commend him frequently, in his private letters, as a servant upright and zealous, as a living register,‖ without whose universal knowledge of things and persons he should hardly know which way to turn. The President, however, was

---

* Correspondance de Philippe II., ii. 970.   † Ibid.

‡ "Vale tan poco como V. M. sabe.—Ibid., ii. 951.   § Ibid.

‖ Ibid., ii. 824.

growing weary of his own sycophancy. He begged his friend Joachim to take his part, if his Excellency should write unfavorably about his conduct to the King. He seemed to have changed his views of the man concerning whose "prudence and gentleness" he could . once turn so many fine periods. He even expressed some anxiety lest doubts should begin to be entertained as to the perfect clemency of the King's character. "Here is so much confiscation and bloodshed going on," said he, "that some taint of cruelty or avarice may chance to bespatter the robe of his Majesty." He also confessed that he had occasionally read in history of greater benignity than was now exercised against the poor Netherlanders. Had the learned Frisian arrived at these humane conclusions at a somewhat earlier day, it might perhaps have been better for himself and for his fatherland. Had he served his country as faithfully as he had served Time, and Philip, and Alva, his lands would not have been so broad, nor his dignities so numerous, but he would not have been obliged, in his old age, to exclaim, with whimsical petulance, that " the faithful servant is always a perpetual ass."[*]

It was now certain that an act of amnesty was in contemplation by the King. Viglius had furnished several plans, which, however, had been so much disfigured by the numerous exceptions suggested by Alva, that the President could scarce recognize his work. Granvelle, too, had frequently urged the pardon on the attention of Philip.[†] The Cardinal was too astute not to perceive that the time had arrived when a continued severity could only defeat its own work. He felt that the country could not be rendered more abject, the spirit of patriotism more apparently extinct. A show of clemency, which would now cost nothing, and would mean nothing, might be more effective than this profuse and wanton bloodshed.

He saw plainly that the brutality of Alva had already over-

---

[*] Epist .ad Joach.　Hop. 62–82.　"Fidus servus perpetuus asinus," etc., etc.
[†] Correspondance de Philippe II., ii. 815.

shot the mark. Too politic, however, openly to reprove so powerful a functionary, he continued to speak of him and of his administration to Philip in terms of exalted eulogy. He was a " sage seignior," a prudent governor, one on whom his Majesty could entirely repose. He was a man of long experience, trained all his life to affairs, and perfectly capable of giving a good account of everything to which he turned his hands.* He admitted, however, to other correspondents, that the administration of the sage seignior, on whom his Majesty could so implicitly rely, had at last " brought the provinces into a deplorable condition."†

Four different forms of pardon had been sent from Madrid, toward the close of 1569.‡ From these four the Duke was to select one, and carefully to destroy the other three. It was not, however, till July of the following year that the choice was made, and the Viceroy in readiness to announce the pardon. On the 14th of that month a great festival was held at Antwerp, for the purpose of solemnly proclaiming the long expected amnesty.§ In the morning, the Duke, accompanied by a brilliant staff, and by a long procession of clergy in their gorgeous robes, paraded through the streets of the commercial capital, to offer up prayers and hear mass in the cathedral. The Bishop of Arras then began a sermon upon the blessings of mercy, with a running commentary upon the royal clemency about to be exhibited. In the very outset, however, of his discourse, he was seized with convulsions, which required his removal from the pulpit ;‖ an incident which was not considered of felicitous augury. In the afternoon, the Duke with his suite appeared upon the square in front of the Town House. Here a large scaffolding or theatre had been erected. The platform and the steps which led to it were covered with scarlet cloth. A throne, covered with cloth of gold, was arranged in the most

---

* Correspondance de Philippe II., ii. 792, 809, 844, etc., etc.

† Ibid., ii. 832.   Letter to Treasurer Schetz.

‡ Ibid., ii. 914.   § Bor, v. 319.   Hoofd, v 201.

‖ Strada, de Bell. Belgic., lib. vii. 353, 354.

elevated position for the Duke.* On the steps immediately below him were placed two of the most beautiful women in Antwerp,† clad in allegorical garments to represent righteousness and peace. The staircase and platform were lined with officers, the square was beset with troops, and filled to its utmost verge with an expectant crowd of citizens. Toward the close of a summer's afternoon, the Duke wearing‡ the famous hat and sword of the Pope, took his seat on the throne with all the airs of royalty. After a few preliminary ceremonies, a civil functionary, standing between two heralds, then recited the long-expected act of grace. His reading, however, was so indistinct, that few save the soldiers in the immediate vicinity of the platform could hear a word of the document.§

This effect was, perhaps, intentional. Certainly but little enthusiasm could be expected from the crowd, had the text of the amnesty been heard. It consisted of three parts—a recitation of the wrongs committed, a statement of the terms of pardon, and a long list of exceptions. All the sins of omission and commission, the heresy, the public preaching, the image-breaking, the Compromise, the confederacy, the rebellion, were painted in lively colors. Pardon, however, was offered to all those who had not rendered themselves liable to positive impeachment, in case they should make their peace with the Church before the expiration of two months, and by confession and repentance obtain their absolution.|| The exceptions, however, occupied the greater part of the document. When the general act of condemnation had been fulminated by which all Netherlanders were sentenced to death, the exceptions had been very few, and all the individuals mentioned by name.¶ In the act of pardon, the exceptions comprehended so many classes of inhabitants, that it was impossible for any individual to escape a place in some

---

* Bor, v. 319. Hoofd, v. 201. Strada, lib. vii. 354.
† Bor, v. 319. Hoofd, v. 201. ‡ Strada, lib. vii. 354.
§ Ibid. || See the document in Bor, v. 320, 321.
¶ Bor, v. 320, 321.

one of the categories, whenever it should please the government to take his life. Expressly excluded from the benefit of the act were all ministers, teachers, dogmatizers, *and all who had favored and harbored such dogmatizers and preachers ;* all those in the least degree implicated in the image-breaking ; all who had ever *been individually suspected of heresy or schism ;* all who had *ever signed or favored the Compromise* or the Petition to the Regent ; all those who had taken up arms, contributed money, distributed tracts ; all those in any *manner chargeable with misprision,* or who had failed to denounce *those guilty of heresy.* All persons, however, who were included in any of these classes of exceptions might report themselves within six months, when, upon confession of their crime, *they might hope for a favorable consideration of their case.*[*]

Such, in brief, and stripped of its verbiage, was this amnesty for which the Netherlands had so long been hoping. By its provisions, not a man or woman was pardoned who had ever committed a fault. The innocent alone were forgiven. Even they were not sure of mercy, unless they should obtain full absolution from the Pope. More certainly than ever would the accustomed rigor be dealt to all who had committed any of those positive acts for which so many had already lost their heads. The clause by which a possibility of pardon was hinted to such criminals, provided they would confess and surrender, was justly regarded as a trap. No one was deceived by it. No man, after the experience of the last three years, would voluntarily thrust his head into the lion's mouth, in order to fix it more firmly upon his shoulders. No man who had effected his escape was likely to play informer against himself, in hope of obtaining a pardon from which all but the most sincere and zealous Catholics were in reality excepted.

The murmur and discontent were universal, therefore, as soon as the terms of the act became known. Alva wrote to the King, to be sure, " that the people were entirely satisfied,

---

* Bor, v. 320, 321.

save only the demagogues, who could tolerate no single exception from the amnesty ;"* but he could neither deceive his sovereign nor himself by such statements. Certainly, Philip was totally disappointed in the effect which he had anticipated from the measure. He had thought "it would stop the mouths of many people."† On the contrary, every mouth in the Netherlands became vociferous to denounce the hypocrisy by which a new act of condemnation had been promulgated under the name of a pardon. Viglius, who had drawn up an instrument of much ampler clemency, was far from satisfied with the measure which had been adopted. "Certainly," he wrote to his confidant, "a more benignant measure was to be expected from *so merciful a Prince*. After four years have past, to reserve for punishment and for execution all those who during the tumult did not, through *weakness of mind, render as much service to government* as brave men might have offered, is altogether unexampled."‡

Alva could not long affect to believe in the people's satisfaction. He soon wrote to the King, acknowledging that the impression produced by the pardon was far from favorable. He attributed much evil effect to the severe censure which was openly pronounced upon the act by members of the government, both in Spain and the Netherlands.§ He complained that Hopper had written to Viglius, that "the most severe of the four forms of pardon transmitted had been selected ;" the fact being, that the most lenient one had been adopted.‖ If this were so, whose imagination is powerful enough to portray the three which had been burned, and which, although more severe than the fierce document promulgated, were still entitled acts of pardon ? The Duke spoke bitterly

---

* Correspondance de Philippe II., ii. 965.—"Con gran contentamiento de pueblo, aunque los que el gobiernan no le han tenido tanto, porque no quisieron excepcion ninguna."

† "Cierto seria ya tiempo de dar esta perdon y taparia la boca á muchos."— Marginal note by Philip on a letter from Granvelle. Correspondance de Philippe II., ii. 815.

‡ Epist. ad Hopp., 110.

§ Correspondance de Philippe II., ii. 980.   ‖ Ibid., ii. 1007.

of the manner in which influential persons in Madrid had openly abominated the cruel form of amnesty which had been decreed.* His authority in the Netherlands was already sufficiently weakened, he said, and such censure upon his actions from head-quarters did not tend to improve it. " In truth," he added, almost pathetically, " it is not wonderful that the whole nation should be ill-disposed towards me, for I certainly have done nothing to make them love me. At the same time, such language transmitted from Madrid does not increase their tenderness."†

In short, viewed as a measure by which government, without disarming itself of its terrible powers, was to pacify the popular mind, the amnesty was a failure. Viewed as a net, by which fresh victims should be enticed to entangle themselves, who had already made their way into the distant atmosphere of liberty, it was equally unsuccessful. A few very obscure individuals made their appearance to claim the benefit of the act, before the six months had expired. With these it was thought expedient to deal gently, but no one was deceived by such clemency. As the common people expressed themselves, the net was not spread on that occasion for finches.‡

The wits of the Netherlands, seeking relief from their wretched condition in a still more wretched quibble, transposed two letters of the word Pardona, and re-baptized the new measure Pandora.§ The conceit was not without meaning. The amnesty, descending from supernal regions, had been ushered into the presence of mortals as a messenger laden with heavenly gifts. The casket, when opened, had diffused curses instead of blessings. There, however, the classical analogy ended, for it would have puzzled all the pedants of Louvain to discover Hope lurking, under any disguise, within the clauses of the pardon.

---

* "Los Españoles en el consejo abominaron de tal forma de perdon."—Correspondance de Philippe II., ii. 885.   † Ibid., ii. 1007.

‡ Zynde terstondt het zeggen, dat men dit niet voor de vinken maar voor grooter vooghelen gespreyt had."—Hoofd, v. 202.   See also Bor. v. 321.

§ Ibid.

Very soon after the promulgation of this celebrated act, the new bride of Philip, Anne of Austria, passed through the Netherlands, on her way to Madrid. During her brief stay in Brussels, she granted an interview to the Dowager Countess of Horn.* That unhappy lady, having seen her eldest son, the head of her illustrious house, so recently perish on the scaffold, wished to make a last effort in behalf of the remaining one, then closely confined in the prison of Segovia. The Archduchess solemnly promised that his release should be the first boon which she would request of her royal bridegroom, and the bereaved countess retired almost with a hope.†

A short digression must here be allowed, to narrate the remaining fortunes of that son, the ill-starred Seigneur de Montigny. His mission to Madrid in company of the Marquis Berghen has been related in a previous volume. The last and most melancholy scene in the life of his fellow-envoy has been described in a recent chapter. After that ominous event, Montigny became most anxious to effect his retreat from Spain. He had been separated more than a year from his few months' bride. He was not imprisoned, but he felt himself under the most rigid although secret inspection. It was utterly impossible for him to obtain leave to return, or to take his departure without permission. On one occasion, having left the city accidentally for a ride on horseback to an adjoining village, he found himself surrounded by an unexpected escort of forty troopers. Still, however, the King retained a smiling mien. To Montigny's repeated and urgent requests for dismissal, Philip graciously urged his desire for a continuance of his visit. He was requested to remain in order to accompany his sovereign upon that journey to the Netherlands which would not be much longer delayed.‡ In his impatience anything seemed preferable to the state of suspense in which he was made to linger. He eagerly offered, if he were accused or suspected of crime, to surrender himself

---

* Hoofd, v. 172.   † Ibid., v. 172, 173.   Meteren, iii. 54.
‡ Meteren, iii. 54.

to imprisonment if he only could be brought to trial.* Soon
after Alva's arrival in the Netherlands, the first part of this
offer was accepted. No sooner were the arrests of Egmont
and Horn known in Madrid, than Montigny was deprived of
his liberty, and closely confined in the *alcazar* of Segovia.†
Here he remained imprisoned for eight or nine months in a
high tower, with no attendant save a young page, Arthur de
Munter, who had accompanied him from the Netherlands.‡
Eight men-at-arms were expressly employed to watch over
him and to prevent his escape.

One day towards the middle of July, 1568, a band of
pilgrims, some of them in Flemish attire, went through
the streets of Segovia. They were chanting, as was customary on such occasions, a low, monotonous song, in which
Montigny, who happened to be listening, suddenly recognized the language of his fatherland. His surprise was
still greater when, upon paying closer attention, he distinguished the terrible meaning of the song. The pretended
pilgrims, having no other means of communication with
the prisoner, were singing for his information the tragic
fates of his brother, Count Horn, and of his friend, Count
Egmont. Mingled with the strain were warnings of his own
approaching doom, if he were not able to effect his escape before it should be too late. Thus by this friendly masquerade
did Montigny learn the fate of his brother, which otherwise,
in that land of terrible secrecy, might have been concealed
from him for ever.§

The hint as to his own preservation was not lost upon
him, and he at once set about a plan of escape. He succeeded in gaining over to his interests one of the eight
soldiers by whom he was guarded, and he was thus enabled to
communicate with many of his own adherents without the
prison walls. His major-domo had previously been permitted
to furnish his master's table with provisions dressed by his
own cook. A correspondence was now carried on by means of

---

* Meteren, f. 53–54.   † Ibid., 54.   ‡ Ibid.   § Hoofd, v. 172.

letters concealed within the loaves of bread sent daily to the prisoner.[*] In the same way files were provided for sawing through his window-bars.[†] A very delicate ladder of ropes, by which he was to effect his escape into the court below, was also transmitted. The plan had been completely arranged. A certain Pole employed in the enterprise was to be at Hernani, with horses in readiness to convey them to San Sebastian.[‡] There a sloop had been engaged, and was waiting their arrival. Montigny accordingly, in a letter enclosed within a loaf of bread—the last, as he hoped, which he should break in prison—was instructed, after cutting off his beard and otherwise disguising his person, to execute his plan and join his confederates at Hernani.[§] Unfortunately, the major-domo of Montigny was in love. Upon the eve of departure from Spain, his farewell interview with his mistress was so much protracted that the care of sending the bread was left to another. The substitute managed so unskilfully that the loaf was brought to the commandant of the castle, and not to the prisoner. The commandant broke the bread, discovered the letter, and became master of the whole plot. All persons engaged in the enterprise were immediately condemned to death, and the Spanish soldier executed without delay. The others being considered, on account of their loyalty to their master as deserving a commutation of punishment, were sent to the galleys. The major-domo, whose ill-timed gallantry had thus cost Montigny his liberty, received two hundred lashes in addition. All, however, were eventually released from imprisonment.[||]

The unfortunate gentleman was now kept in still closer confinement in his lonely tower. As all his adherents had been disposed of, he could no longer entertain a hope of escape. In the autumn of this year (1568) it was thought expedient by Alva to bring his case formally before the Blood Council. Montigny had committed no crime, but

---

* Meteren, iii. 54.   Hoofd, v. 172.   † Ibid.
‡ Correspondance de Philippe II., ii. 775.   § Ibid.
|| Hoofd, Meteren, ubi sup.

he was one of that band of popular nobles whose deaths had been long decreed. Letters were accordingly sent to Spain, empowering certain functionaries there to institute that preliminary examination, which, as usual, was to be the only trial vouchsafed. A long list of interrogatories was addressed to him on February 7th, 1569, in his prison at Segovia. A week afterwards, he was again visited by the *alcalde*, who read over to him the answers which he had made on the first occasion, and required him to confirm them. He was then directed to send his procuration to certain persons in the Netherlands, whom he might wish to appear in his behalf. Montigny complied by sending several names, with a clause of substitution. All the persons thus appointed, however, declined to act, unless they could be furnished with a copy of the procuration, and with a statement of the articles of accusation. This was positively refused by the Blood Council. Seeing no possibility of rendering service to their friend by performing any part in this mockery of justice, they refused to accept the procuration. They could not defend a case when not only the testimony, but even the charges against the accused were kept secret. An individual was accordingly appointed by government to appear in the prisoner's behalf.*

Thus the forms of justice were observed, and Montigny, a close prisoner in the tower of Segovia, was put upon trial for his life in Brussels. Certainly nothing could exceed the irony of such a process. The advocate had never seen his client, thousands of miles away, and was allowed to hold no communication with him by letter. The proceedings were instituted by a summons, addressed by the Duke of Alva to Madame de Montigny in Brussels. That unhappy lady could only appeal to the King. "Convinced," she said

---

* Gachard, notes page 123. Correspondance de Philippe II., ii.

Antoine de Penin, one of those nominated by Montigny, was the person selected by the government.—Correspondance de Philippe II., ii. 870; and note by Gachard on p. 90.

"that her husband was innocent of the charges brought against him, she threw herself, overwhelmed and consumed by tears and misery, at his Majesty's feet. She begged the King to remember the past services of Montigny, her own youth, and that she had enjoyed his company but four months. By all these considerations, and by the passion of Jesus Christ, she adjured the monarch to pardon any faults which her husband might have committed."* The reader can easily judge how much effect such a tender appeal was like to have upon the heart of Philip. From that rock, thus feebly smitten, there flowed no fountain of mercy. It was not more certain that Montigny's answers to the interrogatories addressed to him had created a triumphant vindication† of his course, than that such vindication would be utterly powerless to save his life. The charges preferred against him were similar to those which had brought Egmont and Horn to the block, and it certainly created no ground of hope for him, that he could prove himself even more innocent of suspicious conduct than they had done. On the 4th March, 1570, accordingly, the Duke of Alva pronounced sentence against him. The sentence declared that his head should be cut off, and afterwards exposed to public view upon the head of a pike.‡ Upon the 18th March, 1570, the Duke addressed a requisitory letter to the alcaldes, corregidors, and other judges of Castile, empowering them to carry the sentence into execution.§

On the arrival of this requisition there was a serious debate before the King in council.‖ It seemed to be the general opinion that there had been almost severity enough in the Netherlands for the present. The spectacle of the public execution of another distinguished personage, it was thought,

---

* Correspondance de Philippe II., ii. 879. Letter of Helen de Melun, Dame de Montigny.

† Gachard, note to page 123. Correspondance de Philippe II., ii.

‡ Correspondance de Philippe II., ii. 937.   § Ibid., ii. 938, 939.

‖ Relation transmitted by Philip to Alva. Correspondance de Philippe II., i. 996.

might now prove more irritating than salutary.* The King was of this opinion himself. It certainly did not occur to him or to his advisers that this consideration should lead them to spare the life of an innocent man. The doubts entertained as to the expediency of a fresh murder were not allowed to benefit the prisoner, who, besides being a loyal subject and a communicant of the ancient Church, was also clothed in the white robes of an envoy, claiming not only justice but hospitality as the deputy of Philip's sister, Margaret of Parma. These considerations probably never occurred to the mind of His Majesty. In view, however, of the peculiar circumstances of the case, it was unanimously agreed that there should be no more blood publicly shed. Most of the councillors were in favor of slow poison.† Montigny's meat and drink, they said, should be daily drugged, so that he might die by little and little.‡ Philip, however, terminated these disquisitions by deciding that the ends of justice would not thus be sufficiently answered. The prisoner, he had resolved, should be regularly executed, but the deed should be secret, and it should be publicly announced that he had died of a fever.§

This point having been settled, the King now set about the arrangement of his plan with all that close attention to detail which marked his character. The patient industry which, had God given him a human heart and a love of right, might have made him a useful monarch, he now devoted to a scheme of midnight murder with a tranquil sense of enjoyment which seems almost incredible. There is no exaggeration in calling the deed a murder, for it certainly was not sanctioned by any law, divine or human, nor justified or excused by any of the circumstances which are supposed to palliate homicide. Nor, when the elaborate and superfluous luxury of arrangements made by Philip for the accomplishment of his design

---

* Relation transmitted by Philip to Alva.   Corresp. de Philippe II., ii. 996.
† Ibid.
‡ Ibid. "—— Parescia à los mas que era bien darle un bocado, ò echar alyun gènero de venen en la comida ò bebida, con que sa fuese moriendo poco à poco."
§ Relation transmitted to Philip, etc.

is considered, can it be doubted that he found a positive pleasure in his task. It would almost seem that he had become
jealous of Alva's achievements in the work of slaughter. He
appeared willing to prove to those immediately about him,
that however capable might be the Viceroy of conducting public executions on a grand and terrifying scale, there was yet a
certain delicacy of finish never attained by Alva in such business, and which was all his Majesty's own. The King was resolved to make the assassination of Montigny a masterpiece.

On the 17th August, 1570, he accordingly directed Don
Eugenio de Peralta, concierge of the fortress of Simancas, to
repair to Segovia, and thence to remove the Seigneur Montigny to Simancas.* Here he was to be strictly immured, yet
was to be allowed at times to walk in the corridor adjoining
his chamber. On the 7th October following, the licentiate
Don Alonzo de Avellano, alcalde of Valladolid, was furnished
with an order addressed by the King to Don Eugenio de Peralta, requiring him to place the prisoner in the hands of the
said licentiate, who was charged with the execution of
Alva's sentence.† This functionary had, moreover, been provided with a minute letter of instructions, which had been
drawn up according to the King's directions, on the 1st October.‡ In these royal instructions, it was stated that, although
the sentence was for a public execution, yet the King had
decided in favor of a private one within the walls of the fortress. It was to be managed so that no one should suspect
that Montigny had been executed, but so that, on the contrary, it should be universally said and believed that he had
died a natural death. Very few persons, all sworn and threatened into secrecy, were therefore to be employed. Don
Alonzo was to start immediately for Valladolid, which was
within two short leagues of Simancas. At that place he

---

* Relation sent by Philip. Correspondance de Philippe II., ii. 996.
† Correspondance de Philippe II., ii. 982.
‡ See its analysis in Correspondance de Philippe II., ii. 983.

would communicate with Don Eugenio, and arrange the mode, day, and hour of execution. He would leave Valladolid on the evening before a holiday, late in the afternoon, so as to arrive a little after dark at Simancas. He would take with him a confidential notary, an executioner, and as few servants as possible. Immediately upon his entrance to the fortress, he was to communicate the sentence of death to Montigny, in presence of Don Eugenio and of one or two other persons. He would *then console him*, in which task he would be assisted by Don Eugenio.* He would afterwards leave him with the religious person who would be appointed for that purpose. That night and the whole of the following day, which would be a festival, till after midnight, would be allotted to Montigny, that he might have time to confess, to receive the sacraments, to convert himself to God, and to repent. Between one and two o'clock in the morning the execution was to take place, in presence of the ecclesiastic, of Don Eugenio de Peralta, of the notary, and of one or two other persons, who would be needed by the executioner. The ecclesiastic was to be a wise and prudent person, and to be informed how little confidence Montigny inspired in the article of faith. If the prisoner should wish to make a will, it could not be permitted. As all his property had been confiscated, he could dispose of nothing. Should he, however, desire to make a memorial of the debts which he would wish paid, he was to be allowed that liberty. It was, however, to be stipulated that he was to make no allusion, in any memorial or letter which he might write, to *the execution* which was about to take place. He was to use the language of *a man seriously ill, and who feels himself at the point of death.*† By this infernal ingenuity it was proposed to make the victim an accomplice in the plot, and to place a false exculpation of his assassins in his dying lips. The execution having been fulfilled, and the death having been announced with the dissimulation prescribed, the burial was to take place in the

---

* Correspondance de Philippe II., iii. 983.   † Ibid.

church of Saint Saviour, in Simancas. A moderate degree of pomp, such as befitted a person of Montigny's quality, was to be allowed, and a decent tomb erected. A grand mass was also to be celebrated, with a respectable number, " say seven hundred," of lesser masses. As the servants of the defunct were few in number, continued the frugal King, they might be provided each with a suit of mourning.* Having thus personally arranged all the details of this secret work, from the reading of the sentence to the burial of the prisoner ; having settled not only the mode of his departure from life, but of his passage through purgatory, the King despatched the agent on his mission.

The royal program was faithfully enacted. Don Alonzo arrived at Valladolid, and made his arrangements with Don Eugenio. It was agreed that a paper, prepared by royal authority, and brought by Don Alonzo from Madrid, should be thrown into the corridor of Montigny's prison. This paper, written in Latin, ran as follows : " In the night, as I understand, there will be no chance for your escape. In the daytime there will be many ; for you are then in charge of a single gouty guardian, no match in strength or speed for so vigorous a man as you. Make your escape from the 8th to the 12th of October, at any hour you can, and take the road contiguous to the castle gate through which you entered. You will find Robert and John, who will be ready with horses, and with everything necessary. May God favor your undertaking.—R. D. M."†

The letter, thus designedly thrown into the corridor by one confederate, was soon afterwards picked up by the other, who immediately taxed Montigny with an attempt to escape.‡ Notwithstanding the vehement protestations of innocence naturally made by the prisoner, his pretended project was made the pretext for a still closer imprisonment in the

---

* Correspondance de Philippe II., ii. 983.
† Gachard, note to page 156 of Correspondance de Philippe II., ii.
‡ Ibid., ii. 986–988.

" Bishop's Tower."*   A letter, *written at Madrid,* by Philip's orders, *had been brought by Don Alonzo to Simancas, narrating by anticipation these circumstances, precisely as they had now occurred.*† It moreover stated that Montigny, in consequence of his close confinement, had *fallen grievously ill,* and that he would receive all the attention compatible with his safe keeping.   This letter, according to previous orders, was *now signed by Don Eugenio de Peralta,* dated 10th October, 1570, *and publicly despatched to Philip.*‡ It was thus formally established that Montigny was seriously ill.   A physician, thoroughly instructed and sworn to secrecy, was now ostentatiously admitted to the tower, bringing with him a vast quantity of drugs.   He duly circulated among the townspeople, on his return, his opinion that the illustrious prisoner was afflicted with a disorder from which it was almost impossible that he should recover.§   Thus, thanks to Philip's masterly precautions, not a person in Madrid or Simancas was ignorant that Montigny was dying of a fever, with the single exception of the patient himself.

On Saturday, the 14th of October, at nightfall, Don Alonzo de Avellano, accompanied by the prescribed individuals, including Fray Hernando del Castillo, an ecclesiastic of high reputation, made their appearance at the prison of Simancas. At ten in the evening the announcement of the sentence was made to Montigny.   He was visibly agitated at the sudden intelligence, for it was entirely unexpected by him.‖ He had, on the contrary, hoped much from the intercession of the Queen, whose arrival he had already learned.¶   He

---

* Ibid., ii. 988 ; and Gachard, Introduction to Correspondance de Philippe II., i. 39.

† Relation, etc.   Correspondance de Philippe II., ii. 996.

‡ Correspondance de Philippe II., ii. 988.

§ Relation, etc.   Correspondance de Philippe II., ii. 996.

‖ Ibid.   Also Letter of Fray Hernando del Castillo to Doctor Velasco, in Correspondance de Philippe II., ii. 992.

¶ Ibid.—It will be perceived that Philip had taken precautionary measures against the request which his young bride, according to her promise to the Dowager Countess of Horn, had promised to prefer in behalf of Montigny.

soon recovered himself, however, and requested to be left alone with the ecclesiastic. All the night and the following day were passed in holy offices. He conducted himself with great moderation, courage, and tranquillity. He protested his entire innocence of any complicity with the Prince of Orange, or of any disloyal designs or sentiments at any period of his life. He drew up a memorial, expressing his strong attachment to every point of the Catholic faith, from which *he had never for an instant swerved*.[*] His whole demeanor was noble, submissive, and Christian. "In every essential," said Fray Hernando, "he conducted himself so well that we who remain may bear him envy."[†] He wrote a paper of instructions concerning his faithful and bereaved dependents. He placed his signet ring, attached to a small gold chain, in the hands of the ecclesiastic, to be by him transmitted to his wife. Another ring, set with turquois, he sent to his mother-in-law, the Princess Espinoy, from

---

According to Meteren, who upon this occasion has been followed by Bor and Hoofd, as well as by later historians, Philip determined to despatch the prisoner before the arrival of the Queen, in order that he might not be obliged to refuse her first request. They add, that Montigny was accordingly poisoned in a pottage which his own page was compelled to administer to him. The page was threatened with death if he revealed the secret, says Hoofd; but according to Meteren, he did discover the deed to his intimate friends. A burning fever was said to have been produced by the poison, which carried off the victim on the 1st October. The Queen sailed from Flushing on the 25th September, and although these writers are mistaken as to the exact date and manner of the murder, yet they were certainly well informed as to the general features of the mysterious transaction. Their statement, that Montigny was dead before the Queen left the ship, is manifestly a mistaken one, for it appears by the letter of Fray Hernando that the prisoner had already learned the news of her arrival. Still he was, without doubt represented by Philip to the Queen as already dead or dying, and the masterly precautions taken rendered contradiction impossible. He had already been removed to Simancas on the 1st October, and was reported grievously ill on the 10th. These contemporaries may be forgiven for having given the poisoned pottage instead of the "garote," as the real instrument of death; and this is almost the only mistake which they have made, now that the narration is compared with the detailed statement made by Philip himself.— V. Meteren, iii. 54. Hoofd, v. 172, 173. Compare Wagenaer, Vaderl. Hist., Deel. vi. 246; Bor, iv. 182 (255).

  [*] Correspondance de Philippe II., ii. 990.   [†] Letter of Fray Hernando, etc.

whom he had received it. About an hour after midnight, on the morning, therefore, of the 16th of October, Fray Hernando gave notice that the prisoner was ready to die. The alcalde Don Alonzo then entered, accompanied by the executioner and the notary. The sentence of Alva was now again recited, the alcalde adding that the King, "out of his clemency and benignity," had substituted a secret for a public execution. Montigny admitted that the judgment would be just and the punishment lenient, if it were conceded that the charges against him were true. His enemies, however, while he had been thus immured, had possessed the power to accuse him as they listed. He ceased to speak, and the executioner then came forward and strangled him. The alcalde, the notary, and the executioner then immediately started for Valladolid, so that no person next morning knew that they had been that night at Simancas, nor could guess the dark deed which they had then and there accomplished.* The terrible secret they were forbidden, on pain of death, to reveal.

Montigny, immediately after his death, was clothed in the habit of Saint Francis, in order to conceal the marks of strangulation. In the course of the day the body was deposited, according to the King's previous orders, in the church of Saint Saviour. Don Eugenio de Peralta, who superintended the interment, uncovered the face of the defunct to prove his identity, which was instantly recognised by many sorrowing servants. The next morning the second letter, *prepared by Philip long before, and brought by* Don Alonzo de Avellano to Simancas, received the date of 17th October, 1570, together with the signature of Don Eugenio de Peralta, keeper of Simancas fortress, and was then *publicly despatched* to the King.* It stated that, notwithstanding the care given to the Seigneur de Montigny in his severe illness by the physicians who had attended him, he had continued to grow worse and worse until the previous morning between three and four o'clock, when he had expired. The Fray Hernando del Castillo,

---

* Letter of Fray Hernando.   Correspondance de Philippe II., ii. 992–996.

who had accidentally happened to be at Simancas, had performed the holy offices, at the request of the deceased, who had died in so catholic a frame of mind, that great hopes might be entertained of his salvation. Although he possessed no property, yet his burial had been conducted very respectably.*

On the 3rd of November, 1570, these two letters, ostensibly written by Don Eugenio de Peralta, were transmitted by Philip to the Duke of Alva. They were to serve as evidence of the statement which the Governor-General was now instructed to make, that the Seigneur de Montigny had died a natural death in the fortress of Simancas. By the same courier, the King likewise forwarded a secret memoir, containing the exact history of the dark transaction, from which memoir the foregoing account has been prepared. At the same time the Duke was instructed publicly to exhibit the lying letters of Don Eugenio de Peralta,† as containing an authentic statement of the affair. The King observed, moreover, in his letter, that there was not a person in Spain who doubted that Montigny had died of a fever. He added that if the sentiments of the deceased nobleman had been at all in conformity with his external manifestations, according to the accounts received of his last moments, it was to be hoped that God would have mercy upon his soul. The secretary who copied the letter, took the liberty of adding, however, to this paragraph the suggestion, that " if Montigny were really a heretic, the devil, who always assists his children in such moments, would hardly have failed him in his dying hour." Philip, displeased with this flippancy, caused the passage to be erased. He even gave vent to his royal indignation in a marginal note, to the effect that we should always express favorable judgments concerning the dead‡—a pious sentiment always dearer to writing masters than to historians. It seemed never

---

* Correspondance de Philippe II., ii. 994–996.

† "Mostrando descuidada y dissimuladamente."—Correspondance de Philippe II., ii. 997.

‡ " Esto mismo borrad de la cifra, que de los muertos no hay que hacer, sino buen juicio."—Correspondance de Philippe II., ii. 997.

to have occurred however to this remarkable moralist, that it was quite as reprehensible to strangle an innocent man as to speak ill of him after his decease.*

Thus perished Baron Montigny, four years after his arrival in Madrid as Duchess Margaret's ambassador, and three years after the death of his fellow-envoy Marquis Berghen. No apology is necessary for so detailed an account of this dark and secret tragedy. The great transactions of a reign are sometimes paltry things ; great battles and great treaties, after vast consumption of life and of breath, often leave the world where they found it. The events which occupy many of the statelier pages of history, and which have most lived in the mouths of men, frequently contain but commonplace lessons of philosophy. It is perhaps otherwise when, by the resuscitation of secret documents, over which the dust of three centuries has gathered, we are enabled to study the internal working of a system of perfect tyranny. Liberal institutions, republican or constitutional governments, move in the daylight ; we see their mode of operation, feel the jar of their wheels, and are often needlessly alarmed at their apparent tendencies. The reverse of the picture is not always so easily attainable. When, therefore, we find a careful portrait of a consummate tyrant, painted by his own hand, it is worth our while to pause for a moment, that we may carefully peruse the lineaments. Certainly, we shall afterwards not love liberty the less.

Towards the end of the year 1570, still another and a terrible misfortune descended upon the Netherlands. It was now the hand of God which smote the unhappy country, already so tortured by the cruelty of war. An inundation, more tremendous than any which had yet been recorded in those annals so prolific in such catastrophes, now swept the

---

* On the 22nd March, 1571, a decree condemning the memory of Montigny and confiscating all his estates, was duly issued by the Duke of Alva, "in consequence of information then just received that the said seigneur had departed life by a natural death in the fortress of Simancas."—Correspondance de Philippe II., ii. 1016.

whole coast from Flanders to Friesland.* Not the memorable deluge of the thirteenth century, out of which the Zuyder Zee was born ; not that in which the waters of the Dollart had closed for ever over the villages and churches of Groningen ; not one of those perpetually recurring floods by which the inhabitants of the Netherlands, year after year, were recalled to an anxious remembrance of the watery chaos out of which their fatherland had been created, and into which it was in daily danger of resolving itself again, had excited so much terror and caused so much destruction. A continued and violent gale from the north-west had long been sweeping the Atlantic waters into the North Sea, and had now piled them upon the fragile coasts of the provinces. The dykes, tasked beyond their strength, burst in every direction. The cities of Flanders, to a considerable distance inland, were suddenly invaded by the waters of the ocean.† The whole narrow peninsula of North Holland was in imminent danger of being swept away for ever.‡ Between Amsterdam and Meyden, the great Diemer dyke was broken through in twelve places. The Hand-bos, a bulwark formed of oaken piles, fastened with metal clamps, moored with iron anchors, and secured by gravel and granite, was snapped to pieces like packthread. The "Sleeper," a dyke thus called, because it was usually left in repose by the elements, except in great emergencies, alone held firm, and prevented the consummation of the catastrophe.§ Still the ocean poured in upon the land with terrible fury. Dort, Rotterdam, and many other cities were, for a time, almost submerged. Along the coast, fishing vessels, and even ships of larger size, were floated up into the country, where they entangled themselves in groves and orchards, or beat to pieces the roofs and walls of houses.‖ The destruction of life and of property was enormous throughout the maritime provinces, but in Friesland the desolation was complete. There nearly all the dykes and sluices were dashed to fragments ; the country, far and wide, converted into an angry sea. The

* Bor, v. 329. Hoofd, vi. 205, 206.   † Ibid., vi. 205.

‡ Hoofd, ubi sup.   § Ibid.   ‖ Ibid.

steeples and towers of inland cities became islands of the ocean. Thousands of human beings were swept out of existence in a few hours. Whole districts of territory, with all their villages, farms, and churches, were rent from their places,* borne along by the force of the waves, sometimes to be lodged in another part of the country, sometimes to be entirely engulfed. Multitudes of men, women, children, of horses, oxen, sheep, and every domestic animal, were struggling in the waves in every direction. Every boat, and every article which could serve as a boat, were eagerly seized upon. Every house was inundated ; even the grave-yards gave up their dead. The living infant in his cradle, and the long-buried corpse in his coffin, floated side by side. The ancient flood seemed about to be renewed. Everywhere, upon the top of trees, upon the steeples of churches, human beings were clustered, praying to God for mercy, and to their fellow-men for assistance.† As the storm at last was subsiding, boats began to ply in every direction, saving those who were still struggling in the water, picking fugitives from roofs and tree-tops, and collecting the bodies of those already drowned. Colonel Robles, Seigneur de Billy, formerly much hated for his Spanish or Portuguese blood, made himself very active in this humane work. By his exertions, and those of the troops belonging to Groningen, many lives were rescued, and gratitude replaced the ancient animosity. It was estimated that at least twenty thousand persons were destroyed in the province of Friesland alone. Throughout the Netherlands, one hundred thousand persons perished. The damage done to property, the number of animals engulfed in the sea, were almost incalculable.‡

These events took place on the 1st and 2nd November, 1570. The former happened to be the day of All Saints, and the Spaniards maintained loudly that the vengeance of

---

* Hoofd, vi. 205, 206.   Bor, vi. 329.
† Hoofd, Bor, ubi sup.   Strada, lib. vii. 355, 356.
‡ Hoofd, vi. 206.   Meteren, iii. 59.

Heaven had descended upon the abode of heretics.* The Netherlanders looked upon the catastrophe as ominous of still more terrible misfortunes in store for them. They seemed doomed to destruction by God and man. An overwhelming tyranny had long been chafing against their constitutional bulwarks, only to sweep over them at last ; and now the resistless ocean, impatient of man's feeble barriers, had at last risen to reclaim his prey. Nature, as if disposed to put to the blush the feeble cruelty of man, had thus wrought more havoc in a few hours, than bigotry, however active, could effect in many years.

Nearly at the close of this year (1570) an incident occurred, illustrating the ferocious courage so often engendered in civil contests. On the western verge of the Isle of Bommel, stood the castle of Lowestein. The island is not in the sea. It is the narrow but important territory which is enclosed between the Meuse and the Waal. The castle, placed in a slender hook, at the junction of the two rivers, commanded the two cities of Gorcum and Dorcum, and the whole navigation of the waters.† One evening, towards the end of December, four monks, wearing the cowls and robes of Mendicant Grey Friars, demanded hospitality at the castle gate.‡ They were at once ushered into the presence of the commandant, a brother of President Tisnacq. He was standing by the fire, conversing with his wife. The foremost monk approaching him, asked whether the castle held for the Duke of Alva or the Prince of Orange. The castellian replied that he recognized no prince save Philip, King of Spain. Thereupon the monk, who was no other than Herman de Ruyter, a drover by trade, and a warm partisan of Orange, plucked a pistol from beneath his robe, and shot the commandant through the head. The others, taking advantage of the sudden panic, overcame all the resistance offered by the feeble garrison, and made themselves masters of the place.§ In the course of the

---

* Meteren, Hoofd, ubi sup. † Bentivoglio, lib. v. 87. Guicciardini, x.
‡ Mendoza, v. 109, 110. Hoofd, vi. 207.
§ Mendoza, Hoofd, ubi sup. Bor, vi. 331.

next day they introduced into the castle four or five and twenty men, with which force they diligently set themselves to fortify the place, and secure themselves in its possession.* A larger reinforcement which they had reckoned upon, was detained by the floods and frosts, which, for the moment, had made the roads and rivers alike impracticable.

Don Roderigo de Toledo, governor of Bois le Duc, immediately despatched a certain Captain Perea, at the head of two hundred soldiers, who were joined on the way by a miscellaneous force of volunteers, to recover the fortress as soon as possible.† The castle, bathed on its outward walls by the Waal and Meuse, and having two redoubts, defended by a double interior foss, would have been difficult to take by assault‡ had the number of the besieged been at all adequate to its defence. As matters stood, however, the Spaniards, by battering a breach in the wall with their cannon on the first day, and then escalading the inner works with remarkable gallantry upon the second, found themselves masters of the place within eight and forty hours of their first appearance before its gates. Most of the defenders were either slain or captured alive. De Ruyter alone had betaken himself to an inner hall of the castle, where he stood at bay upon the threshold. Many Spaniards, one after another, as they attempted to kill or to secure him, fell before his sword, which he wielded with the strength of a giant.§ At last, overpowered by numbers, and weakened by the loss of blood, he retreated slowly into the hall, followed by many of his antagonists. Here, by an unexpected movement, he applied a match to a train of powder, which he had previously laid along the floor of the apartment. The explosion was instantaneous. The tower, where the contest was taking place, sprang into the air, and De Ruyter with

---

* Bor, vi. 331.

† Bor, Mendoza, Hoofd, ubi sup. Correspondance de Philippe II., ii. 1004.

‡ Mendoza, v. 109, 110.

§ Bor, Hoofd, ubi sup. Meteren, iii. 60. The last writer, who never omits an opportunity to illustrate the prowess of his countrymen, whose courage certainly needs no exaggeration, assures his readers that *three boat-loads of the corpses* of those who had fallen by de Ruyter's arm were carried from the castle.

his enemies shared a common doom.* A part of the mangled remains of this heroic but ferocious patriot were afterwards dug from the ruins of the tower, and with impotent malice nailed upon the gallows at Bois le Duc.† Of his surviving companions, some were beheaded, some were broken on the wheel, some were hung and quartered—all were executed.‡

---

* Bor, Hoofd, ubi sup.   † Bor, Hoofd, Meteren.

‡ "Twee daar af geraabraakt," says Hoofd, vi. 208. "Gefanghen, gepijnigt ende geexecuteert," says Meteren, iii. 60; "desquartizando los soldados que se tomaron bivos en Anvers," says Mendoza.

CHAPTER VI.

WHILE such had been the domestic events of the Netherlands during the years 1569 and 1570, the Prince of Orange, although again a wanderer, had never allowed himself to despair. During this whole period, the darkest hour for himself and for his country, he was ever watchful. After disbanding his troops at Strasburg, and after making the best arrangements possible under the circumstances for the eventual payment of their wages, he had joined the army which the Duke of Deux Ponts had been raising in Germany to assist the cause of the Huguenots in France.[*] The Prince having been forced to acknowledge that, for the moment, all open efforts in the Netherlands were likely to be fruitless, instinctively turned his eyes towards the more favorable aspect of the Reformation in France. It was inevitable that, while he was thus thrown for the time out of his legitimate employment, he should be led to the battles of freedom in a neighbouring land. The Duke of Deux Ponts, who felt his own military skill hardly adequate to the task which he had assumed, was glad, as it were, to put himself and his army under the orders of Orange.[†]

Meantime the battle of Jarnac had been fought ; the Prince of Condé, covered with wounds, and exclaiming that it was sweet to die for Christ and country, had fallen from his saddle ; the whole Huguenot army had been routed by the royal forces under the nominal command of Anjou, and the body of Condé, tied to the back of a she ass, had been paraded through the streets of Jarnac in derision.[‡] Affairs had already grown almost as black for the cause of freedom in France as in the provinces. Shortly afterwards William of Orange, with a band of twelve hundred horsemen, joined the banners of Coligny. His two brothers accompanied him.[§] Henry, the stripling, had left the university to follow the fortunes of the Prince. The indomitable Louis, after seven thousand of his army had been slain, had swum naked across the Ems, exclaiming " that his courage,

---

[*] Bor, v. 269.   Archives et Correspondance, iii. 316.

[†] Langueti, Epist. Secr. i. 95.   Archives et Correspondance, iii. 317.

[‡] De Thou, t. v. liv. xlv. 570–573.   [§] Ibid., 584.

thank God, was as fresh and lively as ever,"[*] and had lost not a moment in renewing his hostile schemes against the Spanish government. In the meantime he had joined the Huguenots in France. The battle of Moncontour had succeeded, Count Peter Mansfeld, with five thousand troops sent by Alva, fighting on the side of the royalists, and Louis Nassau on that of the Huguenots, atoning by the steadiness and skill with which he covered the retreat, for his intemperate courage, which had precipitated the action, and perhaps been the main cause of Coligny's overthrow.[†] The Prince of Orange, who had been peremptorily called to the Netherlands in the beginning of the autumn, was not present at the battle. Disguised as a peasant, with but five attendants, and at great peril, he had crossed the enemy's lines, traversed France, and arrived in Germany before the winter.[‡] Count Louis remained with the Huguenots. So necessary did he seem to their cause, and so dear had he become to their armies, that during the severe illness of Coligny in the course of the following summer all eyes were turned upon him as the inevitable successor of that great man,[§] the only remaining pillar of freedom in France.

Coligny recovered. The deadly peace between the Huguenots and the Court succeeded. The Admiral, despite his sagacity and his suspicions, embarked with his whole party upon that smooth and treacherous current which led to the horrible catastrophe of Saint Bartholomew. To occupy his attention, a formal engagement was made by the government to send succor to the Netherlands. The Admiral was to lead the auxiliaries which were to be despatched across the frontier to overthrow the tyrannical government of Alva. Long and anxious were the colloquies held between Coligny and the Royalists.[||] The monarch requested a detailed opinion, in writing, from the Admiral, on the most advisable plan for invading the Nether-

---

* Groen v. Prinst., Archives et Correspondance, etc., iii. 272, 273.

† De Thou, liv. xlvi. t. v. 638, 639.

‡ Groen v. Prinst., Archives et Correspondance, iii. 322. De Thou, t. v. iv. xlvi. 627. Bor, v. 269.

§ De Thou, t. vi. liv. xlvii. 32–36. || Ibid., 279, 280.

lands. The result was the preparation of the celebrated memoir, under Coligny's directions, by young De Mornay, Seigneur de Plessis. The document was certainly not a paper of the highest order. It did not appeal to the loftier instincts which kings or common mortals might be supposed to possess. It summoned the monarch to the contest in the Netherlands that the ancient injuries committed by Spain might be avenged. It invoked the ghost of Isabella of France, foully murdered, as it was thought, by Philip. It held out the prospect of re-annexing the fair provinces, wrested from the King's ancestors by former Spanish sovereigns. It painted the hazardous position of Philip, with the Moorish revolt gnawing at the entrails of his kingdom, with the Turkish war consuming its extremities, with the canker of rebellion corroding the very heart of the Netherlands. It recalled, with exultation, the melancholy fact that the only natural and healthy existence of the French was in a state of war—that France, if not occupied with foreign campaigns, could not be prevented from plunging its sword into its own vitals. It indulged in refreshing reminiscences of those halcyon days, not long gone by, when France, enjoying perfect tranquillity within its own borders, was calmly and regularly carrying on its long wars beyond the frontier.*

In spite of this savage spirit, which modern documents, if they did not scorn, would at least have shrouded, the paper was nevertheless a sagacious one; but the request for the memoir, and the many interviews on the subject of the invasion, were only intended to deceive. They were but the curtain which concealed the preparations for the dark tragedy which was about to be enacted. Equally deceived, and more sanguine than ever, Louis Nassau during this period was indefatigable in his attempts to gain friends for his cause. He had repeated audiences of the King, to whose court he had come in disguise.† He made a strong and warm impression upon Elizabeth's envoy at the French Court,

---

* De Thou, t. vi. liv. li. 342–357.　　　　† Ibid., t. vi. 279, 280.

Walsingham. It is probable that in the Count's impetuosity to carry his point, he allowed more plausibility to be given to certain projects for subdividing the Netherlands than his brother would ever have sanctioned.* The Prince was a total stranger to these inchoate schemes. His work was to set his country free, and to destroy the tyranny which had grown colossal. That employment was sufficient for a lifetime, and there is no proof to be found that a paltry and personal self-interest had even the lowest place among his motives.

Meantime, in the autumn of 1569, Orange had again reached Germany. Paul Buys, Pensionary of Leyden, had kept him constantly informed of the state of affairs in the provinces.† Through his means an extensive correspondence was organized and maintained with leading persons in every part of the Netherlands. The conventional terms by which different matters and persons of importance were designated in these letters were familiarly known to all friends of the cause, not only in the provinces, but in France, England, Germany, and particularly in the great commercial cities. The Prince, for example, was always designated as Martin Willemzoon, the Duke of Alva as Master Powels van Alblas, the Queen of England as Henry Philipzoon, the King of Denmark as Peter Peterson. The twelve signs of the zodiac were used instead of the twelve months, and a great variety of similar substitutions were adopted.‡ Before his visit to France, Orange had, moreover, issued commissions, in his capacity of sovereign, to various seafaring persons, who were empowered to cruise against Spanish commerce.§

The "beggars of the sea," as these privateersmen designated themselves, soon acquired as terrible a name as the wild beggars, or the forest beggars ;‖ but the Prince, having had many conversations with Admiral Coligny on the important benefits to be derived from the system, had faithfully set him-

* Groen v. Prinst., Archives et Correspondance, iii. 404, 405. Mem. of Walsingham, 143.

† Bor, v. 280.   ‡ Ibid., v. 310.   § Ibid., v. 289.   Hoofd, v. 197.
‖ Bor, v. 289.   Hoofd, v. 198.

self to effect a reformation of its abuses after his return from
France. The Seigneur de Dolhain, who, like many other
refugee nobles, had acquired much distinction in this roving
corsair life, had for a season acted as Admiral for the Prince.
He had, however, resolutely declined to render any accounts
of his various expeditions, and was now deprived of his command in consequence.* Gillain de Fiennes, Seigneur de
Lumbres, was appointed to succeed him. At the same time
strict orders were issued by Orange, forbidding all hostile
measures against the Emperor or any of the princes of the
empire, against Sweden, Denmark, England, or against any
potentates who were protectors of the true Christian religion.†
The Duke of Alva and his adherents were designated as the
only lawful antagonists. The Prince, moreover, gave minute
instructions as to the discipline to be observed in his fleet.
The articles of war were to be strictly enforced. Each commander was to maintain a minister on board his ship, who was
to preach God's word, and to preserve Christian piety among
the crew.‡ No one was to exercise any command in the fleet
save native Netherlanders, unless thereto expressly commissioned by the Prince of Orange. All prizes were to be divided
and distributed by a prescribed rule. No persons were to be received on board, either as sailors or soldiers, save "folk of good
name and fame." No man who had ever been punished of justice was to be admitted.§ Such were the principal features in
the organization of that infant navy which, in course of this
and the following centuries, was to achieve so many triumphs,
and to which a powerful and adventurous mercantile marine
had already led the way. "Of their ships," said Cardinal Bentivoglio, "the Hollanders make houses, of their
houses schools. Here they are born, here educated, here they
learn their profession. Their sailors, flying from one pole to
the other, practising their art wherever the sun displays itself
to mortals, become so skilful that they can scarcely be

---

* Bor, v. 289.

† Ibid., v. 333, 334. Archives et Correspondance, iii. 363, 364.

§ Bor, v. 324, 325.   ‡ Ibid., v. 324, 325, 326. Hoofd, v. 198.

equalled, certainly not surpassed, by any nation in the civilized world."*

The Prince, however, on his return from France, had never been in so forlorn a condition. "Orange is plainly perishing," said one of the friends of the cause.† Not only had he no funds to organize new levies, but he was daily exposed to the most clamorously-urged claims, growing out of the army which he had been recently obliged to disband. It had been originally reported in the Netherlands that he had fallen in the battle of Moncontour. "If he have really been taken off," wrote Viglius, hardly daring to credit the great news, "we shall all of us have less cause to tremble."‡ After his actual return, however, lean and beggared, with neither money nor credit, a mere threatening shadow without substance or power, he seemed to justify the sarcasm of Granvelle. "*Vana sine viribus ira,*" quoted the Cardinal,§ and of a verity it seemed that not a man was likely to stir in Germany in his behalf, now that so deep a gloom had descended upon his cause. The obscure and the oppressed throughout the provinces and Germany still freely contributed out of their weakness and their poverty, and taxed themselves beyond their means to assist enterprizes for the relief of the Netherlands. The great ones of the earth, however, those on whom the Prince had relied ; those to whom he had given his heart ; dukes, princes, and electors, in this fatal change of his fortunes "fell away like water."||

Still his spirit was unbroken. His letters showed a perfect appreciation of his situation, and of that to which his country was reduced ; but they never exhibited a trace of weakness or despair. A modest, but lofty courage ; a pious, but unaffected

---

* Bentivoglio, Guerra di Fiandra, lib., v. 89.

† "Orangius plane periit."—Languet. ad Caner., 101.

‡ Viglii Epist. ad Joach. Hopp., 79.

§ Correspondance de Philippe II., ii. 743.

|| Hoofd, v. 199. Bor, v. 312.—See also Alva's fierce complaints that the people who refused his tenth and twentieth pence contributed voluntarily far greater sums to support the schemes of the Prince of Orange.—Correspondance de Philippe II., ii. passim. Archives et Corresp., iii. passim.

resignation, breathed through every document, public or private, which fell from his pen during this epoch. He wrote to his brother John that he was quite willing to go to Frankfort, in order to give himself up as a hostage to his troops for the payment of their arrears.* At the same time he begged his brother to move heaven and earth to raise at least one hundred thousand thalers. If he could only furnish them with a month's pay, the soldiers would perhaps be for a time contented.† He gave directions also concerning the disposition of what remained of his plate and furniture, the greater part of it having been already sold and expended in the cause. He thought it would, on the whole, be better to have the remainder sold, piece by piece, at the fair. More money would be raised by that course than by a more wholesale arrangement.‡

He was now obliged to attend personally to the most minute matters of domestic economy. The man who had been the mate of emperors, who was himself a sovereign, who had lived his life long in pomp and luxury, surrounded by countless nobles, pages, men-at-arms, and menials, now calmly accepted the position of an outlaw and an exile. He cheerfully fulfilled tasks which had formerly devolved upon his grooms and valets. There was an almost pathetic simplicity in the homely details of an existence which, for the moment, had become so obscure and so desperate. "Send by the bearer," he wrote, " the little hackney given me by the Admiral ; send also my two pair of trunk hose ; one pair is at the tailor's to be mended, the other pair you will please order to be taken from the things which I wore lately at Dillenburg. They lie on the table with my accoutrements. If the little hackney be not in condition, please send the grey horse with the cropped ears and tail."§

He was always mindful. however, not only of the great cause to which he had devoted himself, but of the wants experienced by individuals who had done him service. He

---

* Archives et Correspondance, iii. 355-360.   † Ibid.
‡ Archives et Correspondance de la Maison d'Orange, iii. 355-360.
§ Ibid. iii. 349, 350.

never forgot his friends. In the depth of his own misery he remembered favors received from humble persons. " Send a little cup, worth at least a hundred florins, to Hartmann Wolf," he wrote to his brother ; "you can take as much silver out of the coffer, in which there is still some of my chapel service remaining."* " You will observe that Affenstein is wanting a horse," he wrote on another occasion ; "please look him out one, and send it to me with the price. I will send you the money. Since he has shown himself so willing in the cause, one ought to do something for him."†

The contest between the Duke and the estates, on the subject of the tenth and twentieth penny had been for a season adjusted. The two years' term, however, during which it had been arranged that the tax should be commuted, was to expire in the autumn of 1571.‡ Early therefore in this year the disputes were renewed with greater acrimony than ever. The estates felt satisfied that the King was less eager than the Viceroy. Viglius was satisfied that the power of Alva was upon the wane. While the King was not likely openly to rebuke his recent measures, it seemed not improbable that the Governor's reiterated requests to be recalled might be granted. Fortified by these considerations, the President, who had so long been the supple tool of the tyrant, suddenly assumed the character of a popular tribune. The wranglings, the contradictions, the vituperations, the threatenings, now became incessant in the council. The Duke found that he had exulted prematurely, when he announced to the King the triumphant establishment, in perpetuity, of the lucrative tax. So far from all the estates having given their consent, as he had maintained, and as he had written to Philip, it now appeared that not one of those bodies considered itself bound beyond its quota for the two years. This was formally stated in the council by Berlaymont and other members.§ The wrath of the Duke blazed forth at this announcement. He

---

* Archives et Correspondance, iii. 339.   † Ibid., 349, 350.

‡ Viglii Comm. super imp. Dec. Den., s. 10.

§ Viglii Comm. Dec. Den., s. 27.

berated Berlaymont for maintaining, or for allowing it to be maintained, that the consent of the orders had ever been doubtful. He protested that they had as unequivocally agreed to the perpetual imposition of the tax as he to its commutation during two years. He declared, however, that he was sick of quotas. The tax should now be collected forthwith, and Treasurer Schetz was ordered to take his measures accordingly.*

At a conference on the 29th May, the Duke asked Viglius for his opinion. The President made a long reply, taking the ground that the consent of the orders had been only conditional, and appealing to such members of the finance council as were present, to confirm his assertion. It was confirmed by all. The Duke, in a passion, swore that those who dared maintain such a statement should be chastised.† Viglius replied that it had always been the custom for councillors to declare their opinion, and that they had never before been threatened with such consequences. If such, however, were his Excellency's sentiments, councillors had better stay at home, hold their tongues, and so avoid chastisement.‡ The Duke, controlling himself a little, apologized for this allusion to chastisement, a menace which he disclaimed having intended with reference to councillors whom he had always commended to the King, and of whom his Majesty had so high an opinion. At a subsequent meeting the Duke took Viglius aside, and assured him that *he was quite of his own way of thinking. For certain reasons, however, he expressed himself as unwilling that the rest of the council should be aware of the change in his views. He wished, he said, to dissemble.*§ The astute President, for a moment, could not imagine the Governor's drift. He afterwards perceived that the object of this little piece of deception had been to close his mouth. The Duke obviously conjectured that the President, lulled into security by this secret assurance, would be silent; that the other councillors, believing the President to have adopted the Governor's views, would alter their opinions; and that the opposition of the estates, thus losing its support in the council, would likewise

---

* Viglii Comm. Dec. Den., s. 27.　　　† Ibid., s. xxviii.
‡ Ibid.　　　§ Ibid., s. xxx

very soon be abandoned.* The President, however, was not to be entrapped by this falsehood. He resolutely maintained his hostility to the tax, depending for his security on the royal opinion, the popular feeling, and the judgment of his colleagues.

The daily meetings of the board were almost entirely occupied by this single subject. Although since the arrival of Alva the Council of Blood had usurped nearly all the functions of the state and finance-councils, yet there now seemed a disposition on the part of Alva to seek the countenance, even while he spurned the authority, of other functionaries. He found, however, neither sympathy nor obedience. The President stoutly told him that he was endeavouring to swim against the stream, that the tax was offensive to the people, and that the voice of the people was the voice of God.† On the last day of July, however, the Duke issued an edict, by which summary collection of the tenth and twentieth pence was ordered.‡ The whole country was immediately in uproar. The estates of every province, the assemblies of every city, met and remonstrated. The merchants suspended all business, the petty dealers shut up their shops. The people congregated together in masses, vowing resistance to the illegal and cruel impost.§ Not a farthing was collected. The "seven stiver people,"‖ spies of government, who for that paltry daily stipend were employed to listen for treason in every tavern, in every huckster's booth, in every alley of every city, were now quite unable to report all the curses which were hourly heard uttered against the tyranny of the Viceroy. Evidently, his power was declining. The councillors resisted him, the common people almost defied him. A mercer to whom he was indebted for thirty thousand florins' worth of goods, refused to open his shop, lest the tax should be collected on his merchandize.¶ The Duke confiscated his debt, as the mercer had foreseen, but this being

* Viglii Com. Dec. Den. s. xxx.   † Ibid., s. xxxv.
‡ Ibid., s. xxxviii.   § Ibid., s. xli. Bor, v. 345-348.   ‖ Hoofd, v. 197.
¶ Letter of Comte de Bergh to Prince of Orange in Arch. et Corresp. de la Maison d'Oran. Nass., iii. 409, 410.

a pecuniary sacrifice, seemed preferable to acquiescence in a measure so vague and so boundless that it might easily absorb the whole property of the country.

No man saluted the governor as he passed through the streets.* Hardly an attempt was made by the people to disguise their abhorrence of his person. Alva, on his side, gave daily exhibitions of ungovernable fury. At a council held on 25th September, 1571, he stated that the King had ordered the immediate enforcement of the edict. Viglius observed that there were many objections to its form. He also stoutly denied that the estates had ever given their consent. Alva fiercely asked the President if he had not himself once maintained that the consent had been granted! Viglius replied that he had never made such an assertion. He had mentioned the conditions and the implied promises on the part of government, by which a partial consent had been extorted. He never could have said that the consent had been accorded, for he had never believed that it could be obtained. He had not proceeded far in his argument when he was interrupted by the Duke—"But you said so, you said so, you said so," cried the exasperated Governor, in a towering passion, repeating many times this flat contradiction to the President's statements.† Viglius firmly stood his ground. Alva loudly denounced him for the little respect he had manifested for his authority. He had hitherto done the President good offices, he said, with his Majesty, but certainly should not feel justified in concealing his recent and very unhandsome conduct.‡

Viglius replied that he had always reverently cherished the Governor, and had endeavoured to merit his favor by diligent obsequiousness. He was bound by his oath, however, to utter in council that which comported with his own sentiments and his Majesty's interests. He had done this heretofore in presence of Emperors, Kings, Queens, and Regents, and they had not taken offence. He did not, at this hour, tremble for

---

* Letter of Comte de Bergh to Prince of Orange in Arch. et Corresp. de la Maison d'Oran. Nass., iii. 409, 410.

† Viglii Com., etc., s. xlv. xlvi.   ‡ Ibid., s. xlvii.

his grey head, and hoped his Majesty would grant him a hearing before condemnation.* The firm attitude of the President increased the irritation of the Viceroy. Observing that he knew the proper means of enforcing his authority— he dismissed the meeting.†

Immediately afterwards, he received the visits of his son, Don Frederic of Vargas, and other familiars. To these he recounted the scene which had taken place, raving the while so ferociously against Viglius as to induce the supposition that something serious was intended against him. The report flew from mouth to mouth. The affair became the town talk, so that, in the words of the President, it was soon discussed by every barber and old woman in Brussels.‡ His friends became alarmed for his safety, while, at the same time, the citizens rejoiced that their cause had found so powerful an advocate. Nothing, however, came of these threats and these explosions. On the contrary, shortly afterwards the Duke gave orders that the tenth penny should be remitted upon four great articles—corn, meat, wine, and beer.§ It was also not to be levied upon raw materials used in manufactures.‖ Certainly, these were very important concessions. Still the constitutional objections remained. Alva could not be made to understand why the *alcabala*, which was raised without difficulty in the little town of Alva, should encounter such fierce opposition in the Netherlands. The estates, he informed the King, made a great deal of trouble. They withheld their consent at command of their satrap. The motive which influenced the leading men was not the interest of factories or fisheries, but the fear *that for the future they might not be able to dictate the law to their sovereign.* The people of that country, he observed, had still the same character which had been described by Julius Cæsar.¶

The Duke, however, did not find much sympathy at Madrid. Courtiers and councillors had long derided his schemes. As

---

* Viglii. Com., etc., xlvii.   † Ibid., s. xlviii.

‡ Ibid., l.   § Ibid., s. vi. See Bor, v. 345–348.

‖ Ibid.   ¶ Correspondance de Philippe II., ii. 1063.

for the King, his mind was occupied with more interesting matters. Philip lived but to enforce what he chose to consider the will of God. While the duke was fighting this battle with the Netherland constitutionalists, his master had engaged at home in a secret but most comprehensive scheme. This was a plot to assassinate Queen Elizabeth of England, and to liberate Mary Queen of Scots, who was to be placed on the throne in her stead. This project, in which was of course involved the reduction of England under the dominion of the ancient Church, could not but prove attractive to Philip. It included a conspiracy against a friendly sovereign, immense service to the Church, and a murder. His passion for intrigue, his love of God, and his hatred of man, would all be gratified at once. Thus, although the Moorish revolt within the heart of his kingdom had hardly been terminated—although his legions and his navies were at that instant engaged in a contest of no ordinary importance with the Turkish empire— although the Netherlands, still maintaining their hostility and their hatred, required the flower of the Spanish army to compel their submission, he did not hesitate to accept the dark adventure which was offered to him by ignoble hands.

One Ridolfi, a Florentine, long resident in England, had been sent to the Netherlands as secret agent of the Duke of Norfolk. Alva read his character immediately, and denounced him to Philip as a loose, prating creature,* utterly unfit to be entrusted with affairs of importance. Philip, however, thinking more of the plot than of his fellow-actors, welcomed the agent of the conspiracy to Madrid, listened to his disclosures attentively, and, without absolutely committing himself by direct promises, dismissed him with many expressions of encouragement.

On the 12th of July, 1571, Philip wrote to the Duke of Alva, giving an account of his interview with Roberto Ridolfi.† The envoy, after relating the sufferings of the Queen of Scot-

---

* "Un gran parlanchin."—Correspondance de Philippe II., ii. 180, note, and 1035.   † Ibid., ii. 1038.

land, had laid before him a plan for her liberation. If the Spanish monarch were willing to assist the Duke of Norfolk and his friends, it would be easy to put upon Mary's head the crown of England. She was then to intermarry with Norfolk. The kingdom of England was again to acknowledge the authority of Rome, and the Catholic religion to be everywhere restored. The most favorable moment for the execution of the plan would be in August or September. As Queen Elizabeth would at that season quit London for the country, an opportunity would be easily found *for seizing and murdering her.* Pius V., to whom Ridolfi had opened the whole matter, highly approved the scheme, and warmly urged Philip's co-operation. Poor and ruined as he was himself, the Pope protested that he was ready to sell his chalices, and even his own vestments, to provide funds for the cause.* Philip had replied that few words were necessary to persuade him. His desire to see the enterprize succeed was extreme, notwithstanding the difficulties by which it was surrounded. He would reflect earnestly upon the subject, in the *hope that God, whose cause it was,* would enlighten and assist him. Thus much he had stated to Ridolfi, but he had informed his council afterwards that he was determined to carry out the scheme by certain means of which the Duke would soon be informed. The end proposed *was to kill or to capture Elizabeth,* to set at liberty the Queen of Scotland, and to put upon her head the crown of England. In this enterprize he instructed the Duke of Alva secretly to assist, without however resorting to open hostilities in his own name or in that of his sovereign. He desired to be informed how many Spaniards the Duke could put at the disposition of the conspirators. They had asked for six thousand arquebusiers for England, two thousand for Scotland, two thousand for Ireland. Besides these troops, the Viceroy†

---

* " Y offresciendome su assistencia en general, sin descender à cosa particular, mas de que, siendo necessario, *aunque estava muy pobre* y gastado, ponria hasta los calices y su propria veste."—Correspondance de Philippe II., 1038.

† The title of Viceroy, occasionally given to the Duke, is, of course, not strictly correct—the Netherlands not constituting a kingdom.

was directed to provide immediately four thousand arque-
buses and two thousand corslets. For the expenses of the
enterprize Philip would immediately remit two hundred
thousand crowns. Alva was instructed to keep the affair a
profound secret from his councillors. Even Hopper at Madrid
knew nothing of the matter, while the King had only expressed
himself in general terms to the nuncio and to Ridolfi, then
already on his way to the Netherlands. The King concluded
his letter by saying, that from what he had *now written with
his own hand*, the Duke could infer how much he *had this affair
at heart*. It was unnecessary for him to say more, persuaded
as he was that the Duke would take as profound an interest
in it as himself.*

Alva perceived all the rashness of the scheme, and felt how
impossible it would be for him to comply with Philip's orders.
To send an army from the Netherlands into England for the
purpose of dethroning and killing a most popular sovereign,
and at the same time to preserve the most amicable relations
with the country, was rather a desperate undertaking. A
force of ten thousand Spaniards, under Chiappin Vitelli, and
other favorite officers of the Duke, would hardly prove a trifle
to be overlooked, nor would their operations be susceptible of
very friendly explanations. The Governor therefore assured
Philip† that he " highly applauded his master for his plot.
*He could not help rendering infinite thanks to God for having
made him vassal to such a Prince.*" He praised exceedingly
the resolution which his Majesty had taken.‡ After this preamble, however, he proceeded to pour cold water upon his
sovereign's ardor. He decidedly expressed the opinion that
Philip should not proceed in such an undertaking until at
any rate the party of the Duke of Norfolk had obtained
possession of Elizabeth's person. Should the King declare
himself prematurely, he might be sure that the Venetians,

---

* Correspondance de Philippe II., 1038.   † Ibid., ii. 1041.

‡ *Yo no puedo dexar de dar le (a Dios) infinitas gracias que me haya hecho
vasallo de tal principe,* y alabar mucho la resolucion que V. M. ha tomado."—
Ibid., ii. 1041.

breaking off their alliance with him, would make their peace with the Turk; and that Elizabeth would, perhaps, conclude that marriage with the Duke of Alençon which now seemed but a pleasantry. Moreover, he expressed his want of confidence in the Duke of Norfolk, whom he considered as a poor creature with but little courage.* He also expressed his doubts concerning the prudence and capacity of Don Gueran de Espes, his Majesty's ambassador at London.

It was not long before these machinations became known in England. The Queen of Scots was guarded more closely than ever, the Duke of Norfolk was arrested; yet Philip, whose share in the conspiracy had remained a secret, was not discouraged by the absolute explosion of the whole affair. He still held to an impossible purpose with a tenacity which resembled fatuity. He avowed that his obligations in the sight of God were so strict that he was still determined to proceed in the sacred cause.† He remitted, therefore, the promised funds to the Duke of Alva, and urged him to act with proper secrecy and promptness.

The Viceroy was not a little perplexed by these remarkable instructions. None but lunatics could continue to conspire, after the conspiracy had been exposed and the conspirators arrested. Yet this was what his Catholic Majesty expected of his Governor-General. Alva complained, not unreasonably, of the contradictory demands to which he was subjected.‡ He was to cause no rupture with England, yet he was to send succor to an imprisoned traitor; he was to keep all his operations secret from his council, yet he was to send all his army out of the country, and to organize an expensive campaign. He sneered at the flippancy of Ridolfi, who imagined that it was the work of a moment to seize the Queen of England, to liberate the Queen of Scotland, to take possession of the Tower of London, and to burn the fleet in the Thames. *"Were your Majesty and the Queen of England acting together,"*

---

* "Al duque tengo le por flaco y de poco animo."—Correspóndance de Philippe II., ii. 1041.   † Ibid., ii. 1043.   ‡ Ibid., 1045.

he observed, "it would be impossible to execute the plan proposed by Ridolfi."* The chief danger to be apprehended was from France and Germany. Were those countries not to interfere, he would undertake to make Philip sovereign of England before the winter.† Their opposition, however, was sufficient to make the enterprise not only difficult, but impossible. He begged his master not to be precipitate in the most important affair which had been negotiated by man *since Christ came upon earth*. Nothing less, he said, than the existence of the Christian faith was at stake, for, should his Majesty fail in this undertaking, not one stone of the *ancient religion would be left upon another*.‡ He again warned the King of the contemptible character of Ridolfi, who had spoken of the affair so freely that it was a common subject of discussion on the Bourse at Antwerp,§ and he reiterated in all his letters his distrust of the parties prominently engaged in the transaction.

Such was the general tenor of the long despatches exchanged between the King and the Duke of Alva upon this iniquitous scheme. The Duke showed himself reluctant throughout the whole affair, although he certainly never opposed his master's project by any arguments founded upon good faith, Christian charity, or the sense of honor. To kill the Queen of England, subvert the laws of her realm, burn her fleets, and butcher her subjects, while the mask of amity and entire consideration was sedulously preserved—all these projects were admitted to be strictly meritorious in themselves, although objections were taken as to the time and mode of execution.

Alva never positively refused to accept his share in the enterprise, but he took care not to lift his finger till the catastrophe in England had made all attempts futile. Philip,

---

* Correspondance de Philippe II., ii. 1045.   † Ibid.

‡ Por amor de Dios pido à V. M. que su gran celo no le lleve à errar el mayor negotio de Dios que se ha tratado despues que el vino à la tierra, porque no pende menos que acabarse su religion, que errandole V. M. no queda en toda la Cristianidad piedra sobre piedra en ella."—Ibid.   § Ibid., ii. 1049.

on the other hand, never positively withdrew from the conspiracy, but, after an infinite deal of writing and intriguing, concluded by leaving the whole affair in the hands of Alva.* The only sufferer for Philip's participation in the plot was the Spanish envoy at London, Don Gueran de Espes. This gentleman was formally dismissed by Queen Elizabeth, for having given treacherous and hostile advice to the Duke of Alva and to Philip, but her Majesty at the same time expressed the most profound consideration for her brother of Spain.†

Towards the close of the same year, however (December, 1571), Alva sent two other Italian assassins to England, bribed by the promise of vast rewards, to attempt the life of Elizabeth, quietly, by poison or otherwise.‡ The envoy, Mondoucet, in apprizing the French monarch of this scheme, added that the Duke was so ulcerated and annoyed by the discovery of the previous enterprise, that nothing could exceed his rage. These ruffians were not destined to success, but the attempts of the Duke upon the Queen's life were renewed from time to time. Eighteen months later (August, 1573), two Scotchmen, pensioners of Philip, came from Spain, with secret orders to consult with Alva. They had accordingly much negotiation with the Duke and his secretary, Albornoz. They boasted that they could easily capture Elizabeth, but said that the King's purpose was to kill her.§ The plan, wrote Mondoucet, was the same as it had been before, namely, to murder the Queen of England, and to give her crown to Mary of Scotland, who would thus be in their power, and whose son was to be seized, and bestowed in marriage in such a way as to make them perpetual masters of both kingdoms.‖

It does not belong to this history to discuss the merits, nor

---

* Correspondance de Philippe II., ii. 1051.

† Letter of Queen Elizabeth to Philip II., in Correspondance de Philippe, II. ii. 1069.

‡ Correspondance Charles IX. et Mondoucet. Com. Roy. de l'Hist., iv. 340, sqq.

§ " Mon maistre a bien eu moyen de faire prisonnier la royne d'Angleterre, mais il la voulloit tuer," etc., etc.—Ibid.   Ibid.

to narrate the fortunes, of that bickering and fruitless alliance which had been entered into at this period by Philip with Venice and the Holy See against the Turk. The revolt of Granada had at last, after a two years' struggle, been subdued, and the remnants of the romantic race which had once swayed the Peninsula been swept into slavery. The Moors had sustained the unequal conflict with a constancy not to have been expected of so gentle a people. "If a nation meek as lambs could resist so bravely," said the Prince of Orange, "what ought not to be expected of a hardy people like the Netherlanders?"* Don John of Austria having concluded a series of somewhat inglorious forays against women, children, and bed-ridden old men, in Andalusia and Granada, had arrived, in August of this year, at Naples, to take command of the combined fleet in the Levant.† The battle of Lepanto had been fought,‡ but the quarrelsome and contradictory conduct of the allies had rendered the splendid victory as barren as the waves upon which it had been won. It was no less true, however, that the blunders of the infidels had previously enabled Philip to extricate himself with better success from the dangers of the Moorish revolt than might have been his fortune. Had the rebels succeeded in holding Granada and the mountains of Andalusia, and had they been supported, as they had a right to expect, by the forces of the Sultan, a different aspect might have been given to the conflict, and one far less triumphant for Spain. Had a prince of vigorous ambition and comprehensive policy governed at that moment the Turkish empire, it would have cost Philip a serious struggle to maintain himself in his hereditary dominions. While he was plotting against the life and throne of Elizabeth, he might have had cause to tremble for his own. Fortunately, however, for his Catholic Majesty, Selim was satisfied to secure himself in the possession of the Isle of Venus, with its fruitful vineyards. "To shed the

* Archives et Correspondance, iii. 362.
† De Thou, liv. l. t. vi. 226, et seq. Cabrera, ix. xxiii. 678, et seq.
‡ De Thou, t. vi. 238, et seq. Cabrera, ix. 23, 692, 693.

blood" of Cyprian vines, in which he was so enthusiastic a connoisseur, was to him a more exhilarating occupation than to pursue, amid carnage and hardships, the splendid dream of a re-established Eastern caliphate.*

On the 25th Sept. 1571, a commission of Governor-General of the Netherlands was at last issued to John de la Cerda, Duke of Medina Cœli.† Philip, in compliance with the Duke's repeated requests, and perhaps not entirely satisfied with the recent course of events in the provinces, had at last, after great hesitation, consented to Alva's resignation. His successor, however, was not immediately to take his departure, and in the meantime the Duke was instructed to persevere in his faithful services. These services had, for the present, reduced themselves to a perpetual and not very triumphant altercation with his council, with the estates, and with the people, on the subject of his abominable tax. He was entirely alone. They who had stood unflinchingly at his side when the only business of the administration was to burn heretics, turned their backs upon him now that he had engaged in this desperate conflict with the whole money power of the country. The King was far from cordial in his support, the councillors much too crafty to retain their hold upon the wheel, to which they had only attached themselves in its ascent. Viglius and Berlaymont, Noircarmes and Aerschot, opposed and almost defied the man they now thought sinking, and kept the King constantly informed of the vast distress which the financial measures of the Duke were causing.‡

Quite at the close of the year, an elaborate petition from the estates of Brabant was read before the State Council.§ It contained a strong remonstrance against the tenth penny. Its repeal was strongly urged, upon the ground that its collection

* De Thou, vi. 1. 50.   Cabrera, lib. ix. etc.
† Correspondance de Philippe II., ii.1055.
‡ Ibid. ii. 1056.   Letter from Bishop of Ypres to Philip, 1073, 1074.   Reports drawn up by Don Francis de Alava on the state of the provinces, 1097.   Letters from Bishops of Ypres, Ghent, Bruges.
§ Viglii Comm. Dec. Den., s. lx.

would involve the country in universal ruin. Upon this, Alva burst forth in one of the violent explosions of rage to which he was subject. The prosperity of the Netherlands, he protested, was not dearer to the inhabitants than to himself. He swore by the cross, and by the most holy of holies, preserved in the church of Saint Gudule, that had he been but a private individual, living in Spain, he would, out of the love he bore the provinces, have rushed to their defence had their safety been endangered.* He felt therefore deeply wounded that malevolent persons should thus insinuate that he had even wished to injure the country, or to exercise tyranny over its citizens. The tenth penny, he continued, was necessary to the defence of the land, and was much preferable to quotas. *It was highly improper that every man in the rabble should know how much was contributed, because each individual, learning the gross amount, would imagine that he had paid it all himself.*† In conclusion, he observed that, broken in health and stricken in years as he felt himself, he was now most anxious to return, and was daily looking with eagerness for the arrival of the Duke of Medina Cœli.‡

During the course of this same year, the Prince of Orange had been continuing his preparations. He had sent his agents to every place where a hope was held out to him of obtaining support. Money was what he was naturally most anxious to obtain from individuals ; open and warlike assistance what he demanded from governments. His funds, little by little, were increasing, owing to the generosity of many obscure persons, and to the daring exploits of the beggars of the sea. His mission, however, to the northern courts had failed. His envoys had been received in Sweden and Denmark with barren courtesy.§ The Duke of Alva, on the other hand, never alluded to the Prince but with contempt ; knowing not that the ruined outlaw was slowly undermining the very ground beneath the monarch's feet ; dreaming not that the feeble

---

* Viglii Comm. Dec. Den. **s. lx.**   † Ibid.

‡ Ibid. lxi.   § Bor, v. 334–340. Hoofd, vi. 210

strokes which he despised were the opening blows of a century's conflict ; foreseeing not that long before its close the chastised province was to expand into a great republic, and that the name of the outlaw was to become almost divine.

Granvelle had already recommended that the young Count de Buren should be endowed with certain lands in Spain, in exchange for his hereditary estates, in order that the name and fame of the rebel William should be forever extinguished in the Netherlands.* With the same view, a new sentence against the Prince of Orange was now proposed by the Viceroy. This was, to execute him solemnly in effigy, to drag his escutcheon through the streets at the tails of horses, and after having broken it in pieces, and thus cancelled his armorial bearings, to declare him and his descendants, ignoble, infamous, and incapable of holding property or estates.† Could a leaf or two of future history have been unrolled to King, Cardinal, and Governor, they might have found the destined fortune of the illustrious rebel's house not exactly in accordance with the plan of summary extinction thus laid down.

Not discouraged, the Prince continued to send his emissaries in every direction. Diedrich Sonoy, his most trustworthy agent, who had been chief of the legation to the Northern Courts, was now actively canvassing the governments and peoples of Germany with the same object.‡ Several remarkable papers from the hand of Orange were used upon this service. A letter, drawn up and signed by his own hand, recited, in brief and striking language, the history of his campaign in 1568, and of his subsequent efforts in the sacred cause.§ It was now necessary, he said, that others besides himself should partake of his sacrifices. This he stated plainly and eloquently. The document was in truth a letter asking arms for liberty. " For although all things," said the Prince, " are in the hand of God, and although he has created all things out of nought, yet hath he granted to different

---

* Correspondance de Philippe II., ii. 959.   † Ibid., 1027.
‡ Bor, vi. 362.   § See it in Bor, vi. 362, 363.

men different means, whereby, as with various instruments, he accomplishes his almighty purposes. Thereto hath he endowed some with strength of body, others with worldly wealth, others with still different gifts, all of which are to be used by their possessors to His honor and glory, if they wish not to incur the curse of the unworthy steward, who buried his talent in the earth. . . . .
Now ye may easily see," he continued, " that the Prince cannot carry out this great work alone, having lost land, people, and goods, and having already employed in the cause all which had remained to him, besides incurring heavy obligations in addition."*

Similar instructions were given to other agents, and a paper called the Harangue, drawn up according to his suggestions, was also extensively circulated. This document is important to all who are interested in his history and character.† He had not before issued a missive so stamped with the warm, religious impress of the reforming party. Sadly, but without despondency, the Harangue recalled the misfortunes of the past, and depicted the gloom of the present. Earnestly, but not fanatically, it stimulated hope and solicited aid for the future. " Although the appeals made to the Prince," so ran a part of the document, " be of diverse natures, and various in their recommendations, yet do they all tend to the advancement of God's glory, and to the liberation of the fatherland. This it is which enables him and those who think with him to endure hunger, thirst, cold, heat, and all the misfortunes which Heaven may send. . . . . . . Our enemies spare neither their money nor their labor ; will ye be colder and duller than your foes ? Let, then, each church congregation set an example to the others. We read that King Saul, when he would liberate the men of Jabez from the hands of Nahad, the Ammonite, hewed a yoke of oxen in pieces, and sent them as tokens over all Israel, saying, ' Ye who will not follow Saul and Samuel, with them shall be dealt even as with these oxen. And the fear of the Lord came upon

---

* Bor, ubi sup. † See the Harangue in Bor, vi. 363–365.

the people, they came forth, and the men of Jabez were delivered.' Ye have here the same warning, look to it, watch well ye that despise it, lest the wrath of God, which the men of Israel by their speedy obedience escaped, descend upon your heads. . . . . . Ye may say that ye are banished men. 'Tis true : but thereby are ye not stripped of all faculty of rendering service ; moreover, your assistance is asked for one who will restore ye to your homes. Ye may say that ye have been robbed of all your goods ; yet many of you have still something remaining, and of that little ye should contribute, each his mite. Ye say that you have given much already. 'Tis true : but the enemy is again in the field, fierce for your subjugation, sustained by the largess of his supporters. Will ye be less courageous, less generous, than your foes."*

These urgent appeals did not remain fruitless. The strength of the Prince was slowly but steadily increasing. Meantime the abhorrence with which Alva was universally regarded had nearly reached to frenzy. In the beginning of the year 1572, Don Francis de Alava, Philip's ambassador in France, visited Brussels.† He had already been enlightened as to the consequences of the Duke's course by the immense immigration of Netherland refugees to France, which he had witnessed with his own eyes. On his journey towards Brussels he had been met near Cambray by Noircarmes. Even that "cruel animal," as Hoogstraaten had called him, the butcher of Tournay and Valenciennes, had at last been roused to alarm, if not to pity, by the sufferings of the country. "The Duke will never disabuse his mind of this filthy tenth penny,"‡ said he to Alava. He sprang from his chair with great emotion as the ambassador alluded to the flight of merchants and artisans from the provinces. "Señor Don Francis," cried he, "there are ten thousand more who are on the point of leaving the country, if the Governor does not pause in his career. God

---

* Harangue of the Commissioners of my Lord the Prince of Orange, ubi sup.
† Correspondance de Philippe II., ii. 1073, 1074.
‡ "Desta negra decima."—Ibid., ii. 1073.

grant that no disaster arise beyond human power to remedy."*

The ambassador arrived in Brussels, and took up his lodgings in the palace. Here he found the Duke just recovering from a fit of the gout, in a state of mind sufficiently savage. He became much excited as Don Francis began to speak of the emigration, and he assured him that there was gross deception on the subject.† The envoy replied that he could not be mistaken, for it was a matter which, so to speak, he had touched with his own fingers, and seen with his own eyes. The Duke, persisting that Don Francis had been abused and misinformed, turned the conversation to other topics. Next day the ambassador received visits from Berlaymont and his son, the Seigneur de Hierges. He was taken aside by each of them, separately. "Thank God, you have come hither," said they, in nearly the same words, "that you may fully comprehend the condition of the provinces, and without delay admonish his Majesty of the impending danger."‡ All his visitors expressed the same sentiments. Don Frederic of Toledo furnished the only exception, assuring the envoy that his father's financial measures were opposed by Noircarmes and others, only because it deprived them of their occupation and their influence.§ This dutiful language, however, was to be expected in one of whom Secretary Albornoz had written, that he was the greatest comfort to his father, and the most divine genius ever known.‖ It was unfortunately corroborated by no other inhabitant of the country.

On the third day, Don Francis went to take his leave. The Duke begged him to inform his Majesty of the impatience with which he was expecting the arrival of his successor.¶ He then informed his guest that they had already begun to collect the tenth penny in Brabant, the most obstinate of all the provinces. "What do you say to that, Don Francis?" he cried, with exultation. Alava

* Correspondance de Philippe II., ii. 1073.

† Ibid.   ‡ Ibid   § Ibid.

‖ "El mas divino ingenio."—Letter to Cayas. Correspondance de Philippe II., ii. 886.   ¶ Ibid., 1073.

replied that he thought, none the less, that the tax would encounter many obstacles, and begged him earnestly to reflect. He assured him, moreover, that he should, without reserve, express his opinions fully to the King. The Duke used the same language which Don Frederic had held, concerning the motives of those who opposed the tax. " It may be so," said Don Francis, " but at any rate, all have agreed to sing to the same tune." A little startled, the Duke rejoined, " Do you doubt that the cities will keep their promises ? Depend upon it, I shall find the means to compel them." " God grant it may be so," said Alava, " but in my poor judgment you will have need of all your prudence and of all your authority."[*]

The ambassador did not wait till he could communicate with his sovereign by word of mouth. He forwarded to Spain an ample account of his observations and deductions. He painted to Philip in lively colors the hatred entertained by all men for the Duke. The whole nation, he assured his Majesty, united in one cry, " Let him begone, let him begone, let him begone !" As for the imposition of the tenth penny, that, in the opinion of Don Francis, was utterly impossible. He moreover warned his Majesty that Alva was busy in forming secret alliances with the Catholic princes of Europe, which would necessarily lead to defensive leagues among the Protestants.[‡]

While thus, during the earlier part of the year 1572, the Prince of Orange, discouraged by no defeats, was indefatigable in his exertions to maintain the cause of liberty, and while at the same time the most stanch supporters of arbitrary power were unanimous in denouncing to Philip the insane conduct of his Viceroy, the letters of Alva himself were naturally full of complaints and expostulations. It was in vain, he said, for him to look for a confidential councillor, now that matters which he had wished to be kept so profoundly secret that the very earth should not hear of them, had been proclaimed aloud above the tiles of every housetop.[§] Nevertheless, he would

---

[*] Correspondance de Philippe II., ii. 1073.
[†] "Todo el pueblo esta en *vaya, vaya, vaya!*—Ibid., 1074.
[‡] Ibid   [§] Ibid., ii. 1095.

be cut into little pieces but his Majesty should be obeyed,
while he remained alive to enforce the royal commands.*
There were none who had been ever faithful but Berlaymont,
he said, and even *he* had been neutral in the affair of the tax.
He had rendered therein neither good nor bad offices, but, as
his Majesty was aware, Berlaymont was entirely ignorant of
business, and "knew nothing more than to be a good fellow."†
That being the case, he recommended Hierges, son of the
"good fellow," as a proper person to be governor of Friesland.‡

The deputations appointed by the different provinces to
confer personally with the King received a reprimand upon
their arrival, for having dared to come to Spain without permission. Farther punishment, however, than this rebuke was
not inflicted. They were assured that the King was highly
displeased with their venturing to bring remonstrances against
the tax, but they were comforted with the assurance that his
Majesty would take the subject of their petition into consideration.§ Thus, the expectations of Alva were disappointed,
for the tenth penny was not formally confirmed ; and the
hopes of the provinces frustrated, because it was not distinctly
disavowed.

Matters had reached another crisis in the provinces. "Had
we money now," wrote the Prince of Orange, "we should,
with the help of God, hope to effect something. This is
a time when, with even small sums, more can be effected than
at other seasons with ampler funds."‖ The citizens were in
open revolt against the tax. In order that the tenth penny
should not be levied upon every sale of goods, the natural but
desperate remedy was adopted—no goods were sold at all.
Not only the wholesale commerce of the provinces was suspended, but the minute and indispensable traffic of daily life
was entirely at a stand. The shops were all shut. "The
brewers," says a contemporary, "refused to brew, the bakers

---

* Correspondance de Philippe II., ii. 1095.

† "Y no sabe mas que ser buen hombre."—Ibid ii. 1103.　　　　‡ Ibid.

§ "Relation of what passed from the arrival of the deputies at Madrid till
20th April, 1572."—Ibid., ii. 1105.　　　　　　　　　　‖ Bor, vi. 362.

to bake, the tapsters to tap."* Multitudes, thrown entirely out of employment, and wholly dependent upon charity, swarmed in every city. The soldiery, furious for their pay, which Alva had for many months neglected to furnish, grew daily more insolent ; the citizens, maddened by outrage and hardened by despair, became more and more obstinate in their resistance ; while the Duke, rendered inflexible by opposition and insane by wrath, regarded the ruin which he had caused with a malignant spirit which had long ceased to be human. " The disease is gnawing at our vitals," wrote Viglius ;† " everybody is suffering for the want of the necessaries of life. Multitudes are in extreme and hopeless poverty. My interest in the welfare of the commonwealth," he continued, " induces me to send these accounts to Spain. For myself, I fear nothing. Broken by sickness and acute physical suffering, I should leave life without regret."

The aspect of the capital was that of a city stricken with the plague. Articles of the most absolute necessity could not be obtained. It was impossible to buy bread, or meat, or beer. The tyrant, beside himself with rage at being thus braved in his very lair, privately sent for Master Carl, the executioner.‡ In order to exhibit an unexpected and salutary example, he had determined to hang eighteen of the leading tradesmen of the city in the doors of their own shops, with the least possible delay and without the slightest form of trial.§ Master Carl was ordered, on the very night of his interview with the Duke, to prepare eighteen strong cords, and eighteen ladders twelve feet in length.‖ By this simple arrangement, Alva was disposed to make manifest on the morrow, to the burghers of Brussels, that justice was thenceforth to be carried to every man's door. He supposed that the spectacle of a dozen and a half of butchers and bakers suspended in front

---

* " De Brouwers en wilden niet brouwen, de Backers en wilden niet backen, noch Tappers niet tappen."—Bor, vi. 361.

† Viglii Epist. ad Joach. Hopper, 126.

‡ Bor, vi. 361.   § Ibid. Strada, lib. vii. 357. Hoofd, vi. 216.

‖ Bor, Hoofd, ubi sup.

of the shops which they had refused to open, would give a more effective stimulus to trade than any to be expected from argument or proclamation. The hangman was making ready his cords and ladders ; Don Frederic of Toledo was closeted with President Viglius,* who, somewhat against his will, was aroused at midnight to draw the warrants for these impromptu executions ; Alva was waiting with grim impatience for the dawn upon which the show was to be exhibited, when an unforeseen event suddenly arrested the homely tragedy. In the night arrived the intelligence that the town of Brill had been captured. The Duke, feeling the full gravity of the situation, postponed the chastisement which he had thus secretly planned to a more convenient season, in order without an instant's hesitation to avert the consequences of this new movement on the part of the rebels. The seizure of Brill was the *Deus ex machinâ* which unexpectedly solved both the inextricable knot of the situation and the hangman's noose.†

Allusion has more than once been made to those formidable partisans of the patriot cause, the marine outlaws. Cheated of half their birthright by nature, and now driven forth from their narrow isthmus by tyranny, the exiled Hollanders took to the ocean. Its boundless fields, long arable to their industry, became fatally fruitful now that oppression·was transforming a peaceful seafaring people into a nation of corsairs. Driven to outlawry and poverty, no doubt many Netherlanders plunged into crime. The patriot party had long since laid aside the respectful deportment which had provoked the sarcasms of the loyalists. The beggars of the sea asked their alms through the mouths of their cannon. Unfortunately, they but too often made their demands upon both friend and foe.‡ Every ruined merchant, every banished lord, every reckless mariner, who was willing to lay the commercial

---

* Bor, vi. 361.   Hoofd, vi. 216.

† Strada, lib. vii. 357.   Bor, Hoofl, suprâ.

‡ Letter of Prince of Orange to the refugee church at London, 26th February, 1573.—Archives de la Maison d'Orange Nassau, iv. 63–66.

world under contribution to repair his damaged fortunes, could, without much difficulty, be supplied with a vessel and crew at some northern port, under color of cruising against the Viceroy's government.* Nor was the ostensible motive simply a pretext. To make war upon Alva was the leading object of all these freebooters, and they were usually furnished by the Prince of Orange, in his capacity of sovereign, with letters of marque for that purpose.† The Prince, indeed, did his utmost to control and direct an evil which had inevitably grown out of the horrors of the time. His Admiral, William de la Marck, was, however, incapable of comprehending the lofty purposes of his superior. A wild, sanguinary, licentious noble, wearing his hair and beard unshorn, according to ancient Batavian custom, until the death of his relative, Egmont, should have been expiated, a worthy descendant of the Wild Boar of Ardennes, this hirsute and savage corsair seemed an embodiment of vengeance. He had sworn to wreak upon Alva and upon popery the deep revenge owed to them by the Netherland nobility, and in the cruelties afterwards practised by him upon monks and priests, the Blood Council learned that their example had made at least one ripe scholar among the rebels.‡ He was lying, at this epoch, with his fleet on the southern coast of England, from which advantageous position he was now to be ejected in a summary manner.§

* "Nam audacissimus quisque Belgica extorres et inops exilium metuentes, in naves se conjecerant, aliasque complures obvias per vim, nacti, aucto numero, prædabundi oceano et per oram maritimam vagabantur. In hanc multitudinem Aurasionensis, quanquam jus et regimen aberant, speciem imperii retinebat, distributis per codicillos potestatibus."—Grotii Annal. lib. ii. 49.   † Ibid.

‡ Vide Bor, vi. 365.   V. Meteren, 64.   Hoofd, 216 seq.—See also Van Wyn of Wagenaer, vi. 86; Van der Vynckt, ii. 127; Grotii Ann., lib. ii. 49; Ulloa, Comment., i. 60.

§ The practice of effecting marine insurances took a great and rapid extension from these and similar piracies. Renom de France MS. (ii. 12) supposes the system to have been invented by the Antwerp merchants at this epoch. The custom, however, was doubtless established at an earlier period in Flanders, England, Italy and Spain. The statute 43 Eliz. c. 12, on the subject, speaks of the immemorial usage among merchants, both English and foreign, to procure

The negotiations between the Duke of Alva and Queen Elizabeth had already assumed an amicable tone, and were fast ripening to an adjustment. It lay by no means in that sovereign's disposition to involve herself at this juncture in a war with Philip, and it was urged upon her government by Alva's commissioners, that the continued countenance afforded by the English people to the Netherland cruisers must inevitably lead to that result. In the latter days of March, therefore, a sentence of virtual excommunication was pronounced against De la Marck and his rovers. A peremptory order of Elizabeth forbade any of her subjects to supply them with meat, bread, or beer.* The command being strictly complied with, their farther stay was rendered impossible. Twenty-four vessels accordingly, of various sizes, commanded by De la Marck, Treslong, Adam van Haren, Brand, and other distinguished seamen, set sail from Dover† in the very last days of March.‡ Being almost in a state of starvation, these adventurers were naturally anxious to supply themselves with food. They determined to make a sudden foray upon the coasts of North Holland, and accordingly steered for Enkbuizen, both because it was a rich sea-port and because it contained many secret partisans of the Prince. On Palm Sunday they captured two Spanish merchantmen. Soon afterwards, however, the wind becoming contrary, they were unable to double the Helder or the Texel, and on Tuesday, the

---

insurance on ships and goods. The Duke of Alva, at this time, after consultation with the merchants, drew up an edict regulating contracts of assurance; stipulating that the sum insured should be less than the just and common value of the property insured, one-tenth at least remaining at the risk of the insurer, and prescribing the forms for the policies. A public officer was appointed to keep register of these contracts, which, without such registration, were to be invalid. Masters, pilots, and sailors were not allowed to insure their wages, or anything belonging to them. Fraud on the part of the insurers or the insured was punished with death and confiscation. These contracts were, however, entirely insufficient to protect vessels, which were plundered daily by " ce canaille de corsaires," which infested every sea and bay.—Renom de France MS. ii. c. 12.

   * Bor, vi. 365, 366.

   † Probably Dover. See in particular Van Wyn op Wagr. vi. 77; also Meteren, 68.   ‡ Bor, ubi sup. Wagenaer, vi. 340, seq.

1st of April, having abandoned their original intention, they dropped down towards Zealand, and entered the broad mouth of the river Meuse. Between the town of Brill, upon the southern lip of this estuary, and Maaslandsluis, about half a league distant, upon the opposite side, the squadron suddenly appeared at about two o'clock of an April afternoon, to the great astonishment of the inhabitants of both places.* It seemed too large a fleet to be a mere collection of trading vessels, nor did they appear to be Spanish ships. Peter Koppelstok, a sagacious ferryman, informed the passengers whom he happened to be conveying across the river, that the strangers were evidently the water beggars.† The dreaded name filled his hearers with consternation, and they became eager to escape from so perilous a vicinity. Having duly landed his customers, however, who hastened to spread the news of the impending invasion, and to prepare for defence or flight, the stout ferryman, who was secretly favorable to the cause of liberty, rowed boldly out to inquire the destination and purposes of the fleet.

The vessel which he first hailed was that commanded by William de Blois, Seigneur of Treslong. This adventurous noble, whose brother had been executed by the Duke of Alva in 1568,‡ had himself fought by the side of Count Louis at Jemmingen, and although covered with wounds, had been one of the few who escaped alive from that horrible carnage. During the intervening period he had become one of the most famous rebels on the ocean, and he had always been well known in Brill, where his father had been governor for the King.§ He at once recognized Koppelstok, and hastened with him on board the Admiral's ship, assuring De la Marck that the ferryman was exactly the man for their purpose. It was absolutely necessary that a landing should be effected, for the people were without the necessaries of life. Captain Martin Brand had visited

---

* Bor. ubi sup.   Hoofd, p. 216, 217.   † Bor, Hoofd, Wagenaer, ubi sup.
‡ Sententien van Alva, 73, 74.
§ Bor, vi. 366.

the ship of Adam Van Haren, as soon as they had dropped anchor in the Meuse, begging for food. "I gave him a cheese," said Adam, afterwards relating the occurrence," and assured him that it was the last article of food to be found in the ship."* The other vessels were equally destitute. Under the circumstances, it was necessary to attempt a landing. Treslong, therefore, who was really the hero of this memorable adventure, persuaded De la Marck to send a message to the city of Brill, demanding its surrender. This was a bold summons to be made by a handful of men, three or four hundred at most,† who were both metaphorically and literally beggars. The city of Brill was not populous, but it was well walled and fortified. It was moreover a most commodious port. Treslong gave his signet ring to the fisherman, Koppelstok, and ordered him, thus accredited as an envoy, to carry their summons to the magistracy.‡ Koppelstok, nothing loath, instantly rowed ashore, pushed through the crowd of inhabitants, who overwhelmed him with questions, and made his appearance in the town-house before the assembled magistrates. He informed them that he had been sent by the Admiral of the fleet and by Treslong, who was well known to them, to demand that two commissioners should be sent out on the part of the city to confer with the patriots. He was bidden, he said, to give assurance that the deputies would be courteously treated. The only object of those who had sent him was to free the land from the tenth penny, and to overthrow the tyranny of Alva and his Spaniards. Hereupon he was asked by the magistrates, how large a force De la Marck had under his command. To this question the ferryman carelessly replied, that there might *be some five thousand in all*.§ This enormous falsehood

---

* Van Wyn op Wagenr. vi. 78, from a MS. journal kept by Adam van Haren himself.

† Bor states their numbers at two hundred and fifty, vi. 366. Hoofd follows Bor. Mendoza, f. 111, says there were eleven hundred in all. The Duke of Alva in his letter of 26th April, 1572 (No. 1107, Correspondance de Philippe II.), estimates them at between seven and eight hundred. Bentivoglio, lib. v. 88, says one thousand.

‡ Bor, Hoofd, Van Wyn.   § Hoofd. vi. 218.

produced its effect upon the magistrates. There was now no longer any inclination to resist the invaders ; the only question discussed being whether to treat with them or to fly. On the whole, it was decided to do both. With some difficulty, two deputies were found sufficiently valiant to go forth to negotiate with the beggars, while in their absence most of the leading burghers and functionaries made their preparations for flight. The envoys were assured by De la Marck and Treslong that no injury was intended to the citizens or to private property, but that the overthrow of Alva's government was to be instantly accomplished. Two hours were given to the magistrates in which to decide whether or not they would surrender the town and accept the authority of De la Marck as Admiral of the Prince of Orange. They employed the two hours thus granted in making an ignominious escape. Their example was followed by most of the townspeople. When the invaders, at the expiration of the specified term, appeared under the walls of the city, they found a few inhabitants of the lower class gazing at them from above, but received no official communication from any source.[*]

The whole rebel force was now divided into two parties, one of which under Treslong made an attack upon the southern gate, while the other commanded by the Admiral advanced upon the northern. Treslong after a short struggle succeeded in forcing his entrance, and arrested, in doing so, the governor of the city, just taking his departure. De la Marck and his men made a bonfire at the northern gate, and then battered down the half-burned portal with the end of an old mast.[†] Thus rudely and rapidly did the Netherland patriots conduct their first successful siege. The two parties, not more perhaps than two hundred and fifty men in all, met before sunset in the centre of the city, and the foundation of the Dutch Republic was laid. The weary spirit of freedom, so long a fugitive over earth and sea, had at last found a resting-place, which rude and even ribald hands had prepared.

---

[*] Bor, vi. 366. Hoofd, vi. 218.　　　　[†] Bor, vi. 366. Hoofd, Wagenaer.

The panic created by the first appearance of the fleet had been so extensive that hardly fifty citizens had remained in the town. The rest had all escaped, with as much property as they could carry away. The Admiral, in the name of the Prince of Orange, as lawful stadholder of Philip, took formal possession of an almost deserted city. No indignity was offered to the inhabitants of either sex, but as soon as the conquerors were fairly established in the best houses of the place, the inclination to plunder the churches could no longer be restrained. The altars and images were all destroyed, the rich furniture and gorgeous vestments appropriated to private use. Adam van Haren appeared on his vessel's deck attired in a magnificent high mass chasuble. Treslong thenceforth used no drinking cups in his cabin save the golden chalices of the sacrament. Unfortunately, their hatred to popery was not confined to such demonstrations. Thirteen unfortunate monks and priests, who had been unable to effect their escape, were arrested and thrown into prison, from whence they were taken a few days later, by order of the ferocious Admiral, and executed under circumstances of great barbarity.*

The news of this important exploit spread with great rapidity. Alva, surprised at the very moment of venting his rage on the butchers and grocers of Brussels, deferred this savage design in order to deal with the new difficulty. He had certainly not expected such a result from the ready compliance of Queen Elizabeth with his request. His rage was excessive ; the triumph of the people, by whom he was cordially detested, proportionably great. The punsters of Brussels were sure not to let such an opportunity escape them, for the name of the captured town was susceptible of a quibble, and the event had taken place upon All Fools' Day.

> "On April's Fool's Day,
>   Duke Alva's spectacles were stolen away,"

---

* Bor, vi. 366, 367. Van Wyn op Wagenaer, vi. 84, note 10.

became a popular couplet.* The word *spectacles*, in Flemish, as well as the name of the suddenly surprised city, being Brill, this allusion to the Duke's loss and implied purblindness was not destitute of ingenuity. A caricature, too, was extensively circulated, representing De la Marck stealing the Duke's spectacles from his nose, while the Governor was supposed to be uttering his habitual expression whenever any intelligence of importance was brought to him : *No es nada, no es nada*—'Tis nothing, 'tis nothing.†

The Duke, however, lost not an instant in attempting to repair the disaster. Count Bossu, who had acted as stadholder of Holland and Zealand, under Alva's authority, since the Prince of Orange had resigned that office, was ordered at once to recover the conquered sea-port, if possible.‡

Hastily gathering a force of some ten companies from the garrison of Utrecht, some of which very troops had recently and unluckily for government, been removed from Brill to that city, the Count crossed the Sluis to the island of Voorn upon Easter day, and sent a summons to the rebel force to surrender Brill. The patriots being very few in number, were at first afraid to venture outside the gates to attack the much superior force of their invaders. A carpenter, however, who belonged to the city, but had long been a partisan of Orange, dashed into the water with his axe in his hand, and swimming to the Niewland sluice, hacked it open with a few vigorous strokes. The sea poured in at once, making the approach to the city upon the north side impossible. Bossu then led his Spaniards along the Niewland dyke to the southern gate, where they were received with a warm discharge of artillery, which completely staggered them. Meantime Treslong and Robol had, in the most daring manner, rowed out to the ships which had brought the enemy to the island, cut some adrift, and set others on fire. The

---

* Bor, vi. 366:—"Den eersten dag van April
      Verloos Duc d'Alva zijnen Bril."
† Vie du Duc d'Albe, i. 403.   Van der Vynckt, ii. 142.   ‡ Bor, vi. 367.

Spaniards at the southern gate caught sight of their blazing vessels, saw the sea rapidly rising over the dyke, became panic-struck at being thus enclosed between fire and water, and dashed off in precipitate retreat along the slippery causeway and through the slimy and turbid waters, which were fast threatening to overwhelm them.* Many were drowned or smothered in their flight, but the greater portion of the force effected their escape in the vessels which still remained within reach. This danger averted, Admiral de la Marck summoned all the inhabitants, a large number of whom had returned to the town after the capture had been fairly established, and required them, as well as all the population of the island, to take an oath of allegiance to the Prince of Orange as stadholder for his Majesty.†

The Prince had not been extremely satisfied with the enterprise of De la Marck.‡ He thought it premature, and doubted whether it would be practicable to hold the place, as he had not yet completed his arrangements in Germany, nor assembled the force with which he intended again to take the field. More than all, perhaps, he had little confidence in the character of his Admiral. Orange was right in his estimate of De la Marck. It had not been that rover's design either to take or to hold the place ; and after the descent had been made, the ships victualled, the churches plundered, the booty secured, and a few monks murdered, he had given orders for the burning of the town, and for the departure of the fleet.§ The urgent solicitations of Treslong, however, prevailed, with some difficulty, over De la Marck's original intentions. It is to that bold and intelligent noble, therefore, more than to any other individual, that the merit of laying this corner-stone of the Batavian commonwealth belongs.|| The enterprise itself was

---

* "Door slyk, door slop, door dik en dun," are the homely but vigorous expressions of the Netherland chronicler.—Bor, vi. 367.

† Ibid., vi. 368. Hoofd, vi. 220.

‡ Bor, vi. 367. Hoofd, vi. 221. Wagenaer, vi. 348.

§ Bor, vi. 366. Hoofd, v. 219. Wagenaer, vi. 345, 346.

|| Hoofd, vi. 219.

an accident, but the quick eye of Treslong saw the possibility of a permanent conquest, where his superior dreamed of nothing beyond a piratical foray.

Meantime Bossu, baffled in his attempt upon Brill, took his way towards Rotterdam. It was important that he should at least secure such other cities as the recent success of the rebels might cause to waver in their allegiance. He found the gates of Rotterdam closed. The authorities refused to comply with his demand to admit a garrison for the King. Professing perfect loyalty, the inhabitants very naturally refused to admit a band of sanguinary Spaniards to enforce their obedience. Compelled to parley, Bossu resorted to a perfidious stratagem. He requested permission for his troops to pass through the city without halting. This was granted by the magistrates, on condition that only a corporal's command should be admitted at a time. To these terms the Count affixed his hand and seal.* With the admission, however, of the first detachment, a violent onset was made upon the gate by the whole Spanish force. The townspeople, not suspecting treachery, were not prepared to make effective resistance. A stout smith, confronting the invaders at the gate, almost singly, with his sledge-hammer, was stabbed to the heart by Bossu with his own hand.† The soldiers having thus gained admittance, rushed through the streets, putting every man to death who offered the slightest resistance. Within a few minutes four hundred citizens were murdered. The fate of the women, abandoned now to the outrage of a brutal soldiery, was worse than death. The capture of Rotterdam is infamous for the same crimes which blacken the record of every Spanish triumph in the Netherlands.‡

The important town of Flushing, on the Isle of Walcheren, was first to vibrate with the patriotic impulse given by the success at Brill. The Seigneur de Herpt, a warm partisan of Orange, excited the burghers assembled in the market-place

---

* Bor, vi. 368.   † Ibid.   Hoofd, vi. 220, 221.
‡ Meteren, 66.   Bor, Hoofd, ubi sup.

to drive the small remnant of the Spanish garrison from the city. A little later upon the same day a considerable reinforcement arrived before the walls. The Duke had determined, although too late, to complete the fortress which had been commenced long before to control the possession of this important position at the mouth of the western Scheld. The troops who were to resume this too long intermitted work arrived just in time to witness the expulsion of their comrades. De Herpt easily persuaded the burghers that the die was cast, and that their only hope lay in a resolute resistance. The people warmly acquiesced, while a half-drunken, half-witted fellow in the crowd valiantly proposed, in consideration of a pot of beer, to ascend the ramparts and to discharge a couple of pieces of artillery at the Spanish ships. The offer was accepted, and the vagabond merrily mounting the height, discharged the guns. Strange to relate, the shot thus fired by a lunatic's hand put the invading ships to flight. A sudden panic seized the Spaniards, the whole fleet stood away at once in the direction of Middelburg, and were soon out of sight.*

The next day, however, Antony of Bourgoyne, governor under Alva for the Island of Walcheren, made his appearance in Flushing. Having a high opinion of his own oratorical powers, he came with the intention of winning back with his rhetoric a city which the Spaniards had thus far been unable to recover with their cannon. The great bell was rung, the whole population assembled in the market-place, and Antony, from the steps of the town-house, delivered a long oration, assuring the burghers, among other asseverations, that the King, who *was the best natured prince in all Christendom*, would forget and forgive their offences if they returned honestly to their duties.†

The effect of the Governor's eloquence was much diminished, however, by the interlocutory remarks, of De Herpt and a group of his adherents. They reminded the people of the

---

* Bor, vi. 369, 370. Hoofd, vi. 222.   † Bor, vi. 370. Hoofd, vi. 22?

King's good nature, of his readiness to forget and to forgive, as exemplified by the fate of Horn and Egmont, of Berghen and Montigny, and by the daily and almost hourly decrees of the Blood Council. Each well-rounded period of the Governor was greeted with ironical cheers. The oration was unsuccessful. "Oh, citizens, citizens!" cried at last the discomfited Antony, "ye know not what ye do. Your blood be upon your own heads; the responsibility be upon your own hearts for the fires which are to consume your cities and the desolation which is to sweep your land!" The orator at this impressive point was interrupted, and most unceremoniously hustled out of the city. The government remained in the hands of the patriots.[*]

The party, however, was not so strong in soldiers as in spirit. No sooner, therefore, had they established their rebellion to Alva as an incontrovertible fact, than they sent off emissaries to the Prince of Orange, and to Admiral De la Marck at Brill. Finding that the inhabitants of Flushing were willing to provide arms and ammunition, De la Marck readily consented to send a small number of men, bold and experienced in partisan warfare, of whom he had now collected a larger number than he could well arm or maintain in his present position.[†]

The detachment, two hundred in number, in three small vessels,[‡] set sail accordingly from Brill for Flushing; and a wild crew they were, of reckless adventurers under command of the bold Treslong. The expedition seemed a fierce but whimsical masquerade. Every man in the little fleet was attired in the gorgeous vestments of the plundered churches, in gold-embroidered cassocks, glittering mass-garments, or the more sombre cowls and robes of Capuchin friars.[§] So sped the early standard bearers of that ferocious liberty which had sprung from the fires in which all else for which men cherish their fatherland had been consumed. So swept that resolute but fan-

---

* Bor, vi. 370. Hoofd, vi. 222.   † Bor, vi. 370.   ‡ Wagenaer, vi. 351.
§ Bor, vi. 370. Wagenaer, vi. 351. Van Wyn op Wagen[r]. vi. 84, seq.

tastic band along the placid estuaries of Zealand, waking the stag-
nant waters with their wild beggar songs and cries of vengeance.

That vengeance found soon a distinguished object. Pacheco,
the chief engineer of Alva, who had accompanied the Duke in
his march from Italy, who had since earned a world-wide reputation as the architect of the Antwerp citadel, had been just
despatched in haste to Flushing to complete the fortress
whose construction had been so long delayed. Too late for his
work, too soon for his safety, the ill-fated engineer had arrived
almost at the same moment with Treslong and his crew.* He
had stepped on shore, entirely ignorant of all which had tran-
spired, expecting to be treated with the respect due to the chief
commandant of the place, and to an officer high in the confidence of the Governor-General. He found himself surrounded
by an indignant and threatening mob. The unfortunate Italian
understood not a word of the opprobrious language addressed
to him, but he easily comprehended that the authority of the
Duke was overthrown. Observing De Ryk, a distinguished
partisan officer and privateersman of Amsterdam, whose reputation for bravery and generosity was known to him, he
approached him, and drawing a seal ring from his finger,
kissed it, and handed it to the rebel chieftain.† By this dumb-
show he gave him to understand that he relied upon his honor
for the treatment due to a gentleman. De Ryk understood
the appeal, and would willingly have assured him, at least, a
soldier's death, but he was powerless to do so. He arrested
him, that he might be protected from the fury of the rabble ;
but Treslong, who now commanded in Flushing, was especially
incensed against the founder of the Antwerp citadel, and felt
a ferocious desire to avenge his brother's murder upon the
body of his destroyer's favourite.‡ Pacheco was condemned to
be hanged upon the very day of his arrival. Having been
brought forth from his prison, he begged hard but not

---

* Bor, vi. 370.   Hoofd, vi. 224, 225.

† Hoofd, who afterwards received the ring as a present from Simon de Ryk, son
of the officer to whom it was given by the unfortunate Don Pedro Pacheco.

‡ Bor, vi. 370.

abjectly for his life. He offered a heavy ransom, but his enemies were greedy for blood, not for money. It was, however, difficult to find an executioner. The city hangman was absent, and the prejudice of the country and the age against the vile profession had assuredly not been diminished during the five horrible years of Alva's administration. Even a condemned murderer, who lay in the town-gaol, refused to accept his life in recompence for performing the office. It should never be said, he observed, that his mother had given birth to a hangman. When told, however, that the intended victim was a Spanish officer, the malefactor consented to the task with alacrity, on condition that he might afterwards kill any man who taunted him with the deed.

Arrived at the foot of the gallows, Pacheco complained bitterly of the disgraceful death designed for him. He protested loudly that he came of a house as noble as that of Egmont or Horn, and was entitled to as honorable an execution as theirs had been. "The sword! the sword!" he frantically exclaimed, as he struggled with those who guarded him. His language was not understood, but the names of Egmont and Horn inflamed still more highly the rage of the rabble, while his cry for the sword was falsely interpreted by a rude fellow who had happened to possess himself of Pacheco's rapier, at his capture, and who now paraded himself with it at the gallows' foot. "Never fear for your sword, Señor," cried this ruffian; "your sword is safe enough, and in good hands. Up the ladder with you, Señor; you have no further use for your sword."

Pacheco, thus outraged, submitted to his fate. He mounted the ladder with a steady step, and was hanged between two other Spanish officers. So perished miserably a brave

---

* Bor, vi. 370. Hoofd, vi. 225. Wagenaer, vi. 352. It is erroneously stated by Bentivoglio, lib. v. 92, and Cabrera, lib. ix. 705, that Pacheco was beheaded. Both these writers follow Mendoza. Tassis differs from all other historians. "Sed suspensum sublime pedibus vita privarunt," J. B. de Tassis, Comment. de Tumultibus Belgicis, xxvi. 149. There is no doubt, however, that the unfortunate gentleman was hanged by the neck, and not by the legs.

soldier, and one of the most distinguished engineers of his time; a man whose character and accomplishments had certainly merited for him a better fate.* But while we stigmatize as it deserves the atrocious conduct of a few Netherland partisans, we should remember who first unchained the demon of international hatred in this unhappy land, nor should it ever be forgotten that the great leader of the revolt, by word, proclamation, example, by entreaties, threats, and condign punishment, constantly rebuked, and to a certain extent, restrained the sanguinary spirit by which some of his followers disgraced the noble cause which they had espoused.

Treslong did not long remain in command at Flushing. An officer, high in the confidence of the Prince, Jerome van 't Zeraerts, now arrived at Flushing, with a commission to be Lieutenant-Governor over the whole isle of Walcheren. He was attended by a small band of French infantry, while at nearly the same time the garrison was further strengthened by the arrival of a large number of volunteers from England.†

---

* It was said, in extenuation of the barbarous punishment which was inflicted upon him, that a paper had been found upon his person, containing a list of a large number of persons in the Netherlands whom the Duke of Alva had doomed to immediate execution. The fact is stated in the " Petition to the King."—Bor, vi. 348-369. Hoofd, vi. 225. Meteren, 71.—Compare Wagenaer, vi. 352, 353; Van Wyn op Wagenʳ. vi. 89, 90.

† Bor, vi. 371.

CHAPTER VII.

of the Prince—Mutiny and dissolution of his army—His return to Holland—His steadfastness—Desperate position of Count Louis in Mons—Sentiments of Alva—Capitulation of Mons—Courteous reception of Count Louis by the Spanish generals—Hypocrisy of these demonstrations—Nature of the Mons capitulation—Horrible violation of its terms—Noircarmes at Mons—Establishment of a Blood Council in the city—Wholesale executions—Cruelty and cupidity of Noircarmes—Late discovery of the archives of these crimes—Return of the revolted cities of Brabant and Flanders to obedience—Sack of Mechlin by the Spaniards—Details of that event.

THE example thus set by Brill and Flushing was rapidly followed. The first half of the year 1572 was distinguished by a series of triumphs rendered still more remarkable by the reverses which followed at its close. Of a sudden, almost as it were by accident, a small but important sea-port, the object for which the Prince had so long been hoping, was secured. Instantly afterward, half the island of Walcheren renounced the yoke of Alva. Next, Enkhuizen, the key to the Zuyder Zee, the principal arsenal, and one of the first commercial cities in the Netherlands, rose against the Spanish Admiral, and hung out the banner of Orange on its ramparts.[*] The revolution effected here was purely the work of the people—of the mariners and burghers of the city.[†] Moreover, the magistracy was set aside and the government of Alva repudiated without shedding one drop of blood, without a single wrong to person or property.[‡] By the same spontaneous movement, nearly all the important cities of Holland and Zealand raised the standard of him in whom they recognized their deliverer.[§] The revolution was accomplished under nearly similar circumstances everywhere. With one fierce bound of enthusiasm the nation shook off its chain. Oudewater, Dort, Harlem, Leyden, Gorcum, Loewenstein, Gouda, Medenblik, Horn, Alkmaar, Edam, Monnikendam, Purmerende, as well as Flushing, Veer, and Enkhuizen, all ranged them-

---

[*] Bor, vi. 371–375. Hoofd, vi. 230–236.
[†] Bor, Hoofd, ubi sup.   [‡] Ibid. Van Meteren, 67–69.
[§] Hoofd, vi. 238–240, et seq. Bor, vi. 377, et seq.

selves under the government of Orange, as lawful stadholder for the King.*

Nor was it in Holland and Zealand alone that the beacon fires of freedom were lighted. City after city in Gelderland, Overyssel, and the See of Utrecht ; all the important towns of Friesland, some sooner, some later, some without a struggle, some after a short siege, some with resistance by the functionaries of government, some by amicable compromise, accepted the garrisons of the Prince, and formally recognized his authority.† Out of the chaos which a long and preternatural tyranny had produced, the first struggling elements of a new and a better world began to appear. It were superfluous to narrate the details which marked the sudden restoration of liberty in these various groups of cities. Traits of generosity marked the change of government in some, circumstances of ferocity disfigured the revolution in others. The island of Walcheren, equally divided as it was between the two parties, was the scene of much truculent and diabolical warfare. It is difficult to say whether the mutual hatred of race or the animosity of religious difference proved the deadlier venom. The combats were perpetual and sanguinary, the prisoners on both sides instantly executed. On more than one occasion, men were seen assisting to hang with their own hands and in cold blood their own brothers, who had been taken prisoners in the enemy's ranks.‡ When the captives were too many to be hanged, they were tied back to back, two and two, and thus hurled into the sea.§ The islanders found a fierce pleasure in these acts of cruelty. A Spaniard had ceased to be human in their eyes. On one occasion, a surgeon at Veer cut the heart from a Spanish prisoner, nailed it on a vessel's prow, and invited the townsmen to come and fasten their teeth in it, which many did with savage satisfaction.||

In other parts of the country the revolution was, on the

---

* Bor, Hoofd, ubi sup.   Meteren, 69, et seq.   Wagenaer, vi. 363–370.

† Bor, Meteren, Hoofd, Wagenaer, ubi sup.   ‡ Hoofd, vi. 227.

§ "Vocten spoelen."—Hoofd.   Wagenaer, vi. 355. || Hoofd, vi. 228.

whole, accomplished with comparative calmness. Even traits of generosity were not uncommon. The burgomaster of Gonda, long the supple slave of Alva and the Blood Council, fled for his life as the revolt broke forth in that city. He took refuge in the house of a certain widow, and begged for a place of concealment. The widow led him to a secret closet which served as a pantry. " Shall I be secure there ?" asked the fugitive functionary. " O yes, sir Burgomaster," replied the widow, " 't was in that very place that my husband lay concealed when you, accompanied by the officers of justice, were searching the house, that you might bring him to the scaffold for his religion. Enter the pantry, your worship ; I will be responsible for your safety."* Thus faithfully did the humble widow of a hunted and murdered Calvinist protect the life of the magistrate who had brought desolation to her hearth.

Not all the conquests thus rapidly achieved in the cause of liberty were destined to endure, nor were any to be retained without a struggle. The little northern cluster of republics which had now restored its honor to the ancient Batavian name was destined, however, for a long and vigorous life. From that bleak isthmus the light of freedom was to stream through many years upon struggling humanity in Europe ; a guiding pharos across a stormy sea ; and Harlem, Leyden, Alkmaar—names hallowed by deeds of heroism such as have not often illustrated human annals, still breathe as trumpet-tongued and perpetual a defiance to despotism as Marathon, Thermopylæ, or Salamis.

A new board of magistrates had been chosen in all the redeemed cities, by popular election. They were required to take an oath of fidelity to the King of Spain, and to the Prince of Orange as his stadholder ; to promise resistance to the Duke of Alva, the tenth penny, and the inquisition ; " to support every man's freedom and the welfare of the country ; to protect widows, orphans, and miserable persons, and to maintain justice and truth."†

---

* Hoofd, vi. 242.

† Bor, vi. 374, 375. Hoofd, vi. 230, 236. Wagenaer, vi. 360, 361.

Diedrich Sonoy arrived on the 2nd June at Enkhuizen. He was provided by the Prince with a commission, appointing him Lieutenant-Governor of North Holland or Waterland.* Thus, to combat the authority of Alva was set up the authority of the King. The stadholderate over Holland and Zealand, to which the Prince had been appointed in 1559, he now reassumed. Upon this fiction reposed the whole provisional polity of the revolted Netherlands. The government, as it gradually unfolded itself, from this epoch forward until the declaration of independence and the absolute renunciation of the Spanish sovereign power, will be sketched in a future chapter. The people at first claimed not an iota more of freedom than was secured by Philip's coronation oath. There was no pretence that Philip was not sovereign, but there *was* a pretence and a determination to worship God according to conscience, and to reclaim the ancient political "liberties" of the land. So long as Alva reigned, the Blood Council, the inquisition, and martial law, were the only codes or courts, and every charter slept. To recover this practical liberty and these historical rights, and to shake from their shoulders a most sanguinary government, was the purpose of William and of the people. No revolutionary standard was displayed.

The written instructions given by the Prince to his Lieutenant Sonoy† were to "see that the Word of God was preached, without, however, *suffering any hindrance to the Roman Church in the exercise of its religion ;* to restore fugitives and the banished for conscience sake, and to require of all magistrates and officers of guilds and brotherhoods an oath of fidelity." The Prince likewise prescribed the form of that oath, repeating therein, to his eternal honor, the same strict prohibition of intolerance. "Likewise," said the formula, " shall those of ' the religion' offer no let or hindrance to the Roman churches."‡

The Prince was still in Germany, engaged in raising troops

---

* Bor, vi. 375.

† See them in Bor, vi. 375–376.   ‡ Ibid., vi. 376.

and providing funds. He directed, however, the affairs of the insurgent provinces in their minutest details, by virtue of the dictatorship inevitably forced upon him both by circumstances and by the people. In the meantime, Louis of Nassau, the Bayard* of the Netherlands, performed a most unexpected and brilliant exploit. He had been long in France, negotiating with the leaders of the Huguenots, and, more secretly, with the court. He was supposed by all the world to be still in that kingdom, when the startling intelligence arrived that he had surprised and captured the important city of Mons.† This town, the capital of Hainault, situate in a fertile, undulating, and beautiful country, protected by lofty walls, a triple moat, and a strong citadel, was one of the most flourishing and elegant places in the Netherlands. It was, moreover, from its vicinity to the frontiers of France, a most important acquisition to the insurgent party. The capture was thus accomplished. A native of Mons, one Antony Oliver, a geographical painter, had insinuated himself into the confidence of Alva, for whom he had prepared at different times some remarkably well-executed maps of the country. Having occasion to visit France, he was employed by the Duke to keep a watch upon the movements of Louis of Nassau, and to make a report as to the progress of his intrigues with the court of France. The painter, however, was only a spy in disguise, being in reality devoted to the cause of freedom, and a correspondent of Orange and his family. His communications with Louis, in Paris, had therefore a far different result from the one anticipated by Alva. A large number of adherents within the city of Mons had already been secured, and a plan was now arranged between Count Louis, Genlis, De la Noue, and other distinguished Huguenot chiefs, to be carried out with the assistance of the brave and energetic artist.‡

On the 23rd of May, Oliver appeared at the gates of Mons,

* Groen v. Prinsterer, Archives, etc., iv. liv.

† Hoofd, vi. 237, 238.   Bor, vi. 377, 378.   Mendoza, lib. v. 120, 121.

‡ Bentivoglio, lib. vi. 100.   Hoofd, vi. 237.   Mendoza, lib. v. 120.   Van Meteren, iv. 71.

accompanied by three wagons, ostensibly containing merchandise, but in reality laden with arquebusses. These were secretly distributed among his confederates in the city. In the course of the day Count Louis arrived in the neighbourhood, accompanied by five hundred horsemen and a thousand foot soldiers. This force he stationed in close concealment within the thick forests between Maubeuge and Mons. Towards evening he sent twelve of the most trusty and daring of his followers, disguised as wine merchants, into the city. These individuals proceeded boldly to a public house, ordered their supper, and while conversing with the landlord, carelessly inquired at what hour next morning the city gates would be opened. They were informed that the usual hour was four in the morning, but that a trifling present to the porter would ensure admission, if they desired it, at an earlier hour. They explained their inquiries by a statement that they had some casks of wine which they wished to introduce into the city before sunrise. Having obtained all the information which they needed, they soon afterwards left the tavern. The next day they presented themselves very early at the gate, which the porter, on promise of a handsome "drink-penny," agreed to unlock. No sooner were the bolts withdrawn, however, than he was struck dead, while about fifty dragoons rode through the gate.* The Count and his followers now galloped over the city in the morning twilight, shouting "France ! liberty ! the town is ours !" "The Prince is coming !" "Down with the tenth penny ; down with the murderous Alva !" So soon as a burgher showed his wondering face at the window, they shot at him with their carbines. They made as much noise, and conducted themselves as boldly as if they had been at least a thousand strong.

Meantime, however, the streets remained empty ; not one of their secret confederates showing himself. Fifty men could surprise, but were too few to keep possession of the city. The Count began to suspect a trap. As daylight approached the

---

* Hoofd, vi. 237. Bor, vi. 377. Meteren, 71. Mendoza, v. 120, 121.

alarm spread ; the position of the little band was critical. In his impetuosity, Louis had far outstripped his army, but they had been directed to follow hard upon his footsteps, and he was astonished that their arrival was so long delayed. The suspense becoming intolerable, he rode out of the city in quest of his adherents, and found them wandering in the woods, where they had completely lost their way. Ordering each horseman to take a foot soldier on the crupper behind him, he led them rapidly back to Mons. On the way they were encountered by La Noue, " with the iron arm,"* and Genlis, who, meantime, had made an unsuccessful attack to recover Valenciennes, which within a few hours had been won and lost again. As they reached the gates of Mons, they found themselves within a hair's breadth of being too late ; their adherents had not come forth ; the citizens had been aroused ; the gates were all fast but one—and there the porter was quarrelling with a French soldier about an arquebuss. The drawbridge across the moat was at the moment rising ; the last entrance was closing, when Guitoy de Chaumont, a French officer, mounted on a light Spanish barb, sprang upon the bridge as it rose. His weight caused it to sink again, the gate was forced, and Louis with all his men rode triumphantly into the town.†

The citizens were forthwith assembled by sound of bell in the market-place. The clergy, the magistracy, and the general council were all present. Genlis made the first speech, in which he disclaimed all intention of making conquests in the interest of France. This pledge having been given, Louis of Nassau next addressed the assembly : " The magistrates," said he, "have not understoood my intentions. I protest that I am no rebel to the King ; I prove it by asking

---

* He had been severely wounded in 1570. His arm had been amputated, but "de bons ouvriers lui firent un bras de fer, dont il a porté depuis le nom."—Vie de De la Noue, 63.

† De Thou, vi. 499. Mendoza, v. 121. Dewez Hist. Gén. de la Belg., v. 413-416. Bor, Meteren, Hoofd.

no new oaths from any man. Remain bound by your old oaths of allegiance ; let the magistrates continue to exercise their functions—to administer justice. I imagine that no person will suspect a brother of the Prince of Orange capable of any design against the liberties of the country. As to the Catholic religion, I take it under my very particular protection. You will ask why I am in Mons at the head of an armed force : are any of you ignorant of Alva's cruelties ? The overthrow of this tyrant is as much the interest of the King as of the people, therefore there is nothing in my present conduct inconsistent with fidelity to his Majesty. Against Alva alone I have taken up arms ; 'tis to protect you against his fury that I am here. It is to prevent the continuance of a general rebellion that I make war upon him. The only proposition which I have to make to you is this—I demand that you declare Alva de Toledo a traitor to the King, the executioner of the people, an enemy to the country, unworthy of the government, and hereby deprived of his authority."*

The magistracy did not dare to accept so bold a proposition ; the general council, composing the more popular branch of the municipal government, were comparatively inclined to favor Nassau, and many of its members voted for the downfall of the tyrant. Nevertheless the demands of Count Louis were rejected. His position thus became critical. The civic authorities refused to pay for his troops, who were, moreover, too few in number to resist the inevitable siege. The patriotism of the citizens was not to be repressed, however, by the authority of the magistrates ; many rich proprietors of the great cloth and silk manufactories, for which Mons was famous, raised and armed companies at their own expense ; many volunteer troops were also speedily organized and drilled, and the fortifications were put in order. No attempt was made to

---

* Paridaens. Mons sous les rapports historiques, statistiques, etc., 68–70 (Mons, 1819). The speech is reported from original documents in the Archives of the city : "farde intitulée Pièces relatives à la Surprise de Mons ; déclarations des echevins, etc., etc."—Compare Bor, v. 377. Hoofd, vi. 238.

force the reformed religion upon the inhabitants, and even Catholics who were discovered in secret correspondence with the enemy were treated with such extreme gentleness by Nassau as to bring upon him severe reproaches from many of his own party.*

A large collection of ecclesiastical plate, jewellery, money, and other valuables, which had been sent to the city for safe keeping from the churches and convents of the provinces, was seized, and thus, with little bloodshed and no violence, was the important city secured for the insurgents.† Three days afterwards, two thousand infantry, chiefly French, arrived in the place.‡ In the early part of the following month Louis was still further strengthened by the arrival of thirteen hundred foot and twelve hundred horsemen, under command of Count Montgomery, the celebrated officer,§ whose spear at the tournament had proved fatal to Henry the Second. Thus the Duke of Alva suddenly found himself exposed to a tempest of revolution. One thunderbolt after another seemed descending around him in breathless succession. Brill and Flushing had been already lost ; Middelburg was so closely invested that its fall seemed imminent, and with it would go the whole island of Walcheren, the key to all the Netherlands. In one morning‖ he had heard of the revolt of Enkhuizen and of the whole Waterland ; two hours later came the news of the Valenciennes rebellion, and next day the astonishing capture of Mons. One disaster followed hard upon another. He could have sworn that the detested Louis of Nassau, who had dealt this last and most fatal stroke, was at that moment in Paris, safely watched by government emissaries ; and now he had, as it were, suddenly started out of the earth, to deprive him of this important city, and to lay bare the whole frontier

---

* Paridaens, 76, 77.

† Bor, vi. 378.   Hoofd, vi. 238.—Compare Bentivoglio, vi. 100, et seq.; Men-
'oza, v. 120, 121; Grotius.

‡ Bor, vi. 378.   Hoofd, vi. 238.   § Bor, vi. 378.

‖ Mendoza, v. 120; vi. 122.

to the treacherous attacks of faithless France. He refused to believe the intelligence when it was first announced to him, and swore that he had certain information that Count Louis had been seen playing in the tennis-court at Paris, within so short a period as to make his presence in Hainault at that moment impossible. Forced, at last, to admit the truth of the disastrous news, he dashed his hat upon the ground in a fury, uttering imprecations upon the Queen Dowager of France, to whose perfidious intrigues he ascribed the success of the enterprise, and pledging himself to send her Spanish thistles enough in return for the Florentine lilies which she had thus bestowed upon him.*

In the midst of the perplexities thus thickening around him, the Duke preserved his courage, if not his temper. Blinded, for a brief season, by the rapid attacks made upon him, he had been uncertain whither to direct his vengeance. This last blow in so vital a quarter determined him at once. He forthwith despatched Don Frederic to undertake the siege of Mons, and earnestly set about raising large reinforcements to his army. Don Frederic took possession, without much opposition, of the Bethlehem cloister in the immediate vicinity of the city, and with four thousand troops began the investment in due form.†

Alva had, for a long time, been most impatient to retire from the provinces. Even he was capable of human emotions. Through the sevenfold panoply of his pride he had been pierced by the sharpness of a nation's curse. He was wearied with the unceasing execrations which assailed his ears. "*The hatred which the people bear me,*" said he, in a letter to Philip, "because of the chastisement which it has been necessary for me to inflict, *although with all the moderation in the world,* make all my efforts vain. A successor will meet more sympathy and prove more useful."‡ On the 10th June, the

---

* Bor, vi. 378.   Hoofd, vi. 238.   Van Meteren, iv. 71.
† Bor, vi. 384.   Meteren, iv. 71, 72.
‡ Correspondance de Philippe II., ii. 1107.

Duke of Medina Cœli, with a fleet of more than forty sail, arrived off Blankenburg, intending to enter the Scheld.* Julian Romero, with two thousand Spaniards, was also on board the fleet. Nothing, of course, was known to the new comers of the altered condition of affairs in the Netherlands, nor of the unwelcome reception which they were like to meet in Flushing. A few of the lighter craft having been taken by the patriot cruisers, the alarm was spread through all the fleet. Medina Cœli, with a few transports, was enabled to effect his escape to Sluys, whence he hastened to Brussels in a much less ceremonious manner than he had originally contemplated. Twelve Biscayan ships stood out to sea, descried a large Lisbon fleet, by a singular coincidence, suddenly heaving in sight, changed their course again, and with a favoring breeze bore boldly up the Hond, passed Flushing in spite of a severe cannonade from the forts, and eventually made good their entrance into Rammekens, whence the soldiery, about one-half of whom had thus been saved, were transferred at a very critical moment to Middelburg.†

The great Lisbon fleet followed in the wake of the Biscayans, with much inferior success. Totally ignorant of the revolution which had occurred in the Ise of Walcheren, it obeyed the summons of the rebel fort to come to anchor, and, with the exception of three or four, the vessels were all taken. It was the richest booty which the insurgents had yet acquired by sea or land. The fleet was laden with spices, money, jewellery, and the richest merchandize. Five hundred thousand crowns of gold were taken, and it was calculated that the plunder altogether would suffice to maintain the war for two years at least. One thousand Spanish soldiers, and a good amount of ammunition, were also captured. The unexpected condition of affairs made a pause natural and almost necessary, before the government could be

---

* Van Meteren, iv. 65. Hoofd, vi. 239. Mendoza, vi. 127, 128.

† Meteren, iv. 65, 66. Hoofd, vi. 239, 240. Correspondance de Philippe II., ii. 1133. Archives, etc., de la Maison d'Orange, iii. 437–442. Mendoza vi. 127, 128.

decorously transferred. Medina Cœli, with Spanish grandilo-
quence, avowed his willingness to serve as a soldier, under a
general whom he so much venerated, while Alva ordered that,
in all respects, the same outward marks of respect should be
paid to his appointed successor as to himself. Beneath all
this external ceremony, however, much mutual malice was
concealed.*

Meantime, the Duke, who was literally "without a single
real,"† was forced at last to smother his pride in the matter
of the tenth penny. On the 24th June, he summoned the
estates of Holland to assemble on the 15th of the ensuing
month. In the missive issued for this purpose, he formally
agreed to abolish the whole tax, on condition that the estates-
general of the Netherlands would furnish him with a yearly
supply of two millions of florins. Almost at the same
moment the King had dismissed the deputies of the estates
from Madrid, with the public assurance that the tax was to
be suspended, and a private intimation that it was not
abolished in terms, only in order to save the dignity of
the Duke.‡

These healing measures came entirely too late. The estates
of Holland met, indeed, on the appointed day of July, but
they assembled not in obedience to Alva, but in consequence
of a summons from William of Orange.§ They met, too, not
at the Hague, but at Dort, to take formal measures for re-
nouncing the authority of the Duke.|| The first congress of
the Netherland commonwealth still professed loyalty to the
Crown, but was determined to accept the policy of Orange
without a question.

The Prince had again assembled an army in Germany, con-

---

* Meteren, iv. 66. Archives de la Maison d'Orange, iii. 440, 442. Hoofd,
vi. 240, vii. 257. Correspondance de Philippe II., ii. 1177.

† Mendoza, vi. 122.—"Hallando se sin un real como el Duque lo estara en
esta sazon."

‡ "Garschelyk te quijten aboleren on aftestallen," etc.—Bor, vi. 384, 385, 386.
Correspondance de Philippe II., ii. 1135.

§ Bor, vi. 386. || Ibid.

sisting of fifteen thousand foot and seven thousand horse, besides a number of Netherlanders, mostly Walloons, amounting to nearly three thousand more.* Before taking the field, however, it was necessary that he should guarantee at least three months' pay to his troops. This he could no longer do, except by giving bonds endorsed by certain cities of Holland as his securities.† He had accordingly addressed letters in his own name to all the principal cities, fervently adjuring them to remember, at last, what was due to him, to the fatherland, and to their own character. "Let not a sum of gold," said he in one of these letters, " be so dear to you, that for its sake you will sacrifice your lives, your wives, your children, and all your descendants, to the latest generations ; that you will bring sin and shame upon yourselves, and destruction upon us who have so heartily striven to assist you. Think what scorn you will incur from foreign nations, what a crime you will commit against the Lord God, what a bloody yoke ye will impose forever upon yourselves and your children, if you now seek for subterfuges ; if you now prevent us from taking the field with the troops which we have enlisted. On the other hand, what inexpressible benefits you will confer on your country, if you now help us to rescue that fatherland from the power of Spanish vultures and wolves."‡

This and similar missives, circulated throughout the province of Holland, produced a deep impression. In accordance with his suggestions, the deputies from the nobility and from twelve cities of that province assembled on the 15th July, at Dort. Strictly speaking, the estates or government of Holland, the body which represented the whole people, consisted of the nobles and six great cities. On this occasion, however, Amsterdam being still in the power of the King, could send no deputies, while, on the other hand, all the small towns

---

* Bor.—Compare Hoofd, vii. 259; Meteren, iv. 71; Bentivoglio, v. 104.

† Ibid., vi. 386. Hoofd, vii. 259.

‡ This remarkable letter is published in Kluit, Hist. der Hollandsche Staats-regering, Deel. i. bl. 376–379 (Bijlagen.)

were invited to send up their representatives to the Congress. Eight accepted the proposal; the rest declined to appoint delegates, partly from motives of economy, partly from timidity.*

These estates were the legitimate representatives of the people, but they had no legislative powers.† The people had never pretended to sovereignty, nor did they claim it now. The source from which the government of the Netherlands was supposed to proceed was still the divine mandate. Even now the estates silently conceded, as they had ever done, the supreme legislative and executive functions to the land's master.‡ Upon Philip of Spain, as representative of Count Dirk the First of Holland, had descended, through many tortuous channels, the divine effluence originally supplied by Charles the Simple of France. That supernatural power was not contested, but it was now ingeniously turned against the sovereign. The King's authority was invoked against himself in the person of the Prince of Orange, to whom, thirteen years before, a portion of that divine right had been delegated. The estates of Holland met at Dort on the 15th July, as representatives of the people, but they were summoned by Orange, royally commissioned in 1559 as stadholder, and therefore the supreme legislative and executive officer of certain provinces. This was the theory of the provisional government.§ The Prince represented the royal authority, the nobles represented both themselves and the people of the open country, while the twelve cities represented the whole body of burghers. Together, they were supposed to embody all authority, both divine and human, which a congress could exercise. Thus the whole movement was directed against Alva and against Count Bossu, appointed stadholder by Alva in the place of Orange.‖ Philip's name was destined

---

* Kluit, Hist. der Hol. Staatsreg., i. bl. 46, et seq.; and Bijlagen, bl. 374, et seq   Bor, vi. 381, 386, et seq. Wagenaer, Vad. Hist., vi. 377–380.

† Kluit, Hol. Staatsreg., i. 10–17.   ‡ Ibid., i. 50, 52.

§ Bor, vi. 388. Kluit, Hist. Hol. Staatsreg., i. 48, et seq.·and 374, et seq.

‖ Bor. Kluit, ubi sup. Wagenaer, vi. 377–380.

to figure for a long time, at the head of documents by which
monies were raised, troops levied, and taxes collected, all to be
used in deadly war against himself.

The estates were convened on the 15th July, when Paul
Buys, pensionary of Leyden, the tried and confidential friend
of Orange, was elected Advocate of Holland.* The convention was then adjourned till the 18th, when Saint Aldegonde
made his appearance, with full powers to act provisionally in
behalf of his Highness.†

The distinguished plenipotentiary delivered before the congress a long and very effective harangue. He recalled the
sacrifices and efforts of the Prince during previous years. He
adverted to the disastrous campaign of 1568, in which the
Prince had appeared full of high hope, at the head of a gallant
army, but had been obliged, after a short period, to retire,
because not a city had opened its gates nor a Netherlander
lifted his finger in the cause. Nevertheless, he had not lost
courage nor closed his heart ; and now that, through the
blessing of God, the eyes of men had been opened, and so
many cities had declared against the tyrant, the Prince had
found himself exposed to a bitter struggle. Although his own
fortunes had been ruined in the cause, he had been unable to
resist the daily flood of petitions which called upon him to
come forward once more. He had again importuned his relations and powerful friends ; he had at last set on foot a new
and well-appointed army. The day of payment had arrived.
Over his own head impended perpetual shame, over the
fatherland perpetual woe, if the congress should now refuse
the necessary supplies. "Arouse ye, then," cried the orator,
with fervor, "awaken your own zeal and that of your sister
cities. Seize Opportunity by the locks, who never appeared
fairer than she does to-day."‡

The impassioned eloquence of St. Aldegonde produced a

---

* Resol. Holl., 14th Sept., 1574, bl. 93.   Wagenaer, vi. 376.
† Bor, vi. 386, 387.
‡ Bor, vi. 386–388, and Hoofd, vii. 248, 249, report the speech in full.

profound impression. The men who had obstinately refused the demands of Alva, now unanimously resolved to pour forth their gold and their blood at the call of Orange. "Truly," wrote the Duke, a little later, "it almost drives me mad to see the difficulty with which your Majesty's supplies are furnished, and the liberality with which the people place their lives and fortunes at the disposal of this rebel."* It seemed strange to the loyal governor that men should support their liberator with greater alacrity than that with which they served their destroyer! It was resolved that the requisite amount should be at once raised, partly from the regular imposts and current "requests," partly by loans from the rich, from the clergy, from the guilds and brotherhoods, partly from superfluous church ornaments and other costly luxuries. It was directed that subscriptions should be immediately opened throughout the land, that gold and silver plate, furniture, jewellery, and other expensive articles should be received by voluntary contributions, for which inventories and receipts should be given by the magistrates of each city, and that upon these money should be raised, either by loan or sale.† An enthusiastic and liberal spirit prevailed. All seemed determined rather than pay the tenth to Alva to pay the whole to the Prince.‡

The estates, furthermore, by unanimous resolution, declared that they recognized the Prince as the King's lawful stadholder over Holland, Zealand, Friesland, and Utrecht, and that they would use their influence with the other provinces to procure his appointment as Protector of all the Netherlands during the King's absence.§ His Highness was requested to appoint an Admiral, on whom, with certain deputies from the Water-cities, the conduct of the maritime war should devolve.

---

* "¡Que verdaderamente me hace perder el juicio ver la dificultad cón que à V. M. servera en sussaguda, y la liberalida con que acuden a este rebelde con sus vidas y haciendas."—Correspondance de Philippe II., ii. 1198.

† Bor, vi. 388. Hoofd, vii. 349, 350. Wagenaer, vi. 378–380.

‡ "Tanto flagrabant odio dominatus," says Grotius (Ann., ii. 58), "omnia dabant ne decimam darent."

§ Bor, vi. 388, et seq. Hoofd, vii. 250. Kluit, i. 50, et seq.

The conduct of the military operations by land was to be directed by Dort, Leyden, and Enkhuizen, in conjunction with the Count de la Marck. A pledge was likewise exchanged between the estates and the plenipotentiary, that neither party should enter into any treaty with the King, except by full consent and co-operation of the other. With regard to religion, it was firmly established, that the public exercises of divine worship should be permitted not only to the Reformed Church, but to the Roman Catholic—the clergy of both being protected from all molestation.*

After these proceedings, Count de la Marck made his appearance before the assembly. His commission from Orange was read to the deputies, and by them ratified.† The Prince, in that document, authorized "his dear cousin" to enlist troops, to accept the fealty of cities, to furnish them with garrisons, to re-establish all the local laws, municipal rights, and ancient privileges which had been suppressed. He was to maintain *freedom of religion, under penalty of death to those who infringed it;* he was to restore all confiscated property; he was, with advice of his council, to continue in office such city magistrates as were favorable, and to remove those adverse to the cause.‡

The Prince was, in reality, clothed with dictatorial and even regal powers. This authority had been forced upon him by the prayers of the people, but he manifested no eagerness as he partly accepted the onerous station. He was provisionally the depositary of the whole sovereignty of the northern provinces, but he cared much less for theories of government than for ways and means. It was his object to release the country from the tyrant who, five years long, had been burning and butchering the people. It was his determination to drive out the foreign soldiery. To do this, he must meet his enemy in the field. So little was he disposed to strengthen his own

---

* Bor, vi. 388.   † Ibid., 389. Hoofd, vii. 250, 251.
‡ See the Commission in Bor. vi. 389–391.

individual power, that he voluntarily imposed limits on himself, by an act, supplemental to the proceedings of the Congress of Dort. In this important ordinance made by the Prince of Orange, as a provisional form of government,[*] he publicly announced " that he *would do and ordain nothing* except by the advice of the estates, by reason that they were best acquainted with the circumstances and the humours of the inhabitants." He directed the estates to appoint receivers for all public taxes, and ordained that all military officers should make oath of fidelity to him, as stadholder, and *to the estates* of Holland, to be true and obedient, in order to liberate the land from the Albanian and Spanish tyranny, *for the service of his royal Majesty as Count of Holland.* The provisional constitution, thus made by a sovereign prince and actual dictator, was certainly as disinterested as it was sagacious.

Meanwhile the war had opened vigorously in Hainault. Louis of Nassau had no sooner found himself in possession of Mons than he had despatched Genlis to France, for those reinforcements which had been promised by royal lips.[†] On the other hand, Don Frederic held the city closely beleaguered; sharp combats before the walls were of almost daily occurrence, but it was obvious that Louis would be unable to maintain the position into which he had so chivalrously thrown himself unless he should soon receive important succor. The necessary reinforcements were soon upon the way. Genlis had made good speed with his levy, and it was soon announced that he was advancing into Hainault, with a force of Huguenots, whose numbers report magnified to ten thousand veterans.[‡] Louis despatched an earnest message to his confederate, to use extreme caution in his approach. Above all

---

[*] "Ordonnantie ende Instructie van den Prince van Orange, voor die van Hollandt, om by provisie 't Landt daarovaer geregeerd to werden."—Groot Placcaet Boek, D. iii. bl. 32. Vide Kluit, Hist. der Hol. Staatsreg., i. 69, et seq.

[†] Bor, vi. 397. Hoofd, vi. 251.

[‡] Bor, vi. 397. Hoofd, vi. 251.—Compare Mendoza, vi. 141; Bentivoglio, v. 102

things, he urged him, before attempting to throw reinforcements into the city, to effect a junction with the Prince of
Orange, who had already crossed the Rhine with his new
army.*

Genlis, full of overweening confidence, and desirous of
acquiring singly the whole glory of relieving the city, disregarded this advice.† His rashness proved his ruin, and
the temporary prostration of the cause of freedom. Push-
ing rapidly forward across the French frontier, he arrived,
towards the middle of July, within two leagues of Mons.
The Spaniards were aware of his approach, and well prepared
to frustrate his project. On the 19th, he found himself
upon a circular plain of about a league's extent, surrounded
with coppices and forests, and dotted with farm-houses
and kitchen gardens.‡ Here he paused to send out a
reconnoitring party. The little detachment was, however,
soon driven in, with the information that Don Frederic of
Toledo, with ten thousand men, was coming instantly upon
them. The Spanish force, in reality, numbered four thousand
infantry, and fifteen hundred cavalry ; but three thousand
half-armed boors had been engaged by Don Frederic, to swell
his apparent force.§ The demonstration produced its effect,
and no sooner had the first panic of the intelligence been
spread, than Noircarmes came charging upon them at the
head of his cavalry. The infantry arrived directly afterwards,
and the Huguenots were routed almost as soon as seen. It
was a meeting rather than a battle.‖ The slaughter of the
French was very great, while but an insignificant number of
the Spaniards fell. Chiappin Vitelli was the hero of the day.
It was to his masterly arrangements before the combat, and to
his animated exertions upon the field, that the victory was
owing. Having been severely wounded in the thigh but a
few days previously, he caused himself to be carried upon a

---

* Bentivoglio, v. 102. Bor, vi. 397. Hoofd. vi. 251.

† Bor, Hoofd, Bentivoglio, ubi sup.   ‡ Mendoza, vi. 139.

§ Hoofd, vi. 251. Mendoza, vi. 139.   ‖ Bentivoglio, v. 102.

litter* in a recumbent position in front of his troops, and was everywhere seen, encouraging their exertions, and exposing himself, crippled as he was, to the whole brunt of the battle. To him the victory nearly proved fatal ; to Don Frederic it brought increased renown. Vitelli's exertions, in his precarious condition, brought on severe inflammation, under which he nearly succumbed, while the son of Alva reaped extensive fame from the total overthrow of the veteran Huguenots, due rather to his lieutenant and to Julian Romero.†

The number of dead left by the French upon the plain amounted to at least twelve hundred, but a much larger number was butchered in detail by the peasantry, among whom they attempted to take refuge, and who had not yet forgotten the barbarities inflicted by their countrymen in the previous war.‡ Many officers were taken prisoners, among whom was the Commander-in-chief, Genlis. That unfortunate gentleman was destined to atone for his rashness and obstinacy with his life. He was carried to the castle of Antwerp, where, sixteen months afterwards, he was secretly strangled by command of Alva, who caused the report to be circulated that he had died a natural death.§ About one hundred foot soldiers succeeded in making their entrance into Mons,|| and this was all the succor which Count Louis was destined to receive from France, upon which country he had built such lofty and such reasonable hopes.

While this unfortunate event was occurring, the Prince had already put his army in motion. On the 7th of July he had crossed the Rhine at Duisburg, with fourteen thousand foot, seven thousand horse, enlisted in Germany, besides a force of three thousand Walloons.¶ On the 23rd of July, he took the city of Roermond, after a sharp cannonade, at which place his

---

* Strada, vii. 364.

† Strada, vii. 363–365. Bentivoglio, v. 102.

‡ Bor, vi. 397, 398. Hoofd, vi. 251, 252. Strada, Bentivoglio, ubi sup. Meteren iv. 72. Mendoza, vi. 139, et seq.

§ Correspondance de Philippe II., ii. 1283.

|| Hoofd, vi. 251. Meteren, iv. 71.   ¶ Bor, vi. 398

troops already began to disgrace the honorable cause in which they were engaged, by imitating the cruelties and barbarities of their antagonists. The persons and property of the burghers were, with a very few exceptions, respected ; but many priests and monks were put to death by the soldiery under circumstances of great barbarity.* The Prince, incensed at such conduct, but being unable to exercise very stringent authority over troops whose wages he was not yet able to pay in full, issued a proclamation, denouncing such excesses, and commanding his followers, upon pain of death, to respect the rights of all individuals, whether Papist or Protestant, and to protect religious exercises both in Catholic and Reformed churches.†

It was hardly to be expected that the troops enlisted by the Prince in the same great magazine of hireling soldiers, Germany, from whence the Duke also derived his annual supplies, would be likely to differ very much in their propensities from those enrolled under Spanish banners ; yet there was a vast contrast between the characters of the two commanders. One leader inculcated the practice of robbery, rape, and murder, *as a duty,* and issued distinct orders to butcher " every mother's son" in the cities which he captured ; the other restrained every excess to the utmost of his ability, protecting not only life and property, but even the ancient religion.

The Emperor Maximilian had again issued his injunctions against the military operations of Orange. Bound to the monarch of Spain by so many family ties, being at once cousin, brother-in-law, and father-in-law of Philip, it was difficult for him to maintain the attitude which became him, as chief of that Empire to which the peace of Passau had assured religious freedom. It had, however, been sufficiently proved that remonstrances and intercessions addressed to Philip were but idle breath. It had therefore become an insult to require pacific conduct from the Prince on the ground

---

* Bor, vi. 399. Hoofd, vii. 259, 260.   † Ibid., vi. 399, 400. Ibid., vii. 259, 260.

of any past or future mediation. It was a still grosser mockery to call upon him to discontinue hostilities because the Netherlands were included in the Empire, and therefore ·protected by the treaties of Passau and Augsburg. Well did the Prince reply to his Imperial Majesty's summons in a temperate but cogent letter,* which he addressed to him from his camp, that all intercessions had proved fruitless, and that the only help for the Netherlands was the sword.

The Prince had been delayed for a month at Roermonde, because, as he expressed it, "he had not a single sou,"† and because, in consequence, the troops refused to advance into the Netherlands. Having at last been furnished with the requisite guarantees from the Holland cities for three months' pay, on the 27th of August, the day of the publication of his letter to the Emperor, he crossed the Meuse and took his circuitous way through Diest, Tirlemont, Sichem, Louvain, Mechlin, Termonde, Oudenarde, Nivelles.‡ Many cities and villages accepted his authority and admitted his garrisons. Of these Mechlin was the most considerable, in which he stationed a detachment of his troops. Its doom was sealed in that moment. Alva could not forgive this act of patriotism on the part of a town which had so recently excluded his own troops. "This is a direct permission of God," he wrote, in the spirit of dire and revengeful prophecy, "for us to punish her as she deserves, for the image-breaking and other misdeeds done there in the time of Madame de Parma, which our Lord was not willing to pass over without chastisement."§

Meantime the Prince continued his advance. Louvain purchased its neutrality‖ for the time with sixteen thousand ducats ; Brussels obstinately refused to listen to him, and was too powerful to be forcibly attacked at that juncture ; other important cities, convinced by the arguments and won by the eloquence of the various proclamations which he scattered as

---

* See it in Gachard, Correspondance de Guillaume le Tacit., iii. 63, et seq.
† Groen v. Prinst., Archives, etc., iii. 490.
‡ Bor, vi. 400–402. Hoofd, vii. 260, et seq.
§ Correspondance de Philippe II. 1156.   ‖ Hoofd, vii. 260.

he advanced, ranged themselves spontaneously and even enthusiastically upon his side. How different would have been the result of his campaign but for the unexpected earthquake which at that instant was to appal Christendom, and to scatter all his well-matured plans and legitimate hopes. His chief reliance, under Providence and his own strong heart, had been upon French assistance. Although Genlis, by his misconduct, had sacrificed his army and himself, yet the Prince was still justly sanguine as to the policy of the French court. The papers which had been found in the possession of Genlis by his conquerors all spoke one language. "You would be struck with stupor," wrote Alva's secretary, "could you see a letter which is now in my power, *addressed by the King of France to Louis of Nassau.*"* In that letter the King had declared his determination to employ all the forces which God had placed in his hands to rescue the Netherlands from the oppression under which they were groaning. In accordance with the whole spirit and language of the French government, was the tone of Coligny in his correspondence with Orange. The Admiral assured the Prince that there was no doubt as to the earnestness of the royal intentions in behalf of the Netherlands, and recommending extreme caution, announced his hope within a few days to effect a junction with him at the head of twelve thousand French arquebusiers, and at least three thousand cavalry.† Well might the Prince of Orange, strong, and soon to be strengthened, boast that the Netherlands were free, and that Alva was in his power.‡ He had a right to be sanguine, for nothing less than a miracle could now destroy his generous hopes—and, alas! the miracle took place ; a miracle of perfidy and bloodshed such as the world, familiar as it had ever been and was still to be with massacre, had not yet witnessed. On the 11th of August, Coligny had written thus hopefully of his movements towards the Netherlands, *sanctioned and aided by his King.* A fort-

---

* Correspondance de Philippe II., 1146.
† Groen v. Prinst., Archives, iii. 496–500.   ‡ Ibid., iii. 501–507.

night from that day occurred the "Paris wedding;" and the Admiral, with thousands of his religious confederates, invited to confidence by superhuman treachery, and lulled into security by the music of august marriage bells, was suddenly butchered in the streets of Paris by royal and noble hands.

The Prince proceeded on his march, during which the heavy news had been brought to him, but he felt convinced that, with the very arrival of the awful tidings, the fate of that campaign was sealed, and the fall of Mons inevitable. In his own language, he had been struck to the earth "with the blow of a sledge-hammer,"*—nor did the enemy draw a different augury from the great event.

The crime was not committed with the connivance of the Spanish government. On the contrary, the two courts were at the moment bitterly hostile to each other. In the beginning of the summer, Charles IX. and his advisers were as false to Philip, as at the end of it they were treacherous to Coligny and Orange. The massacre of the Huguenots had not even the merit of being a well-contrived and intelligently executed scheme. We have seen how steadily, seven years before, Catharine de' Medici had rejected the advances of Alva towards the arrangement of a general plan for the extermination of all heretics within France and the Netherlands at the same moment. We have seen the disgust with which Alva turned from the wretched young King at Bayonne, when he expressed the opinion that to take arms against his own subjects was wholly out of the question, and could only be followed by general ruin. " 'Tis easy to see that he has been tutored,"† wrote Alva to his master. Unfortunately, the same mother, who had then instilled those lessons of hypocritical benevolence, had now wrought upon her son's cowardly but ferocious nature with a far different intent. The incomplete assassination of Coligny, the dread of signal vengeance at the hands of the Huguenots, the necessity of taking the

---

* Archives de la Maison d'Orange, iii. 501–507, and iv. 102.

† Correspondance de Philippe II., ii. 1158.   Hoofd, vii. 262.

lead in the internecine struggle, were employed with Medicean art, and with entire success. The King was lashed into a frenzy. Starting to his feet, with a howl of rage and terror, " I agree to the scheme," he cried, " provided not one Huguenot be left alive in France to reproach me with the deed."*

That night the slaughter commenced. The long premeditated crime was executed in a panic, but the work was thoroughly done. The King, who a few days before had written with his own hand to Louis of Nassau, expressing his firm determination to sustain the Protestant cause both in France and the Netherlands, who had employed the counsels of Coligny in the arrangement of his plans, and who had sent French troops, under Genlis and La Noue, to assist their Calvinist brethren in Flanders, now gave the signal for the general massacre of the Protestants, and with his own hands, from his own palace windows, shot his subjects with his arquebuse as if they had been wild beasts.

Between Sunday and Tuesday, according to one of the most moderate calculations, five thousand Parisians of all ranks were murdered. Within the whole kingdom, the number of victims was variously estimated at from twenty-five thousand to one hundred thousand.† The heart of Protestant Europe, for an instant, stood still with horror. The Queen of England put on mourning weeds, and spurned the apologies of the French envoy with contempt.‡ At Rome, on the contrary, the news of the massacre created a joy beyond description. The Pope, accompanied by his cardinals, went solemnly to the church of Saint Mark to render thanks to God for the grace thus singularly vouchsafed to the Holy See and to all Christendom ; and a *Te Deum* was performed in presence of the same august assemblage.§

---

* Von Raumer, Geschichte Europas seit dem Ende des funfzehnten Jahrhunderts (Leipzig, 1833), ii. 256.

† Von Raumer, ii. 260.—Compare de Thou, t. vi. l. ii. 430; Bor, vi. 402, 403 ; Meteren, iv. 74.

‡ Von Raumer, ii. 263.   § De Thou, t. vi. l. liii. 442.

But nothing could exceed the satisfaction which the event occasioned in the mind of Philip the Second. There was an end now of all assistance from the French government to the Netherland Protestants. "The news of the events upon Saint Bartholomew's-day," wrote the French envoy at Madrid, Saint Goard, to Charles IX., "arrived on the 7th September. The King, on receiving the intelligence, showed, contrary to his natural custom, so much gaiety, that he seemed more delighted than with all the good fortune or happy incidents which had ever before occurred to him. He called all his familiars about him in order to assure them that your Majesty was his good brother, and that no one else deserved the title of Most Christian. He sent his secretary Cayas to me with his felicitations upon the event, and with the information that he was just going to Saint Jerome to render thanks to God, and to offer his prayers that your Majesty might receive Divine support in this great affair. I went to see him next morning, and as soon as I came into his presence *he began to laugh*, and with demonstrations of extreme contentment, to praise your Majesty as deserving your title of Most Christian, telling me there was no King worthy to be your Majesty's companion, either for *valor or prudence*. He praised the steadfast resolution and the long dissimulation of so great an enterprise, which all the world would not be able to comprehend." * * * "I thanked him," continued the embassador, "and I said that I thanked God for enabling your Majesty to *prove to his Master that his apprentice had learned his trade*, and deserved his title of most Christian King. I added, that he ought to confess that he owed the preservation of the Netherlands to your Majesty."*

Nothing certainly could, in Philip's apprehension, be more delightful than this most unexpected and most opportune intelligence. Charles IX., whose intrigues in the Netherlands he had long known, had now been suddenly converted by this

---

* Groen v. Prinst., Archives, etc., Supplement, 125.

stupendous crime into his most powerful ally, while at the same time the Protestants of Europe would learn that there was still another crowned head in Christendom more deserving of abhorrence than himself. He wrote immediately to Alva,* expressing his satisfaction that the King of France had disembarrassed himself of such pernicious men, because he would now be obliged to cultivate the friendship of Spain, neither the English Queen nor the German Protestants being thenceforth capable of trusting him. He informed the Duke, moreover, that the French envoy, Saint Goard, had been urging him to command the immediate execution of Genlis and his companions, who had been made prisoners, as well as all the Frenchmen who would be captured in Mons ; and that he fully concurred in the propriety of the measure. " The sooner," said Philip, " these noxious plants are extirpated from the earth, the less fear there is that a fresh crop will spring up." The monarch therefore added, with his own hand, to the letter, *" I desire that if you have not already disembarrassed the world of them, you will do it immediately, and inform me thereof, for I see no reason why it should be deferred."*† This is the demoniacal picture painted by the French ambassador, and by Philip's own hand, of the Spanish monarch's joy that his " Most Christian" brother had just murdered twenty-five thousand of his own subjects. In this cold-blooded way, too, did his Catholic Majesty order the execution of some thousand Huguenots additionally, in order more fully to carry out his royal brother's plans ; yet Philip could write of himself, " that all the world recognized the gentleness of his nature and the mildness of his intentions."‡

In truth, the advice thus given by Saint Goard on the

---

* The letter is published by M. Gachard. " Particularités inédites sur la Saint Barthélémy."—Bulletins de l'Acad. Roy. de Belg., xvi.

† " Y assi holgare que si ya no les ubiere deshechado del mundo lo hagais luego, y me aviseis dello, pues que no veo que aya causa ni la pueda aber por que esto se dexe de hazer."—Letter of Philip, 18th September, 1572, ubi sup.

‡ Letter to the Emperor. Groen v. Prinst., Archives, etc., Suppl., 46.

subject of the French prisoners in Alva's possessions, was a natural result of the Saint Bartholomew. Here were officers and soldiers whom Charles IX. had himself sent into the Netherlands to fight *for the Protestant cause against Philip and Alva*. Already, the papers found upon them had placed him in some embarrassment, and exposed his duplicity to the Spanish government, before the great massacre had made such signal reparation for his delinquency. He had ordered Mondoucet, his envoy in the Netherlands, to use dissimulation to an unstinted amount, to continue his intrigues with the Protestants, and to deny stoutly all proofs of such connivance. "I see that the papers found upon Genlis," he wrote* twelve days before the massacre, "have been put into the hands of Assonleville, and that they know everything done by Genlis to have been committed with my consent. Nevertheless, you will tell the Duke of Alva *that these are lies invented to excite suspicion against me*. You will also give him occasional information of the enemy's affairs, in order to make him believe in your integrity. Even if he does not believe you, my purpose will be answered, provided you do it dexterously.† At the same time you must keep up a *constant communication with the Prince of Orange,* taking great care to *prevent discovery of your intelligence with him*."‡

Were not these masterstrokes of diplomacy worthy of a King whom his mother, from boyhood upwards, had caused to study Macchiavelli's "Prince," and who had thoroughly taken to heart the maxim, often repeated in those days, that the "Science of reigning was the science of lying"?§

The joy in the Spanish camp before Mons was unbounded. It was as if the only bulwark between the Netherland rebels

---

* These remarkable letters exchanged between Charles IX. and Mondoucet have recently been published by M. Emile Gachet (chef du bureau paléographique aux Archives de Belgique) from a manuscript discovered by him in the library at Rheims.—Compte Rendu de la Com. Roy. d'Hist., iv. 340, sqq.

† "Encores qu'il ne y adjouste foy, toutes fois cela servira à mon intention, pourveu que le faciez destrement."—Ibid.

‡ Ibid.   § " Qui nescit dissimulare nescit regnare."

and total destruction had been suddenly withdrawn. With anthems in Saint Gudule,* with bonfires, festive illuminations, roaring artillery, with trumpets also, and with shawms, was the glorious holiday celebrated in court and camp, in honor of the vast murder committed by the Most Christian King upon his Christian subjects ; nor was a moment lost in apprising the Huguenot soldiers shut up with Louis of Nassau in the beleaguered city of the great catastrophe which was to render all their valor fruitless. "'Twas a punishment," said a Spanish soldier, who fought most courageously before Mons, and who elaborately described the siege afterwards, " well worthy of a king whose title is ' The Most Christian,' and it was still more honorable to inflict it with his own hands as he did."† Nor was the observation a pithy sarcasm, but a frank expression of opinion, from a man celebrated alike for the skill with which he handled both his sword and his pen.

The French envoy in the Netherlands was, of course, immediately informed by his sovereign of the great event. Charles IX. gave a very pithy account of the transaction. "To prevent the success of the enterprise planned by the Admiral," wrote the King on the 26th of August, with hands yet reeking, and while the havoc throughout France was at its height, "I have been obliged to permit the said Guises to rush upon the said Admiral,‡ which they have done, the said Admiral having been killed and all his adherents. A very great number of those belonging to the new religion have also been massacred and cut to pieces. It is probable that the fire thus kindled will spread through all the cities of my kingdom, and that all those of the said religion will be made

---

* Letter of Mondoucet, ubi sup.   Strada, vii. 366.—"In Hispanorum castris sub primas tenebras, ingentis lætitiæ signa hostes edere, scloporum explosione ter repetitia, læto tympanorum tubarumque cantu, ac toto circum vallo festis ignibus collucente," etc., etc.

† Mendoza, vii. 146.

‡ "J'ay été constraint permettre et doner moyen ausdits de Guise de courir sus audit Amiral," etc.—Correspondance de Mondoucet, etc., ubi sup.

sure of."* Not often, certainly, in history, has a Christian king spoken thus calmly of butchering his subjects while the work was proceeding all around him. It is to be observed, moreover, that the usual excuse for such enormities, religious fanaticism, can not be even suggested on this occasion. Catharine, in times past had favored Huguenots as much as Catholics, while Charles had been, up to the very moment of the crime, in strict alliance with the heretics of both France and Flanders, and furthering the schemes of Orange and Nassau. Nay, even at this very moment, and in this very letter in which he gave the news of the massacre, he charged his envoy still *to maintain the closest but most secret intelligence with the Prince of Orange ;* taking great care that the Duke of Alva should not discover these relations. His motives were, of course, to prevent the Prince from abandoning his designs, and from coming to make a disturbance in France. The King, now that the deed was done, was most anxious to reap all the fruits of his crime. "Now, M. de Mondoucet, it is necessary in such affairs," he continued, "to have an eye to every possible contingency. I know that this news will be most agreeable to the Duke of Alva, for it is most favorable to his designs. At the same time, I don't desire that he alone should gather the fruit. I don't choose that he should, according to his excellent custom, conduct his affairs in such wise as to throw the Prince of Orange upon my hands, besides sending back to France Genlis and the other prisoners, as well as the French now shut up in Mons."†

This was a sufficiently plain hint, which Mondoucet could not well misunderstand. "Observe the Duke's countenance carefully when you give him this message," added the King, "and let me know his reply." In order, however, that there might be no mistake about the matter, Charles wrote again to his ambassador, five days afterwards, distinctly stating the regret which he should feel if Alva should not take the city of Mons, or if he should take it by composition. "Tell the

---

* Correspondance de Mondoucet.   † Ibid.

Duke," said he, "that it is most important for the service of his master and of God that those Frenchmen and others in Mons should be cut in pieces."* He wrote another letter upon the same day, such was his anxiety upon the subject, instructing the envoy to urge upon Alva the necessity of chastising those rebels to the French crown. "If he tells you," continued Charles, "that this is tacitly requiring him to put to death all the French prisoners now in hand as well to cut in pieces every man in Mons, you will say to him that this is exactly what he ought to do, and that he will be guilty of a great wrong to Christianity if he does otherwise."† Certainly, the Duke, having been thus distinctly ordered, both by his own master and by his Christian Majesty, to put every one of these Frenchmen to death, had a sufficiency of royal warrant. Nevertheless, he was not able to execute entirely these ferocious instructions. The prisoners already in his power were not destined to escape, but the city of Mons, in his own language, "proved to have sharper teeth than he supposed."‡

Mondoucet lost no time in placing before Alva the urgent necessity of accomplishing the extensive and cold-blooded massacre thus proposed. "The Duke has replied," wrote the envoy to his sovereign, "that he is executing his prisoners every day, and that he has but a few left. Nevertheless, for some reason which he does not mention, he is reserving the principal noblemen and chiefs."§ He afterwards informed his master that Genlis, Jumelles, and the other leaders, had engaged, if Alva would grant them a reasonable ransom, to induce the French in Mons to leave the city, but that the Duke, although his language was growing less confident, still hoped to take the town by assault. "I have urged him," he added, "to put them all to death, assuring him that he would be responsible for the consequences of a contrary course." "Why does not your Most Christian master,"

---

* Correspondance de Mondoucet.   † Ibid.
‡ Mondoucet to Charles IX., 15th September, 1572.   § Ibid., (5th Sept.)

asked Alva, " order these Frenchmen in Mons to come to him
under oath to make no disturbance ? Then my prisoners will
be at my discretion and I shall get my city." " Because,"
answered the envoy, " they *will not trust his Most Christian
Majesty, and will prefer to die in Mons.*"*

This certainly was a most sensible reply, but it is instructive
to witness the cynicism with which the envoy accepts this
position for his master, while coldly recording the results of
all these sanguinary conversations.

Such was the condition of affairs when the Prince of
Orange arrived at Péronne, between Binche and the Duke of
Alva's entrenchments.† The besieging army was rich in nota-
bilities of elevated rank. Don Frederic of Toledo had hitherto
commanded, but on the 27th of August, the Dukes of Medina
Cœli and of Alva had arrived in the camp.‡ Directly afterwards came the warlike Archbishop of Cologne,§ at the head
of two thousand cavalry.|| There was but one chance for the
Prince of Orange, and experience had taught him, four years
before, its slenderness. He might still provoke his adversary
into a pitched battle, and he relied upon God for the result. In his own words, " he trusted ever that the great
God of armies was with him, and would fight in the midst
of his forces."¶ So long as Alva remained in his impregnable camp, it was impossible to attack him, or to throw
reinforcements into Mons. The Prince soon found, too,
that Alva was far too wise to hazard his position by a
superfluous combat. The Duke knew that the cavalry
of the Prince was superior to his own.** He expressed
himself entirely unwilling to play into the Prince's hands,
instead of winning the game which was no longer doubtful.
The Huguenot soldiers within Mons were in despair and

---

* Mondoucet to Charles IX., 15th September, 1572.
† Correspondance de Philippe II., ii. 1158. Hoofd. vii. 262.
‡ Ibid., vii. 257.
§ Correspondance de Philippe II., ii. 1158. || Bor, vi. 402.
¶ Letter of John of Nassau. Archives, etc., iii. 461.
** Correspondance de Philippe II., ii. 1158.

mutiny ; Louis of Nassau lay in his bed consuming with a dangerous fever ; Genlis was a prisoner, and his army cut to pieces ; Coligny was murdered, and Protestant France paralyzed ; the troops of Orange, enlisted but for three months, were already rebellious, and sure to break into open insubordination when the consequences of the Paris massacre should become entirely clear to them ; and there were, therefore, even more cogent reasons than in 1568, why Alva should remain perfectly still, and see his enemy's cause founder before his eyes. The valiant Archbishop of Cologne was most eager for the fray. He rode daily at the Duke's side, with harness on his back and pistols in his holsters, armed and attired like one of his own troopers, and urging the Duke, with vehemence, to a pitched battle with the Prince. The Duke commended, but did not yield to, the prelate's enthusiasm. " 'Tis a fine figure of a man, with his corslet and pistols," he wrote to Philip, "and he shows great affection for your Majesty's service."*

The issue of the campaign was inevitable. On the 11th September, Don Frederic, with a force of four thousand picked men, established himself at Saint Florian, a village near the Havrè gate of the city, while the Prince had encamped at Hermigny, within half a league of the same place, whence he attempted to introduce reinforcements into the town. On the night of the 11th and 12th, Don Frederic hazarded an *encamisada* upon the enemy's camp, which proved eminently successful, and had nearly resulted in the capture of the Prince himself. A chosen band of six hundred arquebusiers, attired, as was customary in these nocturnal expeditions, with their shirts outside their armor, that they might recognize each other in the darkness, were led by Julian Romero, within the lines of the enemy. The sentinels were cut down, the whole army surprised, and for a moment powerless, while, for two hours long, from one o'clock in the morning until three, the Spaniards butchered their foes, hardly aroused from their

* Correspondance de Philippe II., ii. 1158.

sleep, ignorant by how small a force they had been thus suddenly surprised, and unable in the confusion to distinguish between friend and foe.* The boldest, led by Julian in person, made at once for the Prince's tent. His guards and himself were in profound sleep, but a small spaniel, who always passed the night upon his bed, was a more faithful sentinel. The creature sprang forward, barking furiously at the sound of hostile footsteps, and scratching his master's face with his paws.† There was but just time for the Prince to mount a horse which was ready saddled, and to effect his escape through the darkness, before his enemies sprang into the tent. His servants were cut down, his master of the horse and two of his secretaries, who gained their saddles a moment later, all lost their lives,‡ and but for the little dog's watchfulness, William of Orange, upon whose shoulders the whole weight of his country's fortunes depended, would have been led within a week to an ignominious death. To his dying day, the Prince ever afterwards§ kept a spaniel of the same race in his bed-chamber. The midnight slaughter still continued, but the Spaniards in their fury, set fire to the tents. The glare of the conflagration showed the Orangists by how paltry a force they had been surprised. Before they could rally, however, Romero led off his arquebusiers, every one of whom had at least killed his man. Six hundred of the Prince's troops had been put to the sword, while many others were burned in their beds, or drowned in the little rivulet which flowed outside their camp. Only sixty Spaniards lost their lives.‖

This disaster did not alter the plans of the Prince, for those plans had already been frustrated. The whole marrow of his enterprise had been destroyed in an instant by the massacre of

---

* Mendoza, vii. 157.   Strada, vii. 367, 368.

† Strada, vii. 368.   Hoofd, vii. 263.   ‡ Hoofd, vii. 264.

§ Hoofd, vii. 263.   In the statues of the Prince, a little dog is frequently sculptured at his feet.

‖ Bentivoglio, v. 106.   Mendoza, vii. 157, et seq.   Hoofd, vii. 263, 264. Bor vii. 408.

Saint Bartholomew. He retreated to Péronne and Nivelles, an assassin, named Heist, a German, by birth, but a French chevalier, following him secretly in his camp, pledged to take his life for a large reward promised by Alva*—an enterprise not destined, however, to be successful. The soldiers flatly refused to remain an hour longer in the field, or even to furnish an escort for Count Louis, if, by chance, he could be brought out of the town.† The Prince was obliged to inform his brother of the desperate state of his affairs, and to advise him to capitulate on the best terms‡ which he could make. With a heavy heart, he left the chivalrous Louis besieged in the city which he had so gallantly captured, and took his way across the Meuse towards the Rhine. A furious mutiny broke out among his troops. His life was, with difficulty, saved from the brutal soldiery—infuriated at his inability to pay them, except in the over-due securities of the Holland cities—by the exertions of the officers who still regarded him with veneration and affection.§ Crossing the Rhine at Örsoy, he disbanded his army and betook himself, almost alone, to Holland.||

Yet even in this hour of distress and defeat, the Prince seemed more heroic than many a conqueror in his day of triumph. With all his hopes blasted, with the whole fabric of his country's fortunes shattered by the colossal crime of his royal ally, he never lost his confidence in himself nor his unfaltering trust in God. All the cities which, but a few weeks before, had so eagerly raised his standard, now fell off at once. He went to Holland, the only province which remained true, and which still looked up to him as its saviour, but he went thither expecting and prepared to perish. "*There I will make my sepulchre,*"¶ was his simple and sublime expression in a private letter to his brother.

---

* Letter of Mondoucet to Charles IX. Comm. Roy. de l'Hist. iv. 340.

† Letter of Prince of Orange to John of Nassau. Archives de la Maison d'Orange, etc., iii. 501–507, and the cypher explained in t. iv. c. ii.

‡ Hoofd, vii. 264. Meteren, iv. 75.

§ Bor, vii. 408. Meteren, iv. 75. || Hoofd, vii. 264.

¶ "Ayant délibéré de faire illecq ma sépultre."—Letter to his brother John of Nassau. Groen v. Prinst., Archives, etc., iv. 4.

He had advanced to the rescue of Louis, with city after city opening its arms to receive him. He had expected to be joined on the march by Coligny, at the head of a chosen army, and he was now obliged to leave his brother to his fate, having the massacre of the Admiral and his confederates substituted for their expected army of assistance, and with every city and every province forsaking his cause as eagerly as they had so lately embraced it. "It has pleased God," he said, "to take away every hope which we could have founded upon man ; the King has published that the massacre was by his orders, and has forbidden all his subjects, upon pain of death, to assist me ; he has, moreover, sent succor to Alva. Had it not been for this, we had been masters of the Duke, and should have made him capitulate at our pleasure."* Yet even then he was not cast down.

Nor was his political sagacity liable to impeachment by the extent to which he had been thus deceived by the French court. "So far from being reprehensible that I did not suspect such a crime," he said, "I should rather be chargeable with malignity had I been capable of so sinister a suspicion. 'Tis not an ordinary thing to conceal such enormous deliberations under the plausible cover of a marriage festival."†

Meanwhile, Count Louis lay confined to his couch with a burning fever. His soldiers refused any longer to hold the city, now that the altered intentions of Charles IX. were known‡ and the forces of Orange withdrawn. Alva offered the most honorable conditions, and it was therefore impossible for the Count to make longer resistance. The city was so important, and time was at that moment so valuable that the Duke was willing to forego his vengeance upon the rebel whom he so cordially detested, and to be satisfied with depriving him of the prize which he had seized with such audacity. "It would have afforded me sincere pleasure," wrote the Duke, "over and above the benefit to God and

---

* Archives de la Maison d'Orange, etc., iii. 501–507.
† Ibid.   ‡ Ibid. Vie De la Noue, 75.

your Majesty, to have had the Count of Nassau in my power. I would overleap every obstacle to seize him, such is the particular hatred which I bear the man."* Under the circumstances, however, he acknowledged that the result of the council of war could only be to grant liberal terms.

On the 19th September, accordingly, articles of capitulation were signed between the distinguished De la Noue with three others on the one part, and the Seigneur de Noircarmes and three others on the side of Spain. The town was given over to Alva, but all the soldiers were to go out with their weapons and property. Those of the townspeople who had borne arms against his Majesty, and all who still held to the Reformed religion, were to retire with the soldiery. The troops were to pledge themselves not to serve in future against the Kings of France or Spain, but from this provision Louis, with his English and German soldiers, was expressly excepted, the Count indignantly repudiating the idea of such a pledge, or of discontinuing his hostilities for an instant. It was also agreed that convoys should be furnished, and hostages exchanged, for the due observance of the terms of the treaty. The preliminaries having been thus settled, the patriot forces abandoned the town.†

Count Louis, rising from his sick bed, paid his respects in person to the victorious generals, at their request. He was received in Alva's camp with an extraordinary show of admiration and esteem. The Duke of Medina Cœli overwhelmed him with courtesies and "*basolomanos*," while Don Frederic assured him, in the high-flown language of Spanish compliment, that there was nothing which he would not do to serve him, and that he would take a greater pleasure in executing his slightest wish than if he had been his next of kin.‡

---

* Letter of Alva to Philippe II.   Correspondance de Philippe II., ii. 1162.

† Bor. vii. 408, 409.   Hoofd, vii. 265.   Meteren, iv. 76.   Mendoza, vii. 158, 159, 160.

‡ " So haten auch Don Frederico, le grand Prieur genañt (which he certainly was not, however) und der Herzog de Medina Celi mit sonder ehrerbie-

As the Count next day, still suffering with fever, and attired in his long dressing-gown, was taking his departure from the city, he ordered his carriage to stop at the entrance to Don Frederic's quarters. That general, who had been standing incognito near the door, gazing with honest admiration at the hero of so many a hard-fought field, withdrew as he approached, that he might not give the invalid the trouble of alighting.* Louis, however, recognising him, addressed him with the Spanish salutation, "*Perdone vuestra Señoria la pesedumbre,*" and paused at the gate.† Don Frederic, from politeness to his condition, did not present himself, but sent an aid-de-camp to express his compliments and good wishes. Having exchanged these courtesies, Louis left the city, conveyed, as had been agreed upon, by a guard of Spanish troops. There was a deep meaning in the respect with which the Spanish generals had treated the rebel chieftain. Although the massacre of Saint Bartholomew met with Alva's entire approbation, yet it was his cue to affect a holy horror at the event, and he avowed that he would "rather cut off both his hands than be guilty of such a deed"‡—as if those hangman's hands had the right to protest against any murder, however wholesale. Count Louis suspected at once, and soon afterwards thoroughly understood, the real motives of the chivalrous treatment which he had received.§ He well knew that these very

---

tung Graf Ludwig in dem Albanischen Lager selbst persönlich angesprochen und haben den Don Fed. viel besolosmanos gemacht und under andern sich erbotten wo er Grf Ludwigen freundschaft und angenehmen willen werde zu erzeigen wissen, soll sein Gnad : sich des zu ihm gewiszlich versehen das er solchs so gern und willig thun wolle als ob er S. Gn. nechster verwandter were."— Schwarz to Landgrave Will. of Hesse. Appendix to vol. iv. Archives de la Maison d'Orange, 17*.

* Archives de la Maison d'Orange, iii. 515, 518.   † Hoofd, vii, 265.

‡ Letter of Louis of Nassau to Charles IX. (1st June, 1573). Groen v. Prinst., Archives de la Maison, etc., iv. 86,* et seq. The letter is taken from the Archives of Simancas.

§ " Et que cà esté la seulle cause de la courtoisie et fidelité dont le Duc d'Albe a ussé envers le Conte à la prinse de la ville de Monts ; comme il a depuis dict a plusieurs que c'estoit pour monstrer qu'il ne vouldroit point avoir faict ung si méchant acte qu'avoit faict le Roy de France." etc., etc.—Ibid.

men would have sent him to the scaffold, had he fallen into their power, and he therefore estimated their courtesy at its proper value.

It was distinctly stated, in the capitulation of the city, that all the soldiers, as well as such of the inhabitants as had borne arms, should be allowed to leave the city, with all their property. The rest of the people, it was agreed, might remain without molestation to their persons or estates.[*] It has been the general opinion of historians that the articles of this convention were maintained by the conquerors in good faith.[†] Never was a more signal error. The capitulation was made late at night, on the 20th September, without the provision which Charles IX. had hoped for : the massacre, namely, of De la Noue and his companions. As for Genlis and those who had been taken prisoners at his defeat, their doom had already been sealed. The city was evacuated on the 21st September. Alva entered it upon the 24th. Most of the volunteers departed with the garrison, but many who had, most unfortunately, prolonged their farewells to their families, trusting to the word of the Spanish Captain Molinos, were thrown into prison.[‡] Noircarmes the butcher of Valenciennes, now made his appearance in Mons. As grand bailiff of Hainault, he came to the place as one in authority, and his deeds were now to complete the infamy which must for ever surround his name. In brutal violation of the terms upon which the town had surrendered, he now set about the work of massacre and pillage. A Commission of Troubles, in close imitation of the famous Blood Council at Brussels, was established,[§] the members of the tribunal being appointed by Noircarmes, and all being inhabitants of the town. The council commenced proceedings by condemning all the volunteers, although expressly included in the capitulation. Their wives

---

[*] Mendoza, vii. 157ʳᵒ, 158ʳᵒ. Bor, vii. 408, 409.

[†] Bor, Le Petit, Guicciardini, et al.

[‡] Mons; sous les Rapports Historiques et Statisques, etc., par F. Paridaens (Mons, 1819), 77, sqq.   [§] Paridaens, 77–87.

and children were all banished ; their property all confiscated.
On the 15th December, the executions commenced. The intrepid De Leste, silk manufacturer, who had commanded
a band of volunteers, and sustained during the siege the
assaults of Alva's troops with remarkable courage at a very
critical moment, was one of the earliest victims.* In consideration " that he was a gentleman, and not among the most
malicious,"† he was executed by sword. "In respect that
he heard the mass, and made a sweet and Catholic end,"
it was allowed that he should be "buried in consecrated
earth."‡ Many others followed in quick succession. Some
were beheaded, some were hanged, some were burned alive.
All who had borne arms or worked at the fortifications were,
of course, put to death. Such as refused to confess and
receive the Catholic sacraments perished by fire. A poor
wretch, accused of having ridiculed these mysteries, had his
tongue torn out before being beheaded.§ A cobbler, named
Blaise Bouzet, was hanged for having eaten meat-soup upon
Friday.‖ He was also accused of going to the Protestant
preachings for the sake of participating in the alms distributed
on these occasions,¶ a crime for which many other paupers were
executed.** An old man of sixty-two was sent to the scaffold
for having permitted his son to bear arms among the volunteers.†† At last, when all pretexts were wanting to justify
executions, the council assigned as motives for its decrees an
adhesion of heart on the part of the victims to the cause of
the insurgents, or to the doctrines of the Reformed Church.‡‡

---

* Paridaens, 77–87.

† Sentence against Pierre de Leste apud Altmeyer—Une Succursale au Tribunal
de Sang, 113, note 3.

‡ Ibid.—"En considération de sa belle fin, doulce et catholique avec grande
recognoissance et repentance, Monsqʳ. de Vaulx accorda la terre saincte et son
corps porté aux cordeliers."

§ Paridaens. Sentence du 6ᵐᵉ Mars, 1573, et autres.

‖ Altmeyer, 120, from the Archives Judiciaires de Hainaut. Régistre contenant
les sentences criminelles.   ¶ Ibid.

** Sentences du 6ᵐᵉ Mars, 1573, et autres, apud Paridaens, 82.

†† Paridaens.   ‡‡ Ibid., Sentences du 6ᵐᵉ Mars, et autres.

Ten, twelve, twenty persons were often hanged, burned, or beheaded in a single day.* Gibbets laden with mutilated bodies lined the public highways, while Noircarmes, by frightful expressions of approbation, excited without ceasing the fury of his satellites.† This monster would perhaps be less worthy of execration had he been governed in these foul proceedings by fanatical bigotry or by political hatred ; but his motives were of the most sordid description. It was mainly to acquire gold for himself that he ordained all this carnage. With the same pen which signed the death-sentences of the richest victims, he drew orders to his own benefit on their confiscated property.‡ The lion's share of the plunder was appropriated by himself. He desired the estate of François de Glarges, Seigneur d'Eslesmes. The gentleman had committed no offence of any kind, and, moreover, lived beyond the French frontier. Nevertheless, in contempt of international law, the neighbouring territory was invaded, and d'Eslesmes dragged before the blood tribunal of Mons. Noircarmes had drawn up beforehand, in his own handwriting, both the terms of the accusation and of the sentence. The victim was innocent and a Catholic, but he was rich. He confessed to have been twice at the preaching, from curiosity, and to have omitted taking the sacrament at the previous Easter. For these offences he was beheaded, and his confiscated estate adjudged at an almost nominal price to the secretary of Noircarmes, bidding for his master.§ "You can do me no greater pleasure," wrote Noircarmes to the council, "than to make quick work with all these rebels, and to proceed with the confiscation of their estates, real and personal. Don't fail to put all those to the torture out of whom anything can be got."‖

Notwithstanding the unexampled docility of the commis-

---

* Paridaens, 83. Sentences des 15me et 31me Dec., 1572, 17me Jan., 1573, 6me Mars, 10me, 11me, 13me Avril, 9me Juillet, 26me et 27me Aout, 1573.

† Ibid.

‡ Ibid., 84. Lettres aux Commissaires des 1er Juin et 24me Nov., 1573.

§ Ibid., 85. Greffe de Mons. Sentence du 24me Fev., 1573. Lettre de Noircarmes à Buzequies de 25me Nov., 1573, cited by Paridaens.

‖ Altmeyer, 115, from the Archives de Hainaut.

sioners, they found it difficult to extract from their redoubted chief a reasonable share in the wages of blood. They did not scruple, therefore, to display their own infamy, and to enumerate their own crimes, in order to justify their demand for higher salaries. "Consider," they said, in a petition to this end, "consider closely all that is odious in our office, and the great number of banishments and of executions which we have *pronounced among all our own relations and friends.*"*

It may be added, moreover, as a slight palliation for the enormous crimes committed by these men, that, becoming at last weary of their business, they urged Noircarmes to desist from the work of proscription. Longehaye, one of the commissioners, even waited upon him personally, with a plea for mercy in favor of "the poor people, even beggars, who, although having borne arms during the siege, might then be pardoned." Noircarmes, in a rage at the proposition, said that "if he did not know the commissioners to be honest men, he should believe *that their palms had been oiled,*"† and forbade any farther words on the subject. When Longehaye still ventured to speak in favor of certain persons "who were very poor and simple, not charged with duplicity, and good Catholics besides," he fared no better. "Away with you!" cried Noircarmes in a great fury,‡ adding that he had already written to have execution done upon the whole of them. "Whereupon," said poor blood-councillor Longehaye, in his letter to his colleagues, "I retired, I leave you to guess how."§

Thus the work went on day after day, month after month. Till the 27th August of the following year (1573) the execu-

---

* "Considérer de près tout l'odieux de nostre charge et le grand nombre de bannissemens et d'exécutions que nous avons pronouncées *au milieu* de tous nos parens et amis."—Lettres des Commissaires du 22me Juin, 1575; apud Parīdaens, 86; from the Greffe de Mons.

† "—— vous avé veu —— la collere de Monseigneur—disant que se ne nous cognoissoit gens de bien, auroit opinion qu'avions heu les mains engraissées."— Letter of Longehaye in Altmeyer, 125, sqq.

‡ "Replicqua, Arrière! par grant furie," etc.—Ibid.

§ "Sur quoy me rethiray, je vous laisse à penser comment."—Ibid.

tioner never rested, and when Requesens, successor to Alva, caused the prisons of Mons to be opened, there were found still seventy-five individuals condemned to the block, and awaiting their fate.*

It is the most dreadful commentary upon the times in which these transactions occurred, that they could sink so soon into oblivion. The culprits took care to hide the records of their guilt, while succeeding horrors, on a more extensive scale, at other places, effaced the memory of all these comparatively obscure murders and spoliations. The prosperity of Mons, one of the most flourishing and wealthy manufacturing towns in the Netherlands, was annihilated, but there were so many cities in the same condition that its misery was hardly remarkable. Nevertheless, in our own days, the fall of a mouldering tower in the ruined Chateau de Naast at last revealed the archives of all these crimes.† How the documents came to be placed there remains a mystery, but they have at last been brought to light.

The Spaniards had thus recovered Mons, by which event the temporary revolution throughout the whole Southern Netherlands was at an end. The keys of that city unlocked the gates of every other in Brabant and Flanders. The towns which had so lately embraced the authority of Orange now hastened to disavow the Prince, and to return to their ancient, hypocritical, and cowardly allegiance.‡ The new oaths of fidelity were in general accepted by Alva, but the beautiful archiepiscopal city of Mechlin was selected for an example and a sacrifice.

There were heavy arrears due to the Spanish troops. To indemnify them, and to make good his blasphemous prophecy of Divine chastisement for its past misdeeds, Alva now abandoned this town to the licence of his soldiery. By his command Don Frederic advanced to the gates and demanded its surrender. He was answered by a few shots from the garrison. Those cowardly troops, however, having thus

---

* Paridaens, 86, sqq.   † Ibid., 279, note E.   ‡ Bor, vi. 415.

plunged the city still more deeply into the disgrace which, in Alva's eyes, they had incurred by receiving rebels within their walls after having but just before refused admittance to the Spanish forces, decamped during the night, and left the place defenceless.*

Early next morning there issued from the gates a solemn procession of priests, with banner and crozier, followed by a long and suppliant throng of citizens, who attempted by this demonstration to avert the wrath of the victor. While the penitent psalms were resounding, the soldiers were busily engaged in heaping dried branches and rubbish into the moat. Before the religious exercises were concluded, thousands had forced the gates or climbed the walls, and entered the city with a celerity which only the hope of rapine could inspire. The sack instantly commenced. The property of friend and foe, of Papist and Calvinist, was indiscriminately rifled. Everything was dismantled and destroyed. "Hardly a nail," said a Spaniard, writing soon afterwards from Brussels, "was left standing in the walls." The troops seemed to imagine themselves in a Turkish town, and wreaked the Divine vengeance which Alva had denounced upon the city with an energy which met with his fervent applause.†

Three days long the horrible scene continued, one day for the benefit of the Spaniards, two more for that of the Walloons and Germans. All the churches, monasteries, religious houses of every kind, were completely sacked. Every valuable article which they contained, the ornaments of altars, the reliquaries, chalices, embroidered curtains, and carpets of velvet or damask, the

---

* Bor, vi. 409. Meteren, iv. 76.

† Bor, vi. 409. Hoofd, vii. 266. 267. Correspondance de Philippe II., ii. 1185. "Bref il n'y ha heu église, ny monastère, soit d'hommes ou de femmes, hospital ny lieu sacré auquel l'on aye porté respect, que tout n'aye esté saccagé jusques aux lianges et deniers d'epargne des povres."—Discours du Pillage de Malines, 2me Oct., 1572, p. 409; apud Willems. Mengelingen van historisch-vaderlandsten inhoud (Antwerpen, 1827–1830). The author of this contemporary account was a citizen of Mechlin, and a Catholic.

golden robes of the priests, the repositories of the host, the precious vessels of chrism and extreme unction, the rich clothing and jewellery adorning the effigies of the Holy Virgin, all were indiscriminately rifled by the Spanish soldiers. The holy wafers were trampled underfoot, the sacramental wine was poured upon the ground, and, in brief, all the horrors which had been committed by the iconoclasts in their wildest moments, and for a thousandth part of which enormities heretics had been burned in droves, were now repeated in Mechlin by the especial soldiers of Christ, by Roman Catholics who had been sent to the Netherlands to avenge the insults offered to the Roman Catholic faith. The motive, too, which inspired the sacrilegious crew was not fanaticism, but the desire of plunder. The property of Romanists was taken as freely as that of Calvinists, of which sect there were, indeed, but few in the archiepiscopal city. Cardinal Granvelle's house was rifled. The pauper funds deposited in the convents were not respected. The beds were taken from beneath sick and dying women, whether lady abbess or hospital patient, that the sacking might be torn to pieces in search of hidden treasure.*

The iconoclasts of 1566 had destroyed millions of property for the sake of an idea, but they had appropriated nothing. Moreover, they had scarcely injured a human being ; confining their wrath to graven images. The Spaniards at Mechlin spared neither man nor woman. The murders and outrages would be incredible, were they not attested by most

---

* Discours du Pillage de Malines, 2me Octobre, 1572, 406, 407. "Voires ne ont esté respectez les repositoires et cyboires, où estoyent les sainctes hostyes et précieux corps de nostre seigneur et rédempteur, ny les vaisseaux des saint chresme et extrêmes onctions, qui ont esté ravis par les soldats Espagnols —— tiré déhors le ciboire, gectant en terre les sainctes hosties," etc., etc.

"Et y a la mater des noires-soeurs ha perdu 6e florins de son espargne —— et pardessus ha esté tiré à la dicte mater, gisant malade, son lict de dessoubz elle ; comme aussi ha este faict avec infinité de femmes accouchées et d'aultre avortées et de malades."—Discours, etc., 409.

respectable Catholic witnesses. Men were butchered in their houses, in the streets, at the altars. Women were violated by hundreds in churches and in grave-yards.* Moreover, the deed had been as deliberately arranged as it was thoroughly performed. It was sanctioned by the highest authority. Don Frederic, son of Alva, and General Noircarmes were both present at the scene, and applications were in vain made to them that the havoc might be stayed. " They were seen whispering to each other in the ear on their arrival," says an eye-witness and a Catholic, " and it is well known that the affair had been resolved upon the preceding day. The two continued together as long as they remained in the city."† The work was, in truth, fully accomplished. The ultra-Catholic, Jean Richardot, member of the Grand Council, and nephew of the Bishop of Arras, informed the State Council that the sack of Mechlin had been so horrible that the poor and unfortunate mothers had not a single morsel of bread to put in the mouths of their children, who were dying before their eyes—so insane and cruel had been the avarice of the plunderers. " He could say more," he added, "if his hair did not stand on end, not only at recounting, but even at remembering the scene."‡

Three days long the city was abandoned to that trinity of furies which ever wait upon War's footsteps—Murder, Lust, and Rapine—under whose promptings human beings become so much more terrible than the most ferocious beasts. In his letter to his master, the Duke congratulated him upon these foul proceedings as upon a pious deed well accomplished. He thought it necessary, however, to excuse himself before the public in a document, which justified the sack of Mechlin by its refusal to accept his garrison a few months before, and by the shots which had been discharged at his troops as they

---

* Discours, etc., 415.   † Ibid., 411, 412.

‡ Letter of Jean Richardot, apud Gachard; Rapport au Ministre de l'Intérieur sur les Archives de Lille, 234.

approached the city.* For these offences, and by his express order, the deed was done. Upon his head must the guilt for ever rest.†

---

* Bor, vi. 409, 410.

† Bor, vi. 409, 410. Meteren, iv. 76. Hoofd, vii. 266, 267.—Compare Bentivoglio, vi. 114. Mendoza, viii. 161. The latter historian endeavors to exonerate the Duke, by imputing all the blame to the insubordination of his soldiers. Unfortunately the Commander's letters show that he had deliberately ordered tho sack, and was highly satisfied with the faithful manner in which it was accomplished: "donde quedan (los soldados) al presente exécutando el castigo que évidentemente parece que *Dios ha sido servido darles.*" With the blasphemy customary upon such occasions, the Almighty was, of course, represented as the chief perpetrator and instigator of these diabolical crimes.—Vide Correspondance de Philippe II., ii. 1165.

CHAPTER VIII.

WHILE thus Brabant and Flanders were scourged back to the chains which they had so recently broken, the affairs of the Prince of Orange were not improving in Zealand. Never was a twelvemonth so marked by contradictory fortune, never were the promises of a spring followed by such blight and disappointment in autumn than in the memorable year 1572. On the island of Walcheren, Middelburg and Arnemuyde still held for the King—Campveer and Flushing for the Prince of Orange. On the island of South Beveland, the city of Goes or Tergoes was still stoutly defended by a small garrison of Spanish troops. As long as the place held out, the city of Middelburg could be maintained. Should that important city fall, the Spaniards would lose all hold upon Walcheren and the province of Zealand.

Jerome de 't Zeraerts, a brave, faithful, but singularly unlucky officer, commanded for the Prince in Walcheren.* He had attempted by various hastily planned expeditions to give employment to his turbulent soldiery, but fortune had refused to smile upon his efforts. He had laid siege to Middelburg and failed. He had attempted Tergoes and had been compelled ingloriously to retreat. The citizens of Flushing, on his return, had shut the gates of the town in his face, and for several days refused to admit him or his troops.† To retrieve this disgrace, which had sprung rather from the insubordination of his followers and the dislike which they bore his person than from any want of courage or conduct on his part, he now assembled a force of seven thousand men, marched again to Tergoes, and upon the 26th of August laid siege to the place in form.‡ The garrison was very insufficient, and although they conducted themselves with great bravery, it was soon evident that unless reinforced they must yield. With their overthrow it was obvious that the Spaniards would lose the important maritime province of Zealand, and the Duke accordingly ordered D'Avila, who commanded in Antwerp, to throw succor into Tergoes without delay. Attempts were made, by sea and by land, to this effect, but were all unsuccessful. The Zealanders commanded the waters with their fleet, and were too much at home among those gulfs and shallows not to be more than a match for their enemies. Baffled in their attempt

---

* Bor, vi. 392.   † Ibid., vi. 394.   ‡ Ibid.

to relieve the town by water or by land, the Spaniards conceived an amphibious scheme. Their plan led to one of the most brilliant feats of arms which distinguishes the history of this war.

The Scheld, flowing past the city of Antwerp and separating the provinces of Flanders and Brabant, opens wide its two arms in nearly opposite directions, before it joins the sea. Between these two arms lie the isles of Zealand, half floating upon, half submerged by the waves. The town of Tergoes was the chief city of South Beveland, the most important part of this archipelago, but South Beveland had not always been an island. Fifty years before, a tempest, one of the most violent recorded in the stormy annals of that exposed country, had overthrown all barriers,* the waters of the German Ocean, lashed by a succession of north winds, having been driven upon the low coast of Zealand more rapidly than they could be carried off through the narrow straits of Dover. The dykes of the island had burst, the ocean had swept over the land, hundreds of villages had been overwhelmed, and a tract of country torn from the province and buried for ever beneath the sea. This "Drowned Land,"† as it is called, now separated the island from the main. At low tide it was, however, possible for experienced pilots to ford the estuary, which had usurped the place of the land. The average depth was between four and five feet at low water, while the tide rose and fell at least ten feet; the bottom was muddy and treacherous, and it was moreover traversed by three living streams or channels, always much too deep to be fordable.‡

Captain Plomaert, a Fleming of great experience and bravery, warmly attached to the King's cause, conceived the plan of sending reinforcements across this drowned district to the city of Tergoes. Accompanied by two peasants of the country, well acquainted with the track, he twice accomplished

---

* Mendoza, viii. 166, et seq.—Compare Guicciardini and Bentivoglio, vii. 109-114

† "Verdronken Land."—Bor, vi. 394

‡ Bor, Hoofd, Mendoza, Bentivoglio, etc., etc.

the dangerous and difficult passage, which, from dry land to dry land, was nearly ten English miles in length. Having thus satisfied himself as to the possibility of the enterprise, he laid his plan before the Spanish colonel, Mondragon.*

That courageous veteran eagerly embraced the proposal, examined the ground, and after consultation with Sancho d'Avila, resolved in person to lead an expedition along the path suggested by Plomaert. Three thousand picked men, a thousand from each nation,†—Spaniards, Walloons, and Germans, were speedily and secretly assembled at Bergen op Zoom, from the neighbourhood of which city, at a place called Aggier,‡ it was necessary that the expedition should set forth. A quantity of sacks were provided, in which a supply of biscuit and of powder was placed, one to be carried by each soldier upon his head. Although it was already late in the autumn, the weather was propitious ; the troops, not yet informed as to the secret enterprise for which they had been selected, were already assembled at the edge of the water, and Mondragon, who, notwithstanding his age, had resolved upon heading the hazardous expedition, now briefly, on the evening of the 20th October, explained to them the nature of the service. His statement of the dangers which they were about to encounter, rather inflamed than diminished their ardor. Their enthusiasm became unbounded, as he described the importance of the city which they were about to save, and alluded to the glory which would be won by those who thus courageously came forward to its rescue. The time of about half ebb-tide having arrived, the veteran, preceded only by the guides and Plomaert, plunged gaily into the waves, followed by his army, almost in single file. The water was never lower than the breast, often higher than the shoulder. The distance to the island, three and a half leagues at least, was to be accomplished within at most, six hours, or the rising tide would overwhelm them for ever. And thus, across the quaking and uncertain slime, which often refused them a footing, that adven-

---

* Hoofd, vii. 270, 271. Bentivoglio, vi 3.
† Bentivoglio, vi. 112.   ‡ Bor, vi. 394

turous band, five hours long, pursued their midnight march, sometimes swimming for their lives, and always struggling with the waves which every instant threatened to engulph them.

Before the tide had risen to more than half-flood, before the day had dawned, the army set·foot on dry land again, at the village of Irseken. Of the whole three thousand, only nine unlucky individuals had been drowned ; so much had courage and discipline availed in that dark and perilous passage through the very bottom of the sea.* The Duke of Alva might well pronounce it one of the most brilliant and original achievements in the annals of war.† The beacon fires were immediately lighted upon the shore, as agreed upon, to inform Sancho d'Avila, who was anxiously awaiting the result at Bergen op Zoom, of the safe arrival of the troops. A brief repose was then allowed. At the approach of daylight, they set forth from Irseken, which lay about four leagues from Tergoes. The news that a Spanish army had thus arisen from the depths of the sea, flew before them as they marched. The besieging force commanded the water with their fleet, the land with their army ; yet had these indomitable Spaniards found a path which was neither land nor water, and had thus stolen upon them in the silence of night. A panic preceded them as they fell upon a foe much superior in number to their own force. It was impossible for 't Zeraerts to induce his soldiers to offer resistance. The patriot army fled precipitately and ignominiously to their ships, hotly pursued by the Spaniards, who overtook and destroyed the whole of their rearguard before they could embark. This done, the gallant little garrison which had so successfully held the city, was reinforced with the courageous veterans who had come to their relief. His audacious project thus brilliantly accomplished, the " good old Mondragon,"‡ as his soldiers called him, returned to the province of Brabant.§

---

* Bentivoglio, Mendoza, Bor, Hoofd, ubi sup.   Meteren, iv. 76, 77.
† Correspondance de Philippe II., ii. 1179.
‡ " El bueno viejo Mondragon."—Ibid.
§ Bentivoglio, Bor, Mendoza, Hoofd, Meteren, ubi sup.

After the capture of Mons and the sack of Mechlin, the Duke of Alva had taken his way to Nimwegen, having despatched his son, Don Frederic, to reduce the northern and eastern country, which was only too ready to submit to the conqueror. Very little resistance was made by any of the cities which had so recently, and with such enthusiasm, embraced the cause of Orange. Zutphen attempted a feeble opposition to the entrance of the King's troops, and received a dreadful chastisement in consequence. Alva sent orders to his son to leave *not a single man alive in the city,* and to burn every house to the ground.* The Duke's command was almost literally obeyed. Don Frederic entered Zutphen, and without a moment's warning put the whole garrison to the sword. The citizens next fell a defenceless prey ; some being stabbed in the streets, some hanged on the trees which decorated the city, some stripped stark naked, and turned out into the fields to freeze to death in the wintry night. As the work of death became too fatiguing for the butchers, five hundred innocent burghers were tied two and two, back to back, and drowned like dogs in the river Yssel. A few stragglers who had contrived to elude pursuit at first, were afterwards taken from their hiding places, and hung upon *the gallows by the feet,* some of which victims suffered four days and nights of agony before death came to their relief. It is superfluous to add that the outrages upon women were no less universal in Zutphen than they had been in every city captured or occupied by the Spanish troops. These horrors continued till scarcely chastity or life remained, throughout the miserable city.†

This attack and massacre had been so suddenly executed, that assistance would hardly have been possible, even had there been disposition to render it. There was, however, no

---

* Correspondance de Philippe II., ii. 1180.

† Ibid.   Bor, vi. 415.   Hoofd, vii. 274. Meteren, iv. 78.—Compare Mendoza, viii. 172, and Bentivoglio, vi. 114, who glides rapidly over these scenes of horror with a smoothness all his own.

such disposition. The whole country was already cowering again, except the provinces of Holland and Zealand. No one dared approach, even to learn what had occurred within the walls of the town, for days after its doom had been accomplished. "A wail of agony was heard above Zutphen last Sunday," wrote Count Nieuwenar, "a sound as of a mighty massacre, but we know not what has taken place."*

Count Van den Bergh, another brother-in-law of Orange, proved himself signally unworthy of the illustrious race to which he was allied. He had, in the earlier part of the year, received the homage of the cities of Gelderland and Overyssel, on behalf of the patriot Prince. He now basely abandoned the field where he had endeavoured to gather laurels while the sun of success had been shining. Having written from Kampen, whither he had retired, that he meant to hold the city to the last gasp, he immediately afterwards fled secretly and precipitately from the country.† In his flight he was plundered by his own people, while his wife, Mary of Nassau, then far advanced in pregnancy, was left behind, disguised as a peasant girl, in an obscure village.‡

With the flight of Van den Bergh, all the cities which, under his guidance, had raised the standard of Orange, deserted the cause at once. Friesland too, where Robles obtained a victory over six thousand patriots, again submitted to the yoke. But if the ancient heart of the free Frisians was beating thus feebly, there was still spirit left among their brethren on the other side of the Zuyder Zee. It was not while William of Orange was within her borders, nor while her sister provinces had proved recreant to him, that Holland would follow their base example. No rebellion being left, except in the north-western extremities of the Netherlands, Don Frederic was ordered to proceed from Zutphen to Amster-

---

* "Aussi dict on que dimanche passé on a ouy ung grand jammergeschrey et tuerie dedans Zutfen, mais on ne sçait ce que c'est."—Comte Nieuwenar to Louis of Nassau. Archives de la Maison d'Orange, etc. iv. 28.

† Bor, vi. 415.   Meteren, iv. 78.   Hoofd, vii. 274.

‡ Correspondance de Philippe II., ii. 1186.

dam, thence to undertake the conquest of Holland. The little city of Naarden, on the coast of the Zuyder Zee, lay in his path, and had not yet formally submitted. On the 22nd of November a company of one hundred troopers was sent to the city gates to demand its surrender. The small garrison which had been left by the Prince was not disposed to resist, but the spirit of the burghers was stouter than their walls. They answered the summons by a declaration that they had thus far held the city for the King and the Prince of Orange, and, with God's help, would continue so to do. As the horsemen departed with this reply, a lunatic, called Adrian Krankhoeft, mounted the ramparts and discharged a culverine among them.* No man was injured, but the words of defiance, and the shot fired by a madman's hand, were destined to be fearfully answered.

Meanwhile, the inhabitants of the place, which was at best far from strong, and ill provided with arms, ammunition, or soldiers, despatched importunate messages to Sonoy, and to other patriot generals nearest to them, soliciting reinforcements. Their messengers came back almost empty handed. They brought a little powder and a great many promises, but not a single man-at-arms, not a ducat, not a piece of artillery. The most influential commanders, moreover, advised an honorable capitulation, if it were still possible.†

Thus baffled, the burghers of the little city found their proud position quite untenable. They accordingly, on the 1st of December, despatched the burgomaster and a senator to Amersfoort, to make terms, if possible, with Don Frederic.‡ When these envoys reached the place, they were refused admission to the general's presence. The army had already been ordered to move forward to Naarden, and they were directed to accompany the advance guard, and to expect their reply at the gates of their own city. This command was sufficiently ominous. The impression which it made upon them was confirmed by the warning voices of their friends in Amersfoort, who entreated

---

* Bor, vi. 417.   † Ibid.   ‡ Ibid.   Hoofd, vii. 276.

them not to return to Naarden. The advice was not lost upon one of the two envoys. After they had advanced a little distance on their journey, the burgomaster Laurents-zoon slid privately out of the sledge in which they were travelling, leaving his cloak behind him. "Adieu; I think I will not venture back to Naarden at present," said he, calmly, as he abandoned his companion to his fate.* The other, who could not so easily desert his children, his wife, and his fellow-citizens, in the hour of danger, went forward as calmly to share in their impending doom.

The army reached Bussem, half a league distant from Naarden, in the evening. Here Don Frederic established his head quarters, and proceeded to invest the city. Senator Gerrit was then directed to return to Naarden and to bring out a more numerous deputation on the following morning, duly em-powered to surrender the place. The envoy accordingly returned next day, accompanied by Lambert Hortensius, rector of a Latin academy, together with four other citizens. Before this deputation had reached Bussem, they were met by Julian Romero, who informed them that he was commissioned to treat with them on the part of Don Frederic. He de-manded the keys of the city, and gave the deputation a solemn pledge that the lives and property of all the inhabitants should be sacredly respected. To attest this assurance, Don Julian gave his hand three several times to Lambert Hortensius. A soldier's word thus plighted, the commissioners, without exchanging any written documents, surrendered the keys, and immediately afterwards accompanied Romero into the city, who was soon followed by five or six hundred musketeers.†

To give these guests a hospitable reception, all the housewives of the city at once set about preparations for a sumptuous feast, to which the Spaniards did ample justice, while the colonel and his officers were entertained by Senator Gerrit at

---

* "Adieu, ik komm niet weder binnen Naarden voor dit pas."—Bor, vi. 417.
† Bor, vi. 417.   Hoofd, vii. 277.

his own house.* As soon as this conviviality had come to an end, Romero, accompanied by his host, walked into the square. The great bell had been meantime ringing, and the citizens had been summoned to assemble in the Gast Huis Church, then used as a town hall.† In the course of a few minutes five hundred had entered the building, and stood quietly awaiting whatever measures might be offered for their delibe- ration. Suddenly a priest, who had been pacing to and fro before the church door, entered the building, and bade them all prepare for death ; but the announcement, the preparation, and the death, were simultaneous.‡ The door was flung open, and a band of armed Spaniards rushed across the sacred threshold. They fired a single volley upon the defenceless herd, and then sprang in upon them with sword and dagger. A yell of despair arose as the miserable victims saw how hopelessly they were engaged, and beheld the ferocious faces of their butchers. The carnage within that narrow space was compact and rapid. Within a few minutes all were despatched, and among them Senator Gerrit, from whose table the Spanish com- mander had but just risen. The church was then set on fire, and the dead and dying were consumed to ashes together.§

Inflamed but not satiated, the Spaniards then rushed into the streets, thirsty for fresh horrors. The houses were all rifled of their contents, and men were forced to carry the booty to the camp, who were then struck dead as their reward. The town was then fired in every direction, that the skulk- ing citizens might be forced from their hiding-places. As fast as they came forth they were put to death by their im- patient foes. Some were pierced with rapiers, some were chopped to pieces with axes, some were surrounded in the blazing streets by troops of laughing soldiers, intoxicated, not with wine but with blood, who tossed them to and fro

---

* Hooft, vii. 278.   † Bor, Hooft.

‡ " Maar, 't aanseggen, bereyden en sterven was een ding."—Hooft, vii. 278.

§ Bor, Hooft, ubi sup.

with their lances, and derived a wild amusement from their dying agonies. Those who attempted resistance were crimped alive like fishes, and left to gasp themselves to death in lingering torture.* The soldiers becoming more and more insane, as the foul work went on, opened the veins of some of their victims, and drank their blood as if it were wine.† Some of the burghers were for a time spared, that they might witness the violation of their wives and daughters, and were then butchered in company with these still more unfortunate victims.‡ Miracles of brutality were accomplished. Neither church nor hearth was sacred. Men were slain, women outraged at the altars, in the streets, in their blazing homes. The life of Lambert Hortensius was spared, out of regard to his learning and genius, but he hardly could thank his foes for the boon, for they struck his only son dead, and tore his heart out before his father's eyes.§ Hardly any man or woman survived, except by accident. A body of some hundred burghers made their escape across the snow into the open country. They were, however, overtaken, stripped stark naked, and hung upon the trees by the feet, to freeze, or to perish by a more lingering death. Most of them soon died, but twenty, who happened to be wealthy, succeeded, after enduring much torture, in purchasing their lives of their inhuman persecutors. The principal burgomaster, Heinrich Lambertszoon, was less fortunate. Known to be affluent, he was tortured by exposing the soles of his feet to a fire until they were almost consumed. On promise that his life should be spared, he then agreed to pay a heavy ransom ; but hardly had he furnished the stipulated sum when, by express order

---

* Hoofd, vii. 279.—"Als visschen gekorven en lankzaamelyk gewentelt in een taaye doodt."   † Hoofd, ubi sup.   ‡ Bor, Hoofd, ubi sup.

§ Bor, vi. 419. Hoofd.—It was even said that they devoured it : nor was this the only act of cannibalism of which they were accused, for it was said and believed by many that the bodies of children were roasted and eaten by the soldiers. These last traits of horror are, however, only mentioned by Hoofd as reports. The tearing out of the heart before the father's eyes is attested both by him and by Bor.

of Don Frederic himself, he was hanged in his own doorway, and his dissevered limbs afterwards nailed to the gates of the city.*

Nearly all the inhabitants of Naarden, soldiers and citizens, were thus destroyed ; and now Don Frederic issued peremptory orders that no one, on pain of death, should give lodging or food to any fugitive. He likewise forbade to the dead all that could now be forbidden them—a grave. Three weeks long did these unburied bodies pollute the streets, nor could the few wretched women who still cowered within such houses as had escaped the flames ever move from their lurking-places without treading upon the festering remains of what had been their husbands, their fathers, or their brethren. Such was the express command of him whom the flatterers called the "most divine genius ever known." Shortly afterwards came an order to dismantle the fortifications, which had certainly proved sufficiently feeble in the hour of need, and to raze what was left of the city from the surface of the earth. The work was faithfully accomplished, and for a long time Naarden ceased to exist.†

Alva wrote, with his usual complacency in such cases, to his sovereign, that "they had cut the throats of the burghers and all the garrison, and that they had not left a mother's son alive."‡ The statement was almost literally correct, nor was the cant with which these bloodhounds commented upon their crimes less odious than their guilt. "It was *a permission of God,*" said the Duke, "that these people should have undertaken to defend a city, which was so weak that no other persons would have attempted such

---

* Hoofd, vii. 280.

† Bor, vi. 419.   Hoofd, vii. 280.   Meteren, iv. 78.

‡ "Degollaron burgeses y soldados, sin escaparse hombre nascido."—Correspondance de Philippe II., ii. 1186. Every inhabitant of Naarden was put to the sword, says the ultra-Catholic Renom de France, except the ecclesiastics and two or three persons of quality who were reserved. Then the city was pillaged, after which a fire was lighted, "qui la *consomma entièrement.*"—Hist. des Causes des Révoltes des Pays Bas, MS., ii. xx.

a thing."* Nor was the reflection of Mendoza less pious. "The sack of Naarden," said that really brave and accomplished cavalier, "was a chastisement which must be believed to have taken place by express permission of a Divine Providence ; a punishment for having been the first of the Holland towns in which heresy built its nest, whence it has taken flight to all the neighboring cities."†

It is not without reluctance, but still with a stern determination, that the historian should faithfully record these transactions. To extenuate would be base ; to exaggerate impossible. It is good that the world should not forget how much wrong has been endured by a single harmless nation at the hands of despotism, and in the sacred name of God. There have been tongues and pens enough to narrate the excesses of the people, bursting from time to time out of slavery into madness. It is good, too, that those crimes should be remembered, and freshly pondered ; but it is equally wholesome to study the opposite picture. Tyranny, ever young and ever old, constantly reproducing herself with the same stony features, with the same imposing mask which she has worn through all the ages, can never be too minutely examined, especially when she paints her own portrait, and when the secret history of her guilt is furnished by the confessions of her lovers. The perusal of her traits will not make us love popular liberty the less.

The history of Alva's administration in the Netherlands is one of those pictures which strike us almost dumb with wonder. Why has the Almighty suffered such crimes to be perpetrated in His sacred name ? Was it necessary that many generations should wade through this blood in order to acquire for their descendants the blessings of civil and

---

* Correspondance de Philippe II., ii. 1186.

† Mendoza, viii. 173.—The details of these acts of iniquity have only been preserved by the Dutch writers. Mendoza, and Cabrera (who always follows Mendoza), dismiss the sacking of each successive city with a phrase and a pious ejaculation. Alva briefly condenses the principal horrors in a few energetic lines.—Compare Wagenaer, Vad. Hist. vi. 403–408; Meteren, iv. 78; Bentivoglio, vi. 115.

religious freedom ?   Was it necessary that an Alva should
ravage a peaceful nation with sword and flame—that desolation
should be spread over a happy land, in order that the pure and
heroic character of a William of Orange should stand forth
more conspicuously, like an antique statue of spotless marble
against a stormy sky ?

After the army which the Prince had so unsuccessfully led
to the relief of Mons had been disbanded, he had himself
repaired to Holland.   He had come to Kampen shortly before
its defection from his cause.   Thence he had been escorted
across the Zuyder Zee to Eukhuyzen.*   He came to that province, the only one which through good and ill report remained entirely faithful to him, not as a conqueror but as an
unsuccessful, proscribed man.   But there were warm hearts
beating within those cold lagunes, and no conqueror returning
from a brilliant series of victories could have been received
with more affectionate respect than William in that darkest
hour of the country's history.   He had but seventy horsemen
at his back, all which remained of the twenty thousand troops
which he had a second time levied in Germany, and he felt
that it would be at that period hopeless for him to attempt
the formation of a third army.   He had now come thither to
share the fate of Holland, at least, if he could not accomplish
her liberation.   He went from city to city, advising with the
magistracies and with the inhabitants, and arranging many
matters pertaining both to peace and war.†   At Harlem the
States of the Provinces, according to his request, had been
assembled.   The assembly begged him to lay before them, if
it were possible, any schemes and means which he might have
devised for further resistance to the Duke of Alva.   Thus
solicited, the Prince, in a very secret session, unfolded his
plans, and satisfied them as to the future prospects of the
cause.‡   His speech has nowhere been preserved.   His strict
injunctions as to secrecy, doubtless, prevented or effaced any

---

* Bor, vi. 414.   Hoofd, vii. 264.
† Letter of St. Aldegonde in Archives de la Maison d'Orange, iv. 22.
‡ Bor, vi. 414.   Wagenaer, Vad. Hist., vi. 396, 397.

record of the session. It is probable, however, that he entered more fully into the state of his negotiations with England, and into the possibility of a resumption by Count Louis of his private intercourse with the French court, than it was safe, publicly, to divulge.

While the Prince had been thus occupied in preparing the stout-hearted province for the last death-struggle with its foe, that mortal combat was already fast approaching ; for the aspect of the contest in the Netherlands was not that of ordinary warfare. It was an encounter between two principles, in their nature so hostile to each other that the absolute destruction of one was the only possible issue. As the fight went on, each individual combatant seemed inspired by direct personal malignity, and men found a pleasure in deeds of cruelty, from which generations not educated to slaughter recoil with horror. To murder defenceless prisoners ; to drink, not metaphorically *but literally*, the heart's blood of an enemy ; to exercise a devilish ingenuity in inventions of mutual torture, became not only a duty but a rapture. The Liberty of the Netherlands had now been hunted to its lair. It had taken its last refuge among the sands and thickets where its savage infancy had been nurtured, and had now prepared itself to crush its tormentor in a last embrace, or to die in the struggle.

After the conclusion of the sack and massacre of Naarden, Don Frederic had hastened to Amsterdam,* where the Duke was then quartered, that he might receive the paternal benediction for his well-accomplished work. The royal approbation was soon afterwards added to the applause of his parent, and the Duke was warmly congratulated in a letter written by Philip as soon as the murderous deed was known, that Don Frederic had so plainly shown himself to be his father's son.† There was now more work for father and son. Amsterdam was the only point in Holland which held for Alva, and from

---

* Bor, vi. 420, 421.
† Correspondance de Philippe II., ii. 1197.

that point it was determined to recover the whole province. The Prince of Orange was established in the southern
district; Diedrich Sonoy, his lieutenat, was stationed in
North Holland.* The important city of Harlem lay between
the two, at a spot where the whole breadth of the territory,
from sea to sea, was less than an hour's walk. With the fall
of that city the province would be cut in twain, the rebellious
forces utterly dissevered, and all further resistance, it was
thought, rendered impossible.

The inhabitants of Harlem felt their danger. Bossu, Alva's
stadholder for Holland, had formally announced the system
hitherto pursued at Mechlin, Zutphen, and Naarden, as the
deliberate policy of the government. The King's representative had formally proclaimed the extermination of man,
woman, and child in every city which opposed his authority,†
but the promulgation and practice of such a system had an
opposite effect to the one intended. The hearts of the Hollanders were rather steeled to resistance than awed into submission by the fate of Naarden.‡ A fortunate event, too,
was accepted as a lucky omen for the coming contest. A
little fleet of armed vessels, belonging to Holland, had been
frozen up in the neighbourhood of Amsterdam. Don Frederic
on his arrival from Naarden, despatched a body of picked
men over the ice to attack the imprisoned vessels. The
crews had, however, fortified themselves by digging a wide
trench around the whole fleet, which thus became from
the moment an almost impregnable fortress. Out of this
frozen citadel a strong band of well-armed and skilful
musketeers sallied forth upon skates as the besieging force
advanced. A rapid, brilliant, and slippery skirmish succeeded, in which the Hollanders, so accustomed to such sports,
easily vanquished their antagonists, and drove them off the
field, with the loss of several hundred left dead upon the ice.§

---

* Bor, vi. 424.   † Ibid., 417.
‡ Ibid., vi. 420.   Hoofd, vii. 280, 281.   Meteren, iv. 78.   Bentivoglio,
vi. 115.   § Mendoza, vii. 173.

" 'T was a thing never heard of before to-day," said Alva, " to see a body of arquebusiers thus skirmishing upon a frozen sea."* In the course of the next four-and-twenty hours a flood and a rapid thaw released the vessels, which all escaped to Enkhuyzen, while a frost, immediately and strangely succeeding, made pursuit impossible.†

The Spaniards were astonished at these novel manœuvres upon the ice. It is amusing to read their elaborate descriptions of the wonderful appendages which had enabled the Hollanders to glide so glibly into battle with a superior force, and so rapidly to glance away, after achieving a signal triumph. Nevertheless, the Spaniards could never be dismayed, and were always apt scholars, even if an enemy were the teacher. Alva immediately ordered seven thousand pairs of skates, and his soldiers soon learned to perform military evolutions with these new accoutrements as audaciously, if not as adroitly, as the Hollanders.‡

A portion of the Harlem magistracy, notwithstanding the spirit which pervaded the province, began to tremble as danger approached. They were base enough to enter into secret negotiations with Alva, and to send three of their own number to treat with the Duke at Amsterdam. One was wise enough to remain with the enemy. The other two were arrested on their return, and condemned, after an impartial trial, to death.§ For, while these emissaries of a cowardly magistracy were absent, the stout commandant of the little garrison, Ripperda, had assembled the citizens and soldiers in the market-place. He warned them of the absolute necessity to make a last effort for freedom. In startling colors he held up to them the fate of Mechlin, of Zutphen, of Naarden, as a prophetic mirror, in which they might read their own fate should they be base enough to surrender the city. There was

---

* Correspondance de Philippe II., ii. 1186.—"Que me parece la mas nueva cosa que hasta oy se ha oido, escaramuzar arcabuzeria sobre la mer alada."

† Hoofd, vij. 281.

‡ Bentivoglio, vii. 122.   Mendoza, viii. 173, et al.

§ Bor, vi. 420, 421.   Hoofd, vii. 282.   Meteren, iv. 78.

no composition possible, he urged, with foes who were as false as they were sanguinary, and whose foul passions were stimulated, not slaked, by the horrors with which they had already feasted themselves.*

Ripperda addressed men who could sympathize with his bold and lofty sentiments. Soldiers and citizens cried out for defence instead of surrender, as with one voice, for there were no abject spirits at Harlem, save among the magistracy ; and Saint Aldegonde, the faithful minister of Orange, was soon sent to Harlem by the Prince to make a thorough change in that body.†

Harlem, over whose ruins the Spanish tyranny intended to make its entrance into Holland, lay in the narrowest part of that narrow isthmus which separates the Zuyder Zee from the German Ocean. The distance from sea to sea is hardly five English miles across. Westerly from the city extended a slender strip of land, once a morass, then a fruitful meadow, maintained by unflagging fortitude in the very jaws of a stormy ocean. Between the North Sea and the outer edge of this pasture surged those wild and fantastic downs, heaped up by wind and wave in mimicry of mountains ; the long coils of that rope of sand, by which, plaited into additional strength by the slenderest of bulrushes,‡ the waves of the North Sea were made to obey the command of man. On the opposite, or eastern side, Harlem looked towards Amsterdam. That already flourishing city was distant but ten miles. The two cities were separated by an expanse of inland water, and united by a slender causeway. The Harlem Lake, formed less than a century before by the bursting of four lesser meres during a storm which had threatened to swallow the whole Peninsula, extended itself on the south and east ; a sea of limited dimensions, being only fifteen feet in depth with seventy square miles of surface, but, exposed as it lay to all the winds of heaven, often lashed into storms as dangerous as

---

* Bor, vi. 420, 421. Hoofd, vii. 283. Meteren, iv. 78.
† Bor, Hoofd, Mendoza, ubi sup.   ‡ Arundo arenaria.

those of the Atlantic.* Beyond the lake, towards the north, the waters of the Y nearly swept across the Peninsula. This inlet of the Zuyder Zee was only separated from the Harlem mere by a slender thread of land. Over this ran the causeway between the two sister cities, now so unfortunately in arms against each other. Midway between the two, the dyke was pierced and closed again with a system of sluice-works, which when opened admitted the waters of the lake into those of the estuary, and caused an inundation of the surrounding country.†

The city was one of the largest and most beautiful in the Netherlands. It was also one of the weakest.‡ The walls were of antique construction, turreted, but not strong. The extent and feebleness of the defences made a large garrison necessary, but unfortunately, the garrison was even weaker than the walls. The city's main reliance was on the stout hearts of the inhabitants. The streets were, for that day, spacious and regular ; the canals planted with limes and poplars. The ancient church 'of Saint Bavon, a large imposing structure of brick, stood almost in the centre of the place, the most prominent object, not only of the town but of the province, visible over leagues of sea and of land more level than the sea, and seeming to gather the whole quiet little city under its sacred and protective wings. Its tall open-work leaden spire was surmounted by a colossal crown, which an exalted imagination might have regarded as the emblematic guerdon of martyrdom held aloft over the city, to reward its heroism and its agony.

It was at once obvious that the watery expanse between Harlem and Amsterdam would be the principal theatre of the operations about to commence. The siege was soon begun.

---

* Bentivoglio, vii. 118. Mendoza, viii, 176. Bor, vi. 422. Meteren, iv. 78.— This lake, the scene of so many romantic events during the period with which we are occupied, has, within the last few years, been converted into dry land. The magnificent undertaking was completed in the year 1853.

† Bor, Meteren, Bentivoglio, Mendoza, ubi sup.   ‡ Bor, vi. 422.

The fugitive burgomaster, De Fries, had the effrontery, with the advice of Alva, to address a letter to the citizens, urging them to surrender at discretion. The messenger was hanged —a cruel but practical answer, which put an end to all further traitorous communications.* This was in the first week of December. On the 10th, Don Frederic sent a strong detachment to capture the fort and village of Sparendam, as an indispensable preliminary to the commencement of the siege. A peasant having shown Zapata, the commander of the expedition, a secret passage across the flooded and frozen meadows, the Spaniards stormed the place gallantly, routed the whole garrison, killed three hundred, and took possession of the works and village. Next day, Don Frederic appeared before the walls of Harlem, and proceeded regularly to invest the place. The misty weather favored his operations, nor did he cease reinforcing himself, until at least thirty thousand men, including fifteen hundred cavalry, had been encamped around the city. The Germans, under Count Overstein, were stationed in a beautiful and extensive grove of limes and beeches, which spread between the southern walls and the shore of Harlem Lake. Don Frederic, with his Spaniards, took up a position on the opposite side, at a place called the House of Kleef, the ruins of which still remain. The Walloons, and other regiments were distributed in different places, so as completely to encircle the town.† On the edge of the mere the Prince of Orange had already ordered a cluster of forts to be erected, by which the command of its frozen surface was at

---

* Hoofd, vii. 284.

† Pierre Sterlinckx: Eene corte Waerachtige Beschryvinghe van alle Geschiedinissen, Anschlagen, Stormen, Schermutsingen oude Schieten voor de vroome Stadt Haerlem in Holland gheschicht, etc., etc.—Delft, 1574.

This is by far the best contemporary account of the famous siege. The author was a citizen of Antwerp, who kept a daily journal of the events as they occurred at Harlem. It is a dry, curt register of horrors, jotted down without passion or comment.—Compare Bor, vi. 422, 423 ; Meteren, iv. 79 ; Mendoza, viii. 174, 175 ; Wagenaer, Vad. Hist., vi. 413, 414.

first secured for Harlem.* In the course of the siege, however, other forts were erected by Don Frederic, so that the aspect of things suffered a change.

Against this immense force, nearly equal in number to that of the whole population of the city, the garrison within the walls never amounted to more than four thousand men.† In the beginning it was much less numerous. The same circumstances, however, which assisted the initiatory operations of Don Frederic, were of advantage to the Harlemers. A dense frozen fog hung continually over the surface of the lake. Covered by this curtain, large supplies of men, provisions, and ammunition were daily introduced into the city, notwithstanding all the efforts of the besieging force.‡ Sledges skimming over the ice, men, women, and even children, moving on their skates as swiftly as the wind, all brought their contributions in the course of the short dark days and long nights of December, in which the wintry siege was opened.§ The garrison at last numbered about one thousand pioneers or delvers, three thousand fighting men, and about three hundred fighting women.‖ The last was a most efficient corps, all females of respectable character, armed with sword, musket, and dagger. Their chief, Kenau Hasselaer, was a widow of distinguished family and unblemished reputation, about forty-seven years of age, who, at the head of her amazons, participated in many of the most fiercely contested actions of the siege, both within and without the walls.¶ When such a spirit animated the maids and matrons of the city, it might be expected that the men would hardly surrender the place without a struggle. The Prince had assembled a force of three or four thousand men at Leyden, which he sent before the middle of December towards the

---

* Bor, Hoofd, Mendoza. Wagenaer, vi. 415.
† Hoofd, vii. 285.   † Hoofd.
§ Mendoza, ix. 190. Hoofd, vii. 285, 286. Meteren, iv. 79, 80.
‖ Wagenaer, vi. 415. Bor. Hoofd, vii. 286.
¶ Wagenaer. Hoofd. Meteren, iv. 79.

city under the command of De la Marck.* These troops
were, however, attacked on the way by a strong detachment
under Bossu, Noircarmes, and Romero. After a sharp action
in a heavy snow-storm, De la Marck was completely routed.
One thousand of his soldiers were cut to pieces, and a large
number carried off as prisoners to the gibbets, which were
already conspicuously erected in the Spanish camp, and which
from the commencement to the close of the siege were never
bare of victims.† Among the captives was a gallant officer,
Baptist van Trier, for whom De la Marck in vain offered two
thousand crowns and nineteen Spanish prisoners. The proposition was refused with contempt. Van Trier was hanged upon
the gallows by one leg until he was dead, in return for which
barbarity the nineteen Spaniards were immediately gibbeted
by De la Marck.‡ With this interchange of cruelties the siege
may be said to have opened.

Don Frederic had stationed himself in a position opposite
to the gate of the Cross, which was not very strong, but
fortified by a ravelin. Intending to make a very short siege
of it, he established his batteries immediately, and on the 18th,
19th, and 20th December directed a furious cannonade against
the Cross-gate, the St. John's-gate, and the curtain between
the two.§ Six hundred and eighty shots were discharged on
the first, and nearly as many on each of the two succeeding
days.‖ The walls were much shattered, but men, women,
and children worked night and day within the city, repairing
the breaches as fast as made. They brought bags of sand,
blocks of stone, cart-loads of earth from every quarter, and
they stripped the churches of all their statues, which they
threw by heaps into the gaps.¶ They sought thus a more
practical advantage from those sculptured saints than they
could have gained by only imploring their interposition. The
fact, however, excited horror among the besiegers. Men who

---

* Bor, vi. 424.   † P. Sterlincx. Corte Beschr., etc.   Bor.   Hoofd, vii. 286.
‡ Hoofd, vii. 286.   P. Sterlincx.
§ Bor, vi. 423.   Meteren, iv. 79.   Hoofd, vii. 287.   Mendoza, ix. 178–180.
‖ Meteren, iv. 79.   Hoofd.   ¶ Bor, Bentivoglio, P. Sterlincx.

were daily butchering their fellow-beings, and hanging their prisoners in cold blood, affected to shudder at the enormity of the offence thus exercised against graven images.*

After three days' cannonade, the assault was ordered, Don Frederic only intending a rapid massacre, to crown his achievements at Zutphen and Naarden. The place, he thought, would fall in a week, and after another week of sacking, killing, and ravishing, he might sweep on to "pastures new" until Holland was overwhelmed. Romero advanced to the breach, followed by a numerous storming party, but met with a resistance which astonished the Spaniards. The church bells rang the alarm throughout the city, and the whole population swarmed to the walls. The besiegers were encountered not only with sword and musket, but with every implement which the burghers' hands could find. Heavy stones, boiling oil, live coals, were hurled upon the heads of the soldiers ; hoops, smeared with pitch and set on fire, were dexterously thrown upon their necks. Even Spanish courage and Spanish ferocity were obliged to shrink before the steady determination of a whole population animated by a single spirit. Romero lost an eye in the conflict, many officers were killed and wounded, and three or four hundred soldiers left dead in the breach, while only three or four of the townsmen lost their lives. The signal of recal was reluctantly given, and the Spaniards abandoned the assault. Don Frederic was now aware that Harlem would not fall at his feet at the first sound of his trumpet. It was obvious that a siege must precede the massacre. He gave orders therefore that the ravelin should be undermined, and doubted not that, with a few days' delay, the place would be in his hands.†

Meantime, the Prince of Orange, from his head-quarters at Sassenheim, on the southern extremity of the mere, made a fresh effort to throw succor into the place.‡ Two thousand

---

* Vide Bentivoglio, vii. 121. Mendoza, passim.
† Bor, vi. 423. Hoofd, vii. 287, 288. Meteren, 79. Mendoza, ix. 178–180.
‡ Hoofd, vii. 290. Bor, vi. 431.

men, with seven field-pieces, and many wagon-loads of munitions, were sent forward under Batenburg. This officer had
replaced De la Marck, whom the Prince had at last deprived
of his commission.* The reckless and unprincipled freebooter
was no longer to serve a cause which was more sullied by his
barbarity than it could be advanced by his desperate valor.
Batenburg's expedition was, however, not more successful than
the one made by his predecessor. The troops, after reaching
the vicinity of the city, lost their way in the thick mists,
which almost perpetually enveloped the scene. Cannons
were fired, fog-bells were rung, and beacon fires were lighted
on the ramparts, but the party was irretrievably lost. The
Spaniards fell upon them before they could find their way to
the city. Many were put to the sword, others made their
escape in different directions ; a very few succeeded in entering
Harlem. Batenburg brought off a remnant of the forces, but
all the provisions so much needed were lost, and the little
army entirely destroyed.†

De Koning, the second in command, was among the
prisoners. The Spaniards cut off his head and threw it
over the walls into the city, with this inscription : "This
is the head of Captain de Koning, who is on his way
with reinforcements for the good city of Harlem." The
citizens retorted with a practical jest, which was still more
barbarous. They cut off the heads of eleven prisoners and
put them into a barrel, which they threw into the Spanish
camp. A label upon the barrel contained these words : "Deliver these ten heads to Duke Alva in payment of his tenpenny
tax, with one additional head for interest."‡ With such
ghastly merriment did besieged and besiegers vary the monotonous horror of that winter's siege. As the sallies and
skirmishes were of daily occurrence, there was a constant supply

---

* See all the proceedings and papers in the case of De la Marck, in Bor, vi.
425–431. See also Hoofd, vii. 288, 289.

† Hoofd, vii. 290.

‡ P. Sterlincx. Corte Beschyr., etc. Bor, vi. 431. Hoofd, vii. 290, 291.

of prisoners, upon whom both parties might exercise their ingenuity, so that the gallows in camp or city was perpetually garnished.

Since the assault of the 21st December, Don Frederic had been making his subterranean attack by regular approaches. As fast, however, as the Spaniards mined, the citizens counter-, mined. Spaniard and Netherlander met daily in deadly combat within the bowels of the earth. Desperate and frequent were the struggles within gangways so narrow that nothing but daggers could be used, so obscure that the dim lanterns hardly lighted the death-stroke. They seemed the conflicts, not of men but of evil spirits. Nor were these hand-to-hand battles all. A shower of heads, limbs, mutilated trunks, the mangled remains of hundreds of human beings, often spouted from the earth as if from an invisible volcano. The mines were sprung with unexampled frequency and determination. Still the Spaniards toiled on with undiminished zeal, and still the besieged, undismayed, delved below their works, and checked their advance by sword, and spear, and horrible explosions.*

The Prince of Orange, meanwhile, encouraged the citizens to persevere, by frequent promises of assistance. His letters, written on extremely small bits of paper, were sent into the town by carrier pigeons.† On the 28th of January he despatched a considerable supply of the two necessaries, powder and bread, on one hundred and seventy sledges across the Harlem Lake, together with four hundred veteran soldiers.‡ The citizens continued to contest the approaches to the ravelin before the Cross-gate, but it had become obvious that they could not hold

---

* P. Sterlincx. Bor, vi. 431. Mendoza, ix. 182.—"Assi mismo consumian las minas mucha gente y soldados——y en las mismas que se labraran, se combatio algunas vezes, por la estrecheza del lugar con espada y rodela, por no poderse aprovechar de otras armas." "Daer onstond dan een ysslyk schonwspel en slaghreegen van hoofden, armen, beenen een sleeteren van ingewant, uit den aarde, naa de lucht."—Hoofd, vii. 291.

† Hoofd, viii. 303. Mendoza, ix. 188, 189. Meteren, iv. 80.

‡ Bor, vi. 432.

it long. Secretly, steadfastly, and swiftly they had, therefore, during the long wintry nights, been constructing a half moon of solid masonry on the inside of the same portal.* Old men, feeble women, tender children, united with the able-bodied to accomplish this work, by which they hoped still to maintain themselves after the ravelin had fallen.†

On the 31st of January, after two or three days' cannonade against the gates of the Cross and of Saint John, and the intervening curtains, Don Frederic ordered a midnight assault.‡ The walls had been much shattered, part of the John's-gate was in ruins; the Spaniards mounted the breach in great numbers; the city was almost taken by surprise; while the Commander-in-chief, sure of victory, ordered the whole of his forces under arms to cut off the population who were to stream panic-struck from every issue. The attack was unexpected, but the forty or fifty sentinels defended the walls while they sounded the alarm. The tocsin bells tolled, and the citizens, whose sleep was not apt to be heavy during that perilous winter, soon manned the ramparts again. The daylight came upon them while the fierce struggle was still at its height. The besieged, as before, defended themselves with musket and rapier, with melted pitch, with firebrands, with clubs and stones. Meantime, after morning prayers in the Spanish camp, the trumpet for a general assault was sounded. A tremendous onset was made upon the gate of the Cross, and the ravelin was carried at last. The Spaniards poured into this fort, so long the object of their attack, expecting instantly to sweep into the city with sword and fire. As they mounted its wall they became for the first time aware of the new and stronger fortification which had been secretly constructed on the inner side.§ The reason why the ravelin had been at last conceded was revealed. The half moon, whose existence they had not suspected, rose before them bristling with cannon. A sharp fire was instantly

---

* Bor, vi. 431, 432. Mendoza, iv. 188.   † Ibid.
‡ Bor, vi. 432. Hoofd, vii. 292, 293.   § Hoofd, vii. 293.

opened upon the besiegers, while at the same instant the ravelin, which the citizens had undermined, blew up with a severe explosion, carrying into the air all the soldiers who had just entered it so triumphantly. This was the turning point. The retreat was sounded, and the Spaniards fled to their camp, leaving at least three hundred dead beneath the walls. Thus was a second assault, made by an overwhelming force and led by the most accomplished generals of Spain, signally and gloriously repelled by the plain burghers of Harlem.*

It became now almost evident that the city could be taken neither by regular approaches nor by sudden attack. It was therefore resolved that it should be reduced by famine. Still, as the winter wore on, the immense army without the walls were as great sufferers by that scourge as the population within. The soldiers fell in heaps before the diseases engendered by intense cold and insufficient food, for, as usual in such sieges, these deaths far outnumbered those inflicted by the enemy's hand. The sufferings inside the city necessarily increased day by day, the whole population being put on a strict allowance of food.† Their supplies were daily diminishing, and with the approach of the spring and the thawing of the ice on the lake, there was danger that they would be entirely cut off. If the possession of the water were lost, they must yield or starve ; and they doubted whether the Prince would be able to organize a fleet. The gaunt spectre of Famine already rose before them with a menace which could not be misunderstood. In their misery they longed for the assaults of the Spaniards, that they might look in the face of a less formidable foe. They paraded the ramparts daily, with drums beating, colors flying, taunting the besiegers to renewed attempts. To inflame the religious animosity of their antago-. nists, they attired themselves in the splendid, gold-embroidered

---

* Hoofd, vii. 293. Mendoza, ix. 184, 185.   Bor, vi. 432.   Bentivoglio, vii. 124.

† Bentivoglio, vii. 125.   Mendoza, ix. 185.   Bor, vi. 436, 437.

vestments of the priests, which they took from the churches, and moved about in mock procession, bearing aloft images bedizened in ecclesiastical finery, relics, and other symbols, sacred in Catholic eyes, which they afterwards hurled from the ramparts, or broke, with derisive shouts, into a thousand fragments.*

It was, however, at that season earnestly debated by the enemy whether or not to raise the siege.† Don Frederic was clearly of opinion that enough had been done for the honor of the Spanish arms. He was wearied with seeing his men perish helplessly around him, and considered the prize too paltry for the lives it must cost. His father thought differently. Perhaps he recalled the siege of Metz, and the unceasing regret with which, as he believed, his imperial master had remembered the advice received from him. At any rate the Duke now sent back Don Bernardino de Mendoza, whom Don Frederic had despatched to Nimwegen, soliciting his father's permission to raise the siege, with this reply :— "Tell Don Frederic," said Alva, "that if he be not decided to continue the siege till the town be taken, I shall no longer consider him my son, whatever my opinion may formerly have been. *Should he fall in the siege*, I will myself take the field to maintain it, and when we have both perished, the Duchess, my wife, shall come from Spain to do the same."‡

Such language was unequivocal, and hostilities were resumed as fiercely as before. The besieged welcomed them with rapture, and, as usual, made daily the most desperate sallies. In one outbreak the Harlemers, under cover of a thick fog, marched up to the enemy's chief battery, and attempted to spike the guns before his face. They were all slain at the cannon's mouth, whither patriotism, not vainglory, had led them, and lay dead around the battery, with their hammers and spikes in their hands.§ The same spirit was daily manifested. As the spring advanced, the kine went

---

* Bentivoglio, vii. 121.

† Mendoza, ix. 185, 186.   Bentivoglio, vii. 124, 125.

‡ Mendoza, ix. 192.   § Ibid., ix. 182.

daily out of the gates to their peaceful pasture, notwithstanding all the turmoil within and around ; nor was it possible for the Spaniards to capture a single one of these creatures, without paying at least a dozen soldiers as its price.*
"These citizens," wrote Don Frederic, "do as much as the best soldiers in the world could do."†

The frost broke up by the end of February. Count Bossu, who had been building a fleet of small vessels in Amsterdam, soon afterwards succeeded in entering the lake with a few gun-boats, through a breach which he had made in the Overtoom, about half a league from that city.‡ The possession of the lake was already imperilled. The Prince, however, had not been idle, and he, too, was soon ready to send his flotilla to the mere.§ At the same time, the city of Amsterdam was in almost as hazardous a position as Harlem. As the one on the lake, so did the other depend upon its dyke for its supplies. Should that great artificial road which led to Muyden and Utrecht be cut asunder, Amsterdam might be starved as soon as Harlem. " Since I came into the world," wrote Alva, " I have never been in such anxiety. If they should succeed in cutting off the communication along the dykes, we should have to raise the siege of Harlem, to surrender, hands crossed, or to starve."‖ Orange was fully aware of the position of both places, but he was, as usual, sadly deficient in men and means. He wrote imploringly to his friends in England, in France, in Germany. He urged his brother Louis to bring a few soldiers, if it were humanly possible. " The whole country longs for you," he wrote to Louis, " as if you were the archangel Gabriel."¶

The Prince, however, did all that it was possible for man, so hampered, to do. He was himself, while anxiously writing, and hoping, and waiting for supplies of troops from Germany

---

* Hoofd, viii. 303.
† " Todo lo que humanamente podian hacer los mejores soldados del mundo."
—Correspondance de Philippe II., ii. 1217.   ‡ Bor, vi. 436.
§ Ibid., vi. 436, 437.   ‖ Correspondance de Philippe II., ii. 1245.
¶ Archives de la Maison d'Orange, iv. 74.

or France, doing his best with such volunteers as he could raise. He was still established at Sassenheim, on the south of the city, while Sonoy with his slender forces was encamped on the north. He now sent that general with as large a party as he could muster to attack the Diemerdyk.* His men entrenched themselves as strongly as they could between the Diemer and the Y, at the same time opening the sluices and breaking through the dyke. During the absence of their commander, who had gone to Edam for reinforcements, they were attacked by a large force from Amsterdam. A fierce amphibious contest took place, partly in boats, partly on the slippery causeway, partly in the water, resembling in character the frequent combats between the ancient Batavians and Romans during the wars of Civilis. The patriots were eventually overpowered.

Sonoy, who was on his way to their rescue, was frustrated in his design by the unexpected faint-heartedness of the volunteers whom he had enlisted at Edam.† Braving a thousand perils, he advanced, almost unattended, in his little vessel, but only to witness the overthrow and expulsion of his band.‡ It was too late for him singly to attempt to rally the retreating troops. They had fought well, but had been forced to yield before superior numbers, one individual of the little army having performed prodigies of valor. John Haring, of Horn, had planted himself entirely alone upon the dyke, where it was so narrow between the Y on the one side and the Diemer Lake on the other, that two men could hardly stand abreast. Here, armed with sword and shield, he had actually opposed and held in check one thousand of the enemy, during a period long enough to enable his own men, if they had been willing, to rally, and effectively to repel the attack. It was too late, the battle was too far lost to be restored; but still the brave soldier held the post, till, by his devotion, he had enabled all those of his compatriots who still remained in the entrenchments to make good their retreat. e then plunged into the sea, and, untouched by spear or

---

* Bor, vi. 437.   † Ibid. Hoofd, viii. 300.   ‡ Bor, Hoofd.

bullet, effected his escape.* Had he been a Greek or a Roman, an Horatius or a Chabrias, his name would have been famous in history—his statue erected in the market-place ; for the bold Dutchman on his dyke had manifested as much valor in a sacred cause as the most classic heroes of antiquity.

This unsuccessful attempt to cut off the communication between Amsterdam and the country strengthened the hopes of Alva. Several hundreds of the patriots were killed or captured, and among the slain was Antony Oliver, the painter, through whose agency Louis of Nassau had been introduced into Mons. His head was cut off by two ensigns in Alva's service, who received the price which had been set upon it of two thousand caroli.† It was then labelled with its owner's name, and thrown into the city of Harlem.‡ At the same time a new gibbet was erected in the Spanish camp before the city, in a conspicuous situation, upon which all the prisoners were hanged, some by the neck, some by the heels, in full view of their countrymen.§ As usual, this especial act of cruelty excited the emulation of the citizens. Two of the old board of magistrates, belonging to the Spanish party, were still imprisoned at Harlem ; together with seven other persons, among whom was a priest and a boy of twelve years. They were now condemned to the gallows.|| The wife of one of the ex-burgomasters and his daughter, who was a beguin, went by his side as he was led to execution, piously exhorting him to sustain with courage the execrations of the populace and his ignominious doom. The rabble, irritated by such boldness, were not satisfied with wreaking their vengeance on the principal victims, but after the execution had taken place they hunted the wife and daughter into the water, where they both perished.¶ It is right to record these instances of

* Hoofd, viii. 300, 301.—Compare Groen v. Prinsterer, Archives de la Maison d'Orange, iv. 80.

† Letter of Alva to Philip. Correspondance de Philippe II., ii. 1231.

‡ Hoofd, viii. 304.   § Ibid. Meteren, iv. 80. P. Sterlincx.

|| P. Sterlincx. Corte Beschr.

¶ P. Sterlincx. Hoofd, viii. 304, 305. Meteren, iv. 80. Brandt, i. x. 541.

cruelty, sometimes perpetrated by the patriots as well as by their oppressors—a cruelty rendered almost inevitable by the incredible barbarity of the foreign invader. It was a war of wolfish malignity. In the words of Mendoza, every man within and without Harlem "seemed inspired by a spirit of special and personal vengeance."[*] The innocent blood poured out in Mechlin, Zutphen, Naarden, and upon a thousand scaffolds, had been crying too long from the ground. The Hollanders must have been more or less than men not to be sometimes betrayed into acts which justice and reason must denounce.

The singular mood which has been recorded of a high-spirited officer of the garrison, Captain Curey, illustrated the horror with which such scenes of carnage were regarded by noble natures. Of a gentle disposition originally, but inflamed almost to insanity by a contemplation of Spanish cruelty, he had taken up the profession of arms, to which he had a natural repugnance. Brave to recklessness, he led his men on every daring outbreak, on every perilous midnight adventure. Armed only with his rapier, without defensive armor, he was ever found where the battle raged most fiercely, and numerous were the victims who fell before his sword. On returning, however, from such excursions, he invariably shut himself in his quarters, took to his bed, and lay for days, sick with remorse, and bitterly lamenting all that bloodshed in which he had so deeply participated, and which a cruel fate seemed to render necessary. As the gentle mood subsided, his frenzy would return, and again he would rush to the field, to seek new havoc and fresh victims for his rage.[†]

The combats before the walls were of almost daily occurrence. On the 25th March, one thousand of the besieged made a brilliant sally, drove in all the outposts of the enemy, burned three hundred tents, and captured seven cannon, nine standards, and many wagon-loads of provisions, all which they succeeded in bringing with them into the city.[‡] Having

---

[*] Mendoza, ix. 191.   [†] Hoofd, viii. 302.   [‡] Ibid.

thus reinforced themselves, in a manner not often practised by the citizens of a beleaguered town, in the very face of thirty thousand veterans—having killed eight hundred of the enemy, which was nearly one for every man engaged, while they lost but four of their own party*—the Harlemers, on their return, erected a trophy of funereal but exulting aspect. A mound of earth was constructed upon the ramparts, in the form of a colossal grave, in full view of the enemy's camp, and upon it were planted the cannon and standards so gallantly won in the skirmish, with the taunting inscription floating from the centre of the mound—" Harlem is the graveyard of the Spaniards."†

Such were the characteristics of this famous siege during the winter and early spring. Alva might well write to his sovereign, that " it was a war such as never before was seen or heard of in any land on earth."‡ Yet the Duke had known near sixty years of warfare. He informed Philip that " *never was a place defended with such skill and bravery as Harlem*, either by rebels or by men fighting for their lawful Prince."§ Certainly his son had discovered his mistake in asserting that the city would yield in a week ; while the father, after nearly six years' experience, had found this " people of butter" less malleable than even those " iron people" whom he boasted of having tamed. It was seen that neither the skies of Greece or Italy, nor the sublime scenery of Switzerland, were necessary to arouse the spirit of defiance to foreign oppression—a spirit which beat as proudly among the wintry mists and the level meadows of Holland as it had ever done under sunnier atmospheres and in more romantic lands.

Mendoza had accomplished his mission to Spain, and had returned with supplies of money within six weeks from the date of his departure.|| Owing to his representations and

---

* Hoofd, viii. 302.   † P. Sterlincx. Hoofd, ubi sup.

‡ " Es guerra que hasta oy se ha visto ny oydo semijante en pais estraño."— Correspondance de Philippe II, ii. 1230.

§ Corresp. de Philippe II., ii. 1198. || Mendoza, ix. 192.

Alva's entreaties, Philip had, moreover, ordered Requesens, governor of Milan, to send forward to the Netherlands three veteran Spanish regiments, which were now more required at Harlem than in Italy.[*] While the land force had thus been strengthened, the fleet upon the lake had also been largely increased. The Prince of Orange had, on the other hand, provided more than a hundred sail of various descriptions,[†] so that the whole surface of the mere was now alive with ships. Seafights and skirmishes took place almost daily, and it was obvious that the life and death struggle was now to be fought upon the water. So long as the Hollanders could hold or dispute the possession of the lake, it was still possible to succor Harlem from time to time. Should the Spaniards overcome the Prince's fleet, the city must inevitably starve.

At last, on the 28th of May, a decisive engagement of the fleets took place. The vessels grappled with each other, and there was a long, fierce, hand-to-hand combat. Under Bossu were one hundred vessels ; under Martin Brand, admiral of the patriot fleet, nearly one hundred and fifty, but of lesser dimensions. Batenburg commanded the troops on board the Dutch vessels. After a protracted conflict, in which several thousands were killed, the victory was decided in favor of the Spaniards. Twenty-two of the Prince's vessels being captured, and the rest totally routed, Bossu swept across the lake in triumph. The forts belonging to the patriots were immediately taken, and the Harlemers, with their friends, entirely excluded from the lake.[‡]

This was the beginning of the end. Despair took possession of the city. The whole population had been long subsisting upon an allowance of a pound of bread to each man, and half-a-pound for each woman ; but the bread was now exhausted, the famine had already begun,[§] and with the loss of the lake starvation was close at their doors. They sent urgent entreaties to the Prince

---

[*] Mendoza. ix. 192.   [†] Bor, vi. 436.

[‡] Bor, vi. 436, 437. Hoofd, viii. 306, 307.   [§] Bor, vi. 437. Hoofd, viii. 309.

to attempt something in their behalf. Three weeks more they assigned as the longest term during which they could possibly hold out.[*] He sent them word by carrier pigeons to endure yet a little time, for he was assembling a force, and would still succeed in furnishing them with supplies.[†] Meantime, through the month of June the sufferings of the inhabitants increased hourly. Ordinary food had long since vanished. The population now subsisted on linseed and rape-seed ; as these supplies were exhausted they devoured cats, dogs, rats, and mice, and when at last these unclean animals had been all consumed, they boiled the hides of horses and oxen ; they ate shoe-leather ; they plucked the nettles and grass from the graveyards, and the weeds which grew between the stones of the pavement, that with such food they might still support life a little longer, till the promised succor should arrive. Men, women, and children fell dead by scores in the streets, perishing of pure starvation, and the survivors had hardly the heart or the strength to bury them out of their sight. They who yet lived seemed to flit like shadows to and fro, envying those whose sufferings had already been terminated by death.[‡]

Thus wore away the month of June. On the 1st of July the burghers consented to a parley. Deputies were sent to confer with the besiegers, but the negotiations were abruptly terminated, for no terms of compromise were admitted by Don Frederic.[§] On the 3rd a tremendous cannonade was re-opened upon the city. One thousand and eight balls were discharged—the most which had ever been thrown in one day since the commencement of the siege.[||] The walls were severely shattered, but the assault was not ordered, because the besiegers were assured that it was physically impossible

---

[*] Letter of Prince of Orange to his brothers, 16th May, 1573.—Archives etc. iv. 95.

[†] Bor, vi. 438, 439. Hoofd, viii. 310.

[‡] Bor, vi. 436, 437. Hoofd, viii. 309, 310. Meteren, iv. 80. Bentivoglio vii. 128.　　　　　　　　　　[§] Hoofd, viii. 310. Mendoza, ix. 202, 203.

[||] Wagenaer, vi. 426.

for the inhabitants to hold out many days longer.* A last letter, written in blood,† was now despatched to the Prince of Orange, stating the forlorn condition to which they were reduced. At the same time, with the derision of despair, they flung into the hostile camp the few loaves of bread which yet remained within the city walls. A day or two later, a second and third parley were held, with no more satisfactory result than had attended the first. A black flag was now hoisted on the cathedral tower, the signal of despair to friend and foe, but a pigeon soon afterwards flew into the town with a letter from the Prince, begging them to maintain themselves two days longer, because succor was approaching.‡

The Prince had indeed been doing all which, under the circumstances, was possible. He assembled the citizens of Delft in the market-place, and announced his intention of marching in person to the relief of the city, in the face of the besieging army, if any troops could be obtained.§ Soldiers there were none ; but there was the deepest sympathy for Harlem throughout its sister cities, Delft, Rotterdam, Gouda. A numerous mass of burghers, many of them persons of station, all people of respectability, volunteered to march to the rescue. The Prince highly disapproved‖ of this miscellaneous army, whose steadfastness he could not trust. As a soldier, he knew that for such a momentous enterprise, enthusiasm could not supply the place of experience. Nevertheless, as no regular troops could be had, and as the emergency allowed no delay, he drew up a commission, appointing Paulus Buys to be governor during his absence, and provisional stadholder, should he fall in the expedition.¶ Four thousand armed volunteers, with six

---

* Hoofd, viii. 310.

† Letter of Don Frederic to Duke of Alva, 8th and 9th June, 1573.—Correspondance de Philippe II., ii. 1239.

‡ Hoofd, viii. 309, 310.   § Bor, vi. 439, 440.

‖ See his letter of 18th July, 1573, in Bor, vi. 440.

¶ This Commission is published in Kluit. Hol. Staatsreg., iii. 425–427 Bijalgen.

hundred mounted troopers, under Carlo de Noot, had been assembled, and the Prince now placed himself at their head.* There was, however, a universal cry of remonstrance from the magistracies and burghers of all the towns, and from the troops themselves, at this project.† They would not consent that a life so precious, so indispensable to the existence of Holland, should be needlessly hazarded. It was important to succor Harlem, but the Prince was of more value than many cities. He at last reluctantly consented, therefore, to abandon the command of the expedition to Baron Batenburg,‡ the less willingly from the want of confidence which he could not help feeling in the character of the forces. On the 8th of July, at dusk, the expedition set forth from Sassenheim.§ It numbered nearly five thousand men, who had with them four hundred wagon-loads of provisions and seven field-pieces.‖ Among the volunteers, Oldenbarneveld, afterwards so illustrious in the history of the Republic, marched in the ranks, with his musket on his shoulder.¶ Such was a sample of the spirit which pervaded the population of the province.

Batenburg came to a halt in the woods of Nordwyk, on the south side of the city, where he remained till midnight.** All seemed still in the enemy's camp. After prayers, he gave orders to push forward, hoping to steal through the lines of his sleeping adversaries and accomplish the relief by surprise.†† He was destined to be bitterly disappointed. His plans and his numbers were thoroughly known to the Spaniards, two doves, bearing letters which contained the details of the intended expedition, having been shot and brought into Don Frederic's camp.‡‡

The citizens, it appeared, had broken through the curtain work on the side where Batenburg was expected, in order that a sally might be made in co-operation with the relieving force, as

---

* Hoofd, viii. 311.   † Bor, vi. 439.   Hoofd.
‡ Bor, Hoofd, ubi sup. Meteren, iv. 80.   § Bor, Hoofd.   ‖ Bor, ubi sup.
¶ Hoofd (viii. 311), to whose father Oldenbarneveld related the anecdote.
** Bor, Hoofd, viii. 311.   †† Bor, vi. 439.   Hoofd, viii. 311.
‡‡ Hoofd, viii. 311.   Mendoza, ix. 203.

soon as it should appear.* Signal fires had been agreed upon, by which the besieged were to be made aware of the approach of their friends. The Spanish Commander accordingly ordered a mass of green branches, pitch, and straw, to be lighted opposite to the gap in the city wall. Behind it he stationed five thousand picked troops.† Five thousand more, with a force of cavalry, were placed in the neighbourhood of the downs, with orders to attack the patriot army on the left. Six regiments, under Romero, were ordered to move eastward, and assail their right.‡ The dense mass of smoke concealed the beacon lights displayed by Batenburg from the observation of the townspeople, and hid the five thousand Spaniards from the advancing Hollanders. As Batenburg emerged from the wood, he found himself attacked by a force superior to his own, while a few minutes later he was entirely enveloped by overwhelming numbers. The whole Spanish army was, indeed, under arms, and had been expecting him for two days.§ The unfortunate citizens alone were ignorant of his arrival. The noise of the conflict they supposed to be a false alarm created by the Spaniards, to draw them into their camp ; and they declined a challenge which they were in no condition to accept.‖ Batenburg was soon slain, and his troops utterly routed. The number killed was variously estimated at from six hundred to two and even three thousand.¶ It is, at any rate, certain that the whole force was entirely destroyed or dispersed, and the attempt to relieve the city completely frustrated. The death of Batenburg was the less regretted, because he was accused, probably with great injustice, of having been intoxicated at

---

* Hoofd, viii. 311.   Mendoza, ix. 203.
† Ibid.   Wagenaer, vi. 428.   ‡ Hoofd, viii. 312.   Wagenaer.
§ Hoofd, Wagenaer.   Bor, vi. 439.   ‖ Hoofd, viii. 312.
¶ Bor, vi. 440.   Hoofd, viii. 312.   Meteren, iv. 80.   Wagenaer, vi. 428, 429.
—Compare Mendoza, ix. 204; Bentivoglio, vii. 128; Correspondance de Philippe II., ii. 1254. The Dutch authorities give four thousand five hundred as the number of the whole force under Batenburg; the Spanish put them as high as eight thousand. The number of the slain, according to the Netherland accounts, were five or six hundred, according to those of the victors from one thousand five hundred to three thousand.

the time of action,[*] and therefore incapable of properly conducting the enterprise entrusted to him.

The Spaniards now cut off the nose and ears of a prisoner and sent him into the city to announce the news, while a few heads were also thrown over the walls to confirm the intelligence.[†] When this decisive overthrow became known in Delft, there was even an outbreak of indignation against Orange. According to a statement of Alva, which, however, is to be received with great distrust, some of the populace wished to sack the Prince's house, and offered him personal indignities.[‡] Certainly, if these demonstrations were made, popular anger was never more senseless ; but the tale rests entirely upon a vague assertion of the Duke, and is entirely at variance with every other contemporaneous account of these transactions. It had now become absolutely necessary, however, for the heroic but wretched town to abandon itself to its fate. It was impossible to attempt anything more in its behalf. The lake and its forts were in the hands of the enemy, the best force which could be mustered to make head against the besieging army had been cut to pieces, and the Prince of Orange, with a heavy heart, now sent word that the burghers were to make the best terms they could with the enemy.[§]

The tidings of despair created a terrible commotion in the starving city. There was no hope either in submission or resistance. Massacre or starvation was the only alternative. But if there was no hope within the walls, without there was still a soldier's death. For a moment the garrison and the able-bodied citizens resolved to advance from the gates in a solid column, to cut their way through the enemy's camp, or to perish on the field.[||] It was thought that the helpless and the infirm, who would alone be left in the city, might be treated with indulgence after the fighting men had all been slain. At any rate, by remaining the strong could neither protect nor comfort them. As soon, however, as this resolve was known, there was such

---

[*] Bor, vi. 440.   [†] P. Sterlincx.   Hoofd, viii. 312.
[‡] Correspondance de Philippe II., ii. 1254.
[§] Hoofd, viii. 312, 313.   Wagenaer, vi. 429.
[||] Bor, vi. 440.   Hoofd, 313.   Meteren. iv. 80.   Mendoza, ix. 204.

wailing and outcry of women and children as pierced the
hearts of the soldiers and burghers, and caused them to forego
the project.* They felt that it was cowardly not to die in
their presence. It was then determined to form all the females,
the sick, the aged, and the children, into a square, to surround
them with all the able-bodied men who still remained, and thus
arrayed to fight their way forth from the gates, and to conquer
by the strength of despair, or at least to perish all together.†

These desperate projects, which the besieged were thought
quite capable of executing, were soon known in the Spanish
camp. Don Frederic felt, after what he had witnessed
in the past seven months, that there was nothing which
the Harlemers could not do or dare. He feared lest they
should set fire to their city, and consume their houses,
themselves, and their children, to ashes together ;‡ and he
was unwilling that the fruits of his victory, purchased at such
a vast expense, should be snatched from his hand as he was
about to gather them. A letter was accordingly, by his order,
sent to the magistracy and leading citizens, in the name of
Count Overstein, commander of the German forces in the besieging army.§ This despatch invited a surrender at discretion, but contained the solemn assurance that no punishment
should be inflicted except upon those who, in the judgment
of the citizens themselves, had deserved it, and promised
ample forgiveness if the town should submit without further
delay.‖ At the moment of sending this letter, Don Frederic

---

* Hoofd, Meteren, Mendoza.

† Bor, vi. 440. Hoofd, viii. 313. Meteren, iv. 80. Mendoza, ix. 204.

‡ Hoofd, viii. 313.   § Bor, vi. 440. Hoofd, viii. 313. Wagenaer, 429, 430.

‖ Bor, vi. 440. Hoofd, viii. 313.—Even Mendoza admits that a message
promising mercy, was sent into the city in order to induce the besieged to
abandon their desperate resolution.—"Se embio aviso del campo que todos los
que quisiessen quedar en la villa à merced, se usaria con ellos de misericordia."
—ix. 204. The assurance in Count Overstein's letter, according to the uniform
testimony of Dutch historians, was to the effect stated in the text, "Dat er
alsnoch vergiffenis ten beste was, Zoo zy tot oovergift verstaan wilden; ende
niemand gestraft zoude worden, oft hy hadde 't naa hun eighen oordeel, verdient."
—Hoofd, viii. 313.

was in possession of strict orders from his father not to leave a man alive of the garrison, excepting only the Germans, and to execute besides a large number of the burghers.* These commands he dared not disobey, even if he had felt any inclination to do so. In consequence of the semi-official letter of Overstein, however, the city formally surrendered at discretion on the 12th July.†

The great bell was tolled, and orders were issued that all arms in the possession of the garrison or the inhabitants should be brought to the town-house.‡ The men were then ordered to assemble in the cloister of Zyl, the women in the cathedral.§ On the same day, Don Frederic, accompanied by Count Bossu and a numerous staff, rode into the city. The scene which met his view might have moved a heart of stone. Everywhere was evidence of the misery which had been so bravely endured during that seven months' siege. The smouldering ruins of houses, which had been set on fire by balls, the shattered fortifications, the felled trunks of trees, upturned pavements, broken images and other materials for repairing gaps made by the daily cannonade, strewn around in all directions, the skeletons of unclean animals from which the flesh had been gnawed, the unburied bodies of men and women who had fallen dead in the public thoroughfares—more than all, the gaunt and emaciated forms of those who still survived, the ghosts of their former selves, all might have induced at least a doubt whether the suffering inflicted already were not a sufficient punishment, even for crimes so deep as heresy and schism. But this was far from being the sentiment of Don Frederic. He seemed to read defiance as well as despair in the sunken eyes which glared upon him as he entered the place, and he took no thought of the pledge which he had informally but sacredly given.

---

* Correspondance de Philippe II., ii. 1253.

† Bor, vi. 440.   Hoofd, viii. 313.   Meteren, iv. 80.   Mendoza says the 14th July.—ix. 205.

‡ P. Sterlincx.   Bor, vi. 441.   Hoofd, viii. 314, 315.

§ P. Sterlincx.   Bor.   Hoofd.   Mendoza, ix. 205.

All the officers of the garrison were at once arrested. Some of them had anticipated the sentence of their conqueror by a voluntary death. Captain Bordet, a French officer of distinction, like Brutus, compelled his servant to hold the sword upon which he fell, rather than yield himself alive to the vengeance of the Spaniards.* Traits of generosity were not wanting. Instead of Peter Hasselaer, a young officer who had displayed remarkable bravery throughout the siege, the Spaniards by mistake arrested his cousin Nicholas. The prisoner was suffering himself to be led away to the inevitable scaffold without remonstrance, when Peter Hasselaer pushed his way violently through the ranks of the captors. "If you want Ensign Hasselaer, I am the man. Let this innocent person depart," he cried.† Before the sun set his head had fallen. All the officers were taken to the House of Kleef, where they were immediately executed.‡ Captain Ripperda, who had so heroically rebuked the craven conduct of the magistracy, whose eloquence had inflamed the soldiers and citizens to resistance, and whose skill and courage had sustained the siege so long, was among the first to suffer.§ A natural son of Cardinal Granvelle, who could have easily saved his life by proclaiming a parentage which he loathed,‖ and Lancelot Brederode, an illegitimate scion of that ancient house, were also among these earliest victims.

The next day Alva came over to the camp. He rode about the place, examining the condition of the fortifications from the outside, but returned to Amsterdam without having entered the city.¶ On the following morning the massacre commenced. The plunder had been commuted for two hundred and forty thousand guilders, which the citizens

---

* Bor, vi. 440. Hoofd, Meteren, Mendoza.—According to Pierre Sterlincx, the instrument of death selected was an arquebuss, Bordet's words to his servant being: "Et toy, mon ami, qui m'avez faict plusieurs services faitez moy astheure la dernière, me donnant un coup d'harquebouze"——"het welcke," continues Sterlincx, "den knegt naar lange weygheren volbragt heeft."—Korte Beschryv., etc., etc.

† Hoofd, viii. 316.   ‡ Bor, vi. 441.   § P. Sterlincx. Hoofd, viii. 315.
‖ Hoofd, viii. 315. Wagenaer, vi. 431.   ¶ Hoofd, viii. 315.

bound themselves to pay in four instalments;* but murder was an indispensable accompaniment of victory, and admitted of no compromise.   Moreover, Alva had already expressed the determination to effect a general massacre upon this occasion.† The garrison, during the siege, had been reduced from four thousand to eighteen hundred.‡   Of these the Germans, six hundred in number, were, by Alva's order, dismissed, on a pledge to serve no more against the King.   All the rest of the garrison were immediately butchered, with at least as many citizens.   Drummers went about the city daily, proclaiming that all who harbored persons having, at any former period, been fugitives, were immediately to give them up, on pain of being instantly hanged themselves in their own doors.   Upon these refugees and upon the soldiery fell the brunt of the slaughter ; although, from day to day, reasons were perpetually discovered for putting to death every individual at all distinguished by service, station, wealth, or liberal principles ; for the carnage could not be accomplished at once, but, with all the industry and heartiness employed, was necessarily protracted through several days.   Five executioners, with their attendants, were kept constantly at work ; and when at last they were exhausted with fatigue, or perhaps sickened with horror, three hundred wretches were tied two and two, back to back, and drowned in the Harlem Lake.§

---

* Bor, vi. 441.   Meteren, iv. 80.

† "Comme le Duc d'Albe me dist *encores hier* se convertira en justice car il n'est pas délibéré d'en *laisser eschapper pas ung.*"—Letter of Mondoucet, 14th July, 1573.   Correspondance Charles IX., and Mondoucet, Com. Roy. de l'Hist., iv. 340, sqq.

‡ Hoofd, viii. 316.

§ P. Sterlincx.—Bor, vi. 441.   Hoofd, viii. 315, 316.   Meteren, iv. 81.

Compare Mendoza, ix. 205 ; Bentivoglio, vii. 129; Correspondance de Philippe II., 1257 ; Cabrera, Filipe Segundo, x. 754–759.—Even Bentivoglio is shocked at the barbarities committed after the surrender of the city.   "Più di 2 mille furono giustiziati, e nell' operatione restarono ò stracchi, ò satii, ò inhorriditi per maniera i carnefici stessi——resto in dubbio, se fossero stati più atroci, ò da una parte i falli commessi ò dall' altra i supplicij eseguiti."—Bentivoglio, ubi sup.

Cabrera, on the contrary, expresses great disgust that any one should be moved to compassion for the fate of these heretics.

At last, after twenty-three hundred human creatures[*] had been murdered in cold blood, within a city where so many thousands had previously perished by violent or by lingering deaths ; the blasphemous farce of a pardon was enacted.[†] Fifty-seven of the most prominent burghers of the place were, however, excepted from the act of amnesty, and taken into custody as security for the future good conduct of the other citizens. Of these hostages some were soon executed, some died in prison, and all would have been eventually sacrificed, had not the naval defeat of Bossu soon afterwards enabled the Prince of Orange to rescue the remaining prisoners.[‡] Ten thousand two hundred and fifty-six shots had been discharged against the walls during the siege.[§] Twelve thousand of the besieging army had died of wounds or disease, during the seven months and two days, between the investment and the surrender.[||] In the earlier part of August,[¶] after the executions had been satisfactorily accomplished, Don Frederic made his triumphal entry, and the first chapter in the invasion of Holland was closed. Such was the memorable siege of Harlem, an event in which we are called upon to wonder equally at human capacity to inflict and to endure misery.

The Spaniards celebrated a victory, while in Utrecht they made an effigy of the Prince of Orange, which they carried about in procession, broke upon the wheel, and burned.[**] It was, however, obvious, that if the reduction of Harlem were a triumph, it was one which the conquerors might well ex-

---

[*] This is the number given by Alva. (Correspondance de Philippe II., ii. 1257.) The Dutch historians make the amount of slaughter less than it is estimated by the Spanish writers who, as usual, exaggerate these achievements, which they think commendable. Only Meteren, among the Netherland authorities, puts the number of the executed as high as two thousand, three hundred less than that stated by Alva, while Carnero raises it to three thousand.—Compare Bor, Hoofd, Meteren, Bentivoglio, et al.

[†] Bor, vi. 442, 443. Meteren, iv. 80, 82.   [‡] Bor, vi. 443. Meteren. [§] Mendoza, ix. 203.

[||] According to Hoofd, viii. 316, and Bor, vi. 444. The Spanish writers estimate the number at four or five thousand.—Mendoza, ix. 206. Cabrera x. 759.   [¶] Wagenaer, vi. 433.   [**] Ibid., vi. 433, 434.

change for a defeat. At any rate, it was certain that the Spanish empire was not strong enough to sustain many more such victories. If it had required thirty thousand choice troops, among which were three regiments called by Alva respectively, the "Invincibles," the "Immortals," and the "None-such,"* to conquer the weakest city of Holland in seven months, and with the loss of twelve thousand men ; how many men, how long a time, and how many deaths would it require to reduce the rest of that little province ? For, as the sack of Naarden had produced the contrary effect from the one intended, inflaming rather than subduing the spirit of Dutch resistance, so the long and glorious defence of Harlem, notwithstanding its tragical termination, had only served to strain to the highest pitch the hatred and patriotism of the other cities in the province. Even the treasures of the New World were inadequate to pay for the conquest of that little sand-bank. Within five years, twenty-five millions of florins had been sent from Spain for war expenses in the Netherlands.† Yet, this amount, with the addition of large sums annually derived from confiscations,‡ of five millions, at which the proceeds of the hundredth penny was estimated, and the two millions yearly, for which the tenth and twentieth pence had been compounded, was insufficient to save the treasury from beggary and the unpaid troops from mutiny.

Nevertheless, for the moment the joy created was intense. Philip was lying dangerously ill at the wood of Segovia,§ when the happy tidings of the reduction of Harlem, with its accompanying butchery, arrived. The account of all this misery, minutely detailed to him by Alva, acted like

---

* Meteren, iv. 81.

† From 1569–1572.—Vide Kluit, Hol. Staatsreg., iv. 512, 513, and Van Wyn op. Wagen., d. i bl. 287, and d. vi. 17. In June, 1559, Philip had to pay his army in the Netherlands, 8,689,581 florins of arrearage.

‡ According to Meteren, iv. 86, eight millions annually ; but the statement is a great exaggeration.

§ Correspondance de Philippe II., ii. 1259.

magic. The blood of twenty-three hundred of his fellow-creatures—coldly murdered, by his orders, in a single city—proved for the sanguinary monarch the elixir of life : he drank and was refreshed. "The *principal medicine which has cured his Majesty,*" wrote Secretary Cayas from Madrid to Alva, "is the joy caused to him by the *good news* which you have communicated of *the surrender of Harlem.*"* In the height of his exultation, the King forgot how much dissatisfaction he had recently felt with the progress of events in the Netherlands ; how much treasure had been annually expended with an insufficient result. " Knowing your necessity," continued Cayas, "his Majesty instantly sent for Doctor Velasco, and ordered him to provide you with funds, if he had to descend into the earth to dig for it."† While such was the exultation of the Spaniards, the Prince of Orange was neither dismayed nor despondent. As usual, he trusted to a higher power than man. "I had hoped to send you better news," he wrote, to Count Louis, "nevertheless, since it has otherwise pleased the good God, we must conform ourselves to His divine will. I take the same God to witness that I have done everything according to my means, which was possible, to succor the city."‡ A few days later, writing in the same spirit, he informed his brother that the Zealanders had succeeded in capturing the castle of Rammekens, on the isle of Walcheren. " I hope," he said, "that this will reduce the pride of our enemies, who, after the surrender of Harlem, have thought that they were about to swallow us alive. I assure myself, however, that they will find a very different piece of work from the one which they expect."§

---

* Correspondance de Philippe II., ii. 1259.   † Ibid.
‡ Groen v. Prinst., Archives, etc., iv. 175.
§ Archives de la Maison d'Orange, iv. 181.

CHAPTER IX.

FOR the sake of continuity in the narrative, the siege of Harlem has been related until its conclusion. This great event constituted, moreover, the principal stuff in Nether-

land history, up to the middle of the year 1573. A few loose
threads must be now taken up before we can proceed farther.

Alva had for some time felt himself in a false and uncomfortable position. While he continued to be the object of a
popular hatred as intense as ever glowed, he had gradually lost
his hold upon those who, at the outset of his career, had been
loudest and lowest in their demonstrations of respect. " Believe me," wrote Secretary Albornoz to Secretary Cayas,
" this people abhor our nation worse than they abhor the
Devil. As for the Duke of Alva, they foam at the mouth
when they hear his name."* Viglius, although still maintaining smooth relations with the Governor, had been, in
reality, long since estranged from him. Even Aerschot, for
whom the Duke had long maintained an intimacy half
affectionate, half contemptuous, now began to treat him with
a contumely which it was difficult for so proud a stomach to
digest.†

But the main source of discomfort was doubtless the
presence of Medina Cœli. This was the perpetual thorn in his
side, which no cunning could extract. A successor who would
not and could not succeed him, yet who attended him as his
shadow and his evil genius—a confidential colleague who betrayed his confidence, mocked his projects, derided his authority, and yet complained of ill treatment—a rival who was
neither compeer nor subaltern, and who affected to be his
censor—a functionary of a purely anomalous character, shelter-
ing himself under his abnegation of an authority which he had
not dared to assume, and criticising measures which he was
not competent to grasp ;—such was the Duke of Medina Cœli,
in Alva's estimation.

The bickering between the two Dukes became unceasing and
disgraceful. Of course, each complained to the King, and
each, according to his own account, was a martyr to the other's
tyranny, but the meekness manifested by Alva, in all his relations with the new comer, was wonderful, if we are to believe

---

* " Escupen en oir su nombre."—Correspond. de Philippe II., ii. 1208.
† Correspondance de Philippe II., ii. 1298, 1177.

the accounts furnished by himself and by his confidential secretary.* On the other hand, Medina Cœli wrote to the King, complaining of Alva in most unmitigated strains, and asserting that he *was himself never allowed to see any despatches*, nor to have the slightest information as to the policy of the government.† He reproached the Duke with shrinking from personal participation in military operations, and begged the royal forgiveness if he withdrew from a scene where he felt himself to be superfluous.‡

Accordingly, towards the end of November, he took his departure, without paying his respects. The Governor complained to the King of this unceremonious proceeding, and assured His Majesty that never were courtesy and gentleness so ill requited as his had been by this ingrate and cankered Duke. " He told me," said Alva, " that if I did not stay in the field, he would not remain with me in peaceful cities, and he asked me if I intended to march into Holland with the troops which were to winter there. I answered, that I should go wherever it was necessary, even should I be obliged to swim through all the canals of Holland."§ After giving these details, the Duke added, with great appearance of candor and meekness, that he was certain Medina Cœli had only been influenced by extreme zeal for His Majesty's service, and that, finding so little for him to do in the Netherlands, he had become dissatisfied with his position.||

Immediately after the fall of Harlem, another attempt was made by Alva to win back the allegiance of the other cities by proclamations. It had become obvious to the Governor that so determined a resistance on the part of the first place besieged augured many long campaigns before the whole province could be subdued. A circular was accordingly issued upon the 26th July from Utrecht, and published immediately afterwards in all the cities of the Netherlands. It was a paper of singular character, commingling an affectation of almost

---

* Correspondance de Philippe II., ii. 1174, 1177, 1178.
† Ibid., ii. 1178.   ‡ Ibid.   § Ibid., ii. 1193. || Ibid.

ludicrous clemency, with honest and hearty brutality. There was consequently something very grotesque about the document.   Philip, in the outset, was made to sustain towards his undutiful subjects the characters of the brooding hen and the prodigal's father ; a range of impersonation hardly to be allowed him, even by the most abject flattery.   "Ye are well aware," thus ran the address, "that the King has, over and over again, manifested his willingness to receive his children, in however forlorn a condition the prodigals might return. His Majesty assures you once more that your sins, however black they may have been, shall be forgiven and forgotten in the plenitude of royal kindness, if you repent and return in season to his Majesty's embrace.   Notwithstanding your manifold crimes, his Majesty still seeks, *like a hen calling her chickens, to gather you all under the parental wing*.   The King hereby warns you once more, therefore, to place yourselves in his royal hands, *and not to wait for his rage, cruelty, and fury*, and the approach of his army."

The affectionate character of the address, already fading towards the end of the preamble, soon changes to bitterness. The domestic maternal fowl dilates into the sanguinary dragon as the address proceeds.   "But if," continues the monarch, "ye disregard these offers of mercy, receiving them with closed ears, as heretofore, then we warn you that there is no rigor, nor cruelty, however great, which you are not to expect by laying waste, starvation, and the sword, in such manner that nowhere shall *remain a relic of that which at present exists*, but his Majesty will strip bare and *utterly depopulate the land*, and cause it to be inhabited *again by strangers ;* since otherwise his Majesty could not believe that the *will of God and of his Majesty* had been accomplished."*

It is almost superfluous to add that this circular remained fruitless. The royal wrath, thus blasphemously identifying itself with divine vengeance, inspired no terror, the royal blandishments no affection.

---

* The document is published in Bor, vi. 445, 446.

The next point of attack was the city of Alkmaar, situate quite at the termination of the Peninsula, among the lagunes and redeemed prairies of North Holland. The Prince of Orange had already provided it with a small garrison.* The city had been summoned to surrender by the middle of July, and had returned a bold refusal.† Meantime, the Spaniards had retired from before the walls, while the surrender and chastisement of Harlem occupied them during the next succeeding weeks. The month of August, moreover, was mainly consumed by Alva in quelling a dangerous and protracted mutiny, which broke out among the Spanish soldiers at Harlem,‡ between three and four thousand of them having been quartered upon the ill-fated population of that city.§ Unceasing misery was endured by the inhabitants at the hands of the ferocious Spaniards, flushed with victory, mutinous for long arrears of pay, and greedy for the booty which had been denied. At times, however, the fury of the soldiery was more violently directed against their own commanders than against the enemy. A project was even formed by the malcontent troops to deliver Harlem into the hands of Orange. A party of them, disguised as Baltic merchants, waited upon the Prince at Delft, and were secretly admitted to his bedside before he had risen. They declared to him that they were Spanish soldiers, who had compassion on his cause, were dissatisfied with their own government, and were ready, upon receipt of forty thousand guilders, to deliver the city into his hands. The Prince took the matter into consideration, and promised to accept the offer if he could raise the required sum. This, however, he found himself unable to do within the stipulated time, and thus, for want of so paltry a sum, the offer was of necessity declined.||

Various were the excesses committed by the insubordinate

---

* Bor, vi. 444.   † Ibid., vii. 444, 445.
‡ Ibid. Hoofd, viii. 317.   § Bor, vi. 449.
|| Meteren, iv. 81. Hoofd (viii. 318) also tells the story, but does not vouch for it.

troops in every province in the Netherlands upon the long-suffering inhabitants. "Nothing," wrote Alva, "had given him so much pain during his forty years of service."* He avowed his determination to go to Amsterdam in order to offer himself as a hostage to the soldiery, if by so doing he could quell the mutiny.† He went to Amsterdam accordingly, where by his exertions, ably seconded by those of the Marquis Vitelli, and by the payment of thirty crowns to each soldier—fourteen on account of arrearages and sixteen as his share in the Harlem compensation money—the rebellion was appeased, and obedience restored.‡

There was now leisure for the General to devote his whole energies against the little city of Alkmaar. On that bank and shoal, the extreme verge of habitable earth, the spirit of Holland's Freedom stood at bay. The grey towers of Egmont Castle and of Egmont Abbey rose between the city and the sea, and there the troops sent by the Prince of Orange were quartered during the very brief period in which the citizens wavered as to receiving them. The die was soon cast, however, and the Prince's garrison admitted. The Spaniards advanced, burned the village of Egmont to the ground as soon as the patriots had left it, and on the 21st of August Don Frederic, appearing before the walls, proceeded formally to invest Alkmaar.§ In a few days this had been so thoroughly accomplished that, in Alva's language, "it was im-

---

* Correspondance de Philippe II., ii. 1260.   † Ibid.

‡ Hoofd, viii. 318.   Correspondance de Philippe II., ii. 1264.

§ Nanning van Foreest. Een Kort Verhael van de strenghe Belegheringe ende Aftrek der Spangiaerden van de Stadt Alckmaar.—Delft, 1573.

This is much the most important and detailed account of the siege of Alkmaar. The story is told with vigor and ferocity, by a man who was daily and nightly on the walls during the whole siege, and who wrote his narrative as soon as the Spaniards had been repulsed.

The author, who was a magistrate and a pensionary of the city, observes that his "slumberous and sleepy fellow burghers were converted into experienced soldiers by the Spaniard, who summoned them every moment out of bed to the walls."—p. 41.

Compare Hooft, viii. 317–319.   Wagenaer, v'. 441.

possible for a sparrow to enter or go out of the city."* The odds were somewhat unequal. Sixteen thousand veteran troops constituted the besieging force.† Within the city were a garrison of *eight hundred*‡ soldiers, together with *thirteen hundred* burghers, capable of bearing arms.§ The rest of the population consisted of a very few refugees, besides the women and children. Two thousand one hundred able-bodied men, of whom only about one-third were soldiers, to resist sixteen thousand regulars !

Nor was there any doubt as to the fate which was reserved for them, should they succumb. The Duke was vociferous at the ingratitude with which his *clemency* had hitherto been requited. He complained bitterly of the ill success which had attended his monitory circulars ; reproached himself with incredible vehemence, for his previous mildness, and protested that, after having executed only twenty-three hundred persons at the surrender of Harlem, besides a few additional burghers since, he had met with no correspondent demonstrations of affection. He promised himself, however, an ample compensation for all this ingratitude in the wholesale vengeance which he purposed to wreak upon Alkmaar. Already he gloated in anticipation over the havoc which would soon be let loose within those walls. Such ravings, if invented by the pen of fiction, would seem a puerile caricature ; proceeding, authentically, from his own, they still appear almost too exaggerated for belief. "If I take Alkmaar," he wrote to Philip, "I am resolved not to leave a single creature alive ; the knife shall be put to every throat. Since the example of Harlem has proved of no use, *perhaps an example of cruelty* will bring the other cities to their senses."||

---

* Correspondance de Philippe II., ii. 1264.

† Wagenaer, vi. 441. Hoofd, viii. 321.   ‡ Wagenaer, viii. 441, 442. Hoofd. § Ibid. Hoofd, viii. 321.

|| "Estoy resuelto en no dexar criatura con la vida, sino hazerlos passar todos à cuchillo quizà con al exemplo de la crueldad, vernan las demas villas."—Correspondance de Philippe II., ii. 1264.

He took occasion also to read a lecture to the party of conciliation in Madrid, whose counsels, as he believed, his sovereign was beginning to heed. Nothing, he maintained, could be more senseless than the idea of pardon and clemency. This had been sufficiently proved by recent events. It was easy for people at a distance to talk about gentleness, but those upon the spot knew better. *Gentleness had produced nothing*, so far; violence alone could succeed in future. "Let your Majesty," he said, "be disabused of the impression, that with kindness anything can be done with these people. Already have matters reached such a point that many of those born in the country, who have hitherto advocated clemency, are now undeceived, and acknowledge their mistake. They are of opinion *that not a living soul should be left in Alkmaar, but that every individual should be put to the sword.*"* At the same time he took occasion, even in these ferocious letters, which seem dripping with blood, to commend his own natural benignity of disposition. "Your Majesty may be certain," he said, "that no man on earth desires the path of clemency more than I do, notwithstanding my particular hatred for heretics and traitors."† It was therefore with regret that he saw himself obliged to take the opposite course, and to stifle all his gentler sentiments.

Upon Diedrich Sonoy, Lieutenant-Governor for Orange in the province of North Holland, devolved the immediate responsibility of defending this part of the country.‡ As the storm rolled slowly up from the south, even that experienced officer became uneasy at the unequal conflict impending. He despatched a letter to his chief, giving a gloomy picture of his position.§ All looked instinctively towards the Prince, as to a God in their time of danger; all felt as if upon his

---

* Correspondance de Philippe II., ii. 1266.

† "V. M. sea cierto que nadie en la tierra desea mas el camino de la blandura que yo; aunque es odio particular el que tengo con los hereges y traidores," etc., etc.—Correspondance de Philippe II., ii. 1266.

‡ Hoofd, viii. 321. Bor, vi. 451, 452.

§ Bor (vi. 446, 447) publishes the letter.

genius and fortitude depended the whole welfare of the father-land. It was hoped, too, that some resource had been pro-vided in a secret foreign alliance. "If your princely grace," wrote Sonoy, "have made a contract for assistance with any powerful potentate, it is of the highest importance that it should be known to all the cities, in order to put an end to the emigration, and to console the people in their affliction."*

The answer of the Prince was full of lofty enthusiasm. He reprimanded with gentle but earnest eloquence the despondency and little faith of his lieutenant and other adherents. He had not expected, he said, that they would have so soon for-gotten their manly courage. They seemed to consider the whole fate of the country attached to the city of Harlem. He took God to witness that he had spared no pains, and would willingly have spared no drop of his blood to save that devoted city. "But as, notwithstanding our efforts," he con-tinued, "it has pleased God Almighty to dispose of Harlem according to His divine will, shall we, therefore, deny and deride His holy word? Has the strong arm of the Lord thereby grown weaker? Has his Church therefore come to nought? You ask if I have entered into a firm treaty with any great king or potentate, to which I answer, that before I ever took up the cause of the oppressed Christians in these provinces, I had entered *into a close alliance with the King of kings;* and I am firmly convinced that all who put their trust in Him shall be saved by His almighty hand. The God of armies will raise up armies for us to do battle with our enemies and His own." In conclusion, he stated his preparations for attacking the enemy by sea as well as by land, and encouraged his lieutenant and the citizens of the northern quarter to maintain a bold front before the advancing foe.†

And now, with the dismantled and desolate Harlem before their eyes, a prophetic phantom, perhaps, of their own im-

---

* Bor, ubi sup.

† See this remarkable and eloquent letter, dated Dort, August 9, 1573, in Bor, vi. 447, 448.

minent fate, did the handful of people shut up within Alkmaar prepare for the worst. Their main hope lay in the friendly sea. The vast sluices called the Zyp, through which an inundation of the whole northern province could be very soon effected, were but a few miles distant. By opening these gates, and by piercing a few dykes, the ocean might be made to fight for them. To obtain this result, however, the consent of the inhabitants was requisite, as the destruction of all the standing crops would be inevitable. The city was so closely invested, that it was a matter of life and death to venture forth, and it was difficult, therefore, to find an envoy for this hazardous mission. At last, a carpenter in the city, Peter Van der Mey by name, undertook the adventure,* and was entrusted with letters to Sonoy, to the Prince of Orange, and to the leading personages in several cities of the province. These papers were enclosed in a hollow walking-staff, carefully made fast at the top.†

Affairs soon approached a crisis within the beleaguered city. Daily skirmishes, without decisive result, had taken place outside the walls. At last, on the 18th of September, after a steady cannonade of nearly twelve hours, Don Frederic, at three in the afternoon, ordered an assault.‡ Notwithstanding his seven months' experience at Harlem, he still believed it certain that he should carry Alkmaar by storm. The attack took place at once upon the Frisian gate and upon the red tower on the opposite side. Two choice regiments, recently arrived from Lombardy, led the onset, rending the air with their shouts, and confident of an easy victory. They were sustained by what seemed an overwhelming force of disciplined troops. Yet never, even in the recent history of Harlem, had an attack been received by more dauntless breasts. Every living man was on the walls. The storming parties were assailed with cannon, with musketry, with pistols. Boiling water, pitch and oil, molten lead, and unslaked lime, were

---

* Bor, vi. 452.   † Ibid.
‡ Bor, vi. 453.   Hoofd, viii. 323.   Mendoza, x. 217—219.

poured upon them every moment. Hundreds of tarred and burning hoops were skilfully quoited around the necks of the soldiers, who struggled in vain to extricate themselves from these fiery ruffs, while as fast as any of the invaders planted foot upon the breach, they were confronted face to face with sword and dagger by the burghers, who hurled them headlong into the moat below.*

Thrice was the attack renewed with ever-increasing rage—thrice repulsed with unflinching fortitude. The storm continued four hours long. During all that period, not one of the defenders left his post, till he dropped from it dead or wounded.† The women and children, unscared by the balls flying in every direction, or by the hand-to-hand conflicts on the ramparts, passed steadily to and fro from the arsenals to the fortifications, constantly supplying their fathers, husbands, and brothers with powder and ball.‡ Thus, every human being in the city that could walk had become a soldier. At last darkness fell upon the scene. The trumpet of recal was sounded, and the Spaniards, utterly discomfited, retired from the walls, leaving at least one thousand dead in the trenches,§ while only thirteen burghers and twenty-four of the garrison lost their lives.‖ Thus was Alkmaar preserved for a little longer—thus a large and well-appointed army signally defeated by a handful of men fighting for their firesides and altars. Ensign Solis, who had mounted the breach for an instant, and miraculously escaped with life, after having been hurled from the battlements, reported that he had seen "neither helmet nor harness," as he looked down into the city : only some plain-looking people, generally dressed like fishermen.¶ Yet these plain-looking fishermen had defeated the veterans of Alva.

The citizens felt encouraged by the results of that day's

---

* Nanning van Foreest, p. 34. Bor, vi. 453. Hoofd, viii. 323.
† Bor, Hoofd.—Compare Mendoza, x. 216–219. N. van Foreest.
‡ Nanning van Foreest, 33. Hoofd, viii. 324.
§ Bor, vi. 453. Hoofd, viii. 324. ‖ Hoofd. Nanning van Foreest, 38
¶ Hoofd, vii. 324. N. van Foreest.

work. Moreover, they already possessed such information concerning the condition of affairs in the camp of the enemy as gave them additional confidence. A Spaniard, named Jeronimo, had been taken prisoner and brought into the city.* On receiving a promise of pardon, he had revealed many secrets concerning the position and intentions of the besieging army. It is painful to add that the prisoner, notwithstanding his disclosures and the promise under which they had been made, was treacherously executed.† He begged hard for his life as he was led to the gallows, offering fresh revelations, which, however, after the ample communications already made, were esteemed superfluous. Finding this of no avail, he promised his captors, with perfect simplicity, to go down on his knees and *worship the Devil precisely as they did,*‡ if by so doing he might obtain mercy. It may be supposed that such a proposition was not likely to gain additional favor for him in the eyes of these rigid Calvinists, and the poor wretch was accordingly hanged.

The day following the assault, a fresh cannonade was opened upon the city. Seven hundred shots having been discharged, the attack was ordered. It was in vain : neither threats nor entreaties could induce the Spaniards, hitherto so indomitable, to mount the breach. The place seemed to their imagination protected by more than mortal powers ; otherwise how was it possible that a few half-starved fishermen could already have so triumphantly overthrown the time-honored legions of Spain. It was thought, no doubt, that the Devil, whom they worshipped, would continue to protect his children. Neither the entreaties nor the menaces of Don Frederic were of any avail. Several soldiers allowed themselves to be run through the body by their own officers, rather than advance to the walls ; and the assault was accordingly postponed to an indefinite period.§

---

* Bor, vi. 453.   Hoofd, viii. 322, 323.
† Bor, vi. 453.   Hoofd, viii. 323.   ‡ Bor, Hoofd, ubi sup.
§ Hoofd, viii. 324.—Compare Mendoza, x. 219, 220.

Meantime, as Governor Sonoy had opened many of the dykes, the land in the neighbourhood of the camp was becoming plashy, although as yet the threatened inundation had not taken place. The soldiers were already very uncomfortable and very refractory. The carpenter-envoy had not been idle, having, upon the 26th September, arrived at Sonoy's quarters, bearing letters from the Prince of Orange. These despatches gave distinct directions to Sonoy to flood the country at all risks, rather than allow Alkmaar to fall into the enemy's hands. The dykes and sluices were to be protected by a strong guard, lest the peasants, in order to save their crops, should repair or close them in the night-time. The letters of Orange were copied, and, together with fresh communications from Sonoy, delivered to the carpenter. A note on the margin of the Prince's letter, directed the citizens to kindle four beacon fires in specified places, as soon as it should prove necessary to resort to extreme measures. When that moment should arrive, it was solemnly promised that an inundation should be created which should sweep the whole Spanish army into the sea. The work had, in fact, been commenced. The Zyp and other sluices had already been opened, and a vast body of water, driven by a strong north-west wind, had rushed in from the ocean. It needed only that two great dykes should be pierced to render the deluge and the desolation complete. The harvests were doomed to destruction, and a frightful loss of property rendered inevitable, but, at any rate, the Spaniards, if this last measure were taken, must fly or perish to a man.*

This decisive blow having been thus ordered and promised, the carpenter set forth towards the city. He was, however, not so successful in accomplishing his entrance unmolested, as he had been in effecting his departure. He narrowly escaped with his life in passing through the enemy's lines, and while occupied in saving himself was so unlucky, or, as it proved, so fortunate, as to lose the stick in which his despatches were

---

* Bor, vi. 454.   Hoofd, viii. 325.   Mendoza, x. 219, 220.

enclosed. He made good his entrance into the city, where, by word of mouth, he encouraged his fellow-burghers as to the intentions of the Prince and Sonoy. In the meantime his letters were laid before the general of the besieging army. The resolution taken by Orange, of which Don Frederic was thus unintentionally made aware, to flood the country far and near, rather than fail to protect Alkmaar, made a profound impression upon his mind. It was obvious that he was dealing with a determined leader and with desperate men. His attempt to carry the place by storm had signally failed, and he could not deceive himself as to the temper and disposition of his troops ever since that repulse. When it should become known that they were threatened with submersion in the ocean, in addition to all the other horrors of war, he had reason to believe that they would retire ignominiously from that remote and desolate sand hook, where, by remaining, they could only find a watery grave. These views having been discussed in a council of officers, the result was reached that sufficient had been already accomplished for the glory of Spanish arms. Neither honor nor loyalty, it was thought, required that sixteen thousand soldiers should be sacrificed in a contest, not with man but with the ocean.*

On the 8th of October, accordingly, the siege, which had lasted seven weeks, was raised,† and Don Frederic rejoined his father in Amsterdam. Ready to die in the last ditch,

---

* Bor and Hoofd, ubi sup.—Compare Mendoza, x. 219, 220.

† Bor, Hoofd, Mendoza. Letter of Noircarmes to his brother De Selles, in Corresp. de Philippe II., ii. 1280. Nanning van Foreest. Cort Verhael, etc. The stout pensionary, after recording the events of the siege, before the smoke had fairly rolled away, gives his readers two ballads; effusions of the same spirit which had pervaded the city during its energetic resistance. They are as usual, martial and jocular; a single verse may be translated as a specimen.

> "De stad van Alkmaer behielt de kroon,
>   Zy gaaven de Spangaeds kranssen,
> Pypen en trommeln gingen daer schoon.
>   Men spelde daer vreemde danssen.
> De Spangaerds stonden daar vergaart
> Zy tansten ecee nieuwe Spaansche galjaert.
> Maar zy vergeten te komen in de schanssen,"—etc., etc.

and to overwhelm both themselves and their foes in a common catastrophe, the Hollanders had at last compelled their haughty enemy to fly from a position which he had so insolently assumed.

These public transactions and military operations were not the only important events which affected the fate of Holland and its sister provinces at this juncture. The secret relations which had already been renewed between Louis of Nassau, as plenipotentiary of his brother and the French court, had for some time excited great uneasiness in the mind of Alva. Count Louis was known to be as skilful a negotiator as he was valiant and accomplished as a soldier. His frankness and boldness created confidence. The "brave spirit in the loyal breast" inspired all his dealing ; his experience and quick perception of character prevented his becoming a dupe of even the most adroit politicians, while his truth of purpose made him incapable either of overreaching an ally or of betraying a trust. His career indicated that diplomacy might be sometimes successful, even although founded upon sincerity.

Alva secretly expressed to his sovereign much suspicion of France.[*] He reminded him that Charles IX., during the early part of the preceding year, had given the assurance that he was secretly dealing with Louis of Nassau, *only that he might induce the Count to pass over to Philip's service.*[†] At the same time Charles had been doing all he could to succor Mons, and had written the memorable letter which had fallen into Alva's hands on the capture of Genlis, and which expressed such a fixed determination to inflict a deadly blow upon the King, whom the writer was thus endeavouring to cajole.[‡]   All

---

> With double-quick time the Spaniard proud
>   Against Alkmaar advances,
> The piping and drumming are merry and loud,
>   We play them the best of dances.
> The Spaniards stop—though they look very big—
> They dance a very new Spanish jig,
>   But forget the use of their lances,—etc., etc.

[*] Correspondance de Philippe II., ii. 1211.   [†] Ibid.
[‡] Corresp. de Philippe II., ii. 269, note.

this the Governor recalled to the recollection of his sovereign. In view of this increasing repugnance of the English court, Alva recommended that fair words should be employed ; hinting, however, that it would be by no means necessary for his master to consider himself very strictly bound by any such pledges to Elizabeth, if they should happen to become inconveniently pressing. " A monarch's promises," he delicately suggested, " were not to be considered so sacred as those of humbler mortals.* Not that the King should directly violate his word, but at the same time," continued the Duke, " I have thought all my life, and I have learned it from the Emperor, your Majesty's father, that the negotiations of kings depend upon different principles from those of us private gentlemen who walk the world ; and in this manner I always observed that your Majesty's father, who was so great a gentleman and so powerful a prince, conducted his affairs."† The Governor took occasion, likewise, to express his regrets at the awkward manner in which the Ridolfi scheme had been managed. Had he been consulted at an earlier day, the affair could have been treated much more delicately ; as it was, there could be little doubt but that the discovery of the plot had prejudiced the mind of Elizabeth against Spain. " From that dust," concluded the Duke, " has resulted all this dirt."‡ It could hardly be matter of surprise, either to Philip or his Viceroy, that the discovery by Elizabeth of a plot upon their parts to take her life and place the crown upon the head of her hated rival, should have engendered unamiable feelings in her bosom towards them. For the moment, however, Alva's negotiations were apparently successful.

On the first of May, 1573, the articles of convention between England and Spain, with regard to the Netherland difficulty,

---

* Correspondance de Philippe II., ii. 1211.

† " Que las negociaciones de los reyes pendrian de muy differentes cabos que los negocios de los particulares cavalleros que andamos por el mundo, y desta manera lo vi tratar à su padre de V. M. que era tan gran cavallero y tan principe."

‡ " Porque V. M. sea cierto que de aquellos polvos han salido todos estos lodos."—Ibid.

had been formally published in Brussels.* The Duke, in communicating the termination of these arrangements, quietly recommended his master thenceforth to take the English ministry into his pay. In particular he advised his Majesty to bestow an annual bribe upon Lord Burleigh, "who held the kingdom in his hand ; for it has always been my opinion," he continued, "that it was an excellent practice for princes to give pensions to the ministers of other potentates, and to keep those at home who took bribes from nobody."†

On the other hand, the negotiations of Orange with the English court were not yet successful, and he still found it almost impossible to raise the requisite funds for carrying on the war. Certainly, his private letters showed that neither he nor his brothers were self-seekers in their negotiations. "You know," said he in a letter to his brothers, "that my intention has never been to seek my private advantage. I have only aspired for the liberty of the country, in conscience and in polity, which foreigners have sought to oppress. I have no other articles to propose, save that religion, reformed according to the Word of God, should be permitted, that then the commonwealth should be restored to its ancient liberty, and, to that end, that the Spaniards and other soldiery should be compelled to retire.‡

The restoration of civil and religious liberty, *the establishment of the great principle of toleration* in matters of conscience, constituted the purpose to which his days and nights were devoted, his princely fortune sacrificed, his life-blood risked. At the same time, his enforcement of toleration to both religions excited calumny against him among the bigoted adherents of both. By the Catholics he was accused of having instigated the excesses which he had done everything in his power to repress. The enormities of De la Marck, which had

---

* Correspondance de Philippe II., ii. 333, 334.   Meteren.
† Correspondance de Philippe II., ii. 1221.
‡ Archives de la Maison d'Orange, iv. 50.

inspired the Prince's indignation, were even laid at the door
of him who had risked his life to prevent and to chastise
them. De la Marck had, indeed, more than counterbalanced
his great service in the taking of Brill, by his subsequent
cruelties. At last, Father Cornelius Musius, pastor of
Saint Agatha, at the age of seventy-two, a man highly
esteemed by the Prince of Orange, had been put to torture
and death by this barbarian, under circumstances of great
atrocity. The horrid deed cost the Prince many tears,
aroused the indignation of the estates of Holland, and produced the dismission of the perpetrator from their service. It
was considered expedient, however, in view of his past services,
his powerful connexions, and his troublesome character, that
he should be induced peaceably to leave the country.*

It was long before the Prince and the estates could succeed
in ridding themselves of this encumbrance. He created
several riots in different parts of the province, and boasted
that he had many fine ships of war and three thousand men
devoted to him, by whose assistance he could make the estates
"dance after his pipe." At the beginning of the following
year (1574), he was at last compelled to leave the provinces,
which he never again troubled with his presence. Some years
afterwards, he died of the bite of a mad dog ; an end not in-
appropriate to a man of so rabid a disposition.†

While the Prince was thus steadily striving for a lofty
and generous purpose, he was, of course, represented by his
implacable enemies as a man playing a game which, unfortunately for himself, was a losing one. "That poor prince,"
said Granvelle, "has been ill advised. I doubt now whether
he will ever be able to make his peace, and I think we shall

---

* Hoofd, vii. 281, 282. Bor. vi. 422. Brandt, Hist. der Ref., x. 538–540.
(d. i.) "De tijding van so vervlockt een handel koste den prince klagten en
traenen: deese onmenschelijkheit deed den Staaten wee, en strekte den pleeger
self een trap tot sijne ondergank."—Brandt. Hoofd.

† Meteren. Strada. Hoofd, vii. 289, 290. Bor, vi. 424–431. Wagenaer, vi.
434–436.

rather *try to get rid of him and his brother as if they were Turks.*
The marriage with the daughter of Maurice, *unde mala et quia
ipse talis,* and his brothers have done him much harm. So
have Schwendi and German intimacies. I saw it all very
plainly, but he did not choose to believe me."[*]

Ill-starred, worse counselled William of Orange! Had he
but taken the friendly Cardinal's advice, kept his hand from
German marriages and his feet from conventicles—had he
assisted his sovereign in burning heretics and hunting rebels,
it would not then have become necessary "to treat him like
a Turk." This is unquestionable. It is equally so that there
would have been one great lamp the less in that strait and
difficult pathway which leads to the temple of true glory.

The main reliance of Orange was upon the secret negotiations which his brother Louis was then renewing with the
French government. The Prince had felt an almost insur-
mountable repugnance towards entertaining any relation with
that blood-stained court, since the massacre of Saint Bartholomew. But a new face had recently been put upon that
transaction. Instead of glorying in their crime, the King
and his mother now assumed a tone of compunction, and
averred that the deed had been unpremeditated ; that it had
been the result of a panic or an ecstasy of fear inspired by the
suddenly discovered designs of the Huguenots ; and that, in
the instinct of self-preservation, the King, with his family
and immediate friends, had plunged into a crime which they
now bitterly lamented.[†] The French envoys at the different
courts of Europe were directed to impress this view upon the
minds of the monarchs to whom they were accredited. It was
certainly a very different instruction from that which they had
at first received. Their cue had originally been to claim a full
meed of praise and thanksgiving in behalf of their sovereign
for his meritorious exploit. The salvos of artillery, the illumi-

---

[*] Cardinal Granvelle to Morillon, 18th March, 1573, in Groen van Prinst.,
Archives, iv. 35[*].

[†] M. Groen van Prinsterer, in the second part of vol. iv. of the Archives de la
Maison d'Orange Nassau.—Compare de Thou, l. lv. t. vi. 590, et seq.

nations and rejoicings, the solemn processions and masses by which the auspicious event had been celebrated, were yet fresh in the memory of men. The ambassadors were sufficiently embarrassed by the distinct and determined approbation which they had recently expressed. Although the King, by formal proclamation, had assumed the whole responsibility, as he had notoriously been one of the chief perpetrators of the deed, his agents were now to stultify themselves and their monarch by representing, as a deplorable act of frenzy, the massacre which they had already extolled to the echo as a skilfully executed and entirely commendable achievement.*

To humble the power of Spain, to obtain the hand of Queen Elizabeth for the Duke d'Alençon, to establish an insidious kind of protectorate over the Protestant princes of Germany, to obtain the throne of Poland for the Duke of Anjou, and even to obtain the imperial crown for the house of Valois—all these cherished projects seemed dashed to the ground by the Paris massacre and the abhorrence which it had created. Charles and Catharine were not slow to discover the false position in which they had placed themselves, while the Spanish jocularity at the immense error committed by France was visible enough through the assumed mask of holy horror.

Philip and Alva listened with mischievous joy to the howl of execration which swept through Christendom upon every wind. They rejoiced as heartily in the humiliation of the malefactors as they did in the perpetration of the crime. "Your Majesty," wrote Louis of Nassau, very bluntly, to King Charles, "sees how the Spaniard, your mortal enemy, feasts himself full with the desolation of your affairs ; how he laughs, to split his sides, at your misfortunes. This massacre has enabled him to weaken your Majesty more than he could have done by a war of thirty years."†

---

* See the letters in the second part of vol. iv. Archives de la Maison d'Orange.

† "Que S. M. voit l'Espagnol, son ennemy mortel, faire ses choux gras de la désolation de ses affaires, se rire à gorge ouverte de ses malheurs, et employer tout son industrie et estude à entretenir les troubles en son royaume ; s'asseu-

Before the year had revolved, Charles had become thoroughly convinced of the fatal impression produced by the event. Bitter and almost abject were his whinings at the Catholic King's desertion of his cause. "He knows well," wrote Charles to Saint Goard, "that if he can terminate these troubles and leave me alone in the dance, he will have leisure and means to establish his authority, not only in the Netherlands but elsewhere, and that he will render himself more grand and formidable than he has ever been. This is the return they render for *the good received from me, which is such* as every one knows."*

Gaspar de Schömberg, the adroit and honorable agent of Charles in Germany, had at a very early day warned his royal master of the ill effect of the massacre upon all the schemes which he had been pursuing, and especially upon those which referred to the crowns of the Empire and of Poland. The first project was destined to be soon abandoned. It was reserved neither for Charles nor Philip to divert the succession in Germany from the numerous offspring of Maximilian; yet it is instructive to observe the unprincipled avidity with which the prize was sought by both. Each was willing to effect its purchase by abjuring what were supposed his most cherished principles. Philip of Spain, whose mission was to extirpate heresy throughout his realms, and who, in pursuance of that mission, had already perpetrated more crimes, and waded more deeply in the blood of his subjects, than monarch had often done before; Philip, for whom his apologists have never found any defence, save that he believed it his duty to God rather to depopulate his territories than to permit a single heretic within their limits—now entered into secret negotiations with the princes of the Empire. He pledged himself, if they would confer the crown upon him, that he would with-

___

rant avec bonne raison que c'est le seul moyen de parvenir à ses fins sans coup frapper, veu que desjà, tant les guerres passées que par le dernier massacre et troubles présens, l'Espagnol a plus affoibli S. M. que s'il eust faict la guerre trente ans."—Archives de la Maison d'Orange, iv. 85*.

* Archives de la Maison d'Orange, iv. 33*.

draw the Spaniards from the Netherlands ; that he would
tolerate in those provinces the exercise of the Reformed religion;
that he would recognize their union with the rest of the German Empire, and their consequent claim to the benefits of the
Passau treaty ; that he would restore the Prince of Orange
" and all his accomplices" to their former possessions, dignities, and condition ; and that he would cause to be observed,
throughout every realm incorporated with the Empire, all the
edicts and ordinances which had been constructed to secure
religious freedom in Germany.* In brief, Philip was willing,
in case the crown of Charlemagne should be promised him,
to undo the work of his life, to reinstate the arch-rebel
whom he had hunted and proscribed, and to bow before that
Reformation whose disciples he had so long burned and butchered. So much extent and no more had that religious conviction by which he had for years had the effrontery to excuse
the enormities practised in the Netherlands. God would
never forgive him so long as one heretic remained unburned
in the provinces ; yet give him the Imperial sceptre, and
every heretic, without forswearing his heresy, should be purged
with hyssop and become whiter than snow.

Charles IX., too, although it was not possible for him to
recal to life the countless victims of the Parisian wedding, was
yet ready to explain those murders to the satisfaction of every
unprejudiced mind. This had become strictly necessary.
Although the accession of either his Most Christian or Most
Catholic Majesty to the throne of the Cæsars was a most
improbable event, yet the humbler elective throne actually

---

* " —— le roy d'Espagne à l'estat de l'Empereur veu les honestes offres qu'il
leur propose, a sçavoir si les princes veulent consentir à l'eslire Empereur, il
promet qu'avant que d'entrer en ceste dignité, il ostera les Espagnols du Pays
Bas; qu'il réunira le dict Pays Bas au corps de l'Empire, qu'il remettera le Prince
d'Orange et tous ses complices en leur bien et premier estat, et qu'il fera observer et maintenir dedans tous les pays de son obeissance, qui auroient esté ou
seront incorporez à l'Empire, les mêmes edicts et ordonnances qui ont été establis
et se gardent par le reste d'Allemagne sur le faict de la religion."—G. de Schomberg au Duc d'Anjou, Paris, 10me Feb. 1573, in Groen v. Prinsterer, Archives,
etc., etc., iv. 30*. See also the same volume, p. 2.

vacant was indirectly in the gift of the same powers. It was possible that the crown of Poland might be secured for the Duke of Anjou.* That key unlocks the complicated policy of this and the succeeding year. The Polish election is the clue to the labyrinthian intrigues and royal tergiversations during the period of the interregnum. Sigismund Augustus, last of the Jagellons, had died on the 7th July, 1572.† The prominent candidates to succeed him were the Archduke Ernest, son of the Emperor, and Henry of Anjou. The Prince of Orange was not forgotten. A strong party were in favor of compassing his election, as the most signal triumph which Protestantism could gain, but his ambition had not been excited by the prospect of such a prize. His own work required all the energies of all his life. His influence, however, was powerful, and eagerly sought by the partisans of Anjou. The Lutherans and Moravians in Poland were numerous, the Protestant party there and in Germany holding the whole balance of the election in their hands.

It was difficult for the Prince to overcome his repugnance to the very name of the man whose crime had at once made France desolate, and blighted the fair prospects under which he and his brother had, the year before, entered the Netherlands. Nevertheless, he was willing to listen to the statements by which the King and his ministers endeavoured, not entirely without success, to remove from their reputations, if not from their souls, the guilt of deep design. It was something, that the murderers now affected to expiate their offence in sackcloth and ashes—it was something that, by favoring the pretensions of Anjou, and by listening with indulgence to the repentance of Charles, the siege of Rochelle could be terminated, the Huguenots restored to freedom of conscience, and an alliance with a powerful nation established, by aid of which the Netherlands might once more lift their heads.‡ The French government, deeply hostile to Spain,

---

* Compare de Thou, t. vi. lib. lv.   † Ibid., t. vi. lib. liii. 448.

‡ Letters in Groen v. Prinst, Archives, etc., iv. part ii., passim.—Compare De Thou, vi. l. 53 and 55 et al.

both from passion and policy, was capable of rendering much assistance to the revolted provinces. "I entreat you most humbly, my good master," wrote Schömberg to Charles IX., "to beware of allowing the electors to take into their heads that you are favoring the affairs of the King of Spain in any manner whatsoever. Commit against him no act of open hostility, if you think that imprudent ; but look sharp ! if you do not wish to be thrown clean out of your saddle. I should split with rage if I should see you, in consequence of the wicked calumnies of your enemies, fail to secure the prize."* Orange was induced, therefore, to accept, however distrustfully, the expression of a repentance which was to be accompanied with healing measures. He allowed his brother Louis to resume negotiations with Schömberg, in Germany. He drew up and transmitted to him the outlines of a treaty which he was willing to make with Charles.† The main conditions of this arrangement illustrated the disinterested character of the man. He stipulated that the King of France should immediately make peace with his subjects, declaring expressly that he had been abused by those, who, under pretext of his service, had sought their own profit at the price of ruin to the crown and people. The King should make religion free. The edict to that effect should be confirmed by all the parliaments and estates of the kingdom, and such confirmations should be distributed without reserve or deceit among all the princes of Germany. If his Majesty were not inclined to make war for the liberation of the Netherlands, he was to furnish the Prince of Orange with one hundred thousand crowns at once, and every three months with another hundred thousand. The Prince was to have liberty to raise one thousand cavalry and seven thousand infantry in France. Every city or town in the provinces which should be conquered by his arms, except in Holland or Zealand, should be placed under the sceptre, and in the hands of the King of France. The provinces of Holland and Zealand should also

---

* Groen v. Prinst., Archives, etc., iv. 15*, 16*.　　† Ibid., iv. 116–118.

be placed under his protection, but should be governed by
their own gentlemen and citizens. Perfect religious liberty
and maintenance of the ancient constitutions, privileges,
and charters were to be guaranteed "without any cavilling
whatsoever."* The Prince of Orange, or the estates of Holland or Zealand, were to reimburse his Christian Majesty for
the sums which he was to advance. In this last clause was the
only mention which the Prince made of himself, excepting in
the stipulation that he was to be allowed a levy of troops in
France. His only personal claims were to enlist soldiers to
fight the battles of freedom, and to pay their expense, if
it should not be provided for by the estates. At nearly the
same period, he furnished his secret envoys, Lumbres and
Doctor Taijaert, who were to proceed to Paris, with similar
instructions.†

The indefatigable exertions of Schömberg, and the almost
passionate explanations on the part of the court of France, at
length produced their effect. "You will constantly assure the
princes," wrote the Duke of Anjou to Schömberg, "that the
things written to you concerning that which had happened in
this kingdom are true ; *that the events occurred suddenly*, without having been in any manner premeditated ; that neither
the King nor *myself have ever had any intelligence with the King
of Spain*, against those of the religion, and that all is utter
imposture which is daily said on this subject to the princes."‡

Count Louis required peremptorily, however, that the royal
repentance should bring forth the fruit of salvation for the
remaining victims. Out of the nettles of these dangerous
intrigues his fearless hand plucked the "flower of safety" for
his down-trodden cause. He demanded not words, but deeds,
or at least pledges. He maintained with the agents of Charles
and with the monarch himself the same hardy scepticism which

* "Sans contredit ou cavillation quelconque."—Groen v. Prinst., Archives,
iv. 118.

† Groen v. Prinst., Archives, etc. iv. 109-124, and 43* to 48*.—Compare
De Thou, vi. liv. lv. 593, et seq.

‡ Groen v. Prinst., Archives, etc., iv. 26* and 27*.

was manifested by the Huguenot deputies in their conferences with Catharine de Medicis. "Is the word of a king," said the dowager to the commissioners, who were insisting upon guarantees, "is the word of a king not sufficient?" "No, madam," replied one of them, "*by Saint Bartholomew*, no!"* Count Louis told Schömberg roundly, and repeated it many times, that he must have in a very few days a categorical response, "not to consist in words alone, but in deeds, and that he could not, and would not, risk for ever the honor of his brother, nor the property, blood, and life of those poor people who favored the cause."†

On the 23rd March, 1573, Schömberg had an interview with Count Louis, which lasted seven or eight hours. In that interview the enterprises of the Count, "which," said Schömberg, "are assuredly grand and beautiful," were thoroughly discussed, and a series of conditions, drawn up partly in the hand of one, partly in that of the other negotiator, definitely agreed upon.‡ These conditions were on the basis of a protectorate over Holland and Zealand for the King of France, with sovereignty over the other places to be acquired in the Netherlands. They were in strict accordance with the articles furnished by the Prince of Orange. Liberty of worship for those of both religions, sacred preservation of municipal charters, and stipulation of certain annual subsidies on the part of France, in case his Majesty should not take the field, were the principal features.§

Ten days later, Schömberg wrote to his master that the Count was willing to use all the influence of his family to procure for Anjou the crown of Poland,‖ while Louis, having thus completed his negotiations with the agent, addressed a long and earnest letter to the royal principal.¶ This remarkable despatch was stamped throughout with the impress of the writer's frank and fearless character. "Thus diddest

---

* Vide Raumer. Gesch. Eur., ii. 265.
† Groen v. Prinst., Archives, etc. iv. 38*.   ‡ Ibid., iv. 43*, et seq.
§ Ibid., iv. 43*–48*.   ‖ Ibid., iv. 53*, 54*.
¶ June 1st, 1573.—Groen v. Prinst., Archives, etc., iv. 81*–90*.

thou" has rarely been addressed to anointed monarch in such unequivocal tones. The letter painted the favorable position in which the king had been placed previously to the fatal summer of 1572. The Queen of England was then most amicably disposed towards him, and inclined to a yet closer connexion with his family. The German princes were desirous to elect him King of the Romans, a dignity for which his grandfather had so fruitlessly contended. The Netherlanders, driven to despair by the tyranny of their own sovereign, were eager to throw themselves into his arms. All this had been owing to his edict of religious pacification. How changed the picture now ! Who now did reverence to a King so criminal and so fallen ? " Your Majesty to-day," said Louis, earnestly and plainly, " is near to ruin. The State, crumbling on every side and almost abandoned, is a prey to any one who wishes to seize upon it ; the more so, because your Majesty, having, by the late excess and by the wars previously made, endeavoured to force men's consciences, is now so destitute, not only of nobility and soldiery but of that which constitutes the strongest column of the throne, the love and good wishes of the lieges, that your Majesty resembles an ancient building propped up, day after day, with piles, but which it will be impossible long to prevent from falling to the earth."[*] Certainly, here were wholesome truths told in straightforward style.

The Count proceeded to remind the King of the joy which the " Spaniard, his mortal enemy," had conceived from the desolation of his affairs, being assured that he should, by the troubles in France, be enabled to accomplish his own purposes without striking a blow.[†] This, he observed, had been the secret of the courtesy with which the writer himself had been treated by the Duke of Alva at the surrender of Mons.[‡]

---

[*] " Qu'elle resemble à ung viel bastiment qu'on appuye tous les jours de quelques pillotis, mais enfin on ne le peult empescher de tomber."—Groen v. Prinst., Archives, etc., iv. 85*.   [†] Ibid.

[‡] Letter of Count Louis to Charles IX., June 1st, 1573. Groen v. Prinst., Archives, etc., iv. 86*.

Louis assured the King, in continuation, that if he persevered in these oppressive courses towards his subjects of the new religion, there was no hope for him, and that his two brothers would, to no purpose, take their departure for England and for Poland, leaving him with a difficult and dangerous war upon his hands. So long as he maintained a hostile attitude towards the Protestants in his own kingdom, his fair words would produce no effect elsewhere. " We are beginning to be vexed," said the Count, " with the manner of negotiation practised by France. Men do not proceed roundly to business there, but angle with their dissimulation as with a hook."*

He bluntly reminded the King of the deceit which he had practised towards the Admiral—a sufficient reason why no reliance could in future be placed upon his word. Signal vengeance on those concerned in the attempted assassination of that great man had been promised, in the royal letters to the Prince of Orange, just before St. Bartholomew. " Two days afterwards," said Louis, " *your Majesty took that vengeance, but in rather ill fashion.*"† It was certain that the King was surrounded by men who desired to work his ruin, and who, for their own purposes, would cause him " *to bathe still deeper than he had done before in the blood of his subjects.*‡ This ruin his Majesty could still avert, by making peace in his kingdom, and by ceasing to torment his poor subjects of the religion."§

In conclusion, the Count, with a few simple but eloquent phrases, alluded to the impossibility of chaining men's thoughts. The soul, being immortal, was beyond the reach of kings. Conscience was not to be conquered, nor the religious spirit imprisoned. This had been discovered by the Emperor Charles, who had taken all the cities and great personages of Germany captive, but who had nevertheless

---

* " Descouvrant qu'on ne procède point rondement et ne sert-on que de dissimulation, comme ung hameçon."—Groen v. Prinst., Archives, etc., iv. 87*.

† " A deux jours de là elle la fist assez mal."—Ibid., 88*.

‡ " Mais pour le faire, plus que devant, baigner au sang de ses subjetstz."—Ibid., 89*. § Ibid.

been unable to take religion captive. " That is a sentiment," said Louis, " *deeply rooted in the hearts of men, which is not to be plucked out by force of arms.* Let your Majesty, therefore not be deceived by the flattery of those who, like bad physicians, keep their patients in ignorance of their disease, whence comes their ruin."*

It would be impossible, without insight into these private and most important transactions, to penetrate the heart of the mystery which enwrapped at this period the relations of the great powers with each other. Enough has been seen to silence for ever the plea, often entered in behalf of religious tyranny, that the tyrant acts in obedience to a sincere conviction of duty ; that, in performing his deeds of darkness, he believes himself to be accomplishing the will of Heaven. Here we have seen Philip, offering to restore the Prince of Orange, and to establish freedom of religion in the Netherlands, if by such promises he can lay hold of the Imperial diadem. Here also we have Charles IX. and his mother—their hands reeking with the heretic blood of St. Bartholomew—making formal engagements with heretics to protect heresy everywhere, if by such pledges the crown of the Jagellons and the hand of Elizabeth can be secured.

While Louis was thus busily engaged in Germany, Orange was usually established at Delft. He felt the want of his brother daily,† for the solitude of the Prince, in the midst of such fiery trials, amounted almost to desolation. Not often have circumstances invested an individual with so much responsibility and so little power. He was regarded as the protector and father of the country, but from his own brains and his own resources he was to furnish himself with the means of fulfilling those high functions. He was anxious thoroughly to discharge the duties of a dictatorship without grasping any more of its power than was indispensable to his purpose. But he was alone on that little isthmus, in single combat with the great Spanish monarchy. It was to him that all eyes turned, during the

---

* Groen v. Prinst., Archives, etc., iv. 90*.
† Archives de la Maison d'Orange, iv. 74, 177, 191.

infinite horrors of the Harlem siege, and in the more prosperous leaguer of Alkmaar. What he could do he did. He devised every possible means to succor Harlem, and was only restrained from going personally to its rescue by the tears of the whole population of Holland. By his decision and the spirit which he diffused through the country, the people were lifted to a pitch of heroism by which Alkmaar was saved. Yet, during all this harassing period, he had no one to lean upon but himself. " Our affairs are in pretty good condition in Holland and Zealand," he wrote, " if I only had some aid. 'Tis impossible for me to support alone so many labors, and the weight of such great affairs as come upon me hourly— financial, military, political. I have no one to help me, not a single man, wherefore I leave you to suppose in what trouble I find myself."*

For it was not alone the battles and sieges which furnished him with occupation and filled him with anxiety. Alone, he directed in secret the politics of the country, and, powerless and outlawed though he seemed, was in daily correspondence not only with the estates of Holland and Zealand, whose deliberations he guided, but with the principal governments of Europe. The estates of the Netherlands, moreover, had been formally assembled by Alva in September, at Brussels, to devise ways and means for continuing the struggle.† It seemed to the Prince a good opportunity to make an appeal to the patriotism of the whole country. He furnished the province of Holland, accordingly, with the outlines of an address which was forthwith despatched in their own and his name, to the general assembly of the Netherlands.‡ The document was a nervous and rapid review of the course of late events in the provinces, with a cogent statement of the reasons which should influence them all to unite in the common cause against the common enemy. It referred to the old affection and true-heartedness with which they had formerly regarded each other, and to the certainty that the

---

* Archives de la Maison d'Orange, iv. 191.   † Bor, vi. 459.
‡ See the Address in Bor, vi. 459–464.

inquisition would be for ever established in the land, upon the ruins of all their ancient institutions, unless they now united to overthrow it for ever. It demanded of the people, thus assembled through their representatives, how they could endure the tyranny, murders, and extortions of the Duke of Alva. The princes of Flanders, Burgundy, Brabant, or Holland, had never made war or peace, coined money, or exacted a stiver from the people without the consent of the estates. How could the nation now consent to the daily impositions which were practised? Had Amsterdam and Middelburg remained true; had those important cities not allowed themselves to be seduced from the cause of freedom, the northern provinces would have been impregnable. "'Tis only by the Netherlands that the Netherlands are crushed," said the appeal. " Whence has the Duke of Alva the power of which he boasts, but from yourselves—from Netherland cities? Whence his ships, supplies, money, weapons, soldiers? From the Netherland people. Why has poor Netherland thus become degenerate and bastard? Whither has fled the noble spirit of our brave forefathers, that never brooked the tyranny of foreign nations, nor suffered a stranger even to hold office within our borders? If the little province of Holland can thus hold at bay the power of Spain, what could not all the Netherlands—Brabant, Flanders, Friesland, and the rest united —accomplish?* In conclusion, the estates-general were earnestly adjured to come forward like brothers in blood, and join hands with Holland, that together they might rescue the fatherland and restore its ancient prosperity and bloom.†

At almost the same time the Prince drew up and put in circulation one of the most vigorous and impassioned productions which ever came from his pen. It was entitled, an " Epistle, in form of supplication, to his royal Majesty of Spain, from the Prince of Orange and the estates of Holland and Zealand."‡ The document produced a profound im-

---

* Address, etc., Bor, vi. 461.   † Ibid., 464.
‡ " Sendbrief in forme van supplicatie aen Coningklijke Majesteit van Spangien, van wegen des Prinzen van Orangien en der Staten van Holland en Zealand." etc., etc., in Bor, vi. 464–472.

pression throughout Christendom. It was a loyal appeal to the monarch's loyalty—a demand that the land-privileges should be restored, and the Duke of Alva removed. It contained a startling picture of his atrocities and the nation's misery, and, with a few energetic strokes, demolished the pretence that these sorrows had been caused by the people's guilt. In this connexion the Prince alluded to those acts of condemnation which the Governor-General had promulgated under the name of pardons, and treated with scorn the hypothesis that any crimes had been committed for Alva to forgive. "We take God and your Majesty to witness," said the epistle, "that if we have done such misdeeds as are charged in the pardon, we neither desire nor deserve the pardon. Like the most abject creatures which crawl the earth, we will be content to atone for our misdeeds with our lives. We will not murmur, O merciful King, if we be seized one after another, and torn limb from limb, if it can be proved that we have committed the crimes of which we have been accused."*

After having thus set forth the tyranny of the government and the innocence of the people, the Prince, in his own name and that of the estates, announced the determination at which they had arrived. "The tyrant," he continued, "would rather stain every river and brook with our blood, and hang our bodies upon every tree in the country, than not feed to the full his vengeance, and steep himself to the lips in our misery. Therefore we have taken up arms against the Duke of Alva and his adherents, to free ourselves, our wives and children, from his bloodthirsty hands. If he prove too strong for us, we will rather die an honorable death and leave a praiseworthy fame, than bend our necks, and reduce our dear fatherland to such slavery. Herein are all our cities pledged to each other to stand every siege, to dare the utmost, to endure every possible misery, yea, rather to set fire to all our homes, and be consumed with them into ashes together, than ever submit to the decrees of this cruel tyrant."†

---

* Sendbrief, etc., Bor, vi., 469.   † Ibid., 471.

These were brave words, and destined to be bravely fulfilled, as the life and death of the writer and the records of his country proved, from generation unto generation. If we seek for the mainspring of the energy which thus sustained the Prince in the unequal conflict to which he had devoted his life, we shall find it in the one pervading principle of his nature—confidence in God. He was the champion of the political rights of his country, but before all he was the defender of its religion. Liberty of conscience for his people was his first object. To establish Luther's axiom, that thoughts are toll-free, was his determination. The Peace of Passau, and far more than the Peace of Passau, was the goal for which he was striving. Freedom of worship for all denominations, toleration for all forms of faith, this was the great good in his philosophy. For himself, he had now become a member of the Calvinist, or Reformed Church, having delayed for a time his public adhesion to this communion, in order not to give offence to the Lutherans and to the Emperor. He was never a dogmatist, however, and he sought in Christianity for that which unites rather than for that which separates Christians. In the course of October he publicly joined the church at Dort.*

The happy termination of the siege of Alkmaar was followed, three days afterwards, by another signal success on the part of the patriots. Count Bossu, who had constructed or collected a considerable fleet at Amsterdam, had, early in October, sailed into the Zuyder Zee, notwithstanding the sunken wrecks and other obstructions by which the patriots had endeavored to render the passage of the Y impracticable.† The patriots of North Holland had, however, not been idle, and a fleet of five-and-twenty vessels, under Admiral Dirkzoon, was soon cruising in the same waters. A few skirmishes took place, but Bossu's ships, which were larger, and provided with heavier cannon, were apparently not inclined for the close quarters which the patriots sought.‡ The Spanish Admiral,

---

* Archives de la Maison d'Orange, iv. 226.
† Bor, vi. 455.   ‡ Ibid., 455, 456.   Hoofd, viii. 326, 327.

Hollander as he was, knew the mettle of his countrymen in a close encounter at sea, and preferred to trust to the calibre of his cannon. On the 11th October, however, the whole patriot fleet, favored by a strong easterly breeze, bore down upon the Spanish armada, which, numbering now thirty sail of all denominations, was lying off and on in the neighbourhood of Horn and Enkhuyzen. After a short and general engagement, nearly all the Spanish fleet retired with precipitation, closely pursued by most of the patriot Dutch vessels. Five of the King's ships were eventually taken, the rest effected their escape. Only the Admiral remained, who scorned to yield, although his forces had thus basely deserted him.[*] His ship, the "Inquisition,"[†] for such was her insolent appellation, was far the largest and best manned of both the fleets. Most of the enemy had gone in pursuit of the fugitives, but four vessels of inferior size had attacked the "Inquisition" at the commencement of the action. Of these, one had soon been silenced, while the other three had grappled themselves inextricably to her sides and prow. The four drifted together, before wind and tide, a severe and savage action going on incessantly, during which the navigation of the ships was entirely abandoned. No scientific gunnery, no military or naval tactics were displayed or required in such a conflict. It was a life-and-death combat, such as always occurred when Spaniard and Netherlander met, whether on land or water. Bossu and his men, armed in bullet-proof coats of mail, stood with shield and sword on the deck of the "Inquisition," ready to repel all attempts to board. The Hollander, as usual, attacked with pitch hoops, boiling oil, and molten lead. Repeatedly they effected their entrance to the Admiral's ship, and as often they were repulsed and slain in heaps, or hurled into the sea. The battle began at three in the afternoon, and continued without intermission through the

---

* Bor, vi. 456. Hoofd, viii. 326, 327. Letters of Alva to Philip, and of Bossu to Alva.—Correspondance de Philippe II., ii. 1274, and pp. 420, 421, notes.   † Bor, vi. 456. Hoofd, viii. 326.

whole night. The vessels, drifting together, struck on the shoal called the Nek, near Wydeness. In the heat of the action the occurrence was hardly heeded. In the morning twilight, John Haring, of Horn, the hero who had kept one thousand soldiers at bay upon the Diemer dyke, clambered on board the "Inquisition" and hauled her colors down. The gallant but premature achievement cost him his life. He was shot through the body and died on the deck of the ship, which was not quite ready to strike her flag. In the course of the forenoon, however, it became obvious to Bossu that further resistance was idle. The ships were aground near a hostile coast, his own fleet was hopelessly dispersed, three quarters of his crew were dead or disabled, while the vessels with which he was engaged were constantly recruited by boats from the shore, which brought fresh men and ammunition, and removed their killed and wounded. At eleven o'clock, Admiral Bossu surrendered, and with three hundred prisoners was carried into Holland. Bossu was himself imprisoned at Horn, in which city he was received, on his arrival, with great demonstrations of popular hatred. The massacre of Rotterdam, due to his cruelty and treachery, had not yet been forgotten or forgiven.[*]

This victory, following so hard upon the triumph at Alkmaar, was as gratifying to the patriots as it was galling to Alva. As his administration drew to a close, it was marked by disaster and disgrace on land and sea. The brilliant exploits by which he had struck terror into the heart of the Netherlanders, at Jemmingen and in Brabant, had been effaced by the valor of a handful of Hollanders, without discipline or experience. To the patriots, the opportune capture of so considerable a personage as the Admiral and Governor of the northern province was of great advantage. Such of the hostages from Harlem as had not yet been executed, now escaped with their lives. Moreover, Saint Aldegonde, the eloquent patriot and confidential friend of Orange, who was

---

[*] Bor, Hoofd. Letters of Alva and of Bossu, ubi sup. Mendoza, x. 214.

taken prisoner a few weeks later, in an action at Maeslandsluis,[*] was preserved from inevitable destruction by the same cause. The Prince hastened to assure the Duke of Alva that the same measure would be dealt to Bossu as should be meted to Saint Aldegonde.[†] It was, therefore, impossible for the Governor-General to execute his prisoner, and he was obliged to submit to the vexation of seeing a leading rebel and heretic in his power, whom he dared not strike. Both the distinguished prisoners eventually regained their liberty.

The Duke was, doubtless, lower sunk in the estimation of all classes than he had ever been before, during his long and generally successful life. The reverses sustained by his army, the belief that his master had grown cold towards him, the certainty that his career in the Netherlands was closing without a satisfactory result, the natural weariness produced upon men's minds by the contemplation of so monotonous and unmitigated a tyranny during so many years, all contributed to diminish his reputation. He felt himself odious alike to princes and to plebeians. With his cabinet councillors he had long been upon unsatisfactory terms. President Tisnacq had died early in the summer, and Viglius, much against his will, had been induced, provisionally, to supply his place.[‡] But there was now hardly a pretence of friendship between the learned Frisian and the Governor. Each cordially detested the other. Alva was weary of Flemish and Frisian advisers, however subservient, and was anxious to fill the whole council with Spaniards of the Vargas stamp. He had forced Viglius once more into office, only that, by a little delay, he might expel him and every Netherlander at the same moment. "Till this ancient set of dogmatizers be removed," he wrote to Philip, "with Viglius, their chief, who teaches them all their lessons, nothing will go right. 'Tis of no use adding one or

---

* Hoofd, viii. 331.   Correspondance de Philippe II., ii. 1283.   Meteren, iv. 85. Bor, vi. 472.

† Hoofd, viii. 331.

‡ Correspondance de Philippe II., ii. 1234, p. 359, note.

two Spaniards to fill vacancies ; that is only pouring a flask of good wine into a hogshead of vinegar ; it changes to vinegar likewise.* Your Majesty will soon be able to reorganize the council at a blow ; so that Italians or Spaniards, as you choose, may entirely govern the country."†

Such being his private sentiments with regard to his confidential advisers, it may be supposed that his intercourse with his council during the year was not like to be amicable. Moreover, he had kept himself, for the most part, at a distance from the seat of government. During the military operations in Holland, his head-quarters had been at Amsterdam. Here, as the year drew to its close, he had become as unpopular as in Brussels. The time-serving and unpatriotic burghers, who, at the beginning of the spring, set up his bust in their houses, and would give large sums for his picture in little, now broke his images and tore his portraits from their walls, for it was evident that the power of his name was gone, both with prince and people. Yet, certainly, those fierce demonstrations which had formerly surrounded his person with such an atmosphere of terror had not slackened or become less frequent than heretofore. He continued to prove that he could be barbarous, both on a grand and a minute scale. Even as in preceding years, he could ordain wholesale massacres with a breath, and superintend in person the executions of individuals. This was illustrated, among other instances, by the cruel fate of Uitenhoove.‡ That unfortunate nobleman, who had been taken prisoner in the course of the summer, was accused of having been engaged in the capture of Brill, and was, therefore, condemned by the Duke to be roasted to death before a slow fire. He was accordingly fastened by a chain, a few feet in length, to a stake, around which the fagots

---

* Correspondance de Philippe II., 1234.—"Yendo los poniendo poco à poco, los que estàn gastan á los que entran, que es como hechar un jarro de buen vino en cuba de vinagre, que lo convierte luego en vinagre."

† Correspondance de Philippe II., ii. 1234.

‡ Brandt, Hist. der Ref. in de Nederl., d. i. b. x. 546. Hoofd, viii. 433.

were lighted. Here he was kept in slow torture for a long time, insulted by the gibes of the laughing Spaniards who surrounded him—until the executioner and his assistants, more humane than their superior, despatched the victim with their spears—a mitigation of punishment which was ill received by Alva.[*] The Governor had, however, no reason to remain longer in Amsterdam. Harlem had fallen ; Alkmaar was relieved ; and Leyden—destined in its second siege to furnish so signal a chapter to the history of the war—was beleaguered,[†] it was true, but, because known to be imperfectly supplied, was to be reduced by blockade rather than by active operations. Don Francis Valdez was accordingly left in command of the siege,[‡] which, however, after no memorable occurrences, was raised, as will soon be related.

The Duke had contracted in Amsterdam an enormous amount of debt, both public and private. He accordingly, early in November, caused a proclamation to be made throughout the city by sound of trumpet, that all persons having demands upon him were to present their claims, in person, upon a specified day.[§] During the night preceding the day so appointed, the Duke and his train very noiselessly took their departure, without notice or beat of drum.[||] By this masterly generalship his unhappy creditors were foiled upon the very eve of their anticipated triumph ; the heavy accounts which had been contracted on the faith of the King and the Governor, remained for the most part unpaid, and many opulent and respectable families were reduced to

---

* Brandt, Hoofd, ubi sup.   † Bor, vi. 472.
‡ Ibid. Hoofd, viii. 330.   § Hoofd, viii. 329, 330.

|| Ibid.—Compare Correspondance Charles IX. and Mondoucet; Com. Roy. de l'Hist., iv. 340, sqq.—" Et craignant," says the envoy, "toutes sortes de personnes à qu'il est deu argent que se tenir ainsi reserré ne soit ung commencement pour peu à peu se partir en ung coup sans dire adieu, manquant son credit en Anvers et ailleurs comme ilz voient qu'il faict. Ce que je ne puis croyre qu'il veuille faire, et queavec la disgrace des affaires publicques qu'il laisse en mauvais estat, il veuille ainsi engager son particulier. Nous verrons," etc., etc.

beggary.* Such was the consequence of the unlimited confidence which they had reposed in the honor of their tyrant.

On the 17th of November, Don Luis de Requesens y Cuñiga, Grand Commander of Saint Jago, the appointed successor of Alva, arrived in Brussels, where he was received with great rejoicings. The Duke, on the same day, wrote to the King, "kissing his feet" for thus relieving him of his functions. There was, of course, a profuse interchange of courtesy between the departing and the newly-arrived Governors. Alva was willing to remain a little while, to assist his successor with his advice, but preferred that the Grand Commander should immediately assume the reins of office. To this Requesens, after much respectful reluctance, at length consented. On the 29th of November he accordingly took the oaths, at Brussels, as Lieutenant-Governor and Captain-General, in presence of the Duke of Aerschot, Baron Berlaymont, the President of the Council, and other functionaries.†

On the 18th of December the Duke of Alva departed from the provinces for ever.‡ With his further career this history has no concern, and it is not desirable to enlarge upon the personal biography of one whose name certainly never excites pleasing emotions. He had kept his bed for the greater part of the time during the last few weeks of his government—partly on account of his gout, partly to avoid being seen in his humiliation, but mainly, it was said, to escape the pressing demands of his creditors.§ He expressed a fear of travelling homeward through France, on the ground that he might very probably receive a shot out of a window as he went by. He complained pathetically that, after all his

---

* Hoofd, viii. 329, 330.

† Bor, vi. 474. Hoofd, viii. 331. Corresp. de Philippe II., ii. 1283, 1284.

‡ Correspondance de Philippe II., ii. 1291.

§ "—— il a toujours gardé le lict, soit qu'il a les gouttes, ou bien qu'il ne se veuille monstrer au monde pr mauvais succes qu'il a eus——il laissa le lyct sans encores passer outre, plus a ce que je veois de crainte des importunitez et demandemens d'argent dont il est fort pressé."—Corresp. Charles IX. and Mondoucet. Com. Roy. de l'Hist., iv. 340, sqq.

labors, he had not "gained the approbation of the King," while he had incurred "the malevolence and universal hatred of every individual in the country." Mondoucet, to whom he made the observation, was of the same opinion, and informed his master that the Duke "had engendered such an extraordinary hatred in the hearts of all persons in the land, that they would have fireworks in honor of his departure if they dared."*

On his journey from the Netherlands, he is said to have boasted that he had caused eighteen thousand six hundred inhabitants of the provinces to be executed during the period of his government.† The number of those who had perished by battle, siege, starvation, and massacre, defied computation. The Duke was well received by his royal master, and remained in favor until a new adventure of Don Frederic brought father and son into disgrace. Having deceived and abandoned a maid of honor, he suddenly espoused his cousin, in order to avoid that reparation by marriage which was demanded for his offence.‡ In consequence, both the Duke and Don Frederic were imprisoned and banished, nor was Alva released till a general of experience was required for the conquest of Portugal.§ Thither, as it were with fetters on his legs, he went. After having accomplished the military enterprise entrusted to him, he fell into a lingering fever, at the termination of which he was so much reduced that he was only kept alive by milk, which he drank from a woman's breast.‖ Such was the gentle second childhood of the man who had almost literally been drinking blood for seventy years. He died on the 12th December, 1582.¶

---

* Corresp. de Charles IX. et Mondoucet. Com. Roy. de l'Hist., iv. 340, sqq.—The Duke used nearly the language which the poet, at a little later epoch, was placing in the mouth of another tyrant.

"There is no creature loves me,
And, if I die, no soul will pity me."—*King Richard III.*

† Bor, vi. 474.   Hoofd, viii. 332.   Reidani, l. i. 10.   Apologie d'Orange, 88.
‡ Vie du Duc d'Albe, ii.   Hoofd, 332,   § Vie du Duc d'Albe.   Hoofd, ubi sup.
‖ Von Raumer, Gesch. Europas. iii. 170.   ¶ Vie du Duc d'Albe. Hoofd, ubi sup.

The preceding pages have been written in vain, if an elaborate estimate be now required of his character. His picture
has been painted, as far as possible, by his own hand. His
deeds, which are not disputed, and his written words, illustrate
his nature more fully than could be done by the most eloquent
pen. No attempt has been made to exaggerate his crimes,
or to extenuate his superior qualities. Virtues he had none,
unless military excellence be deemed, as by the Romans, a
virtue. In war, both as a science and a practical art, he excelled all the generals who were opposed to him in the Netherlands, and he was inferior to no commander in the world
during the long and belligerent period to which his life belonged. Louis of Nassau possessed high reputation throughout
Europe as a skilful and daring General. With raw volunteers
he had overthrown an army of Spanish regulars, led by a
Netherland chieftain of fame and experience ; but when Alva
took the field in person the scene was totally changed. The
Duke dealt him such a blow at Jemmingen as would have
disheartened for ever a less indomitable champion. Never
had a defeat been more absolute. The patriot army was
dashed out of existence, almost to a man, and its leader, naked
and beggared, though not disheartened, sent back into Germany to construct his force and his schemes anew.

Having thus flashed before the eyes of the country the full
terrors of his name, and vindicated the ancient military
renown of his nation, the Duke was at liberty to employ the
consummate tactics, in which he could have given instruction
to all the world, against his most formidable antagonist. The
country, paralyzed with fear, looked anxiously but supinely
upon the scientific combat between the two great champions
of Despotism and Protestantism which succeeded. It was
soon evident that the conflict could terminate in but one way.
The Prince had considerable military abilities, and enthusiastic
courage ; he lost none of his well-deserved reputation by the
unfortunate issue of his campaign ; he measured himself in
arms with the great commander of the age, and defied
him, day after day, in vain, to mortal combat ; but it was

equally certain that the Duke's quiet game was played in the most masterly manner. His positions and his encampments were taken with faultless judgment, his skirmishes wisely and coldly kept within the prescribed control, while the inevitable dissolution of the opposing force took place exactly as he had foreseen, and within the limits which he had predicted. Nor in the disastrous commencement of the year 1572 did the Duke less signally manifest his military genius. Assailed as he was at every point, with the soil suddenly upheaving all around him, as by an earthquake, he did not lose his firmness nor his perspicacity. Certainly, if he had not been so soon assisted by that other earthquake, which on Saint Bartholomew's Day caused all Christendom to tremble, and shattered the recent structure of Protestant Freedom in the Netherlands, it might have been worse for his reputation. With Mons safe, the Flemish frontier guarded, France faithful, and thirty thousand men under the Prince of Orange in Brabant, the heroic brothers might well believe that the Duke was "at their mercy." The treason of Charles IX. " smote them as with a club," as the Prince exclaimed in the bitterness of his spirit. Under the circumstances, his second campaign was a predestined failure, and Alva easily vanquished him by a renewed application of those dilatory arts which he so well understood.

The Duke's military fame was unquestionable when he came to the provinces, and both in stricken fields and in long campaigns, he showed how thoroughly it had been deserved ; yet he left the Netherlands a baffled man. The Prince might be many times defeated, but he was not to be conquered. As Alva penetrated into the heart of the ancient Batavian land he found himself overmatched as he had never been before, even by the most potent generals of his day. More audacious, more inventive, more desperate than all the commanders of that or any other age, the spirit of national freedom, now taught the oppressor that it was invincible, except by annihilation. The same lesson had been read in the same thickets by the Nervii to Julius Cæsar, by the Batavians to the legions of Vespasian ; and now a loftier and a purer flame than that which inspired the national struggles against Rome glowed within the breasts of the descendants of the same people, and inspired them with the strength which comes from religious enthusiasm.   More experienced, more subtle, more politic than Hermann ; more devoted, more patient, more magnanimous than Civilis, and equal to either in valor and determination, William of Orange was a worthy embodiment of the Christian, national resistance of the German race to a foreign tyranny.   Alva had entered the Netherlands to deal with them as with conquered provinces.   He found that the conquest was still to be made, and he left the land without having accomplished it.   Through the sea of blood, the Hollanders felt that they were passing to the promised land.   More royal soldiers fell during the seven months' siege of Harlem than the rebels had lost in the defeat of Jemmingen, and in the famous campaign of Brabant.   At Alkmaar the rolling waves of insolent conquest were stayed, and the tide then ebbed for ever.

The accomplished soldier struggled hopelessly with the wild and passionate hatred which his tyranny had provoked.   Neither his legions nor his consummate strategy availed him against an entirely desperate people.   As a military commander, therefore, he gained, upon the whole, no additional laurels during his long administration of the Netherlands.   Of all the other attributes to be expected in a man appointed to deal with a free country, in a state of incipient rebellion, he manifested a signal deficiency.   As a financier, he exhibited a wonderful ignorance of the first principles of political economy.   No man before, ever gravely proposed to establish confiscation as a permanent source of revenue to the state ; yet the annual product from the escheated property of slaughtered heretics was regularly relied upon, during his administration, to replenish the King's treasury, and to support the war of extermination against the King's subjects.   Nor did statesman ever before expect a vast income from the commerce of a nation devoted to almost universal massacre.   During the daily decimation of the people's lives, he thought a daily decimation of their industry possible. His persecutions swept the land of those industrious classes which had made it the rich and prosperous commonwealth it had been so lately ; while, at the same time, he found a " Peruvian mine," as he pretended, in the imposition of a tenth penny upon every one of its commercial transactions. He thought that a people, crippled as this had been by the operations of the Blood Council, could pay ten per cent., not annually but daily ; not upon its income, but upon its capital ; not once only, but every time the value constituting the capital changed hands. He had boasted that he should require no funds from Spain, but that, on the contrary, he should make annual remittances to the royal treasury at home, from the proceeds of his imposts and confiscations ; yet, notwithstanding these resources, and notwithstanding twenty-five millions of gold in five years, sent by Philip from Madrid, the exchequer of the provinces was barren and bankrupt when his successor arrived. Requesens found neither a penny in the public treasury nor the means of raising one.

As an administrator of the civil and judicial affairs of the country, Alva at once reduced its institutions to a frightful simplicity. In the place of the ancient laws of which the Netherlanders were so proud, he substituted the Blood Council. This tribunal was even more arbitrary than the Inquisition. Never was a simpler apparatus for tyranny devised, than this great labor-saving machine. Never was so great a quantity of murder and robbery achieved with such despatch and regularity. Sentences, executions, and confiscations, to an incredible extent, were turned out daily with appalling precision. For this invention, Alva is alone responsible. The tribunal and its councillors were the work and the creatures of his hand, and faithfully did they accomplish the dark purpose of their existence. Nor can it be urged, in extenuation of the Governor's crimes, that he was but the blind and fanatically loyal slave of his sovereign. A noble nature could not have contaminated itself with such slaughter-house work, but might have sought to mitigate the royal policy, without forswearing allegiance. A nature less rigid than iron, would at least have manifested compunction, as it found itself converted into a fleshless instrument of massacre. More decided than his master, however, he seemed, by his promptness, to rebuke the dilatory genius of Philip. The King seemed, at times, to loiter over his work, teasing and tantalising his appetite for vengeance, before it should be gratified. Alva, rapid and brutal, scorned such epicureanism. He strode with gigantic steps over haughty statutes and popular constitutions ; crushing alike the magnates who claimed a bench of monarchs for their jury, and the ignoble artisans who could appeal only to the laws of their land. From the pompous and theatrical scaffolds of Egmont and Horn, to the nineteen halters prepared by Master Karl, to hang up the chief bakers and brewers of Brussels on their own thresholds—from the beheading of the twenty nobles on the Horse-market, in the opening of the Governor's career, to the roasting alive of Uitenhoove at its close—from the block on which fell the honored head of Antony Straalen, to the obscure chair in which the ancient gentlewoman of Amsterdam suffered death for an act of vicarious mercy—from one year's end to another's—from the most signal to the most squalid scenes of sacrifice, the eye and hand of the great master directed, without weariness, the task imposed by the sovereign.

No doubt the work of almost indiscriminate massacre had been duly mapped out. Not often in history has a governor arrived to administer the affairs of a province, where the whole population, three millions strong, had been formally sentenced to death. As time wore on, however, he even surpassed the bloody instructions which he had received. He waved aside the recommendations of the Blood Council to mercy ; he dissuaded the monarch from attempting the path of clemency, which, for secret reasons, Philip was inclined at one period to attempt. The Governor had, as he assured the King, been using gentleness in vain, and he was now determined to try what a little wholesome severity could effect. These words were written immediately after the massacres at Harlem.

With all the bloodshed at Mons, and Naarden, and Mechlin, and by the Council of Tumults, daily, for six years long, still crying from the ground, he taxed himself with a misplaced and foolish tenderness to the people. He assured the King that when Alkmaar should be taken, he would not spare a " living soul among its whole population ;" and, as his parting advice, he recommended that *every city in the Netherlands should be burned to the ground*, except a few which could be occupied permanently by the royal troops.* On the whole, so finished a picture of a perfect and absolute tyranny has rarely been presented to mankind by history, as in Alva's administration of the Netherlands.

The tens of thousands in those miserable provinces who fell victims to the gallows, the sword, the stake, the living grave, or to living banishment, have never been counted ; for those statistics of barbarity are often effaced from human record. Enough, however, is known, and enough has been recited in the preceding pages. No mode in which human beings have ever caused their fellow-creatures to suffer, was omitted from daily practice. Men, women, and children, old and young, nobles and paupers, opulent burghers, hospital patients, lunatics, dead bodies, all were indiscriminately made to furnish food for the scaffold and the stake.† Men were tortured, beheaded, hanged by the neck and by the legs, burned before slow fires, pinched to death with red hot tongs, broken upon the wheel, starved, and flayed alive. Their skins stripped from the living body, were stretched upon drums, to be beaten in the march of their brethren to the gallows ‡ The bodies of many who had died a natural death were exhumed, and their festering remains hanged upon the gibbet, on pretext

---

* Correspondance de Philippe II., ii. 1276.

† "—— plonderen, roven en ruiten, verjagen en verwoesten, in't vangen en spannen, in 't bannen, verdrijven en goederen confisqueren, ja in 't branden en blanken, hangen, koppen, hacken, raeybraken met afgrijselijke tormenten pijnigen en vermoorden de ondersaten, so wel edele als onedele, arme als rijke, jonk als oud, weduwen en weesen, mannen, vrouwen en maegden."—Sendbrief in forme von Supplicatie, etc., in Bor, vi. 467. ‡ Sendbrief, etc, Bor, vi. 467

that they had died without receiving the sacrament, but in reality that their property might become the legitimate prey of the treasury.* Marriages of long standing were dissolved by order of government, that rich heiresses might be married against their will to foreigners whom they abhorred.† Women and children were executed for the crime of assisting their fugitive husbands and parents with a penny in their utmost need, and even for consoling them with a letter in their exile.‡ Such was the regular course of affairs as administered by the Blood Council. The additional barbarities committed amid the sack and ruin of those blazing and starving cities, are almost beyond belief ; unborn infants were torn from the living bodies of their mothers ; women and children were violated by thousands ; and whole populations burned and hacked to pieces by soldiers in every mode which cruelty, in its wanton ingenuity, could devise.§ Such was the administration, of which Vargas affirmed, at its close, that too much mercy, "*nimia misericordia*," had been its ruin.‖

Even Philip, inspired by secret views, became wearied of the Governor, who, at an early period, had already given offence by his arrogance. To commemorate his victories, the Viceroy had erected a colossal statue, not to his monarch, but to himself. To proclaim the royal pardon, he had seated himself upon a golden throne. Such insolent airs could be ill forgiven by the absolute King. Too cautious to provoke an open rupture, he allowed the Governor, after he had done all his work, and more than all his work, to retire without disgrace, but without a triumph. For the sins of that administration, master and servant are in equal measure responsible.

The character of the Duke of Alva, so far as the Netherlands are concerned, seems almost like a caricature. As a creation of fiction, it would seem grotesque : yet even that hardy, historical scepticism, which delights in reversing the judgment of centuries, and in re-establishing reputations long since de-

---

* Sendbrief, etc., Bor, vi. 467.   † Ibid.   ‡ Ibid.
§ Ibid.   ‖ Meteren, iv. 86.

graded to the dust, must find it difficult to alter this man's position.   No historical decision is final ; an appeal to a more remote posterity, founded upon more accurate evidence, is always valid ; but when the verdict has been pronounced upon facts which are undisputed, and upon testimony from the criminal's lips, there is little chance of a reversal of the sentence.* It is an affectation of philosophical candor to extenuate vices which are not only avowed, but claimed as virtues.

---

* The time is past when it could be said that the cruelty of Alva, or the enormities of his administration, have been exaggerated by party violence. Human invention is incapable of outstripping the truth upon this subject. To attempt the defence of either the man or his measures at the present day is to convict oneself of an amount of ignorance or of bigotry against which history and argument are alike powerless.   The publication of the Duke's letters in the correspondence of Simancas and in the Besançon papers, together with that compact mass of horror, long before the world under the title of "Sententien van Alva," in which a portion only of the sentences of death and banishment pronounced by him during his reign, have been copied from the official records— these in themselves would be a sufficient justification of all the charges ever brought by the most bitter contemporary of Holland or Flanders.   If the investigator should remain sceptical, however, let him examine the " Registre des Condamnés et Bannis à Cause des Troubles des Pays Bas," in three, together with the Records of the " Conseil des Troubles," in forty-three folio volumes, in the Royal Archives at Brussels.   After going through all these chronicles of iniquity, the most determined historic doubter will probably throw up the case.

NOTE.

As specimens of the songs made by the people while Alva was making their laws, the author ventures the following translations of popular ballads. The originals may be found, the one in the collection of Ernst Münch ; Niederlandsches Museum, I., 125, 126 : the other in Van Vloten's excellent republication of Netherland Historical Songs.—Nederlandsche Geschiedzangen, i., 393. Professor Altmeyer has also quoted them in his " Succursale du Tribunal de Sang."

"Slaet op den tromele, van dirre dom deyne;
　　Slaet op den tromele, van dirre dom does:
　　Slaet op den tromele, van dirre dom deyne,
　　　Vive le geus! is nu de loes.

" De Spaensche Inquisitie, voor Godt malitie,
　　De Spaensche Inquisitie, als draecx bloet fel;
　　De Spaensche Inquisitie ghevoelt punitie,
　　De Spaensche Inquisitie ontvaelt haer spel.

"Vive le geus! wilt christenlyk leven,
　　Vive le geus! houdt fraeye moet :
　　Vive le geus! Godt behoedt voor sneven,
　　Vive le geus! edel christen bloedt."

TRANSLATION.

Beat the drum gaily, rub a dow, rub a dub;
　　Beat the drum gaily, rub a dub, rub a dow;
　　Beat the drum gaily, rub a dow, rub a dub;—
　　　Long live the Beggars! is the watchword now.

The Spanish Inquisition, without intermission—
　　The Spanish Inquisition has drunk our blood ;
　　The Spanish Inquisition, may God's malediction
　　Blast the Spanish Inquisition and all her brood.

Long live the Beggars! wilt thou Christ's word cherish—
　　Long live the Beggars! be bold of heart and hand;
　　Long live the Beggars! God will not see thee perish;
　　　Long live the Beggars! oh noble Christian band.

"De Paus en Papisten, Gods handt doet beven,
    De Paus en Papisten zyn t' eynden haer raet:
  De Paus en Papisten wreet boven schreven,
    Ghy Paus en Papisten, soet nu oflaet.

" 'T swaert is getrokken, certeyn godts wraec naect,
    'T swaert is getrokken, daer Joannes a schryft;
  'T swaert is getrokken, dat Apocalypsis maect, naect,
    'T swaert is getrokken, ghy wert nu ontlyft.

" 'T onschuldig bloet dat ghy heft vergoten,
    'T onschuldig bloet royt over u wraeck;
  'T onschuldig bloet te storten heeft u niet verdroten,
    'T onschuldig bloet dat dronct ghy met den draeck.

" U vleisschen arm, daer ghy op betroude,
    U vleisschen arm beschwyckt u nu;
  U vleisschen arm die u huys houde,
    U vleisschen arm, wyckt van u schoon."

                    Ernst Münch, Niederlandsches Museum, i. 125, 126.

                        TRANSLATION.

  The Pope and Papists are shivering and shaking;
    The Pope and Papists are at their wits' ends;
  The Pope and Papists at God's right hand are quaking;—
    Pope and Papists, find absolution now, my friends!

  The sword is drawn now, God's wakened vengeance lowers;
    The sword is drawn now, the Apocalypse unrolled;
  The sword is drawn now, God's sword and wrath are ours;
    The sword is drawn now which Apostle John foretold.

  The innocent blood which ye've caused to flow like water;
    The innocent blood which your wicked hands hath stained;
  The innocent blood cries out for blood and slaughter;—
    That innocent blood which, like dragons fell, ye drained.

  Your fleshly arm is withering and shrinking—
    Your fleshly arm which ye trusted fierce and bold;
  Your fleshly arm and the house it built are sinking;
    Your fleshly arm now is marrowless and cold.

The bitter blasphemy of the following is but a faint expression of the hatred which the tyranny of Alva had excited in the popular heart. It is called the Ghent Paternoster (Gentsch Vaderonze), and is addressed to the Duke of Alva.

GENTSCH VADERONZE.

" Helsche duvel, die tot Brussel syt,
Uwen naem ende faem sy vermaledyt,
U ryck vergae sonder respyt,
Want heeft geduyrt te langen tyd.
Uwen willen sal nict gewerden,
Noch in hemel noch op erden:
Ghy beneempt ons huyden ons dagelicx broot,
Wyff ende knyderen hebben 't groote noot:
Ghy en vergeeft niemant syn schult,
Want ghy met haet ende nyt syt vervult:
Ghy en laet niemant ongetempteert,
Alle dese landen ghy perturbeert.
O hemelschen vader, die in den hemel syt,
Maeckt ons desen helschen duvel quyt,
Met synen bloedigen, valschen raet,
Daer hy meede handelt alle quaet,
En syn spaens chrychsvolk allegaer,
'T welck leeft of sy des duvels waer.   Amen!"

Van Vloten, Nederlandsche Geschiedzangen, i. 393.

TRANSLATION.

Our devil, who dost in Brussels dwell,
Curst be thy name in earth and hell:
Thy kingdom speedily pass away,
Which hath blasted and blighted us many a day;
Thy will nevermore be done,
In heaven above nor under the sun;
Thou takest daily our daily bread;
Our wives and children lie starving or dead.
No man's trespasses thou forgivest;
Revenge is the food on which thou livest.
Thou leadest all men into temptation;
Unto evil thou hast delivered this nation.
Our Father, in heaven which art,
Grant that this hellish devil may soon depart—
And with him his Council false and bloody,
Who make murder and rapine their daily study—
And all his savage war-dogs of Spain,
Oh send them back to the Devil, their father, again.   Amen.

PART IV.

ADMINISTRATION OF THE GRAND COMMANDER.

1573—1576.

CHAPTER I.

THE horrors of Alva's administration had caused men to look
back with fondness upon the milder and more vacillating
tyranny of the Duchess Margaret. From the same cause the
advent of the Grand Commander was hailed with pleasure[*] and
with a momentary gleam of hope. At any rate, it was a relief
that the man in whom an almost impossible perfection of cruelty
seemed embodied was at last to be withdrawn. It was certain
that his successor, however ambitious of following in Alva's
footsteps, would never be able to rival the intensity and the

---

[*] Bor, vii. 477.

unswerving directness of purpose which it had been permitted
to the Duke's nature to attain. The new Governor-General
was, doubtless, human, and it had been long since the Netherlanders imagined anything in common between themselves and
the late Viceroy.

Apart from this hope, however, there was little encouragement to be derived from anything positively known of the new
functionary, or the policy which he was to represent. Don
Luis de Requesens and Cuñiga, Grand Commander of Castile and late Governor of Milan, was a man of mediocre
abilities, who possessed a reputation for moderation and
sagacity which he hardly deserved. His military prowess
had been chiefly displayed in the bloody and barren battle of
Lepanto, where his conduct and counsel were supposed to have
contributed, in some measure, to the victorious result.* His
administration at Milan had been characterized as firm and
moderate.† Nevertheless, his character was regarded with
anything but favorable eyes in the Netherlands. Men told
each other of his broken faith to the Moors in Granada, and
of his unpopularity in Milan, where, notwithstanding his
boasted moderation, he had, in reality, so oppressed the people
as to gain their deadly hatred. They complained, too, that it
was an insult to send, as Governor-General of the provinces,
not a prince of the blood, as used to be the case, but a simple
" gentleman of cloak and sword."‡

Any person, however, who represented the royal authority
in the provinces was under historical disadvantage. He was
literally no more than an actor, hardly even that. It was
Philip's policy and pride to direct all the machinery of his
extensive empire, and to pull every string himself. His pup-
pets, however magnificently attired, moved only in obedience to his impulse, and spoke no syllable but with his voice.
Upon the table in his cabinet was arranged all the business of

---

* Strada, viii. 405–408.   Mendoza, x. 222, 223.

† Ibid.   Groen v. Prinsterer, iv. 259, 260.

‡ Correspond. de Mondoucet et Charles IX.   Com. Roy. d'Hist., iv. 340, seq.

his various realms, even to the most minute particulars.*
Plans, petty or vast, affecting the interests of empires and
ages, or bounded within the narrow limits of trivial and evan-
escent detail, encumbered his memory and consumed his time.
His ambition to do all the work of his kingdoms was aided by
an inconceivable greediness for labor. He loved the routine
of business, as some monarchs have loved war, as others have
loved pleasure. The object, alike paltry and impossible, of
this ambition, bespoke the narrow mind. His estates were
regarded by him as private property ; measures affecting
the temporal and eternal interests of millions were regarded as
domestic affairs, and the eye of the master was considered the
only one which could duly superintend these estates and those
interests. Much incapacity to govern was revealed in this
inordinate passion to administer. His mind, constantly
fatigued by petty labors, was never enabled to survey his wide
domains from the height of majesty.

In Alva, certainly, he had employed an unquestionable
reality; but Alva, by a fortunate coincidence of character,
had seemed his second self. He was now gone, however,
and although the royal purpose had not altered, the royal
circumstances were changed. The moment had arrived
when it was thought that the mask and cothurn might again
be assumed with effect ; when a grave and conventional
personage might decorously make his appearance to perform an
interlude of clemency and moderation with satisfactory results.
Accordingly, the Great Commander, heralded by rumors of
amnesty, was commissioned to assume the government which
Alva had been permitted to resign.

---

* Letter of Saint Goard to Charles IX., in Groen v. Prinst., Archives, etc., iv.
330, 331.—" Se reservant," said the French envoy, " toutes choses, qui le rend ex-
trément chargé et travaillé et tient ung procédé qu'il respond et veoit toutes les
affaires et les départ toutes où elles se doibvent respondre *où elles demeurent le
plus souvent immortelles*, où qu'elles soient, ou de grande ou de peu de conséquence
de manière qu'il n'en vient rien mieulx, et sur ca les malintentionnés luy forgent
infinies doubtes et soubçons."

See also Letter of Saint Goard to Charles IX., Madrid, 17th December, 1573,
in Groen v. Prinst., Archives, etc., iv. 27*, et seq.

It had been industriously circulated that a change of policy was intended. It was even supposed by the more sanguine that the Duke had retired in disgrace. A show of coldness was manifested towards him on his return by the King, while Vargas, who had accompanied the Governor, was peremptorily forbidden to appear within five leagues of the court.* The more discerning, however, perceived much affectation in this apparent displeasure. Saint Goard, the keen observer of Philip's moods and measures, wrote to his sovereign that he had narrowly observed the countenances of both Philip and Alva ; that he had informed himself as thoroughly as possible with regard to the course of policy intended ; that he had arrived at the conclusion that the royal chagrin was but dissimulation, intended to dispose the Netherlanders to thoughts of an impossible peace, and that he considered the present merely a breathing time, in which still more active preparations might be made for crushing the rebellion.† It was now evident to the world that the revolt had reached a stage in which it could be terminated only by absolute conquest or concession.

To conquer the people of the provinces, except by extermination, seemed difficult—to judge by the seven years of execution, sieges and campaigns, which had now passed without a definite result. It was, therefore, thought expedient to employ concession. The new Governor accordingly, in case the Netherlanders would abandon every object for which they had been so heroically contending, was empowered to concede a pardon. It was expressly enjoined upon him, however, that no conciliatory measures should be adopted in which the King's absolute supremacy, and the total prohibition of every form of worship but the Roman Catholic, were not assumed as a basis.‡ Now, as the people had been contending at least

---

* Letter of Saint Goard to Charles IX., 4th of April, 1574, Archives, etc., iv. 361.

† Letter of Saint Goard, Archives, etc., iv. 361.

‡ Letter of Philip II. to Requesens, 30th March, 1574. Correspondance de Guillaume le Tacit., iii. 395.

ten years long for constitutional rights against prerogative, and at least seven for liberty of conscience against papistry, it was easy to foretell how much effect any negotiations thus commenced were likely to produce.

Yet, no doubt, in the Netherlands there was a most earnest longing for peace. The Catholic portion of the population were desirous of a reconciliation with their brethren of the new religion. The universal vengeance which had descended upon heresy had not struck the heretics only. It was difficult to find a fireside, Protestant or Catholic, which had not been made desolate by execution, banishment, or confiscation. The common people and the grand seigniors were alike weary of the war. Not only Aerschot and Viglius, but Noircarmes and Berlaymont, were desirous that peace should be at last compassed upon liberal terms, and the Prince of Orange fully and unconditionally pardoned.* Even the Spanish commanders had become disgusted with the monotonous butchery which had stained their swords. Julian Romero, the fierce and unscrupulous soldier upon whose head rested the guilt of the Naarden massacre, addressed several letters to William of Orange, full of courtesy and good wishes for a speedy termination of the war, and for an entire reconciliation of the Prince with his sovereign.† Noircarmes also opened a correspondence with the great leader of the revolt, and offered to do all in his power to restore peace and prosperity to the country. The Prince answered the courtesy of the Spaniard with equal, but barren, courtesy ; for it was obvious that no definite result could be derived from such informal negotiations. To Noircarmes he responded in terms of gentle but grave rebuke,‡ expressing deep regret that a Netherland noble of such eminence, with so many others of rank and authority, should so long have supported the King in his tyranny. He, however, expressed his satisfaction that their eyes, however late, had

---

* Letter of Requesens to Philip II. Gachard, Correspondance de Philippe II., ii. 1293.

† Gachard, Correspondance de Guillaume le Tacit., iii. 81–87.

‡ See the Correspondence in Groen, v. Prinst., Archives, etc., iv. 301, 302.

opened to the enormous iniquity which had been practised in the country, and he accepted the offers of friendship as frankly as they had been made. Not long afterwards, the Prince furnished his correspondent with a proof of his sincerity, by forwarding to him two letters which had been intercepted,* from certain agents of government to Alva, in which Noircarmes and others who had so long supported the King against their own country, were spoken of in terms of menace and distrust. The Prince accordingly warned his new correspondent that, in spite of all the proofs of uncompromising loyalty which he had exhibited, he was yet moving upon a dark and slippery pathway, and might, even like Egmont and Horn, find a scaffold as the end and the reward of his career. So profound was that abyss of dissimulation which constituted the royal policy towards the Netherlands, that the most unscrupulous partisans of government could only see doubt and danger with regard to their future destiny, and were sometimes only saved by an opportune death from disgrace and the hangman's hands.

Such, then, were the sentiments of many eminent personages, even among the most devoted loyalists. All longed for peace ; many even definitely expected it, upon the arrival of the Great Commander. Moreover, that functionary discovered, at his first glance into the disorderly state of the exchequer, that at least a short respite was desirable before proceeding with the interminable measures of hostility against the rebellion. If any man had been ever disposed to give Alva credit for administrative ability, such delusion must have vanished at the spectacle of confusion and bankruptcy which presented itself at the termination of his government. He resolutely declined to give his successor any information whatever as to his financial position.† So far from furnishing a detailed statement, such as might naturally be expected upon so momentous an occasion, he informed the Grand Commander that even a

---

* Gachard, Correspondance de Guillaume le Tacit., iii. 94, et seq.

† Letter of Requesens to Philip II., in Gachard, Correspondance de Philippe II., ii. 1285.

sketch was entirely out of the question, and would require more time and labor than he could then afford.* He took his departure, accordingly, leaving Requesens in profound ignorance as to his past accounts; an ignorance in which it is probable that the Duke himself shared to the fullest extent. His enemies stoutly maintained that however loosely his accounts had been kept, he had been very careful to make no mistakes against himself, and that he had retired full of wealth, if not of honor, from his long and terrible administration.† His own letters, on the contrary, accused the King of ingratitude, in permitting an old soldier to ruin himself, not only in health but in fortune, for want of proper recompense during an arduous administration.‡ At any rate it is very certain that the rebellion had already been an expensive matter to the Crown. The army in the Netherlands numbered more than sixty-two thousand men, eight thousand being Spaniards, the rest Walloons and Germans. Forty millions of dollars had already been sunk,§ and it seemed probable that it would require nearly the whole annual produce of the American mines to sustain the war. The transatlantic gold and silver, disinterred from the depths where they had been buried for ages, were employed, not to expand the current of a healthy, life-giving commerce, but to be melted into blood. The sweat and the tortures of the King's pagan subjects in the primeval forests of the New World, were made subsidiary to the extermination of his Netherland people, and the destruction of an ancient civilization. To this end had Columbus discovered a hemisphere for Castile and Aragon, and the new Indies revealed their hidden treasures?

Forty millions of ducats had been spent. Six and a half millions of arrearages‖ were due to the army, while its current

---

* Letter of Requesens to Philip II., in Gachard, Correspondance de Philippe II., ii. 1285.

† Hoofd, viii. 334.

‡ Letter of Requesens. Correspondance de Philippe II., i. 1288.

§ Meteren, v. 103.

‖ Letter of Requesens to Philip II. Correspondance de Philippe II., ii. 1294.

expenses were six hundred thousand a month.* The military expenses alone of the Netherlands were accordingly more than seven millions of dollars yearly, and the mines of the New World produced, during the half century of Philip's reign, an average of only eleven.† Against this constantly increasing deficit, there was not a stiver in the exchequer, nor the means of raising one.‡ The tenth penny had been long virtually extinct, and was soon to be formally abolished. Confiscation had ceased to afford a permanent revenue, and the estates obstinately refused to grant a dollar. Such was the condition to which the unrelenting tyranny and the financial experiments of Alva had reduced the country.

It was, therefore, obvious to Requesens that it would be useful at the moment to hold out hopes of pardon and reconciliation. He saw, what he had not at first comprehended, and what few bigoted supporters of absolutism in any age have ever comprehended, that national enthusiasm, when profound and general, makes a rebellion more expensive to the despot than to the insurgents. " Before my arrival," wrote the Grand Commander to his sovereign, " I did not understand how the rebels could maintain such considerable fleets, while your Majesty could not support a single one. It appears, however, that men who are fighting for their lives, their firesides, their property, and their false religion, for their own cause, in short, are contented to receive rations only, without receiving pay."§ The moral which the new Governor drew from his correct diagnosis of the prevailing disorder was, not that this national enthusiasm should be respected, but that it should be deceived. He deceived no one but himself, however. He censured Noircarmes and Romero for their intermeddling, but held out hopes of a general pacification.‖ He repudiated the idea of any reconciliation

* Letter of Requesens to Philip II. Correspondance de Philippe II., ii. 1294.

† Humboldt. Essai sur la Nouvelle Espagne, iii. 428 (ed. 2nd).

‡ Letter of Requesens. Correspondance de Philippe II., ii. 1285.

§ Correspondance de Philippe II., ii. 1291.   ‖ Ibid., ii. 1293.

between the King and the Prince of Orange, but proposed at the same time a settlement of the revolt.* He had not yet learned that the revolt and William of Orange were one. Although the Prince himself had repeatedly offered to with-draw for ever from the country, if his absence would expedite a settlement satisfactory to the provinces,† there was not a patriot in the Netherlands who could contemplate his depar-ture without despair. Moreover, they all knew better than did Requesens, the inevitable result of the pacific measures which had been daily foreshadowed.

The appointment of the Grand Commander was in truth a desperate attempt to deceive the Netherlanders. He approved distinctly and heartily of Alva's policy,‡ but wrote to the King that it was desirable to amuse the people with the idea of another and a milder scheme. He affected to believe, and perhaps really did believe, that the nation would accept the destruction of all their institutions, provided that penitent heretics were allowed to be reconciled to the Mother Church, and obstinate ones permitted to go into perpetual exile, taking with them a small portion of their worldly goods. For being willing to make this last and almost incredible concession, he begged pardon sincerely of the King. If censurable, he ought not, he thought, to be too severely blamed, for his loyalty was known. The world was aware how often he had risked his life for his Majesty, and how gladly and how many more times he was ready to risk it in future. In his opinion, religion had, after all, but very little to do with the troubles, and so he confidentially informed his sovereign. Egmont and Horn had died Catholics, the people did not rise to assist the Prince's invasion in 1568, and the new religion was only a lever by which a few artful demagogues had attempted to overthrow the King's authority.§

---

* Correspondance de Philippe II., ii. 1293.

† Correspondance de Guillaume le Tacit., 394–400.

‡ Letter of Requesens. Correspondance de Philippe II., ii. 1291.—"A mi parecer ha tenido mucha razon," etc., etc.

§ Letter of Requesens. Correspondance de Philippe II., ii. 1293.

Such views as these revealed the measures of the new Governor's capacity. The people had really refused to rise in 1568, not because they were without sympathy for Orange, but because they were paralyzed by their fear of Alva. Since those days, however, the new religion had increased and multiplied everywhere, in the blood which had rained upon it. It was now difficult to find a Catholic in Holland and Zealand, who was not a government agent.* The Prince had been a moderate Catholic, in the opening scenes of the rebellion, while he came forward as the champion of liberty for all forms of Christianity. He had now become a convert to the new religion, without receding an inch from his position in favor of universal toleration. The new religion was, therefore, not an instrument devised by a faction, but had expanded into the atmosphere of the people's daily life. Individuals might be executed for claiming to breathe it, but it was itself impalpable to the attacks of despotism. Yet the Grand Commander persuaded himself that religion had little or nothing to do with the state of the Netherlands. Nothing more was necessary, he thought, or affected to think, in order to restore tranquillity, than once more to spread the net of a general amnesty.

The Duke of Alva knew better. That functionary, with whom, before his departure from the provinces, Requesens had been commanded to confer, distinctly stated his opinion that there was no use of talking about pardon. Brutally, but candidly, he maintained that there was nothing to be done but to continue the process of extermination. It was necessary, he said, to reduce the country to a dead level of unresisting misery, before an act of oblivion could be securely laid down as the foundation of a new and permanent order of society.† He had already given his advice to his Majesty, that every town in the country should be burned to the ground, except those which could be permanently occupied by the royal troops. The King, however, in his access of clemency at the appointment

---

* Letter of Prince of Orange, 28th September, 1574, in Groen v. Prinst., Archives, v. 73. † Correspondance de Philippe II., ii. 1293.

of a new administration, instructed the Grand Commander *not to resort to this measure unless it should become strictly necessary.** Such were the opposite opinions of the old and new governors with regard to the pardon. The learned Viglius sided with Alva, although manifestly against his will. "It is both the Duke's opinion and my own," wrote the Commander, "that Viglius does not dare to express his real opinion, and that he is secretly desirous of an arrangement with the rebels."† With a good deal of inconsistency, the Governor was offended, not only with those who opposed his plans, but with those who favored them. He was angry with Viglius, who, at least nominally, disapproved of the pardon, and with Noircarmes, Aerschot, and others, who manifested a wish for a pacification. Of the chief characteristic ascribed to the people by Julius Cæsar, namely, that they forgot neither favors nor injuries, the second half only, in the Grand Commander's opinion, had been retained. Not only did they never forget injuries, but their memory, said he, was so good, that they recollected many which they had never received.‡

On the whole, however, in the embarrassed condition of affairs, and while waiting for further supplies, the Commander was secretly disposed to try the effect of a pardon. The object was to deceive the people and to gain time ; for there was no intention of conceding liberty of conscience, of withdrawing foreign troops, or of assembling the states-general. It was, however, not possible to apply these hypocritical measures of conciliation immediately. The war was in full career and could not be arrested even in that wintry season. The patriots held Mondragon closely besieged in Middelburg,§ the last point in the Isle of Walcheren which held for the King. There was a considerable treasure in money and merchandise shut up in that city ; and, moreover, so deserving and distinguished an officer as Mondragon could not be abandoned to

---

* Correspondance de Philippe II., ii. 1287.   † Ibid., ii. 1293.
‡ Ibid., ii. 1291, and p. 443, note.
§ Bor, vii. 479.   Meteren, v. 88.

his fate. At the same time, famine was pressing him sorely, and, by the end of the year, garrison and townspeople had nothing but rats, mice, dogs, cats, and such repulsive substitutes for food, to support life withal.* It was necessary to take immediate measures to relieve the place.

On the other hand, the situation of the patriots was not very encouraging. Their superiority on the sea was unquestionable, for the Hollanders and Zealanders were the best sailors in the world, and they asked of their country no payment for their blood, but thanks. The land forces, however, were usually mercenaries, who were apt to mutiny at the commencement of an action if, as was too often the case, their wages could not be paid. Holland was entirely cut in twain by the loss of Harlem and the leaguer of Leyden, no communication between the dissevered portions being possible, except with difficulty and danger.† The estates, although they had done much for the cause, and were prepared to do much more, were too apt to wrangle about economical details. They irritated the Prince of Orange by huckstering about subsidies to a degree which his proud and generous nature could hardly brook.‡ He had strong hopes from France. Louis of Nassau had held secret interviews with the Duke of Alençon and the Duke of Anjou, now King of Poland, at Blamont.§ Alençon had assured him secretly, affectionately, and warmly, that he would be as sincere a friend to the cause as were his two royal brothers. The Count had even received one hundred thousand livres in hand, as an earnest of the favorable intentions of France,‖ and was now busily engaged, at the instance of the Prince, in levying an army in Germany for the relief of Leyden and the rest of Holland, while William, on his part, was omitting nothing, whether by representations to the estates or by secret foreign

* Letter of De la Klunder in Groen v. Prinst., Archives, etc., iv. 307, 308.
† Bor, vii. 478.
‡ Bor, vii. Kluit, Hist. Holl. Staatsreg., vi., Hoofdst. and Bijlage, i. 401–415.
§ Groen v. Prinst., iv. 263–278. De Thou, t. vii. liv. vii. 28–37. Hoofd, ix. 343, 344.
‖ Archives et Correspondance, iv. 281

missions and correspondence, to further the cause of the suffering country.[*]

At the same time, the Prince dreaded the effect of the promised pardon. He had reason to be distrustful of the general temper of the nation when a man like Saint Aldegonde, the enlightened patriot and his own tried friend, was influenced, by the discouraging and dangerous position in which he found himself, to abandon the high ground upon which they had both so long and so firmly stood. Saint Aldegonde had been held a strict prisoner since his capture at Maeslandsluis, at the close of Alva's administration.[†] It was, no doubt, a predicament attended with much keen suffering and positive danger. It had hitherto been the uniform policy of the government to kill all prisoners, of whatever rank. Accordingly, some had been drowned, some had been hanged, some beheaded, some poisoned in their dungeons—all had been murdered. This had been Alva's course. The Grand Commander also highly approved of the system,[‡] but the capture of Count Bossu by the patriots had necessitated a suspension of such rigor.[§] It was certain that Bossu's head would fall as soon as Saint Aldegonde's, the Prince having expressly warned the government of this inevitable result.[||] Notwithstanding that security, however, for his eventual restoration to liberty, a Netherland rebel in a Spanish prison could hardly feel himself at ease. There were so many foot-marks into the cave and not a single one coming forth. Yet it was not singular, however, that the Prince should read with regret the somewhat insincere casuistry with which Saint Aldegonde sought to persuade himself and his fellow-countrymen that a reconciliation with the monarch was desirable, even upon unworthy terms. He was somewhat shocked that so valiant and eloquent a supporter of the Reformation should coolly express his opinion that the King would probably refuse liberty of con-

---

* Bor, viii. 479, 488, 490. Hoofd, ix. 334, 344.
† Bor, vii. 481, 482. Archives et Correspondance, iv. 237.
‡ Correspondance de Philippe II., ii. 1291, 445.
§ Ibid. || Bor, vii. 482.

science to the Netherlanders, but would, no doubt, permit heretics to go into banishment. " Perhaps, after we have gone into exile," added Saint Aldegonde, almost with baseness, " God may give us an opportunity of doing such good service to the King, that he will lend us a more favorable ear, and, peradventure, permit our return to the country."[*]

Certainly, such language was not becoming the pen which wrote the famous Compromise. The Prince himself was, however, not to be induced, even by the captivity and the remonstrances of so valued a friend, to swerve from the path of duty. He still maintained, in public and private, that the withdrawal of foreign troops from the provinces, the restoration of the old constitutional privileges, and the entire freedom of conscience in religious matters, were the indispensable conditions of any pacification. It was plain to him that the Spaniards were not ready to grant these conditions ; but he felt confident that he should accomplish the release of Saint Aldegonde without condescending to an ignominious peace.

The most pressing matter, upon the Great Commander's arrival, was obviously to relieve the city of Middelburg. Mondragon, after so stanch a defence, would soon be obliged to capitulate, unless he should promptly receive supplies. Requesens, accordingly, collected seventy-five ships at Bergen op Zoom, which were placed nominally under the command of Admiral de Glimes, but in reality under that of Julian Romero. Another fleet of thirty vessels had been assembled at Antwerp under Sancho d'Avila. Both, amply freighted with provisions, were destined to make their way to Middelburg by the two different passages of the Honde and the Eastern Scheld.[†] On the other hand, the Prince of Orange had repaired to Flushing to superintend the operations of Admiral Boisot, who already, in obedience to his orders, had got a powerful squadron in readiness at that place. Late in

---

[*] See the Letter of Ste. Aldegonde, in Correspondance de Guillaume le Tacit., iii. 78, et seq.

[†] Bor, vii. 479. Hoofd, ix. 335. Meteren, v. 88.

January, 1574, d'Avila arrived in the neighbourhood of Flushing, where he awaited the arrival of Romero's fleet. United, the two Commanders were to make a determined attempt to reinforce the starving city of Middelburg.* At the same time, Governor Requesens made his appearance in person at Bergen op Zoom to expedite the departure of the stronger fleet,† but it was not the intention of the Prince of Orange to allow this expedition to save the city. The Spanish generals, however valiant, were to learn that their genius was not amphibious, and that the Beggars of the Sea were still invincible on their own element, even if their brethren of the land had occasionally quailed.

Admiral Boisot's fleet had already moved up the Scheld and taken a position nearly opposite to Bergen op Zoom.‡ On the 20th of January the Prince of Orange, embarking from Zierick Zee, came to make them a visit before the impending action. His galley, conspicuous for its elegant decorations, was exposed for some time to the artillery of the fort, but providentially escaped unharmed. He assembled all the officers of his armada, and, in brief but eloquent language, reminded them how necessary it was to the salvation of the whole country that they should prevent the city of Middelburg—the key to the whole of Zealand, already upon the point of falling into the hands of the patriots—from being now wrested from their grasp. On the sea, at least, the Hollanders and Zealanders were at home. The officers and men, with one accord, rent the air with their cheers. They swore that they would shed every drop of blood in their veins but they would sustain the Prince and the country ; and they solemnly vowed not only to serve, if necessary, without wages, but to sacrifice all that they possessed in the world rather than abandon the cause of their fatherland.§ Having by his pre-

---

* Bor, Hoofd, Meteren, ubi sup.
† Mendoza, xi. 225. Bor, Meteren, ubi sup.   ‡ Bor, vii. 479.
§ Letter of De la Klunder in Archives de la Maison d'Orange, iv. 307.
—"Tellement encouragea les soldats que tous d'une même voix respon-

sence and his language aroused their valor to so high a pitch of enthusiasm, the Prince departed for Delft, to make arrangements to drive the Spaniards from the siege of Leyden.*

On the 29th of January, the fleet of Romero sailed from Bergen, disposed in three divisions, each numbering twenty-five vessels of different sizes. As the Grand Commander stood on the dyke of Schakerloo to witness the departure, a general salute was fired by the fleet in his honor, but with most unfortunate augury. The discharge, by some accident, set fire to the magazines of one of the ships, which blew up with a terrible explosion, every soul on board perishing. The expedition, nevertheless, continued its way. Opposite Romerswael, the fleet of Boisot awaited them, drawn up in battle array.† As an indication of the spirit which animated this hardy race, it may be mentioned that Schot, captain of the flag-ship, had been left on shore, dying of a pestilential fever. Admiral Boisot had appointed a Flushinger, Klaaf Klaafzoon, in his place. Just before the action, however, Schot, "scarcely able to blow a feather from his mouth," staggered on board his ship, and claimed the command.‡ There was no disputing a precedency which he had risen from his death-bed to vindicate. There was, however, a short discussion, as the enemy's fleet approached, between these rival captains regarding the manner in which the Spaniards should be received. Klaafzoon was of opinion that most of the men should go below till after the enemy's first discharge. Schot insisted that all should remain on deck, ready to grapple with the Spanish fleet, and to board them without the least delay.

---

dirent qu'ils étoient prets d'assister à son Exc. jusques à la dernière goutte de leur sang, et que plus tot que d'abandonner la cause, aymeroient mieulx de servir un an sans recevoir maille, voire à enchanger tout ce qu'ils ont en ce monde."

* Archives de la Maison d'Orange, iv. 247, et seq.

† Hoofd, ix. 336.   Bor, vii. 479.   Mendoza, xi. 225.   Meteren, v. 89.

‡ Hoofd, ix. 336.—" Zoo haast als hy een veder vanden mondt blaazen kan quam met noch ungenesen lichaam weeder t'scheep."

The sentiment of Schot prevailed, and all hands stood on deck, ready with boarding-pikes and grappling-irons.*

The first division of Romero came nearer, and delivered its first broadside, when Schot and Klaafzoon both fell mortally wounded. Admiral Boisot lost an eye,† and many officers and sailors in the other vessels were killed or wounded. This was, however, the first and last of the cannonading. As many of Romero's vessels as could be grappled with in the narrow estuary found themselves locked in close embrace with their enemies. A murderous hand-to-hand conflict succeeded. Battle-axe, boarding-pike, pistol, and dagger were the weapons. Every man who yielded himself a prisoner was instantly stabbed and tossed into the sea by the remorseless Zealanders. Fighting only to kill, and not to plunder, they did not even stop to take the gold chains which many Spaniards wore on their necks. It had, however, been obvious from the beginning that the Spanish fleet were not likely to achieve that triumph over the patriots which was necessary before they could relieve Middelburg. The battle continued a little longer ; but after fifteen ships had been taken and twelve hundred royalists slain, the remainder of the enemy's fleet retreated into Bergen.‡ Romero himself, whose ship had grounded, sprang out of a port-hole and swam ashore, followed by such of his men as were able to imitate him. He landed at the very feet of the Grand Commander, who, wet and cold, had been standing all day upon the dyke of Schakerloo, in the midst of a pouring rain, only to witness the total defeat of his armada at last.§ " I told your Excellency," said Romero, coolly, as he climbed, all dripping, on the bank, " that I was a land-fighter and not a sailor. If you were to give me the command of a hundred fleets, I believe that none of them would fare better than this

---

* Hoofd, ubi sup.   † Ibid.   Bor, vii. 479.
‡ Meteren, v. 89.   Hoofd, ix. 336.   Bor, vii. 479.   Mendoza, xi. 226, 227.
§ Cabrera, x. 780.   Hoofd. Meteren, ubi sup.

has done."* The Governor and his discomfited, but philosophical lieutenant, then returned to Bergen, and thence to Brussels, acknowledging that the city of Middelburg must fall,
while Sancho d'Avila, hearing of the disaster which had befal-
len his countrymen, brought his fleet, with the greatest expedition, back to Antwerp. Thus the gallant Mondragon was
abandoned to his fate.†

That fate could no longer be protracted. The city of
Middelburg had reached and passed the starvation point.
Still Mondragon was determined not to yield at discretion,
although very willing to capitulate. The Prince of Orange,
after the victory of Bergen, was desirous of an unconditional
surrender, believing it to be his right, and knowing that he
could not be supposed capable of practising upon Middelburg
the vengeance which had been wreaked on Naarden, Zutfen,
and Harlem. Mondragon, however, swore that he would set
fire to the city in twenty places, and perish with every soldier
and burgher in the flames together, rather than abandon himself to the enemy's mercy.‡ The prince knew that the brave
Spaniard was entirely capable of executing his threat. He
granted honorable conditions, which, on the 18th February,
were drawn up in five articles, and signed.§ It was agreed
that Mondragon and his troops should leave the place, with
their arms, ammunition, and all their personal property. The
citizens who remained were to take oath of fidelity to the
Prince, as stadholder for his Majesty, and were to pay besides
a subsidy of three hundred thousand florins. Mondragon
was, furthermore, to procure the discharge of Saint Aldegonde,
and of four other prisoners of rank, or, failing in the attempt,

---

* "Vide Excellencia bien sabia que yo no era marinero sino infante, no me
entregue mas armadas, porque si ciento me diesse es de temer que las pierda
todas."—Mendoza, xi. 227.

† Bor, vii. 479, 480. Meteren, v. 89 Hoofd, ix. 338.

‡ "Mondragon antwoorde, dat hy en de zynen de staat eer tot twintigh
plaatsen aan brandt zouden steeken, daar naa in eenen uitval zich fechtende
laaten aan stukken haaken."—Hoofd, ix. 339.

§ Bor, vii. 480. Meteren, v. 89. Mendoza, xi. 229.

was to return within two months, and constitute himself prisoner of war. The Catholic priests were to take away from the city none of their property but their clothes.* In accordance with this capitulation, Mondragon, and those who wished to accompany him, left the city on the 21st of February, and were conveyed to the Flemish shore at Neuz. It will be seen in the sequel that the Governor neither granted him the release of the five prisoners, nor permitted him to return, according to his parole. A few days afterwards, the Prince entered the city, re-organized the magistracy, received the allegiance of the inhabitants, restored the ancient constitution, and liberally remitted two-thirds of the sum in which they had been mulcted.†

The Spaniards had thus been successfully driven from the Isle of Walcheren, leaving the Hollanders and Zealanders masters of the sea-coast. Since the siege of Alkmaar had been raised, however, the enemy had remained within the territory of Holland. Leyden was closely invested, the country in a desperate condition, and all communication between its different cities nearly suspended.‡ It was comparatively easy for the Prince of Orange to equip and man his fleets. The genius and habits of the people made them at home upon the water, and inspired them with a feeling of superiority to their adversaries. It was not so upon land. Strong to resist, patient to suffer, the Hollanders, although terrible in defence, had not the necessary discipline or experience to meet the veteran legions of Spain, with confidence, in the open field. To raise the siege of Leyden, the main reliance of the Prince was upon Count Louis, who was again in Germany. In the latter days of Alva's administration, William had written to his brothers, urging them speedily to arrange the details of a campaign, of which he forwarded them a sketch.§ As soon as a sufficient force had been levied in Germany, an attempt

---

* Bor, Meteren, Hoofd, Mendoza, ubi sup.   Cabrera, x. 781.
† Bor, vii. 481.   ‡ Ibid., vii. 478.
§ Archives de la Maison d'Orange, iv. 246, 247, seq.

was to be made upon Maestricht. If that failed, Louis was to cross the Meuse, in the neighbourhood of Stochem, make his way towards the Prince's own city of Gertruidenberg, and thence make a junction with his brother in the neighbourhood of Delft. They were then to take up a position together between Harlem and Leyden. In that case it seemed probable that the Spaniards would find themselves obliged to fight at a great disadvantage, or to abandon the country. " In short," said the Prince, " if this enterprise be arranged with due diligence and discretion, I hold it as the only certain means for putting a speedy end to the war, and for driving these devils of Spaniards out of the country, before the Duke of Alva has time to raise another army to support them."*

In pursuance of this plan, Louis had been actively engaged all the earlier part of the winter in levying troops and raising supplies. He had been assisted by the French princes with considerable sums of money, as an earnest of what he was in future to expect from that source. He had made an unsuccessful attempt to effect the capture of Reque-sens, on his way to take the government of the Netherlands. He had then passed to the frontier of France, where he had held his important interview with Catharine de' Medici and the Duke of Anjou, then on the point of departure to ascend the throne of Poland. He had received liberal presents, and still more liberal promises. Anjou had assured him that he would go as far as any of the German princes in rendering active and sincere assistance to the Protestant cause in the Netherlands. The Duc d'Alençon—soon, in his brother's absence, to succeed to the chieftainship of the new alliance between the "politiques" and the Huguenots—had also pressed his hand, whispering in his ear, as he did so, that the government of France now belonged to him, as it had recently done to Anjou, and that the Prince might reckon upon his friendship with entire security.†

---

* Archives de la Maison d'Orange, iv. 246, 247, seq.
† Letter of Count Louis to Prince of Orange, Archives, etc., iv. 278–281.

These fine words, which cost nothing when whispered in secret, were not destined to fructify into a very rich harvest, for the mutual jealousy of France and England, lest either should acquire ascendency in the Netherlands, made both governments prodigal of promises, while the common fear entertained by them of the power of Spain rendered both languid, insincere, and mischievous allies. Count John, however, was indefatigable in arranging the finances of the proposed expedition, and in levying contributions among his numerous relatives and allies in Germany, while Louis had profited by the occasion of Anjou's passage into Poland, to acquire for himself two thousand German and French cavalry, who had served to escort that Prince,* and who, being now thrown out of employment, were glad to have a job offered them by a general who was thought to be in funds. Another thousand of cavalry and six thousand foot were soon assembled,† from those ever-swarming nurseries of mercenary warriors, the smaller German states. With these, towards the end of February, Louis crossed the Rhine in a heavy snow-storm, and bent his course towards Maestricht. All the three brothers of the Prince accompanied this little army, besides Duke Christopher, son of the elector Palatine.‡

Before the end of the month the army reached the Meuse, and encamped within four miles of Maestricht, on the opposite side of the river.§ The garrison, commanded by Montesdoca, was weak, but the news of the warlike preparations in Germany had preceded the arrival of Count Louis. Requesens, feeling the gravity of the occasion, had issued orders for an immediate levy of eight thousand cavalry in Germany, with a proportionate number of infantry. At the same time he had directed Don Bernardino de Mendoza, with some companies of

---

* Hoofd, ix. 334. Mendoza, xi. 231.

† Meteren, v. 90.—Compare Bor, vii. 489 ; Mendoza, xi. 231.

‡ Bor, vii. 489, 490.

§ Bor, vii. 490. Mendoza, xi. 231, 233. Archives et Correspondance, iv. 327.

cavalry, then stationed in Breda, to throw himself without
delay into Maestricht. Don Sancho d'Avila was entrusted
with the general care of resisting the hostile expedition.
That general had forthwith collected all the troops which
could be spared from every town where they were stationed,
had strengthened the cities of Antwerp, Ghent, Nimwegen,
and Valenciennes, where there were known to be many secret
adherents of Orange ; and with the remainder of his forces
had put himself in motion, to oppose the entrance of Louis
into Brabant, and his junction with his brother in Holland.
Braccamonte had been despatched to Leyden, in order instantly to draw off the forces which were besieging the city.
Thus Louis had already effected something of importance by
the very news of his approach.*

Meantime the Prince of Orange had raised six thousand
infantry, whose rendezvous was the Isle of Bommel. He
was disappointed at the paucity of the troops which Louis
had been able to collect, but he sent messengers immediately to him, with a statement of his own condition, and
with directions to join him in the Isle of Bommel, as
soon as Maestricht should be reduced. It was, however,
not in the destiny of Louis to reduce Maestricht. His
expedition had been marked with disaster from the beginning. A dark and threatening prophecy had, even before its
commencement, enwrapped Louis, his brethren, and his little
army, in a funeral pall. More than a thousand of his men
had deserted before he reached the Meuse. When he
encamped, opposite Maestricht, he found the river neither
frozen nor open, the ice obstructing the navigation, but being
too weak for the weight of an army.† While he was thus
delayed and embarrassed, Mendoza arrived in the city with
reinforcements. It seemed already necessary for Louis to
abandon his hopes of Maestricht, but he was at least desirous

---

* Mendoza, xi. 232, 233. Hoofd. ix. 344. Bor, vii. 488–490. Meteren,
v. 90.   † Bor, vii. 490. Mendoza, xi. 233.

of crossing the river in that neighbourhood, in order to
effect his junction with the Prince at the earliest possible
moment. While the stream was still encumbered with ice,
however, the enemy removed all the boats. On the 3rd of
March, Avila arrived with a large body of troops at Maestricht, and on the 18th Mendoza crossed the river in the
night, giving the patriots so severe an *encamisada,* that seven
hundred were killed, at the expense of only seven of his own
party. Harassed, but not dispirited by these disasters, Louis
broke up his camp on the 21st, and took a position farther
down the river, at Fauquemont and Gulpen, castles in the
Duchy of Limburg. On the 3rd of April, Braccamonte arrived
at Maestricht, with twenty-five companies of Spaniards
and three of cavalry, while on the same day Mondragon
reached the scene of action with his sixteen companies of
veterans.*

It was now obvious to Louis, not only that he should not
take Maestricht, but that his eventual junction with his
brother was at least doubtful, every soldier who could possibly
be spared seeming in motion to oppose his progress. He was,
to be sure, not yet outnumbered, but the enemy was increasing,
and his own force diminishing daily. Moreover, the Spaniards
were highly disciplined and experienced troops ; while his own
soldiers were mercenaries, already clamorous and insubordinate.† On the 8th of April he again shifted his encampment, and took his course along the right bank of the
Meuse, between that river and the Rhine, in the direction of
Nimwegen.‡ Avila promptly decided to follow him, upon the
opposite bank of the Meuse, intending to throw himself between
Louis and the Prince of Orange, and by a rapid march to give
the Count battle, before he could join his brother. On the 8th
of April, at early dawn, Louis had left the neighbourhood of
Maestricht,§ and on the 13th he encamped at the village of

---

* Mendoza, xi. 234, 236, 237.   Hoofd, ix. 346.   Bor, vii. 490.
⌐ Meteren, v. 90, 91.   ‡ Bor, vii. 490.   § Mendoza, xi. 238.

Mook, on the Meuse, near the confines of Cleves.* Sending
out his scouts, he learned, to his vexation, that the enemy had
outmarched him, and were now within cannon-shot. On the
13th, Avila had constructed a bridge of boats, over which he
had effected the passage of the Meuse with his whole army,†
so that on the Count's arrival at Mook, he found the enemy
facing him, on the same side of the river, and directly in his
path.‡ It was, therefore, obvious that, in this narrow space
between the Waal and the Meuse, where they were now all
assembled, Louis must achieve a victory, unaided, or abandon
his expedition, and leave the Hollanders to despair. He was
distressed at the position in which he found himself, for he
had hoped to reduce Maestricht, and to join his brother in
Holland. Together, they could, at least, have expelled the
Spaniards from that territory, in which case it was probable
that a large part of the population in the different provinces
would have risen. According to present aspects, the destiny
of the country, for some time to come, was likely to hang
upon the issue of a battle which he had not planned, and
for which he was not fully prepared. Still he was not the
man to be disheartened, nor had he ever possessed the courage
to refuse a battle when offered. Upon this occasion, it would
be difficult to retreat without disaster and disgrace, but it
was equally difficult to achieve a victory. Thrust, as he was,
like a wedge into the very heart of a hostile country, he was
obliged to force his way through, or to remain in his enemy's
power. Moreover, and worst of all, his troops were in a state
of mutiny for their wages.§ While he talked to them of
honor, they howled to him for money. It was the custom of
these mercenaries to mutiny on the eve of battle—of the
Spaniards, after it had been fought. By the one course, a
victory was often lost which might have been achieved ; by
the other, when won, it was rendered fruitless.

---

* Mendoza, xi. 239. Bor, vii. 490.   † Ibid. xi. 238, 239.
‡ Ibid., vi. 239. Bor, vii. 490. Hoofd, ix. 347.   § Meteren, v. 91.

Avila had chosen his place of battle with great skill. On the right bank of the Meuse, upon a narrow plain which spread from the river to a chain of hills within cannon-shot on the north, lay the little village of Mook.* The Spanish general knew that his adversary had the superiority in cavalry, and that within this compressed space it would not be possible to derive much advantage from the circumstance.

On the 14th, both armies were drawn up in battle array at earliest dawn,† Louis having strengthened his position by a deep trench, which extended from Mook, where he had stationed ten companies of infantry, which thus rested on the village and the river. Next came the bulk of his infantry, disposed in a single square. On their right was his cavalry, arranged in four squadrons, as well as the narrow limits of the field would allow. A small portion of them, for want of space, were stationed on the hill side.*

Opposite, the forces of Don Sancho were drawn up in somewhat similar fashion. Twenty-five companies of Spaniards were disposed in four bodies of pikemen and musketeers ; their right resting on the river. On their left was the cavalry, disposed by Mendoza in the form of a half moon—the horns garnished by two small bodies of sharpshooters. In the front ranks of the cavalry were the mounted carabineers of Schenk ; behind were the Spanish lancers. The village of Mook lay between the two armies.§

The skirmishing began at early dawn, with an attack upon the trench, and continued some hours, without bringing on a general engagement. Towards ten o'clock, Count Louis became impatient. All the trumpets of the patriots now rang out a challenge to their adversaries,‖ and the Spaniards were just returning the defiance, and preparing a general onset,

---

* Mendoza, xi. 239. Bentivoglio, viii. 142, 143.
† Mendoza, xi. 241. Bor, vii. 491.
‡ Mendoza, xi. 239, 240. Bentivoglio, viii. 142, 143. Bor, vii. 491, 492.
§ Mendoza, Bentivoglio, Bor, ubi sup. Hoofd, ix. 347, 348.
‖ Mendoza, xi. 241.

when the Seigneur de Hierges and Baron Chevreaux arrived on the field. They brought with them a reinforcement of more than a thousand men, and the intelligence that Valdez was on his way with nearly five thousand more.[*] As he might be expected on the following morning, a short deliberation was held as to the expediency of deferring the action. Count Louis was at the head of six thousand foot and two thousand cavalry. Avila mustered only four thousand infantry and not quite a thousand horse.[†] This inferiority would be changed on the morrow into an overwhelming superiority. Meantime, it was well to remember the punishment endured by Aremberg at Heiliger Lee, for not waiting till Meghen's arrival. This prudent counsel was, however, very generally scouted, and by none more loudly than by Hierges and Chevreaux, who had brought the intelligence. It was thought that at this juncture nothing could be more indiscreet than discretion. They had a wary and audacious general to deal with. While they were waiting for their reinforcements, he was quite capable of giving them the slip. He might thus effect the passage of the stream and that union with his brother which had been thus far so successfully prevented. This reasoning prevailed,[‡] and the skirmishing at the trench was renewed with redoubled vigour, an additional force being sent against it. After a short and fierce struggle it was carried, and the Spaniards rushed into the village, but were soon dislodged by a larger detachment of infantry, which Count Louis sent to the rescue.[§] The battle now became general at this point.

Nearly all the patriot infantry were employed to defend the post ; nearly all the Spanish infantry were ordered to assail it. The Spaniards, dropping on their knees, according to custom,

---

* Mendoza, ubi sup.   Hoofd, ix. 348.

† Mendoza, xi. 240.   Bentivoglio, viii. 141.

‡ Hoofd, ix. 348.   Bentivoglio, Mendoza, ubi sup.   Bor, vii. 491, 492.   Cabrera, x. 784, 785.

§ Mendoza, xi. 242.   Hoofd.

said a Paternoster and an Ave Mary, and then rushed, in mass, to the attack. After a short but sharp conflict, the trench was again carried, and the patriots completely routed. Upon this, Count Louis charged with all his cavalry upon the enemy's horse, which had hitherto remained motionless. With the first shock the mounted arquebusiers of Schenk, constituting the vanguard, were broken, and fled in all directions. So great was their panic, as Louis drove them before him, that they never stopped till they had swum or been drowned in the river, the survivors carrying the news to Grave and to other cities that the royalists had been completely routed. This was, however, very far from the truth. The patriot cavalry, mostly carabineers, wheeled after the first discharge, and retired to reload their pieces, but before they were ready for another attack, the Spanish lancers and the German black troopers, who had all remained firm, set upon them with great spirit. A fierce, bloody, and confused action succeeded, in which the patriots were completely overthrown.*

Count Louis, finding that the day was lost, and his army cut to pieces, rallied around him a little band of troopers, among whom were his brother, Count Henry, and Duke Christopher, and together they made a final and desperate charge.† It was the last that was ever seen of them on earth. They all went down together, in the midst of the fight, and were never heard of more. The battle terminated, as usual in those conflicts of mutual hatred, in a horrible butchery, hardly any of the patriot army being left to tell the tale of their disaster. At least four thousand were killed, including those who were slain on the field, those who were suffocated in the marshes or the river, and those who were burned in the farm-houses where they had taken refuge.‡ It

* Mendoza, xi. 242-244.   Hoofd, ix. 350.   Meteren, v. 91.
† Hoofd, ix, 350, 351.   Mendoza, xi. 244.   Bentivoglio, viii. 145.
‡ Bentivoglio, viii. 145.—Compare Cabrera, x. 781-786: Mendoza, Hoofd, ubi sup. According to Mendoza, but forty of the Spanish army were killed; according to the Dutch historians, about two hundred.

was uncertain which of those various modes of death had been the lot of Count Louis, his brother, and his friend. The mystery was never solved. They had, probably, all died on the field; but, stripped of their clothing, with their faces trampled upon by the hoofs of horses, it was not possible to distinguish them from the less illustrious dead. It was the opinion of many that they had been drowned in the river ; of others, that they had been burned.* There was a vague tale that Louis, bleeding but not killed, had struggled forth from the heap of corpses where he had been thrown, had crept to the river-side, and, while washing his wounds, had been surprised and butchered by a party of rustics.† The story was not generally credited, but no man knew, or was destined to learn, the truth.

A dark and fatal termination to this last enterprise of Count Louis had been anticipated by many. In that superstitious age, when emperors and princes daily investigated the future, by alchemy, by astrology, and by books of fate, filled with formulæ, as gravely and precisely set forth as algebraical equations ;‡ when men of every class, from monarch to peasant, implicitly believed in supernatural portents and prophecies, it

---

* Meteren, v. 91. Bor, vii. 491, 492. Hoofd, Bentivoglio, ubi sup. The Walloon historian, occasionally cited in these pages, has a more summary manner of accounting for the fate of these distinguished personages. According to his statement, the leaders of the Protestant forces dined and made merry at a convent in the neighbourhood •upon Good Friday, five days before the battle, using the sacramental chalices at the banquet, and mixing consecrated wafers with their wine. As a punishment for this sacrilege, the army was utterly overthrown, and the Devil himself *flew away with the chieftains, body and soul*.

"Oires Dieu permit que cinq jours après ne restait de leurs principaulx chefs ung seul vif; que plus est, entre les corps morts plusieurs de ces seigneurs n'ont été retrouvés nonobstant toute curieuse recherche; à ceste cause lon creut du comenchement que ils estoient eschappes, et depuis que ils étoient emportés en corps et en âme."—Renom de France, MS., ii. c. xxx.

† Francisci Haraei. Ann. Tumult. Belg., iii, 203. Strada alludes to the story without confirming it.—viii. 383.

‡ The conjuring books, in many folio volumes, containing the tables of wizard logarithms, by which Augustus of Saxony was accustomed to steer his course upon the sea of life, and by the aid of which he considered himself com-

was not singular that a somewhat striking appearance, observed in the sky some weeks previously to the battle of Mookerheyde, should have inspired many persons with a shuddering sense of impending evil.

Early in February five soldiers of the burgher guard at Utrecht, being on their midnight watch, beheld in the sky above them the representation of a furious battle. The sky was extremely dark, except directly over their heads, where, for a space equal in extent to the length of the city, and in breadth to that of an ordinary chamber, two armies, in battle array, were seen advancing upon each other. The one moved rapidly up from the north-west, with banners waving, spears flashing, trumpets sounding, accompanied by heavy artillery and by squadrons of cavalry. The other came slowly forward from the south-east, as if from an entrenched camp, to encounter their assailants. There was a fierce action for a few moments, the shouts of the combatants, the heavy discharge of cannon, the rattle of musketry, the tramp of heavy-armed foot soldiers, the rush of cavalry, being distinctly heard. The firmament trembled with the shock of the contending hosts, and was lurid with the rapid discharges of their artillery. After a short, fierce engagement, the north-western army was beaten back in disorder, but rallied again, after a breathing-time, formed again into solid column, and again advanced. Their foes, arrayed, as the witnesses affirmed, in a square and closely serried grove of spears and muskets, again awaited the attack. Once more the aerial cohorts closed upon each other, all the signs and sounds of a desperate encounter being distinctly recognised by the eager witnesses. The struggle seemed but short. The lances of the south-eastern army seemed to snap "like hemp-stalks," while their firm columns all went down

---

petent to ascertain all future events, and their effect upon his destiny, may still be seen in the library of Dresden. No doubt the Elector consulted these tables most anxiously at the time when Count Louis and Duke Christopher were marching towards the Meuse. With still more intensity he studied their combinations when the projected marriage between the Prince of Orange and Charlotte of Bourbon was first announced to him.

together in mass, beneath the onset of their enemies. The overthrow was complete, victors and vanquished had faded, the clear blue space, surrounded by black clouds, was empty, when suddenly its whole extent, where the conflict had so lately raged, was streaked with blood, flowing athwart the sky in broad crimson streams ; nor was it till the five witnesses had fully watched and pondered over these portents that the vision entirely vanished.*

So impressed were the grave magistrates of Utrecht with the account given next day by the sentinels, that a formal examination of the circumstances was made, the deposition of each witness, under oath, duly recorded,† and a vast deal of consultation of soothsayers' books and other auguries employed to elucidate the mystery. It was universally considered typical of the anticipated battle between Count Louis and the Spaniards. When, therefore, it was known that the patriots, moving from the south-east, had arrived at Mookerheyde, and that their adversaries, crossing the Meuse at Grave, had advanced upon them from the north-west, the result of the battle was considered inevitable ; the phantom battle of Utrecht its infallible precursor.

Thus perished Louis of Nassau in the flower of his manhood, in the midst of a career already crowded with events such as might suffice for a century of ordinary existence. It is difficult to find in history a more frank and loyal character. His life was noble ; the elements of the heroic and the genial so mixed in him that the imagination contemplates him, after three centuries, with an almost affectionate interest. He was not a great man. He was far from possessing the subtle genius or the expansive views of his brother ; but, called as he was to play a prominent part in one of the most complicated and imposing dramas ever enacted by man, he, never-

---

* Bor, vii. 492.

† Ibid. Hoofd also relates the story, premising that he could hardly omit doing so, since the magistrates of Utrecht considered the subject worthy of a formal investigation.—ix. 352.

theless, always acquitted himself with honor. His direct, fearless and energetic nature commanded alike the respect of friend and foe. As a politician, a soldier, and a diplomatist, he was busy, bold, and true. He accomplished by sincerity what many thought could only be compassed by trickery. Dealing often with the most adroit and most treacherous of princes and statesmen, he frequently carried his point, and he never stooped to flattery. From the time when, attended by his "twelve disciples," he assumed the most prominent part in the negotiations with Margaret of Parma, through all the various scenes of the revolution, through all the conferences with Spaniards, Italians, Huguenots, Malcontents, Flemish councillors, or German princes, he was the consistent and un-flinching supporter of religious liberty and constitutional law. The battle of Heiliger Lee and the capture of Mons were his most signal triumphs, but the fruits of both were annihilated by subsequent disaster. His headlong courage was his chief foible. The French accused him of losing the battle of Moncontour by his impatience to engage ; yet they acknow-ledged that to his masterly conduct it was owing that their retreat was effected in so successful, and even so brilliant a manner.* He was censured for rashness and precipitancy in this last and fatal enterprise, but the reproach seems entirely without foundation. The expedition as already stated, had been deliberately arranged, with the full co-operation of his brother, and had been preparing several months. That he was able to set no larger force on foot than that which he led into Gueldres was not his fault. But for the floating ice which barred his passage of the Meuse, he would have sur-prised Maestricht ; but for the mutiny, which rendered his mercenary soldiers cowards, he might have defeated Avila at Mookerheyde. Had he done so he would have joined his brother in the Isle of Bommel in triumph ; the Spaniards

---

* "Car ce fut luy qui fit cette belle retraite à la bataille de Moncontour, secon-dant fort à propos Monsieur l'Admiral qui avoit été blesseé."—Brantome, Grands Capitaines, etc., P. d'Orange et Comte L. de Nassau.

would, probably, have been expelled from Holland, and Leyden saved the horrors of that memorable siege which she was soon called upon to endure. These results were not in his destiny. Providence had decreed that he should perish in the midst of his usefulness ; that the Prince, in his death, should lose the right hand which had been so swift to execute his various plans, and the faithful fraternal heart which had always responded so readily to every throb of his own.

In figure, he was below the middle height, but martial and noble in his bearing. The expression of his countenance was lively ; his manner frank and engaging. All who knew him personally loved him, and he was the idol of his gallant brethren. His mother always addressed him as her dearly beloved, her heart's-cherished Louis. " You must come soon to me," she wrote in the last year of his life, "for I have many matters to ask your advice upon ; and I thank you beforehand, for you have loved me as your mother all the days of your life ; for which may God Almighty have you in his holy keeping."*

It was the doom of this high-born, true-hearted dame to be called upon to weep oftener for her children than is the usual lot of mothers. Count Adolphus had already perished in his youth on the field of Heiliger Lee, and now Louis and his young brother Henry, who had scarcely attained his twenty-sixth year, and whose short life had been passed in that faithful service to the cause of freedom which was the instinct of his race, had both found a bloody and an unknown grave. Count John, who had already done so much for the cause, was fortunately spared to do much more. Although of the expedition, and expecting to participate in the battle, he had, at the urgent solicitation of all the leaders, left the army for a brief season, in order to obtain at Cologne a supply of money for the mutinous troops. He had started upon this mission two days before the action† in which he, too, would otherwise have been sacrificed. The young Duke Christopher,

---

* Archives et Correspondance, iv. 174.   † Ibid., iv. 369.

" optimæ indolis et magnæ spei adolescens,"* who had perished on the same field, was sincerely mourned by the lovers of freedom. His father, the Elector, found his consolation in the Scriptures, and in the reflection that his son had died in the bed of honor, fighting for the cause of God. " 'T was better thus," said that stern Calvinist, whose dearest wish was to " Calvinize the world,"† " than to have passed his time in idleness, which is the Devil's pillow."‡

Vague rumors of the catastrophe had spread far and wide. It was soon certain that Louis had been defeated, but, for a long time, conflicting reports were in circulation as to the fate of the leaders. The Prince of Orange, meanwhile, passed days of intense anxiety, expecting hourly to hear from his brothers, listening to dark rumors, which he refused to credit and could not contradict, and writing letters, day after day, long after the eyes which should have read the friendly missives were closed.§

The victory of the King's army at Mookerheyde had been rendered comparatively barren by the mutiny which broke forth the day after the battle.‖ Three years' pay were due to the Spanish troops, and it was not surprising that upon this occasion one of those periodic rebellions should break forth, by which the royal cause was frequently so much weakened, and the royal governors so intolerably perplexed. These mutinies were of almost regular occurrence, and attended by as regular a series of phenomena. The Spanish troops, living so far from their own country, but surrounded by their women, and constantly increasing swarms of children, constituted a locomotive city of considerable population, permanently established on a foreign soil. It was a city walled in by bayonets,

---

* Archives et Correspondance, iv. 367.   † Ibid., iv. 71.
‡ Ibid., iv. 367.   § Ibid., iv. 372.
‖ Bor, vii. 494, et seq. Meteren, v. 91. Hoofd, ix. 352-359. Mendoza, xi. xii. 246, 247. Bentivoglio, viii. 146-149.—The account given by the last-mentioned historian is the clearest and most elegantly written account of this

and still further isolated from the people around by the impassable moat of mutual hatred. It was a city obeying the articles of war, governed by despotic authority, and yet occasionally revealing, in full force, the irrepressible democratic element. At periods which could almost be calculated, the military populace were wont to rise upon the privileged classes, to deprive them of office and liberty, and to set up in their place commanders of their own election. A governor-in-chief, a sergeant-major, a board of councillors and various other functionaries, were chosen by acclamation and universal suffrage. The Eletto, or chief officer thus appointed, was clothed with supreme power, but forbidden to exercise it. He was surrounded by councillors, who watched his every motion, read all his correspondence, and assisted at all his conferences, while the councillors were themselves narrowly watched by the commonalty. These movements were, however, in general, marked by the most exemplary order. Anarchy became a system of government ; rebellion enacted and enforced the strictest rules of discipline ; theft, drunkenness, violence to women, were severely punished.* As soon as the mutiny broke forth, the first object was to take possession of the nearest city, where the Eletto was usually established in the town-house, and the soldiery quartered upon the citizens. Nothing in the shape of food or lodging was too good for these marauders. Men who had lived for years on camp rations—coarse knaves who had held the plough till compelled to handle the musket, now slept in fine linen, and demanded from the trembling burghers the daintiest viands. They ate the land bare, like a swarm of locusts. " Chickens and partridges," says the thrifty chronicler of Antwerp, " capons and pheasants, hares and rabbits, two kinds of wines ;—for sauces, capers and olives, citrons and

---

mutiny which exists. As a specimen of a system, from which many important consequences were destined to flow at different periods, the subject demands especial attention.

* Bentivoglio, viii. 147.

oranges, spices and sweetmeats ; wheaten bread for their dogs, and even wine, to wash the feet of their horses ;*—such was the entertainment demanded and obtained by the mutinous troops. They were very willing both to enjoy the luxury of this forage, and to induce the citizens, from weariness of affording compelled hospitality, to submit to a taxation by which the military claims might be liquidated.

A city thus occupied was at the mercy of a foreign soldiery, which had renounced all authority but that of self-imposed laws. The King's officers were degraded, perhaps murdered ; while those chosen to supply their places had only a nominal control. The Eletto, day by day, proclaimed from the balcony of the town-house the latest rules and regulations. If satisfactory, there was a clamor of applause ; if objectionable, they were rejected with a tempest of hisses, with discharges of musketry. The Eletto did not govern ; he was a dictator who could not dictate, but could only register decrees. If too honest, too firm, or too dull for his place, he was deprived of his office and sometimes of his life. Another was chosen in his room, often to be succeeded by a series of others, destined to the same fate. Such were the main characteristics of those formidable mutinies, the result of the unthriftiness and dishonesty by which the soldiery engaged in these interminable hostilities were deprived of their dearly earned wages. The expense of the war was bad enough at best, but when it is remembered that of three or four dollars sent from Spain, or contributed by the provinces for the support of the army, hardly one reached the pockets of the soldier,† the frightful expenditure which took place may be imagined. It was not surprising that so much peculation should engender revolt.

The mutiny which broke out after the defeat of Count Louis was marked with the most pronounced and inflammatory of these symptoms. Three years' pay was due to

---

* Meteren, v. 103.
† Requesens to Philip. Correspondance de Philippe II., ii. 1292, p. 457.

the Spaniards, who, having just achieved a signal victory,
were disposed to reap its fruits, by fair means or by force.
On receiving nothing but promises, in answer to their
clamorous demands, they mutinied to a man, and crossed
the Meuse to Grave,* whence, after accomplishing the usual
elections, they took their course to Antwerp. Being in
such strong force, they determined to strike at the capital.
Rumour flew before them. Champagny, brother of Granvelle,
and royal governor of the city, wrote in haste to apprise
Requesens of the approaching danger. The Grand Commander, attended only by Vitelli, repaired instantly to
Antwerp. Champagny advised throwing up a breastwork with
bales of merchandize, upon the esplanade, between the citadel
and the town,† for it was at this point, where the connection between the fortifications of the castle and those of the
city had never been thoroughly completed,‡ that the invasion
might be expected. Requesens hesitated. He trembled at a
conflict with his own soldiery. If successful, he could only be
so by trampling upon the flower of his army. If defeated,
what would become of the King's authority, with rebellious
troops triumphant in rebellious provinces ? Sorely perplexed,
the Commander could think of no expedient. Not knowing
what to do, he did nothing. In the meantime, Champagny,
who felt himself odious to the soldiery, retreated to the New-
town, and barricaded himself, with a few followers, in the
house of the Baltic merchants.§

On the 26th of April, the mutinous troops in perfect order,
marched into the city, effecting their entrance precisely at the
weak point where they had been expected. Numbering at
least three thousand, they encamped on the esplanade, where
Requesens appeared before them alone on horseback, and
made them an oration. They listened with composure, but
answered briefly and with one accord, " Dineros y non palabras," dollars not speeches. Requesens promised profusely,

---

* Mendoza, Bentivoglio, Bor, Hoofd, Meteren, ubi sup.
† Bor, vii. 494.   ‡ Bentivoglio, Bor, Meteren, et al.
§ "Oostersfe Huis."—Bor. vii. 494. Meteren. Hoofd.

but the time was past for promises. Hard silver dollars would alone content an army which, after three years of bloodshed and starvation, had at last taken the law into their own hands. Requesens withdrew to consult the Broad Council of the city. He was without money himself, but he demanded four hundred thousand crowns of the city.* This was at first refused, but the troops knew the strength of their position, for these mutinies were never repressed, and rarely punished. On this occasion the Commander was afraid to employ force, and the burghers, after the army had been quartered upon them for a time, would gladly pay a heavy ransom to be rid of their odious and expensive guests. The mutineers foreseeing that the work might last a few weeks, and determined to proceed leisurely, took possession of the great square. The Eletto, with his staff of councillors, was quartered in the town-house, while the soldiers distributed themselves among the houses of the most opulent citizens, no one escaping a billet who was rich enough to receive such company : bishop or burgomaster, margrave or merchant.† The most famous kitchens were naturally the most eagerly sought, and sumptuous apartments, luxurious dishes, delicate wines, were daily demanded. The burghers dared not refuse.‡

The six hundred Walloons, who had been previously quartered in the city, were expelled, and for many days the mutiny reigned paramount. Day after day the magistracy, the heads of guilds, all the representatives of the citizens were assembled in the Broad Council. The Governor-General insisted on his demand of four hundred thousand crowns, representing, with great justice, that the mutineers would remain in the city until they had eaten and drunk to that amount, and that there would still be the arrearages, for which the city would be obliged to raise the funds. On the 9th of May, the authorities made an offer, which was duly communicated to

---

* Meteren, v. 92. Hoofd, Bor, ubi sup.

† Bor, vii. 494, 495. Hoofd. Meteren.

‡ Meteren, v. 92. Bor, vii. 494, 495. Hoofd, ix. 355, 356. Bentivoglio, viii. 148.

the Eletto. That functionary stood forth on a window-sill of the town-house, and addressed the soldiery. He informed them that the Grand Commander proposed to pay ten months' arrears in cash, five months' in silks and woollen cloths, and the balance in promises, to be fulfilled within a few days.* The terms were not considered satisfactory, and were received with groans of derision. The Eletto, on the contrary, declared them very liberal, and reminded the soldiers of the perilous condition in which they stood, guilty to a man of high treason, with a rope around every neck. It was well worth their while to accept the offer made them, together with the absolute pardon for the past, by which it was accompanied. For himself, he washed his hands of the consequences if the offer were rejected. The soldiers answered by deposing the Eletto and choosing another in his room.†

Three days after, a mutiny broke out in the citadel—an unexampled occurrence.‡ The rebels ordered Sancho d'Avila, the commandant, to deliver the keys of the fortress. He refused to surrender them but with his life. They then contented themselves with compelling his lieutenant to leave the citadel, and with sending their Eletto to confer with the Grand Commander, as well as with the Eletto of the army. After accomplishing his mission, he returned, accompanied by Chiappin Vitelli, as envoy of the Governor-General. No sooner, however, had the Eletto set foot on the drawbridge than he was attacked by Ensign Salvatierra of the Spanish garrison, who stabbed him to the heart and threw him into the moat. The ensign, who was renowned in the army for his ferocious courage, and who wore embroidered upon his trunk hose the inscription, " El castigador de los Flamencos,"§ then rushed upon the sergeant-major of the mutineers, despatched him in the same way, and tossed him likewise into the moat.‖ These preliminaries being

---

* Bor, Meteren, Hoofd, ubi sup.   † Hoofd, ix. 359.

‡ "Los soldados del Castillo se amotinaron, alteracion que jamas ha hecho la nacion Española, hallandose en Castillo."—Mendoza, xii. 247.

§ Meteren, v. 92. Hoofd, ix. 359. "The chastiser of the Flemings."

‖ Mendoza, Meteren, Hoofd.

settled, a satisfactory arrangement was negotiated between
Vitelli and the rebellious garrison. Pardon for the past, and
payment upon the same terms as those offered in the city, were
accepted, and the mutiny of the citadel was quelled.* It was,
however, necessary that Salvatierra should conceal himself for
a long time, to escape being torn to pieces by the incensed
soldiery.

Meantime, affairs in the city were more difficult to adjust.
The mutineers raised an altar of chests and bales upon
the public square, and celebrated mass under the open sky,
solemnly swearing to be true to each other to the last.†
The scenes of carousing and merry-making were renewed at
the expense of the citizens, who were again exposed to nightly
alarms from the boisterous mirth and ceaseless mischief-making
of the soldiers. Before the end of the month, the · Broad
Council, exhausted by the incubus which had afflicted them so
many weeks, acceded to the demand of Requesens. The four
hundred thousand crowns were furnished, the Grand Commander accepting them as a loan, and giving in return bonds
duly signed and countersigned, together with a mortgage upon
all the royal domains.‡ The citizens received the documents,
as a matter of form, but they had handled such securities before, and valued them but slightly. The mutineers now agreed
to settle with the Governor-General, on condition of receiving
all their wages, either in cash or cloth, together with a solemn
promise of pardon for all their acts of insubordination. This
pledge was formally rendered with appropriate religious ceremonies, by Requesens, in the cathedral.§ The payments were
made directly afterwards, and a great banquet was held on the
same day, by the whole mass of the soldiery, to celebrate the
event. The feast took place on the place of the Meer, and
was a scene of furious revelry. The soldiers, more thought-
less than children, had arrayed themselves in extemporaneous
costumes, cut from the cloth which they had at last received

---

* Mendoza, Meteren, Hoofd.   † Hoofd, ix. 359.
‡ Bor, vii. 494, 495.   § Bentivoglio, viii. 149.

in payment of their sufferings and their blood. Broadcloths, silks, satins, and gold-embroidered brocades, worthy of a queen's wardrobe, were hung in fantastic drapery around the sinewy forms and bronzed faces of the soldiery, who, the day before, had been clothed in rags. The mirth was fast and furious ; and scarce was the banquet finished before every drum-head became a gaming-table, around which gathered groups eager to sacrifice in a moment their dearly-bought gold.*

The fortunate or the prudent had not yet succeeded in entirely plundering their companions, when the distant booming of cannon was heard from the river. Instantly, accoutred as they were in their holiday and fantastic costumes, the soldiers, no longer mutinous, were summoned from banquet and gaming-table, and were ordered forth upon the dykes. The patriot Admiral Boisot, who had so recently defeated the fleet of Bergen, under the eyes of the Grand Commander, had unexpectedly sailed up the Scheld, determined to destroy the fleet of Antwerp, which upon that occasion had escaped. Between the forts of Lillo and Callao, he met with twenty-two vessels under the command of Vice-admiral Haemstede. After a short and sharp action, he was completely victorious. Fourteen of the enemy's ships were burned or sunk, with all their crews, and Admiral Haemstede was taken prisoner. The soldiers opened a warm fire of musketry upon Boisot from the dyke, to which he responded with his cannon. The distance of the combatants, however, made the action unimportant, and the patriots retired down the river, after achieving a complete victory. The Grand Commander was farther than ever from obtaining that foothold on the sea, which as he had informed his sovereign, was the only means by which the Netherlands could be reduced.†

---

* Hoofd, ix. 359, 360.

† Bor, vii. 495, 496.   Hoofd, ix. 359, 360.   Bentivoglio, viii. 149.   Letter of the Prince of Orange, in Archives, etc., v. 11, 12.

CHAPTER II.

THE invasion of Louis of Nassau had, as already stated, effected the raising of the first siege of Leyden. That leaguer had lasted from the 31st of October, 1573, to the 21st of March, 1574,* when the soldiers were summoned away to defend the frontier. By an extraordinary and culpable carelessness, the citizens, neglecting the advice of the Prince, had not taken advantage of the breathing time thus afforded them to victual the city and strengthen the garrison.† They seemed to reckon more confidently upon the success of Count Louis than

---

* Bor, vii. 502.   † Bor, vii. 502.

he had even done himself; for it was very probable that, in case of his defeat, the siege would be instantly resumed. This natural result was not long in following the battle of Mooker-heyde.

On the 26th of May, Valdez reappeared before the place, at the head of eight thousand Walloons and Germans,[*] and Leyden was now destined to pass through a fiery ordeal. This city was one of the most beautiful in the Netherlands. Placed in the midst of broad and fruitful pastures, which had been reclaimed by the hand of industry from the bottom of the sea, it was fringed with smiling villages, blooming gardens, fruitful orchards. The ancient and, at last, decrepit Rhine, flowing languidly towards its sandy death-bed, had been multiplied into innumerable artificial currents, by which the city was completely interlaced. These watery streets were shaded by lime trees, poplars, and willows, and crossed by one hundred and forty-five bridges, mostly of hammered stone. The houses were elegant, the squares and streets spacious, airy and clean, the churches and public edifices imposing, while the whole aspect of the place suggested thrift, industry, and comfort. Upon an artificial elevation, in the centre of the city, rose a ruined tower of unknown antiquity. By some it was considered to be of Roman origin, while others preferred to regard it as a work of the Anglo-Saxon Hengist, raised to commemorate his conquest of England.[†] Surrounded by fruit trees, and overgrown in the centre with oaks, it afforded, from its mouldering battlements, a charming prospect over a

---

* Ibid., 504.

† Guicciardini, Descript. Holl. et Zelandiæ. Bor, vii. 502. Bentivoglio, viii. 151.

"Putatur Engistus Britanno
Orbe redux posuisse victor," etc., etc.

according to the celebrated poem of John Van der Does, the accomplished and valiant Commandant of the city. The tower, which is doubtless a Roman one, presents, at the present day, almost precisely the same appearance as that described by the contemporaneous historians of the siege. The verses of the Commandant show the opinion, that the Anglo-Saxon conquerors of Britain went from Holland, to have been a common one in the sixteenth century.

wide expanse of level country, with the spires of neighbouring cities rising in every direction. It was from this commanding height, during the long and terrible summer days which were approaching, that many an eye was to be strained anxiously seaward, watching if yet the ocean had begun to roll over the land.

Valdez lost no time in securing himself in the possession of Maeslandsluis, Vlaardingen, and the Hague. Five hundred English, under command of Colonel Edward Chester, abandoned the fortress of Valkenburg, and fled towards Leyden. Refused admittance by the citizens, who now, with reason, distrusted them, they surrendered to Valdez, and were afterwards sent back to England.* In the course of a few days, Leyden was thoroughly invested, no less than sixty-two redoubts, some of them having remained undestroyed from the previous siege, now girdling the city, while the besiegers already numbered nearly eight thousand, a force to be daily increased. On the other hand, there were no troops in the town, save a small corps of "freebooters," and five companies of the burgher guard. John Van der Does, Seigneur of Nordwyck, a gentleman of distinguished family, but still more distinguished for his learning, his poetical genius, and his valor, had accepted the office of military commandant.†

The main reliance of the city, under God, was on the stout hearts of its inhabitants within the walls, and on the sleepless energy of William the Silent without. The Prince, hastening to comfort and encourage the citizens, although he had been justly irritated by their negligence in having

---

* Mendoza, xii. 251, who says that the lives of these English prisoners were spared at his express solicitation. He was at that juncture sent by the Grand Commander on a mission to Queen Elizabeth, and obtained this boon of his superior as a personal favour to himself.

† Hoofd, ix. 362. Bor, vii. 505. Guicciardini.—"Janum Dousam, virum nobilem, Toparcham Nordovicenum, utraque lingua doctissimum, et poetam egregium."—Desc. Holl., ed. usa., 238, 239. "Juan Duse, Señor de Nortwyck—gentil poeta en la lengua Latina."—Mendoza, xii. 254. "Giovanni Douza poeta nobile di quel tempo ne componimenti latini e molto nobile ancora per qualità di sangue e per altre prerogative di merito."—Bentivoglio, viii. 153.

omitted to provide more sufficiently against the emergency
while there had yet been time,* now reminded them that they
were not about to contend for themselves alone, but that the
fate of their country and of unborn generations would, in all
human probability, depend on the issue about to be tried.
Eternal glory would be their portion if they manifested a
courage worthy of their race and of the sacred cause of religion
and liberty. He implored them to hold out at least three
months, assuring them that he would, within that time, devise
the means of their deliverance.† The citizens responded,
courageously and confidently, to these missives, and assured
the Prince of their firm confidence in their own fortitude and
his exertions.‡

And truly they had a right to rely on that calm and un-
flinching soul, as on a rock of adamant. All alone, without
a being near him to consult, his right arm struck from him
by the death of Louis, with no brother left to him but the
untiring and faithful John, he prepared without delay for the
new task imposed upon him. France, since the defeat and death
of Louis, and the busy intrigues which had followed the accession
of Henry III., had but small sympathy for the Netherlands.
The English government, relieved from the fear of France, was
more cold and haughty than ever. An Englishman, employed
by Requesens to assassinate the Prince of Orange, had been
arrested in Zealand, who impudently pretended that he had
undertaken to perform the same office for Count John, with
the full consent and privity of Queen Elizabeth.§ The pro-

---

* Archives et Correspondance, v. 10.

† Letter of Orange in Bor, vii. 505.   ‡ Ibid.   Hoofd. ix. 363, 364.,

§ The story was incredible, so far as the Queen was implicated. but its invention by the assassin indicated the estimate entertained, in general, of her
sentiments towards the Netherlands. "Depuis ceste escripte," wrote the
Prince to his brother, "l'on m'a icy envoyé de Zealande ung Anglois prisonnier, lequel entre aultres confesse d'avoir esté apporté du nouveau Gouverneur
pour me tuer. Et avoit aussi, par charge du dit Gouverneur, entreprins de
vous tuer à Couloigne, passé dix ou douze jours. Et toutes fois il dict le tout
avoir esté faict par consentement et avec intelligence de la Royne d'Angleterre,
pour tant mieux descouvrir les desseings des ennemis."—Archives de la
Maison d'Orange, v. 12. 13.

vinces of Holland and Zealand were stanch and true, but the
inequality of the contest between a few brave men, upon that
handsbreadth of territory, and the powerful Spanish Empire,
seemed to render the issue hopeless.

Moreover, it was now thought expedient to publish the
amnesty which had been so long in preparation, and this time
the trap was more liberally baited. The pardon, which had
passed the seals upon the 8th of March, was formally issued
by the Grand Commander on the 6th of June.[*] By the
terms of this document the King invited all his erring and
repentant subjects to return to his arms, and to accept a full
forgiveness for their past offences, upon the sole condition that
they should once more throw themselves upon the bosom of
the Mother Church. There were but few exceptions to the
amnesty, a small number of individuals, all mentioned by name,
being alone excluded ;[†] but although these terms were ample,
the act was liable to a few stern objections. It was easier
now for the Hollanders to go to their graves than to mass, for
the contest, in its progress, had now entirely assumed the aspect
of a religious war. Instead of a limited number of heretics
in a state which, although constitutional was Catholic, there
was now hardly a Papist to be found among the natives. To
accept the pardon then was to concede the victory, and the
Hollanders had not yet discovered that they were conquered.
They were resolved, too, not only to be conquered, but annihilated, before the Roman Church should be re-established on
their soil, to the entire exclusion of the Reformed worship.
They responded with steadfast enthusiasm to the sentiment
expressed by the Prince of Orange, after the second siege of
Leyden had been commenced ; "As long as there is a living
man left in the country, we will contend for our liberty and
our religion."[‡] The single condition of the amnesty assumed,

---

[*] Bor, vii. 510.　Meteren, v. 93.　Hoofd, ix. 368.

[†] The pardon is given in full by Bor, vii. 510–513.

[‡] "Comme aussi de nostre costel nous sommes icy resoluz de ne quitter la
deffense de sa Parolle et de nostre liberté jusques au dernier homme."—Archives
de la Maison d'Orange, v. 27.

in a phrase, what Spain had fruitlessly striven to establish by a hundred battles, and the Hollanders had not faced their enemy on land and sea for seven years to succumb to a phrase at last.

Moreover, the pardon came from the wrong direction. The malefactor gravely extended forgiveness to his victims. Although the Hollanders had not yet disembarrassed their minds of the supernatural theory of government, and felt still the reverence of habit for regal divinity, they naturally considered themselves outraged by the trick now played before them. The man who had violated all his oaths, trampled upon all their constitutional liberties, burned and sacked their cities, confiscated their wealth, hanged, beheaded, burned, and buried alive their innocent brethren, now came forward, not to implore, but to offer forgiveness. Not in sackcloth, but in royal robes ; not with ashes, but with a diadem upon his head, did the murderer present himself vicariously upon the scene of his crimes. It may be supposed that, even in the sixteenth century, there were many minds which would revolt at such blasphemy. Furthermore, even had the people of Holland been weak enough to accept the pardon, it was impossible to believe that the promise would be fulfilled.* It was sufficiently known how much faith was likely to be kept with heretics, notwithstanding that the act was fortified by a papal Bull, dated on the 30th of April, by which Gregory XIII. promised forgiveness to those Netherland sinners who duly repented and sought absolution for their crimes, even although they had sinned more than seven times seven.†

For a moment the Prince had feared lest the pardon might produce some effect upon men wearied by interminable suffering, but the event proved him wrong. It was received with universal and absolute contempt. No man came forward to take advantage of its conditions, save one brewer in Utrecht, and

* See letter of the Secretary of Requesens in Archives de la Maison d'Orange, v. 31.

† The Bull is given at length in Bor, vii. 513–515.

the son of a refugee pedler from Leyden. With these exceptions, the only ones recorded, Holland remained deaf to the royal voice.[*] The city of Leyden was equally cold to the messages of mercy, which were especially addressed to its population by Valdez and his agents. Certain Netherlanders, belonging to the King's party, and familiarly called "Glippers," despatched from the camp many letters to their rebellious acquaintances in the city. In these epistles the citizens of Leyden were urgently and even pathetically exhorted to submission by their loyal brethren, and were implored "to take pity upon their poor old fathers, their daughters, and their wives." But the burghers of Leyden thought that the best pity which they could show to those poor old fathers, daughters, and wives, was to keep them from the clutches of the Spanish soldiery; so they made no answer to the Glippers, save by this single line, which they wrote on a sheet of paper, and forwarded, like a letter, to Valdez :

"Fistula dulce canit, volucrem cum decipit auceps."[†]

According to the advice early given by the Prince of Orange, the citizens had taken an account of their provisions of all kinds, including the live stock. By the end of June, the city was placed on a strict allowance of food, all the provisions being purchased by the authorities at an equitable price. Half a pound of meat and half a pound of bread was allotted to a full grown man, and to the rest, a due proportion. The city being strictly invested, no communication, save by carrier pigeons, and by a few swift and skilful messengers, called jumpers, was possible. Sorties and fierce combats were, however, of daily occurrence, and a handsome bounty was offered to any man who brought into the city gates

---

[*] Bor, vii. 516.

[†] Jan Fruytiers. Corte Beschryvinghe van der strenghe Belegeringhe en wondebaerlijcke Verlossinge der stadt Leyden——met byvoeghing alle der Brieven die an de van der Stadt geschreven zijn.—Ghedruckt tot Delf., A. D. 1577. This contemporary and very rare volume is much the best authority for the details of the memorable siege which it describes. It was the main source of the historian Pieter Bor. Compare Meteren, v. 94. Hoofd, x. 364.

the head of a Spaniard. The reward was paid many times, but the population was becoming so excited and so apt, that the authorities felt it dangerous to permit the continuance of these conflicts. Lest the city, little by little, should lose its few disciplined defenders, it was now proclaimed, by sound of church bell, that in future no man should leave the gates.*

The Prince had his head-quarters at Delft and at Rotterdam. Between those two cities, an important fortress, called Polderwaert, secured him in the control of the alluvial quadrangle, watered on two sides by the Yssel and the Meuse. On the 29th June, the Spaniards, feeling its value, had made an unsuccessful effort to carry this fort by storm. They had been beaten off, with the loss of several hundred men, the Prince remaining in possession of the position, from which alone he could hope to relieve Leyden.† He still held in his hand the keys with which he could unlock the ocean gates and let the waters in upon the land, and he had long been convinced that nothing could save the city but to break the dykes. Leyden was not upon the sea, but he could send the sea to Leyden, although an army fit to encounter the besieging force under Valdez could not be levied. The battle of Mookerheyde had, for the present, quite settled the question of land relief, but it was possible to besiege the besiegers with the waves of the ocean. The Spaniards occupied the coast from the Hague to Vlaardingen, but the dykes along the Meuse and Yssel were in possession of the Prince. He determined that these should be pierced, while, at the same time, the great sluices at Rotterdam, Schiedam, and Delftshaven should be opened.‡ The damage to the fields, villages, and growing crops would be enormous, but he felt that no other course could rescue Leyden, and with it the whole of Holland from destruction. His clear expositions and impassioned eloquence at last overcame all resistance. By the middle of July the estates fully

---

* Jan Fruytiers. Bor, vii. 552. Meteren, v. Hoofd, ix. 366.
† Bor, vii. 548.
‡ Bor, vii. 548. Meteren, v. 94. Hoofd, ix. 370.

consented to his plan, and its execution was immediately undertaken. "Better a drowned land than a lost land,"* cried the patriots, with enthusiasm, as they devoted their fertile fields to desolation. The enterprise for restoring their territory, for a season, to the waves, from which it had been so patiently rescued, was conducted with as much regularity as if it had been a profitable undertaking. A capital was formally subscribed, for which a certain number of bonds were issued, payable at a long date.† In addition to this preliminary fund, a monthly allowance of forty-five guldens was voted by the estates, until the work should be completed, and a large sum was contributed by the ladies of the land, who freely furnished their plate, jewellery, and costly furniture to the furtherance of the scheme.‡

Meantime, Valdez, on the 30th July, issued most urgent and ample offers of pardon to the citizens, if they would consent to open their gates and accept the King's authority, but his overtures were received with silent contempt, notwithstanding that the population was already approaching the starvation point. Although not yet fully informed of the active measures taken by the Prince, yet they still chose to rely upon his energy and their own fortitude, rather than upon the honied words which had formerly been heard at the gates of Harlem and of Naarden. On the 3rd of August, the Prince, accompanied by Paul Buys, chief of the commission appointed to execute the enterprise, went in person along the Yssel, as far as Kappelle, and superintended the rupture of the dykes in sixteen places. The gates at Schiedam and Rotterdam were opened, and the ocean began to pour over the land. While waiting for the waters to rise, provisions were rapidly collected, according to an edict of the Prince, in all the principal towns of the neighbourhood, and some two hundred vessels, of various sizes, had also been got ready at Rotterdam, Delfthaven, and other ports.§

---

* "Liever bedorven dan verloren land."—Fruytiers, 16. Meteren, Hoofd, ubi sup.   † Bor, vii. 549. Hoofd, ix. 370, 371.   ‡ Hoofd, ix. 370.
§ Jan Fruytiers. Bor, vii. 549, 550. Hoofd, ix. 371.

The citizens of Leyden were, however, already becoming impatient, for their bread was gone, and of its substitute malt cake, they had but slender provision. On the 12th of August they received a letter from the Prince, encouraging them to resistance, and assuring them of a speedy relief, and on the 21st they addressed a despatch to him in reply, stating that they had now fulfilled their original promise, for they had held out two months with food, and another month without food.* If not soon assisted, human strength could do no more ; their malt cake would last but four days, and after that was gone, there was nothing left but starvation. Upon the same day, however, they received a letter, dictated by the Prince, who now lay in bed at Rotterdam with a violent fever, assuring them that the dykes were all pierced, and that the water was rising upon the " Land-scheiding," the great outer barrier which separated the city from the sea. He said nothing however of his own illness, which would have cast a deep shadow over the joy which now broke forth among the burghers.†

The letter was read publicly in the market-place, and to increase the cheerfulness, burgomaster Van der Werf, knowing the sensibility of his countrymen to music, ordered the city musicians to perambulate the streets, playing lively melodies and martial airs.   Salvos of cannon were likewise fired, and the starving city for a brief space put on the aspect of a holiday, much to the astonishment of the besieging forces, who were not yet aware of the Prince's efforts. They perceived very soon, however, as the water everywhere about Leyden had risen to the depth of ten inches, that they stood in a perilous position. It was no trifling danger to be thus attacked by the waves of the ocean, which seemed about to obey with docility the command of William the Silent. Valdez became anxious and uncomfortable at the strange aspect of affairs ; for the be-

---

* " Te weten, de eerste twe maendern met brood, en de derde maend met armoede."—Jan Fruytiers.

† Letter of Fl. de Nuynhem and N. Brunynck to Count John of Nassau, in Archives de la Maison d'Orange, v. 38–40. Bor, vii. 550.

sieging army was now in its turn beleaguered, and by a stronger power than man's. He consulted with the most experienced of his officers, with the country people, with the most distinguished among the Glippers, and derived encouragement from their views concerning the Prince's plan. They pronounced it utterly futile and hopeless. The Glippers knew the country well, and ridiculed the desperate project in unmeasured terms.*

Even in the city itself, a dull distrust had succeeded to the first vivid gleam of hope, while the few royalists among the population boldly taunted their fellow-citizens to their faces with the absurd vision of relief which they had so fondly welcomed. "Go up to the tower, ye Beggars," was the frequent and taunting cry, "go up to the tower, and tell us if ye can see the ocean coming over the dry land to your relief"†—and day after day they did go up to the ancient tower of Hengist, with heavy heart and anxious eye, watching, hoping, praying, fearing, and at last almost despairing of relief by God or man. On the 27th they addressed a desponding letter to the estates, complaining that the city had been forgotten in its utmost need, and on the same day a prompt and warm-hearted reply was received, in which the citizens were assured that every human effort was to be made for their relief. "Rather," said the estates, "will we see our whole land and all our possessions perish in the waves, than forsake thee, Leyden. We know full well, moreover, that with Leyden, all Holland must perish also." They excused themselves for not having more frequently written, upon the ground that the whole management of the measures for their relief had been intrusted to the Prince, by whom alone all the details had been administered, and all the correspondence conducted.‡

The fever of the Prince had, meanwhile, reached its height,

---

* Hoofd, ix. 372. Bor, vii. 551.

† "Gaet en op den toren gy Geuskens en siet het Maeswater te gemoot," etc., etc.—Jan Fruytiers. Bor, vii. 551. Hoofd, ix. 374.

‡ See the letter in Bor, vii. 551, 552.

He lay at Rotterdam, utterly prostrate in body, and with mind agitated nearly to delirium, by the perpetual and almost unassisted schemes which he was constructing. Relief, not only for Leyden, but for the whole country, now apparently sinking into the abyss, was the vision which he pursued as he tossed upon his restless couch. Never was illness more unseasonable. His attendants were in despair, for it was necessary that his mind should for a time be spared the agitation of business. The physicians who attended him agreed, as to his disorder, only in this, that it was the result of mental fatigue and melancholy, and could be cured only by removing all distressing and perplexing subjects from his thoughts, but all the physicians in the world could not have succeeded in turning his attention for an instant from the great cause of his country. Leyden lay, as it were, anxious and despairing at his feet, and it was impossible for him to close his ears to her cry. Therefore, from his sick bed he continued to dictate words of counsel and encouragement to the city; to Admiral Boisot, commanding the fleet, minute directions and precautions.[*] Towards the end of August a vague report had found its way into his sick chamber that Leyden had fallen, and although he refused to credit the tale, yet it served to harass his mind, and to heighten fever. Cornelius Van Mierop, Receiver General of Holland, had occasion to visit him at Rotterdam, and strange to relate, found the house almost deserted. Penetrating, unattended, to the Prince's bed-chamber, he found him lying quite alone. Inquiring what had become of all his attendants, he was answered by the Prince, in a very feeble voice, that he had sent them all away. The Receiver-General seems, from this, to have rather hastily arrived at the conclusion that the Prince's disorder was the pest, and that his servants and friends had all deserted him from cowardice.[†]

---

* Letters of N. Brunynck, Arch. et Correspond., v. 39, 46.   Bor, vii. 551, 552.

† Bor, vii. 551. Hoofd, ix. 372, 373.—Such was the information given by him to the historian Bor, whose account is followed by Hoofd and others. The letters of Secretary Brunynck and of Nuynhem prove, on the contrary, the solicitude with which the Prince was attended in his illness.—Archives et Correspond. ace, v. 38–56.

This was very far from being the case. His private secretary and his maître d'hôtel watched, day and night, by his couch, and the best physicians of the city were in constant attendance. By a singular accident, all had been despatched on different errands, at the express desire of their master, but there had never been a suspicion that his disorder was the pest, or pestilential. Nerves of steel, and a frame of adamant could alone have resisted the constant anxiety and the consuming fatigue to which he had so long been exposed. His illness had been aggravated by the rumor of Leyden's fall, a fiction which Cornelius Mierop was now enabled flatly to contradict. The Prince began to mend from that hour. By the end of the first week of September, he wrote a long letter to his brother, assuring him of his convalescence, and expressing, as usual, a calm confidence in the divine decrees—" God will ordain for me," said he, " all which is necessary for my good and my salvation. He will load me with no more afflictions than the fragility of this nature can sustain."*

The preparations for the relief of Leyden, which, notwithstanding his exertions, had grown slack during his sickness, were now vigorously resumed. On the 1st of September, Admiral Boisot arrived out of Zealand with a small number of vessels, and with eight hundred veteran sailors. A wild and ferocious crew were those eight hundred Zealanders. Scarred, hacked, and even maimed, in the unceasing conflicts in which their lives had passed ; wearing crescents in their caps, with the inscription, " Rather Turkish than Popish ;" renowned far and wide, as much for their ferocity as for their nautical skill ; the appearance of these wildest of the " Sea-beggars" was both eccentric and terrific. They were known never to give nor to take quarter, for they went to *mortal* combat only, and had sworn to spare neither noble nor simple, neither king, kaiser, nor pope, should they fall into their power.†

---

* Archives et Correspondance, etc., 53.
† "Liever Turx dan Paus." Jan Fruytiers.—Bor, vii. 552. Hoofd, ix. 374. Meteren, v. 94.

More than two hundred vessels had been now assembled, carrying generally ten pieces of cannon, with from ten to eighteen oars, and manned with twenty-five hundred veterans, experienced both on land and water.* The work was now undertaken in earnest. The distance from Leyden to the outer dyke, over whose ruins the ocean had already been admitted, was nearly fifteen miles. This reclaimed territory, however, was not maintained against the sea by these external barriers alone. The flotilla made its way with ease to the Land-scheiding, a strong dyke within five miles of Leyden, but here its progress was arrested.† The approach to the city was surrounded by many strong ramparts, one within the other, by which it was defended against its ancient enemy, the ocean, precisely like the circumvallations by means of which it was now assailed by its more recent enemy, the Spaniard. To enable the fleet, however, to sail over the land, it was necessary to break through this two-fold series of defences. Between the Land-scheiding and Leyden were several dykes, which kept out the water ; upon the level territory, thus encircled, were many villages, together with a chain of sixty-two forts, which completely occupied the land. All these villages and fortresses were held by the veteran troops of the King ; the besieging force being about four times as strong‡ as that which was coming to the rescue.

The Prince had given orders that the Land-scheiding, which was still one-and-a-half foot above water, should be taken possession of, at every hazard. On the night of the 10th and 11th of September this was accomplished, by surprise, and in a masterly manner.§ The few Spaniards who had been stationed upon the dyke were all despatched or driven off, and the patriots fortified themselves upon it, without the loss of a man. As the day dawned the Spaniards saw the fatal error

---

* Meteren, v. 94. Bor, vii. 552.   † Bor, vii. 552–554.   Hoofd, ix. 375.

‡ The army of Valdez numbered at least ten thousand.—Hoofd, ix. 387.

§ Jan Fruytiers.—Compare Bor, vii. 554.   Hoofd, ix. 375.

which they had committed in leaving this bulwark so feebly defended, and from two villages which stood close to the dyke, the troops now rushed in considerable force to recover what they had lost. A hot action succeeded, but the patriots had too securely established themselves. They completely defeated the enemy, who retired, leaving hundreds of dead on the field, and the patriots in complete possession of the Land-scheiding.* This first action was sanguinary and desperate. It gave an earnest of what these people, who came to relieve their brethren, by sacrificing their property and their lives, were determined to effect. It gave a revolting proof, too, of the intense hatred which nerved their arms. A Zealander, having struck down a Spaniard on the dyke, knelt on his bleeding enemy, tore his heart from his bosom, fastened his teeth in it for an instant, and then threw it to a dog, with the exclamation, "'Tis too bitter."† The Spanish heart was, however, rescued, and kept for years, with the marks of the soldier's teeth upon it,‡ a sad testimonial of the ferocity engendered by this war for national existence.

The great dyke having been thus occupied, no time was lost in breaking it through in several places, a work which was accomplished under the very eyes of the enemy. The fleet sailed through the gaps ; but, after their passage had been effected in good order, the Admiral found, to his surprise, that it was not the only rampart to be carried. The Prince had been informed, by those who claimed to know the country, that, when once the Land-scheiding had been passed, the water would flood the country as far as Leyden, but the "Green-way," another long dyke, three-quarters of a mile farther inward, now rose at least a foot above the water, to

---

* Bor, vii. 554. Hoofd, ix. 375, 376.

† Bor, vii. 554. Meteren, v. 94. Hoofd, ix. 376.

‡ "Dit gebeten herte met den tekenen der tanden is binnen Delf daer na van vele lofwaerdige luiden gesien en zijn daer na ook, eeinige carmina nitgegeven." etc.—Bor, vii. 554.

One of the "carmina" thus alluded to by the historian, was a Latin poem by the Commandant Van der Does, in which the progress of the siege is described with much spirit and elegance.

oppose their further progress. Fortunately, by a second and still more culpable carelessness, this dyke had been left by the Spaniards in as unprotected a state as the first had been. Promptly and audaciously Admiral Boisot took possession of this barrier also, levelled it in many places, and brought his flotilla, in triumph, over its ruins. Again, however, he was doomed to disappointment. A large mere, called the Fresh-water Lake, was known to extend itself directly in his path about midway between the Land-scheiding and the city. To this piece of water, into which he expected to have instantly floated, his only passage lay through one deep canal. The sea which had thus far borne him on, now diffusing itself over a very wide surface, and under the influence of an adverse wind, had become too shallow for his ships. The canal alone was deep enough, but it led directly towards a bridge, strongly occupied by the enemy. Hostile troops, moreover, to the amount of three thousand occupied both sides of the canal.* The bold Boisot, nevertheless, determined to force his passage, if possible. Selecting a few of his strongest vessels, his heaviest artillery, and his bravest sailors, he led the van himself, in a desperate attempt to make his way to the mere. He opened a hot fire upon the bridge, then converted into a fortress, while his men engaged in hand-to-hand combat with a succession of skirmishers from the troops along the canal. After losing a few men, and ascertaining the impregnable position of the enemy, he was obliged to withdraw, defeated, and almost despairing.†

A week had elapsed since the great dyke had been pierced, and the flotilla now lay motionless in shallow water, having accomplished less than two miles. The wind, too, was easterly, causing the sea rather to sink than to rise. Everything wore a gloomy aspect, when, fortunately, on the 18th, the wind shifted to the north-west, and for three days blew a gale. The waters rose rapidly, and before the second day

---

* Bor, vii. 555. Hoofd, ix. 376.
† Bor, Hoofd, ubi sup.—compare Mendoza, xii. 260–262.

was closed the armada was afloat again. Some fugitives from Zoetermeer village now arrived, and informed the Admiral that, by making a detour to the right, he could completely circumvent the bridge and the mere. They guided him, accordingly, to a comparatively low dyke, which led between the villages of Zoetermeer and Benthuyzen. A strong force of Spaniards was stationed in each place, but, seized with a panic, instead of sallying to defend the barrier, they fled inwardly towards Leyden, and halted at the village of North Aa.* It was natural that they should be amazed. Nothing is more appalling to the imagination than the rising ocean tide, when man feels himself within its power ; and here were the waters, hourly deepening and closing around them, devouring the earth beneath their feet, while on the waves rode a flotilla, manned by a determined race, whose courage and ferocity were known throughout the world. The Spanish soldiers, brave as they were on land, were not sailors, and in the naval contests which had taken place between them and the Hollanders had been almost invariably defeated. It was not surprising, in these amphibious skirmishes, where discipline was of little avail, and habitual audacity faltered at the vague dangers which encompassed them, that the foreign troops should lose their presence of mind.

Three barriers, one within the other, had now been passed, and the flotilla, advancing with the advancing waves, and driving the enemy steadily before it, was drawing nearer to the beleaguered city. As one circle after another was passed, the besieging army found itself compressed within a constantly contracting field. The "Ark of Delft," an enormous vessel, with shot-proof bulwarks, and moved by paddle-wheels† turned by a crank, now arrived at Zoetermeer, and was soon followed by the whole fleet. After a brief delay, sufficient to allow the few remaining villagers to escape, both Zoetermeer and Benthuyzen, with the fortifications, were set on fire, and abandoned

---

* Bor, Hoofd, ubi sup. Mendoza, xii. 262.
† Jan Fruytiers. Bor, vii. 556. Hoofd, ix. 377. Mendoza, xii. 262.

to their fate. The blaze lighted up the desolate and watery waste around, and was seen at Leyden, where it was hailed as the beacon of hope. Without further impediment, the armada proceeded to North Aa ; the enemy retreating from this position also, and flying to Zoeterwoude, a strongly fortified village but a mile and three quarters from the city walls. It was now swarming with troops, for the bulk of the besieging army had gradually been driven into a narrow circle of forts, within the immediate neighbourhood of Leyden. Besides Zoeterwoude, the two posts where they were principally established were Lammen and Leyderdorp, each within three hundred rods of the town. At Leyderdorp were the head-quarters of Valdez ; Colonel Borgia commanded in the very strong fortress of Lammen.[*]

The fleet was, however, delayed at North Aa by another barrier, called the " Kirk-way." The waters, too, spreading once more over a wider space, and diminishing under an east wind, which had again arisen, no longer permitted their progress, so that very soon the whole armada was stranded anew. The waters fell to the depth of nine inches, while the vessels required eighteen and twenty. Day after day the fleet lay motionless upon the shallow sea. Orange, rising from his sick bed as soon as he could stand, now came on board the fleet. His presence diffused universal joy ; his words inspired his desponding army with fresh hope. He rebuked the impatient spirits who, weary of their compulsory idleness, had shown symptoms of ill-timed ferocity, and those eight hundred mad Zealanders, so frantic in their hatred to the foreigners, who had so long profaned their land, were as docile as children to the Prince. He reconnoitred the whole ground, and issued orders for the immediate destruction of the Kirkway, the last important barrier which separated the fleet from Leyden. Then, after a long conference with Admiral Boisot, he returned to Delft.[†]

Meantime, the besieged city was at its last gasp. The

---

[*] Bor, Hoofd, ubi sup. Mendoza. [†] Bor, vii. 556. Hoofd, ix. 380.

burghers had been in a state of uncertainty for many days ; being aware that the fleet had set forth for their relief, but knowing full well the thousand obstacles which it had to surmount. They had guessed its progress by the illumination from the blazing villages ; they had heard its salvos of artillery, on its arrival at North Aa ; but since then, all had been dark and mournful again, hope and fear, in sickening alternation, distracting every breast. They knew that the wind was unfavorable, and at the dawn of each day every eye was turned wistfully to the vanes of the steeples. So long as the easterly breeze prevailed, they felt, as they anxiously stood on towers and housetops, that they must look in vain for the welcome ocean. Yet, while thus patiently waiting, they were literally starving ; for even the misery endured at Harlem had not reached that depth and intensity of agony to which Leyden was now reduced. Bread, malt-cake, horse-flesh, had entirely disappeared ; dogs, cats, rats, and other vermin, were esteemed luxuries. A small number of cows, kept as long as possible, for their milk, still remained ; but a few were killed from day to day, and distributed in minute proportions, hardly sufficient to support life among the famishing population. Starving wretches swarmed daily around the shambles where these cattle were slaughtered, contending for any morsel which might fall, and lapping eagerly the blood as it ran along the pavement ; while the hides, chopped and boiled, were greedily devoured. Women and children, all day long, were seen searching gutters and dunghills for morsels of food, which they disputed fiercely with the famishing dogs. The green leaves were stripped from the trees, every living herb was converted into human food, but these expedients could not avert starvation. The daily mortality was frightful—infants starved to death on the maternal breasts, which famine had parched and withered ; mothers dropped dead in the streets, with their dead children in their arms. In many a house the watchmen, in their rounds, found a whole family of corpses, father, mother, and children, side by side, for a disorder called the plague, naturally engendered of hardship and famine, now came, as if in kindness, to abridge the agony of the people. The pestilence stalked at noonday through the city, and the doomed inhabitants fell like grass beneath its scythe. From six thousand to eight thousand human beings sank before this scourge alone, yet the people resolutely held out—women and men mutually encouraging each other to resist the entrance of their foreign foe—an evil more horrible than pest or famine.*

The missives from Valdez, who saw more vividly than the besieged could do, the uncertainty of his own position, now poured daily into the city, the enemy becoming more prodigal of his vows, as he felt that the ocean might yet save the victims from his grasp. The inhabitants, in their ignorance, had gradually abandoned their hopes of relief, but they spurned the summons to surrender. Leyden was sublime in its despair. A few murmurs were, however, occasionally heard at the steadfastness of the magistrates, and a dead body was placed at the door of the burgomaster, as a silent witness against his inflexibility.†
A party of the more faint-hearted even assailed the heroic Adrian Van der Werf with threats and reproaches as he passed through the streets. A crowd had gathered around him, as he reached a triangular place in the centre of the town, into which many of the principal streets emptied themselves, and upon one side of which stood the church of Saint Pancras, with its high brick tower surmounted by two pointed turrets, and with two ancient lime trees at its entrance. There stood the burgomaster, a tall, haggard, imposing figure, with dark visage, and a tranquil but commanding eye. He waved his broad-leaved felt hat for silence, and then exclaimed, in language which has been almost literally preserved, "What would ye, my friends ? Why do ye murmur that we do not break our vows and surrender the city to the Spaniards ? a fate more

---

* Jan Fruytiers.   Bor, vii. 557.   Hoofd, ix. 381.   Meteren, v. 94.   Mendoza's estimate of the entire population, as numbering only fourteen thousand before the siege (xii. 256), is evidently erroneous. It was probably nearer fifty thousand.

† Hoofd, ix. 381, 382.   Bor, vii. 557.

horrible than the agony which she now endures. I tell you
I have made an oath to hold the city, and may God give me
strength to keep my oath! I can die but once; whether by
your hands, the enemy's, or by the hand of God. My own
fate is indifferent to me, not so that of the city intrusted to
my care. I know that we shall starve if not soon relieved;
but starvation is preferable to the dishonored death which is
the only alternative. Your menaces move me not; my life
is at your disposal; here is my sword, plunge it into my breast,
and divide my flesh among you. Take my body to appease
your hunger, but expect no surrender, so long as I remain
alive."*

The words of the stout burgomaster inspired a new courage
in the hearts of those who heard him, and a shout of applause
and defiance arose from the famishing but enthusiastic crowd.
They left the place, after exchanging new vows of fidelity
with their magistrate, and again ascended tower and battle-
ment to watch for the coming fleet. From the ramparts they
hurled renewed defiance at the enemy. "Ye call us rat-
eaters and dog-eaters," they cried, "and it is true. So long,
then, as ye hear dog bark or cat mew within the walls, ye
may know that the city holds out. And when all has
perished but ourselves, be sure that we will each devour our
left arms, retaining our right to defend our women, our liberty,
and our religion, against the foreign tyrant. Should God, in
his wrath, doom us to destruction, and deny us all relief, even
then will we maintain ourselves for ever against your entrance.
When the last hour has come, with our own hands we will set
fire to the city and perish, men, women, and children together
in the flames, rather than suffer our homes to be polluted and
our liberties to be crushed."† Such words of defiance, thundered
daily from the battlements, sufficiently informed Valdez as
to his chance of conquering the city, either by force or fraud,
but at the same time, he felt comparatively relieved by the

---

* Jan Fruytiers. Hoofd, ix. 379. Meteren, v. 94.
† Jan Fruytiers, 25. Meteren, v. 94. Hoofd, ix. 379, 380.

inactivity of Boisot's fleet, which still lay stranded at North Aa. "As well," shouted the Spaniards, derisively, to the citizens, "as well can the Prince of Orange pluck the stars from the sky as bring the ocean to the walls of Leyden for your relief."*

On the 28th of September, a dove flew into the city, bringing a letter from Admiral Boisot.† In this despatch, the position of the fleet at North Aa was described in encouraging terms, and the inhabitants were assured that, in a very few days at furthest, the long-expected relief would enter their gates. The letter was read publicly upon the market-place, and the bells were rung for joy. Nevertheless, on the morrow, the vanes pointed to the east, the waters, so far from rising, continued to sink, and Admiral Boisot was almost in despair. He wrote to the Prince, that if the spring-tide, now to be expected, should not, together with a strong and favorable wind, come immediately to their relief, it would be in vain to attempt anything further, and that the expedition would, of necessity, be abandoned. The tempest came to their relief. A violent equinoctial gale, on the night of the 1st and 2nd of October, came storming from the north-west, shifting after a few hours full eight points, and then blowing still more violently from the south-west. The waters of the North Sea were piled in vast masses upon the southern coast of Holland, and then dashed furiously landward, the ocean rising over the earth, and sweeping with unrestrained power across the ruined dykes.‡

In the course of twenty-four hours, the fleet at North Aa,

---

* "Dat hat den Prinse so onmogelijk was om Leyden te ontsetten als het henluiden mogelijk was te sterren metter hand te reiken en grijpen."—Bor, vii. 557.

† Bor, vii. 557.—See also the text of the letter transmitted on the same day and in the same manner, from the Admiral to the Commandant Nordtwyck, in Groen v. Prinsterer. The tone of the letter is spirited, cheerful, and almost jocular. The writer claims the hospitality of the Commandant, assuring him that he shall soon arrive in Leyden, to be a guest in his house.—Archives de la Maison d'Orange, v. 67, 68.

‡ Bor, vii. 557.

instead of nine inches, had more than two feet of water. No time was lost. The Kirk-way, which had been broken through according to the Prince's instructions, was now completely overflowed, and the fleet sailed at midnight, in the midst of the storm and darkness. A few sentinel vessels of the enemy challenged them as they steadily rowed towards Zoeterwoude. The answer was a flash from Boisot's cannon, lighting up the black waste of waters. There was a fierce naval midnight battle; a strange spectacle among the branches of those quiet orchards, and with the chimney stacks of half-submerged farm houses rising around the contending vessels.* The neighboring village of Zoeterwoude shook with the discharges of the Zealanders' cannon, and the Spaniards assembled in that fortress knew that the rebel Admiral was at last afloat and on his course. The enemy's vessels were soon sunk, their crews hurled into the waves. On went the fleet, sweeping over the broad waters which lay between Zoeterwoude and Zwieten. As they approached some shallows, which led into the great mere, the Zealanders dashed into the sea, and with sheer strength shouldered every vessel through. Two obstacles lay still in their path—the forts of Zoeterwoude and Lammen, distant from the city five hundred and two hundred and fifty yards respectively. Strong redoubts, both well supplied with troops and artillery, they were likely to give a rough reception to the light flotilla, but the panic, which had hitherto driven their foes before the advancing patriots, had reached Zoeterwoude. Hardly was the fleet in sight when the Spaniards, in the early morning, poured out from the fortress, and fled precipitately to the left, along a road which led in a westerly direction towards the Hague. Their narrow path was rapidly vanishing in the waves, and hundreds sank beneath the constantly deepening and treacherous flood. The wild Zealanders, too, sprang from their vessels upon the crumbling dyke and drove their retreating foes into the sea. They hurled their harpoons at them, with an accuracy ac-

---

* Bor, vii. 557. Hoofd, ix. 382. Meteren, v. 95. Mendoza, xii. 263.

quired in many a polar chase; they plunged into the waves in the keen pursuit, attacking them with boat-hook and dagger. The numbers who thus fell beneath these corsairs, who neither gave nor took quarter, were never counted, but probably not less than a thousand perished. The rest effected their escape to the Hague.[*]

The first fortress was thus seized, dismantled, set on fire, and passed, and a few strokes of the oars brought the whole fleet close to Lammen. This last obstacle rose formidable and frowning directly across their path. Swarming as it was with soldiers, and bristling with artillery, it seemed to defy the armada either to carry it by storm or to pass under its guns into the city.[†] It appeared that the enterprise was, after all, to founder within sight of the long expecting and expected haven. Boisot anchored his fleet within a respectful distance, and spent what remained of the day in carefully reconnoitring the fort, which seemed only too strong. In conjunction with Leyderdorp, the head-quarters of Valdez, a mile and a half distant on the right, and within a mile of the city, it seemed so insuperable an impediment that Boisot wrote in despondent tone to the Prince of Orange. He announced his intention of carrying the fort, if it were possible, on the following morning, but if obliged to retreat, he observed, with something like despair, that there would be nothing for it but to wait for another gale of wind. If the waters should rise sufficiently to enable them to make a wide detour, it might be possible, if, in the meantime, Leyden did not starve or surrender, to enter its gates from the opposite side.[‡]

Meantime, the citizens had grown wild with expectation. A dove had been despatched by Boisot, informing them of his precise position, and a number of citizens accompanied the burgomaster, at nightfall, toward the tower of Hengist— "Yonder," cried the magistrate, stretching out his hand to-

---

* Jan Fruytiers.   Bor, vii. 558.   Hoofd, ix. 383.   Mendoza, xii. 264.
† Bor, vii. 559.   Hoofd, ix. 384.   Meteren, v. 95.
‡ Bor, vii. 559.   Hoofd, ix. 385.

wards Lammen, " yonder, behind that fort, are bread and meat, and brethren in thousands. Shall all this be destroyed by the Spanish guns, or shall we rush to the rescue of our friends ?" " We will tear the fortress to fragments with our teeth and nails," was the reply, " before the relief, so long expected, shall be wrested from us."* It was resolved that a sortie, in conjunction with the operations of Boisot, should be made against Lammen with the earliest dawn. Night descended upon the scene, a pitch dark night, full of anxiety to the Spaniards, to the armada, to Leyden. Strange sights and sounds occurred at different moments to bewilder the anxious sentinels. A long procession of lights issuing from the fort was seen to flit across the black face of the waters, in the dead of night, and the whole of the city wall, between the Cow-gate and the Tower of Burgundy, fell with a loud crash. .The horror-struck citizens thought that the Spaniards were upon them at last ; the Spaniards imagined the noise to indicate a desperate sortie of the citizens.† Everything was vague and mysterious.

Day dawned, at length, after the feverish night, and the Admiral prepared for the assault. Within the fortress reigned a death-like stillness, which inspired a sickening suspicion. Had the city, indeed, been carried in the night; had the massacre already commenced ; had all this labor and audacity been expended in vain ? Suddenly a man was descried, wading breast-high through the water from Lammen towards the fleet, while at the same time, one solitary boy was seen to wave his cap from the summit of the fort. After a moment of doubt, the happy mystery was solved. The Spaniards had fled, panic struck, during the darkness. Their position would still have enabled them, with firmness, to frustrate the enterprise of the patriots, but the hand of God, which had sent the ocean and the tempest to the deliverance of Leyden, had struck her enemies with terror likewise. The lights which had been seen moving during the night were the lanterns of

---

* Bor, vii. 559.

† Jan Fruytiers. Bor, vii. 559. Meteren, v. 95. Mendoza, xii. 265.

the retreating Spaniards, and the boy who was now waving his triumphant signal from the battlements had alone witnessed the spectacle. So confident was he in the conclusion to which it led him, that he had volunteered at daybreak to go thither all alone. The magistrates, fearing a trap, hesitated for a moment to believe the truth, which soon, however, became quite evident.* Valdez, flying himself from Leyderdorp, had ordered Colonel Borgia to retire with all his troops from Lammen. Thus, the Spaniards had retreated at the very moment that an extraordinary accident had laid bare a whole side of the city for their entrance. The noise of the wall, as it fell, only inspired them with fresh alarm ; for they believed that the citizens had sallied forth in the darkness, to aid the advancing flood in the work of destruction. All obstacles being now removed, the fleet of Boisot swept by Lammen, and entered the city on the morning of the 3rd of October. Leyden was relieved.†

The quays were lined with the famishing population, as the fleet rowed through the canals, every human being who could stand, coming forth to greet the preservers of the city. Bread was thrown from every vessel among the crowd. The poor creatures who, for two months had tasted no wholesome human food, and who had literally been living within the jaws of death, snatched eagerly the blessed gift, at last too liberally bestowed. Many choked themselves to death, in the greediness with which they devoured their bread ; others became ill with the effects of plenty thus suddenly succeeding starvation ;—but these were isolated cases, a repetition of which was prevented. The Admiral, stepping ashore, was welcomed by the magistracy, and a solemn procession was immediately formed. Magistrates and citizens, wild Zealanders, emaciated burgher guards, sailors, soldiers, women, children,— nearly every living person within the walls, all repaired without delay to the great church, stout Admiral Boisot leading

---

* Jan Fruytiers.   Bor, vii. 559.   Hoofd, ix. 385.
† Jan Fruytiers.   Bor, vii, 560.   Hoofd, Meteren, ubi sup.

the way. The starving and heroic city, which had been so
firm in its resistance to an earthly king, now bent itself in
humble gratitude before the King of kings. After prayers,
the whole vast congregation joined in the thanksgiving hymn.
Thousands of voices raised the song, but few were able to carry
it to its conclusion, for the universal emotion, deepened by the
music, became too full for utterance. The hymn was abruptly
suspended, while the multitude wept like children. This scene
of honest pathos terminated, the necessary measures for dis-
tributing the food and for relieving the sick were taken by
the magistracy. A note dispatched to the Prince of Orange,
was received by him at two o'clock, as he sat in church at
Delft. It was of a somewhat different purport from that of
the letter which he had received early in the same day from
Boisot ; the letter in which the admiral had informed him
that the success of the enterprise depended, after all, upon the
desperate assault upon a nearly impregnable fort. The joy of
the Prince may be easily imagined, and so soon as the sermon
was concluded, he handed the letter just received to the minister, to be read to the congregation. Thus, all participated
in his joy, and united with him in thanksgiving.*

The next day, notwithstanding the urgent entreaties of
his friends, who were anxious lest his life should be endangered by breathing, in his scarcely convalescent state, the
air of the city where so many thousands had been dying of
the pestilence, the Prince repaired to Leyden. He, at least,
had never doubted his own or his country's fortitude. They
could, therefore, most sincerely congratulate each other, now
that the victory had been achieved. "If we are doomed to
perish," he had said a little before the commencement of the
siege,† "in the name of God, be it so ! At any rate, we
shall have the honor to have done what no nation ever did
before us, that of having defended and maintained ourselves,
unaided, in so small a country, against the tremendous efforts

---

* Jan Fruytiers..   Hoofd, ix. 386.   Bor, vii. 560.   Meteren, v. 95.
† Letter to Count John, 7th May, 1574.   Archives, etc., iv. 385–398.

of such powerful enemies. So long as the poor inhabitants here, though deserted by all the world, hold firm, it will still cost the Spaniards the half of Spain, in money and in men, before they can make an end of us."

The termination of the terrible siege of Leyden was a convincing proof to the Spaniards that they had not yet made an end of the Hollanders. It furnished, also, a sufficient presumption that until they *had* made an end of them, even unto the last Hollander, there would never be an end of the struggle in which they were engaged. It was a slender consolation to the Governor-General, that his troops had been vanquished, not by the enemy, but by the ocean. An enemy whom the ocean obeyed with such docility might well be deemed invincible by man. In the head-quarters of Valdez, at Leyderdorp, many plans of Leyden and the neighbourhood were found lying in confusion about the room. Upon the table was a hurried farewell of that General to the scenes of his discomfiture, written in a Latin worthy of Juan Vargas: "Vale civitas, valete castelli parvi, qui relicti estis propter aquam et non per vim inimicorum!" In his precipitate retreat before the advancing rebels, the Commander had but just found time for this elegant effusion, and for his parting instructions to Colonel Borgia that the fortress of Lammen was to be forthwith abandoned. These having been reduced to writing, Valdez had fled so speedily as to give rise to much censure and more scandal. He was even accused of having been bribed by the Hollanders to desert his post, a tale which many repeated, and a few believed. On the 4th of October, the day following that on which the relief of the city was effected, the wind shifted to the north-east, and again blew a tempest. It was as if the waters, having now done their work, had been rolled back to the ocean by an Omnipotent hand, for in the course of a few days, the land was bare again, and the work of reconstructing the dykes commenced.*

---

* Bor, vii. 560. Meteren, v. 95. Hoofd, ix. 383. Mendoza, xii. 265.— The best authority, after Fruytiers, for the history of this memorable siege,

After a brief interval of repose, Leyden had regained its former position. The Prince, with advice of the estates, had granted the city, as a reward for its sufferings, a ten days' annual fair, without tolls or taxes,* and as a further manifestation of the gratitude entertained by the people of Holland and Zealand for the heroism of the citizens, it was resolved that an academy or university should be forthwith established within their walls.† The University of Leyden, afterwards so illustrious, was thus founded in the very darkest period of the country's struggle.

The university was endowed with a handsome revenue, principally derived from the ancient abbey of Egmont,‡ and was provided with a number of professors, selected for their genius, learning, and piety among all the most distinguished scholars of the Netherlands. The document by which the institution was founded was certainly a masterpiece of ponderous irony, for

---

is Bor, who was living at Utrecht at the time. He afterwards, in writing his Chronicle, used the account drawn up by Jan Fruytiers from information and documents furnished by the magistrates and many persons present at the siege. Bor had also enjoyed frequent communications with the Seigneur de Nordtwyck, Commandant of the city during the siege, with Dirk de Montfort, at whose house the Prince of Orange lodged on the 4th of October, and with other individuals. He had read in the original every letter which he quotes in his history. He cites, also, with amusing gravity, a variety of acrostics, anagrams, and other poetical effusions, wonderful specimens all, of the uncouth gambols by which the poets of that day and country were in the habit of exhibiting their enthusiasm. Among other productions of the muse elicited by the triumphant termination to the siege, he alludes with emotion to a poem which he hoped was soon to see the light. This was an Ode on the Siege of Leyden, " in six hundred and eleven stanzas of eight lines each"—which the suffering reader was at liberty " to sing or to read," as best suited him. To sing six hundred and eleven stanzas, eight lines each, of a Dutch poem, one would think almost as formidable a doom as to endure the horrors of the siege which it celebrated.—Bor, vii. 561. Don Bernardino de Mendoza is the chief Spanish authority.—Compare Bentivoglio, lib. viii. 151–156; and Cabrera, Hist. Don Filipe Segundo, lib. x. cap. xvii. xix. xxi. The last historian sees nothing worthy of admiration or respect in the conduct of the Hollanders, and he is incensed with Geronimo Franchi for having wasted nearly the whole of one book on an account of the memorable relief.

* Bor, vii. 561.   † Bor, viii. 593. Meteren, v. 95.
‡ Bor, viii. 503.

as the fiction of the King's sovereignty was still maintained, Philip was gravely made to establish the university, as a reward to Leyden for rebellion to himself. " Considering," said this wonderful charter,* " that during these present wearisome wars within our provinces of Holland and Zealand, all good instruction of youth in the sciences and liberal arts is likely to come into entire oblivion. . . . *Considering the differences of religion*—considering that we are inclined to gratify *our city of Leyden, with its burghers, on account of the heavy burthens sustained by them during this war with such faithfulness*—we have resolved, after *ripely deliberating with our dear cousin, William, Prince of Orange*, stadholder, to erect a free public school and university," etc., etc., etc. So ran the document establishing this famous academy, all needful regulations for the government and police of the institution being entrusted by Philip to his " above-mentioned dear cousin of Orange."

The university having been founded, endowed, and supplied with its teachers, it was solemnly consecrated in the following winter, and it is agreeable to contemplate this scene of harmless pedantry, interposed, as it was, between the acts of the longest and dreariest tragedy of modern time. On the 5th of February, 1575, the city of Leyden, so lately the victim of famine and pestilence, had crowned itself with flowers. At seven in the morning, after a solemn religious celebration in the Church of St. Peter,† a grand procession was formed. It was preceded by a military escort, consisting of the burgher militia and the five companies of infantry stationed in the city. Then came, drawn by four horses, a splendid triumphal chariot, on which sat a female figure, arrayed in snow-white garments. This was the Holy Gospel. She was attended by the Four Evangelists, who walked on foot at each side of her chariot. Next fol-

---

* See the text of the Octroy by which the university was established, in Bor, viii. 593, 591.

† Bor, viii. 594.

lowed Justice, with sword and scales, mounted, blindfold, upon a unicorn, while those learned doctors, Julian, Papinian, Ulpian, and Tribonian, rode on either side, attended by two lackeys and four men at arms. After these came Medicine, on horseback, holding in one hand a treatise of the healing art, in the other a garland of drugs. The curative goddess rode between the four eminent physicians, Hippocrates, Galen, Dioscorides, and Theophrastus, and was attended by two footmen and four pike-bearers. Last of the allegorical personages came Minerva, prancing in complete steel, with lance in rest, and bearing her Medusa shield. Aristotle and Plato, Cicero and Virgil, all on horseback, with attendants in antique armor at their back, surrounded the daughter of Jupiter, while the city band, discoursing eloquent music from hautboy and viol, came upon the heels of the allegory. Then followed the mace-bearers and other officials, escorting the orator of the day, the newly-appointed professors and doctors, the magistrates and dignitaries, and the body of the citizens generally completing the procession.

Marshalled in this order, through triumphal arches, and over a pavement strewed with flowers, the procession moved slowly up and down the different streets, and along the quiet canals of the city. As it reached the Nuns' Bridge, a barge of triumph, gorgeously decorated, came floating slowly down the sluggish Rhine. Upon its deck, under a canopy enwreathed with laurels *and oranges,* and adorned with tapestry, sat Apollo, attended by the Nine Muses, all in classical costume ; at the helm stood Neptune with his trident. The Muses executed some beautiful concerted pieces ; Apollo twanged his lute. Having reached the landing-place, this deputation from Parnassus stepped on shore, and stood awaiting the arrival of the procession. Each professor, as he advanced, was gravely embraced and kissed by Apollo and all the Nine Muses in turn, who greeted their arrival besides with the recitation of an elegant Latin poem. This classical ceremony terminated, the whole procession marched together to the cloister of Saint

Barbara, the place prepared for the new university, where they listened to an eloquent oration by the Rev. Caspar Kolhas, after which they partook of a magnificent banquet. With this memorable feast, in the place where famine had so lately reigned, the ceremonies were concluded.*

* Bor, viii. 594, 595.

END OF VOL. II.